Emergent Information Technologies and Enabling Policies for Counter-Terrorism

IEEE Press
445 Hoes Lane
Piscataway, NJ 08854

IEEE Press Editorial Board
Mohamed E. El-Hawary, *Editor in Chief*

J. B. Anderson	S. V. Kartalopoulos	N. Schulz
R. J. Baker	M. Montrose	C. Singh
T. G. Croda	M. S. Newman	G. Zobrist
R. J. Herrick	F. M. B. Pereira	

Kenneth Moore, *Director of IEEE Book and Information Services (BIS)*
Catherine Faduska, *Senior Acquisitions Editor, IEEE Press*
Jeanne Audino, *Project Editor, IEEE Press*

IEEE Computational Intelligence Society, *Sponsor*
IEEE CI-S Liason to IEEE Press, David B. Fogel

Books in the IEEE Press Series on Computational Intelligence

Emergent Information Technologies and Enabling Policies for Counter-Terrorism

Edited by

Robert L. Popp
John Yen

IEEE Computational Intelligence Society, *Sponsor*

IEEE Press Series on Computational Intelligence
David B. Fogel, *Series Editor*

IEEE PRESS

A JOHN WILEY & SONS, INC., PUBLICATION

For general information on our other products and services or for technical support, please contact our Customer Care Department within the United States at (800) 762-2974, outside the United States at (317) 572-3993 or fax (317) 572-4002.

Wiley also publishes its books in a variety of electronic formats. Some content that appears in print may not be available in electronic format. For information about Wiley products, visit our web site at www.wiley.com.

Library of Congress Cataloging-in-Publication Data is available.

ISBN-13 978-0-471-77615-4
ISBN-10 0-471-77615-7

Contents

Foreword

The terrorist attacks of September 11, 2001 transformed America like no other event since Pearl Harbor. The all-out battle against terrorism has become a national obsession, and much of our budget and patriotic resolve have been redirected to address the new threat.

Our government has struggled to transform the national security institutions created at the dawn of the Cold War for this new era. Sweeping legislative changes have restructured the government, creating a new Department of Homeland Security and a director for National Intelligence. These structural changes were accompanied by significant new legal authorities in the "Patriot Act" and the Intelligence Reporting and Terrorist Prevention Act of 2003. And the Executive Branch has promulgated new strategies and policies, embodied in the National Security Strategy of 2002, the National Intelligence Strategy of 2004, and the Department of Defense Directive 3001 adopted in 2005.

By any measure, these are landmark changes in the political and security history of the country. Underlying all of these changes has been a constant leitmotiv—America must harness the powers of advanced technologies to defeat this new enemy. Simple in concept, this mandate is devilishly complex in reality. New technologies offer great promise, but challenge fundamental assumptions and premises embedded in current policy and statute. Americans want the government to protect them, but fear the implications of new technology inadequately harnessed by regulation and oversight.

This timely volume deals with the technical challenges accompanying emerging technologies introduced to combat the asymmetric twenty-first century terrorist threat. More important, it grounds the search for practical solutions in a policy framework that insures their disciplined and legitimate use.

JOHN HAMRE
President and CEO, Center for Strategic and International Studies
(former) Deputy Secretary of Defense

March 2006

Preface

The idea for this book germinated, in part, from the controversy surrounding the U.S. government's response to the tragic events of September 11, 2001. In a democracy with extraordinary population diversity, citizens are frequently moved to speak out on every imaginable opinion. Predictably, the views expressed by our citizens toward our government's actions taken in response to the 9/11 attacks span the spectrum from "not strong enough" through "about right" to "draconian."

Wherever the reader may be on this spectrum, the acts of terrorism committed against the United States on September 11, 2001, constitute an intolerable threat to our government and our way of life. In response to this threat, the focus of national defense efforts is upon identifying and pre-empting planned acts of terrorism—counter-terrorism. In the months and years ahead, terrorists may well try to bring even more catastrophic destruction down upon us. Acts of terrorism may expand from bombings, hostage-takings, airline hijackings, and even 9/11-like events to much larger-scale attacks using weapons of mass destruction such as "dirty nukes," biological weapons including anthrax, smallpox, or botulinum toxin, and cyberweapons of enormous destructive power. The spectre of any such catastrophe forces us now to invent a new way of dealing with our enemies. We must craft a collection of sophisticated technology tools and policies that will effectively foil—neutralize if not outright defeat—attempted attacks. We must do all in our power to discover and to preempt if possible terrorist attacks before they can be launched. This is the objective of counter-terrorism.

The way of dealing with our terrorist enemies must be radically new. In 1990, IBM was more profitable than ever before in its history. However, just three years later it was poised on the edge of ruin as it bled tens of billions of dollars from its bottom line. Lou Gerstner took control of the company and turned it around quickly. He understood that IBM's prior success had lulled the company into becoming complacent. His mantra became, in effect "It is a new day, and we need to compete in a new way." So it is with our nation's defense.

But there remains a deeply felt issue that must be captured and remembered in all that we do to bolster our defensive capability. That issue concerns the delicacy of the balance between our nation's security and our citizens' expectation of freedoms and liberties provided under the Constitution. Just as we expect our government to protect us against enemy attack, so we also expect our government to safeguard our treasured freedoms including our civil liberties and especially our right to privacy. Is it possible for us to invent a new and effective way of dealing with our enemies, providing protection against enemy attack while simultaneously respecting our citizens' privacy and providing assurance against unreasonable search and seizure?

We believe the delicate balance between national security for the country and the freedoms and liberties expected by its citizenry are not dichotomous or conflicting, and that the solution lies in developing critical advanced technologies simultaneously with enlightened policies that would guide the implementation of those technologies. Countering terrorism in today's world calls for the development of innovative technologies, together with enlightened, coordinated policies that bind the technologies to their intended use.

This book consists of 22 chapters organized into seven broad areas. They are authored by nationally recognized experts on counter-terrorism, information technology, and policy development. The opening few chapters begins with a discussion of several modeling approaches to counter-terrorism, and the final three chapters discusses issues surrounding the development of policy specifically for guiding the implementation of advanced information technologies in the counter-terrorism domain. The chapters between these deal, respectively, with: information management and signal processing—ingesting and analyzing massive volumes of data; knowledge management—moving from raw *data* through *information* into computer-accessible *knowledge*; collaborative technologies—allowing teams whether located on "the edge" or in "the center" of the problem space to share views and exchange ideas; text and data processing—technologies facilitating analysis across multiple languages, permitting the rapid location and identification of relevant information in a multilingual dataspace; and social and network link analysis—developing advanced tools to analyze social networks leading to the clarification of known or the identification of previously unknown terrorist networks (section six).

Those readers willing to struggle through the sometimes dense thicket of technical prose found in these pages will gain a better understanding of many advanced information technology tools currently under development. If we have succeeded, then the need for developing in parallel a collection of enabling policies that will provide the context and the ground rules for using advanced technology will be clarified as well. We hope these 22 chapters will not only help the reader develop a vision of the capability of emergent technologies to counter-terrorism, but will also facilitate the understanding of complex policy/privacy issues determining the success of implementing such technologies for our national defense.

ACKNOWLEDGMENTS

We would like to acknowledge chapter authors, reviewers, and our colleagues from the broader counter-terrorism community—both technical and policy—who made this book possible. We are also indebted to Catherine Faduska, Lisa Morano Van Horn, and Jeanne Audino at IEEE Press and Wiley for their support, patience, and commitment to the book project. Bob would like to thank his dear friends and colleagues John Poindexter, David Allen, Lucille Cepeda, Jim Lewis, Mary DeRosa, Jason Keiber, and most especially his wife Joanne and children George, Robert Jr. and Sarah for their dedication and steadfast support. John would like to thank his wife Michelle and children Philip and Angela for their love and encouragement throughout his career.

ROBERT L. POPP
JOHN YEN

Woburn, Massachusetts
University Park, Pennsylvania
March, 2006

Contributors

Jeffrey Allanach, University of Connecticut, Storrs, Connecticut

David Allen, SRS Technologies, Arlington, Virginia

Reda A. Ammar, University of Connecticut, Storrs, Connecticut

Devaisis Bassu, Telcordia Technologies, Piscataway, New Jersey

Clifford Behrens, Telcordia Technologies, Piscataway, New Jersey

Chris Boner, Metron Incorporated, Reston, Virginia

Isaac Brewer, The Pennsylvania State University, University Park, Pennsylvania

John Byrnes, Fair Isaac Corporation, San Diego, California

Fred H. Cate, Indiana University, Bloomington, Indiana

Nazli Choucri, Massachusetts Institute of Technology, Cambridge, Massachusetts

Claudio Cioffi-Revilla, George Mason University, Fairfax, Virginia

Thayne Coffman, 21st Century Technologies, Austin, Texas

Erik S. Connors, The Pennsylvania State University, University Park, Pennsylvania

David Cousins, Bolt, Beranek and Newman (BBN), Cambridge, Massachusetts

Steven. A. Demurjian, Sr., University of Connecticut, Storrs, Connecticut

Gary Edwards, ISX Corporation, Arlington, Virginia

Stephen Eick, SSS Research Incorporated, Naperville, Illinois

Xiaocong Fan, The Pennsylvania State University, University Park, Pennsylvania

Aaron B. Frank, BAE Systems Advanced Information Technology, Arlington, Virginia

Greg Godfrey, Metron Incorporated, Reston, Virginia

Linda Gohari, Lockheed Martin Corporation, Bethesda, Maryland

Jennifer Golbeck, University of Maryland, College Park, Maryland

Michael Greenblatt, Metron Incorporated, Reston, Virginia

Seth A. Greenblatt, 21st Century Technologies, Austin, Texas

Ian R. Greenshields, University of Connecticut, Storrs, Connecticut

James Hendler, University of Maryland, College Park, Maryland

Mark Hoffman, ISX Corporation, Marietta, Georgia

Marecki Janusz, University of Southern California, Los Angeles, California

Jeff Jonas, IBM Corporation, Las Vegas, Nevada

Rashaad E. T. Jones, The Pennsylvania State University, University Park, Pennsylvania

John Karat, IBM Corporation, Las Vegas, Nevada

Brian Kettler, ISX Corporation, Arlington, Virginia

Paul Kogut, Lockheed Martin, Philadelphia, Pennsylvania

Mieczyslaw M. Kotar, Versatile Information Sytems, Inc., Framingham, Massachusetts

Mark Lazeroff, BAE Systems Advanced Information Technology, Arlington, Virginia

Jerzy J. Letkowski, Versatile Information Sytems, Inc., Framingham, Massachusetts

Yui Leung, Lockheed Martin, Philadelphia, Pennsylvania

John W. Lockwood, Washington University in St. Louis, St. Louis, Missouri

Ron Loui, Washington University, St. Louis, Missouri

Stuart E. Madnick, Massachusetts Institute of Technology, Cambridge, Massachusetts

Aaron Mannes, University of Maryland, College Park, Maryland

Sherry E. Marcus, 21st Century Technologies, Austin, Texas

Michael McNeese, The Pennsylvania State University, University Park, Pennsylvania

Tom Mifflin, Metron Incorporated, Reston, Virginia

Michael Nicholletti, Bolt, Beranek and Newman (BBN), Cambridge, Massachusetts

Douglas W. Oard, University of Maryland, College Park, Maryland

Krishna Pattipati, University of Connecticut, Storrs, Connecticut

Robert L. Popp, Aptima Incorporated, Woburn, Massachusetts, and formerly at Defense Advanced Research Projects Agency (DARPA)

Sanguthevar Rajasekaran, University of Connecticut, Storrs, Connecticut

Richard Rohwer, Fair Isaac Corporation, San Diego, California

Paul Rosenzwig, Heritage Foundation, Washington, DC

Kathleen M. Ryan, Lockheed Martin, Philadelphia, Pennsylvania

Desmond Saunders-Newton, BAE Systems Advanced Information Technology, Arlington, Virginia

Nathan Schurr, University of Southern California, Los Angeles, California

Brian J. Sharkey, Science Applications International Corporation, Arlington, Virginia

Hyong-Sop Shim, Telcordia Technologies, Piscataway, New Jersey

Michael D. Siegel, Massachusetts Institute of Technology, Cambridge, Massachusetts

Satnam Singh, University of Connecticut, Storrs, Connecticut

David B. Skillicorn, Queen's University, Kingston, Ontario, Canada

Shuang Sun, The Pennsylvania State University, University Park, Pennsylvania

Kim A. Taipale, Center for Advanced Studies in Science and Technology Policy, New York, New York

Milind Tambe, University of Southern California, Los Angeles, California

Haiying Tu, University of Connecticut, Storrs, Connecticut

Doyle Weishar, Science Applications International Corporation, Arlington, Virginia

Peter Willett, University of Connecticut, Storrs, Connecticut

John Yen, The Pennsylvania State University, University Park, Pennsylvania

Chapter 1

Utilizing Information and Social Science Technology to Understand and Counter the Twenty-First Century Strategic Threat

Robert L. Popp, David Allen, and Claudio Cioffi-Revilla

1.1. INTRODUCTION[1]

The world has changed dramatically since the Cold War, when there were only two super powers. During those years, the enemy was clear, and the United States was well-postured around a relatively long-term stable threat. The United States responded clearly, with a policy toward the Soviet threat that centered on deterrence, containment, and mutually assured destruction. To enforce this policy, the United States created a strategic triad comprised of nuclear intercontinental ballistic missiles, Trident nuclear submarines, and long-range strategic bombers.

Today, we are faced with a new world in which change is very rapid, and the enemy is asymmetric and poses a very different challenge: The threats today range from irregular adversaries to catastrophic weapons to rogue states. We believe there is a twenty-first-century analog of the strategic triad comprised of failed states, Weapons of Mass Destruction (WMD) proliferation, and global terrorism—the convergence of which represents the greatest modern-day strategic threat to our national security interests (see Figure 1.1).

In this new century, the adversaries seek to paralyze nation states by employing unconventional methods and WMD (nuclear, biological, chemical). These new adversaries are asymmetric, transnational terrorists, insurgents, criminals, warlords, smugglers, drug syndicates and rogue WMD proliferators. They are indistinguishable from, as well as intermingled among, the local civilian population. They are not part of an organized conventional military force, but instead are collections of loosely organized people who have

---

[1]This section is based on a speech given by Dr. Robert Popp at DARPATech 2005 (http://www.darpa.mil/darpatech2005/presentations/ixo/popp.pdf) and published in: Popp, R. (2005), "Utilizing Social Science Technology to Understand and Counter the 21st Century Strategic Threat," *IEEE Intelligent Systems*, vol. 20, no. 5, pp. 77–79.

Emergent Information Technologies and Enabling Policies for Counter-Terrorism. Edited by Popp and Yen
Copyright © 2006 The Institute of Electrical and Electronics Engineers, Inc.

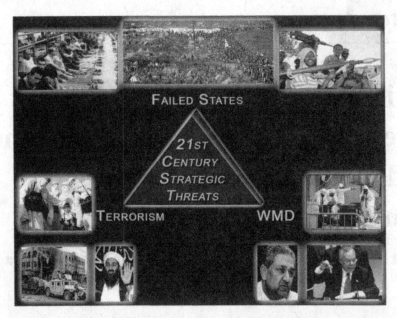

Figure 1.1. Twenty-first-century strategic threat triad.

formed highly adaptive (and difficult to identify) webs based on tribal, cultural or religious affinities. These new adversaries move freely throughout the world, hide when necessary, and conduct quasi-military operations using instruments of legitimate activity found in any open or modern society. They make extensive use of the Internet, cell phones, the press, schools, mosques, hospitals, commercial vehicles, and financial systems. These new adversaries do not respect the Geneva Conventions or the time-honored rules of war. They see WMD not as a weapon of last resort, but instead as an equalizer and a weapon of choice. These new adversaries perpetuate religious radicalism, violence, hatred, and chaos. They find unpunished and oftentimes unidentifiable sponsorship and support, operate in small independent cells, strike infrequently, and utilize weapons of mass effect and the media's response to influence governments. And, finally, they seek safe haven and harbor in weak, failing, and *failed* states (Benjamin and Simon, 2002).

What do we mean by failed states? Failed states have cultures and world views that are vastly different from those of the rest of the world. In today's increasingly interconnected world, they pose an acute risk to world security. Failed states facilitate the routine brutalization and repression of their own people. They reject basic human values and are less concerned with international order and more with lawlessness, demagoguery, hatemongering and thuggery. Failed states are internally divided along ethnic, religious and ideological lines, and they are ruled by thugs who act not in the interests of their citizenry but instead to settle scores, kill those who oppose them, and retaliate against perceived humiliations. Failed states, like the threats they harbor, see the acquisition of WMD technology as empowering and essential to their own prestige on the world stage. Failed states provide breeding grounds for terrorists, narcotics trade, black marketeering, human slavery, weapons trafficking, and other forms of nefarious activity. In failed states, the population suffers in a climate of fear, institutional deterioration, social deprivation, and economic despair (Rotberg, 2004).

With the emergence of this new strategic triad comes the need to understand the dynamics of the nexus among failed states, WMD, and global terrorism. It is not sufficient to simply predict where a nation might fight next and how a future conflict might unfold. The United States can no longer simply prepare for wars it would prefer to fight, but must now prepare for those it will need to fight. The new strategy requires that nations make every effort to prevent hostilities and disagreements from developing into a full scale armed confrontation. This in turn requires applying political, military, diplomatic, economic, and numerous other social options to gain the necessary understanding of the cultures and motivations of potential adversaries and noncombatants. Indeed, nations need to be able to shape the attitudes and opinions of entire societies, with predictable outcomes. Recent experience in Iraq and Afghanistan has shown that military success in pre- and post-conflict stability operations requires a deep social awareness of the threat and of the operational environments in which they reside. Indeed, managing successful stability and reconstruction operations requires just as much social awareness as it does military combat savvy.

The ballistic missiles and conventional intelligence, surveillance and reconnaissance (ISR) systems that were so effective at ending the Cold War are no longer sufficient, nor well-suited, to countering the new twenty-first-century strategic threat. These new threats, who are willing to accept almost any degree of risk to achieve their objectives—often under the false pretext of religion—are able to foil conventional surveillance systems. In many instances, the decisive terrain in twenty-first-century warfighting is the vast majority of noncombatants who are not directly involved in the fighting, but whose support, willing or coerced, is critical to influence. Winning over the hearts and minds of the local population by providing aid to improve their lives is equally as important (and can no longer be subordinated) to projecting military force or capturing and killing the enemy.

How does the United States implement this new strategy? We believe the way forward is clear. It does not involve spending hundreds of billions of dollars procuring more conventional Cold War oriented ISR or high-profile weapons systems to gain incremental improvements in precision, speed, or bandwidth. What is needed is a strategy that leads to a greater cultural awareness and thorough social understanding of the threats comprising the new strategic triad as well as the surrounding environment for which they reside.

What technologies must we then develop to understand and influence nation states, societies, thugs and terrorists, WMD proliferators, and zealots in failed states? We believe two of the key emergent (and strategic) technology areas lies in the (i) information technologies, and (ii) interdisciplinary quantitative and computational social science (Q/CSS) technologies from political science, economics, mathematics, statistics, operations research, computer science, cultural anthropology, psychology, and sociology. The focus of this chapter is to survey some of the recent research and development (R&D) work in these two areas; the remaining chapters provide much more detail on these technologies.

One of the major technical challenges today involves detecting terrorists, terrorist cells, and WMD proliferators whose identities and whereabouts we do not always know a priori. In order to preempt terrorists or WMD proliferators from engaging in adverse actions against the United States, we believe they must be detected and identified by looking for instances of known or emerging patterns (signatures) that are indicative of their plans, plots, and activities. Terrorism and WMD proliferation are considered a low-intensity/low-density form of warfare; however, terrorist plots and WMD proliferation will leave an information signature, albeit not one that is easily detected. As it has been widely reported about the 9/11 plot and the misdeeds of the Pakistani WMD scientist A.Q.

Khan, detectable clues have been left in the information space—the significance of which, however, is generally not understood until after the fact (Popp, 2004). The goal then is to empower intelligence analysts with information technologies and tools to detect and understand these clues long before the fact so that appropriate measures can be taken by decision- and policy-makers to preempt them.

Another major technical challenge today involves assessing, anticipating and forecasting the onset of instability and conflict within nation states. A prime safe haven and breeding ground for terrorists, WMD proliferation and other forms of nefarious activity are weak, fragile and failed states. As the Administration has clearly indicated in its national security strategy, ". . . we will pursue nations that provide aid or safe haven to terrorism . . . any nation that continues to harbor or support terrorism will be regarded by the United States as a hostile regime" (Bush, 2006). The preconditions, root causes and symptoms that give rise to instability and conflict within nation states are inherently dynamic, non-linear, and non-deterministic; understanding and modeling these dynamics is not easily reduced or amenable to classical analytical methods. To date, very little R&D in this area has been utilized by intelligence analysts and military planners to mitigate the deleterious effects that weak, fragile and failed states have on our national security interests. We believe there is a wide range of non-linear and non-deterministic Q/CSS models and tools that can be meaningfully applied in an objective, unbiased, systematic and methodological approach to investigate human social phenomena and understand the preconditions that give rise to instability and conflict within nation states. The goal is to provide intelligence analysts, regional planners and country desk officers with Q/CSS technologies to anticipate the onset of instability and conflict—long before it occurs—so that appropriate measures can be taken by decision-makers to mitigate their effects.

The rest of this chapter is organized as follows. In Section 1.2, we discuss a variety of information technologies we consider critical for counter-terrorism. In Section 1.3, we discuss a variety of Q/CSS technologies we consider critical for nation state instability and conflict analysis. In Section 1.4 we provide a summary.

1.2. INFORMATION TECHNOLOGIES FOR COUNTER-TERRORISM[2]

There are many technology challenges, but perhaps few are more important than how to make sense out of and connect the relatively few and sparse "dots" embedded within massive amounts of information flowing into the government's intelligence and counter-terrorism agencies. Information technology plays a crucial role in overcoming this challenge and is a major tenet of our national and homeland security strategies. The United States government's intelligence and counter-terrorism agencies are responsible for absorbing this massive amount of information, processing and analyzing it, converting it to actionable intelligence, and disseminating it, as appropriate, in a timely manner. It is vital that the United States enhance its Cold War capabilities by exploiting its superiority in information technology by creating vastly improved tools to find, translate, link, evaluate, share, analyze and act on the relevant information faster than ever.

Figure 1.2 identifies some of the key information technology areas we consider crucial for counter-terrorism, namely: collaboration; analysis and decision aides; foreign lan-

[2]This section is based on work published in Popp et al. (2004).

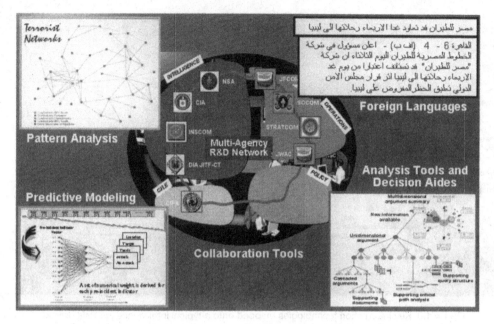

Figure 1.2. Critical information technology thrust areas for counter-terrorism.

guages; pattern analysis; and predictive (or anticipatory) modeling. In this chapter we will only highlight these areas; however, the other chapters in this book as well as Popp et al. (2004; 2005) provides much more discussion on these technology areas.

Figure 1.3 shows how the information technology areas map onto a typical intelligence analysis process. These technologies will (a) allow analysts to (i) search, query, and exploit vastly more foreign (multi-lingual) speech and text than would otherwise be possible by human transcribers and translators alone, (ii) automatically extract entities and entity-relationships from massive amounts of unstructured data, (iii) create models (and discover instances) of terrorist-related relationships and patterns of activities among those entities, and (iv) collaborate, reason, and share information and analyses so that analysts can hypothesize, test, and propose theories and mitigating strategies about plausible futures so that (b) decision- and policy-makers can effectively evaluate the impact of current or future policies and prospective courses of action.

To motivate the critical importance (and promise) of these information technologies, we describe some R&D work and results recently obtained through experiments via partnerships between DARPA and several entities within the United States intelligence and counter-terrorism community. The purpose of the experiments was for intelligence analysts to assess the merits of several DARPA-sponsored advanced information technology developments applied to various foreign intelligence problems. The experiments involved real intelligence analysts solving real foreign intelligence problems using their own lawfully collected foreign intelligence data. DARPA provided several information technology tools to be evaluated, namely, a peer-to-peer collaboration tool, several structured argumentation modeling and decision aides, foreign language tools for audio searching/indexing and text and audio filtering/categorization, and statistical graph-based pattern analysis tools.

As Figure 1.4 shows, when doing traditional intelligence analysis, an analyst spends

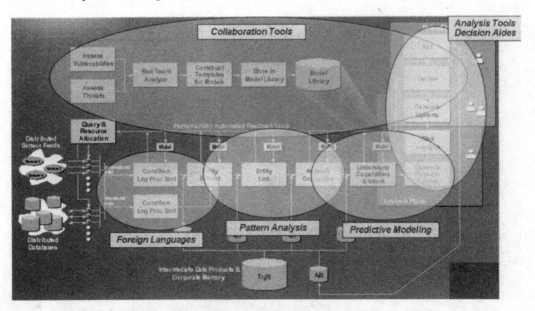

Figure 1.3. Key information technologies mapped onto a typical intelligence analysis process.

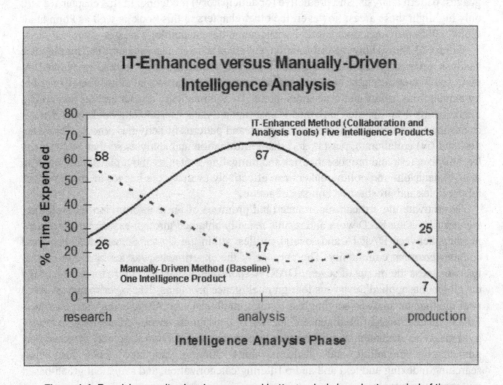

Figure 1.4. Promising results showing more and better analysis in a shorter period of time.

most of his time on the major processes broadly defined as research, analysis, and production. The dotted "bathtub curve" represents the distribution of time one typically sees.[3] This shows that analysts spend too much time doing research (i.e., searching, harvesting, reading, and preprocessing data for analysis), too much time doing production (i.e., turning analytical results into reports and briefings for the decision-maker), and too little time doing analysis (i.e., thinking about the problem). The objective of the experiment was to see if intelligence analysis could be improved through information technology by reversing this trend and inverting the bathtub curve.

In this experiment, the intelligence question the analysts were tasked to analyze was "What is the threat posed by Al Qaeda's WMD capabilities to several cities in the United States?" The data were drawn from a variety of classified intelligence sources, foreign news reports, and Associated Press (AP) and other wire services.

The results of the experiment show an inverted bathtub curve, allowing for more and better analysis in a shorter period of time, as a result of analysts using the information technologies we indicated above to aid their analysis. The results also included an impressive savings in analyst labor (i.e., half as many analysts were used for the analysis), and five reports were produced in the time it ordinarily took to produce just one. The time spent in the research phase was dramatically reduced by using the collaboration tool across multiple agencies to harvest and share pertinent data for the intelligence question at hand, as well as using foreign language tools to transcribe and translate the foreign news and wire service data.

1.2.1. Collaboration Tools

Collaboration tools allow humans and machines to analyze (think) and solve complicated and complex problems together more efficiently and effectively. Combating the terrorist threat requires all elements and levels of the government to share information and coordinate operations—no one organization now has or will ever have all the needed information or responsibility for countering terrorism. Besides breaking down stovepipes, collaboration is also about sharing information (as applicable and allowable), sharing of thinking, and sharing of analyses. This entails sharing multiple perspectives and conflictive argument, and embracing paradox—all of which enable humans to "think outside of the box" to find the right perspective lenses through which to properly understand the contextual complexity where correct meaning is conveyed to data.

A key purpose for collaboration tools is to permit the formation of high-performance agile teams from a wide spectrum of organizations. These tools support both top-down, hierarchically-organized and directed, "center-based" teams, as well as bottom-up, self-organized and directed ad-hocracies—"edge-based' collaboration. An emergent capability is for these two modes of operation to seamlessly co-exist and interoperate—"center-edge" hybrid collaboration—overcoming difficult semantic challenges in data consistency and understanding, and the personal preferences, intellectual capital, multi-dimensional knowledge and tacit understanding of a problem by numerous analysts.

Spurred on by recent intelligence failures, an "emergent" function for collaboration tools is to enable and reinvent the intelligence analyst—policy-maker interface: As Secretary of Defense Rumsfeld has indicated, policy-makers must not simply be passive con-

---

[3]To interpret the curve, each value denotes the percentage of time—out of 100% total—an analyst spends on the three processes of research, analysis, and production.

sumers of intelligence. Instead, senior policy-makers must "engage analysts, question their assumptions and methods, seek from them what they know, what they don't know, and ask them their opinions" (Shanker, 2003). Because the current policy/intelligence interface model was developed in the Cold War era during a time of information scarcity (unlike today's information abundant environment), some of the basic assumptions that underlie it are no longer valid. Novel technology is needed to reinvent the interface, allowing for intelligence that is aggressive vice cautious, intuitive vice simply fact-based, metaphor-rich vice concrete, peer-to-peer vice hierarchical, precedent-shattering vice precedent-based, and opportunistic vice warning-based.

Chapters 6–14 of this book address these and many others aspects of collaboration, and we encourage the readers to peruse these chapters.

1.2.2. Analysis Tools and Decision Aides

Analysis tools and decision aides are what transform the massive amounts of data flowing into the government's intelligence and counter-terrorism community into intelligence. Many of these tools ostensibly address some aspect of the "cognitive hierarchy," the goal being to transform data (discriminations between states of the world) into information (dots or evidence which is data put into context by analysts) into knowledge (useful and actionable information to decision-makers).

A fundamental purpose for these tools is to amplify the human intellect. To deal effectively with the terrorist threat, it is not sufficient for well-informed analysts to simply communicate and share data. The counter-terrorism problem is an intrinsically difficult one that is only compounded by an unaided human intellect. Analysts and analytical teams are beset by cognitive biases and limitations that have been partially responsible for some serious intelligence failures (Heuer, 1999). Analysts must be given assistance in the form of structured argumentation tools and methodologies to amplify their cognitive abilities and allow them to think better (Schum, 1994).

Another purpose for these tools is to understand the present, imagine the future and generate plausible scenarios and corresponding actionable options for the decision-maker. It is not enough to simply "connect the dots." The fact that the dots are indeed connected must be persuasively explained and communicated to decision-makers. Traditional methods—briefings and reports—lack on both counts, and they demand a significant amount of analysts' time to produce (recall the bathtub curve in Figure 1.4). Explanation-generation and storytelling technology is critical to producing traditional products as well as making possible newer forms of intelligence products.

Again, spurred on by recent intelligence failures, an "emergent" need for analysis tools and decision aides is to work within a virtual organizational and team framework where concomitant policies and supporting processes are automatically generated, enforced and managed. The United States is a nation of laws, and all activities of government are conducted within the bounds of existing laws, policies, processes and procedures. But this regime of regulation and procedures varies across the wide variety of organizations that must work together "virtually" to counter today's threats. Tools are needed to allow policy to be unambiguously defined and understood at all levels, to permit virtual organizations and teams—especially ad-hoc peer teams—to reconcile their differing policies into a single coherent policy regime, to consistently and reliably apply that policy regime to its operations, and to identify any deviations from policy to prevent abuses.

The body of work on analysis tools and decision aides is vast and beyond the scope of this book to address at a sufficient level of detail, consequently we omitted it as a focus of the book. However, Chapters 20–22 touch on some of the policy challenges associated with analysis, and we encourage the readers to peruse these chapters.

1.2.3. Pattern Analysis

Many terrorist activities consist of illegitimate combinations of otherwise legitimate activities. For example, acquisition of demolition/construction site explosives, renting of vehicles, visiting high profile landmarks or other public building, and financing by external parties are all legitimate activities in some contexts. However, if combined together or performed by individuals known to be associated with terrorist groups, further investigation may be warranted. While examples of terrorist activities are rare, examples of the component activities are not. Pattern analysis tools, therefore, must be able to detect instances of the component activities involving suspicious people, places, or things and then determine if the other components are present or not in order to separate those situations warranting further investigation from the far larger number that do not.

One key pattern analysis concept that enables "connecting the dots" is representing both data and patterns as graphs. Evidence and (terrorist plot) pattern graphs can be specified as graphs with nodes representing entities such as people, places, things, and events; edges representing meaningful relationships between entities; and attribute labels amplifying the entities and their connecting links. These highly-connected evidence and pattern graphs also play a crucial role in constraining the combinatorics and thereby overcoming the computational explosion challenges associated with iterative graph-processing algorithms such as directed search, matching, and hypothesis evaluation.

Advanced pattern analysis techniques allow for entity-relationship discovery, extraction, linking and creation of initial evidence graphs, which are typically sparse and comprised of entities and relationships extracted from textual narratives about suspicious activities, materials, organizations or people contained in large amounts of unclassified data sources such as public news and/or classified intelligence reports. From known or suspected suspicious entities, terrorist plot pattern graphs are created and used to guide a search through the evidence graph. Patterns can be obtained from intelligence analysts, subject matter experts, red teaming activities, or intelligence or law enforcement tips. Emergent statistical, knowledge-based, and graph-theoretic pattern analysis techniques are used to infer implicit links and to evaluate their significance. Search is constrained by expanding and evaluating partial matches from known starting points, rather than the alternative of considering all possible combinations. The high probability that linked entities will have similar class labels (often called autocorrelation or homophily) can be used to increase classification accuracy.

Complementing pattern analysis, knowledge discovery and pattern learning techniques can induce a pattern description from a set of exemplars. Such pattern descriptions can assist an analyst to discover unknown terrorist activities in data. These patterns can then be evaluated and refined before being considered for use to detect potential terrorist activity. Pattern learning techniques are also useful to enable adaptation to changes in terrorist behavior over time.

Chapters 4, 5 and 17–19 of this book address various aspects of pattern analysis, and we encourage the readers to peruse these chapters. In addition, interested readers can also find a good overview of some of the key technologies in Jensen and Goldberg (1998).

1.2.4. Foreign Languages

Foreign language speech and text are indispensable sources of intelligence. Foreign language data and their corresponding data providers are massive and growing in numbers every day; moreover, because the time to transcribe and translate foreign documents is so labor intensive, compounded by the lack of linguists with suitable language skills to review it all, much foreign language speech and text are never exploited for intelligence and counter-terrorism purposes. Considering it would be impossible to find, train, or pay enough qualified linguists given the sheer volume of data, the only feasible solution is to use new and powerful foreign language technology to allow English-speaking analysts to exploit and understand vastly more foreign speech and text than is possible today.

One of the key foreign language processing technologies is automatic transcription to produce rich, readable transcripts of foreign news broadcasts and conversations (over noisy channels and/or in noisy environments) despite widely-varying pronunciations, speaking styles, and subject matter. The two basic components of rich transcription are speech-to-text conversion (finding words) and metadata extraction (pulling out more information). Interested readers can find more information on basic speech-to-text technology in Young (1996). Recent achievements include word error rates of 26.3% and 19.1% at processing speeds of 7 and 8 times slower than real-time on Arabic and Chinese news broadcasts.

Another key foreign language processing technology is automatic translation. A key intelligence failure finding post 9/11 was the ill preparedness of the intelligence community to handle the challenge it faced in translating the vast amounts of foreign language data it collected. The challenges are numerous and daunting, and includes processing massive volumes of foreign text from an ever growing number of foreign data sources, large unconstrained vocabularies across languages, and numerous domains and languages with limited linguistic resources.

Other key emerging technologies include cross-lingual—language independent information retrieval to detect and discover the exact data in any language that an analyst seeks quickly, accurately (as well as monolingual retrieval), and to flag new data that may be of interest; automatic name extraction (or tagging) for any entity type; automatic summarization such as headline generation to substantially reduce the amount of text that an analyst has to read; and representational techniques that allow technology to be ported cheaply and easily to other languages and domains.

Chapter 15 of this book touches on some aspects of foreign languages, and we encourage the readers to peruse this chapter.

1.2.5. Predictive Modeling

There is a plethora of literature on predictive modeling as related to elements of the new strategic triad (Figure 1.1), such as predicting future terrorist group behaviors and terrorist plots, WMD proliferation, failed states and conflict analysis, and so on. Much of this work is based on exploiting a variety of promising approaches in statistics, neural networks, market-based techniques, artificial intelligence, Bayesian and Hidden Markov Model (HMM) approaches, system dynamics, multi-agent systems, behavioral sciences, red teams, and so on. Instead of tackling this subject here, we encourage interested readers to peruse chapters 1–3 and 16 of this book which cover this subject in more detail. We also encourage readers to read the next section of the book which is based on using quantitative and computational social science (Q/CSS) technologies for assessing and forecasting (predicting) nation state instability and conflict.

1.3. Q/CSS TECHNOLOGIES FOR NATION STATE INSTABILITY AND CONFLICT ANALYSIS

What is "quantitative/computational social science" (Q/CSS) and what new insights does it bring to the area of nation state instability and conflict analysis? How do we develop a sharper focus on "sociocultural awareness" of the adversaries of the twenty-first-century strategic triad and the corresponding operational environments with an emphasis on how Q/CSS can help accomplish this higher level of understanding? Specifically, how can Q/CSS facilitate an understanding of the adversary's societal interests, ideals, habits, beliefs, motives, intentions, social organizations, culture, political and religious symbols and icons? What kind of mission-critical "multidisciplinary research" is being performed by the Q/CSS community to help us understand, anticipate, and forecast the pre-conditions that give rise to instability, conflict, and failure within societies or nation states? The purpose of this section is to define, clarify, and dispel some common misconceptions about Q/CSS; and to describe some recent research and contributions from applying Q/CSS technologies to failed states and conflict analysis.

1.3.1. Social Science Background for Nation State Instability and Conflict Analysis

The main social science disciplines are anthropology, economics, political science, sociology, and psychology (Smelser and Baltes, 2001). Other social science specialties include communication, linguistics, international relations, social geography, management and organization, ethnography, environmental studies, public policy, and some parts of operations research. Social science investigates patterns of human phenomena that range—according to increasing scale or levels of analysis—from cognitive systems to groups, organizations, societies, nations, civilizations, and world systems (Singer, 1961; Wilemski and Resnick, 1999). Besides this range in "patterns of human phenomena"— microsocial to the macrosocial, or what some have called "consilience" (Day, 2004)—social science also employs multiple time scales ranging from milliseconds (brain activity) to many hundreds of thousands of years (human origins).

The rich knowledge base provided by modern social science means that several social sciences and subfields investigate multiple aspects of the twenty-first-century strategic threat triad (Figure 1.1). For instance, terrorism is investigated by political scientists, and similarly for state stability as described in Popp et al. (2006), and WMD proliferation (Berkowitz, 1985). Moreover, all three elements of the twenty-first-century strategic threat triad are also jointly investigated, such as the terrorism-WMD connection (Blum, 2005) or the terrorism-state failure link (Rotberg, 2003). Among the three elements, the theme of state performance/failure is arguably the most investigated (and challenging) component of the triad, based on the pioneering work of Easton (1979), and more recently O'Brien (2002) and Popp et al. (2006).

Nation state instability and conflict analysis is an interdisciplinary, multidisciplinary, and relatively more recent specialization across all the social sciences, such that each social science discipline comprises a practicing community of analysts. The terms "nation

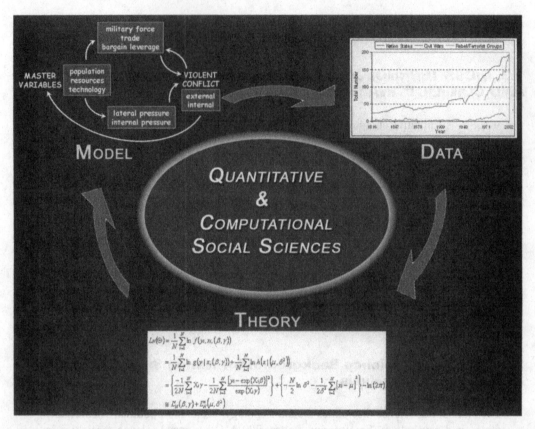

Figure 1.5. Quantitative and computational social sciences are based on fundamental theories, models and data.

state instability" and "conflict analysis" refer to the socio-cultural awareness of an adversary and/or their overall operational environment. Nation state instability and conflict analysis—especially the quantitative and mathematical approaches—have benefited from numerous contributions by scientists outside the social sciences, such as applied mathematics, physics, chemistry, biology, and computer science (Rapoport, 1983). All social science, whether quantitative or computational or not, includes both pure and applied variations, just like any other scientific discipline. Applied social science is focused on modeling, modifying or shaping the social world in one or more respects. As discussed next, Q/CSS also comprises pure and applied research exploiting a variety of theories, models, and data (see Figure 1.5).

1.3.2. Quantitative and Computational Social Science (Q/CSS) Primer

Q/CSS refers to the branch of science that investigates human social phenomena (cognition, conflict, decision-making, cooperation), at all levels of data aggregation (individual, group, societal, global), and is based on direct and intensive application of quantitative and computational theories, models, and methods (see Figure 1.5). Methodologically, Q/CSS refers to the investigation of social phenomena using the tools of modern comput-

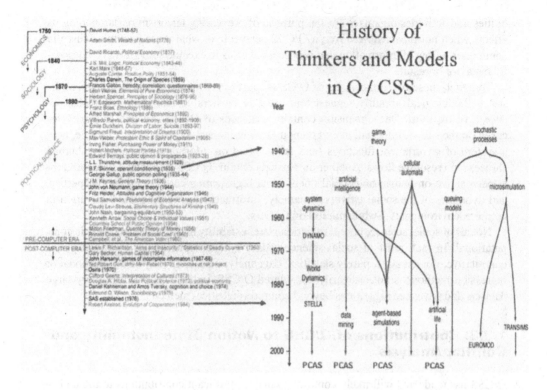

Figure 1.6. History of critical social science thinkers and recent Q/CSS developments.

ing or quantification methods in a mission-critical role for advancing the frontiers of knowledge about the social universe. Taken in this methodological sense, Q/CSS is any branch of social science that exploits the many quantification- and computer-based tools that exist today, including advanced quantitative statistical and econometric methods, event history analysis, artificial neural networks, wavelet analysis, content analysis, systems dynamics, geographic information systems (GIS), social network analysis (SNA), and multi-agent systems (MAS) or agent-based modeling (ABM). Figure 1.6 shows a nice history of some of the critical social science thinkers and recent Q/CSS developments. Today, these Q/CSS technologies also include social simulation and artificial societal environments for small- and large-scale systems limited only by available computing power.

Historically and substantively, Q/CSS refers to the rigorous and systematic analysis of information processing, data structures, control mechanisms, coordination strategies, optimization, energy budgets, behavioral variety, internal architecture, scheduling, implementation, adaptation and other computationally significant processes in human and social systems viewed as artificial systems on various scales (Simon, 1957). Some recent Q/CSS modeling applications include: (i) a national system of government as a complex adaptive societal system for dealing with emerging issues through policy and other measures; (ii) an extremist belief system as a cognitive structure that uses radical notions arrayed as concepts and associations to interpret information and assign meaning; (iii) an election, on any scale, as a computation of political preferences among a group of voters; and (iv) a counter-terrorism system as a set of computational information processes, capabilities and activities organized for the purpose of preventing terrorism or dampening its effects when not preventable. From a Q/CSS perspective, what these examples share in common is a flow of information that is processed so as to execute some form of purposeful behavior or result.

Together, these two dimensions of Q/CSS—pure versus applied, and substantive versus methodological—readily suggest four areas or clusters of computational social science investigations. One dimension contains instances of Q/CSS that are primarily focused on the role of information and computation in human societies—for example, how a system of government functions (and fails) based on information processing, human choices, and resource flows. Another dimension contains Q/CSS that offer a computational perspective on human and social phenomena highlighting certain entities, properties, and dynamics of the social universe—namely, information processing and adaptation in complex environments—while minimizing others.

Not all of social science, nor all of nation state instability and conflict analysis, is computational. In fact, most of social science today is noncomputational, even when it is quantitative. For example, purely statistical data analysis based mostly on correlational or regression methods is not ordinarily considered Q/CSS, unless it is based on very large datasets and advanced algorithms beyond common statistical methods.

1.3.3. Contributions of Q/CSS to Nation State Instability and Conflict Analysis

Q/CSS has made and will likely continue to make significant contributions to the understanding of nation state instability and conflict behavior as posed by the threats of the twenty-first-century strategic triad (Figure 1.1). Such knowledge is essential for understanding and anticipating the preconditions, root causes and symptoms that give rise to instability and conflict with nation states, and then mitigating their deleterious effects through shaping and other strategies by decision- and policy-makers. Just as in any other field of scientific inquiry, past contributions provide useful foundations for present and future research and capabilities.

1.3.3.1. Past Contributions for Nation State Instability and Conflict Analysis

Q/CSS contributions to nation state instability and conflict analysis during the past fifty years include the following:

- *Early-warning* (EW) *indicators* of warfare and potential conflict, based on quantitative information found in open source statistical datasets (O'Brien, 2002)
- Low-dimensionality *dynamical systems* of competing adversaries based on differential or difference equations (Turchin, 2003)
- *Markov models* to understand the structure, relative stability and long-term social dynamics of conflict processes (Schrodt, 2000)
- *Events data analysis,* based on abstracting and coding high-frequency streams of short-term interaction occurrences exchanged among adversaries (Hayes, 1973)
- *Semantic components analysis,* based on decomposition by evaluation, potency and activity in semantic EPA-space, by itself as content analysis, or paired with event data analysis (Osgood, 1975)

- *Large-scale econometric and system dynanmics models* of states and regions in the international systems (Choucri and North, 1975; Forrester, 1973)
- *Probabilistic models* of conflict processes, such as escalation, crises, onset, diffusion and termination of warfare and forms of violence (Dietrich, 2004)
- *Game-theoretic models,* based on the application of 2-person and n-person games to social situations with strategic interdependence (von Neumann and Morgenstern, 1944; Brams and Kilgour, 1988)
- *Expected utility models* based on Bayesian decision theory (Bueno de Mesquita and Lalman, 1994)
- *Control-theoretic models,* applying models from optimal control in dynamical systems (Simaan and Cruz, 1973)
- *Survival models* and *event history analysis,* based on modeling the hazard rate or intensity function of a social process, which are capable of integrating stochastic and causal variables into unified models of social dynamics (King, 1990)
- *Boolean models* based on often complex systems of necessary and sufficient triggers of conflict (Chan, 2003)

1.3.3.2. Recent Contributions for Nation State Instability and Conflict Analysis

There has been recent research to determine the utility and payoff of applying quantitative and computational social science (Q/CSS) models and tools to assess and forecast nation state instability and conflict. The motivation is "failed states"—a prime safe haven and breeding ground for terrorists, WMD proliferators, drug traffickers, arms dealers, black marketeers and other forms of nefarious activity. As the Administration has clearly indicated in its national security strategy, ". . . we will pursue nations that provide aid or safe haven to terrorism . . . any nation that continues to harbor or support terrorism will be regarded by the United States as a hostile regime" (Bush, 2006). This section describes the motivation and rationale for the Q/CSS models and mechanisms, and presents results from some of the models.

The preconditions, root causes and symptoms that give rise to instability and conflict with nation states are inherently dynamic, non-linear, and non-deterministic; understanding and modeling these dynamics is not easily reduced or amenable to classical analytical methods. To date, very little work within the DoD has been focused on addressing this problem, particularly, from an objective, unbiased, systematic and methodological approach.

In some of this research, Q/CSS researcher and practitioner teams developed and applied nation state instability models for different countries to assess their current stability levels as well as forecast their stability levels 6–12 months hence. The models ranged from systems dynamics, structural equations, cellular automata, Bayesian networks and hidden Markov models, and multi agent-based systems. In an effort to ensure the teams' assessments and forecasts were objective, unbiased, systematic and methodological (vice expert opinion elicitation), each team needed to develop a basic theory of nation state instability, build and refine their instability models based on those theories, process in their models a wide range of open-source text-based multi-lingual data, and then provide an interpretation of the model outputs and results. Recall Figure 1.5 illustrates the theory/mod-

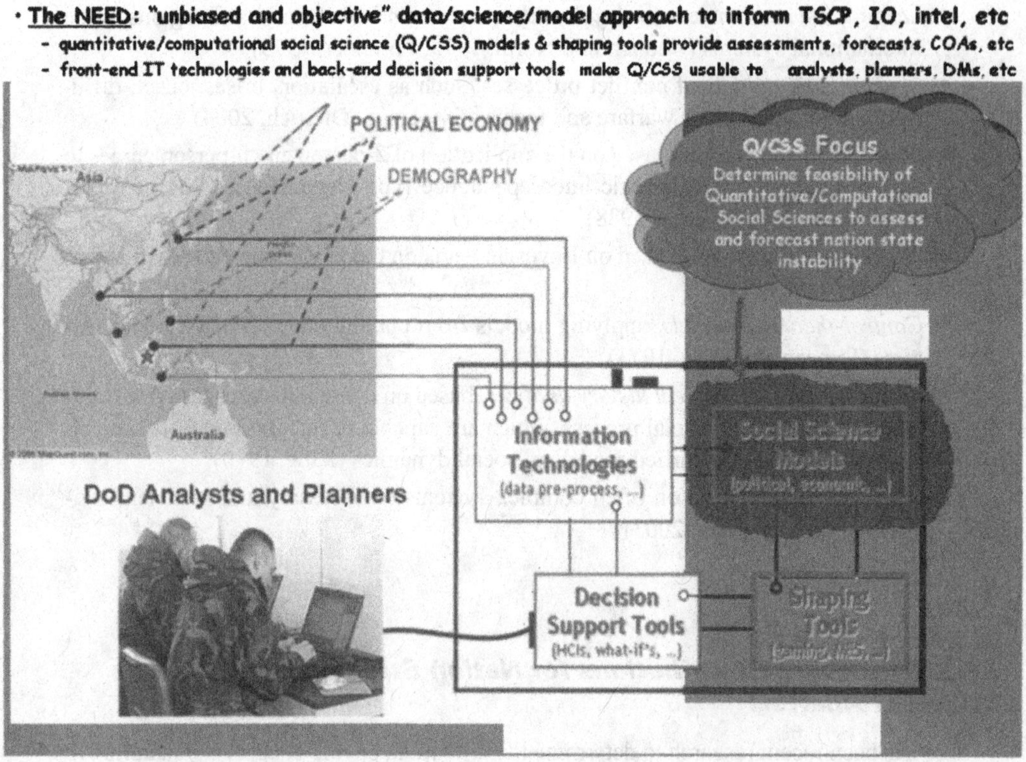

· **The NEED**: "unbiased and objective" data/science/model approach to inform TSCP, IO, intel, etc
   - quantitative/computational social science (Q/CSS) models & shaping tools provide assessments, forecasts, COAs, etc
   - front-end IT technologies and back-end decision support tools make Q/CSS usable to   analysts, planners, DMs, etc

Figure 1.7. Q/CSS focus and need in the context of a decision support framework.

el/data approach—this approach is paramount to assess the S&T merits and utility (or lack thereof) of the Q/CSS technology.

As depicted in Figure 1.7, operationally, the Q/CSS technologies would provide the intelligence community and/or the planning staff of a Regional Combatant Commander (RCC) with a decision support framework comprised of various Q/CSS models to assess, forecast, and ultimately inform the decision-makers about causes and events that may threaten United States interests abroad. Because the analysis of conflict and nation state instability is inherently complex and deeply uncertain, no one social science theory or Q/CSS model is sufficient. An ensemble of models—which contain more information than any single model—must be integrated within a single decision support framework to generate a range of plausible futures. Robust adaptive strategies—vice optimal ones—that hedge across these plausible futures will provide practical options for the decision-maker to consider. Within the right theoretical framework these models and decision support tools will provide strategic early warning capability and actionable options for the decision-maker.

Nor do we think it wise to define a universally accepted or consensus definition of state failure. Different social science perspectives yield different definitions, and as noted in Rotberg (2002), ". . . failed states are not homogeneous. The nature of state failure varies from place to place." Also pointed out in Rotberg (2002) is the problem of nation-state instability and failure as one of assessing the governance ability of a nation-state. By governance is meant the ability of a nation-state to provide the services its citizens and constituents require and expect in order to maintain order and conduct their daily lives. Such services include security, law enforcement, basic services and infrastructure, defense, education, and observation of human rights.

This research has explored a breadth of Q/CSS modeling techniques to see which ones had the greatest promise for assessing and forecasting a nation state's fragility. Again, the modeling approaches ranged from regressive and structural equations, cellular automata, politico-econometric models, Bayesian networks and Hidden Markov Models (HMMs), system dynamics, and agent-based models. In this section we will not provide a comprehensive description of all the Q/CSS models developed; instead, we will describe several models and refer interested readers to Popp et al. (2006) which provides a general survey of the models from several dimensions.

MIT System Dynamics Model: MIT developed a nation state fragility model using a System Dynamics approach (Forrester, 1958). Figure 1.8 depicts the top-level of their model. MIT's model is based on the theory of loads versus capacities. The problem is to determine and 'predict' when threats to stability override the resilience of the state and, more important, to anticipate propensities for 'tipping points', namely conditions under which small changes in anti-regime activity can generate major disruptions. Dissidents and insurgents create loads on the state, e.g., they draw down disproportionate amounts of resources that could otherwise be used to perform the governance functions.

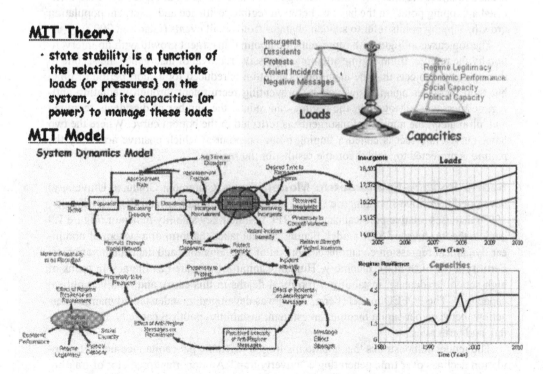

Figure 1.8. MIT systems dynamics model.

As people perceive this reduction in governance, they protest and, perhaps, riot or engage in acts of violence. These acts undermine overall political support for the government or regime, which shifts power balances. Counterbalancing the dissidents is regime resilience, which is the regime's ability to withstand shocks that lead to fragility and instability, and, possibly, dissolution of the state.

Increasingly, the evolution of thinking on sources of state stability and instability has converged on the critical importance of insurgents and the range of anti-regime activities that they undertake. The escalation of dissidents and insurgence is usually a good precursor to propensities for large scale instability if not civil war. By the same token, to the extent that the resilience of the regime is buttressed by requisite capabilities and attendant power and performance, the expansion of insurgency can be effectively limited. MIT focused on the problem of modeling the factors affecting the size of the insurgent population. They hypothesized that some portion of the population becomes disgruntled with the regime and turns to dissidence. Some smaller proportion is dissatisfied with regime appeasement and turns to insurgency and commits acts of violence. To reduce insurgent population, the regime needs to either remove the insurgents or reduce their recruitment rate.

Insurgents attempt to create more dissidents who become potential recruits for the insurgency. Through acts of violence and other incidents, insurgents send anti-regime messages to the population, which increases civil unrest and disgruntlement and leads to further disruption. Effective anti-regime messages reduce the capacity of a regime to govern. Such messages also create more disgruntlement by reinforcing the fervor of those who are already dissatisfied as well as encouraging the perception of those tending towards insurrection. To reduce the increase in recruitment of dissidents, MIT found that the regime needed to affect the intensity of the message rhetoric as depicted in Figure 1.8. MIT identified a "tipping point" in the balance between regime resilience and insurgent population growth. Tipping points refer to sudden changes from small events (Gladwell 2002).

The top curve in Figure 1.8 represents the nominal insurgent growth with no intervention by the regime. If the regime attempts aggressive removal of insurgents, the second to the top curve projects that the insurgent population is reduced for a short period of time, but then increases again. However, by preventing recruitment through mediating anti-regime messages all together, the regime can reduce the number of dissidents recruited and, ultimately, the number of insurgents as reflected in the bottom curve. Where the two latter curves intersect is called a tipping point—a point at which positive action by the regime is projected to yield favorable results for the regime.

Sentia Politico-Econometric Model: Sentia (Claremont Graduate University) developed a Politico-Econometric nation state fragility model termed POFED (Kugler, 1997) that uses relative political capacity (RPC) as their key stability indicator. Figure 1.9 depicts the top-level of their model. Sentia's model takes the form of a system of nonlinear dynamical regression equations comprised of five equations and dependent variables: Fertility b (or birth rate), Income y, Human Capital h (measured as literacy in terms of high school graduates), instability S (political deaths in this case), and relative political capacity X. The POFED model (Feng, 2000) was developed to understand dynamic interactions between per capita income, investment, instability, political capacity, human capital, and birth rates.

The model demonstrates that a nation is fragile when the per capita income of its population declines over time generating a "poverty trap." An important predictor of fragility is the extent to which government extracts resources from its population. Weak govern-

POFED Theory

- Economic Fragility is self reinforcing
- Growth leads to stability creating further growth
- Relative Political Capacity (RPC) is the key metric for (in)stability and growth
  - High and rising RPC insures stability
  - Low and declining RPC creates instability

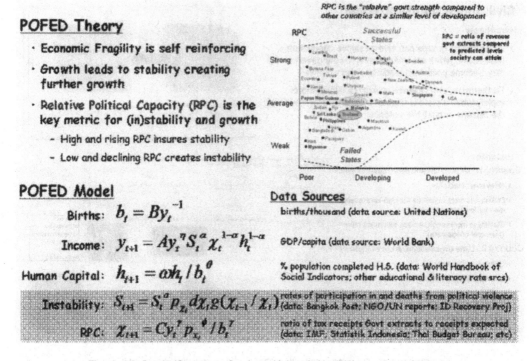

POFED Model

Births: $b_t = By_t^{-1}$

Income: $y_{t+1} = Ay_t^\eta S_t^a \chi_t^{1-\alpha} h_t^{1-\alpha}$

Human Capital: $h_{t+1} = \alpha h_t / b_t^\theta$

Instability: $S_{t+1} = S_t^a p_{z_t} d\chi_t g(\chi_{t-1} / \chi_t)$

RPC: $\chi_{t+1} = Cy_t^\phi p_{x_t}^\phi / b_t^\gamma$

Data Sources

births/thousand (data source: United Nations)

GDP/capita (data source: World Bank)

% population completed H.S. (data: World Handbook of Social Indicators; other educational & literacy rate srcs)

rates of participation in and deaths from political violence (data: Bangkok Post; NGO/UN reports; ID Recovery Proj)

ratio of tax receipts Govt extracts to receipts expected (data: IMF; Statistik Indonesia; Thai Budget Bureau; etc)

Figure 1.9. Sentia (Claremont Graduate University) politico-econometric model.

ments fall below average extraction levels obtained by similarly endowed societies, while robust societies extract more than one would anticipate from their economic endowment and allocate such resources to advance the government's priorities. Instability results from the interaction between economic and political performance. Weakening states decline in their ability to extract resources but still perform above expectations while fragile states under-perform relative to others at comparable levels of development, continuing to lose ground in relative terms. Finally, strengthening states are still relatively weak but begin to gain in relation to their relative cohort. In general assistance provided to strong or strengthening states will have positive effects on stability, while similar contributions to weak and to a lesser degree weakening states will be squandered.

The RPC X is the ability of the government to extract resources (usually measured in dollars, for example) from the country through various means taxes, labor, military service, etc. The instability S, measured in deaths, reflects the level of political violence and anti-regime sentiment in the country. An RPC of zero is the norm, e.g., it indicates the government is acting in a nominal capacity compared to other countries that have been assessed using these techniques. A negative RPC indicates that a government is underperforming and weak, while a positive RPC indicates that a government is efficiently extracting resources. Figure 1.9 depicts the RPC computed over numerous countries.

Computing the RPC for a country allows us to determine the tendency of a particular country toward behavior that could lead to state failure. The accompanying instability metric, based on violent incidents, provides a metric for assessing the resilience of the country to insurgency and to natural disaster events that undermine the state's ability to govern. In country A, we determined that a decline in political capacity or income can

Civil Unrest Diffusion Model

Hypothesis

▶ When salient groups perceive a relative deprivation, grievances, which are unaddressed by the government, may become politicized leading to civil violence

▶ Furthermore, civil violence is likely to diffuse more rapidly when a state is unable to satisfy the demands of the citizens or quell the violence

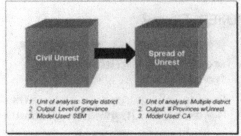

Insights

Country 1: A Lot of Organization, Little Violence

▶ Grievance: Inequality

▶ Diffusion is more important for high-level events than for low-intensity events

▶ Stability is increasing (perhaps becoming more Democratic/legitimate)

Country 2: Little Organization, A Lot of Violence

▶ Grievance: Diversity

▶ Events are highly volatile

   – Rate of diffusion is high regardless of event intensity

▶ Stability is decreasing (moving from a multi-party to a single party system)

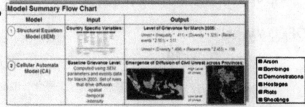

Figure 1.10. Booz Allen Hamilton (BAH) civil unrest diffusion model.

have damaging effects on accelerating instability, however these effects will be minimal. The model anticipates a threshold effect: if the economy falters, instability is expected to rise swiftly but then halt. Long-term serious instability is associated with political rather than economic decline. In country B, declines in current levels of political capacity could have a very large impact on instability. POFED shows that positive political actions and economic advancement have marginal effects on stability, while potential declines will accelerate the decline of stability—consistent with the political assessment that country B is a strengthening society that is improving a weak political base.

Booz Allen Hamilton (BAH) Civil Unrest Diffusion Model: BAH developed a Structural Equation and Cellular Automata model for nation state fragility that simulated how civil unrest diffuses through a population. Figure 1.10 depicts the top-level of their model. When salient groups within a population perceive deprivation, their grievances, when unaddressed by the government, can lead to riots, intense protests, and ultimately to political violence. If the state is unable to meet the demands of the populace, the unrest will spread. The speed and breadth with which the unrest spreads across the state can affect state stability. To model the level of civil unrest, a set of structural equations describing civil unrest at the district level were developed that yielded six key parameters (see Figure 1.10).

The structural equation models were derived by first characterizing prior acts of civil unrest. Multiple data sets and series of violent events from over fifty sources, including newspapers and news reports, were collected and coded. The event intensities (e.g., nonviolent demonstrations, bombings, riots, hostage takings, shootings, etc.) were scored for each data item used in the subsequent model, and then an overall grievance score was cal-

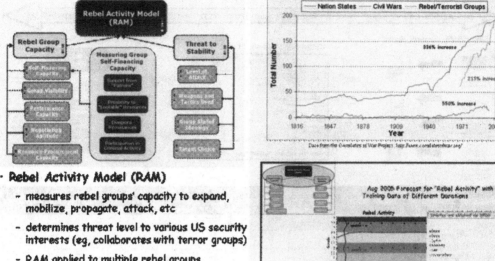

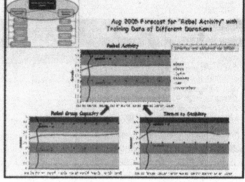

- **Rebel Activity Model (RAM)**

  - measures rebel groups' capacity to expand, mobilize, propagate, attack, etc

  - determines threat level to various US security interests (eg, collaborates with terror groups)

  - RAM applied to multiple rebel groups

    - communists, socialists, separatists (GAM, GMIP, PULO, BRN), Islamic extremist (JI), ...

  - RAM indicators are both quantitative and qualitative; indicators and state stability propagated via HMMs and Bayesian Nets

Figure 1.11. Qualtech Systems—SAIC rebel activity model.

culated for each district. These scores (and parameters) were then used to seed a cellular automata model that estimates the probability of diffusion of unrest across the population. It yields a probability of occurrence of the types of events depicted in Figure 1.10. In the simulation BAH, in general, unrest intensifies and spreads the more violent its events become.

Qualtech Systems—SAIC Rebel Activity Model: This team developed a Rebel Activity Model (RAM) for nation state fragility that is based on Bayesian networks (BN) and Hidden Markov Models (HMMs). Figure 1.11 depicts the top-level of their model. The RAM model ostensibly measures the amount of rebel activity by separatist groups, insurgent and terrorist groups, Islamic extremists, and other nefarious groups within a country.

As depicted in Figure 1.11, the RAM model postulates that the level of rebel activity in a nation state is influenced by two higher level indicators: Rebel Group Capacity, and Threat to Stability. These two higher-level indicators are modeled as discrete-state HMM random processes with five states: (calm, noteworthy, caution, severe, critical). The Rebel Group Capacity sub-indicator is influenced by five lower level indicators: Self-Financing Capacity, Group Visibility, Performance Capacity, Negotiating Aptitude, and Resource Procurement Capacity (e.g., weapons, WMD, etc). The Threat to Stability sub-indicator is influenced by four lower level indicators: Level of Attack, Weapons and Tactics Used, Group Stated Ideology, and Target Choice (e.g., US targets, local targets, etc). The dynamics of each of the nine lower level indicators is modeled as a discrete-state HMM random process with the same five states as mentioned. The observation at each sampling

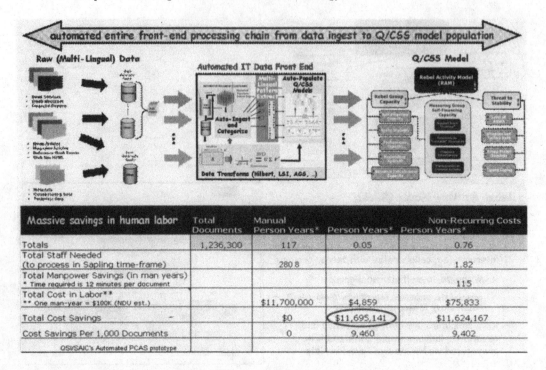

Figure 1.12. Automated front-end data processing pipeline.

time (e.g., daily, weekly, monthly, etc) is one of six-values (corresponding to the same five states as above plus one additional state that corresponds to insufficient data). The probabilistic relationships among the three top nodes (Rebel Activity, Rebel Group Capacity, Threat to Stability) is modeled as a Bayesian network. The HMMs and BNs compute posterior probability mass functions for each of the indicators as they process data over time.

This team also developed a novel emergent IT-based multi-lingual front-end system that automatically ingests, transforms, extracts, and auto-populates the RAM model from massive amounts of text data (i.e., over 1 million English documents and 2300 foreign documents) in near real-time (six documents per second). Figure 1.12 provides a description of the architecture and some of the results.

The HMMs in the RAM model automatically receive their data from a Linguistic Pattern Analyzer (LPA) after the data is first ingested, transformed and categorized into a numerically-encoded language independent format based on a Hilbert engine. Each data item is probabilistically rated by the LPA for relevance to an HMM indicator based on a set of pre-defined phrases. To determine an indicator value, the LPA searches through a document for the set of phrase (or a subset of it) associated with the indicator. Based on the subset of phrases present in the document, a preliminary indicator value is computed. This value is later updated via weighted averaging and quantized into six levels, ranging from 0–5. The weights associated with the phrases are context-dependent, and also depend on the frequencies of occurrence. The quantization levels of indicator ratings are as described previously: insufficient data, calm, noteworthy, caution, severe, critical. The documents can be processed and analyzed on daily basis, weekly, monthly, and so on.

To wrap up this section, recent research has demonstrated the utility of Q/CSS models to address nation state instability, and a variety of Q/CSS models at different levels of granularity and drawn from different social science disciplines were useful to represent and model the numerous causes and effects affecting nation state fragility. An access-controlled website for some of this research exists that archives the extensive amount of work and documentation created in the program. For those readers interested in the material they should contact the first author of this chapter to get an account.

SUMMARY

In this chapter we surveyed a variety of information and quantitative/computational social science (Q/CSS) technologies for counter-terrorism and failed states analysis, respectively, both of which are key elements of the new twenty-first-century strategic triad. Research and experiments such as those described in this chapter will help validate the merits and utility of these technologies. Ultimately, these technologies will enable analysts, planners, decision- and policy-makers to come together to collaborate, translate, find, link, evaluate, share, model, analyze, and act on the right information faster than ever before to detect and prevent terrorist attacks against the United States, as well as mitigate the deleterious effects that failed states have on U.S. national security interests.

National and homeland security institutions have yet to systematically exploit the extant and emergent body of information and Q/CSS technologies that exist for combating elements of the twenty-first-century strategic threat triad (Figure 1.1). From a national security perspective—given sufficient resources as well as a coordinated design—the combined application of these and other mature components of information and Q/CSS technologies could provide government with an unprecedented technical capability for understanding the world and enlightening our policy towards it. Such a capability could be arguably comparable for the post-Cold War world as the physical sciences were during the Cold War.

REFERENCES

Benjamin, D., and Simon, S. (2002). *The Age of Sacred Terror*. New York, Random House.

Berkowitz, B. (1985). Proliferation, deterrence, and the likelihood of nuclear war. *Journal of Conflict Resolution* 29(1):112–136.

Blum, A., Asal, V., and Wilkenfeld, J. (2005). Nonstate actors, terrorism, and weapons of mass destruction. *International Studies Review* 7(1):133–170.

Brams, S. J., and Kilgour, D. M. (1988). *Game Theory and National Security*. New York: Basil Blackwell.

Bueno de Mesquita, B., and Lalman, D. (1994). *War and Reason : Domestic and International Imperatives*. New Haven, CT: Yale University Press.

Bush, G. (2006). Address to a Joint Session of Congress and the American People, United States Capitol, Washington, D.C.

Chan, S. (2003). Explaining War Termination: A Boolean Analysis of Causes. *Journal of Peace Research* 40:49–66.

Choucri, N., and North, R. C. (1975). *Nations in Conflict: National Growth and International Violence*. San Francisco: W. H. Freeman and Company.

Day, R. H. (2004). Consilience, Economic Theory, and the Legacy of Herbert A. Simon. *Models of a Man: Essays in Memory of Hebert A. Simon,* M. Augier and J. G. March (eds.). Cambridge, MA: MIT Press.

Dietrich, F. (2004). Terrorism Prevention: A General Model. Konstanz, Germany. University of Konstanz.

Easton, D. (1979). *A Systems Analysis of Political Life.* Chicago: University of Chicago Press.

Feng, Y, Kugler, J., and Zak, P. (2000). "The Politics of Fertility and Economic Development," International Studies Quarterly (44, 2).

Forrester, J.W. (1958). "Industrial Dynamics—A Major Breakthrough for Decision Makers" Harvard Business Review, 36(4), 37-66.

Forrester, J. W. (1973). *World Dynamics.* Cambridge, MA: Wright-Allen Press.

Gladwell, M. (2002). "The Tipping Point," Little Brown.

Hayes, R. E. (1973). Identifying and measuring changes in the frequency of event data. *International Studies Quarterly* 17 (4):471–493.

Heuer, R. Jr. (1999). *Psychology of Intelligence Analysis.* Center for the Study of Intelligence, Central Intelligence Agency.

Jensen, D., and Goldberg, H. (eds.) (1998). *Artificial Intelligence and Link Analysis: Papers from the 1998 AAAI Fall Symposium,* Menlo Park, CA: AAAI Press.

King, G., Alt, J. E., Burn, N. E., and Laver, M. (1990). A unified model of cabinet dissolution in parliamentary democracies. *American Journal of Political Science* 34 (3):846-871.

Kugler, J., and Arbetman, M. (eds.) (1997). *Political Capacity and Economic Behavior.* Boulder, CO: Westview Press.

O'Brien, S. P. (2002). Anticipating the Good, the Bad, and the Ugly: An Early Warning Approach to Conflict and Instability Analysis. *Journal of Conflict Resolution* 46(6):808–828.

Osgood, C. E., May, W. H., and Miron, M. S. (1975). *Cross-Cultural Universals of Affective Meaning.* Urbana, Illinois: University of Illinois Press.

Popp, R. L., Armour, T., Senator, T., and Numrych, K. (2004). "Countering Terrorism through Information Technology," *Communications of the ACM,* vol. 47, no. 3, pp. 36–43.

Popp, R. L. (2005). "Exploiting AI, Information and Computational Social Science Technology to Understand the Adversary," *AAAI Spring Symposium on AI Technologies for Homeland Security,* Stanford University, CA.

Popp, R., Kaisler, S., Allen, D., Cioffi-Revilla, C., Carley, K., Azam,, Russell, A., Choucri, N, and Kugler, J. (2006). " Assessing Nation-State Instability and Failure," IEEE Aerospace Conference, Big Sky, MO.

Rapoport, A. (1983). *Mathematical Models in the Social and Behavioral Sciences.* New York: John Wiley & Sons.

Report of the Joint Inquiry into the Terrorist Attacks of September 11, 2001, House Permanent Select Committee on Intelligence (HPSCI) and the Senate Select Committee on Intelligence (SSCI), July 2003.

Rotberg, R. L. (2002). "Failed States in a World of Terror," Foreign Affairs, 81(4):127–133.

Rotberg, R. L. (ed.) (2003). *State Failure and State Weakness in a Time of Terror.* Washington, D.C.: Brookings Institution Press.

Rotberg, R. L. (ed.) (2004). "The Failure and Collapse of Nation-States: Breakdown, Prevention, and Repair," *When States Fail: Causes and Consequences,* R. Rotberg , Princeton University Press, pp. 1 – 49.

Schrodt, P. A. (2000). Pattern Recognition of International Crises using Hidden Markov Models. In *Political Complexity,* edited by D. Richards. Ann Arbor, MI: University of Michigan Press.

Schum, D. (1994). *The Evidential Foundations of Probabilistic Reasoning,* Wiley, New York.

Shanker, T. (2003). "For Military Intelligence, a New Favorite Commando," *New York Times,* April 11.

Simaan, M., and Cruz, J. B. Jr. (1973). A Multistage Game Formulation of Arms Race and Control and its Relationship to Richardson's Model. In *Modeling and Simulation,* edited by W. G. Vogt and M. H. Mickle. Pittsburgh, Penn.: Instruments Society of America.

Simon, H. (1957). *Models of Man.* New York: John Wiley & Sons.

Singer, J. D. (1961). The Level of Analysis Problem in International Relations. In *The International System: Theoretical Essays,* K. Knorr and S. Verba (eds.). Princeton, N.J.: Princeton University Press.

Smelser, N. J., and Baltes, P. B. (eds.) (2001). *International Encyclopedia of the Social and Behavioral Sciences.* Oxford, UK: Pergamon.

Turchin, P. (2003). *Historical Dynamics: Why States Rise and Fall.* Princeton, NJ: Princeton University Press.

von Neumann, J., and Morgenstern, O. (1947). *The Theory of Games and Economic Behavior.* Princeton, N. J.: Princeton University Press.

Young, S. (1996). "Large Vocabulary Continuous Speech Recognition: A Review," Technical Report, Cambridge University Engineering Department, Cambridge, UK.

Chapter 2

Hidden Markov Models and Bayesian Networks for Counter-Terrorism

Krishna Pattipati, Peter Willett, Jeffrey Allanach, Haiying Tu, and Satnam Singh

2.1. INTRODUCTION

Information concerning the potential whereabouts and activities of terrorists can be extrapolated from the massive amount of intelligence reported daily to U.S. intelligence agencies. The events encapsulated in these reports—and, in particular, the sequence of these events—can be used to probabilistically infer the activities of terrorists. In this chapter, we are particularly interested in those events that pose a threat to our national security. Our purpose is, therefore, to detect and track likely instances of terrorist activities by analyzing the sources of data that contain partial and/or imperfect information about the identities of actors involved and their actions.

Throughout the chapter, we will refer to these types of data as "transactions." The most evident example—and likely the greatest source of information—is financial. Say, for example:

> A person makes repeated withdrawals of large sums of cash from the same bank but from different tellers. The money withdrawn was not only wired from a few small banks in different countries, but was deposited only a few hours prior. This person's identification revealed that he/she was a citizen of a foreign country known to harbor terrorists.

Note that the transactions themselves are not uncommon, but the fact that the same person is continually withdrawing money from different tellers may be suspicious. In addition, the repeated sequence of events, money deposited and then money withdrawn, implies that an even larger amount of money is potentially being transferred without being noticed. So, it is the sequence of transactions that suggests a reason to be concerned; it may or may not arise from nefarious activity, but ought to be flagged for more careful scrutiny. In this chapter, we discuss a novel approach to modeling terrorist activities such as these, and we introduce methods by which we can detect and track them.

Real-world processes, such as terrorist plots, are characterized as partially observable and uncertain signals. Their signals, or electronic signature, are a series of transactions such as those cited in the previous example. We assume here that the activities of terrorists are only partially observable for good reason, considering that they are able to blend in with civilians, maintain a low profile, and adapt their operations so as to evade detection by law enforcement. In this way, terrorists can limit the "strength" of their signals by limiting the number of transactions that can be traced, and therefore they can achieve their goals without being caught.

It is our purpose here to develop a signal model that can be used to distinguish between suspicious patterns of activity and real instances of terrorist activities. In doing so, our model must be able to (1) detect potential terrorist threats in a highly cluttered environment, (2) efficiently analyze large amounts of data, and (3) generate hypotheses with only partial and imperfect information. Note that the number of instances of terrorism is (thankfully) very low, and hence designing a model from a "learning from data" approach is problematic: Some exogenous information about the likely structure of a terrorist cell is required. This information will be required to filter out unlikely data that appear to be potentially threatening. We have consequently chosen to apply hidden Markov models (HMMs), because they have had much success in a wide variety of applications (the most celebrated being speech recognition) and since they constitute a principal method for modeling partially observed stochastic processes. HMMs provide a systematic way to make inferences about the evolution of terrorist activities. The premise behind an HMM is that the true underlying process (represented as a series of Markov chain states) is not directly observable (hidden), but it can be probabilistically inferred through another set of stochastic processes (observed transactions, for example). In our problem, the "hidden" process refers to a series of true transactions that describe the behavior of a particular terrorist group, and the observation process is an intelligence database containing any information that can be represented as observed transactions. HMMs are perhaps a natural choice for this problem, because we can evaluate the probability of a sequence of events given a specific model, determine the most likely evolution of a terrorist activity based on data, and estimate new HMM parameters that produce the best representation of the most likely path. These traditional HMM problems help satisfy the first and third requirements mentioned above, but we will also consider some methods to efficiently analyze enormous amounts of data and, in particular, to detect the existence of HMMs in the presence of ambient background noise ("irrelevant transactions") and in the presence of other HMMs.

As we will discuss in the following sections, HMMs can be used as "sensors" in an intrusion detection system, whose goal is to detect the presence of an unwanted entity or process as quickly as possible. Similarly, in the war against terrorism, we wish to detect the presence of terrorist activity so that we can prevent it. Given a number of different terrorist HMMs, which for example are monitoring different sources of transaction-based data within our system, we can determine if any of those sources reveal suspicious activity—similar to the behavior described by the HMM monitoring that source—and, in addition, determine how the intrusion will impact our system.

In addition to using HMMs, we also consider the use of Bayesian networks (BNs) as an efficient means of incorporating "higher-level" information and policy decisions. BNs, also known as probabilistic networks, causal networks, or belief networks, are formalisms for representing uncertainty in a way that is consistent with the axioms of probability theory. In our approach, we will combine the sensing capabilities of HMMs with a network of BN nodes that describe their probabilistic relationships to form an intrusion detection system. As will be described in greater detail later, the BN nodes in this system receive information from HMMs in the form of probabilities ("soft evidence"), and then they combine all of this information to evaluate the likelihood of a terrorist attack.

In this chapter, we will discuss the following topics: (1) HMMs and Bayesian networks (BNs), (2) modeling terrorist activities with HMMs and BNs, and (3) detecting and tracking terrorist activities.

2.2. BACKGROUND

The purpose of this section is to familiarize the reader with HMMs and BNs, which are the foundations for our modeling approach.

2.2.1. Hidden Markov Models

A hidden Markov model is a stochastic signal model used to evaluate the probability of a sequence of events, determine the most likely state transition path, and estimate parameters which produce the best representation of the most likely path. An excellent tutorial on HMMs can be found in Rabiner and Juan (1986). The Baum–Welch re-estimation algorithm (Baum et al., 1970), which is in fact an application of the EM algorithm (Moon, 1996), makes it a convenient tool for modeling dependent observations. HMMs may be best known for their application to speech recognition; however, here we propose their use as discrete-time finite-state representations of transactional data that may arise from terrorist activity.

A discrete HMM is parameterized by

$$\Lambda = (A, B, \pi) \tag{2.1}$$

where

$$A = [a_{ij}] = [p(s_{t+1} = j \mid s_t = i)] \tag{2.2}$$

$(i, j = 1, \ldots, N)$ is the transition probability matrix of the underlying Markov chain,

$$B = [b_{ij}] = [p(x_t = j \mid s_t = i)] \tag{2.3}$$

$(i = 1, \ldots, N; j = 1, \ldots, M)$ is the emission matrix (also known as confusion and observation matrix), and

$$\pi = [\pi_i = p(s_1 = i)] \tag{2.4}$$

$(i = 1, \ldots, N)$ is the initial probability distribution of the underlying Markov states s at time $t = 1$. A graphical model of an HMM is shown in Figure 2.1a for $N = 3$ and its dependence on the observation process x_t is shown in Figure 2.1b. Implicit to the above notation is the finite number of states (N) and finite alphabet of observations (M). The HMMs can be generalized to allow for continuous emissions, implying that b_{ij} in Eq. (2.3) is a probability density function. A convenient choice of the initial probability is the stationary distribution of the underlying Markov states, so that the resulting sequence can be regarded as stationary. The joint probability of an HMM sequence is

$$p(s_1, \ldots, s_n, x_1, \ldots, x_n) = \pi_{s_1} \left[\prod_{t=1}^{n-1} a_{s_t s_{t+1}} \right] \left[\prod_{t=1}^{n} b_{s_t x_t} \right] \tag{2.5}$$

and this can be considered its defining property.

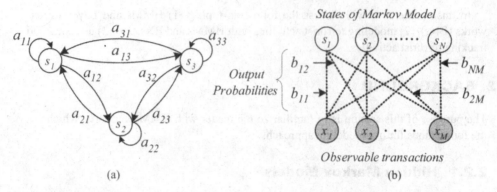

Figure 2.1. (a) A three-state HMM; (b) The N-states of an HMM are coupled to an observation process x of cardinality M.

In terms of a terrorist activity model, A, B, and π represent, respectively, the probability of moving from the current state of terrorist activity to another (usually denoting an increase in terrorist threat), the probability of observing a new suspicious transaction given the current state, and the likelihood of initial threat, respectively. The forward variable will be used to evaluate the probability of terrorist activity, because it is an efficient way to compute the likelihood of a sequence of observations. The forward variable of an HMM is defined as

$$\alpha_t(i) = p(x_1, x_2, \ldots, x_t, s_t = i \mid \lambda) \tag{2.6}$$

λ is the set of HMM parameters (A, B, π). It is easily checked that the following recursion holds for the forward variable

$$\alpha_{t+1}(j) = \left[\prod_{i=1}^{N} \alpha_t(i) a_{ij} \right] b_{jx_{t+1}} \tag{2.7}$$

with the initial condition

$$\alpha_1(j) = \pi(j) b_{jx_1} \tag{2.8}$$

Additional details on HMMs including the backward algorithm, the Viterbi algorithm for finding the most likely sequence of hidden states which could have generated an observed sequence, and the Baum–Welch algorithm for learning HMM parameters may be found in Rabiner and Juang (1986).

2.2.2. Bayesian Networks

A BN can be visualized as a direct acyclic graph (DAG), as shown in Figure 2.2. It consists of a set of variables and a set of directed edges between variables. Variables could be entities or events of interest such as "terrorist organization X is recruiting new members" or "a new attack is being planned." The link between nodes denotes that there is a causal relationship between the corresponding variables. Consider a set V of N variables (nodes): $V = \{V_1, V_2, L, V_N\}$. Each variable may be discrete having a finite or countable number of

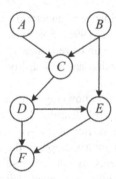

Figure 2.2. A directed acyclic graph (DAG).

exclusive states, or continuous. Given these nodes, one can compute the joint probability of variables in the network via

$$P(V_1, V_2, \mathrm{L}, V_N) = \prod_{i=1}^{N} P(V_i \mid pa(V_i)) \qquad (2.9)$$

where $pa(V_i)$ is the possible instantiation of the parent nodes of V_i. This equation is derived based on the chain rule of probability and the assertions of conditional independence (Heckerman and Breese, 1996). Thus, the causal relationships represented by the Bayesian network structure, shown in Figure 2.2, simplifies computation of the joint probability of variables as

$$P(A, B, C, D, E, F) = P(A)P(B)P(C \mid A, B)P(D \mid C)P(E \mid B, D)P(F \mid D, E) \qquad (2.10)$$

Here, the set of local conditional probability density functions (pdf), also known as conditional probability distributions (CPD) or conditional probability tables (CPT) in the discrete case (e.g., $p(C \mid A, B)$), are the Bayesian network parameters.

Denote hypothesis A (i.e., a hypothesized configuration of variables in certain states), evidence E (a set of variables that are observed to be in certain states), and background context M (domain model). The probabilistic inference in BNs has four types of tasks (Rish and Singh, 2000):

1. Belief update (compute the posterior probability): $BEL(V_i) = P(V_i = v_i \mid E)$.
2. Find the most probable explanation (MPE): $\bar{v}* = \arg \max_{\bar{v}} P(\bar{v}, E)$, where $\bar{v}$ is the instantiation of the variables of interest.
3. Finding the maximum *a posteriori* (MAP) hypothesis: $\bar{a}* = \arg \max_{\bar{a}} \Sigma_{V/A} P(\bar{v}, E)$, where A is the set of hypothesis variables, and $\bar{a}$ is the corresponding instantiations.
4. Find the maximum expected utility (MEU): $\bar{d}* = \arg \max_{\bar{d}} \Sigma_{V/D} P(\bar{v}, E) U(\bar{v})$, where the set D represents the decision variables and $U(\bar{v})$ is the utility function for a particular $\bar{v}$.

In this chapter, we address the problem of belief updating that a certain terrorist activity is active, given certain evidence at the HMM level. Sometimes, the evidence for a particular node at the BN level is observed as being in one of its states, called "hard" evidence. More often, however, the evidence is uncertain, referred to as "soft" evidence, or virtual evidence (Huang and Darwiche, 1996). Soft evidence on a variable V_i (i.e., a node in Bayesian networks, BNs) at time t can be represented by a reported state $v_{ik}(t)$ together with a vector proportional to its conditional probability (can be a distribution after normalization).

In spite of the remarkable power for knowledge representation and dynamic inference, BNs have several limitations. First, while learning the BN parameters (CPDs and CPTs) from data is feasible when we have sufficient training data and the network structure is fixed, learning the structure itself is nontrivial, given the combinatorial explosion of possible topologies. While a BN represents knowledge in a fixed format, it is usually infeasible to respond to some previously unforeseen event (Niedermayer, 1998). Another problem centers on the quality and extent of the prior beliefs used in BN inference. A BN is only as useful as the reliability of this prior knowledge, namely, network parameters of prior beliefs of leaf nodes. Either an excessively optimistic or pessimistic expectation of the quality of these prior beliefs will distort the entire network and invalidate the results (Niedermayer, 1998).

2.2.3. Hybrid and Hierarchal BNs with HMMs

In this section, we will consider the fusion of these two probabilistic models. In our theoretical framework, HMMs are hosted in lower-level (sensing) agencies that serve as information filters; that is, they take transactions as inputs and provide local assessments in the form of soft evidence (i.e., local decisions and the concomitant confidence levels). BNs are maintained by higher-level (decision-making) agencies functioning as fusion centers; they pool the summarized information (in the form of soft evidence) to support global decisions. BNs and HMMs are therefore graphically constructed in a hierarchical fashion.

Theoretically, a hierarchical combination of BNs and HMMs can be arranged in multiple layers. We demonstrate our key ideas of information integration with a two-layer model. A typical model for information fusion is shown in Figure 2.3. It consists of a BN model (with N BN nodes defined as $\{V_i \mid i = 1, 2, \ldots, N\}$ in which each node has $\{Q_i \mid i = 1, 2, \ldots, N\}$ number of states) that serves as the top layer and several HMMs (defined as $\{HMM_i \mid i = 1, 2, \ldots, M\}$) at the bottom layer. The HMMs function as information filters in that they can process raw information and provide soft evidence to the corresponding BN node, where the BN is maintained by the fusion agency. A relation R provides the bridge between the top layer BN and the bottom layer HMMs. R is a set of associations $\{R_{ijk} \mid i = 1, 2, K, M\}; j \in (1, 2, K, N); k \in (1, 2, K, Q)$ with R_{ijk} implying that HMM_i is assigned to state k of BN node V_j. In Figure 2.3, HMM_1 (parameterized by Λ_1) is assigned to one of the states of the BN node V_1 and HMM_2 (parameterized by Λ_2) is assigned to one of the states of the BN node V_4. The information flow associated with the hierarchical model is also shown in the figure. Raw information arrives as sequences of transactions, which constitute the inputs to the HMMs. HMMs, based on the partition of the observation space, detect the "signal" transactions (if any), and they report the local decisions and the corresponding confidences to higher layer BN nodes. Since only the active HMMs will report their findings and trigger the BN inference, the HMMs are essentially running in a faster time scale compared to the BN. The confidence estimates from the active HMMs are then transformed into soft evidence and are used to update the evidential nodes (BN nodes assigned by R). Newly arriving evidence is thus propagated through the BN structure using the inference scheme of the BN.

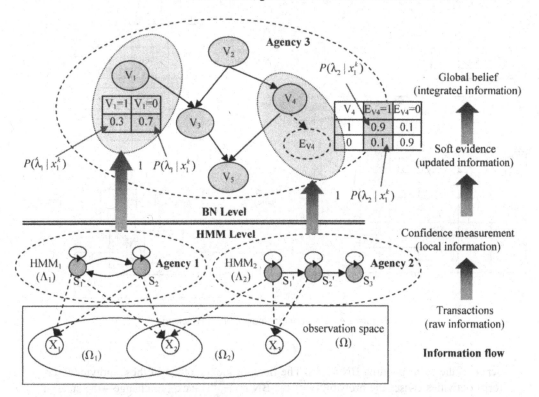

Figure 2.3. Hierarchical structure with HMMs and BN.

2.3. MODELING TERRORIST ACTIVITIES WITH HMMs AND BNs

In this section, we will explain how to model terrorist activities using a real scenario. On December 24, 1999, Indian Airlines (IA) flight IC-814, flying from Kathmandu to New Delhi with 180 persons on board, was hijacked by a group of terrorists. The standoff ended on December 31st when the Indian government released three high-profile terrorists from Kashmir jail. Our Indian Airline Hijacking model abstracts the IA flight IC-814 hijacking event, and it is created based on open source information from the Embassy of India[1] and Frontline Magazine (2000). The model contains patterns of terrorist activities that are present in the actual hijacking. The people, places and things involved in the IA hijacking events are encapsulated in non-specific nodes in an attempt to develop a canonical representation of any airline hijacking.

Figure 2.4 shows the BN model with representative prior probabilities and conditional probability tables. The Bayesian node labeled "PU" depicts the level of political unrest between India and Pakistan over the issue of Kashmir. Another Bayesian node labeled "Activity" represents the activity level of terrorist organizations in Kashmir. In the following simulations, the prior probabilities associated with the BN nodes are held constant, while the statistical inferences calculated by the underlying HMMs ("Planning and Strategy", "Collect Resources," and "Preparations for Hijacking") update the soft evi-

[1]Hijacking of Indian Airlines Flight IC-814. Available at http://www.indianembassy.org/archive/IC_814.htm.

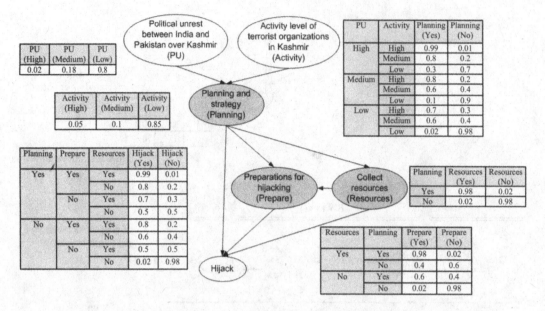

Figure 2.4. BN model for Indian Airline Hijacking.

dence of the corresponding BN nodes. The final, or global, effect of these individual terrorist activities causes the probability of the BN node, "Hijack", to change—the state of which (in the form of a probability mass function) shows the likelihood of a hijacking taking place as a function of time.

In this model, there are three HMMs (assumed to be independent) that symbolize planning and strategy, resource collection, and preparations for hijacking. The likelihoods of these events are associated with the Boolean BN node state: "Yes." The Markov chains of these three HMMs are shown in Figures 2.5, 2.6, and 2.7, respectively.

The evolution of planning activities, political ideology and general goals of the terrorist organization are depicted in a generic HMM: "Planning and Strategy." Political instability associated with a terrorist organization induces them to set up bases/cells in the country X. Parallel to this, fundamentalists and separatists also declare war against the country X. Headquarters personnel of terrorist organizations recruit and train new members with particular talents that can be employed in the attack. Planners analyze the tar-

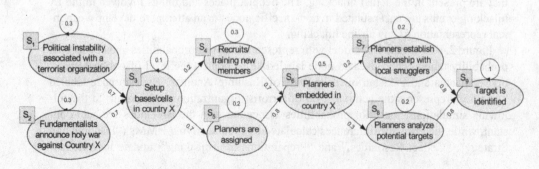

Figure 2.5. Markov chain for the HMM "Planning and Strategy."

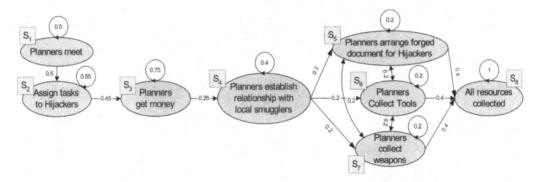

Figure 2.6. Markov chain for the HMM "Collect Resources."

gets and, in selecting the target, attention is given to seize installations that are highly visible and, consequently, would warrant extensive media coverage. As shown in Figure 2.5, this HMM model has nine states ($N = 9$) with state transition probabilities (which form matrix A) labeled next to the feasible transitions. The transaction network snapshots corresponding to S_1, S_2, and S_9 are shown in Figure 2.8. The other states have the same set of nodes, but different links. The transactions of solid lines in S_9 represent the signal transactions of this state, and the transactions with dashed lines superimpose possible signal transactions accumulated from the state transitions (those are the transactions that occurred before reaching the absorbing states). A transaction links two nodes of the network, but each state may introduce more than one new signal transaction. For instance, the assertion that this HMM is in state S_1 is denoting the network state that "there is a political intent from certain terrorist organizations"; the assertion that this HMM is in state S_2 corresponds to the event "enroll fundamentalists from the target country into the terrorist organizations." A possible state sequence of a HMM is essentially a concatenation of all the transactions in its previous state(s) with the current set of transactions—that is, a snapshot of a pattern. The prior probability Π for this model is set as [0.5, 0.5, 0, 0, 0, 0, 0,

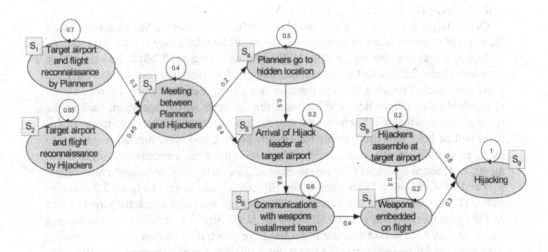

Figure 2.7. Markov chain for the HMM "Preparations for Hijacking."

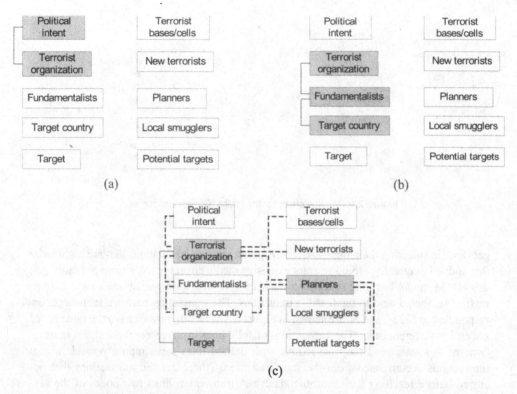

Figure 2.8. Transaction network snapshots for the HMM "Planning and Strategy." (a) Network of S_1. (b) Network of S_2. (c) Network of S_9.

0, 0]. This implies that, at the time this HMM is detected, it will be in state S_1 or S_2 with a probability of 0.5. The state evolution with the structure in Figure 2.5 implies that these two steps (S_1 and S_2) of terrorist planning and strategy process can be performed simultaneously. The emission probabilities are assigned by comparing the observation to the state model via the specified probabilities of false alarm and missed detection associated with the model (Allanach et al., 2004).

Once a target is identified, a detailed plan of attack is developed. Such a plan includes the kinds of demands that will be made and the means by which they will be communicated to authorities and the media. The HMM corresponding to "Collect Resources," as shown in Figure 2.6, tracks the transactions that involve collecting resources to carry out a terrorist attack. Terrorists begin to function as a group, once their organizational identity is established. The tactical and logistical requirements of the operation, such as the types of weapons that will be employed, the means by which the target (an airplane in this case) will be held, the requirements for satellite phones, and other miscellaneous equipment, are established. Planners acquire and transport the arms, ammunition, forged documents, and related equipment through interconnections with local organized crime cells.

The HMM, denoting "Preparations for Hijacking," as shown in Figure 2.7, demonstrates all the exercises for the hijacking. Planners and hijackers check the target airport and the target airline. They repeatedly visit the target airline to estimate the actions and measures they need to take in order to neutralize or penetrate whatever security measures have been established to protect the target. Each hijacker has an organizational affiliation and identity. The organizational identities of the hijackers enable them to get more quickly into the roles that they will play throughout the preparation and duration of the attack. Sometime before the hijacking, planners hide in secret locations, so that security personnel cannot capture them after the hijacking. The hijack leader communicates with the weapons team sometime before the flight departure. When the weapons team informs the hijack leader that weapons are installed on the plane, the hijack leader initiates the actual hijacking of plane with his team. (Due to space limitations, only the terminal states for the latter two HMMs are shown in Figure 2.9.)

2.4. DETECTING AND TRACKING TERRORIST NETWORK HMMs

One of the key capabilities of the proposed use of HMMs and BNs is the ability to continually track many instantiations of terrorist activity in a cluttered environment. While the detection and tracking of a single terrorist activity using an HMM involves the forward or forward–backward algorithm, the competition amongst HMMs for the observations (i.e., the association of transaction observations to the HMMs whence they come) suggests that the inference becomes essentially a multiple-target tracking (MTT) problem (Moon, 1996). In this section, we will discuss the design of an MTT for tracking multiple terrorist network HMMs, but before fully engaging in this, we will first consider some considerably easier methods for detecting HMMs using a Page-like test (Page, 1954). Page's test [a series of sequential probability ratio tests (Page, 1954)] is an efficient change detection scheme and is optimal for detecting conditionally independent and identically distributed HMMs. We will then introduce a method for detecting HMMs whose observation processes are conditionally dependent. To be more specific, suppose we want to detect the presence of either of two HMMs discussed in the previous section. The problem is complicated because it requires checking the existence of both HMMs. While we can assume that the HMMs describing these two terrorist activities are conditionally independent, we must, however, consider that their observation processes are strongly dependent (see Figure 2.10).

In order to compute the likelihood of multiple HMMs, we invoke a target tracking algorithm that assumes the HMM state sequences to be conditionally independent and their likelihoods to be conditionally dependent due to overlapping observations. We will conclude this section by describing a suitable multiple hypothesis tracker (MHT) and some simulation results using the examples introduced in the last section.

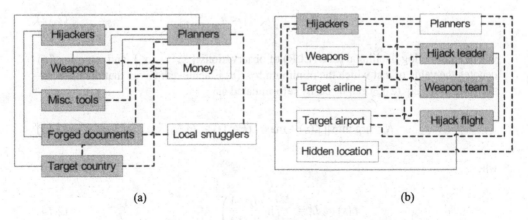

(a)   (b)

Figure 2.9. Transaction network snapshots for the terminal states

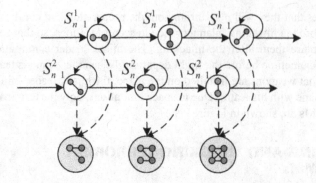

Figure 2.10. Two independent HMMs with conditionally dependent observation processes. In order to evaluate the likelihood equation for this model, we must invoke MTT.

2.4.1. Page's Test

Page's test (Page, 1954), also known as the cumulative sum or CUSUM procedure, is an efficient change detection scheme. A change detection problem is such that the distribution of observations is different before and after an unknown time n_0; and we want to detect the change, if it exists, as soon as possible. Casting it into a standard inference framework, we have the following hypothesis testing problem:

$$
\begin{aligned}
H:\ & x(k) = v(k), \quad 1 \le k \le n \\
K:\ & x(k) = v(k), \quad 1 \le k \le n_0 \\
& x(k) = z(k), \quad n_0 \le k \le n
\end{aligned}
\tag{2.11}
$$

where $x(k)$ are observations and $v(k)$ and $z(k)$ are independent identically distributed (i.i.d.), with probability density functions (pdf) denoted by f_H and f_K, respectively. Note that under K the observations are no longer a stationary random sequence: Their distribution has a switch at n_0 from f_H to f_K.

The Page decision rule, which can be derived from the generalized likelihood ratio (GLR) test (Basseville and Nikiforov, 1993), amounts to finding the stopping time

$$
N = \arg \min_{n} \left\{ \left(\max_{1 \le k \le n} L_k^n \right) \ge h \right\}
\tag{2.12}
$$

where L_k^n is the log likelihood ratio (LLR) of observations $\{x_k, \ldots, x_n\}$, and $\arg \min_n f(n)$ denotes the value of n at which the minimum for $f(n)$ is achieved. Given that the observations are i.i.d., Eq. (2.12) can be easily reformulated as

$$
N = \arg \min_{n} \left\{ \left(L(n) - \max_{1 \le k \le n} L(k-1) \right) \ge h \right\}
\tag{2.13}
$$

where

$$
L(k) @ L_1^k = \sum_{i=1}^{k} \left(\ln \frac{f_K(x_i)}{f_H(x_i)} \right)
\tag{2.14}
$$

with $L(0) = 0$. This is based on the fact that, given independence, we have

$$L_1^n = L_1^{k-1} + L_k^n \tag{2.15}$$

Equation (2.13) allows us to write down the standard recursion for the Page's test

$$N = \arg \min_n \{S_n \geq h\} \tag{2.16}$$

in which

$$S_n = \max\{0, S_{n-1} + g(x_n)\} \tag{2.17}$$

and

$$g(x_n) = \ln\left(\frac{f_K(x_n)}{f_H(x_n)}\right) \tag{2.18}$$

is the update nonlinearity.

Page's recursion ensures that the test statistic is "clamped" at zero; that is, whenever the LLR of current observation would make the test statistic S_n negative (which happens more often when H is true), Page's test resets to zero. As shown in Figure 2.11, the procedure continues until it crosses the upper threshold h and a detection is declared. Thus, operationally, Page's test is equivalent to a series of sequential probability ratio tests (SPRTs) with upper and lower thresholds h and 0, respectively. Whenever the lower threshold 0 is crossed, a new SPRT is initiated from the next sample until the upper threshold h is crossed.

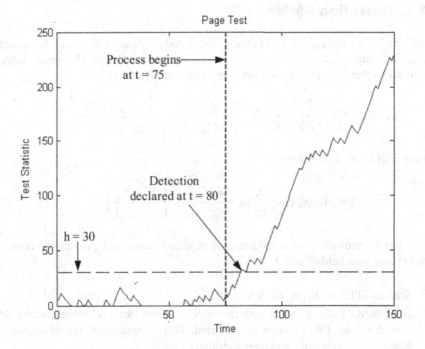

Figure 2.11. A traditional Page test.

In practice, the update nonlinearity $g(x_i)$ need not be an LLR as in Eq. (2.18), since this might not be available as in the case when dealing with composite hypotheses or with hypotheses involving nuisance parameters. For a nonlinearity other than the LLR, a critical requirement for the corresponding CUSUM procedure to work is the "antipodality" condition:

$$E(g(x_n) \mid H) < 0$$
$$E(g(x_n) \mid K) > 0 \tag{2.19}$$

There is no false alarm rate or probability of detection involved, since we see from the implementation that, sooner or later, a detection is always claimed as long as the test is "closed" [i.e., $P(N < \infty) = 1$ under both hypotheses]. The performance of Page's test is therefore measured in terms of average run length (ARL, the average number of observations it takes before declaring detection) under K and H. It is always desired to have a small delay to detection, usually denoted as D, while keeping the average number of samples between false alarms, denoted as T, as large as possible. Analogous to the conventional hypothesis testing problem, where we wish to maximize the probability of detection while keeping the false alarm rate below a fixed level, the tradeoff here amounts to the choice of the upper threshold h. The relationship between h and the ARL is often calculated in an asymptotic sense using first- or second-order approximations, usually credited to Wald (1947) and Sigmund (1995).

As a final note, Page's test using the LLR nonlinearity has minimax optimality in terms of ARL; that is, given a constraint on the average delay between false alarms, the Page's test minimizes the worst-case delay to detection (Lorden, 1971).

2.4.2. Detecting HMMs

Consider a Page's test (in Eq. 2.11) except that f_H and f_K are general non-i.i.d. probability measures. Assume that under K the observations before and after the change are independent of each other. The likelihood ratio (parameterized by n_0) is then

$$\Lambda(n; n_0) = \frac{f(X_1^n \mid K)}{f(X_1^n \mid H)} = \frac{f_H(X_1^{n_0-1}) f_K(X_{n_0}^n)}{f_H(X_1^{n_0-1}) f_H(X_{n_0}^n \mid X_1^{n_0-1})} = \frac{f_K(X_{n_0}^n)}{f_H(X_{n_0}^n \mid X_1^{n_0-1})} \tag{2.20}$$

The log likelihood ratio is then

$$L_k^n = \ln(\Lambda(n; k)) = \sum_{i=k}^{n} \ln\left(\frac{f_K(x_i \mid x_{i-1} = 1, \ldots, x_k)}{f_H(x_i \mid x_{i-1} = 1, \ldots, x_1)} \right) \tag{2.21}$$

Page's test is equivalent to a sequence of repeated sequential probability ratio tests (SPRTs) with thresholds h and 0.

1. Start an SPRT with thresholds 0 and h.
2. If the SPRT ends at time k with test statistic below zero, reinitiate another SPRT from $k + 1$ as if no previous data existed. That is, recalculate the likelihood ratio based on the stationary marginal distribution.
3. Repeat the above procedure until h is crossed.

In compact form, we can write, in a manner similar to the standard Page recursion (Eq. 2.16),

$$S_n = \max\{0, S_{n-1} + g(n; k)\} \tag{2.22}$$

where

$$g(n; k) = \ln\left(\frac{f_K(x_n \mid x_{n-1}, \ldots, x_k)}{f_H(x_n \mid x_{n-1}, \ldots, x_k)}\right) \tag{2.23}$$

and x_k is the first sample after the last reset, that is, $S_{k-1} = 0$. The difference with Eq. (2.21) is that the conditional densities of both numerator and denominator in the logarithm of $g(n; k)$ depend on the same set of random variables, which make a Page-like recursion possible by utilizing the stationarity assumption of hidden Markov models. Note also that such a scheme reduces to the standard Page test with a LLR nonlinearity when the observations both before and after the change are i.i.d. Furthermore, if the observations before the change are independent, we need only replace $f_H(x_n \mid x_{n-1}, \ldots, x_k)$ with $f_H(x_n)$ for the scheme to work.

The scheme presented here is in the same form as the sequential detector proposed in (Bansal and Papantoni-Kazakos, 1986). It was shown that this procedure is in fact asymptotically optimal in Lorden's sense (Lorden, 1971); that is, as $h \to \infty$, it minimizes the worst delay to detection given a constraint on the average time between false alarms, among all possible sequential schemes.

So far, we have proposed a CUSUM procedure that is applicable to the case of dependent observations, *provided* that we have an efficient means to calculate the likelihood function. This is not always a reasonable assumption. Fortunately, for the hidden Markov model, the existence of the forward variable, together with its recursive formula as discussed in this section, enables efficient computation of the likelihood function of an HMM. Specifically, the likelihood function of an HMM with parameter triple Λ could be written as

$$f(x_1, x_2, L, x_t \mid \Lambda) = \sum_{i=1}^{N} \alpha_t(i) \tag{2.24}$$

where N is the total number of states and the α_t's are the forward variables defined in Eq. (2.6). Now the conditional probability in Eq. (2.21) is readily solved as

$$f_j(x_t \mid x_{t-1}, L, x_1) = f(x_{t-1} \mid x_{t-1}, x_{t-2}, L, x_1, \Lambda_j) = \frac{\displaystyle\sum_{i=1}^{N} \alpha_t(i)}{\displaystyle\sum_{i=1}^{N} \alpha_{t-1}(i)} \tag{2.25}$$

where $j = H; K$.

Although we have followed the proposed procedure to find the conditional pdf as in Eq. (2.25), this step can in fact be avoided since the likelihood function, defined as the sum of $\alpha_t(i)$, can be used directly by each individual sequential likelihood ratio test. But in practice, it is found that the direct use of the likelihood function as defined in Eq. (2.24) will cause numerical underflow as the number of observations increases. For discrete HMMs, it is easily seen from the definition of the forward variable that the likelihood decreases monotonically (and generally geometrically) with the number of observations. The conditional likelihood function defined in Eq. (2.25) does not suffer from such a numerical problem. We need therefore to develop a way of recursively computing the conditional likelihood function in (Eq. 2.25) without the direct use of the forward variable. This can be achieved by scaling. Define α_t' such that $\alpha_1'(i) = \alpha_1(i)$, but for $t > 1$

$$\alpha_{t+1}'(j) = \frac{\left[\sum_{i=1}^{N} \alpha_t'(i) a_{ij}\right] b_{j x_{t+1}}}{\sum_{i=1}^{N} \alpha_t'(i)} \tag{2.26}$$

It is easily checked that $\sum_{i=1}^{N} \alpha_t'(i)$ is identical to $f_j(x_t \mid x_{t-1}, L, x_1)$ with $j = H, K$ as defined in Eq. (2.25). Thus, the updating nonlinearity $g(n; k)$ can be obtained recursively without computing explicitly the exact likelihood function at each time.

To summarize, for the quickest detection of HMMs, we propose the following procedure:

1. Set $t = 1$, $l_0 = 0$, where l_t denotes the LLR at time t.
2. Initialize the (scaled) forward variable α_t' using

$$\alpha_t'(j) = \pi(j) b_{j x_t} \tag{2.27}$$

   for each possible state j and for both hypotheses H and K.
3. Update the log likelihood ratio

$$l_t = l_{t-1} + \ln\left(\frac{\sum_{i=1}^{N} \alpha_t'(i \mid K)}{\sum_{i=1}^{N} \alpha_t'(i \mid H)}\right) \tag{2.28}$$

4. If $l_t > h$, declare detection of a change, stop;
   If $l_t < 0$, set $l_t = 0$; $t = t + 1$; then go to 2;
   If $0 < l_t < h$, continue.
5. Set $t = t + 1$;
   Update the scaled forward variable using α_t' in Eq. (2.26);
   then go to 3.

2.4.3 Tracking Multiple HMMs

The detection scheme proposed in the previous section assumes that multiple terrorist networks are independent of each other. This assumption is not always appropriate. In this section, we propose a scheme for tracking multiple terrorist networks where there can be competition for the observations.

Before we begin with multiple HMMs, consider first the case of a single HMM. The forward variables, after suitable normalization, define the posterior probability of state occupancy given observations up to the current time. Specifically, we have

$$p(s_t = i \mid x_1, \ldots, x_t) = \frac{\alpha_t(i)}{\sum_{j=1}^{N} \alpha_t(j)} \tag{2.29}$$

where N is the total number of states, and we have suppressed the dependence on the HMM parameter Λ. In a sense, the HMM state is being "tracked." By extension, the direct model expansion approach suggests optimal (multiple) target tracking, as we now discuss.

Let us denote $s_1(n)$ and $s_2(n)$ as the underlying states of HMM$_1$ and HMM$_2$ at time n, and denote Z_1^n as the superimposed observations $z(1)$ through $z(n)$. The goal of the tracking algorithm is to obtain the likelihood function $p(Z_1^n)$ given that both HMM$_1$ and HMM$_2$ are active. Assume we have obtained $p(Z_1^n, s_1(n), s_2(n))$, and consider the one-step update of $p(Z_1^{n+1}, s_1(n + 1), s_2(n + 1))$. This can be written as

$$p(Z_1^{n+1}, s_1(n + 1), s_2(n + 1)) = p(Z_1^n, z(n + 1), s_1(n + 1), s_2(n + 1))$$

$$= p(z(n + 1) \mid s_1(n + 1), s_2(n + 1), Z_1^n) \times p(s_1(n + 1), s_2(n + 1), Z_1^n) \tag{2.30}$$

$$= p(z(n + 1) \mid s_1(n + 1), s_2(n + 1)) \times p(s_1(n + 1), s_2(n + 1), Z_1^n)$$

where the last identity follows from the fact that given $s_1(n + 1)$ and $s_2(n + 1)$, $z(n + 1)$ is independent of the previous observations. Computation of the first term is essentially the same as obtaining the observation matrix B in the model expansion approach. The derivation of this algorithm can be found in Chen and Willett (2001), the result of which produces the posterior probability of each state.

$$p(s_1(n + 1) \mid Z_1^{n+1}) = \frac{p(s_1(n + 1), Z_1^{n+1})}{\sum_{s_1(n + 1)} p(s_1(n + 1), Z_1^{n+1})}$$

$$p(s_2(n + 1) \mid Z_1^{n+1}) = \frac{p(s_2(n + 1), Z_1^{n+1})}{\sum_{s_2(n + 1)} p(s_2(n + 1), Z_1^{n+1})} \tag{2.31}$$

The derivation of the likelihood function (Chen and Willett, 1998, 2001) of the observation (which after all is the goal here) follows from

$$p(Z_1^{n+1}) = \sum_{s_1(n+1)} p(s_1(n + 1), Z_1^{n+1}) \tag{2.32}$$

$$p(Z_1^{n+1}) = \sum_{s_2(n+1)} p(s_2(n + 1), Z_1^{n+1}) \tag{2.33}$$

requiring $\min(N_1, N_2)$ operations.

Given the output of the likelihood function of the tracker as in Eq. (2.32) or Eq. (2.33), a Page-like test is easily constructed. Under H, we use forward recursion to compute the likelihood given only HMM$_1$ is present. Under K, the target tracker is used to compute the likelihood given both HMM$_1$ and HMM$_2$ are present. The output likelihood functions under both H and K are used to run a sequential test; and whenever the test statistic falls below zero, it is reset to zero and the procedure restarts from the next observation.

Algorithmically, the detector operates as follows:

1. Set $t = 1$, $l_0 = 0$, where l_t denotes the LLR at time t.
2. Set $t = t + 1$; $t_0 = t$. Under H, initialize the forward variable $\alpha(g \mid H)$ using (Eq. 2.8); under K, initialize a multiple target tracker using Eq. (2.8). Compute the likelihood function under both hypotheses.
3. Update the log likelihood ratio

$$l_t = l_{t-1} + \ln\left(\frac{p(Z_{t_0}^t \mid K)}{\sum_{i=1}^{N} \alpha_t(i \mid H)} \right) \tag{2.34}$$

4. If $l_t > h$, declare detection of a change, stop;

   If $l_t < 0$, set $l_t = 0$; then go to 2;

   If $0 < l_t < h$, continue.
5. Set $t = t + 1$; update the forward variable using $\alpha_t(g)$ using Eq. (2.25); and update the "tracker" with either Eq. (2.32) or Eq. (2.33); then go to 3.

If under H more than one HMM is present, then the above procedure may be modified such that the "tracking" approach is used under both hypotheses. It is often necessary to use scaled versions of the forward variables to avoid numerical underflow; consult Chen and Willett (2000) or any standard HMM reference for details.

2.4.4. Multiple Hypothesis Tracking

When there is data association uncertainty (i.e., the observations are not labeled, and it is not known from which source, if any, a given transaction emanates), correct statistical inference requires the evaluation of all possibilities. An MHT (in the kinematic target context) is a type of target tracking system that forms alternative data association hypotheses every time an observation-to-track conflict arises; a special case of this, also known as Reid's algorithm, is presented in Blackman and Popoli (1999). After a new observation is made, a new set of hypotheses is created and is then propagated to the next scan. It is important to properly form and maintain track hypotheses, since their number can increase exponentially with each additional observation. In this section, we present an algorithm similar to Reid's, but from a track-oriented approach, and naturally we adapt it from tracking targets to tracking transaction patterns.

For example, consider only two HMMs that describe the activities associated with HMM_1 and HMM_2. As shown in Figure 2.12, the MHT begins under the assumption that the two HMMs are independent. H_0 represents the null hypothesis, and H_1 and H_2 represent active hypotheses in a conventional detection problem. For example, our first test, "Test #1," is trying to determine if HMM_1 or HMM_2 is active. If HMM_1 is active, then the next test will be "Test #2," where the NULL hypothesis becomes the existence of HMM_1 and the new active hypotheses are as follows: (1) HMM_1 and HMM_2 are both active, and (2) nothing is active. If our detection algorithm receives a few transactions that strongly imply that HMM_1 is currently active, then HMM_1 will be confirmed (statistically) and our new hypothesis will become the following: HMM_1 and HMM_2 are active versus only HMM_1 is active. There are of course many different transitions between tests, and these are represented by the arrows in Figure 2.12.

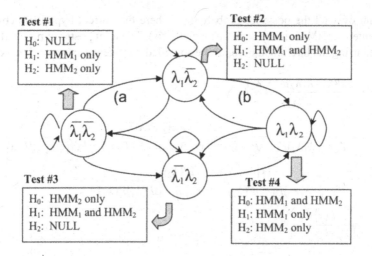

Figure 2.12. MHT for two HMMs.

One of the benefits to this implementation of an MHT is that it is not susceptible to exponential complexity. This is because the number of hypotheses is limited by the number of HMMs that need to be tracked, and hypothesis generation is based on a logical combination of previous knowledge.

2.5. HMM AND BN INFORMATION FUSION

As discussed earlier in Section 2.2.3, our basic model consists of HMMs acting as sensors to a BN, or hierarchical combination of BNs. In this section we will develop an approximate method of computing the posterior probability of a particular hypothesis, as defined in the last section, and how it can be used to update the belief probability mass function of a higher-level BN node.

The MHT discussed earlier yields the likelihood function of the observation sequence given multiple HMMs to be detected (Chen and Willett, 2001), for example, $P(x_1^k \mid \lambda_1, \lambda_2)$. However, we require the marginal posterior probabilities of individual HMMs to be reported to BN, that is, $P(\lambda_i \mid x_1^k) \; \forall i$. Suppose that we are currently testing hypothesis test #2 in Figure 2.12 and that both HMMs are detected (namely, accept "H_1"). The marginal probabilities can then be approximated by

$$P(\lambda_1 \mid x_1^k) \approx P(\lambda_1 \overline{\lambda}_2 \mid x_1^k) + P(\lambda_1 \lambda_2 \mid x_1^k) \tag{2.35}$$

$$P(\lambda_2 \mid x_1^k) \approx P(\lambda_1 \lambda_2 \mid x_1^k) \tag{2.36}$$

The first and second posterior probabilities in Eq. (2.35) come from the hypotheses H_0 and H_1 in test #2, respectively. Generally, this marginal posterior probability is approximated via

$$P(\lambda_i \mid x_1^n) \approx \sum_{\lambda_i \in H_j} P(H_j \mid x_1^k) \qquad \forall i \tag{2.37}$$

that is, sum over all the posterior probabilities where the current hypothesis covers the HMM of interest (HMMi is active in this hypothesis). The joint posterior probabilities are determined using the likelihood ratio, or the so-called confidence estimate. For example,

$$P(\lambda_1\lambda_2 \mid x_1^k) = \frac{P(x_1^k \mid \lambda_1\lambda_2)P(\lambda_1\lambda_2)}{P(x_1^k)}$$

$$= \frac{P(x_1^k \mid \lambda_1\lambda_2)P(\lambda_1)P(\lambda_2)}{P(x_1^k \mid \lambda_1\lambda_2)P(\lambda_1)P(\lambda_2) + P(x_1^k \mid \lambda_1\bar{\lambda}_2)P(\lambda_1)P(\bar{\lambda}_2) + P(x_1^k \mid \bar{\lambda}_1\bar{\lambda}_2)P(\bar{\lambda}_1)P(\bar{\lambda}_2)}$$

$$\approx \frac{P(x_1^k \mid \lambda_1\lambda_2)P(\lambda_1)P(\lambda_2)}{P(x_1^k \mid \lambda_1\lambda_2)P(\lambda_1)P(\lambda_2) + P(x_1^k \mid \lambda_1\bar{\lambda}_2)P(\lambda_1)P(\bar{\lambda}_2)}$$

$$= \frac{L(x_1^k)L_0}{L(x_1^k)L_0 + 1} \tag{2.38}$$

where

$$L(x_1^k) = \frac{P(x_1^k \mid \lambda_1\lambda_2)}{P(x_1^k \mid \lambda_1\bar{\lambda}_2)} \quad \text{and} \quad L_0 = \frac{p(\lambda_1)p(\lambda_2)}{p(\lambda_1)p(\bar{\lambda}_2)} = \frac{p(\lambda_2)}{p(\bar{\lambda}_2)} = \frac{p(\lambda_2)}{1 - p(\lambda_2)}$$

HMMs are assumed to be marginally independent (independent in the absence of observations). When HMMs are functioning independently, similar results will be concluded. Take HMM_1 as an example:

$$P(\lambda_1 \mid x_1^k) = \frac{P(x_1^k \mid \lambda_1)P(\lambda_1)}{P(x_1^k)}$$

$$= \frac{P(x_1^k \mid \lambda_1)P(\lambda_1)}{P(x_1^k \mid \bar{\lambda}_1)P(\bar{\lambda}_1) + P(x_1^k \mid \lambda_1)P(\lambda_1)}$$

$$= \frac{L(x_1^k)L_0}{L(x_1^k)L_0 + 1} \tag{2.39}$$

with

$$L(x_1^k) = \frac{P(x_1^k \mid \lambda_1)}{P(x_1^k \mid \bar{\lambda}_1)} \quad \text{and} \quad L_0 = \frac{p(\lambda_1)}{p(\bar{\lambda}_1)} = \frac{p(\lambda_1)}{1 - p(\lambda_1)}$$

The marginalized posterior probability is the agency's belief on the existence of HMMi based on the observations up to time index k. If the HMM reports to a root node of the BN, since the HMM is the only source of the information for this node, the marginalized posterior probability will be used to update the prior distribution of the root node (i.e., "always trust the sensor"). For non-root nodes, since we should also consider information from other linked nodes, marginalized posterior probability is the probability of detection in the BN layer, thus forming the soft evidence to update the BN inference. For example, HMM_2 is associated with a binary BN node "V_4" (with state "1" associated with λ_4 and state "0" associated with $\bar{\lambda}_4$), and we will augment the initial BN with a dummy node E_{V4} which has the same set of states as V_4 and a link from node V_4 when HMM_2 is detected. The BN belief updating is triggered by a hard evidence $E_{V4} = 1$ (since the local agency reports that the HMM_2

is active) with a CPT constructed from $P(\lambda_2 \mid x_1^f)$ and $1 - P(\lambda_2 \mid x_1^f)$ to represent the uncertainties in the evidence. Actually, only the column corresponding to $E_{V4} = 1$ in the CPT will be needed for belief updating. Both cases are illustrated in Figure 2.3.

It is also feasible that multiple HMMs report to different states of the same non-binary BN node. However, the states of a BN node have an assumption that they are mutually exclusive, thus creating a conflict if more than one HMM reports as being active to the same node at the same time. We assume that this issue is resolved in the modeling process, where we design binary BN nodes to collect information from individual HMMs, while adding intermediate nodes to specify the possible relationships and semantics among active HMMs.

2.6. SIMULATION RESULTS

The results shown in this section were compiled using the Indian Airlines Hijacking model discussed earlier. The detection of these modeled HMMs is shown in Figure 2.13 in the form of a CUSUM test statistic. The evolution of the corresponding Bayesian belief that the airline hijacking is in progress is shown in Figure 2.14. We speed up the flow of the new transactions (e.g., every two seconds in the figures) for simulation purposes. The real times associated with the IA hijacking events are labeled for reference. The starting point of each HMM detection curve is associated with the first time this HMM is detected; thus, we believe (with certain probability) that the modeled terrorist activity is in progress. A peak probability usually results when this pattern evolves into the absorbing state of the HMM, and we obtain maximum number of signal transactions for this HMM. Once the

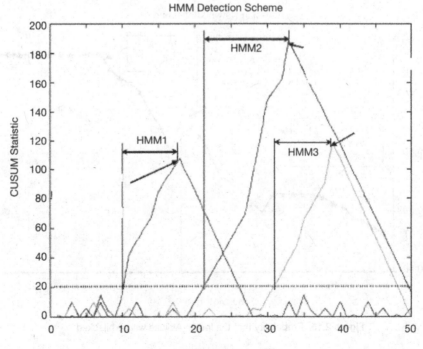

Figure 2.13.

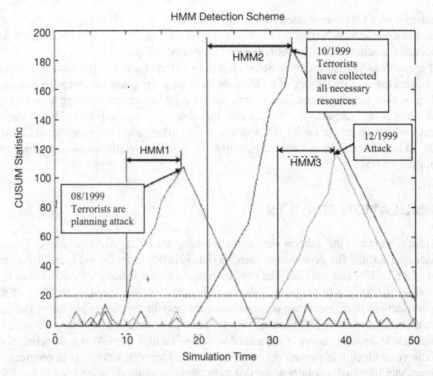

Figure 2.14. Detection of three modeled HMMs in the presence of "noise" background.

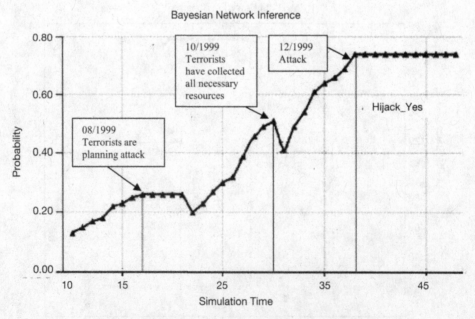

Figure 2.15. Probability that the Indian Airlines will be hijacked.

peak is attained, the numerous unrelated transactions will reduce the confidence in the detection. Thus, there are two reasons for a decrease in the probability of Figure 2.13. They are caused by noise transactions or simply because the terrorist activities have already reached their goal and do not warrant any further transactions. The BN updates its belief only when HMMs detect significant new evidence. Typically, it merges all available information from diverse sources and generates a global alarm.

SUMMARY

In this chapter we introduced a method for modeling terrorist activities and a process for detecting instantiations of those models in a given dataset. The signal model we chose is a hierarchal combination of BNs and HMMs. HMMs are doubly embedded stochastic processes with an underlying stochastic process that, although unobservable (hidden), can be observed through another set of stochastic processes. In the terrorist tracking problem, the true pattern of the transactions are not observable directly; that is, the true pattern of transactions corresponds to the hidden part of the doubly embedded stochastic process or the HMM states. BNs are graphical models that represent randomness in a manner similar to the axioms of probability theory. As described earlier, the highest level BN in our detection system represents an information fusion center in that each BN receives probabilistic inferences (or soft evidence) from one or more HMMs, which function as transaction processors. This signal model can be a very powerful counter-terrorism tool, because it can evaluate the likelihood of a terrorist attack, extrapolate seemingly malignant activities, and identify the persons involved.

ACKNOWLEDGMENT

This work was performed under a contract from the Information Awareness Office of DARPA.

REFERENCES

Allanach, J., Tu, H., Singh, S., Willett, P., and Pattipati, K. R. (2004). Detecting, tracking, and counteracting terrorist networks via hidden Markov models. *Proceedings of the IEEE Aerospace Conference,* Big Sky, MT.

Bansal, R., and Papantoni-Kazakos, P. (1986). An algorithm for detecting a change in a stochastic process. *IEEE Transactions on Information Theory* **32:**227–235.

Bar-Shalom, Y., and Li, X. (1995). *Multitarget-Multisensor Tracking: Principles and Techniques.* YBS Publications.

Basseville, M., and Nikiforov, L. (1993). *Detection of Abrupt Changes,* Englewood Cliffs, NJ: Prentice Hall.

Baum, L., Petrie, T., Soules, G., and Weiss, N. (1970). A maximization technique occurring in the statistical analysis of probabilistic functions of Markov chains. *Annals of Mathematical Statistics* **41:**164–171.

Bethel, R., and Paras, G. (1994). A PDF multitarget tracker. *IEEE Transactions on Aerospace and Electronic Systems* **30:**386–403.

Blackman, S., and Popoli, R. (1999). *Design and Analysis of Modern Tracking Systems.* Boston: Artech House.

Chen, B., and Willett, P. (1998). Quickest detection of superimposed hidden Markov models using a multiple target tracker. In: *Proceedings of the IEEE Aerospace Conference,* Aspen, CO.

Chen, B., and Willett, P. (2000). Detection of hidden Markov model transient signals. *IEEE Transactions on Aerospace and Electronic Systems* 36-4:1253–1268.

Chen, B., and Willett, P. (2001). Superimposed HMM transient detection via target tracking ideas. *IEEE Transactions on Aerospace and Electronic Systems,* **July:** 946–956.

Frontline Magazine (India) **17**(2), January–February 2000. Available at http://www.frontlineonnet.com/fl1702/17020040.htm.

Heckerman, D., and Breese, J. S. (1996). Causal independence for probability assessment and inference using Bayesian networks. *IEEE Transactions on Systems, Man & Cybernetics—Part A: Systems and Humans* **26**(6):826–831.

Huang, C., and Darwiche, A. (1996). Inference in belief networks: A procedural guide. *International Journal of Approximate Reasoning* **15**(3):225–263.

Lorden, G. (1971). Procedures for reacting to a change in distribution. *Annals of Mathematical Statistics* 42, pp. 1897–1908.

Moon, T. (1996). The expectation–maximization algorithm, *IEEE SP Magazine* **13**:47–60.

Niedermayer, D. (1998). An introduction to Bayesian networks and their contemporary applications. Available: http://www.niedermayer.ca/paper/bayesian/bayes.html.

Page, E. (1954). Continuous inspection schemes. *Biometrical,* Volt **41**:100–115.

Pearl, J. (1990). Jeffrey's rule, passage of experience, and neo-Bayesian. In: *Knowledge Representation and Defeasible Reasoning,* H. E. Kyburg, Jr. (ed.), pp. 245–265. Boston: Kluwer Academic Publishers.

Rabiner, L., and Juang, B. (1986). An introduction to hidden Markov models. *IEEE ASSP Magazine,* 4–16. January.

Rish, I., and Singh, M. (2000). A tutorial on inference and learning in Bayesian networks. Available: http//www.research.ibm.com/people/r/rish/talks/BN-tutorial.ppt.

Siegmund, D. (1995). *Sequential Analysis—Tests and Confidence Intervals.* New York: Springer-Verlag.

Streit, R., and Barrett, R. (1990). Frequency line tracking using hidden Markov models. *IEEE Transactions on Acoustics, Speech and Signal Processing* **38**:586–598.

Wald, A. (1947). *Sequential Analysis.* New York: Wiley.

Chapter 3

Anticipatory Models for Counter-Terrorism

Mark Lazaroff and David Snowden

3.1. INTRODUCTION TO ANTICIPATORY MODELING

President Abraham Lincoln (Lincoln, 1862), struggling with the gravest issues of his time, during arguably the greatest crisis in the history of the United States, stated:

> The dogmas of the quiet past are inadequate to the stormy present. The occasion is piled high with difficulty, and we must rise with the occasion. As our case is new, so we must think and act anew.

At the time of this writing, we are almost four years on from the tragic events of the tempestuous day that has become known as "9/11." Over that time, we too have struggled with the implications of the profound changes that face the world in this time. For us, "9/11" should be a turning point to *think and act anew.*

This chapter provides an overview of new thinking about "predictive models" for counter-terrorism that is focused on *multi-ontology sensemaking* in a complex world perplexed by emergent threats. The chapter is not only intended to provide the reader with a context and background that will inform and support many of the issues to be considered regarding "predictive modeling" approaches, but also presents a new paradigm for thinking about intelligence problems and particularly the interaction between intelligence and operational/policy planning and decision making under conditions of ambiguity and uncertainty. We use the term *anticipatory* instead of predictive, because the term *predictive* connotes a level of omniscience that does not exist—and, given new scientific understanding of systems and the functioning of the human brain, can never exist—and thus represents a danger inherent in traditional approaches. A cursory discussion of "traditional" approaches is given in order to contrast these approaches with "new" approaches to modeling. Pros and cons and the assumptions intrinsic to these approaches are addressed.

Predictive modeling techniques that have their roots in the physical problem domain alone (e.g., tracking ground targets) are not adequate for counter-terrorism applications. Yet such models remain pervasive in the community's thinking and restrict their openness to "think anew." We use the "connect the dots" metaphor to lay the groundwork to illustrate this point and to explain the criticality of context in interpretation. We also use the "connect the dots" paradigm as an example for discourse on surprise and complexity. We

Emergent Information Technologies and Enabling Policies for Counter-Terrorism. Edited by Popp and Yen
Copyright © 2006 The Institute of Electrical and Electronics Engineers, Inc.

introduce a sensemaking framework for understanding contextual complexity as a basis for new thinking regarding counter-terrorism models.

In this section, we present information pertaining to issues in modeling to provide the reader with both background and foundational information, in addition to establishing a baseline to contrast with new methods presented later in the chapter.

3.1.1. Role of Modeling in Intelligence Analysis and Synthesis

"*Intelligence*" is the product of a knowledge creation process from denied access information sources. This knowledge creation process involves multiple forms of reasoning by which information is used to describe and/or infer important aspects of the intelligence objective. At the core of the intelligence reasoning process is the formation of hypotheses supported by evidence. "*Evidence*" is information, in context, that changes beliefs about hypotheses. Waltz (2003, p. 163) describes intelligence analysis as the combined process of analysis and synthesis:

- *Analysis* is the process of decomposing intelligence data (evidence) into constituent parts to examine relationships and discover missing data.
- *Synthesis* is the process of assembling feasible solutions (hypotheses) from components of evidence.

The purpose of the intelligence analysis process is to organize and evaluate data (analyze) and then to construct hypotheses (synthesize). *Models* are used as tools to marshal and structure evidence, evaluate logical arguments, capture the analysts' rationale for accepting and/or rejecting information as evidence, and provide a mechanism for explanation of how the evidence supports the hypothesis conclusion. Models are *abstract representations* of the objective of the intelligence investigation, thus they constitute a tradeoff within the representational model space.

3.1.2. Modeling Considerations and Tradeoffs

Given the infinite complexity of the real world and the requirement for models to be simpler than the systems being modeled, special attention must be given to the tradeoffs pertaining to model design and implementation, including codification, abstraction, granularity, assumptions, and other key issues.

Codification. Codification is the process of standardizing an explicit language about a topic of interest and, as such, requires a common context not only of language but also of experience between message creator and message receiver. It is associated with linguistic aspects of essential parts of the model. As such, it forms the basis of communication about the semantics of the model.

Abstraction. Abstraction, as a process, is about representing the essential features of something without including background or nonessential detail (Graham, 1991). Abstraction, as an object (noun), is a simplified description, or specification, of a model that emphasizes key system details or properties while suppressing others. A good abstraction is one that emphasizes details that are significant to the domain of interest and suppresses details that are immaterial or diversionary (Shaw, 1984). In Sickels (2001), abstractions can refer to physical things, processes, or relationships and the *properties* of these things. Analysts are concerned about *patterns* of activity (abstractions), but *not* about *all* the details of a particular process. In other words, models help to bridge an abstraction gap. Another, more familiar term that arises from the abstraction gap concept is *pattern recognition*. The user is interested in gaining knowledge about the real world, but not at the detailed level. In order to recognize a pattern, a "gap" between the concrete (the real world) and the abstract (the pattern) must be bridged in such a way as to take account of the past patterns of success and failure in the decision-making group. Patterns are not limited to just physical things: that is, patterns of activity are also considered. Whether the goal is to confirm or deny a pattern hypothesis, or to learn more about a pattern that that has been detected, the abstraction gap must be bridged—that is, to see real-world details as potential instantiations of some more general, and therefore abstract, pattern.

Granularity. Hobbs (1985) formally defines granularity in terms of simplification, idealization, and articulation. A key consideration of model granularity is the *lower bound* of model representation granularity (McKelvy, 1999). The model lower bound is the lowest level of detail. Below the lower bound, things are assumed to be either uniform or stochastic in nature. In seeking an explanation for any observed or hypothesized relationship, scientists tend to stay at or above the conventional lower bounds of their respective disciplines, so the granularity chosen for any particular model tends to be based on disciplinary traditions as well as on the purpose the model is expected to serve (Sickels, 2001). A related issue is the assumption in much modeling that systems are aggregations of unitary parts and processes; we will later look at the way in which an understanding of complex adaptive systems challenges this assumption.

Assumptions. Most modeling assumptions are related to deciding what the essential elements of the model are and how they are to be represented. Regarding the essential elements, later in the chapter we will make a distinction between modeling of *ordered* systems and *unordered* systems. Associated with this differentiation are *reductionist* and *emergent* approaches. With respect to modeling assumptions, reductionist models emphasize the system's *properties,* whereas in emergent approaches, *interactions* are viewed as key (Cruthchfield, 1995). As a general rule (Sickels, 2001):

- Models that make *simplifying assumptions* at the lower bound tend to be high-level.
- Models that are *more detailed* (less abstract) at the lower bound tend to be reductionist (where the focus is on the properties at the lower bound).
- Emergent models tend to be simple at the lower bound, like the high-level models. But unlike the high-level models, these fine-grained entities are represented individually (rather than in aggregate), *and* the models provide for rich interactions among the independent entities.

Relationship Between Abstraction and Granularity. Abstraction and granularity are interrelated but distinct concepts. Abstraction is a lack of detail, specificity, or "concreteness." As models become finer-grained, the level of detail increases, thereby decreasing abstraction. Thus, abstraction and granularity are correlated. But abstraction can vary without varying granularity; for example, "M1 tank" is far more abstract than "M1 tank, serial number xyz123," which refers to a specific instantiation of the "M1 tank" abstraction, but both are of the same granularity. Similarly, we can vary granularity without varying abstraction: A coarse-grained entity (such as "tank") is not inherently more abstract than a fine-grained entity (such as "tank tread"). It is only when we decompose something into its constituent finer-grained parts—thereby providing detail—that abstraction becomes linked to granularity. It turns out that lower model bounds can be more precisely viewed as granularity/abstraction lower bounds, rather than just lower bounds on granularity. For example, both psychologists' and economists' lower bounds are human beings, but by comparison with the relatively concrete concerns of psychologists, economists often deal with highly abstracted models of humans. (Sickels, 2001).

3.1.3. Predictive Models

We previously stated that intelligence is the product of a knowledge creation process. Intelligence products can be described by the analytic method categories of *descriptive* analysis and *inferential* analysis. As shown in Figure 3.1, inferential analysis includes:

- Inference of the past
- Inference of the present
- Inference of the future

Predictive models are in the later category (highlighted by the shaded box) and are used to predict future events germane to the intelligence objective. Predicting future events with sufficient specificity is key to enabling preemption of terrorist attacks. Examples of predictive products include forecasts (e.g., probability of a state to fail and the implications to national security strategy, proliferation of WMD from North Korea) and indications and warnings (e.g., warning of an imminent terrorist attack against the United States).

In general, predictive models are used to *predict* future system states and to understand

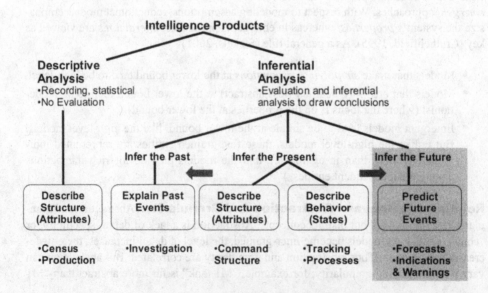

Figure 3.1. Intelligence products by analytic methods.

the implications of changes. In predictive modeling, data are collected, a model is synthesized, predictions are made, and the model is validated as additional data are collected. Models can take many forms, including simple linear equations or complex agent-based systems.

Quoting from Waltz (2003, p. 160), the fundamental problem-solving reasoning process is described as bidirectional, moving between known evidence (*causes*) and desired solutions (*effects*):

- Analysis proceeds from a presumed *effect* (solution) backward searching for the sequence of antecedent *causes* that would bring about that effect. An effect-to-cause sequence that leads backward to a complete set of known causes (axioms or assumptions) is a proven hypothesis.
- Synthesis, in contrast, proceeds from known antecedent causes forward toward a solution by linking them, in a construction process, to assemble a cause–effect chain that leads to the solution.

Cause-and-effect chains are the basis of traditional prediction of future events. For example, Indications and Warning (I&W) systems are deeply rooted in this model. Warning (of effects) is linked to observation of known indicators causally linked to those effects. It is also important to note here that this form of analysis is *outcome-based*. Later we will challenge the underlying assumptions of this *model*.

Reductionism is the analytic approach whereby a problem is *decomposed* into its constituent parts. Problem solution proceeds by solving the parts. Engineering is dominated by reductionist approaches—and for good reason. The problem decomposition is motivated by an implicit requirement to maintain causal chains *or explanation* throughout all levels of decomposition. A key underlying assumption is that the problem (or system) equals the sum of the parts. Thus, we can analyze properties of component parts specifically to explain the whole. From our knowledge of the components, we can *synthesize* a model of the whole. We can also target intelligence collection to fill known knowledge gaps at any level of the decomposition.

Chattoe (2000) describes equation based high-level models as useful for *prediction* but not useful for *explanation*. We have stated that reductionist models are generally focused on causality. High-level equation-based prediction models tend to capture only *correlations,* not causal relationships among system attributes. The correlations *may* correspond to causal relationships, but correlation doesn't always imply causation. In many cases the correlation of two variables may be caused by some other "hidden" variable, rather than by any causal relationship between the variables themselves, or there may be no actual cause (if by *cause* we assume intentionality), just opportunism. Likewise, correlation may imply spurious causal relationships. For theses reasons, high-level models generally don't have explanatory power, and they are used only for prediction. Crutchfield (1993) also addresses the general differences between explanatory and predictive models in stating that in high-level approaches a system's behavior is modeled by observing and capturing (via mathematical equations) *correlations* among aggregate-level attributes of the system. The goal of these models tends to be *prediction,* rather than explanation.

3.1.4. Static Versus Dynamic Models

Here we introduce another modeling consideration: static and dynamic modeling approaches. Static approaches, such as deductive pattern matching models, are inherently reductionist and are based on assumptions that the system being represented by the model has *observable static properties* that can be collected and matched against the model. Thus, to the degree to which the data match the static model, the model provides the estimate of the system being observed. As such, static models are "predictive" only when the *causal observables* match the *effect mechanisms* (cause and effect or indications and warning) within the model.

In contrast, dynamic models are employed for representing systems that exhibit *emergent behavior,* especially complex adaptive systems behavior, where reductionist modeling approaches fail to capture the key system properties—that is, the system interactions. *Emergence* occurs when elements of a system interact over time. Emergent phenomena often exhibit surprise. As shown in Figure 3.2, what distinguishes a *complex* system from a *complicated* system is that in a complex system patterns emerge from the interaction between the systems elements. Associated with the concept of emergence are the linked ideas of co-evolution and irreversability, that is, as the various agents interact and patterns form, those patterns influence the nature of the agents and create change which can stabilize and may not then reverse. Such changes are not always apparent until after they have occurred and for that reason represent catastropic change. One example of that is the switch of a civilian population to active support for a terrorist group or the willingness of a population to accept draconian measures to prevent future outrages.

Complex systems are often confused with chaotic systems because both exhibit emergence and are both unordered in nature, something to which we will return later. However, they are different, and that difference is usefully summarized by Axelrod and Cohen (1999) as follows:

> Chaos deals with situations such as turbulance that rapidly become highly disordered and unmanageable. On the other hand complexity deals with systems compromising many interacting agents. While complex systems may be hard to predict, they may also have a good deal of structure and permit improvement by thoughtful intervention.

Although we separate chaotic from complex systems, they also share much in common, not least their difference from the ordered domains of simple and complicated systems, in that neither of them exhibits the predictable patterns of cause and effect that we see in order. All four domains have different relationships between cause and effect and therefore require different approaches to analysis and decision-making; this is managed through the *Cynefin* framework, described later, which allows for what is known as *multi-ontology sensemaking*.

Unordered systems, both complex and chaotic, exhibit the following key properties:

- Order is *emergent* (contrast with planned or determinant).
- Order arises as a result of co-evolutionary processes, but when patterns form, they are irreversible, thereby creating a strong demand for weak signal detection.
- Retrospective coherence: Cause and effect are discernible only in retrospect if at all (when the context is known for proper interpretation of the data), and there is a danger that correlation will be confused with causation.
- Patterns generally are not repeatable except by accident.
- The future of the system is not knowable (i.e., not "predictable").

3.1.5. Anticipatory Models

When referring to models that deal with inference of future events, we use the term *anticipatory* instead of predictive, because the term *predictive* connotes a level of omni-

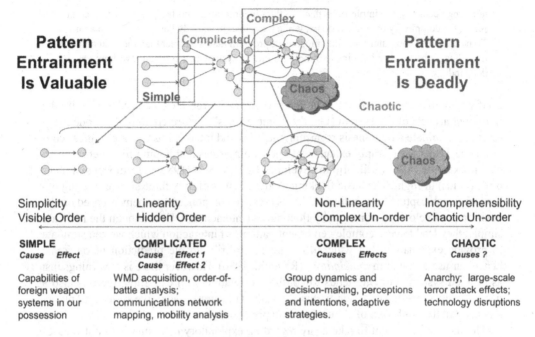

Figure 3.2. Four levels of system complexity.

science that does not usually exist and thus represents a danger inherent in traditional approaches. The issue is not that predictive models should not be used, but rather that one should understand their limitations and apply them in those domains for which they have great utility and not in those domains where they can actually set up conditions for surprise. If we can match data against known *patterns* (models) we have seen before, then our models can be predictive. But if we are dealing with emerging patterns, then the patterns we know can actually blind us and prevent us from "seeing" the new patterns. We also have a strong tendency to attribute "cause" where it may not exist: a variant of the fundamental attribution error. This phenomenon is rife throughout the great surprises in history. We refer to this phenomenon as *pattern entrainment.* This distinction is highlighted in Figure 3.2. We will come back to this point later in the chapter. To avoid pattern entrainment, we need a way to "*anticipate*" new patterns to enable us to "see" those patterns as they emerge and to understand the key changes of the situation which will almost certainly also require a way to disrupt the pattern entrainment of intelligence analysts. Thus, anticipatory models must both be dynamic and have emergent properties.

Thomas Schelling said "One thing a person cannot do, no matter how rigorous his analysis or heroic his imagination, is to draw up a list of things that would never occur to him." So how then do we develop models that have dynamic and emergent properties with a requirement for fidelity and anticipatory power *and* which have the goal of presenting us with information that we do not anticipate (i.e., surprise us)?

Quoting from Pagels (1988), who captures the fundamental challenge:

Usually in computer modeling scientists are trying to model a rather complex system (otherwise why bother to use a computer). The fundamental hypothesis behind simulating complex systems is that the apparent complexity of the system is due to a few simple components interacting according to simple rules that are then incorporated into the program. In a certain sense, the complexity of some systems, while real enough, actually has a simple explanation. To be effective, computer modeling must use a program that is simpler than the system one is modeling. Otherwise on is trying to blindly mimic the system on a computer, without any understanding.

So if we are to avoid modeling a system using trial and error, then we need to identify the important aspects of the system (i.e., the "simple rules") *before* creating the model. It is essential to initiate a hypothesis regarding the rules and interactions that are of great consequence, rather than simply exhaustively generating rules and hoping for emergence. A classic example is Boid's algorithm developed by Reynolds (1986). The model simulates birds (boids) in flight. The basic flocking model consists of only three simple steering behaviors which capture how individual boids (system components) maneuver based on the positions and velocities of its nearby flockmates (interactions). Even though the rules are simple, they lead to very complex emergent patterns of interaction which we can simulate to provide explanation, but which does not necessarily enable prediction of outcome, hence our use of the term *anticipatory* (Reynold, 1986). However there is a warning: Just as ordered systems thinking tends to confuse correlation with causation, there is also a danger in the modeling community that have adopted complex adaptive systems thinking, namely that the confusion of simulation with prediction.

The most salient point to take away regarding exploratory modeling is that it focuses on *possibility and plausibility,* not accuracy and probability. As such, anticipatory modeling provides insight into emergent patterns of "system" behavior for which accurate, predictive, validated models can't be created. Thus, questions regarding validation (validation in the classic sense) of anticipatory models reflect a lack of understanding regarding the utility of such models.

3.1.6. The Importance of Context in Modeling

Humans are influenced by many factors in their analysis and decision-making. The *context* of a human actor's analysis and decision-making (including historical context, other players surrounding the actor, the actor's goals, beliefs, perceptions, and decision-making styles) all play a role in the analysis and decision-making process and its outcome. That said, for human agents, context is critical in the interpretation of data or, stated differently, in the conveyance of meaning to data. The description of an *agent system* that models these factors is given below. In these systems, we need to establish symbolic contextual representations for tacit/prior knowledge and for its use within an analytic process to frame hypotheses (conjectures) and construct beliefs:

$$C \models S$$

The symbols, S, in any communication are interpreted by the receiver's context, C. C cannot be completely represented symbolically. For example:

- Question: Why did you take Interstate 66 today on your way into work?
- Answer: I came in after 9:00 A.M.
- Context: High occupancy vehicle restrictions are lifted after morning rush hour. This is not a reasoning tree, but the most salient response.

Boisot (2002, 2004) depicts a "cognitive hierarchy" as shown in Figure 3.3. In this model, *data* are discriminations between states of the world. *Information* is "data in context." The "lenses" used to put data in context drive what becomes information. Information activates agents. *Knowledge* is a property of agents predisposing them to act according to particular patterns. Note that when we are dealing with intelligence targets in the physical domain, we can use physics (sensor phenomenology) to convey meaning to the data. It is important to realize that Boisot's model departs from the conventional view which sees data, information, knowledge, and wisdom as a form of linear progression. With Snowden (2002) it establishes that knowledge as a shared context is a key aspect of the construction of information from data.

Since the terrorist attack on the United States on September 11th 2001, there has been much written about the reason for the "surprise." A popular metaphor concerns issues about the U.S. Intelligence Community's inability at "connecting the dots." To understand the criticality of context in analysis, we need to take the "connect the dots" discussion to a deeper level than the conventional wisdom so often reported in the popular press. According to Gladwell (2003):

> To read the Shelby report . . . is to be convinced that if the C.I.A. and the F.B.I. had simply been able to connect the dots, [then] what happened on September 11th should not have been a surprise at all. Is this a fair criticism or is it just a case of creeping determinism?

Dots are a metaphor for "signals" in a background of noise. Data become *dots* based on relevance. Relevance is a function of context. So an essential part of the problem is how relevance is determined. So it follows in evidential reasoning that data become relevant *evidence* only when it changes beliefs or perceptions about hypotheses. It is also true that beliefs and perceptions largely drive the search for and determination of evidence.

The question of Weapons of Mass Destruction and how the Intelligence Community (almost unanimously) reached the erroneous conclusions that it did are perhaps even more immediately illustrative of the issue of context than the similar factors which contributed to the intelligence failures of 9/11. The irony of the Iraq WMD intelligence failure is that the accepted wisdom—"Saddam Hussein has WMD"—was in fact a perfectly reasonable conclusion based on the range of information on which the various intelligence analysts made their conclusion. They used a 10-year-old baseline established following the first

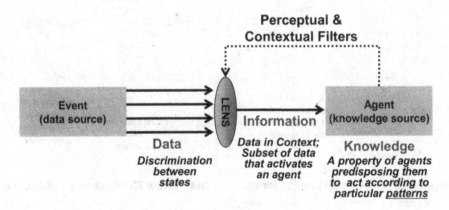

Figure 3.3. Importance of context in knowledge formation.

Gulf War, added to it voluminous information from UN inspections that took place in the immediate aftermath of the war and, finally, fragmentary data from a variety of sources. To the extent that this represented the totality of the data they considered, and because of the context in which the data were obtained and understood, "Saddam Hussein has WMD" was a perfectly legitimate conclusion. Those "dots" were connected properly. The problem was both that they did not have enough "dots' or the right dots and that the dots that they had were firmly embedded in a context that led them inexorably to their erroneous conclusion. So, contrary to common wisdom, the problem was not one of "dot connection," but rather one of "dot production." Or put another way, the worst thing an intelligence analyst can do is to draw conclusions on the basis of too few and too old dots without proper understanding of the context in which they exist. The final, and most terrible, irony is that this intelligence failure and attendant loss and sacrifice could have been avoided in at least two ways. On the one hand, a truly rigorous examination of the available dots and an appreciation of the impact of the context of those dots should have given both analyst and policy-maker pause. On the other hand, new dots (and discovery of new contexts) could still have been obtained by probing actions by American and British authorities to determine whether the too few, too old dots and their associated context really survived scrutiny based on new dots and amended context (MacGaffin and Kay, personal communication).

The critical role of context in detection and discovery processes is shown in Figure 3.4 (Waltz, 2004). In *detection,* the hypothesis sets the contextual lens for viewing data. That context is used to qualify evidence to be fitted to a known hypothesis. In *discovery,* data reveals a new context which in turn reveal a new hypothesis or explanation.

It is important to point out the implicit assumption and the resultant misconception that all the dots are unambiguously "preexisting," rather than a significant portion of dots which are created by some *a priori* context that may or may not be correct. As soon as an event shifts into the past, and is therefore subject to the wisdom of hindsight or "creeping

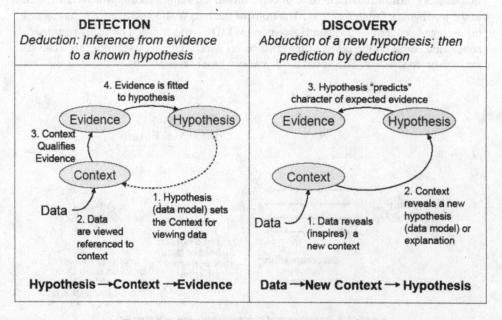

Figure 3.4. Role of Context in detection and discovery.

determinism" (as Gladwell puts it), context becomes clear due to the luxury of retrospection. Because we know the precise context, we can see the dots. At the same time, it appears that the dots were *preexisting*! But that is just an illusion. To make matters worse, in anticipating the future, someone has to make assumptions about what is and what isn't a dot (i.e., imposing a contextual lens), and those assumptions may well "filter out" critical information. Improper filtering of critical information creates the conditions for surprise.

This phenomenon is known as *retrospective coherence*. When you look backwards, everything makes perfect sense, but there was no way at the time to predict that particular outcome. What happens is that "patterns of interaction" stabilize and you can now understand how this occurred and it is explainable, but it could not be predicted in advance. Causality is apparent only after the event. These are key attributes of a complex system.

The conventional wisdom is that "big events lead to big changes and small events lead to small changes." Thus small events (i.e., weak signals) can be ignored. However, complexity science (often referred to as the "science of surprise") teaches us that small events can lead to big changes, and do so *very quickly*. This is essentially the thesis of Gladwell's tipping point concept (Gladwell, 2000), although a weakness of Gladwell's thesis is that he fails to recognize that some events are noncausal. What this all means is that in order to avoid surprise, we must find solutions to weak signal detection and to achieving the agility required to adapt to emerging threats.

3.1.7. Shared Context and its Implications on Collaboration

Knowledge is the way in which we construct information from data, so knowledge is about creating shared context (Snowden, 2002). Here we introduce the importance in recognizing different contexts and why the whole *sensemaking* process is about creating a shared context.

This begs the question: *How then is "context" different from "content."* If the two sides of a communication do not share any context, then no information can be created and everything remains data. Because context is used to convey meaning to data, then shared context creates shared meaning. Content is abstracted from context, and specifically from people. Information is created from data by the provision of shared context which contrasts with the simplistic but all-to-common linear model of data–information–knowledge–wisdom.

Collaboration is well known as one of the key solution elements to intelligence reform. To most, collaboration is about breaking down stovepipes, sharing data, and seeking consensus. In fact, most collaboration systems provide mechanisms for managing and sharing data. *The real value of collaboration is about sharing context (thinking), not data.* This becomes clear when you consider Figure 3.3 and what it really means. Sharing context is all about multiple perspectives, conflictive argument, and embracing paradox—all which enable humans to find the right perspective lenses in which to properly understand the contextual complexity though which correct meaning is conveyed to data. Consider the Gladwell quote (which in part motivates this work):

Twenty years after Pearl Harbor, the United States suffered another catastrophic intelligence failure, at the Bay of Pigs: The Kennedy Administration grossly underestimated the Cubans' capacity to fight and their support for Fidel Castro. This time, however, the diagnosis was completely different. As Irving L. Janis concluded in his famous study of "groupthink," the root cause of the Bay of Pigs fiasco was that the operation was conceived by a small, highly cohesive group whose close ties inhibited the beneficial effects of argument and competition.

Centralization was now the problem. One of the most influential organizational sociologists of the postwar era, Harold Wilensky, went out of his way to praise the "constructive rivalry" fostered by Franklin D. Roosevelt, which, he says, is why the President had such formidable intelligence on how to attack the economic ills of the Great Depression.

3.2. THE NEED FOR ANTICIPATORY MODELS

The Global War on Terrorism represents a major shift in the need to cope with a fundamentally different threat than the one faced in the Cold War. Fifty years of Cold War has created a bureaucratic paradigm optimized for dealing with the Soviet threat. As shown in Figure 3.5, during this period, the national security strategy was one of global surveillance with a sensor-centric intelligence competition. As such, predictive warning was focused on Soviet capability and intent, where capability (e.g., detection of capital assets such as missiles, and tanks on the battlefield) was estimated from sensor data (the context of which was driven by sensor phenomenology and physics) and intent was based largely on ideology. The Cold War was dominated by *symmetric warfare* and the doctrine of *mutual assured destruction*. Maintaining international stability was the foundation of policy.

The recent report of the *National Commission on Terrorist Attacks Upon the United States* (2004) investigates how the U.S. Government failed to anticipate and prevent the terrorist attacks on 11 September 2001 and emphasizes the need for *transformation* in dealing with the terrorism threat. The 9/11 Commission report illustrates *retrospective coherence*—that is in hindsight, the outcome makes sense (i.e., is coherent) but at the time prior to the event it was not possible to predict that particular outcome (e.g., "connect the

	Cold War 1950-1990	Transition- Proliferation 1990-200?	Global Future 200?-2020
Global Situation	Bipolar World	World in Transition	Globalized World
National Security Strategy	Global Surveillance Mutual Destruction (Heavy Response)	Information Dominance Precision Retaliation (Rapid Response)	Knowledge Dominance Precision Coercion (Proactive Persuasion)
Deterrent Factor	Mass Destructive Power	Information plus Destructive Power	Pure Intellectual Capital
The Intelligence Competition	Sensor-Centric Competition for surveillance (to see, synoptically)	Network-Centric Competition for bandwidth and connectivity (to tell, rapidly)	Knowledge-Centric Competition for knowledge, foreknowledge (to know, deeply)
Key Intelligence Technologies	Space sensors	Information Nets Visualization ChemBio Sensing	Complexity Science Neuroscience Quantum Computing Bio, Nano-technology Computer Intelligence
Security Policy Environment	Contain 3rd World Communism Treaty-based Internationalism Institutions to maintain world order (UN, World Bank, IMF)		"Coalitions of the Willing" Demise of Institutionalism World "Disorder" Globalized Complexity

Toffler's Third Wave?
- 1st Wave - Agricultural Revolution
- 2nd Wave - Industrial Revolution
- 3rd Wave – Knowledge Revolution

Key technology Investments in methods to sense, model, and influence human dynamic behavior.

Figure 3.5. Changes in the national security environment.

dots") because causality is apparent only after the full and proper context needed to interpret the data is understood. It is important to point out that retrospective coherence does not occur in tracking physical targets where the dynamics of context are based on physical kinematics—this is contrasted with the ability of humans and human systems to construct reality through language and the co-evolution of language with practice.

During the Cold War, intelligence targets were generally about finding hidden equipment, hidden places and hidden material processes. These targets are largely in the *physical* domain. Because of the shift in the threat and the needed emphasis on counter terrorism and winning "hearts and minds," new intelligence targets must be addressed. These new targets are about *hidden people, social processes and networks*. These targets require much more focus on the *cognitive* and *symbolic* domains. Waltz (2003, pp. 186–190) states the importance of integrated modeling, evidential reasoning, and data fusion across all three of the domains of reality: the physical domain (e.g., vehicles, facilities—governed by the laws of physics), the symbolic domain (e.g., information artifacts, packets, sessions), and the cognitive domain (e.g., intent, mental states, ideas). The three domains are shown in Figure 3.6.

3.3. RETHINKING THE PREDICTION PROBLEM

The CIA's Consumer's Guide to Intelligence (Central Intelligence Agency, 1999) states:

> Reduced to its simplest terms, intelligence is knowledge and foreknowledge of the world around us—the prelude to decision and action by US policymakers.

Foreknowledge requires prediction of future events. The dominant ideology in organizations assumes that in any "system" there are underlying relationships between cause

DOMAIN	CHARACTERISTICS
COGNITIVE ·Human Cognition-emotion ·Perception ·Conception ·Intention	
·SYMBOLIC ·Explicit information ·Communication and Media content	
PHYSICAL ·Mass and energy ·Human bodies, Infrastructure, Weapon systems	

Intelligence targets exist as objects in three fundamental domains of reality – *and should be modeled as such*:

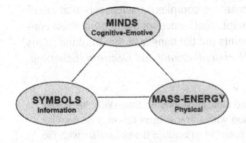

Figure 3.6. Three domains of reality.

and effect which can be discovered or estimated in such a way that the future can be predicted and planned on the basis of desired outcomes. Examples include investigations of past failures (9/11, Pearl Harbor). This paradigm assumes that the future can be *predicted and controlled on the basis of an understanding of the past;* in effect, it is assumed that there is a correct answer and that a failure to achieve the desired outcome is a failure of analysis, data capture/distribution, or execution. The human desire for order is understandable and has historically been contrasted with chaos as an "either–or" alternative. Thus, the function of strategy is to reduce the potential exposure to chaos by reducing uncertainty. This dichotomy between order and chaos is both wrong and of itself an incomplete statement of the various types of possible systems. In management science we see this evidenced in the heavy reliance on case studies and consultancy recipes, seeking to replicate best practice by studying the practices of successful organizations and seeking to identify aspects of those practices which can be imitated by others. While many organizations have benefited from these approaches, such approaches confuse *correlation* with *causation* and, if improperly applied, can lead to disaster.

Consider, for example, the best practices of Jack Welsh as the successful CEO of General Electric. Based on the popularity of recent books and adoption by business management consultants, one is compelled to believe that all that is needed is for one to follow Welsh's recipe and a company will be as successful as General Electric under Welsh. Such thinking assumes that the underlying organization (in General Electric and the target company) are predictable ordered systems when they are complex systems. Anyone who has been through a reorganization can appreciate complex system behaviors.

3.3.1. Surprise and Complexity

In the year 2000, Eliot Cohen (Cohen, 2000) pointed out the following:

> The common use of the term 'post-Cold War era' indicates a failure by students of international affairs to characterize today's world . . . one might usefully call the past dozen years 'the age of surprises.' The U.S. Government has been surprised by the end of the Warsaw Pact, the disintegration of the Soviet Union, the Iraqi invasion of Kuwait. . . . There is no reason to think the age of surprises is over, and there are many reasons to think we are still at it's beginning.

Since then a key tenant underlying causation (cause and effect relationships) is the notion that big events lead to big changes and small events lead to small changes, thus small changes can be ignored. In contrast, a key tenant of complexity science is that small events can lead to big changes. This is the principle that underlies the *tipping point* concept previously discussed. Thomas Schelling points out the danger in this thinking in his Foreword to Wohlstetter's classic work *Pearl Harbor: Warning and Decision* (Schelling, 1962):

> The danger is not that we shall read the signals and indicators with too little skill; the danger is in a poverty of expectations—a routine obsession with a few dangers that may be familiar rather than likely. . . . There is a tendency in our planning to confuse the unfamiliar with the improbable. The contingency we have not considered seriously looks strange; what looks strange is thought improbable; what is improbable need not be considered seriously.

Systems displaying surprising (i.e., unpredictable) behavior are the same as with those we consider to be in some way complex. Complexity is called the *"science of surprise"* (Casti, 1995). Complex systems have the following properties:

- *Unstable*: Small changes can produce large effects.
- *Chaotic*: Simple rules can produce seemingly random outcomes.
- *Irreducible*: System cannot be understood by decomposition.
- *Paradoxical*: More than one 'right' (or wrong) answer.
- *Emergence*: Patterns form from interactions and self-organization, not plans.
- *Co-evolutionary*: As patterns coalescence and achieve stability they can be irreversible (e.g., civilian support of terrorism).

The goal of anticipatory modeling is to anticipate future event dynamics and patterns, for the purpose of avoiding surprise. This is quite different from predicting the future. Thus any approach to anticipatory modeling must consider complexity.

3.3.2. Ordered and Unordered Systems

Earlier we established a difference between ordered and unordered systems. *Ontology* is derived from the Greek word for *being,* and it is the branch of metaphysics which concerns itself with the nature of things. In this context we are using it to understand different types of system based on the nature of causality that underpins the reality of those systems. We earlier (Section 3.1.4) established a difference between ordered and unordered systems, and we further distinguished simple from complicated order and complex from chaotic unorder; and the ability to distinguish between these ontologies and to act accordingly we term *multi-ontology sensemaking*. The basic insight of multi-ontology sensemaking is that the way in which we know things, the study of which is called *epistemology,* differs according to the underlying ontology; therefore there are different approaches to, and possibilities for, both prediction and anticipation.

Traditional approaches to intelligence tools and methodologies tend to single ontology sensemaking, assuming an ordered system in which the failure to predict is a failure of intelligence. We challenge this pervasive *assumption of order* and contrast two high-level systems as *ordered* or *unordered*. In ordered systems there are repeating relationships between cause and effect which allow control based on desired outcome and planning. In contrast, unordered systems are either retrospectively coherent or turbulent, but in neither case can we plan on the basis of a precise outcome; *instead we manage the conditions* under which different novel solutions emerge, monitoring carefully for favorable and unfavorable patterns. Ordered systems are the realm of *empirical truth;* here we can exploit patterns we have seen before by pattern matching to data. Order is described in terms of domains of *simple order* (e.g., the domain of linear prediction) and of *complicated order* (e.g., the domain of analysis where continued data collection and analysis leads to uncertainty reduction). In unordered systems we must *discover* emerging patterns (i.e., patterns that we have not seen before and that do not repeat). Unordered systems are the realm of *contextual truth,* where there is no right answer and where management of emerging patterns is the paradigm.

The Cynefin framework emerged from pioneering work in knowledge management (Snowden, 2002) in various commercial and government applications, but during the period from the year 2000 to the current date the authors with others have been develop-

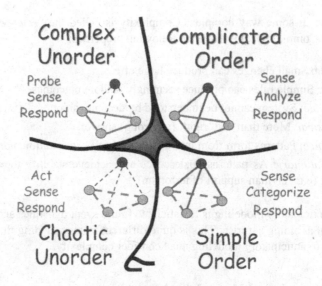

Figure 3.7. Cynefin framework.

ing its use in the context of intelligence. The framework has been taken up in the same field by other authors in related fields such as bioterrorism.

The framework as shown in Figure 3.7 has five domains, two each for order and unorder and a central domain of disorder. The framework allows us to discuss various approaches associated with each domain and why it is important to understand the domain of the problem and the corresponding approaches that are appropriate to dealing with the problem. The sensemaking framework is called *Cynefin*. Cynefin comes from a Welsh word that is inadequately translated into English as "habitats," but is more properly understood as the multiple affiliations that profoundly influence what we are but of which we can only be partly aware. The name seeks to remind us that all human interactions are strongly influenced and frequently determined by the patterns of our multiple experiences, both through the direct influence of personal experience and through collective experience expressed as narratives.

Each of the Cynefin domains carries with it different diagnostic or intervention techniques as well as differing organizational structure. The organizational structure is shown in Figure 3.7 as a series of pyramids in which solid and dotted lines are used to illustrate the network strength between the center (at the top) and the network. Issues can also move between domains as "dynamic" shifts requiring rapid switches in strategic and operational approaches. A detailed treatment of the development and use of the both domains and dynamics can be found in *New Dynamics of Strategy* (Kurtz and Snowden, 2003), but will be summarized here.

Simple Order: Here the relationships between cause and effect are self-evident; having gathered data, then best practice can be applied and a rapid response triggered. We *sense* incoming data, *categorize* it based on our understanding of the past, and then *respond* in a structured and predictable way. Because the cause and effect relationships are self-evident, a hierarchical command and control can be used; in effect, we apply empirically determined *best practice*. Military "rules of engagement" are a classic example of a useful approach for a problem that is in the domain of simple order, but can be disastrous if the problem is complex. For example, during the Cuban missile crisis the military saw the crisis as a problem of simple order and argued "rules of engagement" as the correct approach to the problem—particularly the approach to the blockade. In contrast, the Kennedy administration saw the crisis as a problem of complex unorder (see below) and increased interactions with the Soviets with the hope that a solution to the crisis would emerge.

Complicated Order: In this case the relationships between cause and effect are not self-evident but require some form of expert interpretation. We *sense* incoming data which are then *analyzed* by experts who form conclusions on the basis of which we *respond*. Because of the need of experts, knowledge organization forms tend to require high degrees of consensus between experts that can verge on oligarchic control. The consensus is also more likely to generate pattern entrainment that is difficult to disrupt. There will always be different ways of responding, but such means of response are subject to objective validation, and this is thus a domain in which we can apply *good* but not *best* practice.

Complex Unorder: Here relationships between cause and effect either may not exist or, at best, can only be made coherent in retrospect. Given that there are many possible patterns, before we can sense we must first *probe* to see what patterns are possible, we then sense and *respond* by reinforcing good patterns and disrupting bad ones. Formal structures and processes tend to impose order where no order exists; thus, informal networks, natural leadership, gut feel, experience-based intuition are all indicated in this domain. Applying best or good practice is a mistake, as here appropriate behavior will result from interactions within the system and between the system and ourselves.

Chaotic Unorder: This is the domain where the interactions between agents in the system become chaotic, and there are no perceivable relationships between cause and effect no matter how much data we capture, or what analytical tools are deployed. This is the domain of the opportunist who can *act* to create stable patterns, *sense* the emergence of those patterns, and then *respond*. Practice here is always novel, which is both a threat and an opportunity depending on whether the use of domain is accidental (a rapid and catastrophic descent into a crisis) or deliberate (the breaking of all preexisting patterns) so that *novel* practice can emerge. A classic example is the rise of the dictator Adolph Hitler from the chaos of the economic depression and harsh reparations of post–World War I Germany.

Disorder: This is the central domain of the Cynefin framework and is the state of not knowing what type of system you are in. In practice, this is where most intelligence takes place, and the natural tendency is then to bias your interpretation of events to your personal proclivity for action: Highly structured thinkers will tend to interpret the data as supporting their process to manage simple order; experts will require more time and money to analyze the situation; field agents will make multiple small tests by actions or questions to see what is possible; and the charismatic tyrants will interpret any situation as a crisis so they can be given power to act without reference to other authorities.

A common characteristic of the unordered domains is that the sense-respond mechanism is tightly coupled, while in the ordered domain they are separated by either categorization or analysis. The reason for this is that in every unordered system it is not possible to separate any diagnostic from an intervention; the act of investigating the system changes its nature, and, as such, every diagnostic needs to be designed as an intervention and every intervention designed to create diagnostic properties: Probes can be primarily diagnostic, but they are always interventions, they change the dynamics of the system by their presence alone.

The framework was originally developed to create a simple mechanism and critical language, through which an organization can improve its overall cognitive effectiveness: For example, if the situation is complex, the question is not "What is going to happen?" or "Why are they doing this?" but "What probes are we going to construct?" However, subsequent experimental use has extended the application to a variety of areas including demonstrating and recognizing cognitive bias between agencies. In one experimental government project in Asia, a group of agencies were brought together to socially construct a set of several hundred data items referencing the SARS outbreak which were evenly distributed across the Cynefin framework. Two weeks later the same individuals were brought together but separated into their different agencies working in separate areas to distribute the data items over the same framework. At this point, although it was their material and had been evenly distributed, the material was distributed in different ways by the different agencies—a representation of which is shown in Figure 3.8.

When the groups discussed the different patterns, the reasons were fairly obvious. Agency A was required to produce evidence to prosecute in courts and were thus biased towards evidence and causality, Agency B was "intelligence" with no requirement for concrete evidence before action. The agency most familiar with the model and who also had both training and conceptual awareness of the different domains produced the most even distribution of the material.

The use of this is multifold, but a particular application is to reduce the miscommunication that is often evident in inter-agency collaboration. The use is not to eliminate the differences as they relate to the day-to-day function of the agencies, but to allow them to understand the different frames of reference through which they view data.

The Cynefin framework is one of a category of methods in an emergent field known as *social complexity,* which we describe in the following section.

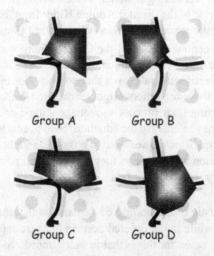

Figure 3.8. Multi-group sensemaking with the Cynefin framework.

3.3.3. Complexity Modeling

We define the position of *social complexity* in the context of the other dominant approaches. In Figure 3.9, the vertical axis contrasts the *ordered* systems with those that are *unordered*. The horizontal axis contrasts two generic approaches: One is based on *rules* and allows a degree of precision over process (in order) or starting conditions and agent behavior (in unorder). Those based on *heuristics* tolerate greater ambiguity, recognizing that precise rules are not always possible, they focus instead in general guidelines and principles. *In effect, this represents a tradeoff between the control of rules and the adaptability of heuristics when the context changes (optimization versus agility).* The tradeoff can also be considered as one between *stability* and *resilience*. In nature, any stable system is not resilient and vice versa. In managing threat, too much stability can reduce the adaptive capacity of an agency or system. One of the insights of complex systems thinking is that frequently a degree of inefficiency in information transfer has to be introduced to enable a system to be *effective*.

This matrix allows us to gain a new understanding of the development of management science over the last century (Snowden and Stanbridge, 2004). We argue that large bureaucracies seek order through imposition of rules; this allows efficiency through optimization on a known problem, but at the expense of agility. Given relative stability over time, bureaucracies form and optimize on a known problem solution. In an extreme form, bureaucracies can become so rule bound that they become fossilized with a complete loss of agility.

The growth of complexity science, particularly associated with the Santa Fe Institute, challenges the basic concept of order as recognizing that in complex systems, "order" emerges from the interaction of agents. As previously described, one of the most commonly quoted examples is Boid's algorithm, which allows the flocking behavior of birds to be modeled through the application of three simple rules. Much work has been done in utilizing complexity principles. The method is to identify the rules (or possible rules) under which individual human agents behave and then to use computer models to simulate the interaction of those agents over time to see what patterns emerge. By implication, operations or policy planners can interact with the modeled system by modifying the rules, observing the effect of those modifications, and then adopting beneficial rules. Considerable benefit has been gained in a variety of areas such as scheduling using these techniques, and more is promised. One key finding in human systems that replicate findings in nature is that suboptimal agent behavior is necessary for system optimization—some-

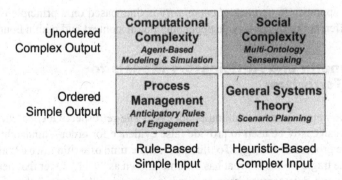

Figure 3.9. Approaches to complexity modeling.

thing that flies in the face of the obsession with efficiency that characterized *Process Reengineering*. This approach is called *Computational Complexity;* although it moves to unorder, it shares the concept of rules with process reengineering—but instead of applying those rules at the level of system, it applies them at the level of agent.

3.3.4. Social Complexity

Social complexity, to which Cynefin belongs, is more recent in origin. It shares with computational complexity the concept of unorder and related ideas such as emergence. However, it argues that there are unique aspects to human systems, which means that we cannot use general biological models for human systems. One of the early thinkers in this field was Ralph Stacy (Stacy, 2001), who is well known for his work to differentiate complexity thinking from that of systems thinking and developed an approach known as participative complexity. The Cynefin approach known as *contingent complexity* argues that human systems are differentiated from biological systems in at least four significant ways:

- First humans do not make decisions based on rules, but on a first-fit pattern they match either with their personal experience or with the narrative experience of the society in which they live or work (at various levels). There are in consequence no rules to model.
- Second, humans have multiple identities that we maintain in parallel and move between according to context. These identities can be individual roles (father, son, brother) or collective (American, social club member, university fraternity). In consequence, there are no agents to model (or at least no simple representation of agency).
- Third, intentionality in human systems is difficult to identify because we are self-aware and capable of opportunistic reinterpretation of accidental events to indicate that they resulted from our planned actions. We find it difficult to distinguish "winks" from "blinks" (to use an old philosophical expression).
- Fourth, humans in their various identities are capable of self-aware action, sometimes known as free will. As a result, humans are capable of creating order or structure in their interactions. This fourth reason leads to one of the key pragmatic aspects of the Cynefin approach which recognizes that most approaches provide benefit and value, *but within context.*

The Cynefin approach to *contextual complexity* is thus based on a principle of bounded diversity: Different things have value depending on the context and within boundaries.

3.3.5. Cynefin and Anticipatory Models for Counter Terrorism

Introducing complex systems thinking is not easy. The retrospective coherence of complex systems can easily be used to provide false evidence for order—hindsight is a common sin in the process of strategy. To illustrate: At the time of writing, we are almost four years since the tragic events of what has become known as "9/11." Over that period, more investigations and data capture have resulted in increasing "evidence" that there was a failure in intelligence—that is, that the various dots were not joined up in time to detect the terrorists' plans which could (it is argued) have been prevented. Increasingly, the failure is being seen as an issue of knowledge management. It is not the intention of this chapter to argue that better intelligence might not have improved the possibility of prevention, although in complex and chaotic systems, *prevention* and *detection* should not be linked, and a focus on detection will detract from prevention because it will lead to a focus on discovering what is going to happen so that it can be prevented, rather than changing the boundary conditions (management of emerging patterns) so that *unknowable* events are less likely to happen. The debate over 9/11 illustrates the way in which the use of retrospective coherence is dangerous:

- No two terrorist outrages are the same, and the system evolves quickly to adapt to detection devices and methods. Similarly, no two actions by a competitor are the same, and the pattern entrainment of human collective decision-making means that an organization's best practice based on past success often hinders, and in many cases distracts from, innovation.

- The mathematics of joining up the dots provides a simple counter: If I have four dots, then there are six possible linkages between those dots and 27 possible patterns arising from those dots and linkages; if the number of dots rises to 10, then the number of possible patterns is over three trillion (Boisot, 2004). (Additionally, the mathematic combinatorics of connecting the dots is explained to illustrate the difficulty and need for new approaches in anticipatory modeling; that is, 4 "dots" leads to 64 possible patterns, 10 "dots" leads to 3.4 trillion patterns. Special consideration is given to understanding contextual complexity and dynamics in anticipation of terrorist threats.) [38]

- Data alone are not informative without (1) a shared context between giver and receiver and (2) an ability to gain attention of the decision-maker. (The most recent space shuttle disaster showed that all the right data were in the right place at the right time, but context and attention issues prevented them from being acted upon.)

By recognizing the importance of different ontologies, the nature of human decision-making, and the nature of noncausal (or only retrospectively coherent) systems, we improve the overall cognitive effectiveness of the symmetric power.

SUMMARY

We have provided an overview of new thinking about "predictive models" for counterterrorism that are focused on sense making in a complex and emergent world. Our intent is to provide the reader with a context and background that will inform and support many of the issues to be considered regarding "predictive modeling" approaches, but also present a new paradigm for thinking about intelligence problems and particularly the interaction between intelligence and operational/policy planning and decision-making under conditions of ambiguity and uncertainty. We have used the term *anticipatory* instead of *predictive,* because the term *predictive* connotes a level of omniscience that represents a danger inherent in traditional approaches. Both "traditional" and "new" approaches to modeling were discussed with pros and cons of the assumptions intrinsic to these approaches addressed.

REFERENCES

Axelrod, R., and Cohen, M. (1999). *Harnessing Complexity.* New York: The Free Press.

Boisot, M. (2002). *Knowledge Assets: Securing Competitive Advantage in the Information Economy,* New York: Oxford University Press, 312 pages.

Boisot, M. (2004). Based on discussions regarding the counter-terrorism problem.

Casti, J. (1995). *Complex-ification: Explaining a Paradoxical World Through the Science of Surprise,* 336 pages. New York: HarperCollins Publishing.

Central Intelligence Agency (Office of Public Affairs) (1999). *A Consumer's Guide to Intelligence,* p. vii. Washington, DC: Central Intelligence Agency,

Chattoe, E. (2000). Why is building multi-agent models of social systems so difficult? A case study of innovation diffusion. (http://www.sociology.ox.ac.uk/chattoe.html).

Cohen, E. A. (2000). *Foreign Affairs,* June.

Crutchfield, J. P. (1993). Observing complexity and the complexity of organization. In: *Inside Versus Outside,* H. Atmanspacher (ed.), Series in Synergetics, pp. 235–272. Berlin: Springer, SFI Technical Report 93-06-035 (http://www.santafe.edu/projects/CompMech/papers/OCACOTitlePage.html).

Crutchfield, J. P. (1995). The evolution of emergent computation. *Proceedings of the National Academy of Sciences, USA* **92**(23):10742–10746 (http://www.santafe.edu/projects/evca/Papers/EvEmComp.html).

Gladwell, M. (2000). *The Tipping Point: How Little Things Can Make a Big Difference.* Boston: Little, Brown, 288 pages.

Gladwell, M. (2003).Connecting the Dots, The Paradoxes of Intelligence Reform. *The New Yorker,* March 10 (http://www.newyorker.com/printable/?critics/030310crat_atlarge).

Graham, I. (1991). *Object-Oriented Methods.* Reading, MA: Addison-Wesley.

Hobbs, J. R. (1985). Granularity. In: *IJCAI-85: Proceedings of the 9th International Conference on Artificial Intelligence,* pp. 432–435. San Mateo, CA: Morgan Kauffman.

Kurtz, C., and Snowden, D. (2003). The new dynamics of strategy: Sense making in a complex-complicated world. *IBM Systems Journal* **42**(3):462–483.

Lincoln, A. (1862). Lincoln's Second Annual Message to Congress, December 1.

MacGaffin, J. and Kay, D. Personal communication.

McKelvey, B. (1999). Complexity theory in organization science: Seizing the promise of becoming a Fad? In: *Emergence: A Journal of Complexity Issues in Organization and Management,* Vol. 1, No. 1, M. R. Lissack (ed.). Hillside, NJ: Lawrence Erlbaum Associates (http://www.emergence.org/Emergence/Archivepage.htm).

Pagels, H. (1988). *The Dreams of Reason: The Computer and the Rise of the Sciences of Complexity,* New York: Simon & Schuster.

Reynolds, C. W. (1986). http://www.red3d.com/cwr/boids/

Schelling, T. (1962). In: Wohlstetter, *R, Pearl Harbor: Warning and Decision.* Stanford, CA: Stanford University Press.

Schelling T. (no attribution)

Shaw, M. (1984). Abstraction techniques in modern programming languages. *IEEE Software* **1**(4):10–26.

Sickels, S. J (2001). Unpublished manuscript.

Snowden, D. (2002). "Complex acts of knowing: Paradox and descriptive self awareness. *Journal of Knowledge Management* **6**(2):100–111.

Snowden, D., and Stanbridge, P. (2004). The landscape of management: Creating the context for understanding social complexity. *Emergence: Complexity and Organisation* **6**(1&2):140–148.

Stacy, R. (2001). *Complex Responsive Processes in Organizations: Learning and Knowledge Creation.* New York: Routledge.

The 9-11 Commission Report. (2004). *Final Report of the National Commission on Terrorist Attacks Upon the United States,* Official Government Edition, 585 pages.

Waltz, E. (2003). *Knowledge Management in the Intelligence Enterprise.* Boston: Artech House.

Waltz, E. (2004). Integrating data fusion and data mining. NSSDF-04, June.

Williams, P. Intelligence requirements for transnational threats: New ways of thinking, alternative methods of analysis, and innovative organizational structures, Unpublished paper for the CIA Global Futures Partnership.

Chapter 4

Information Processing at Very High Speed Data Ingestion Rates

J. Brian Sharkey, D. Weishar, J. W. Lockwood,
R. Loui, R. Rohwer, J. Byrnes, K. Pattipati, S. Eick,
D. Cousins, and M. Nicoletti

4.1. INTRODUCTION

Analysts in the Intelligence Community (IC) must search through massive volumes of data to gather evidence to support or refute their hypotheses. Their effort is made all the more difficult because data appear as unstructured text written in multiple languages and use characters that may have multiple encodings. Furthermore, data processing systems must ingest massive volumes of data at very high data rates.

Existing approaches to analyzing and processing these data have not kept pace with the increasing volume of data that needs to be processed. The IC discards large volumes of data even though they might contain useful information. In this chapter, we explore a new approach for analyzing and organizing intelligence data that provides for categorizing and translating the content of high-speed data streams.

4.1.1. Background

The intelligence analysis problem can be represented as a closed-loop system (Figure 4.1). An analyst selects a hypothesis or argument to be proven from a bank of previously created threat scenarios or generates one in response to an unpredicted event. A hypothesis may affect the parameters used to process incoming data that enter the system either through live data feeds or through queries to databases.

Depending on the situation, data may need to be conditioned, formatted, structured, and, often, converted from one language to another to make it suitable for human interpretation. Humans and algorithms then examine the processed data to detect relevant words, names, places, and events of interest to find associations with the problem being considered. Linked entities can identify activities and describe relationships among the organizations, such as terrorist groups of interest, and uncover other potential leads for continuing the evidence discovery process in light of the investigatory problem undertaken. We refer to the process described, highlighted in Figure 4.1, as the "front end" because it deals with the analysis of data very close to the data ingestion point. The major scientific concern with the front end is that all required processes are human-intensive and

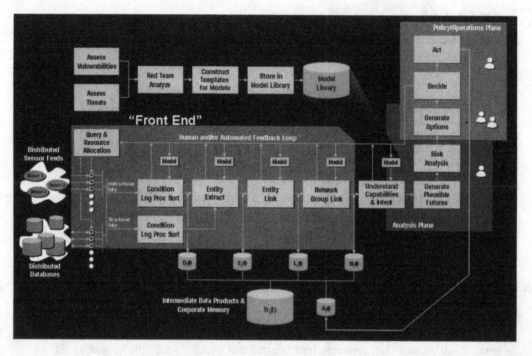

Figure 4.1. A reference model for intelligence analysis.

the rate of data delivered is exceptionally high. Two solutions currently exist for this problem: (1) Store as much raw data as possible for delayed analysis, and (2) make early decisions regarding the value of data to be saved and discard all data that do not satisfy pre-established criteria. Disk capacity doubles approximately yearly, but this increased capacity is quickly offset by the rapid introduction of additional sensors with more aggressive data ingestion rates. In addition, the ability to effectively query these massive archives for relevant data is becoming increasingly difficult. Furthermore, analysts often base the decision to discard data on primitive rules associated with metadata related to data collection methods, matching rules, and/or the physical/temporal aspects of the data itself. This results in increasing difficulty to keep pace with data explosion: Data are discarded before their value can be fully understood. The first step toward solving this problem is to develop high-speed, high-performance document categorization technologies.

Automatic document categorization also has a number of commercial applications. Automatic labeling of newswire articles for distribution purposes and automatic replies to customer e-mail are two of the better-known commercial applications; content-based routing of documents to interested parties is an application we expect to grow as more finely grained categorization becomes available.

Innovative mathematical transformation algorithms implemented in software have shown promise for automatically understanding the content of documents (Papadopoulos, 1998; Dumais et al., 1997). Similarities among content from multiple sources can be computed, but computation can be very expensive—$O(n^2)$ in some cases, where n is the number of documents that contain information. Lengthy computational time limits the amount of information that can be processed.

In this chapter, we propose a radically new approach based on *mathematical transformation algorithms* implemented in reconfigurable hardware to continuously (re)process and (re)interpret high volumes of multilingual, unstructured text data. The system can automatically elicit the semantics of streaming input data, organize the data by concept (regardless of language), and associate concepts with similar concepts needed to parameterize text-processing models. To evaluate the potential of this system, we are building an experimental test bed that enables *rapid implementation of data processing algorithms in hardware.* The system provides a high-performance infrastructure consisting of a hardware-accelerated content processing platform, a mass storage device that holds training data and experimental scenarios, and tools for analyzing and visualizing the data.

In our test bed, we performed experiments in which we implemented three transformation algorithms in hardware. Our platform uses the Field-programmable Port Extender (FPX) modules. Each FPX contains two Field Programmable Gate Arrays (FPGAs): one large FPGA called the Reconfigurable Application Device (RAD) and another, smaller FPGA called the Network Interface Device (NID) (Lockwood, 2001a). Multiple RAD circuits on multiple stacked FPX cards implement semantic processing circuits in reconfigurable hardware to perform "bag of words"-style text analysis. We used NID circuits to route the data through the system at a bandwidth of 2.4 gigabits/second. We use this platform to implement our transformation and perform experiments.

4.1.2. A New Approach to Processing Streaming Data

Today's processing flow involves detecting a context and tracking information that relates to that context. Specifically, the "detect and track" scheme can be described as follows:

1. Filter all information gathered and only save information germane to the immediate problem.
2. Relate atomic facts in the data, including the names of people, places, things, and the relationships among them.
3. Process the results with queries built to uncover "golden nuggets" of useful information.
4. Track and report changes in the status of the information.

As shown in Figure 4.2, the new processing flow *inverts* the mechanism today's processing flow uses. The new process flow proceeds as follows:

1. Catalog and save all information (or as much as possible) gathered based upon atomic facts in the data.
2. Populate many parallel hypotheses (concepts) with facts and data.
3. Use a machine to detect when a hypothesis has sufficient supporting facts (relevance) to warrant evaluation and reinterpretation of data.
4. Aggregate evidence for the hypotheses and report any changes that emerge.
5. Adapt and refine concepts when a concept is deemed either too broad or too specific.

The new processing flow provides substantial cognitive support to the analyst about all data used in all ongoing or past analyses. In other words, the new processing flow keeps track of the original data, the relationships of the data to other information, and the reason

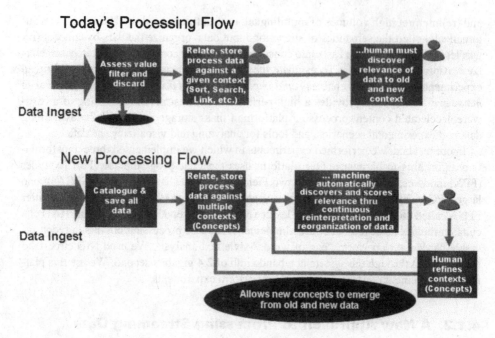

Figure 4.2. A new approach to information management.

why the data were considered important at the time. Additionally, since no analyst could possibly have "seen" *all* data the system collected, the new flow enables analysts to search for related information and discover new associations and patterns in the vast amounts of data.

A *concept-based* storage and retrieval approach enables "track before detect" by reducing the intellectual impedance mismatch between analysts and machines. Special-purpose computing machines that continuously (re)process and (re)interpret extremely large volumes of unstructured multilingual text data enable this process.

As data are streamed into the system, they are transformed by high-speed semantic processing hardware into a multidimensional space, as shown in Figure 4.3. Documents containing similar information—that is, those that relate to similar concepts—will tend to cluster into similar regions of the multidimensional space. A cluster defines a concept. This concept, in turn, is used as a basis to store and receive documents. Clustering self-organizes data. By automatically indexing concepts in distributed databases, servers can automatically and rapidly retrieve data collected from multiple sources. They can score how their position in the multidimensional concept space relates to a new hypothesis. These circuits, implemented as high-speed computing machines in reconfigurable hardware, can rapidly score vast amounts of data to determine what information is relevant to a new concept.

The methodology we describe allows us not only to organize data by concept, but also to continuously scan data and associate it with existing or newly formed hypotheses. Hypotheses can be thought of comprising combinations of concepts. We want to continuously reprocess and reinterpret data to score in real time.

Data can come from various sources that include the Internet, intelligence gathering agencies, and public news feeds. The system instantly processes text for semantic meaning and groups related content together; multiple hypothesis servers process the data in

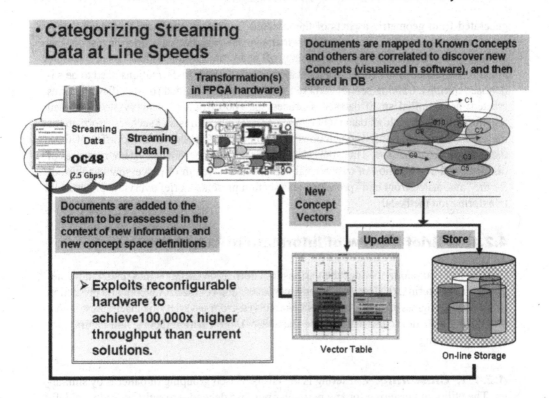

Figure 4.3. Real-time concept-based streaming data processing.

parallel to find new concepts and topics that emerge. Because data are constantly being processed, hypothesis servers can continually aggregate weak information in support for, or rejection of, both new and ongoing concepts. Once a hypothesis gains sufficient support, action can be taken.

4.2. INFORMATION TRANSFORMATIONS FOR CONTENT ANALYSIS

We define information transformations as a class of applications that, through the use of alternative representations of textual (or in some cases multimedia) data, can achieve significant performance improvements over conventional database techniques, especially when performing operations, such as document searching, pattern matching, and hypothesis corroboration. A number of applications are related to the problem of content analysis: data reduction, compression, clustering, categorization, information retrieval, and hypothesis testing.

Transformations are created by identifying a set of *features* in the data, mapping these features into a new coordinate system, and defining appropriate distance measures in these new coordinate spaces. Coordinate systems that uncover hidden relationships among data in the space spanned by the features in the original data are most desirable. Some transformations are engineered directly by choosing statistical relationships that may serve as intuitive measures of similarity (for example, the *mutual information* metric used in Fair Isaac's co-clustering, detailed later in this chapter). Other transformations are generated from geometric aspects of the selected feature set (such as the distance measures in normed spaces). Certain transformations self-organize data upon ingestion, enabling efficient, unsupervised processing of new information—ideal when massive amounts of data need to be ingested and categorized. Some transformations need to be supervised during a training session, where instructions are provided (or specific categories created) as an initial small dataset is processed. The difficulty of applying supervised transformations to the high data rate content analysis problem is that such transformations may not be able to identify connections in the data that are significantly different from those they were trained on. Thus, the selection of features, coordinate system, measures of distance, and combination of transformations provide a wealth of processing capabilities for the "automated front end" problem. This section presents a brief overview of pertinent transformation methods.

4.2.1. A Brief Review of Information Transforms

Our top-level taxonomy divides the various transformation methods into three main categories: (a) clustering, (b) learning-based techniques, and (c) matrix algebra and projection techniques. Progress in these methods has evolved from a variety of disciplines: signal processing, statistics, computer science (databases), information theory, and natural language processing.

4.2.1.1. Clustering. Clustering is the unsupervised grouping of patterns by similarity. The utility of clustering for any particular purpose depends strongly on finding a definition of "similarity" relevant to that purpose. Oftentimes, and particularly in natural language applications, it is best to define "similarity" in terms of the contexts in which a pattern typically appears. This kind of dataset reduction has been done in many ways: using cluster descriptors, centroids, and other methods of describing the central notion that links the clustered data. Jain et al. (1999) provide a comprehensive discussion of clustering techniques based on algorithmic issues, such as whether the algorithms are *agglomerative or divisive, monothetic or polythetic, hard or soft (fuzzy), deterministic or stochastic, and incremental or nonincremental.* Based on these algorithmic issues, they categorize various methods of classifying and organizing clustered data into two categories: *hierarchal* and *partitioning.* Various algorithms, ranging from single-link and complete-link hierarchical clustering approaches to partitioning algorithms—based on hard or soft K-means, minimal spanning trees, order statistics, mixture densities, nearest neighbors, Kohonen's learning vector quantization, self-organizing maps, adaptive resonance theory, evolutionary optimization, Tabu search, simulated annealing, information-theoretic clustering, ant-based clustering, and wavelets—have been developed. Many partitioning algorithms have some chance of working on large datasets as the algorithms compute in $O(n)$ time, while most hierarchal algorithms scale as of $O(n^2)$, where n is the number of data points. Below, we discuss information-theoretic clustering (because it has provided impressive performance in the test bed) and ant-based clustering (because of its potential for massive parallelism). Other techniques are discussed in Cousins et al. (2004a,b) and the companion chapter by Ammar et al (2005).

4.2.1.1.1. Information-Theoretic Co-Clustering. Most clustering algorithms seek to cluster one dimension of the matrix (e.g., documents) based on similarities along the second dimension (e.g., word distribution of documents). For sparse, noisy, and

high-dimensional data, simultaneous clustering ("co-clustering") of both rows and columns is beneficial. For example, given a term-document matrix, co-clustering in two dimensions simultaneously clusters terms and documents. Co-clustering is more robust to sparsity than traditional single-dimensional (e.g., terms or documents) clustering. In addition, unlike traditional matrix approximations, such as the singular value decomposition (SVD) and principal component analysis (PCA), co-clustering preserves the non-negativity of the term-document matrices. Co-clustering can be used as a pre-processor for supervised classification or as a classifier in its own right.

The effectiveness of co-clustering can be quantified in terms of the error between the original data matrix and the approximation matrix based on co-clustering. Recently, it has been shown in Banerjee et al. (2004) that the so-called Bregman divergence measure provides a unified framework for co-clustering. This measure includes a number of widely used divergence measures as special cases, including the squared Euclidean distance [used in k-means clustering (Jain and Dubes, 1982)], the Kullbak–Leibler (K–L) divergence [used in mutual information-based clustering (Dhillon et al., 2003a,b, Rohwer, 2002, 2003)], and Itakuro–Saito distance [used in the LBG vector quantization (Linde et al., 1980)]. The divergence measures can be used to create either hard or soft clusters. One can employ a variety of algorithms, including simulated annealing, genetic algorithms, and sequential row–column clustering, to solve the co-clustering problem. The sequential algorithms used for co-clustering may find a local minimum for the problem. Here, we restrict our attention to the information-theoretic co-clustering problem of maximizing the mutual information between the clustered random variables (or equivalently, minimizing the loss in mutual information between the original random variables and the mutual information between the clustered random variables). Clustering with Bregman divergences may be found in Banerjee et al. (2004).

The reduction in uncertainty due to knowledge of another random variable is called *mutual information (or information gain)*. For two random variables X and Y, mutual information is a non-negative symmetric function in X and Y:

$$I(X; Y) = H(X) - H(X \mid Y) = H(Y) - H(Y \mid X) = H(X) + H(Y) - H(X, Y) = I(Y; X)$$

$$= \sum_{x,y} p(x, y) \log_2 \frac{p(x, y)}{p(x)p(y)} \tag{4.1}$$

where $p(x, y)$ is the probability mass function and $H(X) = E[-\log_2 p(X)] = -\sum_{x \in \{x_1, x_1, \ldots, xm\}} \log_2 p(x)$ is the entropy of random variable, X. Entropy, $H(X)$, measures the amount of *information* (measured in bits per symbol) required to describe sets of symbols from X. $H(X|Y)$ is the conditional entropy of X given Y; it is the expected value of the entropies of the conditional distribution $p(x|y)$, averaged over the conditioning random variable, Y. The mutual information $I(X; Y)$ measures the amount of information from X successfully captured by Y (and thus the degree to which Y predicts X). Evidently, when X and Y are independent—that is, $p(x, y) = p(x) p(y)$—mutual information is zero.

Mutual information is related to the relative entropy or Kullback–Leibler (K–L) divergence measure. The K–L divergence, or relative entropy, is defined as

$$D(p(x) \| q(x)) = E_{p(x)}\left[\log_2 \frac{p(X)}{q(X)}\right] = \sum_{x \in \{x, x_2, \ldots, x_{m_1}\}} p(x) \log_2 \frac{p(x)}{q(x)} \tag{4.2}$$

Thus, the K–L divergence measures the inefficiency of encoding X with probability mass function $p(x)$ using another probability mass function, $q(x)$ (thus providing a measure of the dissimilarity between the two distributions). K–L divergence is non-negative, but not necessarily symmetric for arbitrary distributions $p(x)$ and $q(x)$. The mutual information is the K–L divergence between the joint probability mass function $p(x, y)$ and the product mass function $p(x) p(y)$, that is,

$$I(X, Y) = E_{p(x,y)}\left[\log_2 \frac{p(X, Y)}{p(X)p(Y)} \right] = D(p(x, y) \| p(x)p(y)) = \sum_{x,y} p(x, y) \log_2 \frac{p(x, y)}{p(x)p(y)} \quad (4.3)$$

The objective of co-clustering is to simultaneously cluster rows of $p(X, Y)$ into k disjoint groups and cluster columns of $p(X,Y)$ into l disjoint groups such that loss in mutual information between the original random variables (X,Y) and the mutual information between the clustered random variables is minimal. Let $\hat{X} = R(X)$ $\hat{Y} = C(Y)$ denote the random variables associated with the row and column clusters, that is, $R(X)$: $\{x_1, x_2, \ldots, x_m\} \to \{\hat{x}_1, \hat{x}_2, \ldots, \hat{x}_k\}$ and $C(Y)$: $\{y_1, y_2, \ldots, y_n\} \to \{\hat{y}_1, \hat{y}_2, \ldots, \hat{y}_l\}$. The optimal co-clustering solves the problem

$$\min_{\hat{X}, \hat{Y}} [I(X; Y) - I(\hat{X}; \hat{Y})] \Rightarrow \max_{\hat{X}, \hat{Y}} I(\hat{X}; \hat{Y}) \quad (4.4)$$

subject to the number of row clusters, k, and column clusters, l. A fixed joint probability mass function $p(x, y)$, $I(X; Y)$ is fixed; hence, minimizing the loss in mutual information is equivalent to maximizing the mutual information of the clustered random variables, $I(\hat{X}; \hat{Y})$. Because $\hat{X} = R(X)$ and $\hat{Y} = R(Y)$ are deterministic functions of X and Y, respectively, we have the conditional entropies $H(\hat{X} \mid X) = H(\hat{Y} \mid Y) = 0$. Consequently,

$$I(X; Y) - I(\hat{X}; \hat{Y}) = [H(X) - H(\hat{X})] + [H(Y) - H(\hat{Y})] + [H(\hat{X}, \hat{Y}) - H(X, Y)]$$

$$= H(X \mid \hat{X}) + H(Y \mid \hat{Y}) + H(\hat{X}, \hat{Y}) - H(X, Y)$$

$$= E_{p(x,y)}\left[\log_2 \frac{p(X, Y)}{p(X \mid \hat{X})p(\hat{X}, \hat{Y})p(Y \mid \hat{Y})} \right] = D(p(x, y) \| q(x, y)) \quad (4.5)$$

Here, $q(x, y) = q(x, y, \hat{x}, \hat{y}) = p(x \mid \hat{x})p(\hat{x}, \hat{y})p(y \mid \hat{y})$, where $x \in \hat{x}, y \in \hat{y}$. Thus, co-clustering seeks to decompose the m by n joint probability mass function matrix $[p(x, y)]$ as a product of three matrices: an m by k conditional probability mass function matrix, $[p(x \mid \hat{x})]$; a k by l joint probability mass function matrix for clustered variables, $[p(\hat{x} \mid \hat{y})]$; and an l by n conditional probability mass function matrix, $[p(y \mid \hat{y})]$.

Another way of looking at the co-clustering objective function is

$$I(X; Y) - I(\hat{X}; \hat{Y}) = H(X \mid \hat{X}) + H(Y \mid \hat{Y}) - H(X \mid Y \mid \hat{X}, \hat{Y})$$

$$= E_{p(x,y)}\left[\log_2 \frac{p(X, Y) \mid \hat{X}, \hat{Y}}{p(X \mid \hat{X})p(Y \mid \hat{Y})} \right] = D(p(x, y \mid \hat{x}, \hat{y}) \| p(x \mid \hat{x})p(y \mid \hat{y})) \quad (4.6)$$

An intuitive interpretation of this relation is that, within a cluster denoted by $(\hat{x}, \hat{y})$, minimization of loss in mutual information seeks to approximate $p(x, y \mid \hat{x}, \hat{y})$ by an approximating product distribution of the form $p(x \mid \hat{x})p(y \mid \hat{y})$. Because the marginal probabilities are preserved by clustering—that is, $p(x) = q(x)$, $p(y) = q(y)$, $p(\hat{x}) = q(\hat{x})$, $p(\hat{y}) = q(\hat{y})$—it can be shown (Dhillon et al., 2003b) that $q(x, y) = p(x)q(y \mid \hat{x}(x)) = p(y)q(x \mid \hat{y}(y))$. Consequently,

$$D(p(x, y) \parallel q(x, y)) = E_{p(x)}[D(p(y \mid x) \parallel q(y \mid \hat{x}))] = E_{p(y)}[D(p(x \mid y) \parallel q(x \mid \hat{y}))] \qquad (4.7)$$

Thus, the loss in mutual information can be expressed in either of two ways: as a weighted sum of the K–L divergence measures between row-conditioned probability mass function $p(y \mid x)$ and row-lumped distribution $q(y \mid \hat{x})$ or as a weighted sum of the K–L divergence measures between column-conditioned probability mass function $p(x \mid y)$ and column-lumped distribution $q(x \mid \hat{y})$. This observation leads to an iterative sequential row-column clustering algorithm (Dhillon et al., 2003a,b).

The co-clustering approach in Rohwer, 2002, 2003), termed Association-Grounded Semantics (AGS) and discussed in greater detail in Section 4.2.2, differs from the sequential row–column algorithm in (Dhillon et al. (2003a,b) both in data representation and algorithmic implementation details. Given a set of training documents, the approach seeks to cluster words in these documents such that similar meaning words go into similar clusters. To do this, they define a set of "contexts" in which any given word might appear. For example, if one were to identify names or parts of speech, contexts could be "nearest verb after the nearest name which precedes the given word," "ends with an s," "distance to the end of the sentence," and so on. Evidently, contexts are considered similar when they contain similar words, and words are considered similar when they occur in similar contexts. Thus, the co-occurrence table generated from training documents has words as rows and contexts as columns; the entries are the number of times each word occurred in each context. They divide each of these entries by the sum of all entries to obtain a joint probability mass function $p(x, y)$ over words and contexts. The use of contexts as columns implies that one can experiment with the same document data using different instantiations of contexts ("evolving hypotheses about a situation").

Another interesting feature of the AGS algorithm is that the entries of the word-context joint probability mass function matrix are assumed to be random with Dirichlet prior (a distribution over multinomials). Practical issues, such as discounting to compensate for the overfitting of data and dyadic representation of the Dirichlet prior to significantly reduce the number of parameters, are considered in the estimation process.

Finally, the row and column-clustering steps in AGS use simulated annealing moves. In principle, the Dirichlet parameters should be updated for every trial move, but this is computationally expensive. Instead, they are updated at intervals depending on a heuristic estimate of how much an update would affect the objective function.

So far, we have assumed that the numbers of row and column clusters (k, l) are known. Selecting the number of clusters in a data-driven fashion is still an open research problem that may be approached via information-theoretic criteria (Rissanen, 1978), such as the Minimum Description Length (MDL). Extending co-clustering algorithms to multidimensional data (e.g., term-document matrix evolving over time), although conceptually straightforward, has not been addressed.

4.2.1.1.2. Ant-Based Clustering. Ant-based clustering, a massively parallelizable heuristic for grouping of objects, was inspired by the clustering of corpses observed in real ant colonies (Deneubourg et al., 1991; Lumer and Faieta, 1994; Handl et al., 2005). If corpses are randomly distributed in an area at the beginning of an experiment, the ants form cemetery clusters within a few hours, following a behavior similar to aggregation.

The ant-based clustering algorithms adopt similar basic principles of transporting data items (e.g., paragraphs of text) that are laid out in an artificial environment (e.g., a corpus of documents), and they spatially arrange them in a sorted fashion.

The basic mechanisms of ant-based clustering are straightforward: Simple computational agents that randomly move in a square, toroidal environment model ants. Data items that are to be grouped are initially scattered in this environment. The agents can pick up, transport, and drop the data items. The picking and dropping operations are stochastic; they are biased by the similarity and density of data items within the agent's local neighborhood. Agents are likely to pick up data items that are either isolated or surrounded by dissimilar ones; agents tend to drop the transported items in the vicinity of similar ones. Consequently, a self-organized spatial distribution of data emerges.

Unlike with traditional clustering methods (Jain and Dubes, 1988)—which gradually build or refine clusters based on an explicit representation of data and clusters—with ant-based clustering, clusters emerge in a self-organized fashion as a result of distributed actions and positive feedback only; information on the number of clusters, the size and shape of clusters, and the assignment of data items to clusters is contained in the final spatial distribution of data. Despite its appealing features, real-world applications of ant-based clustering are rare at this time, as are rigorous mathematical proofs of convergence.

4.2.1.2. Learning-Based Techniques.

Several transformation techniques are learning-based, such as parametric density models, hidden Markov models, nonparametric density estimation models, reduced Coulomb energy networks, linear discriminants, multilayer perceptrons, probabilistic neural networks, radial basis function networks, support vector machines (SVM), and context-specific Bayesian networks (Duda et al., 2001; Bishop, 1995). We discuss the SVM below (because it has provided impressive performance on text categorization tasks [e.g., Cooley, 1999; Joachims, 1999; Sun et al., 2002; Namburu et al., 2005)] and context-specific Bayesian networks (because Naïve Bayes algorithm, which is a special case of context-specific Bayesian network, has performed very well on text categorization tasks (McCallum and Nigan, 1998). We discuss other techniques in the references cited earlier and in Ammar et al. (2005).

4.2.1.2.1. Support Vector Machines.

The SVM, as a supervised statistical learning theory, has gained popularity in recent years for text categorization because of its four distinct features. First, SVM is a universal learner by proper selection of the kernel function. Second, it can learn with a small number of training samples, even when the number of features (terms) is large. Because text categorization problems typically have a high-dimensional input space, SVM is naturally suited for this problem. Third, SVM is well-suited for sparse computations, and document vectors in text categorization problems are very sparse. Finally, most text categorization problems are linearly separable. The SVM has been successfully employed in many other applications, such as pattern recognition, multiple regression, nonlinear model fitting, fault diagnosis, and so on.

The essential idea of SVM classification is to transform input data to a higher-dimensional feature space and find an optimal hyperplane that maximizes the margin between the classes. The group of examples that lie closest to the separating hyperplane is referred to as support vectors. Support vectors are obtained by solving a quadratic programming problem (Burges, 1998; Smola, 2000). For multiclass problems, SVM requires a voting scheme based on results of pairwise classification results. For SVM regression, input is first mapped onto high-dimensional feature space using nonlinear mapping, and then a linear regression is performed in this feature space.

4.2.1.2.2. Context-Specific Bayesian Networks.

Bayesian networks (BNs), also known as probabilistic networks, causal networks, or belief networks, are formalisms for representing uncertainty in a way that is consistent with axioms of probability theory (Jorden, 1999; Neapolitan, 2003; Pearl, 1988) and for providing intuitive and modular representation of domain knowledge. BNs represent domain knowledge using two components: a qualitative component and a quantitative component. The qualitative component (the structure) is in the form of a directed acyclic graph, where the nodes represent the probabilistic attributes (e.g., terms in text categorization) in the domain with a finite set of values for each attribute, and the links represent probabilistic dependency relationships among the attributes. The quantitative component (the parameters) is in the form of a conditional probability distribution of each attribute given each combination of the states of its parent attributes.

Given a set of nodes $V = \{1, 2, L, m\}$, a Bayesian network computes the joint probability of attributes $\underline{x} = \{x_1, x_2, L, x_m\}$ in the network via

$$P(\mathbf{x}) = \prod_{i=1}^{m} P(x_i \mid \pi(x_i)) \qquad (4.8)$$

where $\pi(x_i)$ is the possible instantiation of the parent nodes of i.

BNs provide a powerful paradigm for knowledge representation and inference under uncertainty and have been used for classification in the form of the naive Bayes (NB) classifier (Langley et al., 1992). This classifier is a simple BN with a strong assumption of conditional independence among the attribute variables, x given the label $H \in \{H_1, H_2, \ldots, H_c\}$, that is, $P(\mathbf{x} \mid H) = \Pi_{i=1}^{m} P(x_i \mid H)$. The BN classifier selects the class with the maximum posterior probability, $k = \arg \max_{i \in \{1,2,\ldots,c\}} P(H_i \mid \mathbf{x})$. Despite its unrealistic assumption, the performance of BN classifier is surprisingly good in text classification (McCallum and Nigam, 1998; Namburu et al., 2005).

Recent efforts have focused on relaxing the conditional independence assumption and on using flexible structural representations for the BN to improve classification accuracy. BN classifiers (Chen and Greiner, 2001; Friedman et al., 1997) exploit supervised learning algorithms (e.g., Jorden, 1999) to learn the graphical dependency relationships and conditional probability parameters among the attributes from the training data. For example, the Tree Augmented Naive Bayes (TAN) classifier employs a tree-like structure among the attributes. The Bayesian Network Augmented Naive Bayes (BAN) classifier extends the TAN by allowing arbitrary acyclic dependencies among the attributes.

Bayesian Multi-net (BMN) classifier is class-specific in that a local BN is used to represent each class. This representation is more expressive than BNs because it allows different dependency relationships among attributes for different classes. The Recursive Bayesian Multi-net (RBMN) classifier represents the domain knowledge using a decision-tree induction algorithm, with component BN classifiers at the leaves. This allows more flexible partitioning of the attribute space and enables categorization of some nonlinearly separable data.

4.2.1.3. Matrix Algebra and Projection Techniques.

Projection techniques and clustering differ in that data projections are associated with coordinate transforms, whereas clustering is a general description of similar data organized in a multidimensional space. Matrix operations reduce dimensions; this expedites searching within data, because all searching tends to be linear and of the reduced dimension (Berry et al., 1995).

Some projection methods use randomized algorithms to approximate working on the full-dimensioned data and, as a result, are very fast (Achlioptas, 2001; Brin and Page, 1999). Others, such as the Singular Value Decomposition (SVD), project *a priori* selected representation of data [i.e., the terms versus documents matrix of Latent Semantic Indexing (LSI)] onto a lower-dimensional subspace via singular value analysis, where the underlying semantic structure, it is hoped, is evident and pattern matching is performed more efficiently. These kinds of transformations work by removing redundancy in the representation and by removing the "noise" inherent in the data. SVD-based techniques have received a lot of attention and are based on a concrete mathematical background. Cousins et al. (2004a,b) provides a short introduction to SVD, its application to LSI, and computational issues, including randomized algorithms for SVD. Other transformations use an algorithmic convergence technique to find a suitable projection. These include the FastMap and MetricMap approaches (Ammar et al., 2005).

Principle Component Analysis (PCA) is a projection/classification method closely related to SVD. This technique can be used in either an unsupervised or supervised fashion. Partial Least Squares (PLS), also known as Projection to Latent Structures, is a supervised dimensionality reduction technique applicable to the text categorization problem. It has properties similar to those of the SVD and PCA, but with the advantage of being more robust to noise. PLS is applicable when terms are many and redundant, there is no well-understood relationship between the terms and document class variables, categorization is the main goal, and the dataset is missing values. This makes it attractive, but future work must be done to improve computability; PLS is slower than SVM, which has comparable classification accuracy. We single out PLS and describe it briefly because of its exceptional performance on text categorization and robustness to noise (Namburu et al., 2005).

PLS seeks to maximize the covariance between the $n \times m$ independent training data matrix $X = A^T$ (transpose of the term-document matrix) and the $n \times p$ dependent matrix Y (corresponding to p document classes) for each component of the reduced space. Here, Y is formed in such a way that it contains class i information in the ith column of row j of Y if the document in row j of X corresponds to the ith class. PLS builds a regression model between X and Y that consists of three steps. In the first preprocessing step, the X and Y columns are centered so that they have zero mean. In the second step, PLS generates uncorrelated latent variables (concepts), which are linear combinations of the original terms. The basic idea is to select the weights of the linear combination to be proportional to the covariance between the terms and document classes. Once the concepts are extracted, a least squares regression is performed to estimate the document class. Both matrices X and Y are decomposed into a number of concepts (called components in the PLS parlance)—known as the model reduction order—plus residuals. Each concept captures a certain amount of data variation. This reduction order (i.e., number of concepts) is determined by cross-validation. The details of PLS algorithm may be found in Cousins et al. (2004a,b) and Namburu et al. (2005). Noting that for Gaussian X and Y, the mutual information is related to covariance between X and Y, the goal of PLS is similar to that of the mutual information-based algorithm discussed earlier. This may explain its exceptional performance on text categorization and its robustness to noise.

4.2.2. Example Implementation Using Association-Grounded Semantics (AGS)

In this section, we apply the mutual information-based co-clustering algorithm, implementing the principle of Association-Grounded Semantics (AGS) discussed below, for categorizing documents from a stream of Internet Protocol (IP) data that arrives at full rate of a fiber optic link. To operate at such high speeds, machine-learning techniques must be adapted to work in the environment. First, the models should be chosen such that they can be implemented to run at high speed using a practical amount of hardware. A limited number of bits should be used to represent the values of the feature and the model.

4.2.2.1. Word Co-Occurrence Histograms.

We introduce a broad approach to assigning formal semantic representations to data objects that appear without formal structure, such as lexemes in a text document. The goal is to capture the *meaning* of the data object; the intuition behind the solution is that the meaning of the object is based on the objects with which it associates—thus the name *"association-grounded semantics."* Specifically, we represent the semantics of an object by its distribution over the contexts in which the object appears. Contexts can be any features of object occurrences that can be readily determined and counted. The context of a word in text might be the following word or the nearest preceding verb together with all succeeding nouns. The contexts of an image segment might be adjacent segments, words in the caption, or relative size in the image. The context of an audio phoneme could include its duration, adjacent phonemes, and properties of the background noise.

In Figure 4.4, we show histograms that count the number of times each of a given set of keywords was found within some fixed proximity to the target words "dog," "cat," and "computer" in a hypothetical dataset. These histograms convert to probability distributions by simple normalization, and it is clear that the distribution for "cat" is similar to the distribution for "dog" and is quite distinct from the distribution for "computer." We can use mutual information to measure the similarity of two distributions and to measure the relevance of particular pieces of information for obtaining other information.

4.2.2.2. Application of Association-Grounded Semantics.

Given distributions over contexts, as in Figure 4.4, we can use dissimilarity measures such as KL to determine how similar two data objects are: They are similar when they have similar distributions over the same contexts. For concreteness, we will consider lexemes in text documents to be the data objects of interest. Given a set of lexemes and a set of contexts over which they are distributed, we may wish to generalize the above notion of similarity by considering lexemes to be similar when they have similar distributions over groups of *similar* contexts rather than requiring identical contexts. Contexts, dually, will be considered similar when similarly distributed over *similar* lexemes.

These criteria can be simultaneously evaluated by clustering contexts and lexemes at the same time. We apply *co-clustering,* discussed above, introduced by Rohwer (2002, 2003) and independently discovered by Dhillon et al. (2003a,b). Because we wish to cluster lexemes together based on similar distributions over similar contexts, and because we are simultaneously clustering similar contexts, the goal must be to make lexemes as predictive of contexts as possible and vice versa. In other words, we partition both the spaces so as to maximize the mutual information between the resulting partitions. Figure 4.5 illustrates co-clustering. Figure 4.5a presents a matrix of counts of occurrences of a given

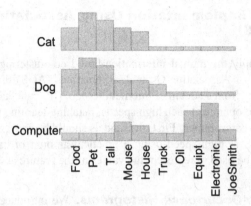

Figure 4.4. Word co-occurrence histograms.

set of lexemes in each of a given set of contexts. Figure 4.5b is obtained by joining (hypothetically) rows 1, 5, and 17 into row 1; joining columns 3, 12, 20, 22, and 23 into column 1; and so on.

4.2.2.3. Lexeme Partition.

For our experiment, the first task was to compress the original vocabulary (1 million possible values) into 4000 variables through a hash function (described in Section 4.3.2.2.1). These variables define the space in which document and category vectors are defined; therefore, we wish to define variables that are as predictive as possible of category labels. It is clear that we wish to preserve as much information as possible, but specifically we wish to preserve as much information *about the category labels* as possible. Having realized this informal goal, the preceding section supplies us with a way to formalize and implement the goal: We will generate variables that have a maximal amount of mutual information with the category labels. Note that once this criterion is settled on, no further work needs to be done. We create a co-occurrence matrix, which counts the number of occurrences of each hash value under each category label, and apply a simulated annealing algorithm to choose the partition of these values that maximizes the mu-

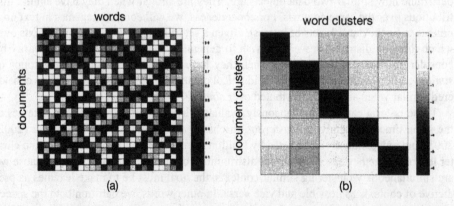

Figure 4.5. Co-clustering. (a) Word/context co-occurrence counts. (b) Unions of rows and unions of columns from (a).

tual information in the compressed table. No stemming is required: If the words "measures" and "measurement" are equally indicative of category, then they will be grouped automatically. If they are not, then they are better separated anyway. We also do not require the removal of stop words: Words that are uniformly distributed across categories will be grouped together in a single class, which will be equally weighted across category vectors. The deployment model will ignore words not seen during training.

The above description does assume a sufficient amount of training data to make the proper determinations. Because this supervised training data requires human labeling, large amounts are not always available.

4.2.2.4. Categorization. As noted in the section outlining the hardware environment, the simplest types of deployment model that fit the given implementation are those that represent each category by a single vector and categorize documents based on the nearest category vector under the cosine measure. When we are also required to recognize when a given document does not belong to any class, we define a threshold for each category and classify a document into a given category only if the cosine exceeds the threshold. Such schemes often make use of a weighting function on the feature vectors, and we will use one here as well.

Let the initial term frequency vector $v = \langle v_1, v_2, K, v_n \rangle$, and suppose we are given a category vector $c = \langle c_1, c_2, K, c_n \rangle$. A weight $w = \langle w_1, w_2, K, w_n \rangle$, which rescales the feature space, can be incorporated by replacing v by $v' = \langle v_1 w_1, v_2 w_2, K, v_n w_n \rangle$ and similarly for c. The cosine between c' and v' is given by

$$\cos[c', v'] = \frac{1}{\|c'\| \, \|v'\|} \sum_k (c_k w_k)(v_k w_k) \tag{4.9}$$

where $\|c'\| = \sqrt{\Sigma_k (c_k w_k)^2}$ and similarly for $\|v'\|$.

We will refer to the original vector v as the document vector and v' as the weighted document vector. The centroid c' to select for each category is the one that is minimally distant from the documents labeled with that category. When distance is measured by cosine, we simply need to average the unit vectors in the direction of each exemplar document vector to obtain a centroid c' in the appropriate direction.

4.3. HARDWARE IMPLEMENTATION OF TRANSFORMATION ALGORITHMS FOR HIGH-SPEED DATA STREAMS

We have developed a test bed that can perform transform algorithms in high-speed, reconfigurable hardware. It enables intelligence analysts to keep pace with data explosion by performing real-time information management and processing. Live data can be processed as it arrives. Data can also be reprocessed as new contexts emerge.

4.3.1. Test Bed Experiments

The overall approach for conducting experiments is shown in Figure 4.6. Reconfigurable hardware is used to rapidly ingest and process data, while software is used to control and manage clusters. Data arrive over a network as text or as HTML documents carried over standard Transmission Control Protocol/Internet Protocol (TCP/IP) packets. A TCP

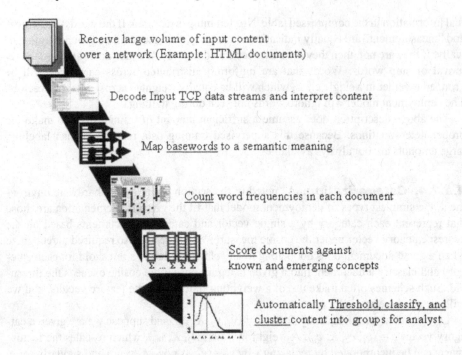

Receive large volume of input content over a network (Example: HTML documents)

Decode Input TCP data streams and interpret content

Map basewords to a semantic meaning

Count word frequencies in each document

Score documents against known and emerging concepts

Automatically Threshold, classify, and cluster content into groups for analyst.

Figure 4.6. Test bed enables real-time, semantic classification of content.

processor decodes the packets that contain the document in one or more TCP/IP input flows. Every word in the document is mapped to a baseword, which in turn is mapped to a semantic meaning. All basewords in each document are then counted to determine their frequencies of occurrence. A document vector is then generated that characterizes occurrences of all basewords in the document. This document vector is then scored against a set of vectors that represent known or emerging concepts. Thresholds are used to determine if content can be classified as an existing concept or if a new cluster should be formed.

The test bed enables computationally intensive semantic processing to be performed in real time. Field Programmable Gate Arrays (FPGAs) perform hardware-accelerated data processing. By using FPGAs, all test bed parts can be dynamically reconfigured or programmed to implement new algorithms for data processing, content classification, and/or concept clustering. Massive volumes of real data can be streamed through the system.

4.3.2. Design of the Experiment Hardware Platform

Our first experimental hardware platform has been prototyped. This system uses Field-programmable Port Extender (FPX) modules developed at Washington University in St. Louis to perform several layers of data processing functions in hardware (Lockwood, 2001a). Multiple FPX modules have been integrated into a Global Velocity GVS-1000 chassis, as shown in Figure 4.7. Each FPX contains two FPGAs: one large FPGA called the Reconfigurable Application Device (RAD) and another, smaller FPGA called the Network Interface Device (NID). In addition to the FPGAs, each FPX card includes two parallel banks of SRAM and two parallel banks of SDRAM. Reconfigurable hardware modules are deployed using logic in the RAD, which is a Xilinx Virtex XCV2000E FPGA.

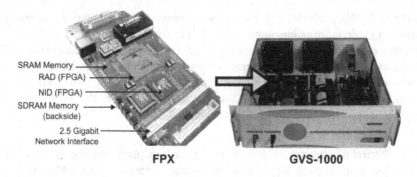

SRAM Memory
RAD (FPGA)
NID (FPGA)
SDRAM Memory
(backside)
2.5 Gigabit
Network Interface

FPX   **GVS-1000**

Figure 4.7. Field-programmable port extender (FPX) modules mount in the GVS-1000 system.

Circuits have been developed on the FPX platform to implement the *TCP processor*, a *Baseword module*, a *Count module*, a *Score module*, and a *Report module*. Circuits are implemented as parallel finite-state machines implemented in modular hardware components that run in FPGAs. High-speed network interfaces enables each FPX module to communicate with other hardware modules within the GVS-1000 system and other software outside of the system using standard IP datagrams. The block diagram of the GVS1000 system that performs semantic processing of TCP/IP traffic passing over a network is shown in Figure 4.8. For this circuit, five FPX cards operated in a pipeline to process content quickly.

4.3.2.1. TCP/IP Processing. More than 85% of all traffic on the Internet uses the TCP/IP. TCP is a stream-oriented protocol providing guaranteed delivery and ordered byte flow services. Today, most Internet backbones operate over communication links ranging in speed from OC-3 (155 Mbps) to OC-192 (10 Gbps) rates. The TCP processor—which is used in this test bed—enables complex network services to operate at gigabit speeds by processing TCP stream data directly in hardware. The TCP processor tracks up to 8 million bidirectional TCP flows on an OC-48 (2.5 Gbps) network link (Schuehler

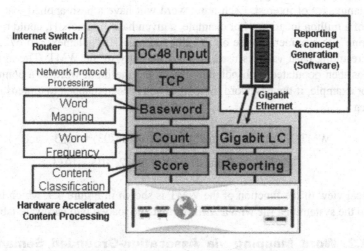

Figure 4.8. Stacks of FPX modules fit into a GVS-1000.

and Lockwood, 2004). Network data packets are annotated with additional control signals, which provide information about which data bytes correspond to the IP header, the TCP header, and the TCP payload section. There are also signals that indicate which TCP data bytes are parts of a consistent stream of data and which bytes should be ignored because they are data retransmissions. Signals that indicate the Start of Flow (SOF) and End of Flow (EOF) are included, along with a unique flow identifier so that the client can independently manage per-flow context (Schuehler et al., 2004).

4.3.2.2. Word Mapping.

The hardware on the FPX platform represents documents and document prototypes as high-dimension feature vectors. A Word Mapping Table (WMT) transforms each word of input text from a universe of 1 million words into one of 4000 dimensions. The WMT is implemented in hardware using a hash table with 1 million entries. Each entry in the lookup table remaps an input word into one of the 4000 dimensions based on the semantics of the word. Three different approaches have thus far been used to generate the content of the WMP using dictionary-based approach, pairwise word differentiation, and automatic selection of features.

4.3.2.2.1. Dictionary-Based Word Mapping.

In the first approach, knowledge about the language itself was used to populate the WMT. Initially, words extracted from an online dictionary were assigned to unique dimensions. Dimensions were then collapsed wherever a synonymous relationship was noted. The dictionary was generated using a combination of automated scripts and human input. AuAtomated scripts were used to apply stemming rules and identify words with common prefix and suffix extensions. Entries in the WMT were grouped with words with similar meaning.

In one experiment, more than 27,000 words were collapsed, including proper nouns, into 6414 dimensions. Further reductions were used to map the table into 4000 dimensions. Hash table entries for words not in the dictionary were mapped to one of the 4000 dimensions.

A sample WMT is shown in Figure 4.9. Two different dimensions are populated with words that represent the meanings of *explosives* and *rockets*. For each dimension, there are several specific words that map to the same dimension. Similar words for explosives include "nitroglycerine," "gelamex," "dynamite," and their equivalents in Arabic, Greek, or other languages of interest. Each input word will have a hash applied that maps it to any one of a million locations. For example, a given hash function, H, could map H ("nitroglycerine") to a numeric value of 101,203 and map H ("gelamex") to 672,101. Each possible resulting hash value is used to index an entry in the WMT. The million-entry WMT was then populated with pointers that remap the input word to a common baseword. For example, if the baseword for explosive has been mapped to dimension number 1033, then

$$\text{WMT}(\text{H}(\text{"nitroglycerine"})) = \text{WMT}(101{,}203) = 1033 \quad \text{and}$$

$$\text{WMT}(\text{H}(\text{"gelamex"})) = \text{WMT}(672{,}101) = 1033$$

A graphical view of the function of the WMT is shown in Figure 4.9, which is itself described to the system in a file with a XML format and loaded into hardware tables.

4.3.2.2.2. Word Mapping via Assocation-Grounded Semantics.

As described in Section 4.2.2.3, AGS techniques can be applied to create a WMT. This

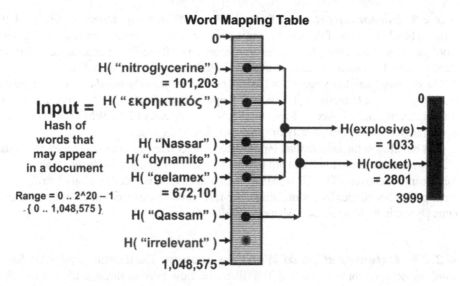

Figure 4.9. Word mapping table (WMT) allows hash of each of 1 million input words to be mapped into any output value in a 4000-dimensional vector.

method entirely bypasses the question of which words should appear in the lexicon and which should not. All words are represented in the million-wide hash. Each of the million buckets is mapped to one of the 4000 dimensions. The mapping is constructed automatically without the need for linguistic resources.

One advantage of this automatic method over one based on linguistic resources is that it can be applied directly to the hash function values rather than to the original text. This is significant because hash collisions can change the meaning of a term. Collisions occur if a lexicon has a large amount of nuisance strings or quasi-words extracted from binary documents that appear as noise. Mapping from the million-wide representation to the 4000-dimensional representation would preserve any ambiguity about what string actually hashed to the original million-wide bucket, so features destroyed by the hash function do not end up contributing erroneously to the classification model.

The second primary advantage of an unsupervised technique such as this is that no expert knowledge of the language is required. Small linguistic communities often develop idiosyncratic usage that might not be anticipated, especially because these change over time. We also can work in any language regardless of what resources are available for that language, and we can learn special technical terms or proper names that may not be available to linguistic experts.

4.3.2.2.3. Word Mapping with Information Retrieval. The third method to populate the WMT used ideas from information retrieval (IR). Words in documents from each training set were studied in order to set categories based on the frequency of occurrence. The most commonly used words, defined as those that occur more than 0.1% of the time, because they typically represent common nouns, verbs, and prepositions that add little meaning to the document, were discarded. Excluding those words, the next most frequent 100 and next most frequent 500 words are assigned to dimensions in the WMT. The background inverse term frequency (ITF) and the inverse document frequency (IDF) were used for weighting of dimensions in dot products between document vectors.

4.3.2.3. Implementation of the Word Mapping Circuit. Figure 4.10 shows a block diagram of the word mapping circuit as it was implemented in FPGA. The word parser includes multiple modules to process text with different encodings, including standard ASCII, Windows 1253/56, and UTF-16 for English, Greek, and Arabic.

Once a word has been parsed, a hash is computed, and the *word-clustering* module generates an index to memory. The Word Mapping Table (WMT) itself is implemented in off-chip Static Random Access Memory (SRAM). Each entry of the WMT returns a value in the range of 0–3999 to identify the base meaning of the word.

It is not always the case that an input packet will contain an integer number of words. It is possible that a word will be split between packets when the data stream is segmented for transmission over a TCP/IP network. The circuit supports identification of strings that cross packet boundaries by maintaining a per-flow context state store in off-chip Synchronous Dynamic Random Access Memory (SDRAM).

4.3.2.4. Determination of Word Frequency. The frequencies of every baseword are counted for every active TCP/IP traffic flow passing through the system. For each traffic flow, a *count circuit* implemented as logic on another FPX platform computes the sum of the basewords that occur in each traffic flow. This circuit counts basewords for each 4000-dimensional vector used by the baseword circuit; the count circuit maintains the state of 4000 parallel counters.

Packets from different flows are generally interleaved as they pass through the network, hindering the determination of word frequency of data that appear on a TCP/IP network backbone link. Each TCP/IP connection (a Web-page download, for example) consists of tens to thousands of packets that are transmitted as an end host transfers data over the network. A network backbone generally carries thousands to millions of parallel TCP/IP connections. Count arrays are tracked individually for each interleaved flow.

As with the baseword circuit, the count circuit uses off-chip SDRAM to maintain multiple contexts that track the state of each flow. The count circuit supports 524,288 (512k) flows, each of which requires storage of 4000 counters. Each counter is represented with

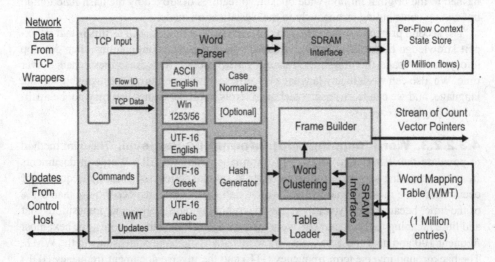

Figure 4.10. Block diagram of the word mapping circuit, as it was implemented in FPGA logic.

a 4-bit (half-byte) value. A total of 512K*2K =1Gbyte of memory is used to store the state of all flows.

4.3.2.5. Scoring. Once a flow has ended, the resulting *document vector* is compared against a set of *concept vectors*. In general, the FPGA could be programmed to compute a score using any distance metric. For the circuit implemented in the existing test bed, a dot product is computed of the *document vector* against a set stored *concept vectors,* as shown in Figure 4.11.

Coefficients can be dynamically loaded into the score table. This *score table* can be formatted in one of two ways. One FPGA circuit was implemented to support 4-bit coefficients for a table of 30 concepts. The other FPGA circuit was implemented for 8-bit coefficients for a table that supports 15 concepts. Both circuits operate on the 4000-dimension vector.

High processing throughput was achieved because the multiplication computation occurs in parallel for each concept. Count values that define the incoming *document vector* arrive at a rate of 8 elements per clock cycle. For the scoring circuit that supports 30 concepts, the system performs 8*30 = 240 parallel multiplications per clock cycle. At a clock rate of 80 MHz, the scoring module performs 80M*240 = 19.2 billion multiplication/accumulate functions per second.

4.4. EXPERIMENTAL RESULTS

The rest of this chapter is an overview of our first experiment and a description of its promising results. We tested the performance of our transformations and hardware platform by analyzing postings to 12 Google groups. The postings were divided into seven known categories, four unknown categories, and a large "chaff" category that we treated as noise. We then compared three transformations with regard to (a) their ability to discover known categories when trained and (b) their ability to discover unknown categories (without training) in the presence of high and low noise levels. For the known categories,

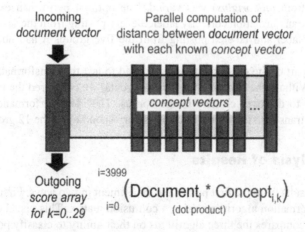

Incoming
document vector

Parallel computation of
distance between *document vector*
with each known *concept vector*

concept vectors   ...

Outgoing
score array
for k=0..29

$$\left(\sum_{i=0}^{i=3999} Document_i * Concept_{i,k}\right)$$

(dot product)

Figure 4.11. Hardware circuits accelerate the classification of documents by computing the least-squares distance (dot product) between an input vector and representative content. At times of peak

all transformations successfully identified and organized documents into known categories. For the unknown categories, two of the transformation algorithms successfully identified some unknown, but pure, categories. This second case is particularly important because it tests the ability of our transformations to self-organize historical data when new issues arise.

A corpus was collected that included 2000 messages from 11 Internet newsgroups, such as *alt.sports.baseball.stl_cardinals, comp.ai.neural_nets,* and so on. The data were human-analyzed for content, and off-topic messages were removed. File headers were stripped so that the machine learning process would not have access to the newsgroup identifier. Training sets were generated through random selection to avoid training only on data that happened to consist of a few large threads. Out-of-class chaff documents were selected from another newsgroup. Tests on the corpus with different amounts of training data and chaff were run. The first set of experiments used no chaff and a training set that consisted of {1%, 33%, and 50%} of the files. The second and third set of tests added random data so that 10% and 90% of the total files were chaff. This latter experiment was run again using {33% and 50%} of the data for training.

In the experiment, we evaluated three mathematical transformation algorithms in terms of their ability to detect known categories when provided with training data on these categories and on their ability to discover unknown categories without training. The first case is intended to model the situation where the transformation organizes material related to a known context. The second case investigates if transforms are able to self-organize and detect new concepts without the benefit of training material.

The three algorithms we investigated were

- K-Means, a standard statistical clustering technique
- Associated Grounded Semantics (AGS)
- Order-ratio of top two order statistics for the document score vector

There were two parts of the experiment. We trained each part of the algorithms using sample data from 7 of the 11 groups. We then applied the algorithms to the remainder of the corpus that contained postings from the seven selected groups and posting from the four other groups. We then conducted experimental runs where the amount of "chaff" (e.g., postings from *talk.origins*) was varied. The optimal performance for these runs would be if the transformation correctly labeled every posting from the seven groups with the appropriate label and labeled posting from the five groups it had not trained on as "chaff."

The second part of the experiment was intended to test the transformation's ability to self-organize. Without the benefit of any training data, we compared the transformations on their ability to discover clusters in the corpus. The ideal performance in this case would be if the transform identified 12 clusters corresponding to the 12 groups.

4.4.1. Analysis of Results

We analyzed results from the first part of the experiment in two ways. First, we compared the three transformation algorithms using a confusion matrix. This visual display, shown in Figure 4.12, compares the three algorithms on their ability to classify posting transformations. The figure shows the results for the run with 90% chaff where 33% of the corpus was used in the training set. This is the most difficult case. The ideal performance would

Detecting Known Content
Training Data: 33%; Amount of Chaff: 90%

true labels	alt.sports	comp.ai	comp. programming	humanities.musics	misc.consumers	misc.writing	rec.equestrian	rejects
alt.sports		2	2	3	7		4	10
comp.al	10	57	12	14	3	2		48
comp.programming	5	8		2	4	7	2	39
humanities.musics		1	1			3	3	21
misc.consumers	5	3	7	7	65	2	8	50
misc.writing	9	2	4	8	7	79	7	56
rec.equestrian	16	6	6	9	14	3	65	92
rec.martial_arts	22	6	7	8	11	6	8	
sci.archeology	26	9	23	54	18	13	13	336
sci.logic	22	5	19	31	1	8	11	69
soc.libraries	6	11	28	5	7	8	4	44
CHAFF	1125	831	1963	2683	1375	945	507	8570

Order Statistic Algorithm
Precision: 6%
Recall: 55%

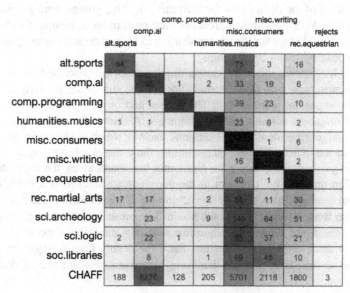

true labels	alt.sports	comp.ai	comp. programming	humanities.musics	misc.consumers	misc.writing	rec.equestrian	rejects
alt.sports	84				75	3	16	
comp.al			1	2	33	19	6	
comp.programming		1			39	23	10	
humanities.musics	1	1			23	6	2	
misc.consumers						1	6	
misc.writing					16		2	
rec.equestrian					40	1		
rec.martial_arts	17	17		2		11	30	
sci.archeology		23		9	145	64	51	
sci.logic	2	22	1			37	21	
soc.libraries		8		1	49	45	10	
CHAFF	188	6876	128	205	5701	2118	1800	3

K-Means Algorithm
Precision: 4%
Recall: 73%

Figure 4.12. Detecting known content.

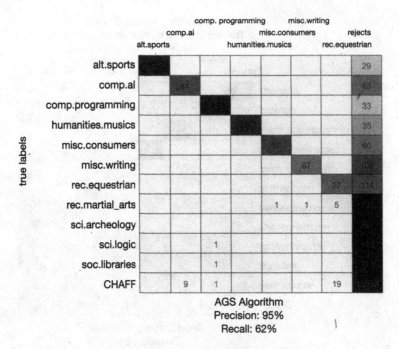

AGS Algorithm
Precision: 95%
Recall: 62%

Figure 4.12. (*continued*).

be if each matrix were diagonal for the first seven categories corresponding to the training data and if all of the documents for the remaining five groups were assigned to the last category. The AGS algorithm approaches ideal performance. It correctly classifies essentially all of the postings for the groups that it was trained on and correctly assigns most of the other postings to the chaff group.

Figure 4.13 shows the ROC curves for the AGS run described above. ROC curves show the ratio type 1 to type 2 errors. These ROC curves are properly shaped, indicated that the algorithm worked well. The second part of the experiment involved the ability to self-organize without training. Figure 4.14 shows the results from a sample run where the algorithm identified 30 clusters, each of which is shown in descending order as rows in the matrix display. The columns show the number of documents from that particular group in the cluster; the horizontal bar charts along the right show the same information graphically. The bars in the bar chart are stacked and shaded to show the number of postings from each of the 12 groups. Thus, an ideal cluster would consist of documents from a single group and would be represented as a "pure" shade in the bar chart. As the figure shows, the algorithm was only somewhat successful at discovering clusters. It discovered several clusters that were cleanly from a single category but also identified several other clusters that were composed of a mixture of documents from various groups.

SUMMARY

We have described a fundamentally new approach for analyzing massive amounts of data in heterogeneous information streams. This approach has the potential to overcome many of the problems with current approaches. The new idea, enabled by hardware-accelerated

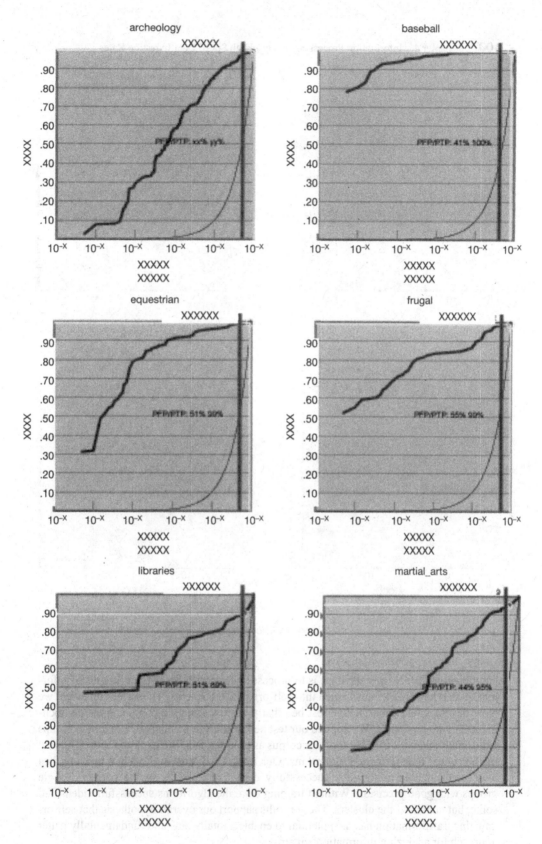

Figure 4.13. ROC curves for AGS.

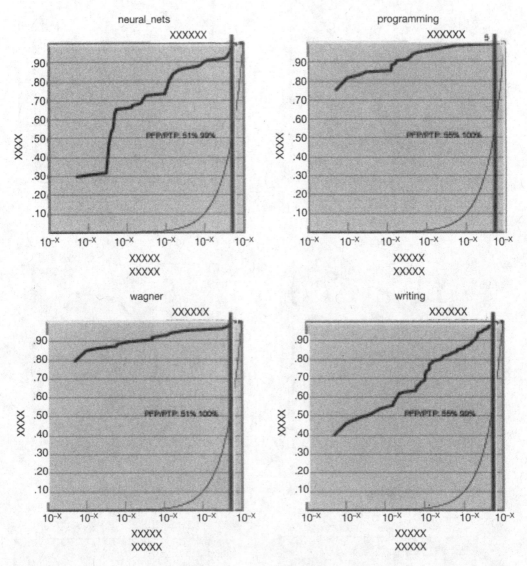

Figure 4.13. (*continued*).

computational processing engines, is to process and reprocess real-time streams of information that have been transformed into self-organized concepts. To explore this idea, we have developed an experimental test bed that performs semantic computations on documents at very high rates. We applied our test bed to analyze postings to 12 Google groups using chaff and various subsets of our corpus as training data. We explored three different mathematical transformation algorithms. Our results are promising. When training data were available, the algorithms successfully classified postings to the correct Google groups with good precision. Without training data, the algorithms successfully identified some, but not all, of the clusters. These results support our overall hypothesis that self-organizing transformation has the potential to enable a totally new and fundamentally better approach for analyzing information streams.

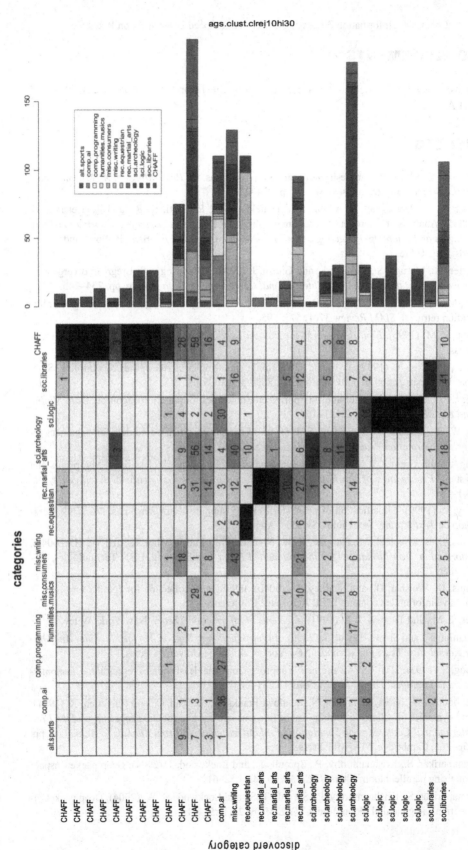

Figure 4.14. Detecting unknown content.

ACKNOWLEDGMENTS

This work was performed under a contract from the Information Awareness Office of DARPA.

REFERENCES

Achlioptas, D. (2001). Database-friendly random projections. In: *Proceedings of ACM Symposium on the Principles of Database Systems,* pp. 274–281.

Ammar, R. A., Demurjian, S. A., Sr., Greenshields, I. R., Pattipati, K. R., and Rajasekaran, S. (2005). Analysis of heterogeneous data in ultrahigh dimensions. In: *Emergent Information Technologies and Enabling Technologies and Policies for Counter-Terrorism,* R. Popp and J. Yen (eds.), IEEE Press.

Banerjee, A., Merugu, S., Dhillon, I., and Ghosh, J. (2004). Clustering with Bregman divergences. *Proceedings of the Fourth SIAM International Conference on Data Mining,* pp. 234–245.

Berry, M. W., Dumais, S. T., and O'Brien, G. W. (1995). Using linear algebra for intelligent information retrieval. *SIAM Review* 37(4):573–595.

Bishop, C. M. (1995). *Neural Networks for Pattern Recognition.* Oxford, UK: Oxford University Press.

Brin, S., and Page, L. (1999). Dynamic data mining: exploring large rule spaces by sampling. Stanford University, http://dbpubs.stanford.edu:8090/pub/1999-68.

Burges, C. J. C. (1998). A tutorial on support vector machines for pattern recognition. *Data Mining and Knowledge Discovery* 2:121–167.

Caid, W. R., Dumais, S. T., Gallant, S. I. (1995). Learned vector-space models for document retrieval. *Information Processing and Management* 31(3).

Cheng, J., and Greiner, R. (2001). Learning Bayesian belief network classifiers: Algorithms and system. *Proceedings of the Fourteenth Canadian Conference on Artificial Intelligence,* pp. 141–151.

Cooley, R. (1999). Classification of news stories using support vector machines. *IJCAI'99 Workshop on Text Mining,* Stockholm, Sweden, August.

Cousins, D. B., Nicoletti, M., Pattipati, K. R., Namburu, M., Luo, J., Choi, K., and Tu, H. (2004a). *Information Transformations for the Automated Front End* Seedling, BBN Technologies, November, 72 pages.

Cousins, D., Weishar, D., and Sharkey, J. (2004b). Intelligence collection for counter terrorism in massive information content. IEEE Aerospace Conference.

Cover, T. M., and Thomas, J. A. (1991). *Elements of Information Theory.* New York: Wiley.

Cristianini, N., and Shawe-Taylor, J. (2000). *An Introduction to Support Vector Machines And Other Kernel-Base Learning Methods.* New York: Cambridge University Press.

de Jong, S. (1993). SIMPLS: An alternative approach to partial least squares regression. *Chemometrics and Intelligent Laboratory Systems* 18:251–263.

Deneubourg, J.-L., Goss, S., Franks, N., Sendova-Franks, A., Detrain, C., and Cheretien, X. (1991). The dynamics of collective sorting: Robot-like ants and ant-like robots. *Proceedings of the First International Conference on Simulation of Adaptive Behavior: From Animals to Animats 1,* pp. 356–365, Cambridge, MA: MIT Press.

Dharmapurikar, S., Krishnamurthy, P., Sproull, T., and Lockwood, J. (2004). Deep packet inspection using parallel bloom filters. *IEEE Micro* 24(1):52–61.

Dharmapurikar, S., Krishnamurthy, P., Sproull, T. S., and Lockwood, J. W. (2004). Deep packet inspection using parallel bloom filters. *IEEE Micro* 24(1):52–61.

Dhillon, S., Mallela, S., and Kumar, R. (2003a). A divisive information-theoretic feature clustering algorithm for text classification. *Journal of Machine Learning Research 3:*1265–1287.

Dhillon, I. S., Mallela, S., and Modha, D. S. (2003b). Information-theoretic co-clustering. *Proceedings of The Ninth ACM SIGKDD International Conference on Knowledge Discovery and Data Mining (KDD),* pp. 89–98, August.

Dietterich, T. G., and Bakiri, G.(1995). Solving multiclass learning problems via error-correcting output codes. *Journal of Artificial Intelligence Research.*

Domingos, P. (2000). Mining high-speed data streams. *Sixth ACM SIGKDD International Conference on Knowledge Discovery and Data Mining (KDD),* Boston, August 20–23, pp. 71–80.

Duda, R. O., Hart, P. E., and Stork, D. G. (2001). *Pattern Classification.* New York: Wiley-Interscience.

Dumais, S. T., Letsche, T. A., Littman, M. L. and Landauer, T. K. (1997). Automatic cross-language retrieval using latent semantic indexing. In: *AAAI Spring Symposuim on Cross-Language Text and Speech Retrieval.*

Fall, C. J., and Benzineb, K. (2002). Literature survey: Issues to be considered in the automatic classification of patents. World Intellectual Property Organization.

Freitag, D. (2004a). Trained named entity recognition using distributional clusters. *Conference on Empirical Methods in Natural Language Processing,* Barcelona.

Freitag, D. (2004b). Toward unsupervised whole-corpus tagging. *20th International Conference on Computational Linguistics,* Geneva.

Friedman, N., Geiger, D., and Goldszmidt, M. (1997). Bayesian Network Classifiers. *Machine Learning 29:*131–161.

Geladi, P., and Kowalski, B (1986). Partial least squares regression: A tutorial. *Analytical Chimica Acta* 185:1–17.

Handl, J., Knowles, J., and Dorigo, M., "Ant-based Clustering and Topographic Mapping", to appear in *Artificial Life.*

Hulten, G., Spencer, L., and Domingos, P. (2001). Mining time-changing data streams. *Sixth ACM SIGKDD International Conference on Knowledge Discovery and Data mining (KDD),* San Francisco, pp. 97–106.

Jain, A. K., and Dubes, R. C. (1988). *Algorithms for Clustering Data.* Englewood Cliffs, NJ: Prentice Hall.

Jain, A. K., Murty, M. N., and Flynn, P. J. (1999). Data clustering: A review. *ACM Computing Surveys 31*(3):

Joachims, T. (1999). Transductive inference for text classification using support vector machines. *Proceedings of the 16th International Conference on Machine Learning,* pp. 200–209.

Jorden, M. I. (1999). *Learning. In: Graphical Models.* Cambridge, MA: MIT Press.

Kumar, S. (2004). Manuscript. Advanced Technologies, Fair Isaac Corporation.

Langley, P., Iba, W., and Thompson, K. (1992). Induction of selective Bayesian classifiers. *Proceedings of the National Conference on Artificial Intelligence,* pp. 223–228. Menlo Park, CA: AAAI Press.

Linde, Y., Buzo, A., and Gray, R. M. (1980). An Algorithm for Vector Quantizer Design. *IEEE Trans. on Communications 28*(1):84–95.

Lockwood, J. (2001a). Evolvable Internet Hardware Platforms. *NASA/DoD Workshop on Evolvable Hardware (EHW'01),* Long Beach, CA, pp. 271–279.

Lumer, E., and Faieta, B. (1994). Diversity and adaptation in populations of clustering ants. *Proceedings of the Third International Conference on Simulation of Adaptive Behavior: From Animals to Animats 1,* pp. 501–508. Cambridge, MA: MIT Press.

Madhusudan, B. and Lockwood, J. (2004). Design of a system for real-time worm detection. *12th Annual Proceedings of IEEE Hot Interconnects (HotI-12),* Stanford, CA, pp. 77–83.

Martens, H., and Naes, T. (1989). *Multivariate Calibration*. New York: John Wiley & Sons.

McCallum, A., and Nigam, K. (1998). A comparison of event models for naive Bayes text classification. *AAAI/ICML-98 Workshop on Learning for Text Categorization*, pp. 41–48. Menlo Park, CA: AAAI Press.

Namburu, S. M., Tu, H., Luo, J., and Pattipati, K. R. (2005). Experiments on supervised learning algorithms for text categorization. *IEEE Aerospace Conference*, Big Sky, Montana.

Neapolitan, R. E. (2003). *Learning Bayesian Networks*. Englewood Cliffs, NJ: Prentice-Hall.

Papadopoulos, G. (1998). *Moore's Law ain't good enough.* Keynote speech at Hot Chips X.

Pearl, J. (1988). *Probabilistic Reasoning in Intelligent Systems: Networks of Plausible Inference.* San Francisco: Morgan Kaufmann.

Rasmus B. (1996). Multiway calibration multilinear PLS", *Journal of Chemometrics*, 10, 47–61.

Reuters (1997). *Reuters Corpus*, Vol. 1, English language, 1996-08-20 to 1997-08-19.

Rissanen, J. (1978). Modeling by shortest data description. *Automatica 14*(5):465–471.

Rohwer, R. (2003). Co-clustering algorithm variations. Internal Memo, HNC Software, June 13.

Rohwer, R., and Freitag. D. (2004). Towards full automation of lexicon construction. *Human Language Technology/North American Chapter of the Association for Computational Linguistics*, Boston, 2004.

Rohwer, R. (2002). The co-clustering algorithm. Internal Memo, HNC Software.

Salton, G. (1991). Developments in automatic text retrieval. *Science*, **253**:974–980.

Salton, G., and McGill, M. (1983). *Introduction to Modern Information Retrieval*. New York: McGraw-Hill.

D. Schuehler, Lockwood, J. W. (2004). A modular system for FPGA-based TCP flow processing in high-speed networks. *14th International Conference on Field Programmable Logic and Applications*, Springer LNCS 3203, Antwerp, Belgium, pp. 301–310.

Schuehler, D., Moscola, J., and Lockwood, J. (2004). Architecture for a hardware-based, TCP/IP content-processing system. *IEEE Micro 24*(1):62–69.

Shannon, C. E. (1948). A mathematical theory of communication. *Bell Systems Technology Journal*, 27.

Smola, A. J., Bartlett, P. L., Scholkopf, B., and Schuurmans, D. (2000). *Advances in Large Margin Classifiers*. Cambridge, MA: The MIT Press.

Sun, A., Lim, E.-P., and Ng, W.-K. (2002). Web classification using support vector machine. *Proceedings of the Fourth International Workshop on Web Information and Data Management*, 96–99. ACM Press.

Indraweb Inc. (2005). White paper, Indraweb's targeted search. Paoli, PA.

Vigna, G., Robertson, W., Kher, V., and Kemmerer R. (2003). A stateful intrusion detection system for world-wide web servers. *Proceedings of the Annual Computer Security Applications Conference (ACSAC 2003)*, pp. 34–43, Las Vegas.

Wang, Y., Hodges, J., and Tang, B. (2003). Classification of Web documents using a naive Bayes method. *IEEE International Conference on Tools with Artificial Intelligence*, Sacramento, CA, p. 560.

Weishar, D., Lockwood, J., Loui, R., Moscola, J., Kastner, C., Levine, A., Attig, M., and Eick, S. (2005). Transformation algorithms for data streams. IEEE Aerospace Conference.

Wold, H. (1975). Soft modeling by latent variables: The nonlinear iterative partial least squares approach. In *Perspectives in Probability and Statistics, Papers in Honor of M.S. Bartlett*, J. Gani (ed.), pp. 520–540, London: Academic Press.

Wold, S., Geladi, P., Esbensen, K., and Ohman, J. (1987). Principal component analysis. *Chemometrics and Intelligent Laboratory Systems* **2**:37–52.

Chapter 5

Analysis of Heterogeneous Data in Ultrahigh Dimensions

R. A. Ammar, S. A. Demurjian, Sr., I. R. Greenshields, K. Pattipati, and S. Rajasekaran

5.1. INTRODUCTION

Counter-terrorism necessarily involves the analysis of massive amounts of data, which can take the form of conventional text data, image data, sound, and so on. Part of the analyst's task is to sift through this mass of data searching for items of specific interest to the counter-terrorism community. For example, it may be valuable to scan an evolving corpus of textual data searching for the occurrence of specific keywords (either alone or in some specific conjunction with other keywords). When the corpus to be searched is itself massive and the number of keywords is also massive, then the problem becomes intractable for humans to tackle in the absence of machine support. An issue of pressing interest, therefore, is the provision of some form of automated search tools which ameliorates the difficulty of the task. The approach discussed here is to convert the heterogeneous data into some analytic space and refer the analysis to that space. Issues which then arise include the transformation itself, the resultant dimensionality of the transformed space, tools for reducing that dimensionality, and tools for extracting information from the transformed data. It is often the latter two steps (reduction of dimensionality and data analysis) which present the greatest difficulties, and the goal of this chapter is to provide a summary of various techniques which address these two critical phases. Generically, we will refer to the notion of data transformed from its original state into a more analytically amenable state as a *transformation space*.

It is likely that issues surrounding transformation spaces not immediately evident at first blush will arise as the work in this area progresses. Nonetheless, it is clear that certain basic issues must be addressed. We list six here:

1. The underlying base dataspace(s) must be characterized in terms of both their syntax and their semantics, and implicit and explicit relationships extant in the base spaces must be understood if any such structures as are deemed valuable are to be carried into the transformed spaces.
2. The nature of the transformations themselves remains a matter of conjecture, and beyond some obvious properties it is not clear what the properties of the transformations should be. One such potential property is that the transform be secure up to inversion by an attacker, and yet remain computationally efficient in the event that

massive quantities of data are to be transformed. Thus, *transformation security* may form a major issue for transformation spaces.

3. The problem of noise, both in terms of the interpretation and characterization of noise in the (untransformed) base spaces and in terms of the transformed spaces must be addressed. Denoising strategies must therefore be sensitized not only to the characterization of noise in the base and transformed dataspaces, but to the intent of the analysis to be performed on the transformed space.

4. Significant ongoing research is exploring the issues surrounding embedding arbitrary metric spaces into more structured spaces (usually of lower dimension). Equivalently, significant efforts are underway in exploring low-distortion embeddings from high-dimension metric spaces into lower-dimensional metric spaces, as well as exploring the role of probabilistic approximations to metric spaces. An issue here is the metric structure of the base and transformed space.

5. Under transform, it is expected that the weight of well-established formal methodologies from analysis, cluster analysis, pattern recognition, signal processing, decision theory, and other domains will be applicable to the transformed data. Issues of dimensionality may play an important role here, depending on the nature of the base spaces and the resultant transformed spaces. Exploring and developing analytic and decision-theoretic tools taking advantage of the structure of the transformed space will be necessary. This links to point 4 above.

6. Large datasets and potentially complex transformations and analytical tools imply that attention will most likely need to be paid both to (a) issues of algorithmic complexity and efficiency and (b) strategies for parallelizing the entire transformation and analytic suite.

One can easily demonstrate simple (if contrived) examples of the ramifications of transformations on the panoply of data analysis tools. For example, standard tristimulus/tricolor imagery is typically represented in red-green-blue (RGB) format, which is usually considered to be unintuitive. Yet it has a Euclidean metric structure, and virtually the entirety of metric classifiers (statistical or nonstatistical) roll into RGB data *mutatis mutandis*. Ignoring for the time being the arguments against the transformation given next, one can trivially effect a transformation of RGB data into a hue/saturation/intensity (HSI) space which some argue is clearly more intuitive. But HSI is demonstrably non-Euclidean; the preferential toolsets come from differential geometry, and (for example) one now has to ask questions about (for example) statistics over manifolds rather than statistics in more flat spaces. Evidently, some clustering processes roll with little difficulty from RGB to HSI. Some do not. More likely, cluster/classification techniques specifically grounded in non-Euclidean geometries will be of the most value. Life with heterogeneous data in ultrahigh-dimensional spaces may not be quite so transparent. Merely because the data are expressed in (for example) R^n (for suitably high n) should not be taken as immediate grounds for assuming that the data (in whole or in part) does not exhibit some geometric structure for which (again, for example) a flat-space metric (such as the Euclidean metric) has *anything other than a purely formal application*.

We might reasonably divide the process of analyzing data embedded in ultrahigh-dimensional spaces into two linked processes, namely, transformation of the original high-dimensional data space into another space which either uncovers structure within the data not immediately evident in the originating space, approximates (perhaps perfectly) the data in a space of lower dimension, permits more efficient computation over the data, or a combination of all of the preceding, followed by data analysis within the transformed space, typically predicated upon some form of cluster analysis. In some senses, these two steps may not be easily differentiated; one thinks, for example (to draw another example from imaging), of the representation of shape by the expansion of some shape-describing function in terms of a harmonic expansion (Fourier series for planar closed curves, or spherical harmonics whenever a spherical map can be adduced from a shape function determined over a surface). In either case, the recognition of two shapes as identical, close or significantly different can be determined by straightforward metric differences between the coefficients of the expansions; *yet it is the approximation properties of the expansions which lend themselves easily to the notion of a continuum of shape classes in a way that is both natural and (in the case of Fourier Shape Descriptors at least) quite successful.*

As one final introductory point about transformations, we note that frequently a transformation may be chosen from a wide library of potential transformations because the transform itself may lend itself naturally to identifying (preserving) some kind of invariance within the data. Returning to classically known transformations (such as Fourier or spherical harmonic expansions), one recalls that both are linked via representation theory to the well-known rotation groups $SO(2)$ and $SO(3)$. To the image, analyst these are critical properties of the transformations; not only (for example) can the Fourier series expansion of a shape function computed over a simple closed planar curve be tuned (by dropping higher-order terms of the expansion) to vary the fidelity by which two curves can be matched, but by its very basis in the representation of $SO(2)$ the expansion also serves to make the recognition of a curve invariant under the action of $SO(2)$ acting on the curve.

In the world of the general (heterogenous) data of the analyst concerned with security, the loss of such invariance can be a source of concern. For example, the notion of *semantic invariance* is (to the best of our knowledge) not easily captured numerically. Indeed, trite analysis mapping textual data to a more amenable numerical form can, notwithstanding the entire machinery (or more likely, the terminology) of real, metric, and functional analysis that gets thrown at it, miss trivially obvious linkages that even the most ill-trained human analyst with a modicum of education could instantly spot. Consider the well-established technique of frequency counts of words (and most extensions thereof). At the same time consider the following sentences:

S1: The Queen of England lives in London.

S2: The Constitutional Monarch of the United Kingdom abides in the capital of Great Britain.

S3: La Reine d'Angleterre demeure à Londres.

Each of these three sentences comprises (essentially) the same semantic unit, and ideally any transformation **T** should take S1, S2 and S3 out to D1, D2, and D3 (respectively) in some "semantic metric space" such that $d(S_i, S_j) = 0$ for any reasonable "semantic metric" d. Now word count.

If it appears at first blush that many of the nicer analytical properties of transformations (such as those outlined above) may be difficult to come by, at least we can directly attack the twin problems of immediate data reduction and computational tractability. At the very least we can attempt to reduce the total volume of data, reduce its dimensionality, and improve computational tractability *while doing as little damage to the original structure of the data* as possible. This is not quite the same as identifying "ideal" transformations; it may be as simple as transforming data having the geometry of some k-dimensional manifold currently embedded in n ($\gg k$) dimensions into essentially the same manifold embedded in m ($\ll n$, $> = k$) dimensions; we may not have uncovered the essential geometry of the data, but at least we have not fundamentally damaged the geometry of the data.

Prohibitively high volumes of data generally cannot be processed in real time, or even near-real time. We might then seek data reduction techniques that preserve all of the relevant information embedded in the higher dimension, with the goal of processing the reduced data in real time. We have broadly categorized data reduction techniques into two techniques: (a) those transformations that reduce the number of data points in the dataset and (b) those transformations that reduce the underlying dimension of the dataset. Any technique that maps points in a higher-dimensional space into points in a lower-dimensional space (preserving certain properties) will fit this category. We can at least begin by identifying the set of techniques that will be most suited for security applications. Exhaustion, of course, is not really practicable. Undoubtedly, favorite technique X will not appear below. Within a broad sampling of well-known techniques, we can nonetheless develop a taxonomy of data reduction techniques. Our expectation is that best-suited techniques for security will be hybrids of the above two techniques.

5.2. DATA CLUSTERING TECHNIQUES: A BRIEF SURVEY

The general goal of data clustering is to partition a set of data points into equivalence classes. Where any equivalence class consists of a class paradigm and variants thereof caused by perturbations due to some noise process, it is probably safe to view the class paradigm as uniquely representative of the equivalence class (e.g., all handwritten "A"s, wetlands observed from a satellite image, etc.). Generally, this is not always the best approach. In this case, the equivalence class stretches the term "equivalence" to encompass wider variations, and indeed perhaps more than one ground truth. In any event, it is reasonable to group clustering techniques into five broad categories: partition clustering, hierarchical clustering, density-based clustering, model-based clustering, and fuzzy clustering. Figure 5.1 below shows a broad taxonomy of data clustering techniques, many of which are discussed here.

Partition clustering is a technique whereby the equivalence classes are constructed such that any object in any given equivalence class has greater similarity to other objects in the same class than to objects in any other class. This is not to be taken to imply that the equivalence classes accurately reflect the true state of nature. They might not. One way to achieve this is by minimizing an objective function iteratively. k-means and k-medoids are two well-known representatives of this form of clustering. In the k-means problem, given a set $P \subset R^d$ of n data points and a number k, we try to partition P into k equivalence classes (clusters) metrically. Each such cluster has a center defined by the centroid (i.e., mean) of the points in the cluster. The clustering should minimize

$$\sum_{x \in P} \|x - K(x)\|^2 \tag{5.1}$$

where $K(x)$ denotes the nearest center to the point x. There are several algorithms proposed for k-means clustering. An example is Lloyd's algorithm (Lloyd, 1982), which initially chooses k centers randomly and repeatedly assigns points to the recomputed nearest

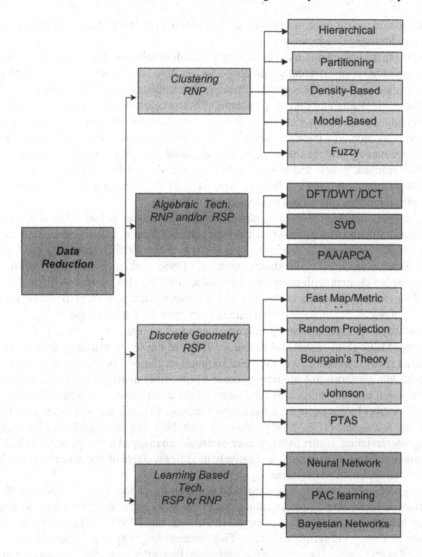

Figure 5.1. Broad taxonomy.

centers until no changes occur. The time complexity is $O(ikn)$, where i is the number of iterations, which is unknown. It has long been recognized that this algorithm may converge to a local minimum with an arbitrarily bad distortion with respect to the optimal solution (Kanungo et al., 2002). Nonetheless, k-means has a surprisingly loyal following, probably because of its simplicity in implementation. Attempts have been conducted to find algorithms with bounded quality, such as $(1 + \varepsilon)$-approximation or constant approximation. Matousek (2000), Kanungo et al. (2000), Har-Peled and Mazumdar (2004), and Kumar et al. (2004) are some examples of these approaches. In the k-medoids clustering strategy we attempt again to find k centers, but in this case these centers are required to form a subset of the original input set. Once we have identified these k centers, they define k clusters in a natural way. Each input point will associate itself with the closest center. Advantages of this method are that there is no limitation on attribute types, and it is less sensitive to outliers. Kaufman and Rousseeuw (1990) and Ng and Han (1994) are among the standard algorithms addressing this technique.

On the other hand, hierarchical clustering builds dendrograms. This allows for a more natural exploration of different granularity levels within the dataset. Here, the running time is quadratic $[O(n^2)]$. Hierarchical clustering techniques are typically grouped into agglomerative clustering and divisive clustering. In the agglomerative clustering approach, the technique proceeds in a bottom-up fashion. Alternatively, divisive clustering uses a top-down approach. For instance, agglomerative clustering starts with single point clusters and recursively merges the most similar two clusters until the requested number of clusters is reached. Sneath and Sokal (1973), Rajasekaran (2004), King (1967), Zhang et al. (1996), Guha et al. (1998, 1999), Karypis et al. (1999), and Boley (1998) represent standard and modern approaches to hierarchical clustering.

A common complaint leveled against clustering techniques is that many will fail to draw decision boundaries around clusters with complex shapes. Clustering techniques in the so-called *density-based clustering* class [Ester et al. (1996), Hinneburg and Keim (1998), Peter et al. (2003), Sheikholeslami et al. (1998), and Agrawal et al. (1998)] are able to resolve clusters with complex boundaries, and they also protect well against the difficulties caused by outliers in the data. The technique is not perfect, as expected; under certain circumstances, adjacent clusters are not separable by the technique.

Model-based clustering techniques have an enormous literature. Maximum likelihood clustering (MLC) (McLachlan and Basford, 1988) and the self-organized map (SOM) of Kohonen (1990) represent two of the more common techniques. In MLC, the expectation is that the data conforms to a mixture model of k probability distributions, and the clustering goal involves estimation of the parameters of the distributions (such as mean and covariance matrix) by maximizing a likelihood function. Perhaps the best-known strategy for accomplishing this is the EM algorithm (op. cit.). MLC is generalizable and has an appealing interpretation. Under SOM, cluster centroids are mapped to the plane, and clustering becomes a learning process that iteratively modifies weights of nodes until there is little or no change between iterations.

Fuzzy techniques seem to enjoy periodic resurgences in popularity. Notwithstanding the debates which still seem to surround fuzzy sets/fuzzy logic, there is at least an engineering validity to its use. Fuzzy c-means (FCM) (Bezdek, 1981) is the *locus classicus* example of a fuzzy clustering technique. This method assigns each point to c clusters up to a membership value. The clustering is performed thereafter by minimizing an objective function with respect to a membership parameter. In fact, the algorithm is perilously close to k-means and EM, employing again an iterative optimization. Since FCM is still sensitive to noise, Dave (1991) proposed a noise clustering (NC) technique wherein the noise is treated as one separate cluster and is represented by a prototype with a constant distance. In yet another approach called PCM (Krishnapuram and Keller, 1993), each cluster has a noise cluster associated with it.

5.3. ALGEBRAIC TRANSFORMATIONS

Algebraic approaches, whether directly associated with linear algebra or having some basis in functional analysis, have made and continue to make impressive contributions to information retrieval and space reduction.

In reviewing the literature, it can appear as if there is a transform for any and all specific problem instances. Often, specific transformations gain their power from specific observations about the originating dataset they are applied to. For example, prior to the ubiquitous use of the wavelet transform in data compression, the Discrete Cosine Transform (DCT) ranked among the best compressing transforms when applied to data having a specific Markovian structure. Equivalently, the Karhunen–Loeve transform (computationally difficult as it might have been to compute) was exploited because of its decorrelating properties. However, the DCT is not so efficient when the underlying dataset lacks Markov-1 structure, and the KLT can be worse than useless when confronted with mixture distributions. And although wavelet transforms can drive dense data to remarkably sparse data (wonderful for compression), they may not be the universal panacea if clustering is the goal (up to the nature of the originating data, naturally). Here we survey the Singular Value Decomposition (SVD), Discrete Fourier Transform (DFT), Discrete Wavelet Transform (DWT), Piecewise Aggregate Approximation (PAA), and Adaptive Piecewise Constant Approximation (APCA).

One of the more celebrated data transforms is the SVD. The essential goal of the SVD (Chandrasekaran et al., 1997) is to reduce the original N-dimensional data to a k-dimensional subspace through the origin. The technique is so established that it does not need elucidation here. The crux of the matter (as far as data compression is concerned) is that one is able to discard components in "negligible dimensions" by observing that if there is a set X of N-dimensional vectors to reduce the dimension of the dataset from N to k, the $(N - k)$ nonsignificant singular values of X are eliminated. What remains is the data in its natural dimensionality. However, computing the SVD requires a very heavy computational effort. Just as the DCT traded the "accuracy" of the KLT for the log-linear computational time expended in its (DCT) computation, one is faced with accepting the benefits of the SVD by trading computational effort. However, there have been some attempts to parallelize the algorithm. Even with its severe penalty in computational costs, the attraction of the SVD has caused many authors (including the authors of this chapter) to consider using the SVD as a post adjunct to some prior dimensionality reducing technique. Later we will consider the computationally efficient random projection (RP); one intriguing possibility is that the RP can be deployed to reduce the dimensionality of the data significantly (efficiently removing, if one can phrase it this way, garbage dimensions) while the SVD can be subsequently employed to refine the reduction further.

A second approach employs the Discrete Fourier Transform (DFT). From a purely computational viewpoint, we can conveniently discard any relationship the DFT might have to the physical interpretation of the Fourier transform. Thus, unless the data warrant, the DFT is no more to us than a morphism with some happy properties. Principal among these is the existence of a fast algorithm (the FFT) and the fact that the morphism exchanges convolution for multiplication. The oft-cited advantage of the DFT is the fact that its expression algorithmically in terms of the FFT allows the calculation of the DFT coefficients in $O(n \log n)$ time. The argument is made that dropping the nonsignificant components of the vectors applied here reduces the data dimensions, but this comes with the caveat that the DFT is not a particularly good compression strategy. Like all other isometries, the DFT does preserve the metric.

Wavelets today are endemic, and with good reason. An entire paper would have to be devoted to the role of the wavelet transform in data compression, and we have a specific interest in its role in this application to be elucidated further in a later publication. Aside from the innate appeal of the time complexity of the transform itself, discrete wavelet transforms (DWTs) based around wavelets of compact support have the added attraction of the very compactness of the wavelets themselves. As is now generally appreciated, the effect of this compactness of support of the underlying basis functions is to limit the ripple effect of changes in subsequences of a datum to a well-defined subsequence of transform coefficients. We have alluded above to the fact that the data of interest to us, although embedded in R^n, might in fact exhibit a more differential-geometric structure (i.e., be a manifold), and this raises the intriguing possibility that wavelets over manifolds may play an important role within this particular problem setting. As an aside, we note that wavelets play an important role in the JPEG 2000 standard (ISO/IEC/JTC1/SC29/WG1, 1997).

Piecewise Aggregate Approximation (PAA) starts with a set X of n-vectors $X = \{X_1, X_2, \ldots, X_m\}$. As in prior approaches, the goal is to reduce the n-dimensional data to k dimensions where $k < n$. First, we divide the data into k equal segments and produce a final data reduced vector which is the vector of the mean values of the data falling within the frame. PAA is both immediately comprehensible and simple to implement. A major advantage of PAA is its ability to provide flexibility within distance measures (such as weighted Euclidean queries). The time for this process is linear. The experimental studies of Keogh and Pazzani (2000) compare PAA to other traditional approaches and demonstrate that PAA outperforms them especially when dealing with long queries.

The variant called Adapted Piecewise Constant Approximation (APCA) is essentially similar to PAA except that it allows the data segments to have arbitrary lengths (Keogh and Pazzani, 2000). This makes APCA a good choice for applications that need metrics other than Euclidean distance.

5.4. DISCRETE GEOMETRY METHODS

Discrete Geometry Methods have recently emerged as a powerful approach for dimensionality reduction. In this section we briefly discuss Random Discrete Geometry Methods including Random Projections (RP), Fast Map, Metric Map, Boost Map, and Locally Linear Embeddings.

The foundation of the Random Projection is the Johnson–Lindenstrauss lemma (Johnson and Lindenstrauss, 1984). Random Projections (Bingham and Mannila, 2001) project original n-dimensional data into a k-dimensional subspace ($k < n$). Under RP, a random matrix R of size $k \times n$ whose columns have unit lengths is employed to achieve this projection. The choice of the random matrix R can be a challenge, particularly when computational effort is considered. The computational difficulties often associated with RPs were mitigated by Achlioptas (2001), who replaced the Gaussian distribution that is normally employed to form the elements of R with elements drawn from simpler distributions. Often, RPs are used as a preprocessing stage prior to data mining, image processing, and clustering algorithms; see, for example, Papadimitriou et al. (1998) who deploy random projections in the preprocessing stage of LSI. We defer further discussion of the RP technique to the experimental section below.

Fast Map (Faloutsos and Lin, 1995) is another discrete geometry technique, in which projection is onto a line (X_a, X_b) in R^n formed by the two pivots X_a and X_b. Given an arbitrary pivot X_b, the pivot X_a is chosen to be as far as possible from X_b. The pivot X_b is then updated to be the farthest object from X_a, and the process iterates k times to eventually map all objects to points in the reduced-dimension space R^k. Computationally linear in the data size N, it is possible to map any new document in $O(k)$ computational steps independent of the original data size N. Tesic et al. (2002) show that Fast Map outperforms SVD for image data sets.

A third discrete geometric approach is that of the Metric Map (Wang et al., 1999). Here, a small sample of the dataset is selected by picking at random $2k$ objects. The pairwise distances among these sampled objects are calculated and used to establish the target space R^k.

Suppose $\mathbf{A} = \{X_0, X_1, \ldots, X_{2k-1}\}$ defines the set of samples. One defines the mapping α such that $\alpha(X_0) = a_0 = (0, 0, \ldots, 0)$ and $\alpha(X_i) = a_i = (0, 0, \ldots, 1(i), \ldots, 0)$. Next, one constructs the matrix $\mathbf{M} = (m_{i,j})$ $(1 \leq i, j \leq 2k - 1)$, where $(m_{i,j}) = (d^2_{0,i} - d^2_{i,j} + d^2_{0,j})/2$. Then the singular value decomposition is deployed to find the singular values of $\mathbf{M}$. Thereafter, one drops the least significant $k - 1$ singular values of $\mathbf{M}$ and chooses the remaining $k + 1$ objects (called reference objects). Finally, each point in the original dataset is mapped to the new target space. Taking $O(Nk)$ units of time (N is the number of points), the algorithm is much faster than traditional approaches. However, its use of the SVD renders it not suitable for online use.

Yet another approach is the so-called Boost Map, which is an embedding approach for dimension reduction (Athisos, 2004). One of the main advantages here is that the proximity structure of the original space is, to a great extent, preserved. The Boost Map approach is based on combining one-dimensional embeddings into a multidimensional embedding. Since each object in the original space can be used as a reference object, the number of one-dimensional embeddings is quadratic in the number of the objects in the original space. Boost Map selectively combines these embeddings into a single, high-dimensional embedding. With the added advantage that Boost Map is formulated as a classifier-combination problem, it can therefore take advantage of existing machine learning techniques.

Its main disadvantage, however, is the large running time needed for the training part of the algorithm. However, experimental results (Athisos, 2004) show that Boost Map achieves a high accuracy when compared against FastMap and MetricMap.

Locally Linear Embedding (LLE) (Roweis and Saul, 2000) is an intriguing quasi-differential-geometric approach that can be used to map points in a higher-dimensional space into points in a lower-dimensional space such that *neighborhoods* of points are preserved. The two stages in the algorithm proceed as follows: Initially, neighborhood information is captured for each input point in the form of certain weights; subsequently, these weights are used to compute the coordinates of the image of each input point in the lower-dimensional space.

In the first stage, one identifies the closest m (a tuning parameter) neighbors of each input point X_i $(1 \leq i \leq N)$. Next, one computes weights $w_{ij}(1 \leq j \leq N; j \neq i)$ such that X_i can be closely reconstructed using only these weights and the points $X_j(1 \leq j \leq N; j \neq i)$. One has that the w_{ij} will be nonzero only for the m neighbors of X_i and, for any i, the following equality is ensured:

$$\sum_j w_{ij} = 1 \tag{5.2}$$

The weights therefore can be construed as information describing the neighborhood of the point X_i, and the best possible values for these weights are obtained minimizing the following error function:

$$\varepsilon(w) = \sum_i \left| X_i - \sum_j w_{ij} X_j \right|^2 \tag{5.3}$$

The second stage of the algorithm then involves computing the coordinates of the projected points in the lower-dimensional space, making use of the weights computed in stage 1.

If $Y_1, Y_2, \ldots, Y_N$ are the points in the lower-dimensional space, then computing these points reduces to the problem of minimizing the following function:

$$\Phi(Y) = \sum_i \left| Y_i - \sum_j w_{ij} Y_j \right|^2 \tag{5.4}$$

Though LLE is simple in implementation it takes more time than the other approaches such as random projections.

5.5. LEARNING TECHNIQUES

We define learning techniques to encompass those such as neural networks and probably approximately correct learning. Here we briefly summarize neural networks, probably approximately correct learning, and Bayesian networks.

A neural network can be considered to be a connected leveled graph where each node corresponds to a (simple) processing element and the (directed) edges correspond to communication links. One expects there to be at least two levels (one for input and another for output), but of course there could be more levels referred to as hidden levels.

Associated with each edge in the network is a weight. Restricting our attention to bilevel nets, let N be any node in the second level (i.e., the output level). Let q be the number of incoming edges into N and let $x_1, x_2, \ldots, x_q$ be the corresponding input values. Suppose the weights on these incoming edges are denoted $w_1, w_2, \ldots, w_q$ and the threshold value of N is denoted by T. If each output is binary, then N outputs one of its two possible outputs dependent on the outcome of

$$\sum w_i x_i > T \tag{5.5}$$

Neural networks have a massive and (now) somewhat antique literature. Representative papers in this area are: Diamantaras and Kung (1996) and Perantois and Virvilis (1999).

Probably Approximately Correct (PAC) learning (Valiant, 1984) is perhaps lesser known. If C is any concept that we are interested in learning and if G is the concept that has been learned, one defines the error in learning $e(G)$ as the probability that $C(x) \neq G(x)$, for an arbitrary element x of the universe under concern. For example, if C is a Boolean formula on n variables, one way of specifying C is with the set C' of satisfying assignments to C. The distance between C and G (or $e(G)$) can then be defined as

$$\frac{|C' - G'| + |G' - C'|}{2^n} \tag{5.6}$$

One states that a learning algorithm is capable of learning a concept C probably approximately with parameters ε and δ if the probability that $e(G)$ is greater than ε is at most δ. Here ε is an accuracy parameter and δ is the confidence. These parameters can either be user-specified or set to default values. It has been shown that PAC learning algorithms can be devised for a variety of concepts (Valiant, 1984).

Suppose F is a length-n Boolean formula to be learned. Input to the learner will be a set of examples that are no more than assignments to the n variables. An exemplar is positive provided the assignment satisfies the formula; it is otherwise negative. A learner might call for exemplars that are positive or negative (or indeed both). Two criteria are used to judge a learning algorithm, namely its sample complexity and run time. The sample complexity of a PAC learner (with parameters ε and δ) is the number of samples required by the algorithm (as a function of ε, δ, n). The run time refers to the amount of time taken by the learner.

Recall that a Boolean formula is said to be in conjunctive normal form (CNF) if it is the conjunction of disjunctions of literals (i.e., variables and their negations). Thus $(x_3 \vee \bar{x}_1) \wedge (\bar{x}_2 \vee x_3 \vee x_4)$ is a formula in CNF and $(x_3 \vee \bar{x}_1)$ and $(\bar{x}_2 \vee x_3 \vee x_4)$ are the clauses of this formula. A Boolean formula is k-CNF if it is CNF and has at most k literals per clause. It is well known that polynomial time learning algorithms exist for various classes of formulas (including k-CNF formulas). A typical learning algorithm for k-CNF formulas might be devised as in the following. Suppose F is the formula to be learned. Using only positive examples, the algorithm commences with a formula G that is the conjunction of all possible clauses of length at most k. Note that each example e can be thought of as a binary sequence $e_1, e_2, \ldots, e_n$, where e_i is the value assigned to the variable x_i, $1 \leq i \leq n$. The algorithm then processes one example at a time, and on being given example e the algorithm deletes all the clauses of G whose values are false under the assignment e. After processing all the examples in this fashion, the output is the resultant formula, which is a very good approximation to F.

The Bayesian Networks (BNs) [as defined, for example, in Bernardo and Smith, 1994)] is a model for representing uncertainty in knowledge using the probability theory. BNs employ Directed Acyclic Graphs (DAG) to represent the conditional dependencies between the different knowledge components. Bayesian Networks can be used for space or data reduction. Like Neural Networks above the Bayesian Network is subject to a massive literature not reviewable in a paper of this size. However, a good example of unsupervised learning in data clustering is given in Cheeseman and Stutz, 1995.

Vapnik (1995) introduced a new supervised learning approach called the Support Vector Machine (SVM). SVM is a learning technique that introduces flexible representations for the knowledge as well as efficient training algorithms. The advantage of SVM is its amenability to generalizations. This advantage is inherited from the Structural Risk Minimization (SRM) principle on which SVM is based. In contrast to the statistical learning methods that minimize the error on the training data, SRM minimizes the generalization error.

5.6. LATENT SEMANTIC INDEXING

As noted above, one of the major difficulties facing counter-terrorism applications is the need to process high volumes of data through the deployment of a variety of information retrieval (IR) techniques. Two critical problems of import to us arise when IR techniques utilize classical lexical matching: *polysemy,* representing the notion that the meaning of individual words are influenced by their context (e.g., surrounding words); and *synonymy,* representing the reality that the same object (term) can be described in different ways. To address these issues, complementing the techniques presented in the prior sections of this chapter, we explore the area of latent semantic indexing (LSI) (Deerwester et al., 1990), which represents an extended vector space IR model.

LSI makes the following assumptions: In any document there is some underlying semantic structure involving the "words" of the text, and this structure can be captured and described (but see the caveats above) while allowing the resulting indexed document to be searched and queried. In terms of counter-terrorism, it seems clear that having information reduced and then indexed via LSI techniques (with the expectation that minimum information is lost), one can significantly reduce processing time that is required to access the documents while still retaining the meaning. Here we review a selective subset of LSI approaches: Latent Semantic Analysis (LSA), probabilistic LSI (PLSI), Unitary Operators for Fast Latent Semantic Indexing (UOFLSI), Polynomial Filtering Latent Semantic Indexing (PFLSI), and Distributed LSI (DLSI).

The classical LSI approach, Latent Semantic Analysis (LSA) (Deerwester et al., 1990), is a technique based on the singular value decomposition (SVD). One supposes that there is a set of documents needing to be indexed for which there is an associated set of terms to be found. Indexable terms are organized into a vector whose entries are the frequencies of occurrence of the term in the original document. Thus, one generates the large term-by-document matrix X, with each position x_{ij} corresponding to the term (row i) in a document (column j). The assumption made in LSI is that there exists an underlying semantic structure of the use of words throughout the collection of documents. The argument then becomes that the resulting document space that is represented by the matrix X can be reduced (via SVD) to a smaller space subtended by the matrix X', which has a lower rank k. The value k represents a threshold that is used to maintain the most significant structural aspects of the document collection while still excluding noise or trivial values as needed to improve retrieval performance. To augment classical LSI, Probabilistic Latent Semantic Indexing (PLSI) (Hoffman, 1999) employs a statistical model that targets domain-specific synonymy and polysemy. The intent of this model is to more precisely characterize the content of the documents (based on the indexes), but, as claimed by Hoffman (1999), more robust and achieves better precision over the classical LSI method.

Clearly, an area of significant concern arises if the database to which LSI is applied is not static—that is, it is subject to addition of (less likely deletion of) documents. Evidently, the major concern is the computation of the SVD. To address this, one approach, the Unitary Operators for Fast Latent Semantic Indexing (UOFLSI) (Hoerkamp, 2001) reduces the computational cost. UOFLSI utilizes a memory-efficient unitary transformation and can be computed in linear to sublinear time. The claim is that UOFLSI can preserve the cohesive nature of the document content and reduce the dimension of the document content, with less computation. Equally, Polynomial Filtering for Latent Semantic Indexing (PFLSI) (Kokiopoulou and Saad, 2004) is a framework for LSI that utilizes polynomial filtering to assist in the calculation of the vector and matrix content. The claim here is that matrix decomposition and its computational cost and storage requirements are substantially reduced when compared to traditional implementations of LSI.

Distributed LSI seeks to address issues related to scalability within a more realistic environment as the quantity of documents increase—while still attempting to maintain the quality of returned documents (Bassu and Behrens, 2003). The objective is to improve the match between a user's query (and its meaning) and the document collection. In this case, distributed LSI (DLSI) addresses scalability by partitioning information sources with respect to different conceptual domains (e.g., counterintelligence, intercepted communications, terrorist activity, etc.), indexing each derived subcollection with LSI. Then queries can be performed over individual domains or indeed the entire space (depending on the specificity of the desired results). For counter-terrorism purposes, partitioning may improve performance and may allow more focused queries to be posed and answered.

5.7. EXPERIMENTAL RESULTS

Our focus in this section is on certain applications of the Random Projection (RP), and in particular that espoused by Achlioptas (2001). Recall that the intent of the Random Projection is to embed data in a high-dimensional space into a lower-dimensional space in such a way as to control distortion (particularly metric distortion) in the lower-dimensional space. Typically, one assumes that there are n points in R^d and the goal is to embed these points into R^k up to some acceptable distortion ($k < d$). It is convenient to consider the n points in R^d as being represented by the $n \times d$ matrix (table) $\mathbf{A}$ such that rows in $\mathbf{A}$ represent data points. One thinks of (for example) frequency counts of documents; here a document is represented by an individual row.

The major assertion of Johnson and Lindenstrauss (1984) is as follows:

For given $\varepsilon > 0$ and integer n, let k be a positive integer such that $k \geq k_0 = O(\varepsilon^{-2} \log n)$. For every set P of n points in R^d, there exists $f: R^d \to R^k$ such that, for all $u, v \in P$

$$(1 - \varepsilon)\|u - v\|^2 \leq \|f(u) - f(v)\|^2 \leq (1 + \varepsilon)\|u - v\|^2 \tag{5.7}$$

Under refinement by Achlioptas, we have

Theorem (Achlioptas). Let P be an arbitrary set of n points in R^d represented as an $n \times d$ matrix A. Given $\varepsilon, \beta > 0$ let

$$k_0 = \frac{4 + 2\beta}{\varepsilon^2/2 - \varepsilon^3/3} \log n \tag{5.8}$$

For integer $k \geq k_0$ let R be a $d \times k$ random matrix with $R_{ij} = r_{ij}$, where $\{r_{ij}\}$ are independent random variables from either one of the following two probability distributions:

$$r_{ij} = \begin{cases} +1 & \text{with probability } 1/2 \\ -1 & \text{with probability } 1/2 \end{cases} \tag{5.9}$$

$$r_{ij} = \begin{cases} +1 & \text{with probability } 1/6 \\ 0 & \text{with probability } 2/3 \\ -1 & \text{with probability } 1/6 \end{cases} \tag{5.10}$$

Let $E = \dfrac{1}{\sqrt{k}} AR$ and let $f: R^d \to R^k$ map the ith row of A to the ith row of E.

With probability at least $1 - n^\beta$ for all $u, v \in P$

$$(1 - \varepsilon)\|u - v\|^2 \leq \|f(u) - f(v)\|^2 \leq (1 + \varepsilon)\|u - v\|^2 \tag{5.11}$$

One sees immediately the attraction of Achlioptas' work, particularly as it applies to computational efficiency. The question then naturally arises as to its performance in real examples. Importantly, we are interested in the behavior of clustering algorithms under RP.

We begin by taking some trivial examples. We generate synthetic data in R^d with $d = 5000$. We partition this data using K-means to derive a *ground truth* for subsequent experiments with RP. (We take the obvious precautions in deploying K-means under different experimental settings.) K-means, as pointed out above, is generally regarded as a weak clustering procedure, but it is in such widespread use that results reported from its use remain of value. Figure 5.2 shows the classification rate of K-means relative to the ground truth developed in the original data space.

It is easy to determine the expected RP dimension for a given ε and n. What one immediately notices is that the performance of the clustering *remains essentially constant throughout a significant decrease in the projected dimension up to what is an obvious heel in the graph.* One sees above that we are able to decrease the projected dimension down to about $k = 20$ prior to any significant classification distortion arising. This has, as expected, an effect on the computational effort expended in classification, as shown in Figure 5.3.

There is evidently no surprise in the reduction of computational costs associated with performing clustering in significantly reduced dimensions *even when the cost of the RP is considered.* It is worth drawing attention to the fact that clustering can incur speedups of about a factor of 700 (in this case) with no discernable difference in cluster quality.

The combination of RP with SVD (or other post-RP data reduction method) has already been discussed. The intention here is usually to deploy RP to prune out the truly insignificant dimensions and let (for example) SVD elucidate the natural (remaining) dimensions within the data. Here we consider RP, SVD, and RP + SVD in combination and explore their behavior relative to distance and similarity metrics.

Figure 5.4 shows the error behavior of RP, SVD, and RP + SVD when the consideration is inter-vector distance. Note that the combined strategy (RP + SVD) involved pro-

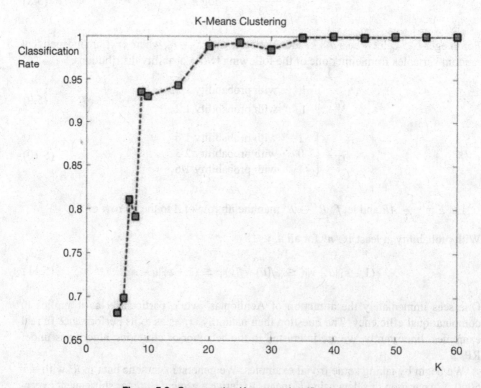

Figure 5.2. Comparative K-means classification rates.

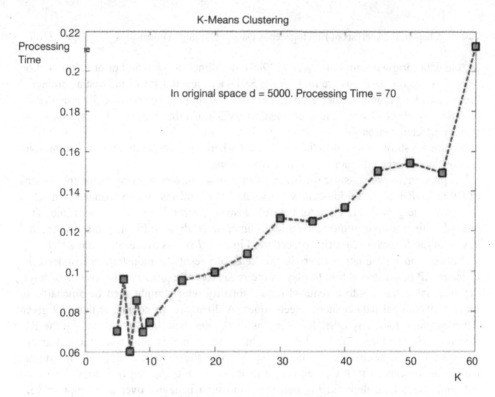

Figure 5.3. Absolute run times.

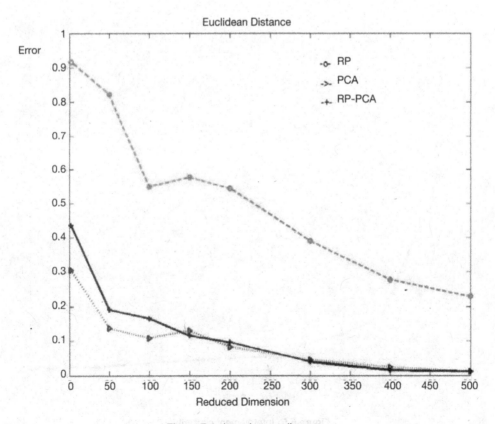

Figure 5.4. Interelement distances.

jecting data (originally in dimension $d = 900$) into dimension $k = 500$ prior to application of SVD. Two observations are immediate: SVD, as expected, performs best as projected dimensions lower; on the other hand, initially deploying RP (computationally much faster than SVD) *followed* by SVD is as efficient as SVD alone for all but the lowest dimension target projected subspaces.

Figure 5.5 shows essentially the same result when the (admittedly weak) inner product is considered as the interelement similarity measure.

As previously, we consider the behavior of simple clustering processes on the options of RP and RP + SVD. In this case we examine both K-means and an unsupervised KNN (K nearest neighbor) strategy. As before, clustering error is relative to an established ground truth produced in the original high-dimensional dataset. Figure 5.6 shows the behavior of the K-means clustering procedure. Figure 5.7 shows the results from KNN.

In common with other workers in the field, our results demonstrate that indeed the efficient RP has a strong role to play in the reduction of expressed dimensions of high-dimensional datasets into a reduced dimensionality which might then be amenable to more conventional data reduction techniques. A difficulty, of course, is that any given RP may outperform any other RP in terms of the net distortion introduced by the RP. Recently (He and Greenshields, 2005), we have shown that judicious selection of an appropriate RP can be deduced by deploying RP over the support vectors of the original dataset as a means whereby an ensemble of RPs can be computed over very few original data points (and their fidelity deduced from their behavior over these support vec-

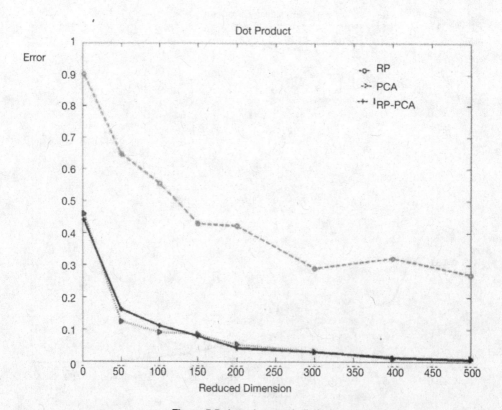

Figure 5.5. Interelement similarity.

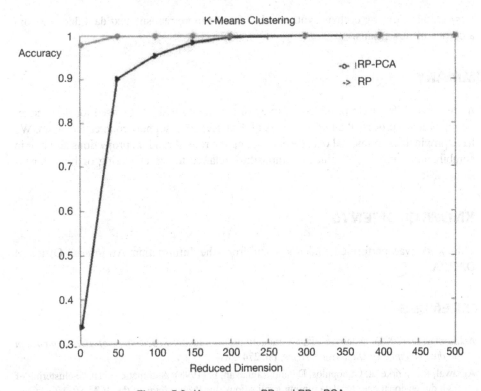

Figure 5.6. K-means over RP and RP + PCA.

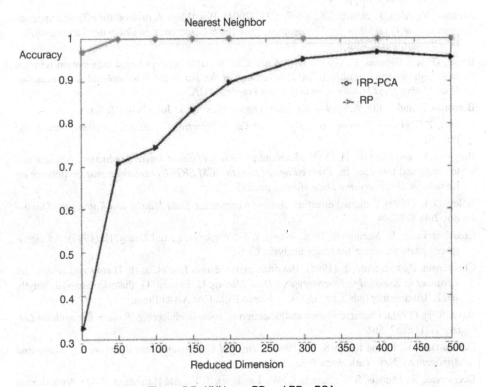

Figure 5.7. KNN over RP and RP + PCA.

tors). In this case, we eschew synthetic data for the more realistic text data derived from a corpus of newgroups.

SUMMARY

In this chapter, we have provided a survey of techniques that can be used for data reduction in order to process the high volumes of data needed to support counter-terrorism. We have provided experimental data demonstrating the role of random projections alone or in combination with single value decomposition relative to the clustering of high-dimensional data.

ACKNOWLEDGMENTS

This work was performed under a grant from the Information Awareness Office at DARPA.

REFERENCES

Achlioptas, D. (2001). Database-friendly random projections. In: *Proceedings of ACM Symposium on the Principles of Database Systems,* pp. 274–281.

Agrawal, R., Gehrke, J., Gunopulos, D., and Raghavan, P. (1998). Automatic subspace clustering of high dimensional data for data mining applications. In: *Proceedings of the ACM SIGMOD Conference,* Seattle, WA, pp. 94–105.

Athitsos, V., Alon, J., Sclaroff, S., Kollios, G. (2004). BosstMap: A method for efficient approximate similarity rankings. In: *Proceedings of the IEEE Conference on Computer Vision and Pattern Recognition* (CVPR).

Bassu, D., and Behrens, C. (2003). Distributed LSI: Scalable concept-based information retrieval with high semantic resolution. In: *Proceedings of the 3rd SIAM International Conference on Data Mining (Text Mining Workshop),* San Francisco, CA.

Bernardo, J., and Smith, A. (1994). *Bayesian Theory.* New York: John Wiley & Sons.

Bezdek, J. C. (1981). *Pattern Recognition with Fuzzy Objective Function Algorithms.* New York: Plenum.

Bingham, E., and Mannila, H. (2001). Random projection in dimensionality reduction: Applications to image and text data. In: *Proceedings of the 7th ACM SIGKDD International Conference on Knowledge Discovery and Data Mining,* pp. 245–250.

Boley, D. L. (1998). Principal direction divisive partitioning. *Data Mining and Knowledge Discovery,* **2**(4):325–344.

Chandrasekaran, S., Manjunath, B. S., Wang, Y. F., Winkeler, J., and Zhang, H. (1997). An eigenspace update algorithm for image analysis. *CVGIP.*

Cheeseman, P., and Stutz, J. (1995). Bayesian classification (AutoClass): Theory and results. In: *Advances in Knowledge Discovery and Data Mining,* U. Fayyad, G. Piatesky-Shapiro, Smyth, and R. Uthurusamy (eds.), pp. 153–180. Menlo Park, CA: AAAI Press.

Dave, R. N. (1991). Characterization and detection of noise in clustering. *Pattern Recognition Letters* **12**(11):657–664.

Diamantaras, K. I., and Kung, S. Y. (1996). *Principal Component Neural Networks: Theory and Applications.* New York: John Wiley & Sons.

Deerwester, S., Dumais, S. T., Furnas, G. W., Landauer, T. K., and Harshman, R. (1990). Indexing by latent semantic analysis. *Journal of American Society for Information Science and Technology* **41**:391–407.

Ester, M., Kriegel, H-P., Sander, J., and Xu, X. (1996). A density-based algorithm for discovering clusters in large spatial databases with noise. In *Proceedings of the 2nd ACM SIGKDD*, pp. 226–231, Portland, Oregon.

Faloutsos, C., and Lin, K. (1995). FastMap: A fast algorithm for indexing, data-mining and visualization of traditional and multimedia datasets. *ACM SIGMOD Proceedings*, pp. 163–174.

Guha, S., Rastogi, R., and Shim, K. (1998). CURE: An efficient clustering algorithm for large databases. In: *Proceedings of the ACM SIGMOD Conference*, Seattle, WA, pp. 73–84.

Guha, S., Rastogi, R., and Shim, K. (1999). ROCK: A robust clustering algorithm for categorical attributes. In: *Proceedings of the 15th ICDE*, Sydney, Australia, pp. 512–521.

Har-Peled, S., and Mazumdar, S. (2004). Coresets for k-means and k-median clustering and their applications. *STOC*.

He, L., and Greenshields, I. R. (2005). Empirical determination of lower bounds on RP embedding. *AI for Homeland Security*.

Hinneburg, A., and Keim, D. (1998). An efficient approach to clustering large multimedia databases with noise. In: *Proceedings of the 4th ACM SIGKDD*, New York, pp. 58–65.

Hoenkamp, E. (2001). Unitary operators for fast latent indexing. In: *Proceedings of 24th Annual International ACM SIGIR Conference on Research and Development in Information Retrieval*, New York, 400–401.

Hofmann, T. (1999). Probabilistic latent semantic indexing. In: *Proceedings of ACM SIGIR 99*, pp. 50–57.

ISO/IEC/JTC1/SC29/WG1 N390R, JPEG 2000 Image Coding System (1997). http://www.jpeg.org/public/wg1n505.pdf.

Johnson, W., and Lindenstrauss, J. (1984). "Extensions of Lipshitz mapping into Hilbert space. In: *Conference in Modern Analysis and Probability*, Contemporary Mathematics, Vol. 26, pp. 189–206. Washington, DC: American Mathematical Society.

Kanungo, T., Mount, D. M., Netanyahu, A. S., Piatko, C. D., Silverman, R., and Wu, A. Y. (2002). An efficient k-means clustering algorithm: Analysis and implementation. *IEEE Transactions on Pattern Analysis and Machine Intelligence* **24**(7):881–892.

Karypis, G., Han, E.-H., and Kumar, V. (1999). CHAMELEON: A hierarchical clustering algorithm using dynamic modeling. *COMPUTER*, **32**:68–75.

Kaufman, L., and Rousseeuw, P. (1990). *Finding Groups in Data: An Introduction to Cluster Analysis*. New York: John Wiley & Sons.

Keogh, E., and Pazzani, M. (2000). Dimensionality reduction for fast similarity search in large time series databases. In: *Pacific-Asia Conference on Knowledge Discovery and Data Mining*.

King, B. (1967). Step-wise clustering procedures. *Journal of the American Statistical Association* **69**:86–101.

Kohonen, T. (1990). The self-organizing map. *Proceedings of the IEEE* **9**:1464–1479.

Kokiopoulou, E., and Saad, Y. (2004). Polynomial filtering in latent semantic indexing for information retrieval. In: *Proceedings of the 27th Annual International Conference on Research and Development In Information Retrieval*, pp. 104–111.

Krishnapuram, R., and Keller, J. M. (1993). A possibilistic approach to cluster-ing. *IEEE Transactions on Fuzzy Systems* **1**:98–110.

Kumar, A., Sabharwal, Y., and Sen, S. (2004). A simple linear time $(1 + \varepsilon)$-approximation algorithm for k-means clustering in any dimensions. In: *Proceedings of the 45th Annual IEEE Symposium on Foundations of Computer Science (FOCS '04)*.

Lloyd, S. P. (1982). Least squares quantization in PCM. *IEEE Transactions on Information Theory* **28**:129–137.

Matousek, J. (2000). On approximate geometric k-clustering. *Discrete and Computational Geometry* **24**:61–84.

McLachlan, G., and Basford, K. (1988). *Mixture Models: Inference and Applications to Clustering.* New York: Marcel Dekker.

Ng, R., and Han, J. (1994). Efficient and effective clustering methods for spatial data mining. In *Proceedings of the 20th Conference on VLDB,* Santiago, Chile, pp. 144–155.

Papadimitriou, C., Raghavan, P., Tamaki, H., and Vempala, S. (1998). Latent semantic indexing: A probabilistic analysis. In: *Proceedings of the 17th ACM Symposium on the Principles of Database Systems,* pp. 159–168.

Perantonis, S. J., and Virvilis, V. (1999). Dimensionality reduction using a novel neural network based feature extraction method of boolean functions. In: *Proceedings of IEEE & INNS International Joint Conference on Neural Networks,* Washington DC.

Peter, W., Chiochetti, J., and Giardina, C. (2003). New unsupervised clustering algorithm for large datasets. *Proceedings of the Ninth ACM SIGKDD International Conference on Knowledge Discovery and Data Mining,* Washington, DC.

Rajasekaran, S. (2004). Efficient parallel hierarchical clustering algorithms. In: *Proceedings of the 17th International Conference on Parallel and Distributed Computing Systems (PDCS),* pp. 27–32.

Roweis, S., and Saul, L. (2000). Nonlinear dimensionality reduction by locally linear embedding, *Science* **290**(5500):2323–2326.

Ruck, D., Rogers, S., and Karisky, M. (1990). Feature selection using a multiplayer perceptron. *Neural Network Comput.,* Vol. 2, pp. 40–48.

Sheikholeslami, G., Chatterjee, S., and Zhang, A. (1998). WaveCluster: A multi-resolution clustering approach for very large spatial databases. In: *Proceedings of the 24th Conference on VLDB,* New York, pp. 428–439.

Sneath, P. H. A., and Sokal, R. R. (1973). *Numerical Taxonomy.* London: Freeman, Taylor, V. York, B. http://www.iaaec.com/projects/coretech/ct3.html.

Tesic, J., Newsam, S., and Manjunath, B. S. (2002). Challenges in mining large image datasets. In: *IPAM Short Program on Mathematical Challenges in Scientific Data Mining,* Los Angeles, CA.

Valiant, L. G. (1984). A theory of the learnable. *Communications of the ACM* **27**:1134–1142.

Vapnik, N. (1995). *The Nature of Statistical Learning Theory.* New York: Springer.

Wang, J. T.-L., et al. (1999). Evaluating a class of distance-mapping algorithms for data mining and clustering. In: *Knowledge Discovery and Data Mining,* pp. 307–311.

Zhang, T., Ramakrishnan, R., and Livny, M. (1996). BIRCH: An efficient data clustering method for very large databases. In: *Proceedings of the ACM SIGMOD Conference,* Montreal, Canada, pp. 103–114.

Chapter 6

Semantic Web Technologies for Terrorist Network Analysis

Jennifer Golbeck, Aaron Mannes, and James Hendler

6.1. INTRODUCTION

The Semantic Web is a new approach to using information online. When the Web was originally created, it was designed as a place where users could store their documents, link them to other documents, and ultimately present them so other web users could read them. The HyperText Markup Language (HTML) designed to create these web pages is infused down to the very name of the tags to present information in a way that is useful for the human reader. As HTML evolved, the added features all helped enhance the web author's ability to create better layouts and present pages that were even more comprehensible by human readers.

As the number of pages on the web increased, so did the number of directories, search engines, and portals that helped people locate useful information more quickly. Improved technology also has facilitated an increase in the number of images, movies, audio clips, and other media, as well as the number of large databases that are accessible online. With the number of web pages approaching the tens of billions, a new problem has arisen to the forefront: How do we use all this information? Information is often spread across many pages in different forms. Search engines are helpful with the text, but are less likely to help users find an image or a movie according to its content.

The Semantic Web is envisioned as the next generation of the web that will help address these problems. New languages—the Resource Description Framework (RDF) and Web Ontology Language (OWL)—support the creation of data models that reflect the knowledge contained in any web resource, be it a text page, a media document, or a database. Unlike HTML, this knowledge is represented in a way that makes it easy for computers to understand and work with the data. It also allows for the integration of data from across the web into a single model.

In this chapter, we will introduce the fundamentals of the Semantic Web with a focus on how it can be used for creating a portal of terrorism-related information. We will describe the ontology developed as part of the MINDSWAP Counter-terror project and will also present a look at the experimental portal developed from our own data input. This leads into a discussion of how this technology can be used as part of the intelligence and counter-terrorism analysis processes.

6.2. SEMANTIC WEB FOUNDATIONS

Just as the World Wide Web, as we know it, is an idea that incorporates many smaller concepts, so is the Semantic Web. This section introduces some of its basic terminology and technology.

6.2.1. Resources, URIs, and Triples

The basic unit we often think of on the World Wide Web is a "document." We most often think of this as a web page made out of HTML, but it can also be an Acrobat PDF Document, an image, a flash movie, or some other document. The web is built on a model where every document has a unique web address (also known as a Uniform Resource Locator, or URL). While there are documents on the Semantic Web, the basic unit is the *resource*. A resource is essentially a representation of a concept. For example, a resource may be a picture or a web page, but it also could be the e-mail address of a person in a social network, or the last known location of a specific terrorist. Each resource is also given an address with a Uniform Resource Indicator, or *URI*. URLs are actually a specific type of URI.

A URI can take many forms, but it generally begins with a protocol (like "http" or "ftp"), followed by a domain name, a path to a file containing a reference to the resource, and then the name of the resource itself. For example, say we have a file called "terrorism.owl," and inside that file is the description of a concept called "IntelligenceReport." A URI could take the following form:

```
http://example.com/terrorism.owl#IntelligenceReport
```

Once the concept of "IntelligenceReport" has been created, we may want to say something about the report. For example, we may want to add a date on which the report was created. This leads into the next Semantic Web fundamental: the *triple*. A triple is how statements are made on the Semantic Web. As one would expect, triples have three parts: the subject, the predicate, and the object. The subject of the triple is the thing being described—in this case, the "IntelligenceReport" resource. The predicate is a descriptor of what is being described about the subject. In this example, the predicate will be the creation date. The predicate itself is named with a URI that indicates where that resource could be defined. The object of the triple is the value given to the predicate. The object can be a literal (like a string of text) or another resource. The triple is often represented as two nodes (representing the subject and the object) connected by an edge representing the predicate. Figure 6.1 shows the triple for stating that the "IntelligenceReport" has a creation date of January 1, 2006.

6.2.2. The Resource Description Framework (RDF) and RDF Graphs

The examples in Section 6.2.1 were limited because we had no way of clearly expressing triples or creating concepts. For that, the syntax of a language is required, and one of the foundational languages on the Semantic Web is the Resource Description Framework (RDF). RDF is designed to allow users to represent information about resources.

Resources are still identified by their URI. In addition, users can create "Properties" in RDF. Properties equate to the predicate of the triple, the predicate is generally a property

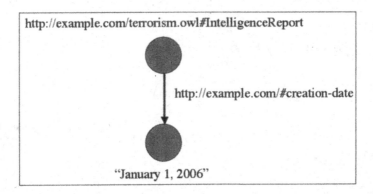

Figure 6.1. The triple created from stating that the Intelligence Report has a creation date of January 1, 2006. Notice that a URI has been created for the "creation-date" predicate. There is no URI for the "January 1, 2006" object because it is a string.

of the subject. To define a property actually requires a triple as well. The URI for the new property is given as the subject. The predicate is "type" and the object is "Property," where both "type" and "Property" are defined as part of the RDF specification. To create a property called "creation-date," the following triple would suffice:

```
<http://example.com/#creation-date>
<http://www.w3.org/1999/02/22-rdf-syntax-ns#type>
<http://www.w3.org/1999/02/22-rdf-syntax-ns#Property>.
```

Notice that the URI for the RDF elements is "http://www.w3.org/1999/02/22-rdf-syntax-ns#" and the names of the resources appear at the end.

The syntax of the previous example, where each URI in the triple is enclosed in "<" and ">" symbols and where the statement is terminated with a period, is actually a valid RDF notation called N-Triples. There are other notations, including RDF/XML, based on the eXtensible Markup Language (XML) meta-language, and Notation3 (commonly called N3), which is a shorthand serialization of RDF that is designed to be more easily human readable. Regardless of the syntax, an RDF file will contain a series of triples and is usually saved with the ".rdf" extension, though that is not required.

Because RDF has the ability to create named properties, this facilitates the process of creating data models. For example, the "IntelligenceReport" of our examples may have several properties; there is a creation date, an author, and perhaps a classification level. There may also be properties about the author, like name, e-mail address, and job title. When making multiple statements about the same resource, that resource is the subject of several triples. This leads to the development of the *RDF graph* where each resource is represented by a node, and each property or predicate is represented by an edge, as in Figure 6.1. The graphs can grow more complex, though. Using the properties mentioned here, the RDF graph can become quite large. Figure 6.2 shows some of this information. Resources are represented as circles, and literal values are represented as squares. The URIs of the resources have been shortened to include just the name for clarity.

An important fact about RDF graphs is that they are models of the *concepts,* not of a specific file. In the example shown in Figure 6.2, information about the IntelligenceReport could be contained in one file, the information about JoeBlog could be in another

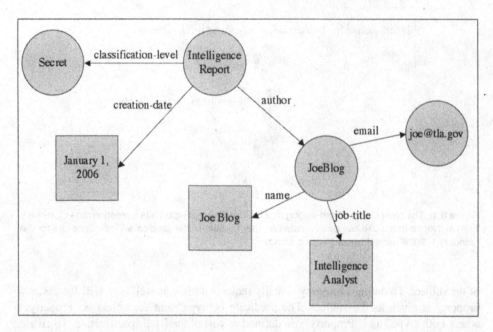

Figure 6.2. A graph showing an IntelligenceReport with a "secret" classification level, a creation date of January 1, 2006, and an author, Joe Blog, who is an Intelligence Analyst with the e-mail address joe@tla.gov. Resources are represented as circles while literal values are represented as squares.

file. To connect them, all that is required is a triple with the URI of the IntelligenceReport as the subject and the URI of JoeBlog as the object.

6.2.3. RDF Schema and the Web Ontology Language (OWL)

To extend the capabilities of RDF, two additional languages add semantic expressivity and power: RDF Schema (RDFS) and the Web Ontology Language (OWL).

6.2.3.1. RDF Schema (RDFS). RDFS is based on RDF, so any valid RDF is also valid RDFS. There are new features available in RDFS. The most important of these are the ability to create classes and to restrict properties.

Classes are general categories of concepts. They essentially provide the ability to add a type to resources in RDF. For example, Section 6.2.2 introduced a resource named "Joe-Blog." Using RDFS, we can create a class called "Person" and use that as the type for the resource. This would make JoeBlog an *instance* of the Person class. Then, in addition to knowing the properties about the resource, we also know the category to which it belongs. In RDFS, classes can also be structured in a hierarchy, using the subClassOf syntax. Multiple inheritance is allowed, so classes can be subclasses of any number of other classes.

Consider the example in Section 6.2.2, and say we want to include information about where Joe Blog works. Taking advantage of the ability to create classes in RDFS, we will state that the resource "JoeBlog" is an instance of the Person class. Furthermore, we will create a class called "Organization." That will allow us to create in instance of that class to represent where Joe works. For this example, we will say that Joe works for the State Department; a resource "StateDepartment" is created with the type "Organization." To connect these two instances, a Property is required. Using RDF, we create a Property called "employed_by". This allows us to finally state the triple JoeBlog employed_by StateDepartment.

With the existence of classes, Properties can be restricted so that they are only used with instances of particular classes. It would be reasonable to restrict the "employed_by" Property such that it could only connect a "Person" to an "Organization." RDFS allows this sort of restriction. There are two special Properties defined as part of RDFS that can only be used with other Properties: domain and range. The domain is used within the definition of a property to restrict the type of instances that can be used as the subject of the property. In this example, we are restricting the domain of "employed_by" to the class "Person." We will assume that all of these concepts are being defined in a file named "intel.rdf" in the example.com domain.

```
<http://example.com/intel.rdf#employed_by>
<http://www.w3.org/1999/02/22-rdf-syntax-ns#domain>
<http://example.com/intel.rdf#Person>.
```

Similarly, the RDFS range property restricts the type of instances that can be used as the object part of the triple with the property. In this example, the range of "employed_by" would be restricted to instances of "Organization":

```
<http://example.com/intel.rdf#employed_by>
<http://www.w3.org/1999/02/22-rdf-syntax-ns#range>
<http://example.com/intel.rdf#organization>.
```

With these restrictions in place, some of the logical reasoning capabilities of RDFS become clear. For example, consider the following triple:

```
<http://example.com/intel.rdf#JoeBlog>
<http://example.com/intel.rdf#employed_by>
<http://example.com/intel.rdf#StateDepartment>.
```

If we were to make that statement *without* first stating that "JoeBlog" was an instance of the "Person" class and without stating that "StateDepartment" was an instance of the "Organization" class, both facts can be *inferred*. Since we know that the subject of "employed_by" must be an instance of the "Person" class, then we know that "JoeBlog" must be a "Person," even if that has not been explicitly stated. The same goes for "StateDepartment"; based on the range restriction, we know it must be an "Organization," even if that has never been stated.

This type of inferencing has numerous benefits. For example, if we had a large knowledge base and we wanted to find all of the instances of "Organization" within it, any resource used as the object of "employed_by" can be identified.

6.2.3.2. Web Ontology Language (OWL).

OWL builds on RDFS and introduces new syntax and expressivity. The new features are numerous, but they can be grouped into several major categories: equality and inequality, property characteristics, property restrictions, and set features.

Equality and inequality expressions allow authors to state that two resources represent the same concept or different concepts. Equivalence can be expressed between two classes, two properties, or two instances. Differences can also be expressed between two individuals or among a set of individuals, indicating that they all are distinct from one another.

Properties could only have domains and ranges with the features of RDFS. In OWL, more information can be given about properties and their relationships to other properties. Authors can describe properties as transitive, symmetric, or the inverse of other properties. The cardinality of properties can also be stated. This can be used to require a minimum and/or maximum number of times that the property must be used on any one instance. For example, every person has a birthday, and a person can have only one birthdate. A property representing that should be restricted such that it is used once and only once for each person (a cardinality of 1). On the other hand, a person may have many e-mail addresses, and such a restriction would not be appropriate.

There are also new ways that the domains and ranges of properties can be restricted in OWL. In RDFS, the domain and range could only be restricted once per property. However, in reality, the range may differ depending on the type used in the domain. A clear example of this is one involving food. If we had a property called "eats," it would be reasonable to restrict the domain to "Person" and the range to "Food." However, if we created a subclass of "Person" called "Vegetarian," the range of "Food" would no longer be specific enough. OWL allows us to add additional restrictions to the range of a property within a class definition. In this example, we would add information within the "Vegetarian" class that stated the range was limited to non-meat foods. These local restrictions on range allow us to ensure that the appropriate values are used with each class.

The set properties allow for the creation of unions, intersections, and complements of classes, and they allow the explicit statement of disjointness among classes. This is particularly useful when creating unnamed classes. For example, a Vegetarian Government Employee could be created by taking the intersection of the "Vegetarian" class and the "GovernmentEmployee" class.

6.3. SEMANTIC WEB PORTALS

6.3.1. Background

Traditional web portals are websites that collect information and links to pages, usually with a common theme or topic. A Semantic Web portal has a slightly different function. Since everything on the Semantic Web is identified by a URI, the notion of linking to files as it is done in hypertext does not translate. Instead, Semantic Web portals collect URIs of files on the Semantic Web, and they allow users to interact with the RDF graph of the statements.

In the context of creating a Semantic Web portal for terrorism, any user would have the ability to submit RDF or the URIs of documents with data.

Using ontologies, the portal can combine statements from multiple files into a single model. Among the implications, this means that users can select sets of statements that reflect their personal interests, even if no one else has had that specific focus. Mapping between concepts to connect items as equivalent also allows statements to be merged into a single model.

Figure 6.3 illustrates a sample page from a Semantic Web portal. It takes a knowledge model written in RDF and OWL, as described above, and presents it in a coherent way. Section 6.4 goes further into depth about how this technology is used.

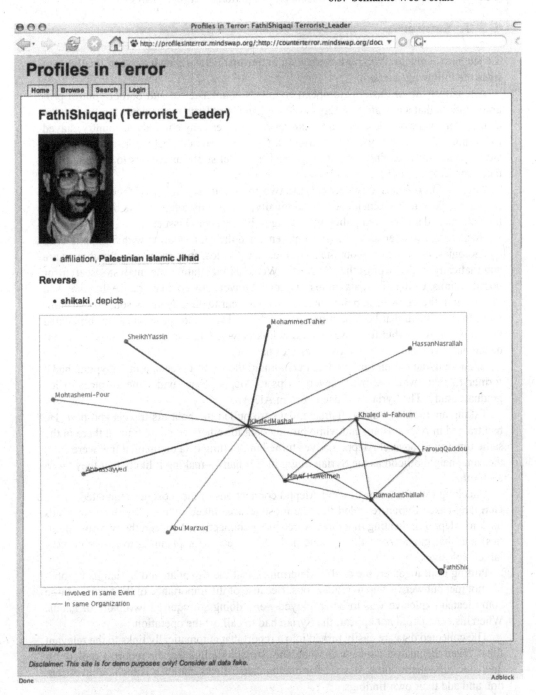

Figure 6.3. The Semantic Web portal page for Fathi Shiqaqi. Information about individuals is often much more extensive than this, but for the brevity of figure size, this more limited example is presented. Please see http://profilesinterror.mindswap.org for further examples.

6.3.2. Scenario

To see how Semantic Web portals may aid in terrorist network analysis specifically, consider the following scenario.

An analyst for an Eastern European country's counter-terror and border control program notices that a day after an Egyptian living in Great Britain was denied entry into the country for suspicious behavior, a Syrian residing in Germany entered the country, stayed in his hotel for a few days, and returned to Germany. His odd behavior, never meeting anyone and rarely leaving the hotel, aroused the hotel staffs suspicions to the point that they contacted the authorities and monitored his activity.

There is no obvious link between the two men, but the timing of their travel plans seems too close to be coincidence. Additionally, it was only a few weeks before the Parliament opened and foreign policy was going to be the central issue.

Because the counter-terror program has encoded their information with Semantic Web technologies, information about the movements, activities, and associates of both men are automatically pulled from other Semantic Websites facilitating the analyst's search for possible links. Comparing data on the two men's travel showed no evidence that they had ever been in the same place before, nor did they appear to directly know someone in common. It was shown that both men had been affiliated with mosques that were implicated in Islamic activity—but there was no direct link between the mosques, nor was there evidence that any members of the two mosques had met.

Expanding the search for any data in common, the analyst sees that the Egyptian had a former flatmate who had made several trips to Aleppo, Syria under the auspices of his graduate study. The Syrian had been born in Aleppo.

Taking another look at the flatmate, data are pulled in about his travels and past. He had trained in Afghanistan, and while pulling data for others who had trained there in the same timeframe, several Aleppo natives turned up. Pulling data on them, a few were from the same neighborhood as the Syrian living in Germany—making it likely that they knew each other.

Checking into the terror ties and Aleppo connections of the mosque frequented by the Germany-based Syrian revealed that the mosque was linked to a charity that sent funds back to Aleppo (indicating that there were strong connections between the two communities) and that members of the mosque had been arrested for planning to assemble very large explosives.

Putting it all together, the analyst determines that the Egyptian and Syrian had probably not met but were set up to rendezvous. Because of the importance of the target, a large complicated explosive was to be employed—and doing so required two pairs of hands. When his contact did not appear, the Syrian had to call off the operation.

The collected data are easily turned into a report that automatically links to the relevant files. When the analyst contacts German and British intelligence, the report is pulled immediately into their online files. These intelligence officers can then launch an investigation and add their own findings.

6.4. TERRORIST NETWORK ANALYSIS ON THE SEMANTIC WEB

> Intelligence work is a little like the unraveling of a knotted skein of wool. You get hold of an end and you have to follow it through until you are near enough to the heart of the knot to see what it consists of.
>
> —Stella Rimington, former head of MI-5, *Wall Street Journal*,
> January 3, 2005, " 'Humint' Begins at Home"

If you get a children's magazine . . . the dots are numbered. . . . Intelligence is nothing like that. There are no numbers on the dots.
>   —James Woolsey, former Director Central Intelligence,
>   at the American Enterprise Institute, June 3, 2004

Whatever metaphor is applied to untangling terrorist activity, the Semantic Web can be a useful technology, for managing and analyzing data about terrorist activities. Terror operations are conspiracies involving a small group of people carrying out a complex chain of actions and bound by an intricate web of relationships. When investigating terrorism, useful information is in short supply, extraneous information is abundant, and separating the two is an enormous challenge. The Semantic Web is not a silver bullet that will identify links that were invisible to analysts. But it can serve as a valuable tool for gathering, organizing, and disseminating information.

After a major crime or terrorist act—and also when potentially interesting intelligence is discovered—diligent investigators examine every possible lead. After 9/11 the National Security Agency's chief of Signals Intelligence, Maureen Baginski set the tone for the investigation, "with an approach familiar to any reader of police procedurals: on a large piece of paper, she wrote the initials 'UBL' and drew a box around them; then she asked her team to come up with any plausible connections, social and otherwise" (Walsh, 2004). The ad hoc databases created from these inquiries become elaborate and are often built around the intuition of the creator or creating team.

But these ad hoc databases are often on paper, are only intelligible to their creators, and are not maintained in a formal manner. The Semantic Web will facilitate the construction and use of this sort of informal database. But perhaps most importantly, a Semantic Web database can be used to share data electronically and show the process of the investigation—the quality of information, the false leads, and even hunches—to people who were not involved in the database's creation.

Mapping a terrorist organization or event requires a series of steps: gathering data, organizing the data and outlining connections, and identifying holes in the connections and developing theories to fill them. The process is then repeated as theories are tested and new leads are generated. In this process, enormous amounts of seemingly irrelevant data are accumulated, but it will need to be organized into the framework as well because it may become relevant in a later stage of the investigation. The Semantic Web can be a useful tool at each stage of an investigation.

In gathering data, traditional search engines have drawbacks for efficiently searching information. Based on natural language, traditional search engines gather data with too broad a net to be useful for the time-pressed investigator. The bulk of the information accumulated is of limited relevance. By conducting smart searches, the Semantic Web can surmount these weaknesses and maximize the amount of relevant data brought to the intelligence analyst's attention.

Search engines gather enormous quantities of information quickly, but search without discrimination. Googling al-Qaeda leader Ayman al-Zawahiri brings over 100,000 results—the vast majority of which are irrelevant and repetitive. A particular fact may be buried within thousands of documents. For example, responding to a query on Zawahiri's activities in 1993, Google provides 5000+ results. Some of these hits are responses to the copyright date on the document's publication or are an article that mentions 1993 peripherally or chatroom discussions in which Zawahiri was praised and another discussant mentioned an event in 1993. This is because the search engine, which is based on natural language, is simply matching characters—the information has no inherent meaning to the search engine.

For the Semantic Web, Zawahiri and 1993 would have a specific meaning, so that a search could focus on information relating to Zawahiri's activities in the appropriate time-frame. The marked-up data could then be pulled into the researcher's Semantic Web portal automatically. This ability to aggregate information could save the researcher hours of scanning documents and, by automatically placing information into a context, possibly reveal connections that the researcher would not have noticed.

A particular area where "smart" searches are essential is on names. In the realm of illicit activity aliases and false identification are commonly employed to deceive law enforcement. In dealing with terrorists from the Middle East, this is exacerbated by the different transliterations used for the non-Latin alphabets of the region. Terrorists on watchlists have evaded detection (sometimes unwittingly) by simply using different Latin alphabet spellings of their names. A Semantic Web portal could be encoded to recognize Osama ben Laden and Usama bin Ladin as the same person—or to compare other information, such as birthdate or nationality. A Semantic Web portal could also be encoded to recognize nicknames and aliases, for example, Abu Ammar is a common nickname for Yasser Arafat. The utility of this feature is not limited to names. Because terrorists frequently travel on fake passports and use stolen credit cards, encoding false information as being connected to a particular individual would be invaluable for tracking individual's movements. This technology could also help avoid false-positive identifications. Because the encoded information would have meaning to the Semantic Web, rather than just matching the letters of a name, the system could evaluate other key personal data and recognize whether an individual was the wanted terrorist or simply unfortunate enough to share a name with one.

The Semantic Web also gives the user the ability to shape the information according to changing needs. A Semantic Web portal can be used to examine information from several different angles. In one context it may be useful to examine a suspect's connections to individuals, and in another it may be useful to examine that suspect's movements over a specific time period. In a different situation the user may need to examine a terrorist network as a whole. A Semantic Web portal can display data in different configurations and be modified to reflect the user's changing needs. This is particularly important for investigating terrorist activity because data are frequently fragmentary and research needs to be structured around whatever data the researchers possess.

At the core of terrorist activity is a network of personal connections that allows the terrorist organization to function. Consequently, looking at who knows whom and how they know each other is central to understanding the extent of a terrorist cell. The Semantic Web can note the various connections between cell members such as shared residences, communal affiliations, places of employment, and birthplace. By allowing the researcher to focus on these connections and organize information according to them, the researcher will be better able to unravel the web of connections underpinning a terrorist cell.

This flexibility in structuring the data is particularly useful for tracking the movement of money and of suspected terrorists. Intelligence on both of these matters provides a crucial window into terrorist goals and operations. According to the *9/11 Commission Report* (page 385), "terrorist travel intelligence collection and analysis . . . has produced disproportionately useful results." Terrorist movements can reflect training needs, assembling for an operation, or planning meetings (crucial for maintaining terrorist networks because operatives try to avoid using communications that can be monitored such as telephones.) The information in a Semantic Web portal can easily be shaped to accommodate this sort of search, showing what links exist between suspected terrorists and a particular place—whether and when they were born there, traveled there, or resided there. Alternately, the information could be quickly reorganized to show a suspect's peregrinations so that their routes could be compared. Because the Semantic Web portal gives meaning to the data, the Semantic Web will be extremely useful for tracking movements in time and space.

On a related issue, the Semantic Web could also be used to track terrorist codes. In telephone and e-mail conversations, terrorists frequently use simple code words to mask their plans. In one case a terror attack was called a wedding; and when one of the speakers asked if the bride was ready, he was actually asking about the status of the bomb the terrorists were building. On a Semantic Web, portal analysts could mark up suspicious statements and link them into the context in which they were used—time, place, and the identity and activities of the participants in the conversation.

The Semantic Web could be similarly helpful in tracking and analyzing financial transactions. For example, all the users of a suspect bank account could be noted and then compared for other connections. The Semantic Web can also be used to study patterns of use of stolen credit and ATM cards. A series of purchases of potential explosive components with stolen credit cards, for example, could indicate that an operation was being planned. Because the Semantic Web encodes data, it can be an effective tool for sorting through masses of details.

Information comes in numerous forms, not just words and numbers. The Semantic Web's ability to include and annotate different forms of data is critical, because sometimes a picture really is worth a thousand words. Photographs placing individuals together have often been invaluable resources for identifying links between individuals. Photographs of graffiti, which is frequently used to communicate and mark territory by terrorists and gangs, can provide a glimpse into relations between terrorist groups. A written report describing the graffiti will not be as useful because the report may have missed a key detail or had a subjective interpretation. On the Semantic Web, the photograph could be annotated to include notes and theories about its meaning and be linked to other relevant information. Maps are another example of a useful image. Simply listing suspect's addresses may not reveal the proximity of their dwellings, whereas a map that could show this might also reveal how terrorist cell members arranged meetings. Photographs of forged documents could be posted and compared for similarities in technique and other crucial details that could reveal their origins. Seamlessly including images in Semantic Web databases vastly increases the user's ability to build models of terrorist networks and activities.

The ability to share and aggregate information electronically is a feature of the Semantic Web that will be invaluable to terrorism researchers. The ad hoc databases created to track terrorist activity are often designed around the immediate needs of the investigator or investigating team and the internal dynamics of the team can mirror the close-knit unique internal culture of the terrorist cell that is being analyzed. Consequently these databases, often paper files, are not readily intelligible to outsiders. The renowned CIA case officer, Robert Baer, who devoted a substantial part of his career to finding out who was behind the 1983 truck-bombing of the U.S. Embassy in Beirut, describes running a half-dozen Lebanese agents who gathered rumors, public records, political membership lists, old newspaper articles, and photos in his book *See No Evil*. He would combine this information with information from the CIA database as well as transcripts from wiretaps. Then, Baer (2002) writes:

> I would spend hours poring over the take, making connections between people, eliminating false leads, adding to my matrices. My makeshift charts started to look like the wiring diagram for a Boeing-747 cockpit.

These charts are familiar to any researcher, but pity the investigator who inherits such a file. Unique abbreviations, cryptic notes, and assumptions about the information and the relationships charted characterize these charts. However, such databases created on the Semantic Web could be marked up to show who had entered data, with notes about how and why they came to their conclusions, thereby providing a window into the thinking of the investigative team. The Semantic Web portals would also transcend limits of time and space. Where only a few people can view a folder or chart at once, a Semantic Web portal can be accessed by multiple people from multiple locations. This would facilitate teams made up of members operating from diverse locations, and it would also allow for easier collaboration between different teams. But, it would also allow investigators of one situation better access to the data of a related investigation. This would facilitate the intuitive processes—the hunches—that help investigators see patterns. A team looking at a new incident might find something useful in the false leads from an earlier stalled investigation.

A particularly compelling example of the importance of sharing these hunches on a database is found in the *9/11 Commission Report* (page 353):

> . . . In late 1999, the National Security Agency (NSA) analyzed communications associated with a man named Khalid, a man named Nawaf, and a man named Salem. Working-level officials in the intelligence community knew little more than this. But they correctly concluded that "Nawaf and "Khalid" might be part of "an operational cadre" and that "something nefarious might be afoot."

The *9/11 Commission Report* goes on to explain how there was information in the NSA's own database and other government databases confirming these suspicions, but because of poor interagency communications the men were not adequately investigated and their movements were not closely tracked. Ultimately the men reached the United States and linked up with the other 9/11 hijackers.

The *9/11 Commission Report* goes on to grant that "it is not likely that watchlisting [these men], by itself, [would] have prevented the 9/11 attacks." The incident also raises issues of organizational culture and procedure far beyond the scope of this chapter. But the Semantic Web could have helped reduce some inherent bureaucratic barriers. A Semantic Web system would have allowed the initial NSA team to post a note to the effect that they thought these men were involved in terrorist activity along with the data—even if they were very limited and fragmentary—that inspired this hunch. Then, if the suspects' activities caught the attention of another analyst there would have been at least some background information. Equally useful, the second analyst could have seen who made the initial note and follow-up with them.

This sharing would probably not have prevented 9/11. But the U.S. intelligence community consists of dozens of agencies with thousands of analysts between them that sift through petabytes of data daily. Operating on this scale, calling to break down bureaucratic barriers to "connect the dots" is easier said than done. Encouraging more communication may result in analysts and teams drowning each other in data. The Semantic Web can help point researchers and analysts toward the information they need.

SUMMARY

The Semantic Web is the next generation of the web, designed to make content and knowledge machine understandable. Based on languages such as the Resource Description Framework (RDF), RDF Schema (RDFS), and the Web Ontology Language (OWL), knowledge models can be built, reasoned upon, and made publicly accessible.

This holds great promise for efforts toward terrorism and counter-terrorism. In a field where there are many specialists with expertise in specific areas. Semantic Web portals offer a way to share information and to extract useful data that may have gone previously unseen. Furthermore, patterns that may not be apparent to any one person can emerge as data is aggregated together.

Countering terrorism, at its core, is about managing information. The Semantic Web has a great deal of potential to facilitate this task for analysts of terrorism. First, the Semantic Web allows information to be encoded so that the processing abilities of the computer can be employed to sift data. This capability will help analysts quickly obtain relevant information, saving them from examining copious quantities of irrelevant responses for the nuggets of crucial information. Second, the Semantic Web will enable the analyst to organize the data around the factors germane to the investigation. This will facilitate an analyst's efforts to follow the chain of events by which a terrorist act is planned and identify the extent of a terrorist cell. Finally, the Semantic Web will allow analysts to share and discuss findings across time and space. Defunct investigations that may hold clues to current issues will be more readily accessible; and, in tracking international activity, analysts located throughout the world will be able to easily share information. The Semantic Web will not be a panacea to the challenges facing terrorism analysts. But, it can effectively multiply the analytical capabilities brought to bear on an investigation by employing a computer's processing capabilities to sift data, freeing analysts to make the connections that will ultimately resolve the investigation and by bringing more analysts into the process. The Semantic Web cannot replace human intuition, but it can effectively augment it.

REFERENCES

Baer, Robert. (2002). *See No Evil.* New York: Crown Publishers.

Becket, Dave (ed.). (2004). *RDF/XML Syntax Specification (Revised),* W3C Recommendation <http://www.w3.org/TR/rdf-syntax-grammar/>

Brickley, Dan (ed.). (2004). *RDF Vocabulary Description Language 1.0: RDF Schema* W3C Recommendation <http://www.w3.org/TR/rdf-schema/>

Dean, Mike, and Schreiber, Guus (eds.). (2004). *OWL Web Ontology Language Reference,* W3C Recommendation <http://www.w3.org/TR/owl-ref/>

National Commission on Terrorist Attacks. (2004). *The 9/11 Commission Report*: Final Report of the National Commission on Terrorist Attacks Upon the United States., New York: W. W. Norton & Company.

Walsh, Elsa. (2004). Learning to spy: Can Maureen Baginski save the F.B.I., *The New Yorker.*

Chapter 7

Improving National and Homeland Security Through Context Knowledge Representation and Reasoning Technologies

Nazli Choucri, Stuart E. Madnick, and Michael D. Siegel

7.1. INTRODUCTION

7.1.1. Emergent Challenges to Effective Use of Information

The convergence of three distinct but interconnected trends—unrelenting globalization, rapidly changing global and regional strategic balances, and increasing knowledge intensity of economic activity—is creating critical new challenges to current modes of information access and understanding. First, the discovery and retrieval of relevant information has become a daunting task due to the sheer volume, scale, and scope of information on the Internet, its geographical dispersion, varying context, heterogeneous sources, and variable quality. Second, the opportunities presented by this transformation are shaping new demands for improved information generation, management, and analysis. Third, more specifically, the increasing diversity of Internet uses and users points to the importance of cultural and contextual dimensions of information and communication. There are significant opportunity costs associated with overlooking these challenges, potentially hindering both (a) empirical analysis and theoretical inquiry so central to many scholarly disciplines and (b) their contributions to national policy. In this chapter, we identify new ways to address these challenges by significantly improving access to diverse, distributed, and disconnected sources of information.

7.1.2. National and Homeland Security

The information needs in the realm of national and homeland security involve emergent risks, threats of varying intensity, and uncertainties of potentially global scale and scope. Specifically, there is need to focus on (a) crisis situations, (b) conflicts and war, and (c) anticipation, monitoring, and early warning. Information needs in these domains are extensive and vary depending on (1) the *salience* of information (i.e. the criticality of the issue), (2) the *extent of customization,* and (3) the *complexity* at hand. More specifically, in:

- **Crisis Situations.** The needs are characteristically immediate and are usually highly customized, and they generally require complex analysis, integration, and manipulation of information. International crises are now impinging more directly than ever before on national and homeland security, thus rendering the information needs and requirements even more pressing.

- **Conflicts and War.** The needs are not necessarily time-critical, are customized to a certain relevant extent, and involve a multifaceted examination of information. Increasingly, it appears that coordination of information access and analysis across a diverse set of players (or institutions) with differing needs and requirements (perhaps even mandates) is more the rule rather than the exception in cases of conflict and war.

- **Anticipation, Monitoring, and Early Warning.** The needs tend to be gradual, but may involve extensive though routine searches and may require extraction of information from sources that may evolve and change over time. Furthermore, in today's global context, "preventative action" takes on new urgency and creates new demands for information services.

Table 7.1 illustrates the types of information needs required for effective research, education, decision-making, and policy analysis on a range of conflict issues. Indeed, "Critical central decisions should flow smoothly downward. Similarly, low-level urgent requests for communication, assistance, or information should flow upward to the

Table 7.1. Illustrating Information Needs in Three Contexts

Illustrative Cases	Information Needs	Intended Use of Information
1. **Strategic Requirements for Managing Cross-Border Pressures in a** *Crisis* UNHCR needs to respond to the internal dislocation and external flows of large numbers of Afghans into neighboring countries, triggered by waves of post-Soviet violence in Afghanistan.	Logistical and infrastructure information for setting up refugee camps, such as potential sites, sanitation, and potable water supplies. Also streamlined information on sabotage.	Facilitate coordination of relief agencies with up-to-date information during a crisis for more rapid response (as close to real time as possible). Reduce vulnerability to disruption.
2. **Capabilities for Management during an Ongoing** *Conflict & War* The UNEP-Balkans group needs to assess whether the Balkan conflicts have had significant environmental and economic impacts. Existing data are extensive, but highly dispersed, presented in different formats and prepared for different purposes.	Environmental and economic data on the region prior to the initiation/escalation of the conflict. Comparison of these data with newly collected data to assess the impacts to environmental and economic viability.	Improved decision-making during conflicts—taking into account contending views and changing strategic conditions—to prepare for and manage future developments and anticipate the need for different modes of action.
3. **Strategic Response to Security Threats for** *Anticipation, Prevention, and Early Warning* The Department of Homeland Security needs to coordinate efforts with local government, private businesses, and foreign governments using information from different regions of the world.	Intelligence data from foreign governments, nongovernmental agencies, U.S. agencies, and leading institutions on international strategy and security here and overseas.	Streamline potentially conflicting information content and sources in order to facilitate coherent interpretation, anticipation, preventive monitoring, and early warning.

appropriate agency and then back to the appropriate operatives" (National Research Council, 2002, p. 160). These issues remain central to matters of security in this increasingly globalized world.

7.1.3. Addressing Information Needs

7.1.3.1. Examples of Information Challenges. There are many important data elements critical to effective national and homeland security, such as place names, geographic locations, people names, and many others. All of these are subject to possible confusion, especially when the information is gathered by many different agencies (possibly from different countries) using different procedures and different standards. Some examples are briefly illustrated below.

Airport Naming. In addition to airport names themselves which are often written in different ways (e.g., "London airport," "London Heathrow Airport," "Heathrow Airport"), there are two major standards for codes designating airports: IATA and ICAO. An example of these differences is:

IATA	ICAO	Location Name	Airport Name	Country
LHR	EGLL	London	Heathrow	United Kingdom

City and Country Names. Is the city "Brussels" or "Bruxelle" or "Brussel"? It depends on whether it is being identified by a U.S., French, or German source.

Geographic Coordinate Systems. Not only are there over 40 different geographic coordinate systems used around the world, there are even differences within the same governmental departments, such as within the U.S. Department of Defense. The Army and Marine Corps use the Universal Transverse Mercator (UTM) Grid and Military Grid Reference System (MGRS), while the U.S. Navy uses latitude and longitude expressed in degrees, minutes and seconds. The Air Force uses latitude and longitude expressed in degrees and decimal degrees.[1]

People Naming. Many problems exist in the identification of person by names in a database. For example, the name

$$\text{قذافي}$$

has been shown to have over 60 romanizations including: Gadaffi, Gaddafi, Gathafi, Kadafi, Kaddafi, Khadafy, Qadhafi, and Qathafi. There are numerous Romanization from Transliteration Standards. But different agencies may choose different standards. For example, from Arabic to English, some examples of romanization standards are:

ALA-LC (library of Congress) 1972[2]

DIN 31636-198 (Germany)

---

[1]From http://www.findarticles.com/p/articles/mi_m0IAU/is_1_8/ai_98123571
[2]See http://www.loc.gov/catdir/cpso/romanization/arabic.pdf

EI (encyclopedia of Islam) 1960
ISO 233-1984
UN 1972
USC—Transliteration of the Quran[3]

Many More. The above examples illustrate just a few of the challenges to using data effectively for national and homeland security.

7.1.3.2. Operational Example.

For illustrative and simplification purposes only, let us consider the types of information illustrated by case 2 in Table 7.1. A specific question is, **To what extent have economic performance and environmental conditions in Yugoslavia been affected by the conflicts in the region?** The answer could shape policy priorities for different national and international institutions, may influence reconstruction strategies, and may even determine which agencies will be the leading players. Moreover, there are potentials for resumed violence, and the region's relevance to overall European stability remains central to the U.S. national interest. This is not an isolated case but one that illustrates concurrent challenges for information compilation, analysis, and interpretation—under changing strategic conditions.

For example, in determining the change of carbon dioxide (CO_2) emissions in the region, normalized against the change in GDP—before and after the outbreak of the hostilities—we need to consider shifts in territorial and jurisdictional boundaries, changes in accounting and recording norms, and varying degrees of decision autonomy. User requirements add another layer of complexity. For example, what units of CO_2 emissions and GDP should be displayed, and what unit conversions need to be made from the information sources? Which Yugoslavia is of concern to the user: the country defined by its year 2000 borders, or the entire geographic area formerly known as Yugoslavia in 1990? One of the effects of war is that the region, which previously was one country consisting of six republics and two provinces, has been reconstituted into five legal international entities (countries), each having its own reporting formats, currency, units of measure, and new socioeconomic parameters. In other words, the meaning of the request for information will differ, depending on the *actors, actions, stakes,* and *strategies* involved.

In this simple case, we suppose that the request comes from a reconstruction agency interested in the following values: CO_2 emission amounts (in tons/yr), CO_2 per capita, annual GDP (in million USD/yr), GDP per capita, and the ratio CO_2/GDP (in tons CO_2/million USD) for the entire region of the former Yugoslavia (see the alternative User 2 scenario in Table 7.2). A restatement of the question would then become, **What is the change in CO_2 emissions and GDP in the region formerly known as Yugoslavia before and after the war?**

7.1.3.2.1. Diverse Sources and Contexts.

By necessity, to answer this question, one needs to draw data from diverse types of sources (we call these differing *domains* of information) such as economic data (e.g., the World Bank, UN Statistics Division), environmental data (e.g., Oak Ridge National Laboratory, World Resources Institute), and country history data (e.g., the CIA Factbook), as illustrated in Table 7.2. Merely combining the numbers from the various sources is likely to produce serious errors due to different sets

[3]See http://www.usc.edu/dept/MSA/quran/transliteration/table.html

Table 7.2. Operational Example: Information Needs in Cases of Conflict

Domain and Sources Consulted	Sample Data Available	Basic Question, Information User Type & Usage
Economic Performance • World Bank's World Development Indicators database • UN Statistics Division's database • Statistics Bureaus of individual counties	A. Annual GDP and Population Data: *GDP in billions local currency per year* *— Population in millions*	Question: How did economic output and environmental conditions change in YUG over time? **User 1:** YUG as a geographic region bounded at T0:
Environmental Impacts • Oak Ridge National Laboratory's CDIAC database • WRI database • GSSD • EPA of individual countries	B. Emissions Data: *Emissions in 1000s tons per year*	**User 2:** YUG as a legal, autonomous state
Country History • CIA • GSSD	$T0.\{YUG\} = T1.\{YUG, BIH, HRV, MKD, SVN\}$ (i.e., geographically, YUG at T0 is equivalent to YUG+BIH+HRV+MKD+SVN at T1)	
Mappings Defined • Country code • Currency code • Historical exchange rates* [As an interesting aside, the country last known as "Yugoslavia,"officially disappeared in 2003 and was replaced by the "Republics of Serbia and Montenegro." For simplicity, we will ignore this extra complexity.] *Note: Hyperinflation in YUG resulted in establishment of a new currency unit in June 1993. Therefore, T1.YUN is completely different from T0.YUN.*		Note (receiver' contexts): *T0: 1990 (prior to breakup)* *T1: 2000 (after breakup)* *CO_2: 1000's tons per year* *CO_2/capita: tons per person* *GDP: billions USD per year* *GDP/capita: 1000's USD per person* *CO_2/GDP: tons per million USD*

A. Annual GDP and Population Data:

Country	T0.GDP	T0.Pop	T1.GDP	T1.Pop
YUG	698.3	23.7	1627.8	10.6
BIH			13.6	3.9
HRV			266.9	4.5
MKD			608.7	2.0
SVN			7162	2.0

B. Emissions Data:

Country	T0	T1
YUG	35,604	15,480
BIH		1279
HRV		5405
MKD		3378

User 1: YUG as a geographic region bounded at T0:

Parameter	T0	T1
CO_2	35,604	29,523
CO_2/capita	1.50	1.28
GDP	66.5	104.8
GDP/capita	2.8	4.56
CO_2/GDP	535	282

User 2: YUG as a legal, autonomous state

Parameter	T0	T1
CO_2	35,604	15,480
CO_2/capita	1.50	1.46
GDP	66.5	24.2
GDP/capita	2.8	1.1
CO_2/GDP	535	640

Country	Code	Currency	Currency Code
Yugoslavia	YUG	New Yugoslavian Dinar	YUN
Bosnia and Herzegovia	BIH	Marka	BAM
Croatia	HRV	Kuna	HRK
Macedonia	MKD	Denar	MKD
Slovenia	SVN	Tolar	SIT

C_From	C_To	T0	T1
USD	YUN	10.5	67.267
USD	BAM		2.086
USD	HRK		8.089
USD	MKD		64.757
USD	SIT		225.93

of assumptions driving the representation of the information in the sources. These assumptions are often not explicit but are an important representation of "reality" (we call these the meaning or *context* of the information, to be explained in more detail later.)

The purpose of Table 7.2 is to illustrate some of the complexities in a seemingly simple question. In addition to variations in data sources and domains, there are significant differences in contexts and formats, critical temporality issues, and data conversions that all factor into a particular user's information needs. As specified in the table, time T0 refers to a date *before the war* (e.g., 1990), when the entire region was a single country (referred to as "YUG"). Time T1 refers to a date *after the war* (e.g., 2000), when the country "YUG" retains its name, but has lost four of its provinces, which are now independent countries. The first column of Table 7.2 lists some of the sources and domains covered by this question. The second column shows sample data that could be extracted from the sources. The bottom row of this table lists auxiliary mapping information that is needed to understand the meanings of symbols used in the other data sources. For example, when the GDP for Yugoslavia is written in YUN units, a currency code source is needed to understand that this symbol represents the Yugoslavian Dinar. The third column lists the outputs and units as requested by the user. Accordingly, for User 1, a simple calculation based on data from country "YUG" will invariably give a wrong answer. For example, deriving the CO_2/GDP ratio by simply summing up the CO_2 emissions and dividing it by the sum of GDP from sources A and B will not provide a correct answer.

7.1.3.2.2. Manual Approach.
Given the types of data shown in Table 7.2, along with the appropriate context knowledge (some of which is shown in italics), an analyst could determine the answer to our question. The proper calculation involves numerous steps, including selecting the necessary sources, making the appropriate conversions, and using the correct calculations. For example:

For Time T0:
1. Get CO_2 emissions data for "YUG" from source B.
2. Convert it to tons/year using scale factor 1000; call the result X.
3. Get GDP data from source A.
4. Convert to USD by looking up currency conversion table, an auxiliary source; call the result Y.
5. No need to convert the scale for GDP because the receiver uses the same scale, namely, 1,000,000.
6. Compute X/Y (equal to 535 tons/million USD in Table 7.2).

For Time T1:
1. Consult source for country history and find all countries in the area of former YUG.
2. Get CO_2 emissions data for "YUG" from source B (or a new source).
3. Convert it to tons/year using scale factor 1000; call the result X1.
4. Get CO_2 emissions data for "BIH" from source B (or a new source).
5. Convert it to tons/year using scale factor 1000; call the result X2.
6. Continue this process for the rest of the sources to get the emissions data for the rest of the countries.
7. Sum X1, X2, X3, and so on, and call it X.

8. Get GDP for "YUG" from source A (or alternative); Convert it to USD using the auxiliary sources.

9. No need to convert the scale factor; call the result Y1.

10. Get GDP for "BIH" from source E; Convert it to USD using the auxiliary sources; call the result Y2.

11. Continue this process for the rest of the sources to get the GDP data for the rest of the countries.

12. Sum Y1, Y2, Y3, and so on, and call it Y.

13. Compute X/Y (equal to 282 tons/million USD in Table 7.2).

The complexity of this task would be easily magnified if, for example, the CO_2 emissions data from the various sources were all expressed in different metrics or, alternatively, if demographic variables were drawn from different institutional contexts (e.g., with or without counting refugees). This example shows some of the operational challenges if a user were to manually attempt to answer this question. This case highlights just some of the common data difficulties where information reconciliation continues to be made "by hand." It is easy to see why such analysis can be very labor-intensive and error-prone. This makes it difficult under "normal" circumstances and possibly impossible under time-critical circumstances. This example may appear to be simple, but it includes major complexities such as reconciling spatial territoriality, currency, and atmospheric measures. Barriers to effective information access and utilization usually involve complexities of this sort.

7.1.3.3. LIGHT: A Better Way. With reference to national and homeland security concerns, a NRC study states: "*Different emergency responders must be able to communicate with each other, but poor interoperability among responding agencies is a well-known problem . . . The fundamental technical issue is that different agencies have different systems, different frequencies and waveforms, different protocols, different databases, and different equipment*" (National Research Council, 2002, p. 159). A key goal of the MIT Laboratory for Information Globalization and Harmonization Technologies (LIGHT) is to automatically determine and reliably perform the steps shown above in response to each user's request. Every user is distinct. LIGHT will be capable of storing the necessary context information about the sources and users, and it will have a reasoning engine capable of determining the sources, conversions, and calculations necessary to meet each user's needs. The COIN and GSSD systems, to be described briefly below, have proven the feasibility of this approach in more limited situations. LIGHT is the next generation: it will combine context and content.

7.1.4. Existing Foundations: COIN and GSSD

Important research in two areas has already been completed that provides essential foundations for addressing the emergent and pressing challenges discussed above: the *COntext INterchange* Project (COIN) and the *Global System for Sustainable Development* (GSSD).

7.1.4.1. COIN. The *COntext INterchange* (COIN) Project has developed a basic theory, architecture, and software prototype for supporting intelligent information integration employing context mediation technology (Madnick, 1999; Goh et al., 1996, 1999;

Goh, 1996; Siegel and Madnick, 1991). We utilize the foundation of COIN to develop theories and methodologies for the new System for Harmonized Information Processing (SHIP). A fundamental concept underlying such a system is the representation of knowledge as **Collaborative Domain Spaces (CDSs)**. A **CDS** is a grouping of the knowledge including source schemas, data context, conversion functions, and source capabilities as related to a single domain ontology. The software components needed to provide harmonized information processing (i.e., through the use of a CDS or collections of linked CDSs) include a context mediation engine (Bressan et al., 2000; Goh, 1996), one or more ontology library systems, a context domain and conversion function management system, and a query execution and planner (Fynn, 1997). In addition, support tools are required to allow for applications' (i.e., receivers') context definition and source definitions to be added and removed easily (i.e., schemas, contexts, capabilities).

7.1.4.2. GSSD. The *Global System for Sustainable Development* serves as an Internet-based platform for exploring the contents transmitted through different forms of information access, provision, and integration across multiple information sources, languages, cultural contexts, and ontologies. GSSD has an extensive, quality-controlled set of ontologies related to system sustainability (specifically, to sources of instability and alternative responses and actions), with reference to a large set of specific domains related to the field of international relations. In addition, GSSD has made considerable gains into understanding and undertaking the organization and management of large-scale, distributed, and diverse research teams, including cross-national (China and Japan, and countries in the Middle East and Europe) and institutional partners (private, public, and international agencies). Designed and implemented by social scientists, GSSD is seen as demonstrating "opportunities for collaboration and new technologies," according to the National Academy of Engineering (Richard et al., 2001, p. viii). GSSD databases cover issues related to dynamics of conflict, as well as other domains relevant to our proposed research, such as population, migration, refugees, unmet human needs, as well as evolving efforts at strategic and coordinated international actions. (As an example, for "population" see Choucri, 1999; pp. 280–282.) GSSD provides a rich ground for the technologies, including automated methods for information aggregation from various sources, context mediation capabilities, customized information retrieval capabilities, and ontology representations.

7.2. IT THEORY AND TECHNOLOGY RESEARCH

7.2.1. Needs for Harmonized Information Processing and Collaborative Domain Spaces

Advances in computing and networking technologies now allow extensive volumes of data to be gathered, organized, and shared on an unprecedented scale and scope. Unfortunately, these newfound capabilities by themselves are only marginally useful if the information cannot be easily **extracted** and **gathered** from **disparate sources**, if the information is represented with **different interpretations**, and if it must satisfy **differing user needs** (March, 2000; Madnick, 1999; Chen et al., 2001). The data requirements (e.g., scope, timing) and the sources of the data (e.g., government, industry, global organizations) are extremely diverse. National and homeland security, by definition, take into account internal as well as external dimensions of relations among actors in both the public and the private domains.

It is necessary to:

1. Analyze the data and technology requirements for the categories of problems described in Section 7.1.
2. Research, design, develop and test extensions and improvements to the underlying COIN and GSSD theory and components.
3. Provide a scalable, flexible platform for servicing the range of applications described in Section 1.
4. Demonstrate the effectiveness of the theories, tools, and methodologies through technology transfer to other collaborating organizations.

7.2.2. Illustrative Example of Information Extraction, Dissemination, and Interpretation Challenges

As an illustration of the problems created by information disparities, let us refer back to the example introduced in Section 7.1.3. The question was, **What are the impacts of CO_2 emissions on economic performance in Yugoslavia**? It is necessary to draw data from diverse sources such as CIA Worldbook (for current boundaries), World Resources Institute (for CO_2 emissions), and the World Bank (for economic data). There are many additional information challenges that had not been explicitly noted earlier, such as:

Information Extraction. Some of the sources may be full relational databases, in which case there is the issue of remote access. In many other cases, the sources may be traditional HTML websites, which are fine for viewing from a browser but not effective for combining data or performing calculations (other than manual "cut and paste"). Other sources might be tables in a text file, Word document, or even a spreadsheet. Although the increasing use of eXtensible Markup Language (XML) will reduce some of these interchange problems (Madnick, 2001), we will continue to live in a very heterogeneous world for quite a while to come. So we must be able to extract information from all types of sources.

Information Dissemination. Different users want the resulting "answers" expressed in different ways. Some will want to see the desired information displayed in their web browser, but others might want the answers to be deposited into a database, spreadsheet, XML document, or application program for further processing.

Information Interpretation. Although the problems of information extraction and dissemination will be addressed in this research, the most difficult challenges involve information interpretation. Specifically, an example question is, What is the change of CO_2 emissions per GDP in Yugoslavia before and after the Balkans war?

Before the war (time T0), the entire region was one country. Data for CO_2 emissions were in thousands of tons/year, and GDP was in billions of Yugoslavian Dinars. *After the war* (time T1), Yugoslavia only has two of its original five provinces; the other three provinces are now four independent countries, each with its own currency. The size and population of the country, now known as Yugoslavia, has changed. Even Yugoslavia has introduced a new currency to combat hyperinflation.

From the perspective of any one agency—UNEP, for example—the question How have CO_2 emissions per GDP changed in Yugoslavia after the war? may have multiple interpretations. Not only does each source have its own context, but so does each user (also referred to as a receiver). For example, does the user mean Yugoslavia as the original geographic area (depicted as *user 1* in Table 7.2) or as the legal entity, which has changed size (*user 2*). To answer the question correctly, we have to use the changing context information. A simple calculation based on the "raw" data will not give the right answer. As seen earlier, the calculation will involve many steps, including selecting necessary sources, making appropriate conversions, and using correct calculations. Furthermore, each receiver context may require data expressed in different ways, such as tons/million USD or kilograms/billion Euro.

Although seemingly simple, this example addresses some of the most complex issues, namely, the impact of changing legal jurisdictions and sovereignties on (a) state performance, (b) salience of sociopolitical stress, (c) demographic shifts, and (d) estimates of economic activity, as critical variables of note. Extending this example to the case of the former Soviet Republics, before and after independence, is conceptually the same type of challenge—with greater complexity. For example, the U.S. Department of Defense may be interested in demographic distributions (by ethnic group) around oil fields and before and after independence. Alternatively, UNEP may be interested in CO_2 emissions per capita from oil-producing regions. Foreign investors, however, may be interested in insurance rates before and after independence. The fact that the demise of the Soviet Union led to the creation of a large number of independent and highly diverse states is a reminder that the Yugoslavia example is far from unique. It highlights a class of increasingly complex information reconciliation problems. Many of the new states in Central Asia may also rank high as potential targets and bases for global terrorism.

The information shown in italics in Table 7.2 (e.g., "population in millions") illustrates **context knowledge**. Sometimes this context knowledge is explicitly provided with the source data (but still must be accessed and processed), but often it must be found from other sources. The good news is that such context knowledge almost always exists, though widely **distributed** within and across organizations. Thus, a central requirement is **the acquisition, organization, and effective intelligent usage of distributed context knowledge to support information harmonization and collaborative domains.**[4]

7.2.3. Research Platform

The MIT COntext INterchange (COIN) project has developed a platform including a theory, architecture, and basic prototype for such intelligent harmonized information processing. COIN is based on database theory and mediators (Wiederhold, 1992, 1999). Context Interchange is a mediation approach for semantic integration of disparate (heterogeneous and distributed) information sources as described in Bressan et al. (2000) and Goh et al. (1999). The Context Interchange approach includes not only the mediation infrastructure and services, but also wrapping technology and middleware services for accessing the source information and facilitating the integration of the mediated results into end-users applications (see Figure 7.1).

[4]See http://www.gao.gov/new.items/d03322.pdf for types of information central to national and homeland security; also see the functionalities listed in http://www.dhs.gov/dhspublic/ for the range of some domain-specific information needs.

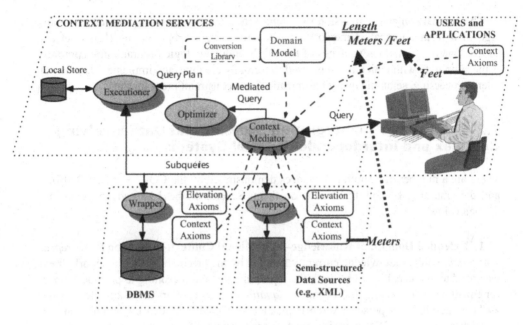

Figure 7.1. The architecture of the context interchange system.

The *wrappers* are physical and logical gateways providing uniform access to the disparate sources over the network (Chen, 1999; Firat et al., 2000a,b). The set of *Context Mediation Services,* comprises a Context Mediator, a Query Optimizer and a Query Executioner. The Context Mediator is in charge of the identification and resolution of potential semantic conflicts induced by a query. This automatic detection and reconciliation of conflicts present in different information sources is made possible by ontological knowledge of the underlying application domain, as well as informational content and implicit assumptions associated with the receivers and sources.

The result of the mediation is a mediated query. To retrieve the data from the disparate information sources, the mediated query is then transformed into a query execution plan, which is optimized, taking into account the topology of the network of sources and their capabilities. The plan is then executed to retrieve the data from the various sources, and then the results are composed and sent to the receiver.

The knowledge needed for harmonization is formally modeled in a COIN framework (Goh, 1996). The COIN framework is a mathematical structure offering a robust foundation for the realization of the Context Interchange strategy. The COIN framework comprises a data model and a language, called COINL, of the Frame-Logic (F-Logic) family (Kifer et al., 1995; Dobbie and Topor, 1995). The framework is used to define the different elements needed to implement the strategy in a given application:

- *The Domain Model* is a collection of rich types (semantic types) defining the domain of discourse for the integration strategy.
- *Elevation Axioms* for each source identify the semantic objects (instances of semantic types) corresponding to source data elements and define integrity constraints specifying general properties of the sources.
- *Context Definitions* define the different interpretations of the semantic objects in the different sources and/or from a receiver's point of view.

The comparison and conversion reasoning procedure is inspired by and takes advantage of a formal logical framework of Abductive Logic Programming (Kakas et al., 1993). One of the main advantages of the COIN abductive logic programming approach is the simplicity with which it can be used to formally combine and implement features of query processing, semantic query optimization, and constraint programming.

7.2.4. Advances in Integrating Systems and Data Involving Complex and Interdependent Social Systems

There are a number of important advances demonstrated by the COIN and GSSD efforts and the emerging LIGHT that builds on them. Several of these key advances are described below.

1. Extended Domain of Knowledge—Equational Context. In addition to the *representational* context knowledge currently handled by the original COIN framework, there was need to add capabilities for both the representation and reasoning to provide support for equational (Firat et al., 2002) context. *Equational context* refers to the knowledge such as "average GDP per person (AGDP)" means "total GDP" divided by "population." In some data sources, AGDP explicitly exists (possibly with differing names and in differing units), but in other cases it may not explicitly exist but could be calculated by using "total GDP" and "population" from one or more sources—if that knowledge existed and was used effectively. The original COIN design has been extended to exploit simultaneous symbolic equation solving techniques through the use of Constraint Handling Rules (CHR) (Frühwirth, 1998), a high-level language extension of constraint logic programming (CLP). This extension, coupled with our context-based reasoning approach to detecting and reconciling data semantics, provides an elegant and powerful solution to the problem of detecting and resolving equational conflicts. This combines the advantages of logic programming and constraint solving by providing a declarative approach to solving problems, while at the same allowing users to employ special purpose algorithms in the subproblems (Firat et al., 2002).

2. Extended Domain of Knowledge—Temporal Context. *Temporal context* refers to variations in context not only across sources but also over time. Thus, the implied currency for France's GDP prior to 2002 might be French Francs, but after 2002 it is Euros. If one were performing a longitudinal study over multiple years from multiple sources, it is essential that variation in context over time be understood and processed appropriately. A seemingly straightforward variable, like the size of 'military expenditures' across countries, is defined differently depending on the rules of inclusion or exclusion (for example, military pensions) used in different jurisdictions. Changes in territorial boundaries signal changes in jurisdiction and often signal changes in modes of information provision and formatting. This is a common problem facing a new government after a revolution. The COIN context knowledge representation has been augmented to include a specification of the history of all contextual attributes in the ontology (Zhu et al., 2004). Mathematically, it is set of *<contextual_attribute, history>* pairs, where history is a set of *<value, valid_interval>* pairs. Then temporal reasoning can be treated as a constraint solving problem, using constraint handling rules similar to those of [Frühwirth, 1994).

3. Extended Domain of Knowledge—Entity Aggregation Context. *Entity aggregation* addresses the reality that we often have multiple interpretations of what constitutes an entity. We have already seen that example in the multiple interpretations of what is meant by "Yugoslavia." This situation occurs even in domestic cases, such as does "IBM" include "Lotus Development Corp" (a wholly owned subsidiary)? The frequent answer is "depends on the context." We have defined this problem as "corporate house-holding" (Madnick et al., 2002). This is also a common occurrence and challenge in many aspects of national and homeland security. Corporate householding entity aggregation problems are very similar to traditional COIN applications in the sense that entity aggregation also involves different source and receiver contexts. Under different contexts, an entity may or may not need to be aggregated. The semantic types in the ontology can be divided into two categories: structure-related and task-related. Structure-related semantic types represent common concepts in organizational structure and entity aggregation, and thus they are useful in any entity aggregation problems; the task-related semantic types are specific to particular applications. The COIN reasoning process has been extended to comprehend the general semantics of the organization hierarchies that must be navigated (Madnick et al., 2003).

4. Linked Collaborative Domain Spaces. The original COIN framework provided representation and reasoning capabilities for a single domain. Although there are a number of ontology library systems that allow for management of multiple ontologies (Duineveld et al., 1999; Ding and Fansel, 2001; Fensel, 2001; Helfin and Hendler, 2000), they have limitations in scalability and dynamically incorporating new ontological knowledge. In particular, they lack the capability of representing rich context knowledge needed for reconciling differences among sources. A primary need is the ability to operate in a multi-disciplinary environment across *multiple-linked collaborative domain spaces*. The representational capabilities to relate concepts across domains and efficiently maintain the effectiveness of these collaborative domain spaces is critically important, especially in an environment where we believe the underlying domains themselves will continually undergo evolution. For some users, the reality of domain shifts itself is the defining feature of interest (Nunamaker, 2001; Kaleem, 2003).

5. Advanced Mediation Reasoning and Services. The COIN abductive logic framework can also be extrapolated to problem areas such as *integrity management, view updates* and *intentional updates,* for databases (Chu, 2000). Because of the clear separation between the generic abductive procedure for query mediation and the declarative logical definition of domain models and source and receiver contexts, we are able to adapt our mediation procedure to new situations such as mediated consistency management across disparate sources, mediated update management of one or more database using heterogeneous external auxiliary information, or mediated monitoring of changes. An update asserts that certain data objects must be made to have certain values in the updater's context. By combining the update assertions with the COIN logical formulation of context semantics, we can determine whether the update is unambiguous and feasible in the target context and, if so, what source data updates must be made to achieve the intended results. If ambiguous or otherwise infeasible, the logical representation may be able to indicate what additional constraints would clarify the updater's intention sufficiently for the update to proceed. We build upon the formal system underlying our framework, abductive reasoning, and extend the expressiveness and the reasoning capabilities leveraging ideas developed in different yet similar frameworks such as Description Logic and classification, as well as ongoing in Semantic Web research. These national security applications, where there are fundamental shifts in relationships, systems, and pressures, is a 'tough test' since the underlying domain is highly dynamic even volatile.

6. Automatic Source Selection. A natural extension is to leverage context knowledge to achieve context-based *automatic source selection*. One particular kind of context knowledge useful to enable automatic source selection is the *content scope of data sources*. Data sources differ either significantly or subtly in their coverage scopes. In a highly diverse environment with hundreds and thousands of data sources, differences of content scopes can be valuably used to facilitate effective and efficient data source selection. Integrity constraints in COINL and the consistency checking component of the abductive procedure provide the basic ingredients to characterize the scope of information available from each source, to efficiently rule out irrelevant data sources and thereby speed up the selection process (Tu and Madnick, 1998). For example, a query requesting information about *companies with assets lower than $2 million* can avoid accessing a particular source based on knowledge of integrity constraints stating that *the source only reports information about companies listed in the New York Stock Exchange* (NYSE) and that *companies must have assets larger than $10 million to be listed in the NYSE*. In general, integrity constraints express necessary conditions imposed on data. However, more generally, a notion of completeness degree of the domain of the source with respect to the constraint captures a richer semantic information and allows more powerful source selection. For instance, a source could contain exactly or at least all the data verifying the constraint (e.g., all the companies listed in the NYSE are reported in the source). The source may be influenced by institutional objectives, resulting in major differences in metrics (for concepts like 'terrorism') due to differences in definitions of the concept itself. In cases of violent conflict, casualty reports vary significantly, largely because of differences in definitions of the variable (i.e., who is being counted).

7. Source Quality. Not only do the sources vary in semantic meaning, they also vary in quality, and they do so in various ways. We must be able to represent and reason about the *quality attributes* of the sources (Wang, et al., 1993; Madnick, 2003).

8. Attribution Knowledge Processing. For quality assessment and other reasons, it is important to know the *attribution of the sources* (Lee et al., 1998, 1999). For example, it can be important to know that although three different sources agree on a controversial piece of the information (e.g., casualties in the Afghanistan war), all three sources acquired that information from the same, maybe questionable, origin source [Lee02].

9. Domain Knowledge Processing—Improving Computer Performance. While *domain and context knowledge processing* has been shown to have considerable conceptual value (Cherniak and Zdonik, 1998; Moulton et al., 1998; Lee et al., 1996; Sheng and Wei, 1992), its application in real situations requires both efficiency and scalability across large numbers of sources, quantities and kinds of data, and demand for services. The scalability and optimization of this mediation processing for large numbers of sources across multiple collaborative domains and contexts is important. In a heterogeneous and distributed environment, the mediator transforms a query written in terms known in the user or application program context (i.e., according to the user's or program's assumptions and knowledge) into one or more queries in terms of component sources. Individual subqueries at this stage may involve one or multiple sources. Subsequent planning, optimization, and execution phases (Arens et al., 1996; Fynn, 1997) take into account the limitations of the sources and the topology and costs of the network (especially when dealing with non-database sources, such as web pages or web services). The execution phase schedules execution of steps in the query execution plan and the realization of the integrative operations not handled by the sources individually (e.g. a join across sources) (Tarik, 2002).

10. Domain Knowledge Acquisition—Improving Human Performance. *Domain and context knowledge acquisition* are also essential. One critical property to be emphasized is the independence of domains and sources. The COIN approach is nonintrusive and respects source and receiver independence (i.e., autonomy). To effectively use the expressive power of the constructs and mechanisms in COIN, it is important that subject matter domain experts be able to easily provide the needed domain and context knowledge. It is therefore essential to have an appropriate flexible methodology and tools supporting this methodology. Where a large number of independent information sources are accessed (as is now possible with the global Internet), flexibility, scalability, and nonintrusiveness will be of primary importance. Traditional tight-coupling approaches to semantic interoperability rely on the *a priori* creation of federated views on the heterogeneous information sources. These approaches do not scale-up efficiently or reliably given the complexity involved in constructing and maintaining a shared schema for a large number of possibly independently managed and evolving sources. Loose-coupling approaches rely on the user's intimate knowledge of the semantic conflicts between the sources and the conflict resolution procedures. This reliance becomes a drawback for scalability when this knowledge grows and changes as more sources join the system and when sources are changing. The COIN approach is a middle ground between these two approaches. It allows queries to the sources to be mediated—that is, allows semantic conflicts to be identified and solved by a context mediator through comparison of contexts associated with the sources and receivers concerned by the queries. It only requires the minimum adoption of a common Domain Model, such as that developed for GSSD, that defines the domain of discourse of the application (Lee, 2003).

11. Relationship with Evolving Semantic Web. Although the initial COIN and GSSD research and theories preceded the emerging activities now described as the Semantic Web, there are many areas of overlap, especially involving the development of the OWL ontology standards and the use of rules and reasoning. The LIGHT research contributes to the maturing of the Semantic Web; at the same time, LIGHT exploits relevant ontologies, standards, and tools that are emerging from the Semantic Web activities.

12. Operational System for Harmonized Information Processing. A key development is the new *System for Harmonized Information Processing* (SHIP), a distributed information infrastructure that will be used to support the types of challenges listed in Section 7.1, incorporating all the components identified above. This system has maximum flexibility and extensibility that permits new and existing applications to seamlessly extract data from an array of changing heterogeneous sources. The utility of many databases in the national priority areas has been seriously constrained by the difficulties of reconciling known disparities and conflicts within and across sources. SHIP directly addresses this problem. (Data reconciliation itself has become an important focus of scholarly inquiry in various parts in political science, as recognized by the NSF.)

13. Policy Implications Regarding Data Use and Reuse. There are widely differing views regarding the use and reuse of even publicly available information. In particular, the United States has taken a largely "laissez faire" approach whereas the European Union is pursuing a much more restrictive policy (as embodied in its "Database Directive"). We have been applying principles from the domain of economics to develop a more scientific approach to studying and evaluating the current and proposed policies and legislation in this area (Zhu et al., 2002).

7.3. NATIONAL AND HOMELAND SECURITY

National and homeland security (NHS) is an important research area. In this section, we describe some of the most fundamental barriers to the reliable use of information systems in this area. *Our goal is to reduce serious barriers, enhance understanding and meaning across substance, topics, and ontologies, and provide new tools for national security analysis in international relations (IR) research.* For example, data on incidences of conflict and war are available on the websites of a wide range of institutions with different capabilities and objectives, such as the U.S. Department of State, the SIPRI in Sweden, the UN HCR, and the Correlates of War Project.[5] Despite all this information, we cannot compute the 'actual' number of deaths and casualties in a conflict—at one point in time, over time, and as the contenders change and reconfigure their own jurisdictions—largely due to differences in definitions of key variables. These are typical questions that have plagued researchers, as far back as 1942, with classics in the field such as Quincy Wright's *A Study of War* (Wright, 1965), and even earlier, with Lewis Fry Richardson's *Statistics of Deadly Quarrels* (1917) (Richardson, 1960).

7.3.1. Pressing Demands on Information Systems

The proliferation of new actors on the international landscape (i.e., new states, nongovernmental organizations, cross-border political groups, non-state actors, international institutions, global firms, etc.) reflects diverse perspectives and creates new sources of data, legacy problems, and new difficulties for access, interpretation, and management. A persistent challenge to national security is to reduce the **distinction between reality and representation**. Reality is the empirical domain and is the referent of representations. Representations (ontologies) are idealized frameworks that identify salient aspects of reality and allow us to organize and manipulate them as information. The properties of the database scheme or application ontology define the domain of analysis, types of inferences, and nature of conclusions drawn. While representations are the interface *to* reality, organizations take action *in* reality. To date, efforts to address the problem of domain-specific representation in international relations remain costly and time-consuming, yet acting without them may be even more costly—or simply impossible.

Indeed, an often-cited recent review of empirical challenges in a noteworthy issue of *International Political Science Review* (2001), devoted to "Transformation of International Relations—Between Change and Continuity," argues that "reconfiguration of the founding concepts of international relations . . . is linked to important paradigmatic changes" (Sjourn, 2001, p. 224) and that state-centric modes of analysis and information configuration must be augmented by methods that help capture changes in both structure and process in the international arena. This is one of the major challenges in the new domain of inquiry, termed CyberPolitics, as noted in the *International Political Science Review* (2000) issue "CyberPolitics in International Relations" (Choucri, 1999, 2000), which identifies new directions of research, research priorities, and critical next steps.

7.3.2. Defining the Research Problem: The Paradox of Plenty

While there exists no "single authoritative view" of the international relations field as a whole, Katzenstein et al. (1999) illustrate dominant trends in the nonquantitative aspects of the field. By contrast, in quantitative international politics (QIP), theory development and analysis is more data-driven and thus invariably more vulnerable to limitations of in-

---

[5]http://www.pcr.uu.se/ research/UCDP/ conflict_dataset_catalog/data_list.htm

formation systems. Earlier quantitative works, such as Hoole and Zinnes (1976) and Russett (1972), as well as the more recent advances by Levy (1989), Choucri and North (1993), Choucri et al. (1992), and Schweller and Pollins (1999), illustrate the general progression in the field and the persistent data representation problems. Concurrently, Alker (1996) highlighted some analogous and fundamental challenges to humanistic approaches to international studies, illustrated by ranges of computer-assisted applications. Further, in the issue of *International Studies Quarterly* (Cioffi-Revilla, 1996) devoted to evolutionary perspectives in international relations, leading scholars such as George Modelski, Robert Gilpin, Cioffi-Revilla, and others articulated the importance of transformation and adaptation over time, as an important departure from the common focus on discrete events, or retrospective case-based interpretation, so dominant in the field. By far the most succinct statement about data reconciliation problems is made by a leading scholar who proceeds to demonstrate in considerable detail the "semantic carelessness . . . [that can] stand in the way of cumulative research" and then identifies a large set of specific examples that may be particular to international relations, but "most seem to be found all across the discipline [of political science]" (Singer, 2002; p. 604).

The *Paradox of Plenty* is this. Despite the *abundance* of existing data and information, there is a *paucity* in the consistency, reliability, and connectivity of the information. For example, in the conflict theory and analysis domain, advances in the long tradition of tracking wars and casualties have been severely hampered by the difficulties of generating an integrated approach to diverse information resources, drawing upon large scale collaborative efforts in the profession and undertaken by a large number of research groups, nationally and internationally. The same point holds for the cooperation theory domain where, for example, efforts to measure "regime formation" and "compliance" in a wide range of specific issue areas are hampered by the diversity of ontologies, data meanings, metrics, and methods.

7.3.3. Context Mediation for National Security

Increasingly, the nation's intelligence agencies rely on information from all over the world to anticipate, identify, and develop strategic responses to security threats. As noted in (National Research Council, 2002, p. 304): "Although there are many private and public databases that contain information potentially relevant to counter terrorism programs, they lack the necessary context definitions (i.e., metadata) and access tools to enable interoperation with other databases and the extraction of meaningful and timely information." The tragic events of 9/11/2001 starkly indicate how changes in the scale, scope, type, and intensity of external threats to national security is surpassing existing practices in information access, interpretation, and utilization—in both the scientific and policymaking communities.

The *Paradox of Plenty* is amply demonstrated by the large number of datasets compiled by international relations scholars on conflict, crises, and war that are now found in central repositories such as the InterUniversity Consortium for Political Science Research (ICPSR), the Harvard–MIT Data Center, and others. Despite decades of painstaking research, cumulativeness remains hampered by barriers to information reconciliation. There are no mechanisms for extracting coherent and integrated information from these datasets, since the variables are defined differently, the formatting varies, and content is represented in different forms and is updated variously. It is nearly impossible to utilize these sets for purposes other than those intended by the initial compilers, and it is even more difficult to merge, streamline, or normalize. The NSF sponsored Data Documentation Initiative (DDI) offers the prospect of formal XML-based documentation of the coding and structure of social science datasets. The Context Mediation research draws on DDI results and enables information extraction and fusion in a collaborative environment hitherto unreachable.[6]

For example, among the most notable datasets of the *Correlates of War Project,* a highly respected and well-structured dataset, wars are reported in dyads—that is, country X–country Y. Data are reported by war-months, for the warring dyads, devoid of context, which means that we cannot determine if it was an offensive or defensive war, nor can we readily extract other salient features of the "situation." These problems could be reduced if systematic comparisons could be made with relevant information from other datasets (such as the CIA Factbook and the Uppsala Conflict Database). Achieving this integration of datasets on attributes and activities of states over time requires the ability to reconcile different coding schemes representing states as well as the ability to track and integrate the impacts of changes in territorial and jurisdictional boundaries (using, for example, the Uppsala Territorial Change dataset). Working from the opposite direction, the CASCON research (Bloomfield and Moulton, 1997) developed a set of policy relevant factors relating to the potential for violence in conflict situations, but requires laborious hand coding of each new conflict that arises. With the context mediation technology, it should be possible to connect many of these factors to available data sources and thereby enable fact patterns to be readily filled in so that the method can be more readily applied to supporting the policy analytic process.

These are the challenges that are being addressed with the development of the next generation of context mediation technologies in LIGHT. New technologies cannot alter shifting realities, but they can provide functionalities to reduce barriers to information access, use, reuse, customization, and interpretation.

7.3.4. Research Design in Practice: Approach, Test Applications, Implementation

7.3.4.1. Approach. This research is based on (a) the structural differentiation among *contextual* conditions and (b) the *type of gap* between the variable of interest, the *referent* (such as actor, issue, institution, etc.), and the information system and its properties, the *representation.* The goal is to reduce the gap between the two and increase the representation power of the information systems. Toward this end, we address the *context* of content, develop specific classes of tools to represent *context types,* and approach these computationally through test applications. For each of the applications, we focus on (i) properties of the *context* situation; (ii) properties of the *data features,* and (iii) properties of the *data collection agencies.*

7.3.4.2. Example Applications. Our focus is on the "tough cases"—that is, reducing barriers to information access and use when the *properties of the problem* themselves are changing as a function of *unfolding* conflicts and contentions and when the *demands* for information change in the course of the contentions. This includes three sets of applications selected because of their known and powerful impediment to national security analysis. (Each of these context problems has some similarities with the Balkans example earlier, but each highlights added complexities.)

[6]see http://www.icpsr.umich.edu/DDI/index.html

1. **Shifts in Spatial Configuration**—for example, the territorial boundaries problem. As any student of international relations knows, the dissolution of the Soviet Union is a major, but far from unique, reconfiguration of territorial boundaries. Several databases seek to capture these changes, and below we refer to one such example with cases spanning well over one century (1816–1996).

2. **Disconnects in Definitions of "Conflict"**—for example, the wars and casualties problem. Of the leading 10 datasets on international conflict and violence over time, no two datasets are synchronized or reconciled (see below for two examples).

3. **Distortions due to Data Temporality**—for example, economic and political "currency" problem. The ongoing experiment in Europe on the formal shift from national currencies to the Euro must be addressed if we are to ask, How extensive are the individual countries' investments in their military systems compared to each other, to the United States, and to past commitments?

7.3.4.3. Implementation and Examples.
To deploy the technical work put forth in Section 7.2 toward solving specific problems in the NHS domain, we proceed in the following steps (with of a degree of overlap as needed): (1) Identify the referent situations, such as shifts in the Balkan countries' boundaries, war casualties in region X, or U.S. troop casualties over the past X years; (2) create the case catalogue; that is, in such cases, list of all spatial reconfigurations over the past 20 years, and verify the degree of congruence among alternative sources for representing the shifts; (3) identify the similarities and differences between the variable definitions of the problem in various information systems or relevant databases and compare these to the topic and/or domain specific ontology in GSSD; (4) use the results to design context features for computational purposes of new context mediation tools; (5) construct the pilot study for the case in point; (6) test viability of specifications against at least three different information systems or databases (see below) and, on this basis, make adjustments, changes, and so on; and (7) undertake the actual test application.

To illustrate parts of the design, we refer below to application Case 2, namely, international conflict and war, so fundamental to the nation's security. For example, the *Correlates of War Project* (*COW*) and the Project on *Assessing Societal and Systemic Impact of Warfare* (*SSIW*) both deal with deaths due to violence and hostility, but they define war (terms and categories) in different ways: COW defines war as "sustained armed combat between two or more state member of the international system which meets the violence threshold" and uses 1000 battle-related fatalities as the threshold, with no fixed time within which these deaths must occur, and proceed to differentiate between intra-state war, interstate war, and extra-state war (each defined specifically). ASSW develops a 10-point scale for assessing magnitude, intensity, and severity of war, differentiating among interstate warfare, wars of independence, civil warfare, ethnic warfare, and genocide. In the absence of a common frame of reference spanning these two information systems, it is extremely difficult to get a sense of what in fact may have taken place (i.e., clarifying the "dependent" variable as a necessary precursor to statistical, simulation, modeling or policy analysis of any type.) For this reason, we use the ontology for the "conflict and war" domain developed for GSSD as our platform, to provide the baseline for developing the new operational ontology. This latter task, of course, is guided by the dominant theories of conflict and war in international relations.[7]

---

[7]See "Using GSSD- GSSD Knowledge Strategy" at http://gssd.mit.edu/GSSD/gssden.nsf

At the same time, however, we know from historical and situational analysis that the very act of war (variously defined) is often preceded by, or results in, territorial shifts in legal political jurisdiction. This means that (a) reconciliation of definitions is only the first step and (b) accounting for spatial reconfiguration is a necessary next step. Both steps must be completed before we can address the question of "how many casualties" Interestingly, the *Territorial Change Coding Manual,* showing the different dimensions across which spatial changes are coded, notes that these include "at least one nation-state" of the COW information system and then identifies six specific procedures by which special changes take place (conquest, annexation, cession, secession, unification, mandated territory)—and as any international lawyer knows, these are contentious conditions.

The current *information base* for the GSSD platform consists of web-based resources from over 250 institutions worldwide, representing a diverse set of datasets by type, scale, and scope that is then cross-referenced and cross-indexed for ease of retrieval and analysis, according to an integrated and coherent conceptual framework covering the knowledge domain (Choucri, 2001). The domain consists of (a) a hierarchical and nested representation spanning 14 key socioeconomic "sectors" of human activities, (b) attendant known problems to date related to each, (c) responses to these problems, in terms of scientific and technological activities, social and regulatory instruments, and (d) modes of international collaboration. GSSD was chosen as our platform because it (1) provides a *domain-specific ontology* based on (a) rigorous applications of social science theories and (b) related domains in science and technology; (2) offers practical reasoning rules for forming additional ontologies; (3) presents scenarios for broad applications of the new technologies to be developed in this project; (4) regularly updates its representation of, and links to, large and important set of information sources; and (5) spans local and global data information sources.

7.3.5. Generalizing the Research Tasks

To illustrate specific aspects of the research design, we note two key issues:

7.3.5.1. Comprehensive Information-Base Survey. First, we want to more fully understand attributes of the data types in the GSSD knowledge base that are relevant to the specific domain selected for a test-application. The outcomes of this phase include: (a) an assessment of the context of data types within the domain, including the following aspects: data source, format, organization, equational and temporality attributes, provision rules, and utility for user-driven query; and (b) typologies of barriers to access, noted above.

7.3.5.2. Multidisciplinary and Distributed User Survey for the Test Applications. Second, we want to develop and apply methods to survey current and future information demands from diverse NHS actors, differentiated in terms of (i) data users, (ii) data providers, and (iii) data intermediaries (or brokers). Test cases to capture the impacts and represent the views of different user types on information and data needs will emerge from this assessment. Specific activities include:

(a) **Multidimensional assessments of information demand** from different user types within the diverse conflict domains noted earlier (e.g., Sections 7.1.2.1 and 7.1.3), based on surveys, workshops, and in-depth interviews.

(b) **Development of new or refined ontologies and a knowledge repository** to represent specific NHS domains and provide a test bed for the emergent information technologies.

(c) **Refined substantive applications of the new technologies for enhancing information capabilities in theory and methods development, and results of tests for effectiveness of the design.** This would demonstrate the performance of the technologies' domain-specific and practical applications test cases, as well as generate some guidelines of relevance for similarly complex domains.

(d) **Collaborative assessments** and evaluations of the technologies' effectiveness to address NHS information issues and LIGHT's capacity for scalability and cross-domain applicability.

7.4. LABORATORY FOR INFORMATION GLOBALIZATION AND HARMONIZATION TECHNOLOGIES

The **Laboratory for Information Globalization and Harmonization Technologies (LIGHT)** has been established to address the strategy, application, development, and deployment of this next generation of intelligent information technologies that are designed to support the national priority areas. Its purpose is to examine 'frontier' issues, such as transformations in patterns of conflict and cooperation, changes in modes of international business, emergent dimensions of globalization and system change, and negotiation systems for new global accords, among others. In addition, LIGHT hosts the technical infrastructure of our System for Harmonized Information Processing (SHIP).

In practice, this multidisciplinary laboratory brings together faculty and students with interdisciplinary interests and activities from a number of departments of MIT, including Information Technologies, Political Science, Management Science, and the Technology, Management, and Policy program.

More specifically, the laboratory is the central entity for developments in four areas: (1) Software Platforms, (2) Knowledge Repositories, (3) Application Demonstrations, and (4) Education and Research. The software platforms include, but are not limited to, SHIP with Collaborative Domains Spaces (CDS) including one or more Ontology Library Systems, Context and Conversion Management Systems, Context Mediation Engine, Execution and Planning Module, and Application and Source Support Tools. The Knowledge Context Repositories include the NHS domain specific knowledge represented in ontologies, context and conversion libraries, source schemas, and capabilities. The Application Demonstrations are being developed at MIT, with the participation of collaborators, nationally and internationally.

SUMMARY

The LIGHT project, building on the COIN and GDSS systems, will lead to major advances in information technology applicable to the national priority areas. The outcomes of this innovative project address many of the challenges facing our nation:

1. Theory and Technology. The LIGHT System for Harmonization of Information Processing (SHIP) provides an effective mechanism for effective and meaningful information interchange among very large-scale (in terms of size and geographical locations) and diversified (in terms of media, schemas, and domains) systems. The reliability of systems is significantly improved by dynamically incorporating semantically equivalent sources into the interconnected system. It allows new applications to be built quickly to facilitate information sharing among diverse groups of people, devices, and software systems. Since it facilitates semantic level information interchange, any information receiver (people, devices, or software) can obtain customized information accurately and in a form and meaning that the receiver prefers.

2. National Priorities. This effort significantly augments the effective use of information in our society and expands the frontiers of political science and information technology. This has important applicability for increasing national security and prevention and attribution of terrorism. These findings help us to meet the goal of improved information utilization that also can be applied and extended to other important areas. Through international collaborators we will be able to obtain a more robust handle on matters of context, culture, multiple interpretations, multilingualism, imperatives of localization, and so on. This also will lead to more effective use of information in society.

3. Knowledge Acquisition and Interpretation. Two of the fundamental goals of this effort are (1) the acquisition of information context knowledge (both for sources and users) and (2) the ability to use our SHIP's reasoning ability about this knowledge to correctly and effectively organize and interpret the information. A third goal will be shaped as a result of work on the fundamental ones, namely, articulating and formalizing logics required for reasoning about emergent knowledge acquisition and interpretation needs in the evolution of a "context" (i.e., situation, conflict, etc.) over time.

The technical infrastructure and intellectual advances developed by the new Laboratory for Information Globalization and Harmonization Technologies (LIGHT) will be shared to encourage collaboration with the broader community. The materials will be made publicly available on the Internet including: literature reviews, survey results, theoretical models, reports, the System for Harmonized Information Processing technology, other analyses conducted during the life cycle of the project, and an evaluative discussion forum. We expect that this effort will generate important impacts for the research and practitioner communities, as well as society, in general.

REFERENCES

Arens, Y., Knoblock, C. and Shen, W. M. (1996). Query reformulation for dynamic information integration. *Journal of Intelligent Information Systems* **6**:99–130.

Alker, H. R. (1996). *Rediscoveries and Reformulations: Humanistic Methodologies for International Studies.* Cambridge, UK: Cambridge University Press.

Bressan, S., Goh, C., Levina, N., Madnick, S., Shah, S., and Siegel, S. (2000) Context knowledge representation and reasoning in the context interchange system. *Applied Intelligence: The International Journal of Artificial Intelligence, Neutral Networks, and Complex Problem-Solving Technologies* **12**(2):165–179.

Bloomfield, L. P., and Moulton, A. (1997). *Managing International Conflict: From Theory to Policy.* New York: St. Martin's Press (supplemented by CASCON web site http://mit.edu/cascon).

Chen, P. (1999). ER model, XML and the Web. In: *18th International Conference on Conceptual Modeling.*

Chen, X., Funk, J., Madnick, S., and Wang, R. (2001). Corporate Household Data: Research Directions. In: *Proceedings of the Americans Conference on Information Systems,* AMCIS'01, Boston.

Cherniak, M., and Zdonik, S. (1998). Inferring function semantics to optimize queries. *VLDB* **0**:239–250.

Choucri, N. (2000). CyberPolitics in international relations. *International Political Science Review* **21**(3):243–264.

Choucri, N. (2001). Knowledge networking for global sustainability: new modes of cyberpartnering. In D. J. Richard, B. R. Allenby, and D. W. Compton, *Information Systems and the Environment*, pp. 195–210. Washington, DC: National Academies Press.

Choucri, N. (1999). *Innovations in uses of cyberspace*. In *Sustainability and the Social Sciences*, E. Becker and T. Jahn (eds.), pp. 274–283. New York: Zed Books–St. Martin's Press.

Choucri, N., and North, R. C. (1993). Growth, development, and environmental sustainablity: Profiles and paradox. *Global Accord: Environmental Challenges and International Responses*, pp. 67–131. Cambridge, MA, MIT Press.

Choucri, N., North, R. C., and Yamakage, S. (1992). *The Challenge of Japan Before World War II and After*. London: Routledge.

Chu, W. (2000). Introduction: Conceptual models for intelligent information systems. *Applied Intelligence* **13**(2).

Cioffi-Revilla, C. (1996). Origins and evolution of war and politics. *International Studies Quarterly* **40**:1–22.

Ding, Y., and Fensel, D. (2001). Ontology library systems: The key to successful ontology reuse. In: *International Semantic Web Working Symposium*, Stanford University, CA.

Dobbie, G., and Topor, R. (1995). On the declarative and procedural semantics of deductive object-oriented systems, *Journal of Intelligent Information Systems* **4**:193–219.

Duineveld, A. J., Stoter, R., Weiden, M. R., Kenepa, B., and Bejamins, V. R. (1999). WonderTools? A Comparative study of ontological engineering tools. In: *Proceedings of the 12th International Workshop on Knowledge Aquisition, Modeling, and Management (KAW'99)*, Banff, Canada.

Fensel, D. (2001). *Ontologies: A Silver Bullet for Knowledge Management and Electronic Commerce*. Berlin: Springer.

Firat, A., Grosof, B., and Madnick, S. (2002). Financial information integration in the presence of equational ontological conflicts. In: *Proceedings of the Workshop on Information Technology and Systems*, Barcelona, Spain, pp. 211–216.

Firat, A., Madnick, S., and Siegel, S. (2000a). The Caméléon Web Wrapper Engine. In: *Proceedings of the VLDB2000 Workshop on Technologies for E-Services*.

Firat, A., Madnick, S., and Siegel, S. (2000b). The Caméléon approach to the interoperability of web sources and traditional relational databases. In: *Proceedings of the Workshop on Information Technology and Systems*.

Frühwirth, T. (1994). Temporal Reasoning with Constraint Handling Rules, ECRC-94-5.

Frühwirth, T. (1998). Theory and practice of constraint handling rules, Special issue on constraint logic programming (P. Stuckey and K. Marriot, eds.). *Journal of Logic Programming* **37**(1–3):95–138.

Fynn, K. D. (1997). *A Planner/Optimizer/Executioner for Context Mediated Queries*. MS Thesis, MIT.

Gamson, W. A. (1968). *Power and Discontent*. Homewood, IL: The Dorsey Press.

Goh, C. H., Bressan, S., Madnick, S., and Siegel, S. (1999). Context interchange: New Features and Formalisms for the Intelligent Integration of Information. *ACM Transactions on Information Systems*, **17**(3):270–293.

Goh, C. H., Bressan, S., Madnick, S. E., and Siegel, M. D. (1996). Context interchange: Representing and reasoning about data semantics in heterogeneous systems. *Sloan School Working Paper #3928*, Sloan School of Management, MIT, 50 Memorial Drive, Cambridge MA 02139.

Goh, C. (1996). *Representing and Reasoning about Semantic Conflicts In Heterogeneous Information System*, PhD Thesis, MIT.

Geller, D. S., and Singer, J. D. (1997). *Nations at War: A Scientific Study of International Conflict*. Cambridge, England: Cambridge University Press.

Helfin, J., and Hendler J. (2000). Dynamic ontologies on the web. In: *Proceedings of the 11th National Conference on Artificial Intelligence* (AAAI-2000), Menlo Park, CA, pp. 443–449.

Hoole, F. W., and Zinnes, D. A. (eds.) (1976). *Quantitative International Politics: an Appraisal.* New York: Praeger.

Kaleem, M. B. (2003). CLAMP: Application Merging in the ECOIN Context Mediation System using the Context Linking Approach, CISL Working Paper 2003-05 and MIT Thesis.

Katzenstein, P., Keohane R., and Krasner, S. (eds.) (1999). *Exploration and Contestation in the Study of World Politics.* Cambridge, MA: The MIT Press.

Kakas, A. C., Kowalski, R. A., and Toni, F. (1993). Abductive logic programming. *Journal of Logic and Computation* **2**(6):719–770.

Kifer, M., Lausen, G., and Wu, J. (1995). Logical foundations of object-oriented and frame-based languages. *JACM* **4**:741–843.

Lasswell, H. D. (1958). *Politics: Who Gets What, When and How.* New York: McGraw-Hill.

Lee, T., Chams, M., Nado, R., Madnick, S., and Siegel, M. (1999). Information integration with attribution support for corporate profiles. In: *Proceedings of the International Conference on Information and Knowledge Management,* pp. 423–429.

Lee, T. (2002). Attribution Principles for Data Integration: Technology and Policy Perspectives—Part 1: Focus on Technology. CISL Working Paper 2002-03 and MIT Thesis.

Lee, P. (2003). Metadata Representation and Management for Context Mediation. CISL Working Paper 2003-01 and MIT Thesis.

Levy, J. S. (1989). The causes of war: A review of theories and evidence. In: *Behavior, Society, and Nuclear War.* Tetlock, Jervis, Stern, and Tilly (eds.) New York: Oxford University Press.

Lee, T., Madnick, S., and Bressan, S. (1998). Source attribution for querying against semi-structured documents. In: *Proceedings of the ACM Workshop on Web Information and Data Management* (WIDM'98), Washington, DC, pp. 33–39.

Lee, J., Madnick, S., and Siegel, M. (1996). Conceptualizing semantic interoperability: A perspective from the knowledge level. *International Journal of Cooperative Information Systems* [Special Issue on Formal Methods in Cooperative Information Systems], **5**(4).

Madnick, S. (2001). The misguided silver bullet: What XML will and will NOT do to help information integration. In: *Proceedings of the Third International Conference on Information Integration and Web-based Applications and Services,* IIWAS2001, Linz, Austria, pp. 61–72.

Madnick, S. (2003). Oh, so that is what you meant! The interplay of data quality and data semantics. In: *Proceedings of the 22nd International Conference on Conceptual Modeling (ER'03),* Chicago, October. Also in: *Conceptual Modeling—ER 2003, pp. 3–13.* New York: Springer-Verlag.

Madnick, S. (1999). Metadata Jones and the Tower of Babel: The challenge of large-scale heterogeneity. In: *Proceedings of the IEEE Meta-data Conference.*

Moulton, A., Bressan, S., Madnick, S., and Siegel, M. (1998). Using an Active Conceptual Model for Mediating Analytic Information Exchange in the Fixed Income Securities Industry. In: *Proceedings of the 17th International Conference on Conceptual Modeling* (ER'98), Singapore.

McNeill, J. R. (2000). *Something New Under the Sun.* New York: W.W. Norton & Company.

March, S., Hevner, A., and Ram, S. (2000). Research commentary: An agenda for information technology research in heterogeneous and distributed environments. *Information Systems Research,* **11**(4):327–341.

Madnick, S., Wang, R., and Xian, X. (2003). The design and implementation of a corporate householding knowledge processor to improve data quality. *Journal of Management Information Systems* **20**(3):

Madnick, S., Wang, R., and Zhang, E. (2002). A framework for corporate householding. In:*Proceedings of the International Conference on Information Quality* Cambridge, pp. 36–46.

National Research Council (2002). *Making the Nation Safer: The Role of Science and Technology in Countering Terrorism."* Washington, DC: National Academy Press. [http://www.nap.edu/ html/stct/index.html]

Nunamaker, J. F. (2001). Collaboration systems and technology track—Introduction. In: *Hawaii International Conference on System Sciences.*

Richard, D. J., Allenby, B. R., and Compton, W. D. (eds.). (2001). *Information Systems and the Environment.* National Academy of Engineering. Washington, DC: National Academy Press.

Richardson, L. F. (1960). *Statistics of Deadly Quarrels.* Pittsburgh: Boxwood Press.

Rosenau, J. N. (1990). *Turbulence in World Politics: A Theory of Change and Continuity.* Princeton, NJ. Princeton University Press.

Russett, B. M. (ed.) (1972). *Peace, War, and Numbers.* Beverly Hills, CA: Sage Publications.

Sindjoun, L. (2001). Transformation of international relations—Between change and continuity. *International Political Science Review* **22**(3):219–228

Siegel, M., and Madnick, S. (1991). Context interchange: Sharing the meaning of data. *SIGMOD RECORD,* **20**(4):77–78.

Singer, J. D. (2002). Accounting for Interstate War: Progress and Cumulation. In B. Brecher and F. P. Harvey (eds.). *Millennial Reflections on International Studies,* pp. 598–615. Ann Arbor, MI: The University of Michigan Press.

Schweller, R. and Pollins B. (1999). Linking the levels: The long wave and shifts in U.S. foreign policy, 1790–1993. *American Journal of Political Science* **43**(2):431–464.

Sheng, O. R. L., and Wei, C.-P. (1992). Object-oriented modeling and design of coupled knowledge-base/database systems. *International Conference on Data Engineering,* pp. 98–105.

Tarik A. (2002). Capabilities Aware Planner/Optimizer/Executioner for COntext INterchange Project. CISL Working Paper 2002-01 and MIT Thesis.

Templeton, M., Brill, D., Dao, S. K., Lund, E., Ward, P., Chen, A. L. P., and MacGregor, R. (1987). Mermaid—a front end to distributed heterogeneous databases. In: *Proceedings of the IEEE,* **75**(5):695–708.

Tu, S. Y., and Madnick, S. (1998). Incorporating generalized quantifiers into description logic for representing data source contents. In: *Data Mining and Reverse Engineering: Searching for Semantics,* New York: Chapman & Hall.

Wang, R., Allen, T., Harris, W., and Madnick, S. (2003). An Information Product Approach for Total Information Awareness" (with R. Wang, T. Allen, W. Harris). In: *Proceedings of the 2003 IEEE Aerospace Conference,* Big Sky, MT.

Wang, R., Kon, H., and Madnick, S (1993). Data quality requirements analysis and modeling. In: *International Conference on Data Engineering,* pp. 670–677

Wiederhold, G. (1992). Mediation in the architecture of future information systems. *IEEE Computer* **25**(3):38–49.

Wiederhold, G. (1999). Mediation to deal with heterogeneous data sources. In: *Proceedings of Interop'99,* Zurich, pp. 1–16.

Wright, Q. (1965). *A Study of War.* Chicago, IL: University of Chicago Press.

Walter, B., and Snyder, J. (1999). *Civil Wars, Insecurity, and Intervention.* New York: Columbia University Press.

Zhu, H., Madnick, S. and Siegel, M. (2002). The interplay of web aggregation and regulations (with H. Zhu and M. Siegel). In: *Proceedings of the IASTED International Conference on Law and Technology (LAWTECH 2002),* Cambridge, MA.

Zhu, H., Madnick, S., and Siegel, M. (2004). Effective Data Integration in the Presence of Temporal Semantic Conflicts. CISL Working Paper.

Chapter 8

Anonymized Semantic Directories and a Privacy-Enhancing Architecture for Enterprise Discovery

Jeff Jonas and John Karat

8.1. INTRODUCTION

Information sharing is being heralded as a silver bullet for solving the pressing security problems of the early twenty-first century. Responding to the events of September 11th, well-intended technologists around the world converged on the notion that something more could be done to detect and preempt such events in the future. They imagined harnessing countless global databases, mining these treasure troves for meaningful clues, and enjoying "Eureka" moments in which they headed off future disasters. They believed that this would be not only an important step in protecting our way of life, but also a powerful capability that could be applied to other pressing societal issues (e.g., conducting medical research).

Evidence suggests that the necessary data did exist to detect and likely disrupt the 19 terrorists prior to September 11th.[1] The problem was that the people who could have used the information to prevent the attack did not have any good method for finding all of the crucial pieces or "connecting the dots." Organizations responsible for security in the United States have argued that we must get access to the information needed to achieve these noble aims.[2] And thus, the government has concluded, we must start "sharing information" across disparate systems, organizations, and, if necessary, countries.[3] How to do this while adhering to principles of privacy protection for the citizens is a difficult challenge (OECD, 1980), and is part of what needs to be considered within the scope of the grand challenges for security and privacy technology (CRA, 2003).

While there are many ways to stop bad things from happening, clearly one of the most effective is to identify and locate the perpetrator before the bad event occurs. How to

---

[1] Protecting America's Freedom in the Information Age, First Report of the Markle Foundation Task Force on National Security in the Information Age (October 2002), pp. 27–31.
[2] See generally, Safeguarding Privacy in the Fight Against Terrorism. Report of the Technology and Privacy Advisory Committee (Mar. 2004)(TAPAC Report).
[3] See generally, TAPAC Report; Executive Order 13356 (September 1, 2004).

achieve this while respecting the rights of the data subjects[4] is a story about information management, knowledge discovery, and collaboration. This chapter captures the dimensions of the problem, identifies feasibility and privacy issues in the solutions discussed to date, introduces an information sharing architecture that solves many of the technical problems, and, lastly, invites a focused debate on the necessary safeguards to our civil liberties and policy issues.

Very few technical approaches exist that will actually perform at scale. This chapter proposes one solution that is asserted to both perform at scale and satisfy reasonable privacy and civil liberties expectations: anonymized semantic directories that are maintained dynamically using accumulation of context at ingestion.

Key attributes of this architecture include:

- Avoidance of a large central data warehouse
- Use of a central index with pointers
- Use of anonymized data for information correlation
- Use of audit logs

In this chapter, we will discuss this solution. We hope that this discussion will stimulate policy-makers so that we can collectively begin to frame, scope, and control such a system.

8.2. DIMENSIONS OF THE INFORMATION SHARING PROBLEM

Nothing is new about information sharing. It occurs today at unprecedented levels. Airlines share data with car rental companies; magazines share subscription data with marketers; data aggregators share public record information with prospective employers for pre-employment background checks. Sharing is commonplace. However, information sharing in the area of homeland security raises new issues (NRC, 2003).

This is a very difficult. In order to achieve this goal, many challenges must be addressed. These include:

- Most data and systems are outside the control of the discovery seekers—little, if anything, can be forced upon legacy structures and operations
- Budgets and time are finite—it is not an option to re-engineer every system from the ground up.
- Information flows must be tethered—changes in one system must appropriately replicate and be reconcilable.
- Systems must be accountable—lack of accountability is a security flaw and an invitation to abuse.
- Systems must be near real time—the best results cannot be achieved with only weekly or hourly updates.
- Scale matters—solutions that only work in the lab have no real-world relevance.
- Results must focus limited investigatory and/or analytic resources on reliable and actionable insights.

---

[4]"[D]ata subject" means an individual who is the subject of personal data.

- Because governments have extraordinary powers to deny one's civil liberties, accurate discovery is paramount.
- Most organizations do not want to share their information because this presents the risk of potential unintended disclosure.

Appropriately, most information systems work in their own unique ways to deliver on a specific mission. The health club management system provides accounting, management reports, and member access controls to the health club facility. The employee of the health club uses the system to find a member by membership number or name, but it is not necessary that he locate members by address. Similarly, employee records typically can be searched by employee ID, employee name, and/or social security number, but not by emergency-contact name. Why? If an employee suffers an on-the-job injury, one need only retrieve the employee's file to access the emergency contact number.

There are many dimensions to the problem of information sharing for knowledge discovery. The solutions proposed so far do not meet the challenges noted above.

8.3. EXISTING SOLUTIONS

So how should information sharing with privacy protection really work? Does every system with information publish its data to every other system? Or does every system simply publish its content to a central, mother-of-all-government-database? In either case, how will published information be kept accurate and current? If information is not centralized, can we expect every user to inquire upon every available system in search of discovery? And what if the user asks a question today that is not a smart question until next week? Can we expect a user to ask every smart question every day?

Since it is commonly understood that leveraging existing operational systems for knowledge discovery will not provide the necessary means to the end,[5] a natural tendency has been to consider the creation of one very large database containing all the data. This is an impractical solution from a technological point of view.[6] Simply put, there is insufficient computing power and storage space. And if that problem were remedied by technological advances, keeping the database current and reconciled with all of the contributing systems would prove equally daunting. Why? Every time a source system is replaced or upgraded, cascading effects are produced that invalidate the content of the large central data warehouse.

8.3.1. Blind Knowledge Exploration

Currently, some initiatives have addressed the problem of interacting with existing systems to find related data points by creating super-users with unprecedented access into countless systems[7] so that the user can blindly query systems for anything related to a piece of information of interest. Though such systems make more data available, this model resembles the popular but inefficient card game called "Go Fish." For example, an analyst might log to each system and ask, "Do you have any records on Khalid Al-Midhar?"

---

[5]See, generally, Creating a Trusted Information Sharing Network for Homeland Security. Second Report of the Markle Foundation (December 2003) (Second Markle Report).
[6]See generally Second Markle Report.
[7]See Second Markle Report.

This is an acceptable system, provided there are only a few such interfaces and only a few items to search for, but when there are many systems and many searches (and many individuals conducting searches) this approach does not scale. Analysts and investigators should not be expected to ask every smart question every moment of every day, which is the only way to have real-time awareness in the "Go Fish" model.

8.3.2. Federated Search

Some technologists have attempted to address the scalability problem with a technique known as "Federated Search."[8] One possible way of helping users search through countless information systems is to implement automated search tools that broadcast each user query automatically across the network to all available and relevant systems.

While this approach scales to a certain extent, as will be illustrated in a moment, there are serious limitations. Additionally, whether a user is using blind knowledge exploration or using a federated search tool, the information retrieved cannot be assured as accurate without substantial processing and latency. This type of search requires one to choose between "inaccurate but fast" or "accurate but slow." The accuracy dilemma is related to both false positives and false negatives. We will explore this issue in more detail.

As discussed earlier in this chapter, source systems may be designed to only permit searches by name, date of birth, or social security number but not phone number. Therefore, a phone number search will not return any matches—even when such records exist! In this case, the user has two choices and both are unsatisfactory: (1) Abort the search and find no records (prone to false negatives), or (2) search by common identifiers such as names and find all the records bearing matching names (prone to false positives). For example, imagine having to look through every record with name Mark Smith, even though the user was only seeking a certain Mark Smith who is known to have a certain phone number. In this case, the only practical thing to do is perform secondary triage using the federated search engine to filter out all records that do not have the same phone number. Of course this will have additional performance consequences.

8.3.3. Just-in-Time Context

To solve the elevated false positives and false negatives problem, some engineers contemplate algorithms to deliver "just-in-time" context.[9] This is the electronic analogue to the old adage: "The more you know, the more you know you don't know."

One way to solve this is to recursively query the network until no new data points are discovered. This approach does not scale.

The best way to explain the problem with this type of context construction is with a real-world story. An organization currently uses federated search to gather data from over 1000 disparate data sources and uses "just-in-time" context to deliver "correct" answers. Notwithstanding significant processing capacity, it takes up to eight minutes to develop each answer. This is unacceptable. Imagine being provided 40,000 names of people and

---

[8]See Second Markle Report.

[9]"Just-in-time" context is first introduced in this chapter and is used to describe the practice of assembling enterprise knowledge about a subject or object only at the moment the context is required. Such a method as will be illustrated is not practical in both computing cost and the elevation of false positives and negatives.

wanting to know what knowledge of them is in the network. Such a search would take over seven months.

Federated search with just-in-time context in environments with more than a few data sources performs very poorly in terms of accuracy as well. For example, consider an analyst who runs a basic name and date of birth (DOB) search. The federated search agent then broadcasts the name and DOB to 1000 disparate systems and awaits a response. Consider further that all systems provide answers within a fraction of a second. Suppose that five addresses, two phone numbers, and one social security number are returned as matching. We have just learned something about this individual. Just to be thorough, the just-in-time context algorithm takes this newly discovered information and fires off the federated search tool again.

It turns out that data were missed because a number of data sources have no DOB but do have addresses and phone numbers. So the federated search agent returns more findings, this time six name variations, two more new addresses, a driver's license and fishing license. Again, we have learned something about this individual. Just to be thorough, the federated search tool is run again and more information is discovered. The processing burden on operational systems of such recursive processes are often unacceptable.

8.3.4. Stored Queries

To address the problem of having to ask every smart question every day, others have tried to fix federated search by allowing the user to store a query. This approach permits the federated query system to re-process all of the prior, historical queries. While an improvement, stored query implementations do not scale well either. This is because it is expensive to repeat hundreds of thousands of queries over and over each and every day against hundreds or thousands of systems. An additional consequence is that such a technique degrades the operational systems being searched, causing other operational problems. One method for dealing with the scaling issue is to run the Stored Queries on a periodic (e.g., once a week) basis. Depending on the mission, even a one-day delay could cause important events to be missed.

The solutions being discussed today are deficient in a variety of respects. They are not scalable, they tax computing resources too heavily yet return results too slowly, and they are heavy on errors, increasing both false positives and false negatives.

8.4. INFORMATION SHARING WITH PRIVACY PROTECTIONS

What is really required to deliver on the information sharing goals can be summed up in just two words: "active awareness." When key data points are introduced or changed anywhere in a network, the data points should become known, be contextualized in relation to all data points previously known, be evaluated for possible disclosure, be published to appropriate subscribers, and be made available for efficient future discovery.

Knowledge discovery is then serving two related but distinct missions:

1. Did something just become known that someone or something needs to know about? If so, tell them.
2. Does any node in the network know anything about this subject matter? If so, who knows what?

There are two critical components needed to achieve information sharing for knowledge discovery and collaboration. We introduce these here as "find" and "fetch." In order to accomplish these, we also introduce "sensing." Users or systems must learn about the existence of another piece of data (the "find") and then determine the process and policy to "fetch" it. The challenge is finding relevant connections between disparate datasets in the first place ("sensing").

8.4.1. The Find

An information sharing solution must not require the re-engineering of every existing system. However, this raises the challenge about how information sharing can be accomplished to allow the user to answer an almost endless set of question from the network about specific queries. Most legacy systems are unable to effectively locate records for a particular search unless it just happens to be on one of the preconceived indexed fields (e.g., attempting to locate a phone number when their system has no phone number index). And even if they could, these systems are unlikely to have the extra processing capacity necessary to answer the mail.

8.4.2. Information Discovery Using Directories

For all these reasons, information sharing seems to necessitate that some information needs to be replicated and restructured. However, there are many open research questions. How much information must flow? What is the minimum amount of transfer? And what means are there to protect the sensitive data from unintended disclosure, misuse, and repurposing? Where would this data flow to?

A goal is to create a system that could access all the necessary data, There are several challenges that must be addressed. First, there is too much data to correlate and assemble. Second, searches across such vast amounts of data produce an explosion of false positives causing users to become overwhelmed with the "possibilities." Third, unassembled data prevent context, and this lack of context blinds one from seeing any relevance.

For example, are we dealing with three people, each entering the country with a visa once or are we dealing with one person who has entered the country three times? The challenge comes from the fact that different operational systems describe the same thing in different ways. Said another way, people, places, and things do not have globally unique serial numbers, which is arguably a good thing. Mark D. Smith at 123 Main Street might be in one system, while M. Dean Smith at PO Box 456 might exist in another system. If you cannot accurately count like things in the information sharing domain, the system will be useless and any large-scale information sharing and knowledge discovery system will break under its own weight. The scope of this problem is generally not fully appreciated, but is in fact one of the largest hurdles to overcome in delivering on the knowledge discovery vision.

8.4.3. Lessons from the Library—Introducing Directory Services

A directory service is like the card file at the Library of Congress. Nobody goes to the library and randomly roams the halls looking for a specific book expecting this to be efficient; rather, they go to the card file. The card file is cross-referenced and represents the current inventory and provides specific pointer information to the exact whereabouts of each inventory item. When new books are put on the shelf, index cards are placed in the card file. Cross-indexing is used for all of the essential search terms (e.g., cross-filed under author, title, subject, etc.). When a user finds a card in the card file, they use something like the Dewey Decimal number to locate the location of the original document. Similarly, a directory service operates like a card file, providing a reference as to which organization and system has the record, and under which reference number.

Let us explore the life and times of a record in this proposed model.

A record is introduced into a system somewhere in the network. After the system of record handles its routine processing and storage activities, the following new events occur:

1. Key data points of the new, changed, or deleted record are published to the semantic directory.
2. The semantic directory has a librarian function; it receives the submission and checks the directory of other like (same) records or related (similar) records.
3. The new record is saved in context.
4. The cross-reference index is updated based on the searchable key data points.
5. Relationships to existing records (not the same but similar) are noted and recorded.

Finally, if the librarian determines if anybody cares about the relevance of this new record, a message is published to each such subscriber.

8.4.4. Accumulating Context at Ingestion

A subtle but most significant aspect of this is the function of step 2. The system concludes that two or more items are the same (entity resolved) when the right combinations of entity attributes are observed based on the decision made by an expert rule system. For example, an expert rule might say that if the name is close and the address and driver's license number are the same, then the entities can be resolved. So to ensure that such resolution is accurate, the number of corroborating attributes must be set high. Said another way, the system is tuned to favor false negatives; that is false positives are really bad and, if not absolutely positive about the accuracy of the match, do not entity resolve the data points.

We will illustrate how this might be implemented manually in a library scenario. Imagine—if the library cards were about the exact same item (i.e., not just related), they would be rubber banded together. In this way, a future search finding any one card would find all enterprise-wide-related context. This means that one can search the directory for a phone number and find all records related to that number, even if some of the records were never described by phone number. For example, a credit card number search would not be able to find a record containing only name and address. However, when using entity-resolved data, it is now quite likely one can find all related records despite the impedance mismatch between the searched data points and the originating data. As more cards (records) are rubber-banded together (matched), we are in fact accumulating context or, put another way, growing understanding.

In a system tuned to favor false negatives over false positives (a smart thing to do technically, but really good news from a civil liberties perspective), future data may provide the insight to correct a previous false negative. This happens when a new data point grows (accumulates context) around an entity one already had on file. Sometimes the newly discovered data point (e.g., an AKA) enables the system to fix a prior inaccuracy. For scaling reasons, this activity of detecting and correcting previous errors must be dealt with at ingestion and must not be handled via a future batch maintenance activity. This entity resolution process produces an outcome such that more hay finds more needles more accurately.[10]

Without context at ingestion, more data makes for lower probability of discovery. In the past, this has been solved using data filters and minimization strategies, leaving much content on the cutting room floor. Using context at ingestion strategies, an otherwise seemingly neutral piece of data produces value by gluing together two otherwise seemingly unrelated records, which, in turn, lowers false negatives and positives. When the significance of this is fully appreciated, interests shift into what is important to collect and catalog.

8.4.5. Persistent Search

Now, let's return again to the issue of having to ask every smart question every day. How could this be more efficiently handled? In our approach, we allow the user to deposit a red card in the card file where they had looked in the past. This red card would contain the contact information of the user. Now, suppose further that as the system is updating the card file in real time (i.e., as new books are being added to the library) the librarian would notice the red card. Observing this red card, the librarian would know in real time who to tell about this new record. Thus, a directory service with persistent search capabilities provides an efficient means for users to be alerted to new relevant records in an accurate and scalable manner, without having to ask every smart question every day. This approach eliminates many of the scaling problems of the Go Fish and federated search models.

8.4.6. Data Anonymization

This architecture also benefits from the ability to accumulate context at ingestion to create a semantic directory of pointers where all of the data points are represented by only anonymized values. To illustrate this, imagine the librarian only receiving anonymized card files—that is, no distinguishable attributes related to persons, places, or things. The values received could be either encrypted (i.e., decryptable) or irreversible (e.g., one-way hashed[11]). The use of the directory would then be limited only to returning knowledge discovery pointers to systems or users. Holders of the source data would determine use rights, policy constraints, legal thresholds, and so on.

The challenge is how to accumulate context in real time on streaming data in a world where entity resolution requires fuzzy logic.[12] In our architecture, this problem has been

---

[10]This notion of context accumulation may in fact have a place in disambiguating other objects (e.g., imagery). Such a technique would theoretically be able to assemble a puzzle without knowing what the puzzle looks like *a priori* and without brute force.

[11]A one-way hash is also known as a "pre-image-resistant hash." In simplistic terms, this is the notion that one cannot turn a sausage into a pig even when provided the grinder. Examples of such algorithms include SHA-1 and MD-5.

[12]See, generally, James X. Dempsey and Jeff Jonas, Technologies That Can Protect Privacy as Information Is Shared to Combat Terrorism. Center for Democracy and Technology/The Heritage Foundation/ (May 26, 2004)(CDT/Heritage Report).

addressed using a one-way hash (also known as a "pre-image-resistant hash"). Examples of such algorithms include SHA-1 (FIPS, 1993) and MD-5 (Rivest, 1992).

As a cryptographic solution, implementation is everything. Thus it should be said that a cryptographic harness and specific deployment models must be used to prevent such basic attacks as dictionary attacks, statistical re-identification, traffic analysis attacks, and man-in-the-middle vulnerabilities. Techniques to harden anonymous semantic directory against cryptographic attack will be the subject of a coming paper.

It is envisioned with high certainty that Anonymous Semantic Directories will not only enhance knowledge discovery potentiality, but also address certain privacy concerns at a level more robust than is capable by today's existing information sharing models.[13]

8.5. INVITATION FOR DEBATE ON THE NECESSARY SAFEGUARDS AND POLICY ISSUES

What about the complex policy issues? Is it likely that every (or actually any) data holder will either publish all their data or provide unfettered access to their data? Information is power, so why would we expect a data holder to share without being compelled by subpoena or other legal instrument? And even if you could access all of the data, what restraints in U.S. law protect privacy by preventing the wholesale convergence of law enforcement and intelligence data with public records and private industry data? What prevents even a card-file system from being overused by authorities?

We believe that Anonymized Semantic Directories solve critical architecture and design challenges necessary to deliver on the information sharing for knowledge discovery and collaboration mission. But how do semantic directories square with responsible notions concerning privacy and civil liberties? What are the pluses and minuses?

A number of plus points are gained by this model. For example:

- Content is left at the edges of the system. Banking transactions, medical records, and communications traffic are not moved to a central database (only a limited number of data points for card file indexing).
- Following knowledge discovery, collaboration is governed by the actual original data holders.
- The system is specifically tuned to err in favor of false negatives over false positives.
- The system is designed for currency, accountability, and reconcilability.[14]
- Audit logs can record how the directory is used, enabling a more practical way to implement oversight than farming hundreds of disparate logs.

One existing privacy challenge posed by central directories is the increased risk of misuse, unintended disclosure, and/or re-purposing of the data. Additional research is needed to determine how a central directory that is essential to deliver an active awareness environment can also prevent these privacy breaches.

[13]See, generally, CDT/Heritage Report for discussion of privacy-enhancing attributes of anonymization; Stewart Baker et al., Anonymization, Data-Matching and Privacy: A Case Study, reprinted as Attachment B to the Testimony of Stewart Baker before the National Commission on Terrorist Attacks Upon the United States (December 8, 2003).
[14]Paul Rosenzweig and Jeff Jonas, Correcting False Positives: Redress and the Watch List Conundrum, The Heritage Foundation (June 17, 2005).

Finally, there are questions about the rules for accessing data the existence of which has been revealed by the directory. Research is needed to determine how the network should be capable of communicating the investigatory basis under which information is being sought, including transfer of a provable valid warrant or subpoena.

8.5.1. Policy Considerations

There are also many policy considerations. As with any transformational technology, the issue suddenly is not solely the technology but also policy issues surrounding appropriate implementation scenarios. What data can be shared in an anonymized form? What third party will control and manage the central directory? Will there be multiple central directories in response to availability requirements? How long is data retained? Who will oversee use? These policy issues must be addressed.

SUMMARY

Information sharing for knowledge discovery and collaboration is a technically challenging mission. Solutions du jour are demonstrably going to under-deliver in the areas of scalability, protections against false negatives, and reluctant willingness to share due to risk of unintended disclosure. Context accumulating strategies and anonymization open the door to transformational capabilities. Yet these new capabilities carry with them privacy and policy concerns. The debate should now be about the responsible use cases, implementation models, controls, and misuse protection mechanisms that are necessary to deliver knowledge discovery and collaboration in a privacy-enhancing manner.

REFERENCES

CRA (2003). Computing Research Association Conference on "Grand Research Challenges in Information Security and Assurance." http://www.cra.org/Activities/grand.challenges/security/.

FIPS (1993). Secure Hash Standard. United States of America, National Institute of Science and Technology, Federal Information Processing Standard (FIPS) 180-1.

National Research Council. (2003). Who Goes There? *Authentication Through the Lens of Privacy.* Washington, D.C: National Academies Press.

OECD (1980). OECD guidelines on the protection of privacy and transborder flows of personal data. http://www.oecd.org/home/

Rivest, R. (1992). The MD5 Message-Digest Algorithm. RFC 1321.

Chapter 9

Facilitating Information Sharing Across Intelligence Community Boundaries Using Knowledge Management and Semantic Web Technologies

Brian Kettler, Gary Edwards, and Mark Hoffman

9.1. INTRODUCTION

In the aftermath of 9/11 Mr. George Tenet, the *Director of Central Intelligence* (DCI), tasked each of the then 13 member organizations of the intelligence community to identify the 3 primary risk areas leading to potential intelligence failures. Of the 13 organizations, 12 included difficulties in collaboration—specifically, information sharing as a critical risk area. This was the single most frequently cited risk area as underscored below:

> In hindsight, it is becoming clear that the C.I.A., F.B.I. and other agencies had significant fragments of information that, under ideal circumstances, could have provided some warning if they had all been pieced together and shared rapidly.
>
> —New York Times, October 7, 2001

Information sharing has become the mantra of reform for the intelligence community, law enforcement, and counterintelligence agencies responsible for terrorist threat analysis and counter-terrorism. "Connecting the dots" and "finding the needles" require that analysts have access to the full range of relevant information and knowledge available. Every information source that is ingested, every analysis that is performed, and every dot that is connected across every agency may hold the key to interdicting a catastrophic event. Despite this need, and despite the deep commitment of involved agencies, barriers to this sharing still dominate.

Common wisdom ascribes the problem to bureaucracy and political turf wars. While such cultural issues can contribute, the underlying fact is simple: Implementing open information sharing with today's technology is very, very difficult. Any solution will require a complex recipe of technical capabilities such as search engines and retrieval tools, Web-based interoperability mechanisms, knowledge extraction and pattern detection algorithms, and so on.

Emergent Information Technologies and Enabling Policies for Counter-Terrorism. Edited by Popp and Yen

To meet enterprise-level information sharing needs, any practical framework will exhibit two critical requirements. First, such a framework must enable interoperability between organizations that can rapidly adapt to meet unanticipated demands and to exploit the best features of changing and emerging organizational knowledge assets. This implies that conventional, long-lead-time approaches depending on extensive co-engineering of data models and interface standards pose unacceptable barriers to the on-demand interoperability that is needed.

Second, such a framework must also maintain and enforce controls on the management of information and services. Assessments of access to services and the releaseability (and releasable form and detail) of information and knowledge products must be made. That automated assessment must be based on machine-understandable representations of the relevant policies and their application in the context at hand. These policies include regulatory constraints as well as organizational and personal sharing policies. For effective information sharing to take place, a "trust chain" must exist and be respected. The analyst must be confident in his understanding of the policies (both those that he "inherits" as well as those he himself levies) to govern the information sharing process. He must trust that the system will implement exactly those policies in its releaseability assessment. Also, he must trust that the recipient of the information will abide by the policies and constraints that are entailed in his acceptance and use of that information.

The right answers to both of these key requirements lies in infrastructure that exposes information, knowledge, and services in a form that is both human understandable *and* machine understandable. It is this machine understandability that enables an analyst's tools encountering a new source to tell what the source contains, map its content into a language the tool and analyst understands, and determine what pieces are likely relevant to the analyst. It is machine understandability of content, services requests, metadata, and policy that enables capabilities like metadata-derived releasability mechanisms to adapt policy-based information management. Techniques that exploit semantic representation and reasoning to achieve the benefits of machine understandability provide the enabling capability for future information sharing architectures.

In this chapter, we will discuss the current barriers to effective knowledge management; discuss desirable attributes of any functional architecture designed to overcome these barriers; examine some key technologies (and their challenges) that could help enable such an architecture; and then discuss some key services, built within that architecture that would help address the two key challenges described above.

9.2. BARRIERS TO EFFECTIVE KNOWLEDGE MANAGEMENT

In the real world, the legacy information resources of intelligence, counterintelligence, and law enforcement agencies are large, often distributed, and extremely complex. Developed independently to unique problem requirements, each typically forms an information stovepipe with unique representation standards and access protocols. New collection activities and methods, new knowledge extraction techniques, and new exploitation capabilities are creating new generations of stovepiped systems, at the same time that new threats and forensic problems are constantly increasing the scope of information and knowledge being developed. Individually, each agency faces an internal struggle to manage this information and knowledge. Faced with constant organizational growth, mission evolution, and technology change, these organizations undergo continuous evolution of their own knowledge management environments and purposes. Collectively, these issues amplify the barriers to

(1) physical access and interoperability (hampered by engineering issues, incompatible tools, security issues, regulatory issues, etc.) and (2) logical access and interoperability (hampered by differing representational formats, localized semantics, and the sheer scope of potentially relevant information). Within today's organizations, management and use of even existing stove-piped systems and processes are already an ongoing problem. Bridging organizational boundaries, where even less co-engineering of the information environment has been possible, has proven a truly daunting technical challenge.

Any solution to these problems must face some basic facts. First, change is inevitable and continuous and is often not easily or accurately forecast far into the future. Second, each organization's knowledge management environments will and must evolve independently to meet the changing mission requirements and growing data sources of that individual organization. And finally, information control policies are important real-world issues that are (a) critical to security, (b) critical to implementing privacy and regulatory standards, and (c) often overlooked or underestimated in system design.

In recognizing these real-world constraints, we expose the complexity of the community's collective information engineering problem. Simplistic approaches, often based on attempts at standardization of tools and content, offer little more than Band-Aids that will quickly obsolesce in the face of rapid change.

The answer lies in technologies that can let organizations gracefully expose their knowledge assets without simply opening the doors and that can expose them is a way that can be exploited in a managed way by the community. We need tools to let analysts look across organizations' information environments to discover these resources. These tools must let the analyst access and retrieve relevant information from the massive content available despite the fact that these are unfamiliar sources, while respecting necessary information controls and policies.

9.3. A FUNCTIONAL ARCHITECTURE FOR KNOWLEDGE MANAGEMENT

The on-demand ability to share information and knowledge across organizational boundaries can be described at the highest level by the architectural model of Figure 9.1. In general, the problem here is modeled as an organization whose enterprise architecture is hosting knowledge generation and capture processes, augmented by a tunnel through which an external client can reach into that enterprise architecture to find and usefully access content and services.

The key elements of such architectures include the following:

- Provider side:
  - The capabilities that generate knowledge assets hosted by the enterprise architecture
  - The means for the organization to selectively expose access to these resources as services to potential clients
  - Mechanisms for the products of these interactions to be retrieved or delivered to the client in useful form
- Client side:
  - The means for the client to discover and access content and capabilities via these exposed services

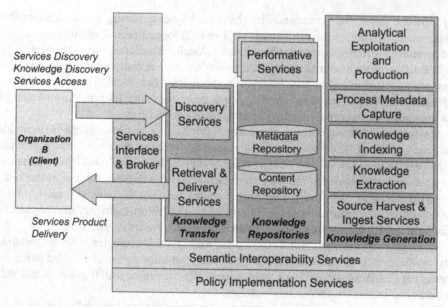

Figure 9.1. KM functional architecture for an enterprise.

- The means for the client to understand the quality and reliability of products and the level of trust in knowledge sources and services
- The means for the client to map delivered products into their work processes

Within the host organization's architecture, knowledge is being made available from multiple sources and in multiple forms. Data and documents may be harvested and ingested from various sources, and they may be used to feed the knowledge processes within the architecture. These will frequently involve more than simply archiving and warehousing this content. It will typically involve multiple layers of activity that extract knowledge from this content. Lower levels may perform direct extraction of knowledge: categorizing documents, extracting entity and relationship references, capturing state data, and so on. Higher-level processes may perform data analysis and fusion tasks, as well as multi-source fusion, and at higher levels they may perform information integration and analysis to produce more integrated knowledge products, feeding these back into the knowledge accretion process to support further analysis.

This architecture may also host performative services, capable of being tasked on demand to perform specific knowledge services, such as a particular integration or analysis activity. For example, a service to extract names, locations, and phone numbers in Arabic languages may provide a high-volume document processing service that reflects a significant investment in building extraction rules that work reliably. A similar but less automated example may simply provide a mechanism to pose a task or analytic question to a specialist within the organization.

9.3.1. Policy-Based Control

All of these capabilities are impacted by a set of overarching requirements. The first and foremost is the need to govern each stage in the sharing of knowledge. Invariably, the level of access to an organization's knowledge assets is a highly sensitized issue. Different client consumers and their permissions, the level of assurance of their identity, the specifics of the content or capabilities being accessed, and the certification of the purpose or need (and adherence to associated certification processes) all may impact what services are exposed, whether access is granted, what level of access is granted, and in what form knowledge is delivered (i.e., what resolution of data, level of information detail, or abstraction of content or metadata is delivered). Guaranteed enforcement of organizational policies, regulatory constraints, and other layers of policy are necessary, both to assure protection of the organization's information and to protect against the liability of improper information collection or disclosure. This issue is perhaps the largest barrier to mechanisms enabling knowledge sharing across organizations.

9.3.2. Information Assurance

A second collection of issues which span the functions of the knowledge sharing architecture fall into the general category of information assurance issues. Some of these issues are widely recognized and addressed by a range of off-the-shelf approaches and best practices in the community. These include authentication of clients, encryption of communications, and assured delivery of products. Other issues are more subtle and more difficult, but may be amenable to emerging techniques based on machine understandable service descriptions and knowledge representations.

9.3.2.1. Trust and Pedigree. Issues of trust and pedigree pose a second set of assurance issues. Pedigree in general refers to the documented history of an information product, or of the knowledge process that creates such a product. Typically, pedigree is represented as metadata associated with a knowledge product or service. More literally, we sometimes distinguish between (a) *pedigree* as describing the component elements, sources, and processes that generated the particular product and (b) *provenance* (as in the art world) as documenting the "chain of custody" of the product and its constituent pedigree elements. (Provenance plays a particularly critical role in establishing trust in a product: Is this document real? Did it really come from this source? Have these data been handled securely, or have they been exposed to corruption or disinformation?) Trust and reputation may be thought of as an analogue of pedigree, used to describe the reliability or performative history of a product or (more typically) a source, expert, or service supplier. In trust and pedigree areas, numerous organizations (both research and operational) are experimenting with practical mechanisms. It should be noted that while useful techniques are being developed and demonstrated, widely recognized best practices are really not yet beginning to emerge.

9.3.2.2. Metadata. In general, pedigree falls into the broad category of metadata that serves as the basis for exploitation and sharing by providing a knowledge-level description of a particular source, content element, or service. These descriptions are used to (a) discover resources and match them to needs, (b) sort and filter resources, and (c) adjudicate trust in those resources. This knowledge-level metadata may be captured automatically, such as capturing pedigree by tracking the processes of product generation and the contributing sources (both data sources and authors), or by tracking how a product has been handled and by whom. Other metadata may be descriptive, using varying degrees of automated or manual processes to characterize a product or service. At its extreme, these descriptions become abstractions of the actual content, made machine-understandable to enhance information discovery and exploitation. Annotative metadata may go beyond description, offering essentially new analysis or assessment of the product or service to support.

Metadata generation and exploitation is critical to providing machine-understandable knowledge about content and services, but there is a fundamental tradeoff in the cost of generating metadata and its utility in enabling effective knowledge management for sharing. High-fidelity metadata generation requires either manual processes (and thus is very expensive) or very advanced knowledge-based mechanisms (which are both expensive to build and limited in their scope of capability). Lower-fidelity metadata can be generated by process tracking and simple classification algorithms that can be largely automated to achieve low cost and high volumes of throughput. A fundamental design issue for these problems is the cost of metadata generation versus the adequacy of the resulting metadata knowledge in supporting (a) effective policy enforcement, (b) effective discovery of relevant knowledge by clients, and (c) mechanisms for trust and pedigree.

9.3.2.3. Consistency and Completeness.
A third area of concern for information assurance lies in the ability of the architecture to guarantee (or at least express some assessment of) both consistency and completeness. Consider a client who has discovered a particular element of knowledge related to her needs. To be confident in her use of this knowledge, she would like a clear answer to several questions. Have I found everything available relevant to my knowledge requirements? Is the knowledge I have found consistent or contradictory? And does knowledge exist that contradicts or refutes this belief? Incomplete, contradictory, and inconsistent information is a particular concern in intelligence domains where one's collection and analysis capabilities may be limited and one's adversary is engaged in denial and deception.

For example, retrieval using metadata might be incomplete. This can occur when a document, for example, is missing metadata or has incorrect metadata supplied by a user or automated tool. In the IC, although metadata are mandated, they are often incomplete or inconsistent. A document might be run through an automated classifier which specifies that the document is about Topic A when it really is about Topic B. Also the composition of services that produces knowledge might be incorrect, leading to an erroneous result (see Section 9.6.4).

In general, we have found that a useful property of a KM architecture is the separation of completeness of content representation from consistency resolution of this content. In other words, we typically desire to capture everything and let the client (user and her tools) determine how best to deal with contradictory or conflicting knowledge.

9.3.2.4. Downstream Assurance.
Finally, the area of information assurance will increasingly face the requirement to manage downstream assurance of information. Some of the capabilities being supported today involve tracking recipient clients, and if a piece of knowledge is changed, updated, or revoked, providing a client notification of the changed status. A category of emerging downstream knowledge management involves electronic watermarking of knowledge elements, guaranteeing that downstream consumers can distinguish valid vs. tampered copies. A more futuristic concern involves propagation of obligations. Obligations emerge when the act of accessing and accepting

delivery of a knowledge element poses entailments, such as required steps in a process or a notification policy. Techniques for tracking downstream obligations are a current knowledge management research topic.

9.3.3. Semantic Interoperability

A third general area of requirements for sharing of knowledge services lies in the general topic of resolution of semantics. While policy enforcement may pose the greatest barrier to an organization's acceptance of knowledge sharing services, bridging the semantic gap between clients and the service provider provides by far the biggest technical hurdle. Discovery of services poses the challenge of understanding what the advertised services of the provider mean, and whether they are relevant to the client. Accessing those services implies decoding the semantics of the services' interface and composing the right service requests. Once "inside" the provider's services environment, semantic matching is necessary at almost every query, navigation or search step, or performative action to match the knowledge search or navigation needs of the client and the representation of knowledge in the host.

Relevant knowledge discovered may require semantic translation to deliver a useful product to the client. The semantic dissonance between client and host must be assumed to enable sharing across organizations without extensive pre-engineering based on static information requirements, and it poses a substantial technical barrier. This barrier becomes more daunting when we realize that the semantics of both knowledge providers and consumers change constantly, and established semantic agreements will require technologies capable of maintaining semantic agreement as the semantics evolve.

The challenge of supporting machine-understandable semantic interoperability is a primary technical challenge that must be addressed to enable sharing, to enable trust and assurance mechanisms, and to enable policy enforcement in knowledge management processes. The application of these technologies will be the primary focus for the remainder of this chapter.

9.4. ENABLING TECHNOLOGIES AND CHALLENGES

Knowledge Management (KM) technologies can help address some of the key technical barriers to sharing knowledge across organizations. They support the generation, capture, discovery, sharing, transfer, and exploitation of an organization's explicit and tacit knowledge. The former exists as structured information codified in written form such as unstructured (text) documents or structured form in databases. The latter includes the mix of facts, knowhow, experience, and wisdom that typically exists in the minds of experts and that is difficult to elicit and codify. KM technologies range from repositories and networks for document management and dissemination (including intranets, extranets, and the Internet) to collaboration tools designed to bring together humans into communities of interest (and communities of practice) and facilitate their creation and exchange of knowledge. Document management systems and intranets support the generation and sharing of explicit information in documents and databases. Collaboration systems help with the sharing of tacit knowledge.

Thus most successful KM efforts thus far have focused the majority of their resources on nontechnical issues involved in getting humans to incorporate KM explicitly into their work processes. One KM expert states that if a project spends more than one-third of its time and budget on technology, it is really an IT project, not a KM project. Many KM efforts have failed due to the social, cultural, political, and organizational policy issues, rather than lack of viable IT tools.

For example, an individual's behavior such as knowledge hoarding (to preserve job security or prestige) can be detrimental to a KM effort. An organizational/cultural issue in the IC has been the "need to know" mindset which is beneficial in protecting sources and methods but can lead to overclassification and hence reduced information sharing. When Intelink, the IC's classified family of intranets, came into being over a decade ago, there was much resistance to publishing intel products accessible to anyone on the networks with a web browser.

However, we believe that many of these basic KM approaches have reached a point of diminishing returns. To go farther than locating experts and interest groups, and to enable cross-organization discovery of relevant information and capabilities, the scale and depth of knowledge management services must expand dramatically. This will require not just new IT capabilities, but new kinds of IT capabilities that rely on machine understanding to provide automation at the scale and with the adaptability needed.

9.4.1. Knowledge Sharing Processes

Assume two organizations wish to share knowledge and each has an enterprise (functional) architecture similar to that in Figure 9.1. The technologies that implement this architecture are discussed in the sections that follow. The Knowledge Generation steps for Organization A to make its knowledge assets available include the following:

1. Organization A collects and augments its content and metadata repository(ies) by harvesting, ingesting, integrating, extracting, and indexing information from sources. Organization A's knowledge workers add value by annotating and expanding this knowledge both manually and through the application of automated and human aided performative services.

2. Organization A puts the information into some explicit form such as a document (e.g., a MS Word document or a web page) or database. Alternatively, an online service (such as a web service) could generate the information on demand. Getting the knowledge into an explicit form may involve eliciting it from the mind of one or more humans. This might also involve validation processes by experts and supervisors to make sure the knowledge is correct, complete, and so on.

3. Organization A assigns (or extracts) metadata for the elicited, captured knowledge to make it easier to find and provide the basis for applying policies to control its distribution, and so on. This may be done by the author or a librarian completely manually or with the aid of automated tools such as a classifier. Services may also be associated with metadata for discovery purposes.

4. Organization A publishes the information (and metadata) in a generally accessible place such as on an extranet or the Web. Organization B must be able to physically access the network and service (i.e., they must be accessible online through any firewalls) and must be allowed to access the information by any applicable security policies (see Policy Interoperability below).

The knowledge transfer steps for Organization B to exploit Organization A's knowledge include:

1. Organization B must discover relevant knowledge. This can be done through manual search (e.g., via search engines) or automated discovery (e.g., via information retrieval software agents). Such search often involves metadata to locate knowledge of potential value. Machine understanding of the search request and the target content metadata enables more precise search and enables other relevant items to be associated with that search.

2. The information products must be retrieved and delivered from Organization A's systems. This may involve returning the results to a search engine query (e.g., a set of documents) or invoking Organization A's service.

3. Once someone in Organization B finds the information, they must make sense out of it. This could be done by a human using visualization tools, a spreadsheet, and so on. When this sensemaking is aided by visualization or analysis tools, translation into a target semantics is required. Software agents can make sense of information that is in machine-understandable form. To truly absorb and exploit the information found, it must be integrated within Organization B's existing knowledge in a form that Organization B's analytic tools and processes can exploit. Throughout this process, the pedigree of the transferred knowledge should be maintained.

9.4.2. Interoperability Challenges

A key technical barrier to knowledge sharing is the lack of interoperability. As Figure 9.2 shows, there are several layers of interoperability ranging from "lower-level" ones such as physical connectivity at the network level to higher-level, "logical" layers of interoperability. This section briefly describes these layers, which significantly impact the design of KM services such as those mentioned in the preceding section.

- **Network Interoperability.** The ability to connect information sources, processes, and knowledge workers within and across organizations. This includes network physical interconnectivity, common protocols, shared data formats (syntax), and so on. This chapter does not address this capability, which is still an active area of research for interconnection challenges involving mobile, wireless devices, for example. A detailed discussion of this is outside the scope of this chapter.

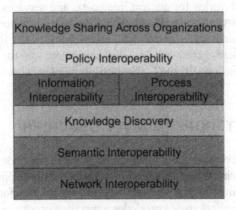

Figure 9.2. Layers of interoperability.

- **Semantic Interoperability.** The ability to represent information content and processes using shared terminology that has explicit semantics. This involves bridging any "semantic gap" that exists between knowledge from heterogeneous sources. Even for knowledge in the same syntactic format (e.g., an XML data file or WSDL service description), different vocabularies may exist. A term or tag in one source might have a different meaning in another. Different sources also use different terms for the same concept. Concepts may be at differing levels of granularity, and so on. This is discussed in more detail in Section 9.5.

- **Knowledge Discovery.** The ability for a person or machine to find relevant information sources, processes, and policies that should be shared. Even for knowledge that has been externalized from human minds, it can be a challenge to locate relevant knowledge across the vast amounts of knowledge distributed across different networks, machines, and data sources. This is discussed in more detail in Section 9.7.1.

- **Policy Interoperability.** The ability to encode policy in a machine-understandable and machine-enforceable manner, combining (potentially conflicting) policies on the fly from multiple organizations. Policies can be proscriptive (i.e., prohibiting or restricting some action) or prescriptive (i.e., prescribing some action should occur). They can be applied to information access, dissemination, and so on. This is discussed in more detail Section 9.8.

- **Information Interoperability.** The ability to integrate relevant information from multiple organizations, sources, and representations into a usable whole that can be processed as a whole. This includes combining data from heterogeneous sources such as databases with different schemas. This is discussed in more detail in Section 9.6.3.

- **Process Interoperability.** The ability to integrate relevant knowledge creation, manipulation, and management processes from multiple organizations into a new workflow that has cross-organizational boundaries. Because knowledge is often wedded to specific processes that generate and manipulate it, it often becomes necessary to combine previously separate workflows into a new workflow. This is discussed in more detail Section 9.6.4.

Achieving interoperability at these layers requires agreements between the parties involved. This can range from the use of common standards (e.g., networking protocols, XML) to shared vocabularies for content, metadata, and services. Agreement is easier when the number of parties involved is small and known in advance and the parties share common interests terminology—for example, establishing a B2B link between a company and its supplier. These agreements are often hard-wired into the IT systems involved. The harder challenge is "on demand" interoperability between two parties that have not interoperated before.

9.5. SEMANTIC INTEROPERABILITY SERVICES

As discussed in the previous section, semantic interoperability underlies many of the other interoperability requirements. This section describes some applicable technologies to the challenge of bridging the gap between diverse vocabularies for representing knowledge, metadata, and descriptions of knowledge generation processes and services. Semantic interoperability is a prerequisite to "on demand" interoperability in which two organizations wish to share information for the first time. Their IT systems and databases might not speak the same language or, worse, may use the same term in different ways. This requires tools that make meanings of data source schemas, service descriptions, and messages explicit and machine-understandable.

Because KM systems are designed primarily to promote knowledge generation, capture, and exchange among humans, their ability to promote information sharing across communities is somewhat limited. KM tools generally lack an understanding of the information they are handling. This means that the bulk of the work to elicit, encode, organize, filter, and digest information must still involve humans. Asking knowledge workers to take on this burden for their own community has had mixed results.

These challenges will only become exacerbated when the requirement to share knowledge across organizational boundaries is added to the knowledge worker's workload. With a better understanding of the content and context of the information they handle, KM tools can help reduce the burden on knowledge workers.

Semantic interoperability supports the machine integration of information from disparate sources. Applicable technologies include standardized knowledge representation languages and translation mechanisms. AI researchers have addressed the former for several decades. The combination of that work with web standards (such as XML) has resulted in more widespread adoption of these techniques. Translation mechanisms have also been the focus of the database community to bridge disparate schemas. Recent standards such as the Extensible Stylesheet Language Transformations (XSLT) have also addressed this for translating to and between XML schemas.

XML does provide a common format for structuring data and is frequently also used as a messaging format for integrating two applications, in addition to representing a collection of information in an XML document. XML has the advantage of extensibility and is really a meta-language for specifying domain-specific vocabularies (sets of tags and how they may be organized in a document or message). XML alone may be insufficient as an "lingua franca" for integrating information unless there is agreement on the precise meaning of the tag set used, and all of the software that processes the XML adheres to this *a priori* agreement. For example, when these applications process the XML element <price>$100</price>, they know, for example, that the tag <price> means retail price (versus wholesale price).

Because the bulk of this information is in human languages and often in unstructured form (e.g., reports), the use of natural language processing (NLP) technology is one approach to extracting machine-processable meaning from text. NLP can be very useful in some limited circumstances (e.g., processing semi-structured message traffic), searching for keywords, and so on. But, in general, understanding of text at any deep level requires not only parsing the contents of a document but doing so in the context of all of the commonsense and specialized knowledge humans bring to bear. Attempts to formalize commonsense knowledge (e.g., the Cycorp's Cyc project[1]) for machines have shown some promise, but general text understanding by machines is still a distant reality.

The Semantic Web is a vision of the World Wide Web in which machines can understand and exploit the vast array of content—including that in web pages and web-accessible databases and other services—created by many organizations and individuals. Machines will help humans publish, share, filter, organize, aggregate, track, and archive this information. The premise of the semantic web is that we can meet the machines

---

[1]http://www.cyc.com/

halfway in terms of requiring them to understand such information. With some semi-automated annotation of content (and metadata) using a machine-understandable language, machines will be able to better understand and process structured and unstructured information.[2]

The technologies behind this vision include next-generation languages that leverage work from Artificial Intelligence on knowledge representation to support the annotation—"mark up"—of web content and services. The World Wide Web Consortium's Web Ontology Language (OWL) is one such language.[3] OWL builds on the foundations of the Resource Description Framework (RDF) language and the Extensible Markup Language (XML). Semantic (web) markup is not just limited to adding metadata tags to documents. OWL uses ontologies—shared, formal conceptualizations of a domain of knowledge that provide explicit semantics and controlled vocabularies (of classes and properties)—to mark up the entities and relationships in a document's content, the content of a database, or the interface for a web service using classes and properties defined in one or more ontologies. A number of tools have been developed for manually and automatically doing markup in OWL using ontologies. These include manual annotation tools; text extraction and web scraping tools; automated classification tools; and tools that convert from structured representations such as XML and relational databases to OWL.[4] Additional tools exist to create, validate, and manage OWL ontologies.[5]

Once encoded, this knowledge can be exploited by machines (e.g., smarter search agents) and humans (e.g., using browsing and query tools). A number of research initiatives such as the DARPA Agent Markup Language (DAML) program and EU's OntoWeb have supported the development of semantic web languages and tools. Government and commercial applications have been developed, and an increasing number of commercial and open source products are being marketed to support this.[6]

The semantic web family of languages including OWL and RDF goes further than XML in making the meaning of tags more explicit and also machine-understandable through the use of ontologies with underlying formalisms (e.g., axiomatic semantics). OWL also supports the sharing and reuse of common ontologies by enabling the linking and extension of ontologies. For example, the Army and Navy might not agree entirely on what constitutes a military unit or weapon. A ship could be viewed as both a weapon system and a military unit (i.e., the members of the ship's crew). If a common ontology defines the concepts of military unit and weapon system as ontology classes with a few core properties, then each service is free to extend these classes as desired in service-specific ontologies. Because the extended classes derive from a common class, some interoperability is possible. To the extent that information producers can link their ontologies in this way, interoperability is promoted without having to have massive, mandatory, "one size fits all" vocabularies.

Semantic mapping technologies can be used to bridge different vocabularies. These include schema and ontology mapping tools for putting two data schemas in correspondence. These techniques are still mainly in the research stage with ontology mapping work building on previous techniques from database schema mapping and leveraging lexical and structural properties of ontologies, using statistical and heuristic matching func-

---

[2]http://www.w3.org/2001/sw/

[3]http://www.w3.org/TR/2004/REC-owl-features-20040210/

[4]For example, www.semwebcentral.org

[5]For example, Stanford's Protégé Ontology Editor (http://protege.stanford.edu/) and ISX's DIONE tools for ontology versioning (http://semanticobjectweb.isx.com).

[6]For example, http://semwebcentral.org, http://www.semanticweb.org

tions.[7] Some commercial ontology mapping tools are emerging.[8] Some ontology mapping tools claim accuracy in the 80–85% range, given some significant assumptions about similarity of the ontologies' domains, and so on. Translation is facilitated if ontologies have common ancestor ontologies, as described above.

Ontology mapping techniques are still largely heuristic (e.g., lexical matching, which is highly dependent on a knowledge engineer's choice of class/property names) and/or computational expensive [e.g., structural (graph) matching]. Investment is needed in hybrid approaches and the use of machine learning to improve mapping over time. Mappings will need to evolve as ontologies evolve. The representation of mappings (e.g., in OWL, etc.) so that they can be efficiently exploited and maintained is an issue.

In sum, the development of shared ontologies and mappings between ontologies is still human labor intensive and can require significant domain and knowledge engineering expertise. Many tools can assist this process but not replace the human in the loop. As ontology mapping technologies evolve, "on demand" interoperability will become increasingly possible in many cases. Shared syntax such as XML and languages supporting ontology reuse and extension (e.g., OWL) can facilitate this.

9.6. KNOWLEDGE GENERATION AND CAPTURE SERVICES

Knowledge generation and capture services (such as those shown in Figure 9.1) enable an organization to pull the information it needs from diverse sources, integrate that information as needed, and make the resulting knowledge available within the organization and to other organizations (via the Knowledge Transfer Services described in Section 9.7).

9.6.1. Source Ingest and Harvesting

Source ingest and harvesting services cull information from large datasets. Data may include raw intelligence such as (translated) message traffic or processed image data abstracted into features by image analysts. An organization typically pulls data from these sets selectively. Pulled data are stored in a content repository for the organization. The mapping between the source databases and the content repository's schema is often hard-coded and may involve the application of federated query/database mediator tools. Organizations may have standing queries or profiles set up to receive updated data from the sources.

9.6.2. Knowledge Extraction

Some source data may need to be processed to extract content, particularly if a structured content repository is used to integrate information from multiple sources. Text extraction tools (e.g., Lockheed's AeroSwarm or Inxight's SmartDiscovery) can be used to mine entities (specific individuals, organizations, countries, etc.) and relationships (facts) from

---

[7]For example, Stanford KSL's Chimaera tool (lexical matching, http://www.ksl.stanford.edu/software/chimaera/); Stanford's PROMPT tool (structural matching, http://protege.stanford.edu/plugins/prompt/prompt.html); Lockheed ATL's Ontrapro (matching using radical interpretation/translation protocol, http://www.atl.external.lmco.com/projects/ontology/), etc.

[8]For example, Network Inference's Cerebra tool (http://www.networkinference.com/Products/Index.html)

multiple documents.[9] Accuracy of these techniques is high for entities and improving for facts.[10] These tools often require a large amount of *a priori* configuration such as the definition of linguistic patterns or extraction rules or the training on documents.

9.6.3. Knowledge Integration and Indexing

Knowledge integration services support the merging of knowledge extracted from multiple sources into one or more content repositories for the organization. This information integration task may require semantic interoperability, as described in Section 9.5, because the sources may use different vocabularies, many of which will lack explicit semantics. Semantic interoperability techniques leverage shared or integrated formal vocabularies such as ontologies.

Knowledge pertaining to a particular entity—for exampke, information on the XYZ terrorist organization—should be integrated. Pulling such information together requires addressing challenges such as entity name aliases (e.g., XYZ might have other names) and handling reports of activities for which the organization is unknown but might potentially be XYZ. In the intelligence domain, an organization may be trying to conceal its identity or even pose as another organization.

Dealing with such uncertainty complicates this general challenge of "co-reference resolution." Linguistic techniques can help with entity name disambiguation, but more sophisticated (matching) techniques may be required to determine that two entities are the same based on the facts known about them at a given time. The semantic web vision includes the use of Uniform Resource Identifier (URIs) to uniquely identify entities. For example, IBM could be identified by the Uniform Resource Locator (URL—a kind of URI) for its website: http://www.ibm.com. For entities without websites, URIs might be assigned (i.e., similar to the way country codes are assigned in the IC). This is harder to do if the set of entities is open-ended: For example, terrorist events may be overlapping (at different levels of granularity) and have many associated names.

Knowledge indexing includes the organization of content using metadata. Metadata can range from administrative metadata (such as a document's title, name and organization of its author, etc.) to content metadata. The latter describes what the content is or what a document is about. This includes topic or subject keywords (or codes) but also more complex abstractions of a document's content such as a summary paragraph or the representation of key assertions in the document using a language such as OWL.

Metadata schemes use structured vocabularies ranging from HTML and XML tags to ontologies. IC metadata may include security classification and related markings to control the information's dissemination. Metadata such as timestamps specifying when a document was created or published and what time period the content of the document is about might improve the precision of that document's retrieval. For example, a recently published document might actually be about an event that occurred 20 years ago. Additional metadata such as subject or topic keywords might be added. A number of standard vocabularies exist for specifying metadata.[11] Despite the existence of this vocabularies, metadata is often omitted or used incorrectly.

---

[9]http://www.aerotext.com; http://www.inxight.com

[10]A recent study by Mark Maybury at MITRE cites entity, relation, and fact extraction accuracies as being 85-90%, 80%, and 60%, respectively. https://analysis.mitre.org///proceedings/Final_Papers_Files/272_Presentation_Slides.pdf

[11]For example, http://dublincore.org/ ; http://schemaweb.org

As mentioned in Section 9.3.2.2, there are a number of tradeoffs associated with meta-data such as the human effort involved, accuracy, expressivity, and usefulness in retrieving relevant information. Text extraction techniques (described in the previous section), automated categorization and classification tools, and form-based tools for manual meta-data annotation/tagging are all applicable to this task. Tools for taxonomy building and ontology authoring are also useful and range in degree of automation.[12]

9.6.4. Process Metadata Capture and Performative Services

The information integration techniques described above may not be sufficient to support the integration of knowledge from multiple sources and its augmentation by an organization. Because not all information resides in documents, process interoperability may be required to access applications and web services (including databases) to find information in harvested sources or from other organizations via Knowledge Transfer services described in Section 9.7. The process by which such information was generated initially may also be important to consider, particularly for information assurance purposes (see Section 9.3.2), and thus needs to be determined and made known (by process metadata capture and representation). To add value to information from sources, an organization may wish to apply performative services that transform knowledge through aggregation, automated analysis, etc. These services might thus need to be composed into (novel) work processes.

Process interoperability may also be required to exploit information found in documents, databases, or services. For example, consider a multi-agency task force being stood up to investigate a cache of documents obtained from a raid on a safe house for a terrorist organization. Participating IC and law enforcement agencies might have to integrate their knowledge management systems and processes rapidly to support the processing, analysis, and exploitation of the found documents.

Process interoperability is concerned with connecting machine-mediated processes together. These processes may be complex ones with intricate information workflows that involve multiple applications and users. They also may involve the use of web services that implement relatively discrete functions—for example, looking up the price of an item on an e-commerce site or finding the zip code for a street address. Combining workflows and services enables the creation of new services.

The connection and creation of services from components may require significant knowledge engineering work *a priori*. The ultimate goal is to support the rapid combination of services and content to support "on demand" interoperability. This requires resolving any semantic gaps at runtime between the pieces combined (see Section 9.5) and some assurance that the resulting composite service or system will produce a correct and consistent result (Section 9.3.2.3) within the criteria for information assurance that apply (Section 9.3.2).

In addition, two communities that wish to share information might want to connect up their existing IT applications and data sources. These existing components do not exist in a vacuum but rather are embedded in existing organizational processes and workflows. These interdependencies often must be taken into account. For example, in a real-world army situation, it was deemed important to connect up two systems for tracking the position of friendly forces. Each system was embedded originally in separate workflows that populated the underlying data sources the system used. When connected, these systems

[12]For example, Stanford's Protégé editor, entrieva's Semio products (www.entrieva.com)

exhibited incorrect behavior which, when gone undetected, may have led to losing track of friendly forces in the battlespace or even friendly fire incidents. These systems both used reference data that identified military units. It turned out that one system was using a much more recent and non-backwards compatible version of these data than the other. The disparity in versions caused units to be misidentified on the map display created from the information pulled from the integrated systems.

For example, consider a notional example of integrating just two route planning systems beyond the challenges of establishing network connectivity between the two potentially distributed systems. The following interoperability challenges might exist:

- Different inputs—origin and destination: coordinate schemes
- Different maps—from different GIS sources, of different scales, different versions of same map
- Different outputs—waypoints versus line segments; coordinate schemes; scale
- Different models and methodologies—route planning algorithms, doctrine/ROEs/ threat models/vehicle capability models (can't cross X, go near Y), and so on.

Resolving the above challenges presupposes that an integrator has access to detailed information on a system's data schema and processes—both the process the system embodies and the process in which it is embedded. This is a large assumption, because often this information—particularly its semantics—often only exists in the mind of original programmers. Where this documentation has been written down, it is often incomplete. For example, often the source code must be consulted to determine the (operational) semantics of an interface.

Process interoperability technologies include the following:

- Process representation/modeling formalisms and languages such as Petri nets, process algebras, and logic-based languages such as the NIST's Process Specification Language (PSL)[13]
- Tools to model existing and desired processes using these languages and formalisms. For example, there are numerous Petri net modeling tools.[14] This modeling is typically done by a programmer or knowledge engineer as it may require some reverse engineering from examination of components' code.
- Knowledge Discovery services to find relevant knowledge and services (discussed in detail below).
- Tools to compose processes discovered.

Representation and modeling formalisms include the Unified Modeling Language (UML) for object-oriented analysis/design, Entity–relationship (E–R) diagrams for database schemas, the Extensible Markup Language (XML) for data exchange, and so on. A number of mature, commercial tools exist such as IBM's Rational Rose for UML modeling, which can generate models from code and vice versa. For the representation of semantics, standard ontology languages are emerging such as the World Wide Web Consortium's (W3C's) Web Ontology Language (OWL), based upon the W3C's Resource Description Framework (RDF) language.

[13]http://www.mel.nist.gov/psl/
[14]For example, http://www.informatik.uni-hamburg.de/TGI/PetriNets/

For modeling the interfaces and interaction protocols between components or systems wrapped as web services, a number of languages exist. These include the W3C's Web Services Description Language (WSDL) for interface modeling, the Simple Object Access Protocol (SOAP) for communication, and Universal Description, Discovery, and Integration (UDDI) for capability description. These languages often lack explicit representation of semantics. The emerging Semantic Web Services Languages such as OWL-S address this need using ontologies (i.e., represented in OWL). A number of new languages exist for modeling the interaction of web services. These include the Business Process Execution Language for Web Services (BPEL4WS), the Web Services Choreography Interface (WSCI), and so on.

More general process modeling formalisms and languages include Petri nets, process algebras, and logics such as National Institute of Standards' Process Specification Language (PSL). Commercial workflow management tools use some of these formalisms, in addition to languages such as XML.

Most of the above modeling languages (and formalisms) have few tools that support automatic model generation. A number of tools exist for manually creating models in these languages and for automatically validating manually generated models. Many of these languages have been well-studied in terms of their properties such as expressivity and computability.

In addition to the dearth of tools for automatically generating models of systems, there is the issue of how to compose and reconcile models using heterogeneous languages—for example, combining a process model in PSL with one in OWL-S or Petri nets. This heterogeneity is desirable because different modeling languages and formalisms can model different aspects of a system and be used to compute different aspects of its behavior.

Tools to compose processes include "glueware"—components that are designed to connect other components. For example, connecting a route planner that requires street addresses for the route's origin and destination to a GIS system that provides map data given input in coordinates would require a translator that converted addresses to coordinates. The models of each component would be used to determine that a gap exists between the output of one component and the input of another.

For component assembly, AI planning technology could be leveraged to decompose a target workflow into its constituent tasks and assign components to tasks and subtasks. This has already been done for the automated composition of web services.[15] Other tools detect gaps between the assembled components.[16] Smart connectors could leverage agent-based technology that maintains an awareness of and adapts to a changing context. For the conversion or translation, simple technologies such Extensible Stylesheet Language Transformations (XSLT) can handle data conversions.

9.6.5. Repository Services

An organization typically hosts one or more repositories to hold knowledge that it has harvested and augmented through its own analysis. These range from data warehouses and data marts that unify (re-host) data from disparate original sources to knowledge bases described by ontologies. Repositories hold both content and metadata (which may

[15]For example, the University of Maryland's composition tool utilizing the SHOP2 planner (http://www.cs.umd.edu/projects/shop/)

[16]For example, the University of Maryland's MINDSWAP Composer (http://www.mindswap.org/~evren/composer/)

overlap) and include a number of APIs. Semantic web repositories—such as ISX's Semantic Indexing Engine—can be thought of as knowledge-rich indices (unlike book indices, which are typically just term hierarchies and associations) for an underlying information space of documents and other content.[17]

Many semantic web repositories leverage OWL ontologies, triple stores such as Sesame, and relational databases. Like relational databases, these repositories support structured queries that return facts. XML repositories, on the other hand, store content using the XML Document Object Model and support queries based on document structure. Text documents may be stored in document management systems, intranets and the Web, or even shared file systems. A comparison of these techniques is beyond the scope of the chapter. Suffice it to say, the choice of a repository can significantly impact the requirements and capabilities of the Knowledge Transfer services described in the next section. Repositories may require some amount of engineering to define schemas (or ontologies).

9.7. KNOWLEDGE TRANSFER SERVICES

Knowledge transfer services support a client—for example, an analyst from another organization or a proxy software agent on her behalf—finding relevant knowledge within her organization and from other organizations. This knowledge was created by the services described above. Knowledge transfer also includes the ability of an analyst or software agent to understand and exploit the knowledge found.

9.7.1. Discovery

This capability includes the finding of information and services across organizational boundaries. This includes the search and discovery of information by humans and machines. It also includes service discovery by machines for invocation or composition (as described in Section 9.6.4).

On the Web, discovery is primarily through search engines and other tools for information pull. Search engines often provide too little or too much information, requiring manual reading of documents in the results list or manual refinement of the search query. Queries may include metadata specifications and constraints. Web search engines are beginning to make increased use of metadata for retrieval and result ranking (e.g., Google's page rank system). Facet search engines can search on metadata (such as an item's price) and group results accordingly.[18] They also help avoid dead-end searches. Online human-readable directories—such as Yahoo.com and the Open Directory Project—often complement search engines when a specific search target or metadata category is vague.

Information push tools may be used to register standing queries through a subscription mechanism. If the published information is in a (online) database, document management system, or service, discovery is complicated. Web crawlers that populate search engines such as Google™ often cannot access this information in the so-called "dark Web". Access requires finding the service and accessing information through some user or application interface. Users are often required to specify queries in the terminology of the specific service. The contents and interfaces for web services can be published using languages such as Web Services Description Language (WSDL). To invoke a web service or to

---

[17]http://semanticobjectweb.isx.com
[18]For example, Endeca's ProFind tool: http://endeca.com/

compose web services together on the fly to answer a query presents additional challenges (see Information Interoperability and Process Interoperability in Section 9.4.2).

For service discovery, there are registries (e.g., directories in UDDI or OWL-S) for services and agent-based matchmaking and brokering technology to match a required capability to a component/service.[19] Currently lookup and discovery is done largely based on a few simple service attributes (e.g., keyword lookup), but more sophisticated matching techniques that take into account additional constraints and handle "near matches" have begun to emerge. Finding "near matches" can involve using an ontology of service attribute values and schemes for automatic query relaxation. Discovery is facilitated by shared service taxonomies and ontologies such as the United Nation's Standard Products and Services Codes (UNSPSC) and the OWL Services Ontology (OWL-S), respectively.[20] These taxonomies and ontologies may require significant knowledge engineering effort to create but have high potential for reuse.

9.7.2. Retrieval and Delivery

This may just involve reading the document or viewing a web page containing the results from a web-based database query or the output of a web service. If that person is using an automated tool, then it must interpret the information in whatever form and language the information is in, resolve any semantic gaps (see Section 9.3.3)m, and then do something useful with it such as integrate it with other information or into an existing work process (see Section 9.6.4). For a user, this is facilitated by visualization, browsing, and other navigation tools. For a software agent, this is facilitated by machine-understandable representations of the knowledge such as used by semantic web tools (see Section 9.3.3). Knowledge transfer tools should support downstream assurance (see Section 9.3.2.4).

9.8. POLICY IMPLEMENTATION SERVICES

One of the most formidable of these barriers to interoperability involves the formal policies and regulations involved in information sharing across the intelligence community. A number of legal and regulatory issues, laws, executive orders, and so on, come into play when considering the sharing of information across intelligence agencies. Recent legislation has made sharing in certain situations where national security is at stake feasible. However, the application of this legislation is ill-specified, context dependent, and complex in practice.

Because of these complexities, assessing the shareability of intelligence information continues to be beyond the normal level of responsibility that an analyst is willing to assume. Legal professionals must become involved to assess releasability of many types of information between various collaboration partners. This retards the collaboration process and, worse yet, often serves as an excuse for continued parochial attitudes and practices. If effective knowledge management across the intelligence community is to be achieved, a dynamic and manageable method for specifying, combining, and implementing these policies must be embedded in the sharing process.

We take a broad view of policy as serving ultimately to discouraging or prohibiting some behaviors (e.g., unauthorized access to information) and encouraging or mandating

---

[19]For example, CMU's RETSINA matchmakers: http://www-2.cs.cmu.edu/~softagents/
[20]For example, http://www.unspsc.com/; http://www.daml.org/services/owl-s/

others (e.g., the inclusion of metadata, digital watermark, etc., in a document posted on the Web). Policy can enforce rules such as access control or regulatory requirements. Policy impacts information assurance areas described in Section 9.3.2. Metadata (Section 9.3.2.2) and pedigree (Section 9.3.2.1) can support the application of policy. The combination of policies may require semantic interoperability mechanisms (Section 9.5).

Current forms of "access control" based on individual or role-based permissions utilizing artifacts such as "certificates" and "keys" of various types, while good for classification/compartment filtering in general, tend to be too monolithic and static in nature to satisfy these broader requirements. The context of the situation must be included in releaseability considerations.

The representation and implementation of policies suffers from some of the same issues as those already discussed related to the meaningful sharing of information content. The "policy language" must be expressive, extensible, and flexible. Several policy representation languages have been developed and are being refined within various applications today. Many of these languages are based on formal logic. Some of these languages are based on OWL. Languages such as Ponder, KAoS, and Rei are examples that provide flexible expressivity based on deontic logic to capture concepts such as "allow," "forbid," and "obligate."[21] This expressivity is required to adequately capture the nuances of today's regulatory policies.

Beyond the requirements of expressivity and flexibility, the policies of tomorrow may differ significantly from those of today—and in ways that we cannot completely predict. In essence, again we face the need for an adaptive and modular policy architecture where the cellular elements of that architecture (locally controlled and managed) may interact with each other over time without the need for extensive enterprise-wide co-engineering, coordination, and synchronization of those policies. For collaborative information sharing to succeed, not only must (1) the information be recognized, (2) the collaboration partners for sharing be identified, (3) the releaseability of the information be assessed, (4) the desire to share that information be established, and (5) the mechanism for sharing be utilized, but there is also the issue of trust.

Once information has been shared, a trust relationship then exists between the collaboration partners such that (1) the party sharing the information has provided all relevant pedigree and vetting metadata related to that piece of information, and (2) the party receiving the information will act in accordance with the guidelines/standards established regarding the use and/or further propagation of that information. Establishing and maintaining that trust relationship is critical to that collaboration process.

The policy language used to capture the nuances of information sharing must fully address these aspects as well or a trust relationship cannot be maintained. Utilizing these emerging languages for policy expression and reasoning coupled with the same OWL-based semantic grounding of the policy structures and primitives, we can envision a flexible and extensible policy framework that could provide the range of capabilities needed to achieve enterprise-wide knowledge management in the intelligence community.

SUMMARY

As we have discussed, the two primary classes of stumbling blocks to effective information sharing across the intelligence community are (1) the technical difficulties in-

---

[21]http://www.doc.ic.ac.uk/~mss/Papers/Ponder-summary.pdf;   http://www.ihmc.us/research/projects/KAoS/; http://rei.umbc.edu/

volved in identifying relevant candidate information for sharing given the disparate and evolving infrastructures across the Intelligence Community and (2) even if we could find the relevant information for sharing, being able to manage that sharing process in order to correctly assess releasability of information and provide a "trust chain" across the community.

While achieving integration across the enterprise described in class 1 above could be achieved using a brute-force approach, we have argued that that sort of heavy weight strongly co-engineered methodology makes it unworkable given real-world dynamics and evolution of information technology infrastructures. However, we have discussed several techniques leveraging emerging semantic technologies as a means to characterize processes, products, and information within an environment that will enable the "understanding" of each of those constituent components. Once these elements are "understood," the semantic reasoning techniques discussed can be applied to manage the integration, search, retrieval, and sharing across the environment—even as these elements evolve over time.

The second class of stumbling blocks involves the assessment of information releaseability and management of the sharing process to enable and maintain a trust chain across the enterprise. That trust chain starts with the confidence by those members in the enterprise that all necessary policies (both those that they "inherit" as well as those they themselves might levy) are accurately characterized and utilized. Those policies must be both machine and human understandable in order to foster human trust and enable machine reasoning. The analyst must trust that the system will accurately implement exactly those policies in its releaseability assessment. And, the analyst must trust that the recipient of the information will abide and/or be made to abide by the policies and constraints that are entailed in their acceptance and use of that information.

In this chapter, we proposed a functional architecture designed to overcome these stumbling blocks by supporting a semantically integrated and coupled environment that would require only a modest level of co-engineered integration and would be flexible and adaptable to dynamic changes in system architectures, users, processes, and data. We have also discussed the use of evolving policy languages and potential services built upon those languages and reasoning engines that could enable the necessary trust relationships to enforce the correct and effective use of information that is shared. Many of the supporting technologies needed to realize this vision remain active areas of research, however, the fulfillment of the architecture described can be fully envisioned and, once envisioned, fulfillment becomes more a matter of serious engineering and cultural acceptance than relying on new basic research.

ACKNOWLEDGMENTS

ISX Corporation remains a groundbreaking participant in many of these fields and a vital partner in these communities. We would like to acknowledge the support of DARPA (the Defense Advanced Research Projects Agency), AFRL (the Air Force Research Laboratory), ARDA (the Advanced Research and Development Activity), and several members of the Intelligence Community for their continued support in many of the areas discussed in the chapter.

Chapter 10

Applying Semantic Web Reasoning to Counter-Terrorism

Paul Kogut, Yui Leung, Kathleen M. Ryan, Linda Gohari,
Mieczyslaw M. Kotar, and Jerzy J. Letkowski

10.1. INTRODUCTION

The Semantic Web provides a foundation for automated reasoning with distributed knowledge. Chapter 6 by Golbeck et al. introduced Semantic Web technology and described terrorism ontologies. Chapter 9 by Kettler et al. introduced a wide variety of tools for applying Semantic Web technology. This chapter focuses on automated reasoning that is enabled by the formal semantics of OWL ontologies. The generation of OWL markup from text via natural language processing (NLP) technology facilitates the creation of large quantities of instance data to feed a reasoner. The approach covered in this chapter complements the approaches described in Chapters 6 and 9.

Analysts are swamped by an ever-increasing volume of various types of collected data, such as intelligence reports, annotated imagery, telephone intercepts and open source data, such as websites and broadcast news (Waltz, 2003). The analyst needs automated tools to help her figure out what to look at first (i.e., filter and prioritize incoming messages). The analyst also needs automated support for evidence marshaling (i.e., putting knowledge together to formulate and support hypotheses). Humans simply cannot be expected to remember large quantities of evidence. The analyst cycles back and forth between filtering (foraging) and marshaling (sensemaking) (Bodnar, 2005). Both filtering and marshaling are facilitated by Semantic Web reasoning. We do not claim that the analyst will be replaced by a computer anytime in the foreseeable future. We do claim that Semantic Web reasoning can automate routine screening and retrieval tasks and will eventually be able to make useful suggestions to the analyst.

The reasoning described in this chapter is mainly description logic subsumption reasoning which means it uses taxonomic relations. The design of OWL was heavily influenced by years of research in description logic reasoning (Baader et al., 2002). Description logic researchers studied the tradeoffs between the expressiveness of knowledge representation languages and computational tractability. Illustrative real-world examples of this type of reasoning can be found in the Lehigh University benchmark (Guo et al., 2004). For example, a query such as *give me all persons who are members of the computer science department at MIT* would cause the reasoner to apply subClassOf relations for *person* and subPropertyOf relations for *memberOf* (e.g., *worksFor*) to make inferences that generate the query response. OWL reasoners also make inferences with other relations such as *transitive, inverseOf,* and cardinality constraints (e.g., *person has only one social security number*). In this chapter, "Semantic Web reasoning" or "OWL reasoning" means that the automated reasoner adheres to the formally defined semantics of OWL (Patel-Schneider et al., 2004). This semantic standard supports reasoning with knowledge from heterogeneous markup generators (manual or automated). The work reported in this chapter was based on a homogeneous markup generator; however, it should work with heterogeneous generators as long as the semantic standard is followed. More powerful reasoning support has recently become feasible with the emergence of the Semantic Web Rule Language (SWRL) (Horrocks et al., 2004) and SWRL first-order logic (SWRL FOL) (Patel-Schneider, 2004).

10.2. AUTOMATED MARKUP GENERATION FROM FREE TEXT

In this chapter we focus on reasoning with text sources such as reports, messages, web pages, and imagery annotations. OWL-based reasoning and fusion of physical sensor data is discussed in Kogut and Heflin (2003) and in Matheus et al. (2003). Text sources must first be converted into markup. The markup process involves linking words in a document to classes and properties in an ontology, thus creating instances (e.g., *Mohammed Zakin is a terrorist person*). Markup can be done manually with drag and drop tools such as OntoMat.[1] Manual markup is tedious and not practical for large volumes of documents. So researchers investigated the application of NLP technologies such as information extraction (IE) to automate the markup process. Early applications of IE for automated markup generation were described in Kogut and Holmes (2001). The *Aero*Text™ *Semantic Web Automated Relation Markup* (AeroSWARM) tool is a good example of current capabilities. AeroSWARM automatically generates OWL markup from web pages for a number of common domain-independent classes and properties.

The basic idea of the IE approach in AeroSWARM is to use linguistic patterns to extract entities and relations in the text. Entities such as *people, places, organizations,* and *artifacts* map to instances in OWL markup. Relations such as *parent of, employed by,* and *purchased* map to object properties in OWL markup. Relations such as *weight* and *age* map to data properties in OWL markup. The linguistic patterns are created and customized by engineers. Entity extraction with patterns customized to a particular domain (e.g., counter-terrorism, weapons of mass destruction) can achieve precision and recall of around 90%. Relation extraction for specific domains has precision and recall of about 80%. Recall and precision degrade in more complex multidomain texts like newspapers or informal communications like e-mail. There is often semi-structured text like resumes and dynamically generated data on the web that also pose a significant challenge to IE techniques (Ciravegna and Chapman, 2005).

The output of this process can be posted as OWL markup on the web or an intranet. For some applications it may be appropriate to store results in a database or an RDF triple store. Commercial products like Cerebra's Product Suite support the mapping of ontologies to database schema which permits reasoning over instance data stored in database tables.[2]

The KIM project uses an approach similar to AeroSWARM to generate markup from

---

[1]OntoMat http://annotation.semanticweb.org/ontomat/index.html
[2]Cerebra http://www.cerebra.com

about 500 to 2000 news stories per day (Kiryakov et al., 2005). IBM's SemTag system has marked up millions of web pages using corpus statistical techniques, but the markup is limited to entities (not relations) (Dill et al., 2003). The METS system uses multiple IE tools to increase precision and recall (Lee, 2005). Researchers are investigating machine learning techniques to reduce the effort to acquire IE linguistic patterns (Ciravegna and Chapman, 2005).

The next three sections describe various Semantic Web reasoning applications relevant to analysts which leverage the automated markup generation capabilities explained above.

10.3. SEMANTIC FILTERING

Analysts spend a large percentage of their time searching for relevant facts in documents, so various forms of information retrieval technology are critical. Current information retrieval engines such as Google and standing query mechanisms do not leverage semantic knowledge. They depend on lists of keywords that must be entered by the analyst. These lists may be long, complex, and difficult to maintain. What we really want is to define a concise semantic query and let reasoning do some of the work. For example, you could say "give me all messages related to a specific terrorist cell." So even if the message did not mention the name of the cell, the reasoner could infer from a distributed dynamically updated knowledge-base that a member of the cell was mentioned in the message and therefore it is relevant. This avoids queries with long lists of names and terms.

Another problem with keyword search is that it returns documents that may have the wrong meaning/sense of the word (e.g., White House the *building* rather than White House the *organization*). This is especially important in the real world of open source intelligence. Also they may return chance co-occurrences of keywords rather than relevant explicit relations. For example, the document may mention an aircraft made by Lockheed and someone named Al Smith, however, what you really want is information about Al Smith the vice president of Lockheed Martin.

A similar problem is found with channel subscription mechanisms such as RDF Site Summary (RSS). The problem is that these channels are too broad, resulting in an overload of information. Semantic filtering approaches could be used to define finer-grained channels where more messages are relevant to the analyst.

In this section we will describe a semantic filtering prototype called GOWLgle. GOWLgle uses keywords chosen from an ontology to semantically filter the list of documents returned by Google. The goal was to improve information retrieval precision by eliminating documents that Google found by chance co-occurrence of keywords. Figure 10.1 shows the GOWLgle architecture.

The analyst enters entity names and selects the corresponding OWL classes from a menu that was generated from an ontology to specify OWL instances. The analyst also chooses the appropriate property from the ontology to specify the desired relation. AeroSWARM generates OWL markup of the N best Google results (N is specified by the analyst). The agent filters out web pages that do not match the semantic query. The markup must contain the appropriate instance–property–instance assertion or else there is no match. Figure 10.2 shows the query at the top and the list of documents that were semantically relevant. The query (at the top) says find documents where the person *Al Smith* is in a *hasEmployrole* relation with an organization called *Lockheed* in the top 30 docu-

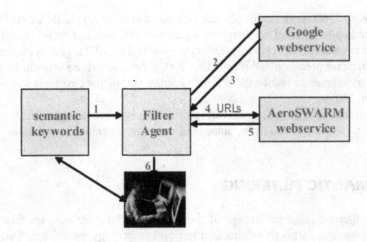

Figure 10.1. GOWLgle architecture.

http://ubot.lockheedmartin.com/ubot/hotdaml/gswarm.html

Argument 1	Predicate	Argument 2
Al Smith	hasEmployRole	Lockheed
Person	30	Organization

Submit   RESET

Found Articles:

Spaceflight Now | Breaking News | Lockheed proposal for next ...
... an NPOESS system which delivers the required environmental data to the user communities," said Al Smith, executive vice president of Lockheed Martin Space ...
http://spaceflightnow.com/news/n0203/21npoess/-19k

News
... to show students an insider view of the stimulating work that the space business affords, said Al Smith, executive vice president of Lockheed Martin Space ...
http://news.spacefoundation.org/index.cfm?releaseid=000CFE6C-8939-1EEF-B4DAA24BD83A365F-17k

VPNAVY - VP-8 Alumni Association Page
... Keith Sharer and Al Smith dubbed the P2V a product of 'The Lockheed Novelty Company.' Ironically, after his Navy retirement, Al worked for Lockheed for many ...
http://www.vpnavy.com/vp8_3.html-29k

Preparing for 'Network-Centric' Warfare (washingtonpost.com)
... President Bush announced in May that he planned to nominate Al Smith, chief of Lockheed Martin Space Systems, for the service's No. 2 post. ...
http://www.washingtonpost.com/wp-dyn/articles/A741-2001Aug26.html-

US Aerospace Prowess Hinges on New Projects, New Hires
... Al Smith, executive vice president of Lockheed Martin Space Systems, said that when it comes the US military might, technology is every bit as important as the ...
http://www.space.com/news/nss_aerospace_030408.html-36k

Lockheed Martin Corp. To Keep Commercial Space Systems Business
... Al Smith, executive vice president of Lockheed Martin Space Systems reaffirmed the company's dedication to mission success: "Our commercial space team ...
http://www.satnews.com/stories2/3jan2003-2.html-7k

Lockheed Martin Unveils Advanced Air-Space Integration Lab
... increasing requirements for horizontally integrated, network- centric solutions," said Al Smith, Executive Vice President, Lockheed Martin Integrated Systems ...
http://www.forrelease.com/D20030929/dcm005.P1.09262003193023.10057.html-6k

National Space Symposium Next Week
... and commander, Air Force Space Command; Jim Albaugh, president of Boeing Space and Communications; Al Smith, Executive Vice President, Lockheed Martin Space ...
http://www.hispanicnews.com/archive/2001/April06/05.htm-13k

Figure 10.2. GOWLgle filtered results.

ments returned by Google from a query *Al Smith Lockheed*. This may involve reasoning about property hierarchies. For example, if the query includes the *employee of* property, the agent will search for subproperties such as *vice president of*. GOWLgle currently uses the Jena inference engine.[3] Figure 10.3 shows results of the same query that were found not to be semantically relevant. Preliminary results show that the current GOWLgle has high precision (most of the found pages are relevant) but low recall (it improperly rejects a significant number of relevant pages). This low recall problem can be reduced by customizing the linguistic patterns used by AeroSWARM for a particular domain. The GOWLgle approach illustrates semantic filtering that can be applied by analysts for searching open source or classified document repositories.

Researchers have used Semantic Web techniques to augment the results of Google searches (Guha et al., 2003). The Swoogle system was developed for Google-like searches of OWL ontologies and markup that is posted on the web (Ding et al., 2004). The Xinfosphere system does semantic filtering based on reasoning similar to GOWLgle, but it focuses on military messages rather than Google result web pages (Uschold et al., 2004; Uschold, 2005). The KIM system is probably the most similar system to GOWLgle, although it uses it own information retrieval system instead of Google (Kiryakov et al., 2005).

[3]Jena http://jena.sourceforge.net/

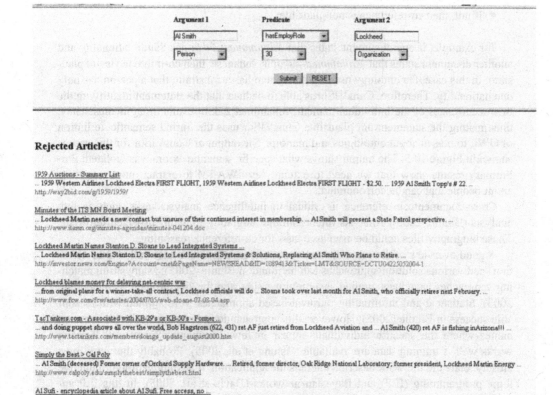

Figure 10.3. GOWLgle filtered-out results.

10.4. CO-REFERENCE REASONING

Another challenge with reasoning with large collections of documents (e.g., open source intelligence) is determining the plausibility of cross document co-reference (e.g., person X in document A is the same as person Y in document B). Linguistic clues can be exploited for intra-document co-reference but not for cross-document co-reference. AeroSWARM can determine co-reference within a document using linguistic patterns. For example, within the same document it is likely that *Dr. Robert Jones* in the first sentence and *Jones* in the second sentence is the same person. For cross-document co-reference the system must use other types of clues. Both kinds of co-reference can be expressed directly in OWL with the *sameAs* language construct.

Our approach was to apply OWL reasoning to determine cross-document co-reference by searching for corroborating assertions. Figure 10.4 shows an experimental prototype architecture for cross-document co-reference. The prototype was based on a similar approach for level 2 fusion in a battlefield domain (Kokar et al., 2004). A set of web pages that mention a person with apparently the same name (i.e., string match) are sent to the OWL markup generator. The agent adds an OWL assertion that person X *sameAs* person Y. The aggregated markup is sent to ConsVISor,[4] an OWL consistency checker (Baclawski et al., 2002). ConsVISor applies logical reasoning to check if all assertions about these persons in the set of documents and constraints in the ontology are consistent.

- If they are consistent, then co-reference is plausible.
- If not, then co-reference is not plausible.

For example, if one document states that *Mohammed Zakin* has Saudi nationality and another document states that *Mohammed Zakin* is Sudanese, then co-reference is not plausible. In this case, the ontology used by the system has a constraint that a person has only one nationality. Therefore, ConsVISor is able to deduce that the statement identifying the two occurrences of the individual named Mohammed Zakin results in an inconsistency, thus making the statement not plausible. ConsVISor uses the formal semantic definition of OWL to reason about ontologies and markup. The output of ConsVISor for this case is shown in Figure 10.5. The output shows what specific semantic axiom was violated. Preliminary results show that we need to extend AeroSWARM to extract more assertions about people that can be corroborated.

Cross-document co-reference is critical to intelligence analysis tasks such as link analysis (Blume, 2005). Analysts often compile biography files on suspected terrorists. These biography files could be used as a basis for co-reference reasoning.

A good overview of the cross-document co-reference problem (also called alias detection) and various solution approaches can be found in Blume (2005). Many string matching approaches have been applied as a preprocessing step for this problem (Cohen et al., 2003). Statistical and information retrieval-based approaches were applied with reasonable success in Blume (2005). However, this approach does not work well with common names where the specific individuals appear in few documents. Supervised learning works well if training data are available (Hsiung et al., 2005). Probably the work most closely related to the work described here is the application of a combination of inductive logic programming (ILP) and Bayesian networks (Davis et al., 2005). In this ILP approach the researchers learn rules and then reason with them. In our approach the rules are

---

[4]ConsVISor http://vistology.com/consvisor

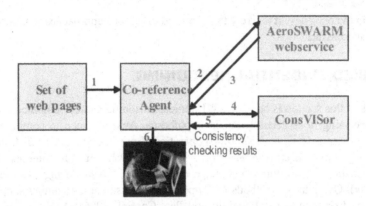

Figure 10.4. Cross-document co-reference.

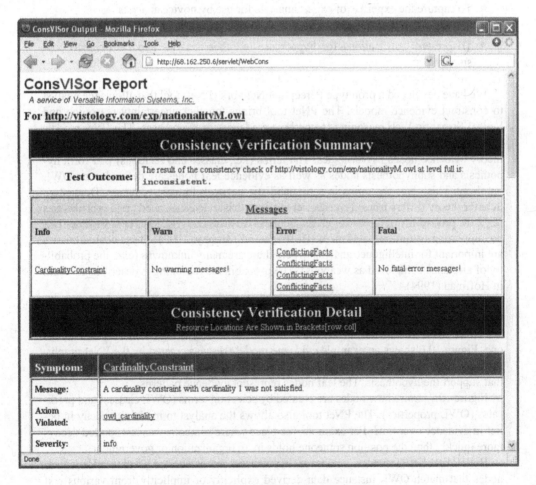

Figure 10.5. ConsVISor output (partial).

encoded in the ontology. It is likely that a hybrid of various approaches will ultimately be the most successful.

10.5. HYBRID EVIDENTIAL REASONING

The focus of this section is on how OWL logical reasoning can be combined with probabilistic reasoning to ascertain belief in hypotheses. Analysts need to combine complex chains of evidence (e.g., *member of organization X purchased ingredient A, member of organization X purchased equipment B . . .*) to ascertain belief in hypotheses about people, organizations, and future events (e.g., *organization X is acquiring weapons of mass destruction*). Quantitative methods for hypothesis assessment are gaining support in the Intelligence Community (McLaughlin and Pate-Cornell, 2005). Analysts need tools to represent evidence models and compute belief in hypotheses based on explicit and implicit evidence. Formal evidence models can be used in a variety of ways:

- To capture the expertise of expert analysts for use by novice analysts
- To define conditions and thresholds for agents to generate alerts
- To present justifications for hypotheses to other analysts and intelligence consumers

We have developed a prototype Perceptual Network (PNet) tool that allows the analyst to construct evidence models. The PNet tool brings together uncertainty reasoning and logical Semantic Web reasoning to combine evidence for hypotheses. The PNet models are a novel hybrid knowledge representation that semantically ground Dempster–Shafer theory evidence nodes in ontologies. The terms (i.e., classes and relations) that form hypothesis and subhypothesis nodes as well as evidence leaf nodes are defined in an OWL ontology. This gives the terms in a probabilistic network formal semantics. Dempster–Shafer theory differs from Bayesian networks in that it does not need prior probabilities (e.g., the probability of a person getting a certain disease) and it allows for ignorance (i.e., no supporting or refuting evidence) (Hoffman and Murphy, 1993). These characteristics are important for intelligence analysis where there are many unknowns (e.g., the probability of airplanes being used as weapons). The probabilistic reasoning is described in detail in Hoffman (1994).

The PNet tool allows the analyst to create, store and browse models. The PNet tool can then calculate belief/disbelief/ignorance values for a hypothesis based on evidence represented as OWL instance data. The sum of belief, disbelief, and ignorance values equals one. Figure 10.6 shows an example evidence model that was created by the PNet graphical tool. The top node is the hypothesis. The middle nodes represent the subhypotheses that support the hypothesis. The leaf nodes represent evidence patterns.

Figure 10.7 shows how nodes are created by selecting terms (OWL classes) and predicates (OWL properties). The PNet tool also allows the analyst to model the decay in belief in evidence over time. For example, the place where someone was last spotted decays more quickly than the position someone holds in an organization or government.

Belief/disbelief/ignorance values of hypotheses are calculated from evidence leaf nodes that match OWL instance data derived explicitly or implicitly from various text sources. For example, AeroSWARM processed a document that explicitly asserts that *Amed Omar* purchased plutonium. Implicit assertions derived from explicit assertions in multiple documents via logical reasoning with ontologies and reference knowledge sup-

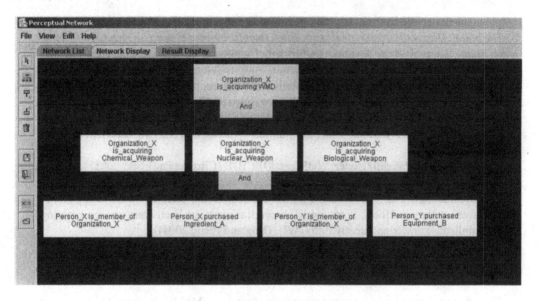

Figure 10.6. PNet tool interface.

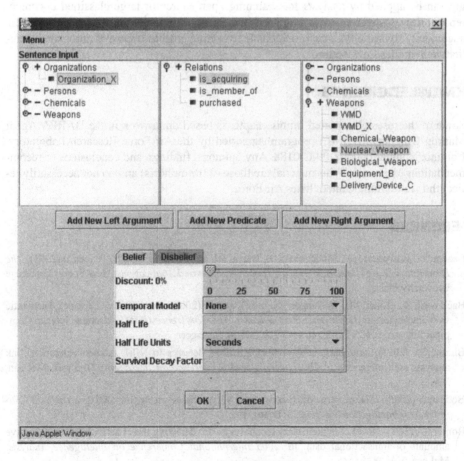

Figure 10.7. PNet node creation.

plements the evidence from explicit assertions. For example, *Amed Omar is a member of Hezbolah, Hezbolah is part of Islamic Jihad, therefore Amed Omar is a member of Islamic Jihad*. The analyst can assign belief/disbelief/ignorance values to text sources (e.g., AP newswire, a specific HUMINT report author) or to individual pieces of evidence data.

The combination of OWL and probabilistic reasoning has two major benefits for analysts. One is that the terms in the network have formal definitions in an ontology that supports human understanding and semantic interoperability with other tools like IE software. Second, OWL reasoning can infer implicit evidence that can help ascertain belief in hypotheses.

Tools such as Paladin (Boner, 2005) and DECIDE (Cluxton and Eick, 2005) are similar to the work described above except that they do not leverage OWL and they are based on Bayesian networks. The OWL approach described in this chapter would be applicable to Bayesian Network tools. Some initial theoretical work has been done on incorporating probabilistic knowledge directly into OWL (Ding and Peng, 2004).

SUMMARY

This chapter focused on automated reasoning which is enabled by the formal semantics of OWL and the generation of OWL markup from text via NLP technology. Semantic filtering can be applied by analysts for searching open source or large classified document repositories. Co-reference reasoning can help connect the dots that come from different documents. Hybrid OWL and probabilistic reasoning enables improved automated quantitative hypothesis evaluation.

ACKNOWLEDGMENTS

Some of the research reported in this chapter is based upon work in the DARPA Agent Markup Language (DAML) program supported by the Air Force Research Laboratory, Contract Number F30602-00-C-0188. Any opinions, findings, and conclusions or recommendations expressed in this material are those of the author(s) and do not necessarily reflect the views of the United States Air Force.

REFERENCES

Baader, F., Calvanese, D., McGuiness, D., Nardi, D., and Patel-Schneider, P. (eds.). (2002). *The Description Logic Handbook: Theory, Implementation and Applications.* New York: Cambridge University Press.

Baclawski, K., Kokar, M., Waldinger, R., and Kogut, P. (2002). Consistency checking of semantic web ontologies. In: *1st International Semantic Web Conference (ISWC),* Lecture Notes in Computer Science, LNCS 2342, pp. 454–459. Berlin: Springer.

Blume, M. (2005). Automatic entity disambiguation: Benefits to NER, relation extraction, link analysis and inference. In: *2005 International Conference on Intelligence Analysis,* McLean, VA.

Bodnar, J. (2005). Making sense of massive data by hypothesis testing. In: *2005 International Conference on Intelligence Analysis,* McLean, VA.

Boner, C. (2005). Novel complementary technologies for detecting threat activities within massive amounts of transactional data. In: *2005 International Conference on Intelligence Analysis,* McLean, VA.

Ciravegna, F., and Chapman, S. (2005). Mining the semantic web: requirements for machine learning. In: *Proceedings of the Dagstuhl Seminar on Machine Learning for the Semantic Web*, Wadern, Germany.

Cluxton, D., and Eick, S. (2005). DECIDE Hypothesis Visualization Tool. In: *2005 International Conference on Intelligence Analysis*, McLean, VA.

Cohen, W., Ravikumar, P., and Fienberg, S. (2003). A comparison of string distance metrics for name-matching tasks. In: *Proceedings of IJCAI-03 Workshop on Information Integration on the Web*, Acapulco, Mexico.

Davis, J., Dutra, I., Page, D., and Santos Costa, V. (2005). Establishing identity equivalence in multi-relational domains. In: *2005 International Conference on Intelligence Analysis*, McLean, VA.

Dill, S., Eiron, N., Gibson, D., Gruhl, D., Guha, R., Jhingran, A., Kanungo, T., Rajagopalan, S., Tomkins, A., Tomlin, J., and Zien, J. (2003). Semtag and seeker: Bootstrapping the semantic web via automated semantic annotation. In: *12th Int. World Wide Web Conference*, Budapest.

Ding, Z., and Peng, Y. (2004). A probabilistic extension to the web ontology language (OWL). In: *37th Hawaii International Conference on System Sciences*, Big Island, Hawaii.

Ding, L., Finin, T., Joshi, A., Peng, Y., Cost, R., Sachs, J., Pan, R., Reddivari, R., and Doshi, V., (2004). Swoogle: A semantic web search and Metadat engine. In: *13th ACM Conference on Information and Knowledge Management*, Washington, DC.

Guha, R., McCool, R., and Miller, E. (2003). Semantic Search. In *12th International World Wide Web Conference*, Budapest.

Guo, Y., Pan, Z., and Heflin, J. (2004). An evaluation of knowledge base systems for large OWL datasets. In: *Third International Semantic Web Conference (ISWC)*, Hiroshima, Japan, LNCS 3298, pp. 274–288. New York: Springer.

Hoffman, J. (1994). A generalization of Dempster's rule for combining belief: A Tutorial, Colorado School of Mines Technical Report.

Hoffman, J., and Murphy, R. (2005). Comparison of Bayesian and Dempster–Shafer theory for sensing. In: *SPIE Proceedings on Neural and Stochastic Methods in Image and Signal Processing*.

Horrocks, I., Patel-Schneider, P., Boley, H., Tabet, S., Grosof, B., and Dean, M. (2004). SWRL: A semantic Web Rule Language combining OWL and RuleML Draft Version 0.7, http://www.daml.org/rules/proposal/

Hsiung, P., Moore, A., Neill, D., and Schneider, J. (2005). Alias detection in link data sets. In: *2005 International Conference on Intelligence Analysis*, McLean, VA.

Kiryakov, A., Popov, B., Terziev, I., Manov, D., and Ognyanoff, D. (2005). Semantic annotation, indexing and retrieval. *Journal of Web Semantics* 2(1).

Kogut, P., and Heflin, J. (2003). Semantic web technologies for aerospace. In: *Proceedings of IEEE Aerospace Conference*, Big Sky, MT.

Kogut, P., and Holmes, W. (2001). AeroDAML: Applying information extraction to generate DAML annotations from web pages. In: *First International Conference on Knowledge Capture (K-CAP 2001) Workshop on Knowledge Markup and Semantic Annotation*, Victoria, BC, Canada.

Kokar, M., Matheus, C., Letkowski, J., Baclawski, K., and Kogut, P. (2004). Association in level 2 fusion. In: *Multisensor, Multisource Information Fusion: Architectures, Algorithms, and Applications*, pp. 228–237. Bellingham, WA: SPIE.

Lee, R. (2005). METS as a tool to support intelligence analysis. In: *2005 International Conference on Intelligence Analysis*, McLean, VA.

Matheus, C., Kokar, M., and Baclawski K. (2003). A core ontology for situation awareness. In: *Proceedings of the Sixth International Conference on Information Fusion*, pp. 545–552.

McLaughlin, J., and Pate-Cornell, M. (2005). A Bayesian approach to Iraq's nuclear program intelligence analysis: A hypothetical illustration. In: *2005 International Conference on Intelligence Analysis,* McLean, VA.

Patel-Schneider, P. (2004). A proposal for a SWRL extension to first order logic, November, http://www.daml.org/2004/11/fol/proposal

Patel-Schneider, P., Hayes, P., and Horrocks, I. (2004). OWL Semantics and Abstract Syntax, http://www.w3.org/TR/owl-semantics/

Uschold, M. (2005). Semantic annotations for semantic filtering. In: *Proceedings Of the Dagstuhl Seminar on Machine Learning for the Semantic Web,* Wadern, Germany.

Uschold, M., Clark, P., Dickey, F., Fung, C., Smith,. S., Uczekaj, S., Wilke, M., Bechofer, S., and Horrocks, I. (2004). A semantic infosphere. In: *2nd International Semantic Web Conference (ISWC),* Sanabel, FL.

Waltz, E., (2003). *Knowledge Management in the Intelligence Enterprise.* Norwood, MA: Artech House.

Chapter 11

Schemer: Consensus-Based Knowledge Validation and Collaboration Services for Virtual Teams of Intelligence Experts

Clifford Behrens, Hyong-Sop Shim, and Devasis Bassu

11.1. INTRODUCTION

A major goal of recent research efforts for the Intelligence Community is developing information technology needed by teams of intelligence analysts, as well as by operations and policy personnel, in attempting to anticipate and preempt terrorist threats to U.S. interests. A key to realizing this goal is greater collaboration among *virtual teams* of subject matter experts (SMEs) in war gaming and decision-modeling activities. The idea here is to involve the brightest and most qualified individuals, regardless of the time or location of their communications, in collaborative modeling activities so as to produce *valid* and *reliable* intelligence in a *timely* manner. To meet these challenges, Telcordia is developing Schemer (Behrens and Kashyap, 2002; Behrens and Shim, 2004), a flexible knowledge-driven technology that motivates collaboration through a heightened awareness of "who knows what." Schemer provides this capability by imposing consensus analysis, a rigorous scientific methodology, on collaborative modeling which yields (1) timely and relevant knowledge validation and collaboration metrics, (2) visual representations of collaboration processes and the distribution of knowledge within expert panels, and (3) real-time model estimation from information provided by virtual panels (or teams) of SMEs. This chapter describes in greater detail how Schemer contributes to improving intelligence by offering a comprehensive Web service for qualifying SMEs and vetting the models they produce, as well as for monitoring consensus and knowledge-building fostered by increased collaboration among panelists.

11.2. CORE CONCEPTS AND SUPPORTING FEATURES

We strongly believe that new collaboration tools will only gain acceptance by users if there is hope that, by collaborating with others, higher-quality intelligence will be produced, and there is also a way to validate the process whereby this intelligence is produced. This goal is achievable if collaboration is supported by sound experimental research design and metrics from both static and longitudinal analysis of panel data, as well as by the models computed from these data. Moreover, teamwork requires efficient communications; that is the cost of collaboration must be low and acceptable to team members. Minimally, our knowledge-driven methodology for collaboration requires four supporting metrics: (1) a measure of the overall saliency of the knowledge domain to SMEs, (2) the level of domain expertise or "competence" for each SME with whom one might interact, (3) the most probable set of "correct answers," derived from the responses of each SME (i.e., the consensus model), and (4) a measure of consensus formation and knowledge-building over the life of the collaboration. This section introduces some of the key concepts behind the knowledge and collaboration frameworks that inform Schemer and its features which it implement these frameworks.

11.2.1. Establish Saliency of Knowledge Domain

Information sharing is critical for knowledge-building. Therefore, it is not surprising that knowledge validation might exploit the degree to which information is agreed upon or found to be salient among a group of SMEs. Schemer's knowledge validation services are built around *consensus analysis*. Consensus analysis is based on a few simple, but powerful, ideas: *Knowledge is both distributed and shared* (Romney et al., 1986). For any knowledge domain and any group of subject "experts" in this domain, these SMEs possess different experiences; hence, they know different things, and some of them know more about the domain than others (see Figure 11.1). Information sharing (e.g., among individuals A-H in the figure) facilitates the availability of a much larger pool of information with nonuniform distribution of knowledge across members of the same *community of interest* (or *COI*).

Along with the differential expertise one typically finds among members of a community of interest, there also exists some knowledge that is widely shared and recognized as being "essential." In fact, this knowledge may be so fundamental and its use so widespread that, over time, it becomes logically well-structured or canonical. This core knowledge is not all that one knows (e.g., the set of knowledge for each individual represented

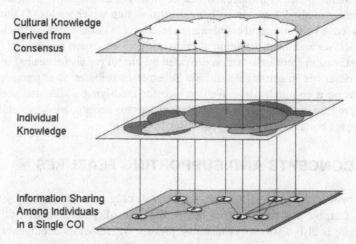

Figure 11.1. Information sharing, individual knowledge, and cultural knowledge derived from consensus.

in the middle layer of Figure 11.1), nor is it the sum total of what everybody knows (e.g., the union of individual knowledge sets in the middle layer). Rather, it is an abstraction, knowledge shared in its "broad design and deeper principles" by members of a community of interest (Behrens and Kashyap, 2002). In other words, while its entire details are not usually known (or cannot always be articulated explicitly) by anyone, core knowledge consists of those things that members of a community of interest understand that all others hold to be true. This conceptual framework provides the rationale for consensus analysis: *Consensus is an indicator of core or "cultural" knowledge.* But before we can apply this framework to provide knowledge validation and consensus modeling services to collaborative modeling efforts, it is important to place expert panels within the larger context of communities of interest.

As the discussion above suggests, communities of interest consist of members who, at a fundamental level, share domain theories, vocabulary, and semantics. For purposes of the present discussion, this shared knowledge constitutes a *bias*. An assumption of consensus analysis is that panelists are drawn from a single community of interest, but this must be confirmed as part of knowledge validation. Since "expert" panelists in particular bring with them the biases of their respective community of interest, it is important to the process of deriving consensus knowledge to identify these biases early on. When significant biases are discovered among panelists, a decision must be made to take action to either (a) mitigate differences between them (through further negotiation or collaboration) or (b) form new panels along the lines of different communities of interest represented on the panel. Consequently, a rigorous methodology capable of supporting knowledge validation and qualification of panelists with metrics is required. With this as motivation, a formal account for consensus analysis, envisioned as a knowledge validation and collaboration framework, is presented. This account is novel in the way it weds the mathematics of consensus analysis with that of measurement theory and recent research in knowledge elicitation from experts.

In the present case the formal model consists of a data matrix X containing the responses X_{ik} of panelists (or team members) $1 \leq i \leq N$ on items $1 \leq k \leq M$. From this matrix another matrix M^* is estimated and it holds the empirical point estimates M_{ij}^*, the amount of agreement in the responses on all items between panelists i and j (with $M_{ij}^* = M_{ji}^*$ for all pairs of SMEs i and j) (Romney et al., 1986). For any instrument with panelists' responses measured on an interval or ratio scale, the M_{ij}^* entries are *concordance correlation coefficients* given by

$$\hat{\rho}_c = \frac{2rs_x s_y}{s_x^2 + s_y^2 + (\bar{x} - \bar{y})^2} \tag{11.1}$$

where s_x^2, and s_y^2 are the variances in the response sets of panelists x and y, respectively, $\bar{x}$ and $\bar{y}$ are their mean response values, and r is the Pearson product moment correlation between their response sets (Lin, 1989). This index has an advantage over the simple Pearson correlation coefficient because it corrects for relative bias and precision (Shoukri, 2004).

To obtain D_i^*, an estimate of the proportion of answers panelist i "actually" knows and the main diagonal entries of M^*, a solution to the following system of equations is sought:

$$M^* = D^* D^{*\prime} \tag{11.2}$$

where D^* is a column vector containing estimates of individual competencies $D_1 \dots D_i \dots D_N$ and $D^{*\prime}$ is merely its transpose. Since Eq. (11.2) represents an overspecified set of equations and because of sampling variability, an exact solution is unlikely. However, an approximate solution yielding estimates of the individual panelist competencies (the D_i^*) can be obtained by applying *Maximum Likelihood Factor Analysis* (MLFA) (Basilevsky, 1994) to fit Eq. (11.2) and solve for the main diagonal values. Schemer uses the *factanal* function in the *R* library for MLFA (The R Development Core Team, 2003). The saliency of the knowledge domain for panelists can be measured by the relative magnitude of eigenvalues: The first eigenvalue λ_1 at least three times greater than the second is used to determine whether a single factor solution was extracted (Romney et al., 1986). All values of the first eigenvector, v_1, should also range between 0 and 1. Exceptions to these criteria suggest that the targeted domain is not salient for a panel, or a panel may actually consist of subgroups (i.e., panelists representing different communities of interest) that introduce significant and detectable biases to the collaborative modeling activity.

Schemer computes a *Knowledge Domain Profile* that, along with other useful metrics, provides a measure of domain saliency, as shown in Figure 11.2. For example, the ratio of the first two eigenvalues reported in the example exceeds 9, which is three times greater than the criterion needed to qualify a domain for a panel. This result suggests that the targeted knowledge domain is familiar to panelists, and they all seem to share a similar theory of the domain. (More will be said later about the Schemer Knowledge Domain Profile.)

11.2.2. Qualify SMEs

Panels may be convened in a number of ways, with their members selected for any number of reasons. Moreover, panel members often bring with them different biases and different levels of domain expertise or "competency." For purposes of this discussion, competency merely refers to the amount of knowledge in a particular domain possessed by a panelist. Viewed in a slightly different way, competency is proportional to the probability that a panelist will provide the consensus answer to a question selected randomly from the knowledge domain. Therefore, it is important to qualify panelists so that their biases and

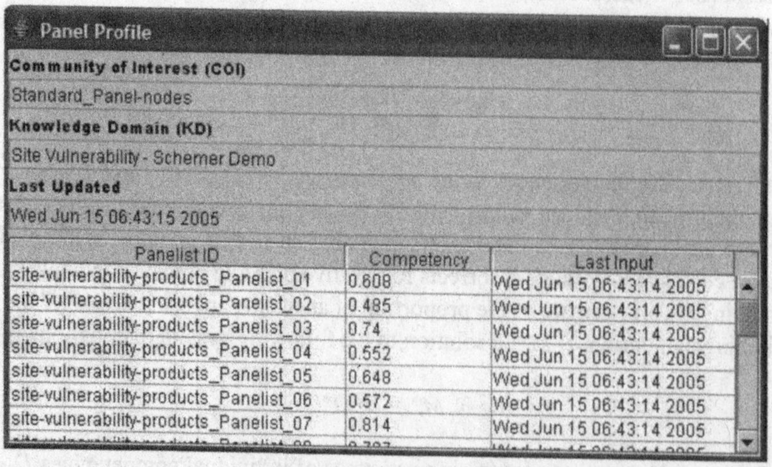

Panelist ID	Competency	Last Input
site-vulnerability-products_Panelist_01	0.608	Wed Jun 15 06:43:14 2005
site-vulnerability-products_Panelist_02	0.485	Wed Jun 15 06:43:14 2005
site-vulnerability-products_Panelist_03	0.74	Wed Jun 15 06:43:14 2005
site-vulnerability-products_Panelist_04	0.552	Wed Jun 15 06:43:14 2005
site-vulnerability-products_Panelist_05	0.648	Wed Jun 15 06:43:14 2005
site-vulnerability-products_Panelist_06	0.572	Wed Jun 15 06:43:14 2005
site-vulnerability-products_Panelist_07	0.814	Wed Jun 15 06:43:14 2005

Figure 11.2. Consensus model and knowledge validation metrics produced by Schemer.

varying degrees of expertise are weighed appropriately when attempting to derive valid knowledge for a domain from the information they provide.

Fortunately, if the domain saliency criteria mentioned above are satisfied, then the individual panelist competencies can be estimated with

$$D_i^* = v_{1i}\sqrt{\lambda_1} \qquad (11.3)$$

The D_i^*, then, are the loadings for all panelists on the first factor. As will be explained below, these estimates are required to complete the analysis—that is, to infer the "best" answers to the items.

Schemer also produces a *Panel Profile* in which an estimate of each panelist's competency is listed, as shown in Figure 11.3. This estimate is computed from the most recent set of information acquired from each SME, and the time of this last acquisition is also listed.

11.2.3. Derive and Validate Consensus Models

Once the validity of the targeted knowledge domain for a panel of experts has been established, along with the competency of each panelist in the domain, a consensus model can be estimated from the set of panelists' responses. While numerous methods have been offered for combining expert opinions (Ayyub, 2001; Cooke, 1991), the general strategy taken here is to combine panelists' responses in a way that weights each response by the estimated competency of the panelist that provided it; that is, the estimated competency values (D_i^*) and the response matrix (X_{ik}) are used to compute the consensus model containing the "correct" answers.

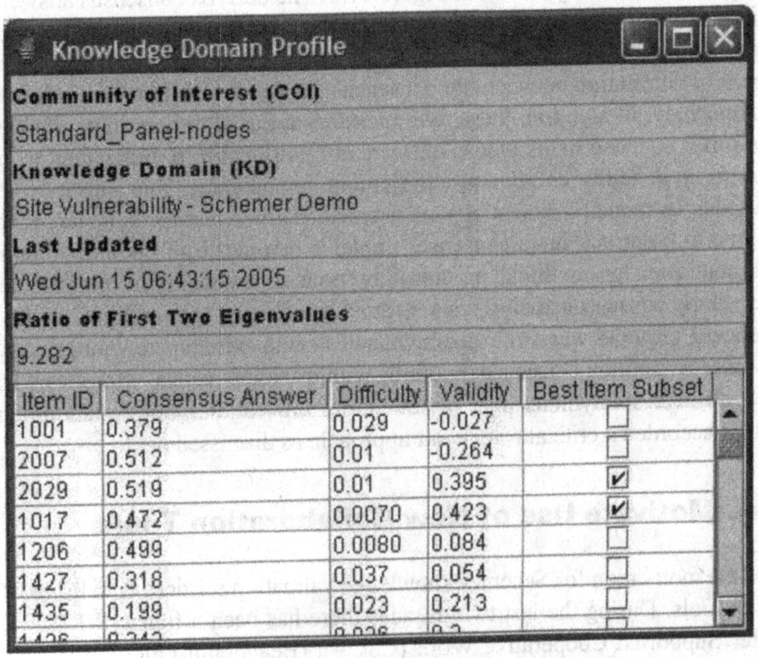

Knowledge Domain Profile

Community of Interest (COI)
Standard_Panel-nodes

Knowledge Domain (KD)
Site Vulnerability - Schemer Demo

Last Updated
Wed Jun 15 06:43:15 2005

Ratio of First Two Eigenvalues
9.282

Item ID	Consensus Answer	Difficulty	Validity	Best Item Subset
1001	0.379	0.029	-0.027	☐
2007	0.512	0.01	-0.264	☐
2029	0.519	0.01	0.395	☑
1017	0.472	0.0070	0.423	☑
1206	0.499	0.0080	0.084	☐
1427	0.318	0.037	0.054	☐
1435	0.199	0.023	0.213	☐
1436	0.343	0.026	0.2	

Figure 11.3. Panel profile produced by Schemer.

The actual model used to compute the consensus model depends on the scale on which panelists' responses are measured. For continuous response data, a weighted average is used:

$$X_k^c = \sum_{i=1}^{N} x_{ik} D_i^* / \sum_{i=1}^{N} D_i^* \tag{11.4}$$

where X_k^c is the consensus or "correct" answer to item k, x_{ik} is the response to item k by panelist i, and D_i^* is the estimate of panelist i's competency (Meyer and Booker, 2001). When response data are measured on a discrete scale (e.g., TRUE/FALSE or multiple-choice), the estimated competency values (D_i^*) and the profile of responses for item k ($X_{ik,l}$) are used to compute the Bayesian *a posteriori* probabilities for each possible answer (Behrens and Kashyap, 2002; Romney et al., 1986). In the case of discrete response data, the formula for the probability that an answer is "correct" follows:

$$\Pr(<X_{ik}> i = 1 \mid Z_k = l) = \prod_{i=1}^{N} [D_i^* + (1 - D_i^*)/L]^{X_{ik,l}} [(1 - D_i^*)(L-1)/L]^{1 - X_{ik,l}} \tag{11.5}$$

where Z_k is the "consensus" answer to item k, l is the lth response to item k, and L is the total number of possible responses ($l_1 \dots l_L$) to item k. Again, it should be mentioned that the "correctness" of an answer is relative to the perspective (or bias) shared by members of a particular community of interest—that is, the one sampled. Equations (11.1)–(11.5) provide formal motivation for the approach taken in this research, and they indicate algorithms that need to be implemented in software as part of a Web-based consensus and knowledge validation server.

The consensus model and other associated statistics are provided as part of a Schemer Knowledge Profile, already shown in Figure 11.2. The derived consensus answer is given for each item, along with an estimate of the item's difficulty and validity. Item difficulty measures the amount of dispersion around the consensus answer, and validity measures the amount of correlation between the consensus answer for an item and estimates of domain competency. In addition, these two measures are used to determine the best subset of items—that is, those items whose answers are not known to either few or many and which seem most highly correlated with domain competency. This subset of best items can be used later to qualify potential panelists who claim expertise in the target domain. It is important to point out that a consensus model is derived from the individual inputs of panelists and is not "group think" produced by force of personality or other social dynamics. If anything, consensus analysis is a means for reducing "group think" in the collaborative process, provides ways of exposing panelists with extreme viewpoints early on, and enables one to monitor consensus-building within expert panels. Moreover, consensus achieved through anonymous peer review and knowledge-driven collaboration among panelists is accorded a critical role in our approach, as discussed next.

11.2.4. Motivate Use of New Collaboration Tools

Much of the motivation for Schemer knowledge validation services is to drive use of collaboration tools. During the last two decades there has been a flurry of R&D activity in Computer Supported Cooperative Work (CSCW) (Beaudouin-Lafon, 1999; Ellis et al., 1991; Mills, 2003). Enthusiasm over the potential of collaboration technologies has caused some to deploy these as a means for improving knowledge creation and management in their work environment. CSCW research has tended to focus on the production of new collaboration tools without concurrently developing new technologies to motivate their use (Grudin, 1994). We believe that some of this motivation might be provided by giving users greater insight into how knowledge is distributed within their work environments along with new communications interfaces which, based on this insight, facilitate interactions between those who possess and those who need knowledge. This perspective is a departure from many process-based collaboration approaches designed to enforce prescribed work flows (Mills, 2003); rather, we propose a more flexible and informal knowledge-driven approach where collaboration grows out of a heightened awareness of "who knows what."

Schemer contributes to heightening awareness by producing a knowledge map (KMap), which is a contour image (analogous to a topographical map) that graphically displays relative distances among panelists in terms of their estimated competencies and differences in their domain knowledge (see Figure 11.4). The x–y coordinates of the panelists plotted on this image are obtained through a metric multidimensional scaling (MDS) of the agreement matrix (M^*), using the ***cmdscale*** function in the ***R*** library (The R Development Core Team, 2003). The typical image resembles a "fried egg," with the most knowledgeable panelists in the center or "yolk" of the egg, and the least knowledgeable panelists plotted toward the edges or "white" of the egg. The closer two panelists are on this image, the more similar they are in the knowledge they possess; conversely, those

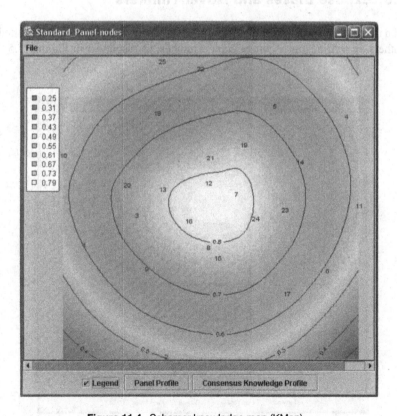

Figure 11.4. Schemer knowledge map (KMap).

panelists plotted most distant from one another have the most different perspectives (Schiffman et al., 1981). In addition, competency contour lines are overlaid on this image to provide references for groups of panelists possessing equivalent knowledge, and a legend is also provided for more detailed visual interpretation of the plot. Again, these competencies are merely estimates of the degree to which a panelist's knowledge contributes to the consensus view and is related to the probability that he would correctly answer any question drawn from the same knowledge domain.

The objects returned by Schemer, particularly the knowledge map, are crucial to our notion of knowledge-driven collaboration. By giving panelists greater insight into the manner in which knowledge is distributed among them, Schemer motivates further collaboration and the formation of advice networks. For example, a panelist with a question might seek an answer from another panelist who seems to be more knowledgeable, but not necessarily one of the so-called "gurus," thus reducing the demand on the most knowledgeable individuals on the panel. One might also wish to use information about other panelists represented on the map to determine those whose perspective seems most different from their own, then initiate further collaboration in attempt to resolve or explain these differences. The critical assumption here is that panelists vary in the knowledge they possess, insight into the distribution of knowledge among panelists will motivate them to collaborate, and this collaboration will, in turn, lead to knowledge-building and model improvement.

11.2.5. Expose Biases and Novel Thinkers

A KMap might also reveal novel thinkers or the so-called "lone wolf," those plotted apart from others or with negative competency estimates, as displayed in Figure 11.5. These

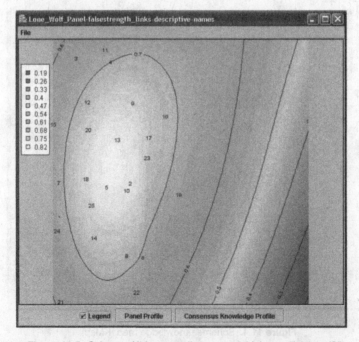

Figure 11.5. Schemer KMap revealing a novel thinker or "lone wolf."

may be panelists with whom others might want to collaborate to determine whether these individuals have new knowledge or unique insights. Such insights could lead some panel members to change their thinking, resulting in revisions to their models. The KMap and knowledge saliency metric can also detect the existence of strong biases within a panel. This might be revealed by the display of more than one point cluster in the KMap or by a small (<3) knowledge saliency value. Any of these insights gained from information provided by Schemer can potentially promote collaboration and peer review, hence contribute to consensus formation.

11.2.6. Monitor Consensus and Knowledge-Building

A KMap is useful as a "snapshot" that provides panelists and panel administrators with a current view of knowledge distribution within a panel. Again, the hope is that this view will motivate panelists to use collaboration tools in their IT environment to exchange ideas and, when appropriate, revise their opinions. This form of knowledge-building, and the role played by collaboration and consensus-building, can actually be monitored by longitudinal analysis of KMaps.

In principle, it should be reasonably easy to compare KMaps to determine whether any panelists have changed their position relative to others. For example, over time a "lone wolf" with keen or deep insights may persuade others to his point of view. In this case, his position would move toward the center of the plot, within the "yolk." In other cases, more knowledgeable panelists may further educate less knowledgeable ones so that the latter are brought closer to the plot's center. The same overall properties should hold true, with the most knowledgeable panelists located in the plot's center and the least knowledgeable panelists located in the plot's periphery. However, if knowledge-building is taking place through collaboration, then one would expect two other patterns to emerge over time. First, the plot of points should become more compact and, second more points should fall within higher competency contours.

Schemer performs longitudinal analysis on a series of KMaps to compute visualizations and metrics useful for assessing the amount of consensus formation and knowledge-building produced by collaboration, as illustrated in Figure 11.6. However, longitudinal analysis is complicated by the fact that the MDS algorithm produces a KMap whose scale is indeterminate. This means that before successive KMaps can be compared, and metrics computed, all KMaps used for longitudinal analysis must be referenced to the same coordinate configuration. Schemer uses the *procrustes* function in the *R* library for this purpose (The R Development Core Team, 2003).

Procrustes analysis refers to a set of strategies used to "rotate" a matrix to maximum similarity with a target matrix (Gower, 1975; Mardia et al., 1975). It is often used to compare ordination results, such as the different point configurations in KMaps computed by Schemer. In a typical Procrustes rotation, the configurations are re-scaled to a common size and jointly centered and, if necessary, mirror reflected so that their orientation is coincident. In order to find the optimal superimposition, one configuration is kept fixed as a reference, while the other is rotated successively until the sum-of-the-squared residuals between corresponding coordinates in both configurations is minimized. In Figure 11.6, each plot in the leftmost column (with the obvious exception of the top one) was rotated using the one above it (from the last time period) as a reference plot. The individual residuals between homologous points are also interpreted separately in the center column of plots. In these plots, the differences between a panelist's current and preceding location is represented by an arrow, with the head of the arrow pointing to his location in the refer-

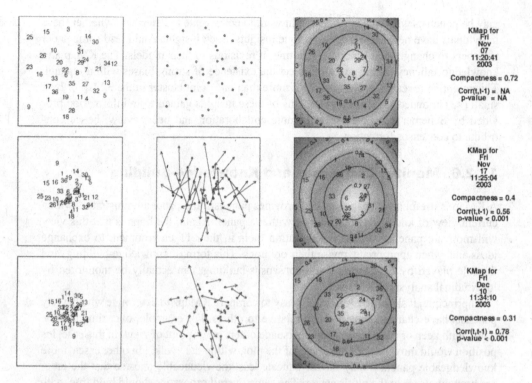

Figure 11.6. Growth in consensus and knowledge-building over time. The leftmost column of plots reveals increasing compactness, suggesting growth in consensus among panelists. The center column of plots shows change in each panelist's knowledge relative to peers from one period to the next; the length of an arrow is proportional to the amount of change, and the head of the arrow indicates the panelist's reference point from the previous KMap. The right column of plots shows a KMap after Procrustes rotation. The statistics on the right report the date/time for each KMap used for longitudinal analysis, the compactness of points (representing the panelists) in each KMap, and the correlation between a KMap configuration and its predecessor along with the associated *p*-value.

ence configuration; the length of the arrow is proportional to the residual distance between these locations.

Greater concordance between datasets after rotation produces a smaller residual sum of squared differences in Euclidean multivariate space. Schemer measures this concordance with a correlation-like statistic (Corr) derived from the symmetric Procrustes sum of squares (SS) as Corr = $\sqrt{1 - SS}$. As the concordance between plots increases, the value of Corr goes to 1.0. The **R** function **protest** computes Corr and then conducts a randomization test to estimate its significance (or *p-value*) by calling the **procrustes** function repeatedly (1000 times), keeping track of the proportion of times the value of Corr obtained for the permuted data is greater than or equal to the observed value (Peres-Neto and Jackson, 2001; The R Development Core Team, 2003). Along with the rotated plots and correlation between each rotated plot and its reference configuration, a Compactness metric, measuring the overall knowledge variability among panelists, is also reported. Based on intra-configuration standard deviation, it is computed as follows:

$$\text{sdev}(X) = \sqrt{\frac{1}{N} \sum_{i=1}^{N} d^2(x_i, \overline{x})} \qquad (11.6)$$

where $d^2(x_i, \overline{x})$ is the squared Euclidean distance between a vector x_i and $\overline{x}$, the centroid of X; and N is the number of points (panelists) in the KMap configuration (Halkidi et al., 2001). The value of compactness goes to 0 as the configuration becomes more compact, indicating greater consensus among panelists.

The reason for providing all of the visualizations and supporting metrics described above is to foster knowledge-building and intelligence improvement through increased collaboration among panelists. Again, our hope is that, by giving panelists greater insight into how knowledge is distributed within a panel, they will be further motivated to share what they know. This includes (a) a heightened awareness of key concepts and the negotiation of their meaning and (b) growing agreement on first principles and assumptions key to the relevant domain theory. Schemer provides a means for actually monitoring this process. For example, the plots and statistics computed from a longitudinal analysis of KMaps, presented in Figure 11.6, indicate a scenario in which collaboration is, indeed, promoting consensus and knowledge-building. As panelists exchange more information and increase their knowledge of the topic domain, they eventually come to share a similar domain theory, and the following pattern emerges. The leftmost column of scatter plots exhibits a single cluster of points, and this cluster of points grows more compact over time, suggesting that panelists are converging on a shared or "consensus" model. This conclusion is further supported by a gradual decrease in the compactness metric over the same time periods. The middle column of plots shows how the knowledge possessed by panelists, with respect to their peers, changes over time. The length of an arrow is directly proportional to the shift in a panelist's position, and the amount of overlap (or "spaghetti") among arrows indicates the degree of uncertainty among panelists. The last plot in this series exhibits relative stability with few panelists having shifted much from their previous position. The rightmost column of plots is a replotting of each KMap after Procrustes rotation, if rotation was applied. The trend in this sequence of plots is for a greater concentration of panelists within higher-valued competency contours. The increase in correlation between successive KMaps in the series also confirms growing consensus and panel convergence on a shared domain theory.

11.3. SCHEMER DESIGN

Even though consensus analysis seems to offer much when it comes to validating and monitoring collaborative model-building activities carried-out by expert panels, deploying consensus analysis as a reliable online service to a wide variety of client modeling tools is nontrivial. While Schemer's knowledge validation service is applicable to a general class of information modeling tools, it is unreasonable to assume that the same input data model would satisfy the data processing requirements of all possible modeling tools. At the same time, support for new modeling tools should not disrupt Schemer's service or require existing tools to change the way they access and use this service. Moreover, with the wide availability of computer-based collaboration tools that exists today, Schemer should not "reinvent" its own. Most groups already have collaboration tools that their members prefer or are required to use by policy. Since these tools are often designed or tailored to meet specific requirements of collaboration groups, it is unreasonable, and even unproductive, to impose an additional set of generic tools on collaborators. Ideally, Schemer should provide a collaboration interface through which users can easily access consensus analysis results and engage in collaboration on an as-needed basis using all (or any) of the existing collaboration tools in their IT environment. Because Schemer cannot (or should not) have any prior knowledge of collaboration groups or their IT environments, this means that its collaboration interface should be able to dynamically discover what tools are deployed and then make them available to local users. Thus, the key ideas behind Schemer design are threefold. First, it should be scalable and extensible, capable of providing generic knowledge validation services to a wide variety of collaborative modeling tools without requiring significant customization, development, and management overhead. Second, Schemer should easily and transparently integrate with collaboration tools that are *locally available.* Third, Schemer should be robust, able to analyze a wide variety of response data over the complete life cycle of an expert panel. These are formidable challenges, so the next few sections describe in some detail the manner in which each of these is addressed in the Schemer data model and architecture.

11.3.1. Data Model

The Schemer data model is the information model that precisely defines the schema (type and structure) for response data submitted by modeling tools to Schemer for consensus analysis and knowledge validation. To support a wide variety of collaborative modeling tools, the design of this data model is intentionally kept simple and is based on the following two principles. First, modeling tools differ only in terms of the fundamental psychometric measurement scales they employ to collect data—that is, nominal, ordinal, interval, and ratio (Stevens, 1946). Second, consensus is derived from a set of responses, made by a group of *panelists,* to any ordered (or IDed) list of questions (or *items*). In the Schemer data model, forms adopted by collaborative modeling tools for collecting panelists' inputs, which differ in their measurement scales, are called *instrument types.*

Distinctions by measurement scale are crucial for selecting appropriate statistical algorithms for deriving consensus from a set of response data supplied by a Schemer client.

For any response set, Schemer requires that each panelist and item be assigned a unique identifier and each tuple of (panelist id, item id) should be unique; that is, a panelist cannot have more than one response to the same item. Furthermore, the response set should be *complete* in the sense that all panelists should have responses to all items. In the future, we intend to relax this completeness requirement so that panelists can submit their responses incrementally at different times and at their convenience (see Section 11.4.3 for more on data imputation).

To address the scalability requirement, we have designed a *hierarchical* data model, which is graphically illustrated in Figure 11.7. This model includes a common data model that defines all data elements and their structure, required for Schemer consensus analysis. As the name implies, the information in this data model is common to all the model-

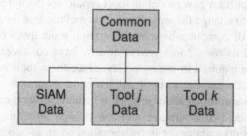

Figure 11.7. Schemer Web Service (WS) data model.

ing tools, regardless of their instrument types, and includes instrument metadata (e.g., instrument type name, domain name, and an ordered list of item identifiers) and panel metadata (e.g., panel name and an ordered list of panelist identifiers). It also defines a data structure for storing values of panelists' responses to instrument items.

Any information specific to a given instrument type is specified in a "child" data model defined for that instrument type by extending and refining a small subset of data elements in the common data model. Instrument-specific information includes data types for an instrument's items and any allowed range or list of values. Any instrument data that conforms to the Schemer data model is collectively referred to as *Schemer response data*.

By encapsulating instrument-specific information in its own data model, the hierarchical data model greatly facilitates Schemer to support new collaborative modeling tools on an as-needed basis without introducing any side effect on existing tools. This property of built-in inheritance also minimizes the effort needed to create and support new data models for specific instrument types. Furthermore, modularity inherent in the hierarchical model leads to a modular architecture, in which individual instrument "adapter" components can be built and deployed incrementally without introducing undue downtime in Schemer's services.

Schemer exploits a platform-independent mechanism for data transfer so that it can interoperate with diverse modeling tools and on a wide variety of operations platforms. Hence, *any tool should be able to submit Schemer response data to Schemer, regardless of the platform on which it is running*. For this purpose, XML Schemas (Biron and Malhotra, no date; Thompson et al., no date) are used to implement Schemer's hierarchical data model. Specifically, the redefine mechanism is used extensively to define instrument-specific schemas by adapting generic XML elements defined in the common schema to specific data types and allowed-value requirements of a particular instrument type. In addition, the *key* and *keyref* mechanisms are used to specify uniqueness constraints in the common schema. This ensures that every instrument-specific schema specifies the same set of constraints. Furthermore, this enables Schemer to delegate the responsibility of validating XML instances of Schemer response data to an XML parser. This greatly helps increase robustness of Schemer by eliminating the need of writing application code to check for uniqueness constraints. The completeness constraint cannot be specified in XML Schemas due to lack of support for cross validation in the current XML Schema specification. Thus Schemer validates XML instances of Schemer response data against this constraint once they are validated against the uniqueness constraints by the XML parser.

11.3.2. Service Architecture

Schemer has been designed and implemented as a Web Service (WS) (W3C, no date). That is, Schemer provides its service interface in WSDL and communicates with client modeling tools by exchanging SOAP messages over HTTP. The Web Service implementation greatly increases interoperability because it can support any Web Service-capable modeling tools, regardless of their implementation and operations platforms. Furthermore, it enables the Schemer WS to update its service interface without affecting the ongoing operation of existing modeling tools, which means that it can incrementally provide advanced features and capabilities on an as-needed basis.

Figure 11.8 shows an architectural overview of the Schemer WS. The current implementation is based on the Java Web Services Developer Pack (JWSDP) (Sun Microsys-

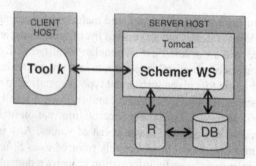

Figure 11.8. Schemer Web Service (WS) architecture.

tems, no date). Specifically, the Schemer WS is implemented as a servlet, which is life cycle-managed by the Tomcat servlet container, included in JWSDP. Schemer WS uses the JAX-RPC package, also included in JWSDP, to create a WSDL interface and to parse and process SOAP request messages from client modeling tools.

To perform consensus analysis, the Schemer WS uses the well-known and widely deployed *R* statistical and graphics environment (The R Development Core Team, 2003). Specifically, it has a script that implements the consensus analysis and knowledge validation methods (see Section 11.2) in the *R* language. It executes this script to derive a consensus model and panelist competencies for each valid Schemer response dataset received from client modeling tools. The results of each execution of the script are asynchronously stored in an internal database and sent to these client tools, through a process that will be described shortly.

The WSDL interface of the Schemer WS is designed to support asynchronous interaction, where client tools make separate requests to submit Schemer response data for consensus analysis and then to retrieve analysis results. In this design, for each request to perform consensus analysis, the Schemer WS returns to the client tool as quickly as possible a token that acknowledges the receipt of the request, *without* completing analysis on the submitted Schemer response data. In turn, the client uses this token in its subsequent request(s) to retrieve analysis results. This way, client tools learn the status of their "perform" requests without significant delay, which is critical in any environment that involves interaction with end users. Furthermore, this design greatly increases the availability of the Schemer WS by maximizing throughput of its "perform" requests. This is a clear advantage over a synchronous design, where a web service processes a "perform" request from a single client tool to completion and returns results before processing other requests, essentially rendering the service unavailable to other client tools. Consequently, in the synchronous design, "downtime" is unpredictable and can be significant, depending on the number of client tools that compete for the service at the same time, limiting both the availability and usability of the service.

11.4. CURRENT IMPLEMENTATION

Currently, Schemer has been implemented to provide knowledge validation services to the SIAM™ Influence Network modeling application, and uses tools in the Groove® environment to provide collaboration services. This section describes in more detail these client-server interactions.

11.4.1. Collaborative INET Modeling with SIAM

The *Situational Influence Assessment Module* (or *SIAM*) is a decision support tool for collaborative Influence Net (INET) modeling (Rosen and Smith, 2000). INET modeling blends two established techniques: (a) influence diagramming for user interaction during model construction; and (b) the Bayesian inference network framework for real-time, rigorous analysis of the constructed model. INET modeling, as implemented in SIAM, enables panelists to create "influence nodes." These influence nodes depict events that form cause–effect relationships within the situation under investigation. Panelists also create "influence links" between cause-and-effect pairs which graphically illustrate the causal relation between the connected events. This cause–effect relationship can be either reinforcing or reversing, as identified by the link "terminator," an arrowhead or a circle. The resulting graph is called the Influence Net's "topology." A sample INET topology is illustrated in Figure 11.9.

From Schemer's point of view, one can think of SIAM as an application for presenting a form containing slots for a panelist's estimates of parameters in their INET model. These answers may be of three types, all measured on a ratio scale: *baseline beliefs* for nodes (having values 0 to 1), and *true strength influences* or *false strength influences* for each link (with values -1 to $+1$). Consequently, the child data in the Schemer data model for the SIAM_INET instrument type specify that panelists' responses should have real values and that they should only range between (0.0, 1.0) for INET node items and between (-1.0, 1.0) for INET link items (see Figure 11.7).

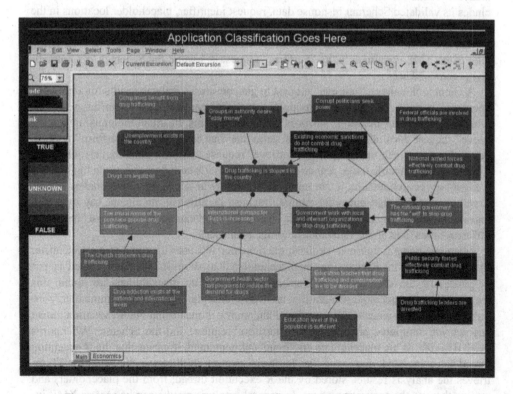

Figure 11.9. Influence network model created with the SIAM™ software application.

In the past, the SIAM application was used primarily in face-to-face meetings to enter a single INET model "coaxed" from panelists by a moderator, one that best represented their consensus view. However, the SIAM team wants to extend its application so that it enables collaborative construction of INET models by virtual panels—that is, panels of experts that may be separated in time and space. Moreover, they also desire to impose greater scientific rigor on the modeling process by identifying biases among panelists, qualifying panelists, deriving valid consensus models, and facilitating incremental improvement in models through further collaboration among panelists, based on their level of knowledge and experience. For these reasons, and to better evaluate the efficacy of our knowledge-driven approach to collaboration, we are providing Schemer knowledge validation and consensus modeling services to SIAM INET panels.

11.4.2. Schemer Knowledge Objects and Collaboration Interface

A "perform" request includes an XML instance (or document) of input Schemer response data and instrument-type information. Upon receiving a "perform" request, the Schemer WS first validates the XML instance against an appropriate schema (e.g., the SIAM INET schema) based on the instrument type information. If valid, it goes on to create a globally unique identifier for the current request, reserves placeholders for analysis results in the database, and notifies a separate R execution thread of the current request. This thread is responsible for executing the aforementioned R script for consensus analysis and storing analysis results for each "perform" request. The notification of the current request includes its validated Schemer response data, request identifier, placeholder locations in the database, and instrument type information. Immediately after notifying the R execution thread, the Schemer WS returns the request identifier to the requesting client modeling tool. If the XML document in the "perform" request is invalid, the Schemer WS immediately returns NULL.

A client tool makes a "retrieve" request to get consensus analysis results for a previous "perform" request. The "retrieve" request includes the same request identifier as the one returned by the corresponding "perform" request. Note that the client tool making the "retrieve" request does not have to be the same one that has made the "perform" request. Also, client tools can make multiple "retrieve" requests with the same request identifier. This allows for flexible usage scenarios. For example, if a collaborative modeling tool has a client–server architecture, it can implement a policy in which the server makes a "perform" request and distributes the returned request identifier to the clients, say by email, instant messaging, or any other method. Then each client can make a "retrieve" request at different times (and at the convenience of the local user).

Upon receiving a "retrieve" request, the Schemer WS uses the input request identifier as a key to search its database for the placeholders that (should) have been created as part of processing the corresponding "perform" request. If no placeholders are found, this means that the input request identifier is invalid, and the Schemer WS immediately returns NULL. If the placeholders are found but empty, it means that the R execution thread has not yet completed processing the "perform" request, and the Schemer WS returns NOT READY. If the placeholders are found and populated, it means that the R execution thread has completed processing the "perform" request. In this case, the Schemer WS retrieves the analysis results, stored by the R execution thread, from the placeholders and returns them to the requesting client. In general, analysis results can be sent as XML instances. For Java-based clients, they are encapsulated in a *Schemer knowledge object* (*SKO*).

In Schemer WS, an SKO refers to a Java object that encapsulates consensus analysis results and has code to render them on client hosts. It also provides a graphical user interface (GUI) through which the local user can engage in collaboration with remote users, using their own collaboration tools. Schemer WS returns an SKO, containing consensus analysis results, to Java-based client tools in response to "retrieve" requests. For any valid Schemer response dataset, these results include a *panelist profile* that provides competency measurements for panelists and a *knowledge domain profile* that includes the consensus values computed for an instrument. Figure 11.10 shows the KMap window (the middle one in the figure) of an example SKO. This window displays the KMap image of panelist competencies. The panelists are represented on this image with identifiers assigned by the Schemer WS. By selecting one of these identifiers, a user reveals the "real" panelist identifier as specified in the Schemer response data set. Our intention is to use this level of indirection for an access control mechanism in the future. Depending on his role in the panel, the local panelist may (or perhaps should) not always have access to entire analysis results, including the identities of other panelists. The KMap window also provides an interface through which the local user can display statistical results in the form of *panel and knowledge domain profiles*. Internally, each profile is represented as an XML document that conforms to a Schemer WS-defined XML schema. The panel profile contains the competency estimates for all panelists, and the knowledge domain profile gives the knowledge validation metric (the ratio of the first two eigenvalues, as characterized in Section 11.2), the consensus knowledge model and other statistics useful for assessing the importance of certain items for consensus derivation and knowledge validation. These include a "best" subset of items for measuring overall competency in a knowledge domain, useful for qualifying potential panelists.

The SKO facilitates knowledge-driven collaboration as follows. To discover collaboration tools that are locally available and used by panelists, the SKO requires a client modeling tool to provide a Java object that implements a Schemer WS-defined Java interface, called *KmapClient*. This interface defines a set of Java methods that the SKO can invoke to

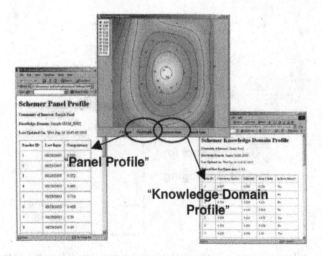

Figure 11.10. KMap window of an example Schemer knowledge object (middle).

query for the names of available collaboration tools and to make a request to initiate collaboration with a certain user of the named tool. The advantage of having individual modeling tools to implement the KMapClient interface is twofold. First, since each modeling tool has the first-hand knowledge of what collaboration tools are being provided to its panelists, the collaboration tools made accessible through the SKO can be exactly the same as those currently in use. This eliminates the need for users to learn and employ new tools when collaborating through the interface of the KMap window, as described shortly. Second, the SKO can discover locally available collaboration tools in a consistent and tool-independent manner, which greatly increases its interoperability with a wide variety of tools.

Currently, we have implemented a KMapClient object designed to integrate with Groove® collaboration tools. Specifically, this object implements the KMapClient interface on the one hand and some application logic to invoke Groove tools per user request on the other. The KMapClient object uses Groove Web Services (Groove, no date) to initiate individual Groove tools.

The SKO makes locally available collaboration tools accessible on the KMap window, as shown in Figure 11.11. When the user selects a panelist identifier on the KMap image, a pop-up menu displays the names of those collaboration tools provided by the KMapClient object. When the user selects a tool name, the SKO notifies the KMapClient to start the corresponding tool for the local user and remote user associated with the selected panelist identifier. Figure 11.11 graphically illustrates the manner in which a Groove tool for instant messaging is invoked from the KMap window.

11.4.3. Data Imputation and Programmed Research Design

Providing support for virtual panels poses many challenges. For example, if information is collected from panelists incrementally and at *their* convenience, this implies that, at any moment in time, the amount of data needed to compute a consensus model may be incom-

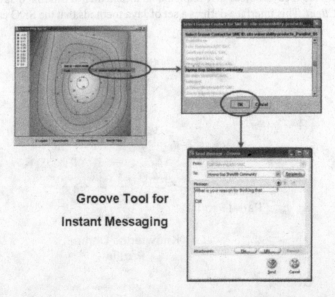

Groove Tool for

Instant Messaging

Figure 11.11. Example of invoking a locally available collaboration tool from the KMap window. The dialog box in the middle asks the user to identify the remote user as known to Groove®.

plete, so missing data must be imputed. Obviously, data imputation methods work best when the existing data they exploit have been collected in a rigorous and systematic manner—that is, according to a data acquisition plan based on sound experimental research design. Otherwise, only a small, unbalanced, and unrepresentative subsample of data may be available for model estimation, which can result in severely biased models or may make consensus model estimation by Schemer computationally intractable. Consequently, incremental and asynchronous data acquisition should be monitored and properly guided in order to ensure balanced data collection, which is critical for meaningful analysis. We address this issue by putting a data acquisition plan in place, which essentially has three primary functions: (1) provide a prioritized data collection strategy given the present cumulative data, (2) provide imputation strategies so that analysis may be carried out on incomplete data, and (3) spread data acquisition evenly over panelists so that no panelist shoulders more of the burden than any other. The data acquisition strategy generated by Schemer (and carried out by the CPA, discussed more in the next section) is based on the principles of "balanced incomplete block design." The idea is to *grow* the incomplete data in a balanced fashion (i.e., each instrument item/data slot and each panelist get proper representation) toward a fully complete dataset.

To impute missing item values in Schemer, we are implementing a *k-NN* (*k* nearest neighbors) imputation scheme with appropriate thresholds (Hastie et al., 1999; Troyanskaya et al., 2001). The underlying principle is that a panelist will tend to respond (for the missing data) in a similar fashion as other panelists who seem to *match on most responses* (for the collected data). Based on the thresholds, the scheme may even choose to drop a panelist or a piece of the panel instrument if the collected data is insufficient to yield any meaningful results. From a Panel Administrators' point of view, having the ability to set these thresholds provides some control over the quality of the collected data and, hence, the quality of the derived consensus model.

11.5. SCHEMER APPLICATIONS AND FUTURE WORK

The results reported in this chapter were obtained for simulated data, assuming model panels with different response distributions; however, we have plans to evaluate Schemer using real-domain experts in a government testbed later this year. Even though our work to this point has involved mostly prototyping, it has given us a better idea about the proper domain of applications for Schemer and has also implicated new information infrastructure for better supporting expert panel life-cycle management.

While developing the data imputation and data acquisition plan capabilities above, it became obvious that there is a need for new middleware that supports the life cycle of expert panels, and provides a generic interface between modeling tools, analytical services, and collaboration tools. We have begun work on this middleware, which we call the *Collaborative Panel Administrator* (or CPA) (Shim et al., 2005). It is not the purpose of this middleware to replace existing modeling and collaboration tools in one's IT environment. Rather, it is to provide intelligent administration of these tools in support of collaborative model-building by expert panels. For example, upon receiving a request from a CPA client, the CPA may apply any one of several algorithms to recruit experts for a panel. But once it has built a list of candidates, local e-mail services will be used to invite experts on this list to participate. Furthermore, the CPA will provide a set of client APIs so that a variety of modeling tools can be used for data acquisition and analysis of these data. This middleware will also push requests for data to panelists, again using available communications infrastructure (e.g., e-mail services) so that data acquisition plans are met on time and then aggregate panel data before requesting analytical services such as those provided by Schemer. Similarly, generic interfaces to collaboration tools will be provided by the CPA so that a wide variety of services are available to panelists to facilitate interaction and knowledge-building. With the CPA, panel recruitment and data acquisition from panelists is automatically guided by experimental research design and the computational requirements of analytical services required for producing a valid and reliable intelligence model.

Together, the Schemer and CPA are capable of yielding valid models much more expeditiously. Figure 11.12 suggests that for any knowledge domain, the amount of knowledge shared among a random sample of individuals drawn from even a single community of interest can range from minimal to maximal. Through information exchange and collaboration between those most knowledgeable and those least knowledgeable, the amount of shared information should increase through time, ultimately resulting in maximal shared knowledge or a "consensus model." This life cycle (i.e., the amount of time required to attain consensus) is significantly reduced by the CPA and Schemer. First, the CPA facilitates more efficient recruitment of potentially larger "virtual" panels consisting of more qualified experts. Hence, less time should be required to bootstrap collaborative model-building since significant knowledge-sharing already exists among the most qualified panelists. Furthermore, the CPA determines what new information is needed from which panelists, and it proactively acquires this information according to a data acquisition plan computed on-the-fly. Second, through the metrics and visualizations derived from longitudinal analyses of Schemer's consensus analysis results, along with the motivation these provide for panelists to make better use of tools in their collaboration environment, it should be possible to demonstrate statistically when a valid consensus model has been produced. This happens when there is little change in knowledge distribution within a panel, and presumably well short of actually achieving "perfect" knowledge-sharing, as depicted in Figure 11.12. Once the desired consensus model has been realized, there is no longer need to maintain the panel, so it may be disbanded, further reducing the time and cost of model development.

SUMMARY

In this chapter we have described Schemer, a new Web Service useful for (a) validating knowledge derived from collaborative modeling by expert panels and (b) promoting col-

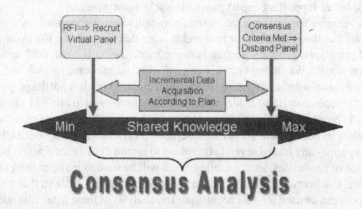

Figure 11.12. Expert panel life cycle and role of consensus analysis for knowledge-building.

laboration leading to consensus formation and knowledge-building. Schemer is based on consensus analysis, a quantitative method for discovering knowledge based on the amount of concordance measured in the response data acquired from experts. The services that Schemer provides to its clients, based on consensus analysis, include computation of consensus models, visualizations and supporting metrics for vetting expert panelists and the models they produce, and tools for monitoring collaboration and its contribution to knowledge-building over the life cycle of a panel.

Critical to the success of Schemer is its support for virtual panels, ones whose members are separated in space and time. This additional capability creates new and complex challenges for expert panel recruitment, timely data acquisition from panelists, and the computation of valid and reliable models from incomplete or incremental data. There also exist issues related to integration with existing modeling and collaboration tools in one's IT environment. To address these issues, we have initiated work on new middleware we call the Collaborative Panel Administrator. With this middleware, along with existing modeling tools and services like Schemer, we believe that we can provide a generic framework making it possible to increase involvement of the best and brightest experts in collaborative war-gaming and decision-modeling panels, with the potential of yielding the best possible models at reduced cost to the Intelligence Community.

REFERENCES

Ayyub, B. (2001). *Elicitation of Expert Opinions for Uncertainty and Risks,* New York: CRC Press.

Basilevsky, A. (1994). *Statistical Factor Analysis and Related Methods.* New York: John Wiley & Sons.

Beaudouin-Lafon, M. (ed.) (1999). *Computer Supported Co-Operative Work.* New York: John Wiley & Sons.

Behrens, C., and Kashyap, V. (2002). The "emergent" semantic web: A consensus approach to deriving semantic knowledge on the web. In: *Real World Semantic Web Applications. Frontiers in Artificial Intelligence Applications,* Vol. 2, V. Kashyap and L. Shklar (eds.), pp. 69–90. Amsterdam: IAO Press.

Behrens, C., and Shim, H.-S. (2004). Web services for knowledge-based collaborative modeling. Paper presented in a session entitled "IT for Counterterrorism," *2004 IEEE Aerospace Conference,* Big Sky, MT.

Biron, Paul V., and Malhotra, A. (no date). XML schema, part 2: Datatypes. W3C Recommendation available at http://www.w3.org/TR/2001/REC-xmlschema-2-20010502/.

Cooke, R. (1991). *Experts in Uncertainty: Opinion and Subjective Probability in Science.* New York: Oxford University Press.

Ellis, C. A., Gibbs, S., and Rein, G. (1991). Groupware: Some issues and experiences. *Communications of the ACM,* **34**(1):38–58.

Gower, J. (1975). Generalized procrustes analysis. *Psychometrika* **40**(1):33–51.

Groove (no date). Web services groove development kit (GDK). Available for download at http://www.groove.net/devzone/default.cfm?pagename=GWS_GDK.

Grudin, J. (1994). Groupware and social dynamics: Eight challenges for developers. *Communications of the ACM,* **37**(1):92–105.

Halkidi, M., Batistakis, Y., and Vazirgiannis, M. (2001). On clustering validation techniques. *Journal of Intelligent Information Systems,* **17**(2–3):107–145.

Hastie, T., Tibshirani, R., Sherlock, G., Eisen, M., Brown, P., and Botstein, D. (1999). *Imputing Missing Data for Gene Expression Arrays.* Stanford University Statistics Department Technical Report, http://www-stat.stanford.edu/~hastie/Papers/missing.pdf.

Lin, L. I. (1989). A concordance correlation coefficient to evaluate reproducibility. *Biometrics* **26:**671–676.

Mardia, K. V., Kent, J. T., and Bibby, J. M. (1979). *Multivariate Analysis.* New York: Academic Press.

Meyer, M., and Booker, J. (2001). *Eliciting and Analyzing Expert Judgment: A Practical Guide,* Philadelphia: SIAM and ASA.

Mills, K. (2003). Computer-supported cooperative work. In: *Encyclopedia of Library and Information Science.* New York: Marcel Dekker.

Peres-Neto, P. R., and Jackson, D. A. (2001). How well do multivariate data sets match? The advantages of a Procrustean superimposition approach over the Mantel test. *Oecologia,* **129:**169–178.

The R Development Core Team (2003). *The R Environment for Statistical Computing and Graphics: Reference Index Version 1.7.0,* R Development Core Team.

Romney, K., Weller, S. C., and Batchelder, W. H. (1986). Culture as consensus: A theory of culture and informant accuracy. *American Anthropologist* **88:**313–338.

Rosen, J., and Smith, W. (2000). Influence net modeling for strategic planning: A structured approach to information operations. *Phalanx,* **33**(4):.

Schiffman, S., Reynolds, M. Lance, and Young, F. (1981). *Introduction to Multidimensional Scaling: Theory, Methods, and Applications.* New York: Academic Press.

Shim, H.-S., Behrens, C., and Bassu, D. (2005). Middleware platform for recruiting and proactively managing virtual panels of intelligence experts. Paper presented in a session entitled *AI Technologies for Homeland Security, 2005 AAAI Spring Symposium Series,* held at Stanford University, Stanford, CA, R. Popp and J. Yen (organizers).

Shoukri, M. M. (2004). *Measures of Interobserver Agreement.* New York: Chapman and Hall/CRC.

Stevens, S. S. (1946). On the theory of scales of measurement. *Science* **103,** 677–680.

Sun Microsystems (no date). "Java web services developer pack. Available for download at http://java.sun.com/webservices/.

Thompson, H. S., Beech, D., Maloney, M., and Mendelsohn, N. (no date). "XML schema, part 1: Structures. W3C Recommendation available at http://www.w3.org/TR/2001/REC-xmlschema-1- 20010502/.

Troyanskaya, O., Cantor, M., Sherlock, G., Brown, P., Hastie, T., Tibshirani, R., Botstein, D., and Altman, R. B. (2001). Missing value estimation methods for DNA microarrays. *Bioinformatics,* 17, 6, 520–525. http://bioinformatics.oupjournals.org/cgi/screenpdf/17/6/520.

W3C (no date). Web services activity. available at http://www.w3.org/2002/ws/#drafts.

Chapter 12

Sharing Intelligence Using Information Supply Chains

Shuang Sun, Xiaocong Fan, and John Yen

12.1. INTRODUCTION

The Markle Foundation Task Force reports (Baird et al., 2003) that the challenges of homeland security raise a critical need to create a decentralized network for information sharing and analysis with key characteristics such as focusing more on preventive strategies. Unfortunately, such an envisioned network is hard to create because the current information sharing systems bear the following limitations. First, the existing systems are susceptible to single point of failure, a problem for typical centralized systems that have no redundant backups. Second, the systems are mostly designed to only flow information up to senior agencies, but not down to operational entities or out to other parties. Third, the information to first responders is oftentimes irrelevant and not actionable (Baird et al., 2003). To overcome these weaknesses, a general design guideline called the System-wide Homeland Analysis and Resource Exchange network (SHARE) is proposed (Baird et al., 2003). SHARE argues for developing loosely coupled architectures that (1) are robust to avoid single point of failure, (2) support directory-based services and real-time operations, and (3) offer security and accountability services to prevent abuse. How to realize a network that meets the SHARE guidelines, however, is still an open issue. Our research goal is to find solutions and design methodologies that can satisfy these guidelines.

To achieve such a goal and enable effective information sharing and analysis, we propose a framework called ISCM (Information Supply Chain Management), drawing upon ideas from the supply chain management (SCM), which has been widely used in business management science. Aiming to satisfy information demand with high responsiveness and efficiency, we designed algorithms (e.g., information requirement planning) in ISCM for information agents to capture, consolidate, investigate, and satisfy dynamic information requirements in a timely manner. The concept of information supply chain not only allows us to take a new perspective to organize information agents and view how information is processed, but also motivates us to produce new solutions for sharing the right information to the right recipients in the right way and at the right time.

In the following, we first examine the information sharing problem and the related subproblems. Then, Section 12.3 describes the ISCM framework. Next, we demonstrate information sharing with an example in Section 12.4. We discuss related issues in Section 12.5, and, finally, Section 12.6 summarizes this chapter.

Emergent Information Technologies and Enabling Policies for Counter-Terrorism. Edited by Popp and Yen **231**
Copyright © 2006 The Institute of Electrical and Electronics Engineers, Inc.

12.2. THE INFORMATION SHARING PROBLEM

Information sharing[1] is a critical issue for developing shared situation awareness and collaboratively making decisions in complex, dynamic, and distributed environments that are often present in current counter-terrorism intelligence analysis tasks. Our investigation on this problem focuses on four aspects: what to share, whom to share with, how to share, and when to share.

1. **What to Share?** Information should be shared in the right *type* and *amount*. Potential terror attack plots or sleep cells' activities are all right types of information to share because they are *directly* needed for early detecting or preventing terrorism attacks. Some types of information can be *indirectly* or *partially* related to a requirement. For example, "current temperature is 7°C" directly satisfies "What is the temperature?" while partially satisfying "What is the weather condition?", which requires other information such as the wind condition, humidity, and so on. When direct information is unavailable, information that indirectly or partially satisfies a requirement can be helpful (Yen et al., 2003b).

In addition, sharing either too much or too little information is undesirable. On one hand, sharing too much information can cause *information overload* (Schick et al., 1990). For example, a piece of crucial information may be easily ignored if it is buried in a large volume of irrelevant information. In a counter-terrorism context, intelligence analysts must be able to distinguish useful signals of potential terrorist activities from useless noise (Baird et al., 2003). On the other hand, sharing too little information can cause *information deficiency*. Every day, intelligence and law enforcement agencies, health care providers, private companies, and numerous other organizations receive information that might be relevant to uncovering a terrorist plot (Baird et al., 2003). Therefore, being able to identify the useful information is critical. In summary, to explore the trade-off and find a way to *balance* sharing of information can greatly improve the outcome of an information sharing operation.

2. **Whom to share with?** Information should be shared with the right *entities*. This is trivial in some cases but becomes an extremely challenging issue when the size of the organization scales up. For instance, intelligence analysis about terrorism requires collaborations among a great number of experts working in different areas such as terrorist organizations, languages, and weapons (Popp et al., 2004). It's no longer easy to identify the right information recipients in such a large virtual organization, especially under time stress situations. Simply broadcasting intelligence is not acceptable because it can easily cause information overload (Baird et al., 2003; Schick et al., 1990).

3. **How to share?** Information should be shared in the right *way*. The teacher can inform the parents about their children's problems *proactively*. Alternatively, the teacher can hold the information until the parents' inquires about their children. In this case, proactive is better than reactive since the parents would rather get timely feedbacks. Nevertheless, proactive is not always better. For instance, when most students are clear about how to do a project and only a few aren't, waiting for students' questions is more efficient for a teacher than giving a lecture to the entire class about the project. Therefore, choosing different information sharing methods, proactive (Yen et al., 2004c) or reactive, can have different results: Either be more *responsive* with faster information sharing or be more *efficient* with lower communication costs.

---

[1]In this chapter, information refers to intelligence information, analyzing reports, or other kinds of information in general.

4. When to share? Information should be shared at the right *time*. It is often easy to tell when to share a piece of information: the sooner the better. However, if the information is changing frequently, it would be better to hold the information until the moment when it is going to be used because otherwise the information will become obsolete. For example, providing information about a sleeper's whereabouts just before a capture operation is better than flooding the information all the time because the location of the sleeper may change from time to time.[2] Sharing a piece of information immediately before one needs it is called "*Just-in-time*", a method that will be explained in Section 12.3.5.

In summary, addressing the above issues can greatly enhance the way to share information: avoiding overload or deficiency, reducing sharing cost, and being more responsive. The issue of information sharing has drawn wide attentions from many areas including information agent, information retrieval, and grid computing. Klusch (2001) classified information agents into three types: to provide resource discovery, to match information consumers with the providers (Sycara et al., 1999), and to offer value-added services. Grid technologies enable large-scale sharing of resources among multiple institutions (Czajkowski et al., 2001) and have been applied to "on demand" services as utility grid computing (Zhang et al., 2004). However, these approaches are incomplete to answer what to share, whom to share with, how to share, or when to share. Our ISCM (Information Supply Chain Management) framework is a synthetic approach that covers information services beyond what the existing approaches can offer.

12.3. THE INFORMATION SUPPLY CHAIN MANAGEMENT FRAMEWORK

Information Supply Chain Management (ISCM) is designed by drawing some ideas from the supply chain management (SCM), which has been widely used in business management science. A supply chain can provide value-added services and fulfill its customer's demands by a network of companies, mainly including (a) suppliers that provide materials, (b) manufactures that make products, and (c) distributors that allocate products to customers. Figure 12.1a shows a typical supply chain.

Similar to a material supply chain, an information supply chain[3] (ISC) can provide *value-added services* to information and fulfill users' information requirements by a network of information sharing agents (ISA) that may include a) scanning agents that gather information and provide information to other agents, b) interpretation agents[4] that analyze the information and make sense of it, and c) broker agents that collect users' requirements and satisfy the requirements with proper information. Figure 12.1b shows an information supply chain.

A material supply chain has two primary targets: to balance demand and supply and to improve efficiency and responsiveness (Chopra and Meindl, 2001). These are also the primary goals for sharing information. So, creating an ICSM framework offers us the opportunity to (a) look at the information sharing problem from a new perspective and (b) better leverage the existing research effort in the SCM framework to find new solutions to information sharing.

---

[2]All examples that are used in this chapter are for idea illustration only. They do not represent any real-life terrorism activities or counter-terrorism operations.
[3]An ISC is different from the information flow of a supply chain.
[4]Scanning and interpretation are from Weick's sensemaking framework (Weick and Daft, 1983).

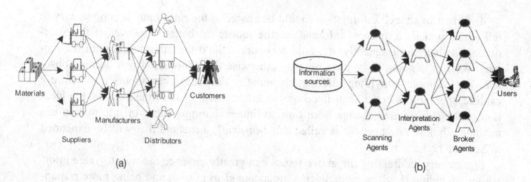

Figure 12.1. (a) A material supply chain. (b) An information supply chain.

Next, we introduce the ISCM framework, which is built upon the key concept of "information supply chain." We establish the mapping from SCM to ISCM in Section 12.3.1. In Section 12.3.2, we explain how the ISCM framework has been implemented using information sharing agents, and then we answer the questions of "What," "Whom," "How," and "When" in Sections 12.3.3 and 12.3.4.

12.3.1. Developing ISCM from SCM

We develop ISCM from SCM from six aspects: goals, problems, concepts, methods, transaction models, and evaluation criteria (as shown in the left two columns of Figure 12.2). First, the ultimate *goal* of both ISCM and SCM is to balance demands and supplies. Unbalanced demands and supplies can lead to poor supply chain performances: either high cost due to oversupplies or poor customer service due to stock-outs. Information

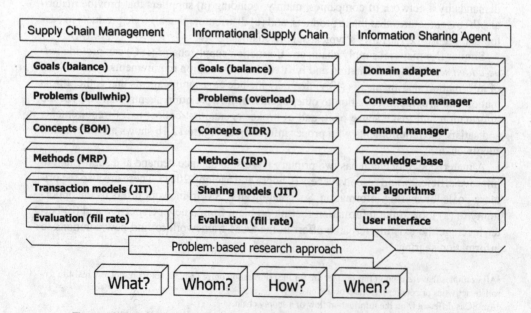

Figure 12.2. From motivation to solution: addressing the information sharing problem

sharing has the same goal: Unbalanced demand and supply can cause problems such as information overload due to supplying too much irrelevant information or information deficiency due to inefficient information investigations.

Second, we can develop a rich set of *concepts* for ISCM by finding a counterpart for each concept of SCM. For example, basic activities and objects (or entities) in SCM such as purchase, sales, product, supplier, customer, and warehouses correspond to those in ISCM: query, inform/answer, information, supplier, requester, and knowledge base, respectively. Even some complex concepts in SCM have their counterpart in ISCM. For example, a bill of materials (BOM) lists the components needed to produce one unit of a product. Checking each component's availability can reveal the shortage for desired productions. Figure 12.3a shows a simple BOM in a tree structure: A computer is composed of a machine, a monitor, and a keyboard. The machine is composed of a main board, a CPU, and a hard disk.

We can find similar composition or *dependency relationships* among information. For example, a piece of information may depend on several supporting evidences, each of which may further depend on other evidences. Such a dependency relationship is called *information dependency relation* (IDR), which can also be represented in a tree-like structure. Figure 12.3b shows an IDR tree about anti-terror intelligence analysis. A group is labeled as "has key insurgents" if the group has a member who is on the wanted list. A group is considered to be "dangerous" if the group has a key insurgent and its size is large. Each node in the tree corresponds to the application of an antecedent-consequent rule.[5] Suppose a group is large and its members are known. Diagnosing the IDR can identify the missing information—"if the members are on the wanted list." Such IDR trees can also be used for information fusion as described in Yen et al. (2003a).

Furthermore, warehouses, machines, or vehicles have capacity limitations for material storage, production, or transportation. Information sharing agents have capacity limitations in a similar way: They have limited memory, time for investigation, reasoning power, or communication bandwidth. In addition, human users have more *cognitive constraints* than agents have. People can only read a very limited amount of information at a time, thus they can be easily overloaded by an overwhelming amount of information from many poorly designed systems.

Third, business models in SCM can be adapted to handle information sharing problems. For example, vendor-managed inventory (VMI) is a business model that specifies that vendors should manage their customers' inventories. After a customer sets its demands over a period of time, the vendor monitors the customer's stock and decides to refill when the stock level is low. It is an effective model that can reduce the workload of a company from inventory management and spend more time for customer service. Similarly, we can adopt the VMI model to share information by subscription, in which an information provider updates its subscribers about any new or changed information. By using a subscription, a user can save time on querying information and spend more time on processing information. We call the subscription model a *counterpart* of the VMI model.

Similar to the VMI model, other business models that have no counterparts for current information sharing solutions can suggest new ways of sharing information. In Section 12.3.5, we introduce a new information sharing method called *Just-in-time* (JIT), which is developed on the basis of Just-in-time in SCM. We should point out that unlike goals or

---

[5]We use logical rules as an example for IDR. However, IDR can also be used to capture other dependences such as the aggregative or selective relations among views and data sources.

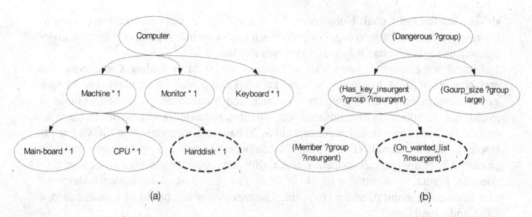

Figure 12.3. (a) A BOM tree. (b) An IDR tree.

terms, developing business models from SCM to ISCM requires a great deal of understanding on information sharing challenges, on differences between handling material and information, and on evaluation criteria. The examples such as subscription or JIT are introduced to inspire readers to pursue new information sharing approaches from an information supply chain perspective.

Finally, criteria such as *fill rate* and *total cost* that are used to evaluate material supply chains can be used to evaluate information supply chains. In ISCM, fill rate (φ) is defined as the ratio between the total number of satisfied requirements (σ) and the total number of requirements (ψ): $\varphi = \delta/\psi$. Fill rates measure responsiveness: The more demands are fulfilled (the higher the fill rate), the better the performance. Total cost measures efficiency by considering the total numbers of information seeking actions and communications. Fill rate and total cost are often contradictory to each other. Oversupplies can often yield a better fill rate. However, oversupplies can cost more and indicate inefficiency. Thus, setting a performance target for an ISC is often a trade off decision: choosing a balanced point between high responsiveness and high efficiency.

Fill rate and total cost are different from precision and recall, two criteria that are used for evaluating information retrieval systems because, in general, precision and recall are used to evaluate individual queries. Precision measures the ratio of relevant information among the total retrieved information. Recall measures the ratio of retrieved relevant information among the total relevant information. In the ISCM framework, precision and recall can be used as "quality control" criteria—to evaluate how well the provided information satisfies each information requirement.

Above, we (a) identified the information sharing problems such as information overload and information deficiency, (b) set goals such as to balance demand and supply and to improve efficiency, (c) defined terms and concepts such as information customer, vendor, and IDR, (d) adapted business models such as subscribe and JIT, and (e) selected evaluation criteria such as fill rate and cost. It is worth to note that SCM differs from ISCM in many ways (explained more detailed in Section 12.5.1). It is unwise to borrow everything from SCM to ISCM in a stiff manner. In spite of the differences, we believe that some *high-level* concepts, goals, methods, and the philosophy of SCM are useful for managing information requirements and improving information sharing results. In the next section, we introduce the design of an information sharing agent (ISA) architecture, which can be used to model information agents for constructing an ISC.

12.3.2. Realizing ISCs Using Information Sharing Agents

Information agents for an ISC should have essential functions such as managing information requirements, planning for information seeking operations, and fulfilling the requirements. We designed an ISA architecture[6] that has all the essential functions. The ISA architecture is composed of a communication manager, a knowledge base, a process manager, a decision model, and an information requirement planning (IRP) module, which interacts with other components through a demand manager and a supply manager. Figure 12.4 gives the interface screenshots for an IRP, a communication manager, a process manager, and a knowledge base. In this section, we will introduce each of these components.

12.3.2.1. Communication Manager. The communication manager governs inter-agent communications. An agent may either initiate a new conversation or simply follow existing ones. The communication manager organizes related messages into a conversation session, and monitors the development of the ongoing conversation according to a conversation protocol. An "inquiry" or "inform" creates a new conversation. An "answer," "acknowledgement," or "reject" may end the current conversation. The communication manager serves as a channel to request and fulfill information requirements between two agents. A screenshot, "a3" in Figure 12.4, shows a monitoring interface of a communication manager.

12.3.2.2. Knowledge Base. Each agent has an internal knowledge base (KB) to maintain what it believes regarding the external world. The KB is a forward-chaining rule-based system that specifies how to represent information,[7] information sources, and information dependency relations. For our research, we use predicates to represent information or information type, and we use rules to represent IDR. Figure 12.5 lists examples for an information type, information, and a rule.

To simplify the representation issues, information will be represented as *facts*. A fact is an instance of a *fact type*. Each fact type describes a common schema for facts of the same type. A fact type is composed of two essential kinds of elements: *predicate* name and *arguments* and four optional kinds of elements: a template, a time duration, sources, and needers. For example, "abnormal-activity (?virus ?location)" in Figure 12.5 is a fact type: "abnormal-activity" is a predicate name; "?virus" and "?location" are arguments. A fact type can have multiple fact instances. For example, "abnormal-activity (hog_virus Chicago)" is a fact, where argument "?virus" is bound to "hog_virus" and "?location" is bound to "Chicago." Similarly, "abnormal-activity (nine_west_virus Louisiana)" is a different fact of the same fact type.

In addition to the two essential elements, a fact type can specify four optional kinds of information: a template, a time duration, sources, and needers. First, each fact type can have a *natural language* mapping template, which can translate a fact from or to natural language sentences. This simple design provides information sharing agents with a basic capability to handle information that is used by human users. Second, facts can be *time-sensitive* because they can become obsolete as time proceeds. The duration of a fact type

---

[6]The ISA architecture that we developed is a prototype for research on information sharing problems, not for real-life applications.

[7]Here, we use the term information and fact interchangeably.

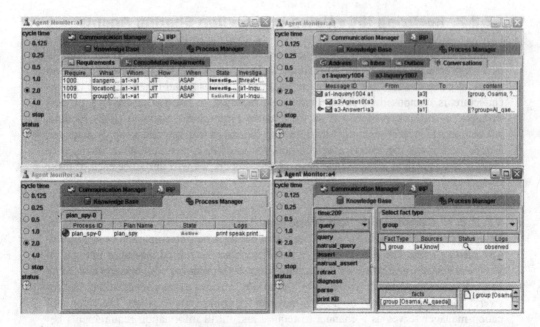

Figure 12.4. The interfaces of information sharing agents.

can be pre-specified according to the nature of the information. Different types of information may vary in their durations. Lastly, *needers and sources* of a fact type specify the "long-term" customers and vendors, respectively. For example, in Figure 12.5, "sources" indicate that an FBI or CIA agent can obtain information about this type of information and the "needer" indicates that CIA headquarters need this type of information. If an agent has multiple customers or vendors, it needs to make decisions on where to "sell" or where to "buy". However, both needers and sources are not fixed because an information sharing agent has an incentive to "sell" information to other potential customers, or to find alternative vendors when the current vendors cannot fulfill a requirement. Such dynamics depend upon an open interaction mechanism such as an *information market*.

Rules will be used to represent relations between fact types. Once fired, a rule can generate an implied fact on the basis of a set of facts called "evidences," which are preserved for each implied fact. This is very useful when information link-analysis is needed: The more evidences, the more credible the information (Sun et al., 2005). In a rule, the dependency relationship between the consequence predicate and the rest (antecedent predicates) forms a dependency relationship for the information type that each predicate represents. The rule, "signs_for_bio_attack" in Figure 12.5, forms a dependency relationship whereby the consequence predicate (bio-terror ?location) depends on antecedent predicates: (abnormal-activity ?virus ?location), (bio-expert ?person ?location), and (symptom ?virus ?location).

Rules can also be used to *interpret* information or *diagnose* missing information. An agent can interpret each piece of new information with rules that contain predicates that match the information. For example, if hog_virus is found in Chicago, the information will be interpreted with the rule "signs_for_bio_attack," and we will try to interpret the information as a hypothesis "bio-terror Chicago." Because some information is not available, the KB will diagnose the missing information by considering the IDR. In the above

```
(FactType abnormal-activity (?virus ?location)
     (template "?location has abnormal activity with ?virus virus")
     (time 10)
     (source (FBI investigation))
     (source (CIA investigation))
     (needer (CIA_headquarters))
)

(Rule "signs_for_bio_attack"
     (abnormal-activity ?virus ?location)
     (bio-expert ?person ?location)
     (symptom ?virus ?location)
     ->
     (bio-terror ?location)
)

(Fact abnormal-activity (hog_virus Chicago)
     (time 10)
     (source (FBI_Chicago informed))
)
```

Figure 12.5. Examples of information type, information, and IDR.

example, two pieces of information, (bio-expert ?person Chicago) and (symptom hog_virus Chicago), are missing for evaluating the hypothesis.

It worth to note that real-life tasks for intelligence sharing and counter-terrorism analysis demand much more than what we designed here mainly because intelligence reports are usually in unstructured natural langrage format, which is difficult to understand by computational systems. Under this situation, explicitly representing information dependencies, information types, or information requirements become a challenging task. In addition, the real-life systems require standardization of a wide range of techniques from natural language processing to information semantics or ontology that are used across all agencies. Without standards, sharing information under the ISCM framework can introduce ambiguity and information lost. In this chapter, we will focus on the issue of information requirement planning and simplify other issues such as those on representation, semantics, and standardization.

12.3.2.3. Process Manager. Processes or predefined *plans* are used to model the procedures for counter-terrorism operations. The process manager manages the templates of the plans, each of which contains preconditions, effects, termination conditions, fail conditions, a contingency plan, and a process body. Upon being requested by the decision-making module or the IRP module, the process manager can instantiate plan instances from appropriate templates. An agent may run multiple plan instances simultaneously, each of which can be in active, suspended, wait, failed, or terminated state. The process manager is responsible for scheduling the execution of plan instances based on the constraints associated with the instances and the current KB state. Figure 12.6 gives a process that specifies how to count numbers from an initial value to a target value.

A process manager has two roles: to model investigation activities and to model the information requirements for a task. Investigation activities can be modeled as processes so that an information sharing agent can not only share information, but also seek information by actions. For example, measurements, scout operations, and search queries are investigation activities.

```
(plan plan_count_from_to(?from ?to)
    (precondition (current_number ?number))
    (failcondition (> ?number ?to))
    (contingency (plan_count_back_to ?number ?to))
    (termcondition (current_number ?to))
    (process
        (plan_count)
        (choice big_or_small
            ((prefcondition (> ?number 7.0))(print "big"))
            ((prefcondition (< ?number 3.0))(print "small"))
            ((default)(print "medium"))
        )
    )
)
```

Figure 12.6. An example of process that count numbers in either ascending or descending.

Additionally, directly capturing an information requirement as part of an operation procedure can overcome the issue that first responders often find that the provided information is irrelevant and not *actionable* (Baird et al., 2003). This is because information that is required for operations is modeled as preconditions, termination conditions, fail conditions, or preference conditions. Thus, information that is useful to evaluate these conditions is relevant to the operations. In addition to information required for operations, an agent can also model the requirements for complex decision making. In order to be relevant and actionable, agents should only share information that fits these requirements. Section 12.3.3.2 introduces how to anticipate these information requirements through a shared mental model (Cannon-Bowers et al., 1993) analysis.

12.3.2.4. The IRP Module. The IRP module coordinates information requirements, launches investigations, and fulfills the requirements. Figure 12.7 shows the steps of this process as numbered labels. First, initial information requirements are collected by a demand manager, which either anticipates others' requirements (1a) or creates requirements upon request (1b). Next, the requirements are consolidated and prioritized by the IRP algorithm (step 2). Then, the IRP investigate each requirement following an investigation strategy, which specifies an order of different investigation methods. An agent has three methods to investigate: taking investigation action (3a), diagnosing a requirement and seeking information for dependent requirements (3b), and querying others who might know or can obtain the required information (3c). Lastly, a supply manager monitors the investigation status and fulfills the requirements when information is available. We will introduce the information requirement representation and how to anticipate information requirements for a task in Section 12.3.3 and give algorithms for IRP in Section 12.3.4.

12.3.3. Information Requirements

To balance the demand and supply, an ISC should manage effectively information requirements. In the flowing subsections, we formally define how to represent information requirements and discussion about why anticipation of requirements and proactive information sharing behavior can help the intelligence analysis and the emergency responses for terror attacks.

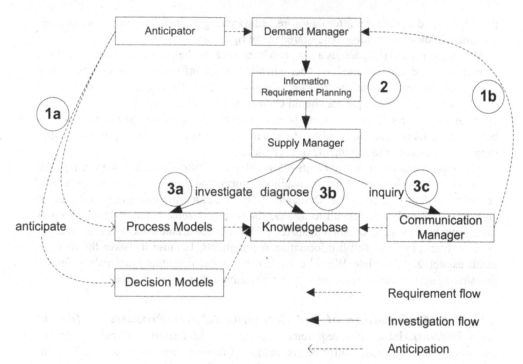

Figure 12.7. The information sharing agent architecture.

12.3.3.1. Definition of Information Requirements.

An information requirement (r) specifies what is required (p), who needs it (a), how to respond (m), and when it is needed (t)—formally denoted as $r = <p, a, m, t>$. **What** is required (p) specifies both an information type and a size limit of expected results. An agent can fulfill a requirement if it knows information i that can satisfy p. How to represent i or p is relevant to problem domains. For example, p can be either a logical condition or an SQL query statement. Likewise, i can be either a logical proposition or a database record. In addition, p also includes a size limit, which specifies a maximum number of results that the needer can process. An agent should be clear about what is required so that it can satisfy the requirements with both the right type and the right amount of information.

Who needs it (a) specifies a requestor and a needer. The requestor may be a different agent from the needer. For instance, agent a_1 may request certain information from a_2 for agent a_3. Then, a_1 is the requestor and a_3 is the needer. The difference between requestor and needer has been incorporated in current business practices for a long time: A sales order normally specifies a sold-to party who placed the order and a ship-to party who get the products. Yet current agent communication methods such as FIPA (FIPA, 1997) or KQML (Finin et al., 1994) have overlooked the deference. They simply specify a requestor or an initiator without explicitly specify who the needer is. This makes an agent unable to identify duplication of information requirements that are from different requestors.

How to respond (m) specifies a protocol such as "one-time query," "third-party subscribe" (J Yen et al., 2004), "protell" (Yen et al., 2001), or "JIT." Each protocol specifies how a provider interprets requirements and how the provider interacts with other agents such as needers or requestors. For example, if an agent subscribes certain information, the provider should update the information regarding changes. Including protocols in a requirement allows information to be shared in the right way.

When it is needed (t) specifies a time condition such as "before certain time," "as soon as possible," "at certain time," or "periodically." Most information requirements may choose "before certain time" or "as soon as possible." Nevertheless, if a requester chooses subscribe or JIT, the requestor should choose "within certain time range" or "periodically" as its time conditions. Whether or not a provider satisfies the time conditions can be used to evaluate its service quality. We can improve the performance of an information supply chain by better satisfying the time conditions.

This representation of requirements allows effective information sharing because the representation can increase demand visibility. Information demands, in current research, are often implicit or incomplete. Demands are often hidden in assumptions, queries, or protocols. This makes it difficult to address the four questions: what to share, whom to share with, how to share, or when to share. With the ISCM framework, it is easy to organize, analyze, plan, and fulfill information requirements, because it makes the requirements explicit and complete. We believe that better demand visibility can make information sharing systems more responsive without causing information overload.

12.3.3.2. Anticipation of Requirements Allows Proactive Information Sharing.
Information requirements come from three sources: direct requests (or independent requirements), collaborative sharing of requests, and *anticipations*. First, an agent or a user can request certain information by directly asking or subscribing. Such requests generate information requirements immediately. After the agent created a new request, it may forward it to other agents who can provide the information or seek information by investigating evidences, which may generate new requirements (or dependent requirements).

Additionally, an agent can anticipate other's needs according to their mutual beliefs (Cannon-Bowers et al., 1993; Orasanu, 1990; Sycara and Lewis, 1991; Yen et al., 2004a). An agent *Alice* can anticipate that another agent *Bob* needs information *I*, if *Alice* believes that (a) *Bob* currently has or about to have a task *T*, (b) *I* is relevant to *T*, and (c) *Bob* does not know *I*. Anticipation of information requirements allows proactive information sharing behavior. In the above example, when *Alice* anticipate that *Bob* needs *I*, she will proactively seek the information that is relevant to *I* and provide it to *Bob*. To further study how to anticipate other's needs, we analyze *T* as three types of tasks: routine operations, complex decision-making tasks, and information analysis tasks.

First, a task can be for *routine operations,* which have well-defined working procedures. For example, a firefighter can put out an ordinary fire by following standard procedures. In our agent architecture, conducting a procedure may require four types of information: preconditions, termination condition, fail conditions, and preference conditions. (1) A precondition specifies whether certain operations can be executed. For example, a fire engine must be in position before it can start to extinguish a fire. (2) A termination condition specifies whether the current goal is achieved or become irrelevant (Cohen & Levesque, 1991). "A fire is extinguished" is a condition that tells firefighters to terminate the current extinguishing operation. Additionally, a termination condition can represent a condition that tells that the current goal is irrelevant, such as when the firefighters learned that the fire is set on purpose for shooting a movie and doesn't need to be put out. (3) A fail condition specifies whether the current operation is failed (Cohen and Levesque, 1991). For example, a fire is out of control. If so, a contingency plan, such as "to evacuate," should be instantiated. (4) A preference condition specified whether to choose an alternative operation among several others. These kinds of information are essential for successful missions. Thus, anticipation for the requirements and proactively sending the relevant information to the mission operators are always desirable.

Next, a task can be for making a complex *decision,* which is difficult to be captured as routine procedures. For example, a terrorism attack usually cannot be addressed simply according to a predefined procedure, but needs collaboration among experts who have rich set of experiences. We use an RPD model (Klein, 1989; Yen et al., 2004b) to capture how domain experts make decisions based on the recognition of similarity between the current situation and past experiences. A decision maker tries to recognize by matching the set of observed cues (synthesized from information describing the current situation) with the pattern of cues considered in past experiences. After recognition, expectancies serve as conditions for continuing working on the current recognition. Due to the dynamic and uncertain nature of the environment, it is important to monitor the status of the expectancies because a decision maker may have misinterpreted a situation but she cannot recognize it until some expectancy is invalidated as the situation further evolves. Therefore, cues and expectancies are the key information requirements for the RPD model. Proactively providing such useful information for the decision maker allows not only fast recognition, but also fast response to adapt current decisions.

Lastly, a task can be for *analyzing information,* a task that requires knowledge about how various types of information are linked and related. We use an Information Dependency Relationship (IDR) to represent such knowledge for interpretation and investigations. For example, in Figure 12.5, the rule "signs_for_bio_attack" captured the information analysis knowledge for information type "(symptom ?virus ?location)." When *Alice* is analyzing a piece of information "symptom hog_virus Chicago," it is useful if *Bob* can proactively inform *Alice* if any bio-experts are around Chicago area.

In summary, anticipation of information requirements allows proactive information sharing behavior. Such a proactive behavior strategy is crucial for effective intelligence analysis that can prevent possible terror attacks and for efficient responses to terror attacks.

12.3.4. Information Requirement Planning (IRP)

Above, we introduced how to manage the information requirements: how to represent and how to capture the requirements. In this section, we will introduce how to plan and satisfy the requirements. When an agent has a few requirements at a time, it may be easy to handle, investigate, and seek required information. However, as the number of requirements increases or as the agent needs to work under significant time pressure, it is necessary to plan and collaborate to make the information investigations and supplies efficient.

To achieve efficient planning, we adopt a commonly used method from the SCM framework—*material requirement planning* (MRP). MRP proposes how to satisfy material requirements by considering type, quantity, and time of the requirements. According to the BOM and available materials, MRP can determine any shortages and creates the appropriate procurement or production plans. On the basis of MRP, we developed *information requirement planning* (IRP) for proposing plans to satisfy information requirements. IRP determines missing information according to the information dependency relation (IDR) and available information. IRP, then, creates information seeking plans accordingly.

SCM uses collaborative planning methods to prevent unstable demand forecast and supply problems, known as "bullwhip" effects. Through collaboration, business partners create a common plan on how to satisfy consumers' demand across the supply chain network. A common plan avoids redundant or deficient supplies. We can apply the same principle in ISC management. Agents can avoid duplications on anticipating, finding, or sending information through collaborations.

Figure 12.8 gives two IRP algorithms: a reactive (*pull*) one and a proactive (*push*) one. The reactive IRP, Pull_IRP, fulfills a requirement by finding or producing information that can satisfy the requirement. Pull_IRP consolidates duplicated requirements from different sources. For example, if an agent gets a requirement that has already been anticipated, the agent should combine the two requirements to avoid duplicated efforts. Step 4 in Pull_IRP, gathering evidences, is based on identifying missing information, which can be obtained by considering the IDR and available information. The Push_IRP algorithm

Pull_IRP()	Push_IRP(information)
1. An agent consolidates all the information requirements from users' requests, indirect requests by an interpretation agent as in step 4, or anticipations of other's needs.	1. An agent obtains a new piece of information by scanning/observing the environment or by implying new information from evidences as in step 4.
2. **For each** unsatisfied new requirement r: Pull_IRP(r)	2. **If** the agent has a requirement that can be satisfied by the information, **then** satisfy the requirement by sending the information to the needer.
3. **If** the agent can obtain the required information directly by observing or querying information sources, **then** satisfy the requirement by sending the information to the needer.	3. **If** the agent knows how to interpret the information, **then** interpret the information.
4. **Else if** the agent knows how to derive the information by necessary evidences $<p_1, p_{2...}, p_n>$, **then** generate new requirements to gather the evidences: Pull_IRP($<p_1, p_{2...}, p_n>$)	4. **If** the agent generates a new information i', **then** push new information to others: Push_IRP(i');
5. **If** the agent cannot get sufficient evidences, **then** go to 7.	5. **Else if** further information is needed: $<p_1, p_{2...}, p_n>$, **then** gather the missing information: Pull_IRP($<p_1, p_{2...}, p_n>$. Then, go to 3.
6. **Else** derive the needed information and go to 3.	
7. **Else if** the agent knows other agents who can obtain/derive the information, **then** pass the requirement to others (copy the original request and set self as the requestor).	
8. **If** all other others declare unable to fulfill the request, **then** go to 10	
9. **Else** derive the needed information and go to 3.	
10. **Else** declare unable to fulfill the request.	

Figure 12.8. Basic IRP algorithms.

proactively scans and interprets new information so that agents fulfill requirements without further delay. To make the algorithms easy to understand, we ignore the time aspect of requirements and assume that each agent keeps an acquaintance model that details others capabilities, such as who can provide what kind of information.

Theses two algorithms are basic skeletons for more complex sharing methods, such as JIT. Moreover, the algorithm Pull_IRP can choose a different order of investigations or investigational strategies. For instance, an agent can investigate in the following order: First, conduct investigation action; then, diagnose to find dependent requirements; and last, query others. Alternatively, the agent can choose to query others first, to find dependent requirements next, and to conduct investigation actions last. How to choose or adapt investigation strategies to optimize an information supply chain is an interesting research topic that deserves further attention.

12.3.5. Sharing Information Using Just-in-Time

The ISCM framework can also lead to new solutions for information sharing because years of research and practice in supply chain management can suggest overlooked problems, concepts, and methods in the field of information sharing. For example, Just-in-Time (JIT) is an efficient supply mode that aims to maintain high-volume productions with minimum inventories (raw materials, work-in-process, or finish goods). Successful JIT productions depend on close collaborations with suppliers. The JIT philosophy, "to avoid over supply," reflects a goal of information sharing: to avoid information overload. We thus propose using the JIT method to handle situations when agents/users are overloaded with frequently changed information. For example, suppose Tom lives in New York and he needs go to London for a conference in one month. He wants to check weather conditions before he leaves. It would be appropriate to pass the local weather forecast of London to Tom just before he leaves, as specified in JIT. Other methods are inappropriate. If Tom requests a forecast now, the information will become obsolete by the time he leaves. If Tom subscribes forecasts regularly (e.g., daily), he has to receive weather information regarding days before he leaves, which he doesn't need. In this case, a JIT request is the most appropriate approach because (a) the information will not become obsolete and (b) Tom will not get overloaded by irrelevant forecasts. The JIT method is suitable for requesting changing information such as weather forecasts, locations of moving objects, exchange rates, prices, and so on.

Figure 12.9 gives the JIT algorithm. First, a broker agent plans how to get the requested information by sending the request to other agents. If a provider can fulfill the request-

---

```
JIT_IRP (requirement)
1.   The user specifies a new information requirement <r> and passes
     it to a broker agent.
2.   The broker schedules a set of requirements <r_k> to agents <a_k>
     who can collaboratively obtain and derive information that can
     satisfy the requirement <r>.
3.   For each agent who belongs to <a_k>, the agent scans, passes, and
     derives information as scheduled: JIT_IRP (<r_k>).
4.   The broker sends the result as its user has scheduled.
```

Figure 12.9. JIT algorithm.

ed information, it will send a confirmation to the requester. When a scheduled time arrives, the provider will scan or derive requested information and deliver the information without further requirements from requestors. Detailed planning process for step 2 can be obtained through the Pull_IRP algorithm.

12.4. AN EXAMPLE OF INFORMATION SUPPLY CHAIN FOR INTELLIGENCE SHARING

In this section, we demonstrate how to use information sharing agents to address a particular intelligence sharing case. We take a bio-terror threat scenario from the Markle report (Baird et al., 2003) to study the problem of information sharing between and within government agencies. It is worth to note that this example is only to illustrate the concept of ISCM, how an ISC can capture the information requirements and how it can identify the information needers that are often neglected by current solutions.

> This scenario begins with a report from a special agent of FBI Chicago field office. A source informs an FBI special agent that there is a plan to spread a sickness with a virus that terrorist scientists have extracted from sick hogs. Someone would drive from Chicago to St. Louis with a cooler containing several packages and would hand the cooler over to someone in St. Louis. The individual would then drive somewhere else and hand the cooler to another operative. The source believes the package could contain the virus.
>
> After about one month, a highly reliable source in Afghanistan informs CIA that "sleepers" had been placed in the U.S. for the purpose of carrying out terrorist attacks. All sleepers have lifescience backgrounds and are working in universities and other facilities in Chicago. One of the sleepers is called "Sadiq", a postdoctoral student in microbiology. This particular group aims to sow panic in the U.S. They were told to scare Americans rather than create a spectacular attack such as the one on September 11.

The Markle report also gives likely information sharing methods that are used today and highlights their problems. Currently, the information will go to Joint Terrorism Task Force (JTTF) and FBI headquarters. FBI will pass the information to Terrorist Threat Integration Center where the information will be analyzed and correlated. A detailed information flow diagram is shown in Figure 12.10. However, the information failed to go to the Chicago police department, other state or local law enforcement, health, and agricultural agencies. The scenario illustrates that without an overall framework to link the regional or local networks, the full potential of state and local governments will never be realized. Poor coordination of information sharing efforts might cause critical clues of impending terrorist attacks to go unnoticed (Baird et al., 2003).

12.4.1. Using an ISC to Share Information

The information supply chain used in this scenario is composed of eight information sharing agents, each of which represents a government agency. Figure 12.11 shows how the information is relayed to the proper agencies. In the following section, we explain the information sharing process step by step.

1. *Share Information from FBI Chicago Field Office to the FBI Headquarters and Local Law Enforcement Agencies.* Assume that the FBI Chicago office only has limited information resources and methods to interpret the information about the suspicious activi-

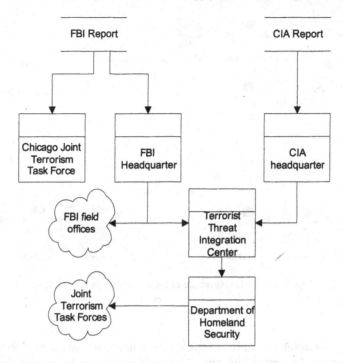

Figure 12.10. A likely as-is information flow of threat information processing.

ties with viruses. Thus, when receiving the information about abnormal activities with hog virus—namely, "abnormal-activity (hog_virus Chicago)"—the office cannot interpret it. However, as a normal practice that presented in the as-is solution, the office may know that the FBI headquarters and the local law enforcement agency need this type of information. So, the office will directly pass the information to the FBI headquarters and Chicago police department.

```
(FactType abnormal-activity (?virus ?location)
        (needer Police-department)
        (needer FBI_headquarters))
```

2. *Share Information from the FBI Headquarters to TTIC Counter Bio-Terror Division.* Similar to step 1, the FBI headquarters further relays the information to TTIC counter-bio-terror division. The information sharing activities are routine because the information needers are regular and are explicitly specified. This type of information sharing is easy, thus they have already been addressed in as-is solutions.

3. *Share information requirements from the TTIC to CIA headquarters and a health agency.* If we assume TTIC has knowledge (a rule) to interpret the information about suspicious activities about virus, TTIC can then initiate a diagnostic investigation.

```
(Rule "signs_for_bio_attack"
        (abnormal-activity ?virus ?location)
        (bio-expert ?person ?location)
        (symptom ?virus ?location)
        ->
        (bio-terror ?location))
```

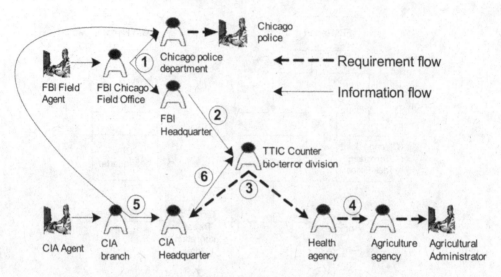

Figure 12.11. The structure of the Information Supply Chain.

The investigation results in a list of dependent requirements, including (bio-expert ?person Chicago) and (symptom hog_virus Chicago), which can be sourced from the CIA headquarters, the health agency. Because TTIC does not have the information, it will dispatch the two dependent requirements to the CIA headquarters and the health agency, respectively.

This step illustrates why the useful information is relayed to the health agency, which was not the case in the as-is intelligence sharing process. The difference is not because we know that the information should be shared with the health agency, but because we let the TTIC has the *knowledge* or capability to relate the two types of different information: "abnormal-activity" and "symptom." When identifying that "(symptom hog_virus Chicago)" is relevant to interpret the abnormal activity, very naturally, TTIC will pass the information to the most likely information vendor—the health agency. Therefore, we believe that, in this example, the knowledge or the information dependency relationship (IDR) is the key for repairing current broken links in information sharing across agencies.

4. *Share Information Requirements from the Health Agency to the Agricultural Agency.* Assume the health agency does not have any cases with hog_virus symptoms but it knows that it is important to monitor if there are any animals cases.

```
(Rule "sign for virus"
      (animal_symptom ?virus ?location)
      ->
      (symptom ?virus ?location))
```

The health agency then will request information about cases regarding animal symptoms from agriculture agency. Similar to step 3, the driving force of this sharing behavior is the information dependency relationship.

Up to this step, the Chicago police department, the CIA headquarters, and the health and agriculture agencies are all aware about the information requirements to interpret situations about suspicious hog virus activities and launch actions to investigate or monitor with focused attention.

5. *Share new information from the CIA branch office to CIA headquarters.* The new information about sleep cell comes in to a CIA branch office: (bio-expert Sadiq Chicago). From step 3, the CIA office knows that the local law enforcement and headquarters needs this information, so, it notifies the information to the needers.

6. *Share information from the CIA headquarters to TTIC.* In step 3, TTIC has posted CIA headquarters about a requirement for bio-expert information in Chicago area. Now, the new information matches the requirement. Naturally, CIA passes the needed information to TTIC. Step 5 and 6 demonstrate that the demand management can effectively organize the requirements such that all requirements will be constantly monitored and will not get off the radar of the investigational agencies before they are satisfied or expired.

12.4.2. How ICSM Responds to the Challenges Raised in SHARE

As demonstrated from the case, the ICSM framework is a promising approach to achieving the goals that are specified in the SHARE network design. First, the ISC structure is *distributed* and loosely coupled. There is no central control in the ISC. The connections for each agent are specified as needers and sources for each information type. If needers and sources are properly maintained, information can be relayed to the needers throughout the network. In addition, the design allows forming multiple paths for each type of information. Therefore, assigning multiple needers and sources to each information type can resist single point failures. Second, directories are maintained locally: information flow to the needers, and requirements flow to providers. A simulated ISC can be used for testing before constructing a real-life ISC so that information or requirements will not flood and overload some agents. In other words, the demand and supply are balanced. An ISC can adjust its information processing or investigation capabilities by adding or removing nodes so as to reduce the nodes that are likely to have unbalanced demand and supply. Sources and needers that are specified for each information type can evolve over time—new sources and needers are added, while some problematic ones are dropped—similar to a company getting or losing customers or vendors. Lastly, the ISCM framework aims to not only promote legitimate information sharing, but also enforce secured access controls and provide an effective way to improve information credibility. The thesis on *secure* and *credible* information sharing using the ISCM framework can be found in Sun et al. (2005).

12.5. DISCUSSIONS

We have introduced how to develop ISCM from SCM, described how to implement ISA, and explained how to formulate information requirements to answer the subproblems of information sharing. Now, we discuss the differences between ISCM and SCM and the relations between ISCM and existing methods. Additionally, we will briefly discuss our future research along the line.

12.5.1. ISCM Differs from SCM

SCM deals with the flow of materials, while ISCM deals with the flow of information. When we borrow strategies and methods from SCM to ISCM, the differences between material and information should be considered. First, *quantity* is used to measure material requirements. One material cannot fulfill demands from two requests. In contrast, we cannot use quantity to describe information. A piece of information can fulfill all demands about this kind of information, no matter how many requests are about it. Furthermore, processing *activities* for handling material and information are different. Material handling includes ordering, producing, packing, loading, and shipping, whereas information processing includes query, observing, reasoning, and transforming. The difference results in different challenges between SCM and ISCM. For example, uncertainties are big challenges for producing and shipping for a material supply chain, whereas uncertainties are not a problem for producing information or transmitting information. Finally, materials have *values,* which can be determined in a market, whereas no market exists for information exchange. Although material differs from information in many ways, we believe that concepts, goals, methods, and the philosophy of SCM can greatly improve information sharing results.

12.5.2. ISCM Unifies Existing Methods

The ISCM framework serves as an information sharing platform regardless of complex information contents. The framework is *general* enough to manage various information sharing activities, from scanning and interpretation to information delivery. Many existing information sharing methods can be unified and incorporated into ISCM by matching a counterpart method in the SCM framework. For example, FIPA "Query Interaction Protocol" (FIPA, 2002) specifies how to handle a query between an initiator and a participant as shown in Figure 12.12a. We can find a counterpart process in SCM, such as PIP-3A1 (Request Quote as shown in Figure 12.12b) from Rosettanet (RosettaNet, 2003) in which a seller can choose to confirm a request or refer other suppliers if it cannot satisfy the request. It is easy to notice that the *referral* option is ignored in FIPA's specification. We thus can extend the current query protocol to incorporate the choice of referring alternative suppliers as third-party query confirmation. The third-party order process and the third-party query process are shown in Figure 12.13. Similar to the query interaction protocol, ISCM is capable of unifying many other information sharing protocols such as

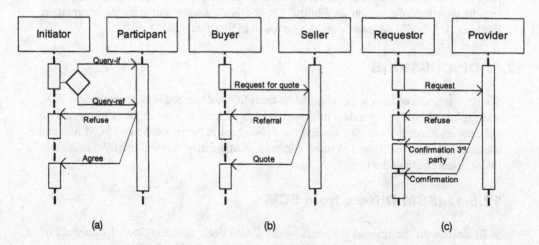

(a)   (b)   (c)

Figure 12.12. (a) FIPA query. (b) PIP FRQ. (c) ISCM query.

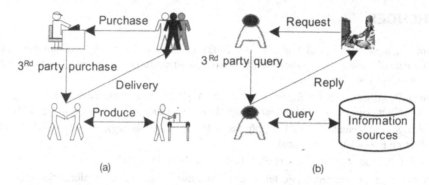

Figure 12.13. (a) Third-party order process. (b) Third-party query.

"subscription," "third-party subscribe" (Yen et al., 2004a), and "protell" (Yen et al., 2001).

12.5.3. Future Research

For the future research along the direction of ISCM, we plan to design a simulated *information market,* model the information overload problem, and conduct comparative experiments for new information sharing methods. First, a simulated information market can serve as a test-bed environment, through which we investigate research issues about information supply chains such as the scalability of the information supply chain approach and the organization and management of information supply chains. Next, we plan to model the information overload constraints that exist among human users. Such constraints are important for us to understand the challenge of the problem of information overload and make information sharing methods more realistic and closer to real-life problems. Then, we can evaluate different information sharing methods, strategies, or ISC configurations by evaluation criteria such as fill rate and total cost. We may also apply the ISC concepts addressing some real-life problems. Finally, economic theories play an important role in the SCM studies. It will be an interesting research idea that brings economic theories or market mechanisms into the field of information sharing.

SUMMARY

In this chapter, we (a) analyzed the problem of information sharing from a perspective that can capture a whole picture of information requirement, (b) developed a framework to study and address these problems, (c) implemented an agent architecture that can capture, consolidate, investigate, and satisfy dynamic information requirements in a timely manner, and (d) tested the framework with a intelligence sharing problem.

The goal of this research is to create a generic framework for information sharing using the SCM metaphor. Sharing information requires a clear understanding about what to share, whom to share with, how to share, and when to share. The information supply chain framework explicitly captures these questions as information requirements, so we expect that the systems developed under the framework will enable the right information to be delivered to the right recipients in the right way and at the right time.

REFERENCES

Baird, Z., Barksdale, J., and Vatis, M. A. (2003). *Creating a Trusted Information Network for Homeland Security* (http://www.markletaskforce.org/reports/TFNS_Report2_Master.pdf). New York City: The Markle Foundation.

Cannon-Bowers, J. A., Salas, E., and Converse, S. A. (1993). Shared mental models in expert team decision making. In: *Individual and Group Decision Making, N. Castellan (ed.), pp. 221–246.*

Chopra, S., and Meindl, P. (2001). *Supply Chain Management: Strategy, Planning, and Operation.* Pearson Education International.

Cohen, P. R., and Levesque, H. J. (1991). Teamwork. *Nous* **25**(4):487–512.

Czajkowski, K., Fitzgerald, S., Foster, I., and Kesselman, C. (2001). Grid information services for distributed resource sharing. Paper presented at the 10th IEEE Symposium on High Performance Distributed Computing (HPDC-10), San Francisco, CA.

Finin, T., Fritzson, R., McKay, D., and McEntire, R. (1994). KQML as an agent communication language. Paper presented at the Third International Conference on Information and Knowledge Management (CIKM'94), Gaithersburg, MD.

FIPA (1997). *Foundation for Intelligent Physical Agents* (PC00089C). Geneva, Switzerland: Foundation for Intelligent Physical Agents.

FIPA (2002). *FIPA Query Interaction Protocol Specification* (SC00027H). Geneva, Switzerland: Foundation for Intelligent Physical Agents.

Klein, G. A. (1989). Recognition-primed decisions. In: *Advances in Man–Machine Systems Research,* Vol. 5, W. B. Rouse (ed.), pp. 47–92. Greenwich, CT: JAI Press.

Klusch, M. (2001). Information agent technology for the internet: A survey. *Journal on Data and Knowledge Engineering, Special Issue on Intelligent Information Integration* **36**(3).

Orasanu, J. (1990). Shared mental models and crew performance. Paper presented at the 34 Annual Meeting of the Human Factors Society, Orlando, FL.

Popp, R., Armour, T., Senator, T., and Numrych, K. (2004). Countering terrorism through information technology. *Communication of ACM* **47**(3).

RosettaNet. (2003). *PIP 3A1 Business Process Model:* Uniform Code Council.

Schick, A. G., Gordon, L. A., and Haka, S. (1990). Information overload: A temporal approach. *Accounting, Organizations and Society* **15**(3):199–220.

Sun, S., Liu, P., Airy, G., Zhu, S., and Yen, J. (2005). Toward secure and credible information sharing using information supply chains. *International Journal of Uncertainty, Fuzziness and Knowledge-Based Systems* (submitted).

Sycara, K., Klusch, M., Widoff, S., and Lu, J. (1999). Dynamic service matchmaking among agents in open information environments. *Journal ACM SIGMOD Record (Special Issue on Semantic Interoperability in Global Information Systems)* **28**(1):47–53.

Sycara, K., and Lewis, M. (1991). *Cooperation of Heterogeneous Agents Through the Formation of Shared Mental Models.* Paper presented at the AAAI-91 Workshop on Cooperation Among Heterogeneous Intelligent Systems, Anaheim, CA.

Weick, K. E., and Daft, R. E. (Eds.). (1983). *The Effectiveness of Interpretation Systems.* New York: Academic Press.

Yen, J., Yin, J., Ioerger, T. R., Miller, M. S., Xu, D., and Volz, R. A. (2001). CAST: Collaborative agents for simulating teamwork. Paper presented at the Seventeenth International Joint Conference on Artificial Intelligence (IJCAI-01), Seattle, WA.

Yen, J., Fan, X., Sun, S., Wang, R., Chen, C., Kamali, K., and Volz, R. A. (2003b). Implementing shared mental models for collaborative teamwork. Paper presented at the the Workshop on Collaboration Agents: Autonomous Agents for Collaborative Environments in the IEEE/WIC Intelligent Agent Technology Conference, Halifax, Canada.

Yen, J., Fan, X., and Volz, R. A. (2003b). Proactive information exchanges based on the awareness of teammates' information needs. Paper presented at the AAMAS 2003 Workshop on Agent Communication Languages and Communication Policies, Melbourne, Australia.

Yen, J., Fan, X., Sun, S., Hanratty, T., and Dumer, J. (2004a). Agents with shared mental models for better tactical decision-makings. *Journal of Decision Support System* (to appear).

Yen, J., Fan, X., Sun, S., McNeese, M., and Hall, D. (2004b). Supporting anti-terrorist analyst teams using agents with shared RPD process. Paper presented at the the IEEE International Conference on Computational Intelligence for Homeland Security and Personal Safety, Venice, Italy.

Yen, J., Fan, X., and Volz, R. A. (eds.). (2004c). *Proactive Communications in Agent Teamwork,* Vol. LNAI-2922. Berlin: Springer.

Zhang, L.-j., Li, H., and Lam, H. (2004). Toward a business process grid for utility computing. *IT Professional.*

Chapter 13

Supporting Knowledge Management in Emergency Crisis Management Domains: Envisioned Designs for Collaborative Work

Michael D. McNeese, Isaac Brewer, Rashaad E. T. Jones, and Erik S. Connors

13.1. INTRODUCTION

Recent political events have emphasized the importance of increased communication, accurate intelligence gathering and analysis, and ubiquitous sharing of information between various government agencies, military groups, and crisis-management organizations for the prediction and prevention of terrorist attacks. As we approach the ultimate system of systems to support national security, there are a plethora of perspectives, approaches, and biases that may be appropriated to understand, predict, and respond to situations that threaten the assets and resources of counter-terrorism efforts. Oftentimes, failure has ensued when the design of complex military systems only enables advanced technology *without* understanding human or team cognitive processes (what is typically referred to as *distributed cognition*). This has been encountered and documented for numerous areas within the areas of military C^{3}I and complex weapons systems (e.g., fighter aircraft). Distributed cognition infers states where information is distributed broadly across time, place, and people. If the socio-cognitive factors surrounding situation assessment, decision-making, and executable actions are given short shrift, then systemsJ260
are designed solely from the limited vision of a designer's own boundary constraints. This narrow approach results in systems that tend to be brittle, fail to adapt under uncertain and ill-defined circumstances, and cause users to be confused, overloaded, or unable to control the technology that is supposedly at their disposal. Researchers have investigated these effects and refer to them under various classifications of errors or maladaptive behavior including clumsy automation, mode failure, channelized attention, information overload, and automation surprises (see Woods et al., 1994).

Many of these problems may be prevented by utilizing a cognitive systems engineering approach to enable user-centric methods in the design and testing of complex systems, intelligent interfaces, and cognitive support tools. National security and counter-terrorism are highly contingent and dependent upon (a) the human element represented by individual operators and users and (b) teams operating in separate cells or in collaboration with other teams as collective counter-terrorism units. In maintaining the importance of this human element, the chapter will describe a number of cogent efforts involving the following *research themes:*

1. Understanding, reasoning, and communicating among team member specialists
2. Recognizing patterns and gradients inherent in situation awareness
3. Comprehending and interacting with intelligent systems and technologies
4. Perceiving ecological information in the context of use

Applying these research themes to counter-terrorism and national security has the potential to lead to the design of advanced information technologies that improve the capabilities of users and teams involved in these fields. In support of these research themes, this chapter describes a cognitive systems approach that emphasizes (1) a human/team-centric focus, (2) predictive/preventative problem states, and (3) envisioned intelligence support.

13.1.1. Problem Domain

There are many domains, and directions within a domain, in which the above research themes can be investigated. However, for the purpose of placing meaningful boundary constraints around our efforts, we will focus primarily on two distinct fields of practice in national security and counter-terrorism: *emergency crisis management* and *intelligence/ image analyst work.* Each of these can be considered a "complex problem domain" because they exhibit what Young and McNeese (1995) have referred to as complex problem domain characteristics. These authors identified multiple characteristics for a related complex field of study, battle management, which are shown in Figure 13.1.

The characteristics represented in Figure 13.1 have many interconnections and interdependencies that blend together to create domains that are unwieldy and difficult to attend to or predict. Domains that exhibit these characteristics are relatively nonroutine and therein require adaptation and timely use of resources in order to reach conditions of suc-

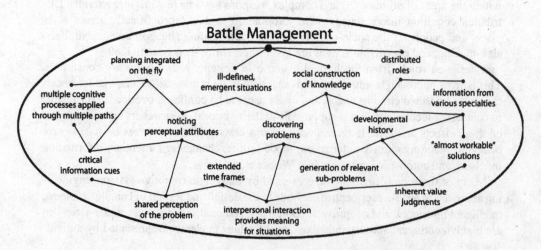

Figure 13.1. Complex problem domain characteristics for battle management.

cess. When a designer proposes advanced information technologies to support such adaptive processes, recognition must be made that political, social, and interagency factors often induce frequent changes (e.g., restrictions on information access, personnel adjustments, etc.) that alter the nature of domain work. Thus, designs cannot be static or brittle; rather, they require an ability to adapt to the changing landscape of the complex domain in question. The next two sections provide descriptions of the domains under discussion in this chapter.

13.1.1.1. Emergency Crisis Management.

Emergency crisis management (ECM) covers a multitude of situations that can arise from a wide range of circumstances including natural disasters (e.g., tornados, wildfires, landslides, thunderstorms, blizzards, and volcanic eruptions) and human-caused mishaps (e.g., mine subsidence, toxic spills, nuclear meltdowns, and even terrorism). Each of these catastrophes manifests itself differently in terms of losses of resources and impact on communities and nations. For instance, hurricanes, earthquakes, and floods have consistently ranked among the worst natural disasters in terms of lives lost and damage induced. Terrorism, on the other hand, attempts to erode patriotism, destroy faith, and threaten national security. Despite these differences, all emergencies require decision-makers to take immediate steps to aid response and recovery. Similarly, these emergencies call for preventative measures, such as planning and preparedness, as well as sustained efforts to reduce long-term risk to hazards or mitigation. ECM takes place in a wide variety of disciplines (e.g., emergency medicine, battle management, hurricane centers, piloting, terrorist activities in cities, bomb threats in schools), emerges in context, and takes different forms across time and space. In most areas, crisis management involves people—individuals, teams, and "teams of teams"—interacting through various levels of technological sophistication under certain levels of stress and emotion.

13.1.1.2. Intelligence/Image Analysts.

The intelligence community is highly diverse, with many individual agencies responsible for selective information gathering. This community is also experiencing rapid changes as a result of improvements to technology, organizational restructuring, and increased knowledge of threats. Intelligence analysts may very well be considered the "frontline" of counter-terrorism efforts in the United States, because their work concerns issues of varying significance from tracking enemy forces, identifying potential targets, and assessing vulnerabilities, to monitoring, intercepting, and decoding communication exchanges between terrorists. The nature of the intelligence analyst domain is thus comparable to related fields that involve intense decision-making processes (e.g., battle management, ECM, etc.). The responsibilities of intelligence analysts (IA) focus upon the evaluation of past and current global events, trends, and activities in an effort to prevent, detect, and respond to terrorist activity. While the function of an IA is inherently an individual knowledge construction process, there is significant social construction of knowledge performed through collaboration and corroboration between analysts. Much of this process is emergent via information gathering, distillation of salient information fragments, and interpretation of these pieces of information via sets of rules, experience, or perhaps doctrine. Thus, we stress that there are several critical characteristics to consider in this field, including multi-source information fusion, cognitive analysis of complex information, and team collaboration in decision-making.

The role of image analysts (ImA) within the intelligence community is unique in that the information gathering process originates with imagery data, rather than reports or cables. Additionally, ImAs are primarily concerned with the tacit and hidden elements of collected imagery data. Instead of examining an image to understand its meaning, image analysts must extract the significance of entities present (or absent) in the image. Although image analysis work may be performed initially within the mind of a single individual, further analysis and use of image information is actually socially constructed across several analysts and settings that mutually inform, back-fill, and constrain each other through means of articulation. Hence, we proffer that image analyst work is facilitated through a community of practice that includes activities performed within a distributed setting amongst a group of analysts/domain experts. We also suggest that training, camaraderie, affiliation, subcultures, standing, role, and rank are additional factors involved within the image analyst work domain. Analysis of intelligence and image analyst work requires domain-specific knowledge elicitation in order to generate relevant testbeds for implementing effective analytic tools and procedures with the intent of aiding the accuracy of modern intelligence reporting.

13.1.2. Goals and Significance

The goal for this chapter is to show how the aforementioned research themes are addressed as they specifically relate to national security and counter-terrorism interests, applications, and resources; our intention is to show how these themes can assist researchers in the development of solutions for the prediction and prevention of threats and future acts of terrorism. Our work applies a broad, interdisciplinary viewpoint to the domains of emergency crisis management and intelligence/image analysts using a cognitive system engineering framework known as the Living Laboratory approach. The motivation of this approach is to gain and apply understanding of the nature of work in these domains in order to design adaptive support systems that are user/team-centered and focus on increasing the success of workers within the domains. This is significant because most design approaches are typically one-dimensional; they can take a theoretical view, a practical view, or a techno-centric view, but rarely is a balanced perspective explored. Additionally, our research is highly participatory; at each stage, human users are integrated into the research process to maximize our understanding of these domains.

An integrative, balanced view of work in national security and counter-terrorism requires that context, knowledge, theory, technology, users, and practice mutually inform one another. Thus, we intend to show in this chapter that such a view can be maintained through the use of the Living Laboratory approach. First, we review the cognitive science foundations upon which the Living Laboratory has been built. A specific emphasis is placed on situated cognition and the related topics of perceptual anchors and distributed cognition. After this review, we discuss the Living Laboratory Approach as a cognitive systems engineering framework for structuring research. We then show how the Living Laboratory approach has guided our research efforts in developing technological solutions for emergency crisis management and intelligence/image analyst work. We conclude with a brief outlook on the implications of the approach to research in national security and counter-terrorism.

13.2. BACKGROUND

Crises such as the terrorist bombing in Oklahoma City and the September 11 attacks on the World Trade Center and Pentagon buildings have called attention to how people and teams use cognition to perform under extreme situations in addition to their daily activities in real-world events. Contemporary approaches to understanding cognition range from an emphasis on situated action (Greeno and Moore, 1993; Lave and Wenger, 1991) and symbolic systems (Vera and Simon, 1993) to how action is limited by context (Rasmussen et al., 1994) and more recent work on how specific knowledge is spontaneously accessed and used in a given context (McNeese, 2001). Oftentimes events are anticipated, considered routine, and proceed in an orderly manner. Responses to these situations rarely affect the cognitive processes of workers in these cases. There are exceptions, however, wherein individuals and groups find themselves in circumstances that are ill-defined, messy, nonroutine, and time-pressured. In these cases, those involved encounter unexpected conditions and complications. In situations where cognition may become overloaded, there exist many challenges to functioning without committing an error. In teamwork, these challenges may be magnified to an even greater degree because activity involves coordination, communication, and articulation of a common ground to facilitate mutual understanding. In crisis management scenarios, errors can "snowball" into larger disasters and even become catastrophic (e.g., the disaster at Three Mile Island; see Woods et al., 1994).

The World Trade Center attacks are salient examples of ill-defined, time-pressured, and multifaceted situations where events are often entangled and hard to differentiate. The September 11 attacks also represent an extreme form of emergency crisis management, and they are categorized in such a manner for a variety of reasons. The most pertinent of these was that people were not prepared for the enormity of what happened. Due to the magnitude of violence, destruction, and disbelief happening in front of them, people experienced a state of shock and panic. This represents a severe kind of stress that can either disable or move people in different ways. Additionally, the very source for responding to crises (i.e., the crisis management headquarters) was eliminated because it was contained within one of the Trade Center buildings that were destroyed. This placed an unseen importance on mobile and distributed command and control in an environment that was undergoing constant upheaval and change with multiple levels of information uncertainties present. Finally, the unanticipated consequences of these attacks were intense owing to the high interconnectedness of events. Their "chain reaction" impact resulted in a number of systems being in a state of crisis and dire circumstances. Even with this extreme situation unfolding, the evidence of people making critical decisions and solving problems with extraordinary risks is documented. These occurrences show that people can and do employ effective cognitive strategies [e.g., cognition in the wild (Hutchins, 1995)] under unbelievable circumstances, constraints, and conflict in order to adapt on the fly to what they may be experiencing. Often the use of experience is how we adapt to barriers or constraints (typically hidden) and managing with what we have ready-at-hand (Vera and Simon, 1993). These types of response are thus rich examples of what has been referred to in the literature as *situated cognition*.

13.2.1. Situated Cognition

Situated cognition is a flexible, adaptive, and unstructured way of thinking and then interacting with others (e.g., as members of a team) while simultaneously interacting with the environment (Bereiter, 1997; Brown et al., 1989; Salomon, 1993; Suchman, 1987). It differs from the more "rules-based" conceptualizations of cognition in its ability to cope with the randomness and seemingly chaotic nature of the world. Rather than relying on cumbersome and lengthy lists of laws and rules to govern interaction, situated cognition relies more on using opportunistic and context specific knowledge as a guide. A less understood and under-studied aspect of situated cognition concerns the idea that cognition is often culturally and historically contingent (Cole and Engstrom, 1993). This suggests that cognitive skills, like mental representations, may be formed according to the specific cultural group or context in which a person develops. This view is especially prevalent in the cultural–historical perspectives of Russian activity theorists, Luria (1979) and Vygotsky (1978). Since culture can be instantiated through mediators along ethnic, political, racial, gender, and religious lines, it may be particularly important to assess cognition with such factors in mind. As related to crisis management, it is increasingly becoming the case that in the distributed global economy, team members from varying, diverse cultures formulate unique multinational teams to perform important duties around the world. Prime examples of this are peacekeeping teams (McNeese, 2001) who are often called upon to perform emergency crisis management activities in global settings.

13.2.2. Perceptual Anchors

When cognition is focused on specific events that emerge through the context of experience within a given environment, situated cognition is said to be present. Situated cognition is thus predicated upon recognizing cues from the environment known as *perceptual anchors*. These cues often provide conceptual links that facilitate spontaneous access of knowledge (Bransford et al., 1988) and in turn help a person or team to orient within their contextual sense surround. When perceptual anchors are recognized, they enable a person to actively generate and construct knowledge in ways that produce effective mental models. When presented with a similar environment or analogous problem, there is an increase in the chance that the person will transfer their prior (anchored) knowledge to the new condition (McNeese, 2000). When an individual or team is perceptually anchored to their environment in a way that affords (1) contrasts and comparisons, (2) exploration of the problem space, or (3) perceptual learning, their degree of realism, joint presence, and individual/team understanding is likely to increase. This in turn provides a positive impact to individual and team performance. Perceptual anchoring is similarly related to naturalistic decision-making. Naturalistic decision-making is defined as an effort to understand and improve decision-making in field settings by helping people to more quickly develop and apply situational expertise (Klein et al., 1993; Salas and Klein, 2001; Zsambok and Klein, 1997). Here, perceptual anchoring refers to the depth, richness, and presentation method of the information available to decision-makers as they deliberate and formulate decisions.

13.2.3. Distributed Cognition

Akin to situated cognition, *distributed cognition* is based upon the premise that cognition is distributed across people, places, and objects rather than resting solely in a single mind (Resnick, 1991). Distributed cognition can also imply that people may not be interacting in the same place (i.e., they are in distributed spaces) or at the same time (asynchronous or synchronous interaction). Past research has often treated cognitive processes such as knowledge acquisition, situation awareness/assessment, knowledge transfer, and even memory of an event, in a very isomorphic fashion. Typically, these views have lacked consideration of an individual's contextual surround. There are exceptions to this such as transactive memory or joint cognitive systems (Hollnagel and Woods, 1983; Liang et al.,

1995). But all too often, the research zeitgeist has approached these phenomena as if they are isolated cognitive streams operating under independent processes. However, examining such topics from a distributed cognition perspective shows that these processes are entwined, critically related and constrained by each other, and heavily dependent on the ecological sense surround [i.e., they ebb and flow with perception–action cycles inherent with what the environment offers and affords an actor (McNeese, 1992)]. A large, and potentially critical, part of situated, distributed cognition that has not been investigated to this point in the literature is how people constantly recognize situations, acquire and assess knowledge, and then use that data (or rather how they spontaneously apply it) for similar events. Looking at the September 11 attacks as an example, it is clear that there were both successes and failures in these specific aspects of distributed cognition. Another feature of distributed cognition that has not been studied much is the extent to which the above processes differ for individuals, teams, or multi-teams [note that the study by Wellens (1993), represents an exception]. It only stands to reason that information use is dependent upon whether cognition is distributed to one versus many.

13.3. METHODOLOGY

When approaching the design of systems intended to provide support for workers of domains such as emergency crisis management or intelligence/image analyst work, designers may take a number of different approaches to generate systems that produce some form of efficiency, effectiveness, or usefulness when it comes to performance. Indeed, what often emerges in the form of artifacts, interfaces, aids, or tools can be the result of design processes and procedures that emphasize alternate and sometimes even conflicting positions. Much of our own work has identified four distinct perspectives (i.e., technology-centric, data-centric, user-centric, and group-centric) in creating systems or designs to support cooperative work (McNeese et al., 1992).

Technology-centric views often reify the intuition of the designer as being correct. Thus, the designer utilizes technology without really knowing the needs, requirements, or constraints of the work setting. Designs are informed through the knowledge of what technology offers, and they are treated as ends unto themselves. Multiple cases exist where designs have emerged because of the "quick rush" to market an innovative idea (e.g., the recent explosion of smart phones and handheld devices). Once introduced, the user is expected to conform and learn the complexities of the design despite a device's clumsy automation or automation surprises (Woods et al., 1994) that may be present. Clearly, this kind of design process results in systems that fail or induce user mistakes. For example, many large group display products in the 1980s were made possible with the introduction of certain kinds of technologies [e.g., gas-plasma displays; refer to McNeese and Brown (1986)]. These displays were at one point put forth as solving many problems of increasing display size without sacrificing resolution. However, the display was not designed specifically for human use and could be subject to actually decreasing human performance because of tradeoffs that actually incurred with the technology. Unfortunately, usability approaches may be "too little, too late" because they are often applied as surface-level analyses only after the "real design" has been conceptualized. Post-hoc usability is better than nothing but is not optimal.

One of the first alternatives to techno-centric approaches was *data-centric* designs. In this approach to design, laboratory experiments are conducted for a given hypothesis for a set of phenomena related to group work (e.g., experiments in social psychology, team performance, or social cognition). Data are collected in controlled research facilities employing sophisticated experimental designs and then analyzed using statistical techniques. Based on the results of these studies, a researcher can generalize findings beyond the locally controlled study. Such generalizations may suggest that specific design concepts or features would improve performance in a given manner. The problem herein is that findings tend to be over-generalized, suggested designs are unproven, and studies often ignore contextual or ecological variables that influence results. This view highlights the role of theory and abstraction in design and certainly can be informative from top-down considerations.

Alternatively, a more viable approach is *user-centered* design. Here, the user is placed in a participatory role alongside the designer to assist with usability. A designer is thus informed as to the users' needs, how they are constrained, and what forms of cognitive processes are used to interpret work. A user-centric design approach acknowledges and incorporates a user's expertise as a potentially useful source to inform the design, often utilizing different forms of knowledge elicitation, cognitive task analysis, or design storyboarding for translating users' knowledge into design.

McNeese et al. (1992) chose a new approach termed *group-centered* design—an adaptation of user-centered design wherein groups and teams (as social units) participate in the design of support systems. Here, groups are used to understand the social construction of knowledge in their workplaces. Knowledge is acquired from the group ethnographically while still utilizing the group as multiple participants involved in improving their work practices. This is similar to many views today that employ in-situ, ecologically valid understanding and development of collaborative systems-products (e.g., Hutchins, 1995; Schmidt and Bannon, 1992).

13.3.1. Philosophy

Assessing the above approaches retrospectively, each has varying elements of value and worth, depending on the researcher's desired outcome. A typical result, however, is that these approaches often are not informed by each other, exist in isolation, and generally distill into a one-dimensional understanding of cognition, work, and technology. McNeese and colleagues have advocated the use of the Living Laboratory approach (McNeese, 1996) to espouse a broader, interdisciplinary view and to produce multidimensional alternatives that are complimentary with one another. Essentially, the Living Laboratory is used to create an understanding of the intentions, goals, values, and beliefs that drive individual behavior in the context of work. The approach also examines how these characteristics alter and influence patterns of behavior and modes of understanding when the situation for interaction involves teamwork. Figure 13.2 illustrates the Living Laboratory framework, which congeals unique dimensions of work and designs from multiple perspectives, shows their interconnections, and depicts how they inform each other, generate feedback and feed-forward loops, and act to integrate theory, models, use, and practice to access multiple levels of analysis. The figure outlines the four major components of the Living Laboratory for assessing workers in context: (1) ethnographic study, (2) knowledge elicitation (sometimes referred to as tool/knowledge development), (3) scaled worlds, and (4) reconfigurable prototypes. These four components can be further categorized into fieldwork (left) and development (right) elements.

Historically, the vision of the Living Laboratory is related to the ideas and research approach of Suchman (1987), who suggested that cognition and collaboration come about

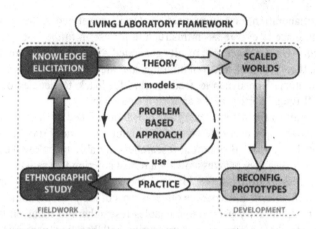

Figure 13.2. The Living Laboratory approach.

not by symbolic systems and plans, but through situated actions that arise during the course of events occurring in a particular context. Specifically, Suchman was referring to cognition that is constructed by social processes and situational contingencies, rather than that which is bounded by the individual brain or mind (Resnick, 1991). This view highlights the *qualitative* and *naturalistic* components of what individuals actually do when they work together and is often referred to as *distributed cognition* (see Salomon, 1993). Thus, the Living Laboratory is necessarily bound to approaches that are described as *ecological, participatory,* and *ethnographic* in nature.

The four elements of the Living Laboratory, working in concert, produce emergent layers of activities that mutually inform technology-, data-, user-, and group-centered elements of cooperative work. Notably, practice and use are tightly interwoven by these four components; the output from one becomes the input for another. The process is cyclic, but flexible enough to move forwards, backwards, and crosswise between components. The value of the Living Laboratory approach resides in its ability to address distributed cognition settings wherein information is dispersed broadly across time, space, and individuals. Typically, these settings require the effective design integration of (1) systems that enhance situation awareness and cognitive readiness, (2) supportive technologies (e.g., information, communication, and collaboration technologies), (3) knowledge management strategies, and (4) safe work practices.

The Living Laboratory, as a research process, revolves around the notion of a problem-based approach (McNeese et al., 2000; McNeese, 1996). Thus, applying the Living Laboratory framework begins with the identification of a problem salient to the domain under study through a method known as problem-finding. Problem-finding is considered one of the core principles of cognitive systems engineering and reflects what cognitive systems must overcome in order to be effective. Once a problem has been identified, the general premise of the Living Laboratory is that both the observations of users or teams in their work domain (ethnography), along with the knowledge acquired from them (knowledge elicitation), provide the basis for ecologically valid simulations. Simulations become synthetic task environments (scaled worlds) that allow for theories of the user(s) to be empirically tested within an actual context of use. These scaled worlds can also incorporate the use of partially defined design prototypes (reconfigurable prototypes) to assess hypotheses formulated on the ability of these prototype environments to enhance or constrain cognition, collaboration, or communication. Designs that evolve from empirical studies may be set in place to evolve lab infrastructure for use in future studies, or tested operationally *in situ*. The feedback and results generated by these studies are additionally useful for future theory, model, and tool building, and they lead to further cycling through the Living Laboratory. The dynamic feed-forward/feedback tendencies of the framework provide the "Living" portion of the approach's moniker.

Owing in part to the natural, everyday constraints faced by most researchers, it may not be possible to apply every element of the Living Laboratory framework in a full-scale development. In an optimal situation, researchers are able to follow the arrows of interconnectivity because they progress toward a robust solution that satisfies the refined problem. The process of utilizing the Living Laboratory is one of learning and discovery wherein answers inform and leverage other aspects of the problem-solution space. Applying the Living Laboratory perspective enables researchers to focus on the mutual interplay of understanding, modeling, and measuring collaboration, perception, and cognition within complex systems.

13.4. APPLICATIONS

Our current research concentrates on the development of computer-supported cooperative work systems, designs, tools, and interfaces to support teamwork in the emergency crisis management and intelligence/image analyst domains. Presently, our projects correspond to a single cycle through the Living Laboratory framework, and they represent our goals of understanding work in these domains and designing appropriate solutions (i.e., the problem-based approach). These projects compare and contrast processes across collocated and distributed teams, and they feature work on information, communication, and collaborative technologies that can enhance team cognitive processes that frequently incur under time pressure, emerge as a function of new information seeking, and are subject to multiple constraints and uncertainties. Specifically, the application of *cognitive engineering techniques* (McNeese et al., 1995; McNeese, 2002), *cognitive field research tools* (Sanderson et al., 1994a; McNeese et al., 1999a), *cognitive modeling methods* (Perusich and McNeese, 1997), *scaled world simulations* (McNeese et al., 1999b; Perusich et al., 1999), and *team schema similarity measurement* (Rentsch et al., 1998; McNeese and Rentsch, 2001) have been at the heart of this research.

In order to better orient the reader, we begin in Section 13.4.1 with the lower-left corner of the Living Laboratory, discussing our work in Ethnographic Study (see Figure 13.2). Following the main arrow pathways, we proceed to the results of Knowledge Elicitation and Cognitive Work/Task Analyses in Section 13.4.2. Section 13.4.3 explains the integration of these fieldwork elements into the Scaled World component known as NeoCITIES. Developments in intelligent group interfaces are introduced in a discussion of Reconfigurable Prototypes in Section 13.4.4. A related project in hurricane management centers is provided in Section 13.4.5 to show an additional example of how the Living Laboratory can be used to structure the research process from start to finish.

13.4.1. Ethnographic Study

Ethnography is a method of studying and learning about a person or group of people. The technique originated in anthropology where anthropologists spent extended periods of time with primitive societies making detailed observations of their activities. When applied to organizations, agencies, and industry, as is the case in computer-supported cooperative work or human–computer interaction research, ethnography involves the study of a small group, or team, of subjects in their own environment. As a mode of social research, it is concerned with producing detailed descriptions of the daily activities of social actors within specific contexts. In a design context, the aim of this technique is to develop a thorough understanding of the subjects under study, particularly their current work practices as the basis for system design. The merit of ethnographic study is its ability to make visible the "real-world" sociality of a particular setting or domain. While ethnographic studies are particularly useful for gathering in-depth information about work domains, technical requirements, and the like, they can be costly and time-consuming.

As a launching point for our progress through the Living Laboratory, an ethnographic research study was performed that focused on the interactions, responsibilities, and responses of emergency dispatch workers in emergency management call centers. This venture has included multiple scenario-based interviews and observation sessions of 911 call center dispatchers as they perform their daily tasks in emergency response. Among the tasks studied is the allocation of resources to various types of emergencies and their associated relay of information to police officers, fire officials, and paramedics during emergency situations. These sessions with 911 dispatchers have resulted in the acquisition of information about possible responses toward various emergencies, the different functions and capabilities of emergency resources, and the development and refinement of emergency scenarios and storylines. We used these results to inform and create realistic scenarios, emergency events, and storylines for the simulation represented the scaled world component of the Living Laboratory (see Section 13.4.3 for more information).

As mentioned previously, it is sometimes difficult to apply each element of the Living Laboratory; our ethnographic studies of 911 call centers are an example of such. Though the results of these studies have focused our knowledge elicitation efforts and mutually informed the design of a scaled world simulation, we recognize that this is an underutilized focus in our research efforts. Thus, we have initiated an additional project that will consist of case studies in two dispatch centers, one in an urban setting and the other in a more suburban/rural community, to strengthen this portion of our efforts.

13.4.2. Knowledge Elicitation

Knowledge elicitation (KE) represents a particular strength in our research efforts. Indeed, we have conducted multiple sessions with intelligence analysts and image analysts in an effort to understand their roles in counter-terrorism and emergency crisis management. Knowledge elicitation sessions are typically rapid and informative, lasting no longer than a few hours, and are extremely user-centric. Most sessions involve either a single subject matter expert (e.g., an intelligence analyst or geographic information scientist) or small groups/teams of experts working in tandem with researchers to produce a representation of the experts' knowledge. Over the course of our research, we have utilized a number of elicitation methods depending on the domains or experts involved.

One such method is adapted from the participatory, user-centered knowledge elicitation framework pioneered by McNeese et al. (1995) called Advanced Knowledge Acquisition and Design Methodology (AKADAM). Over the last decade, this methodology has been tailored, adapted, and put into practice, particularly for complex applications in the Department of Defense (e.g., fighter aircraft cockpits, intelligent associates, management information systems). AKADAM focuses on utilizing cognitive task analysis and function-based decomposition techniques as a basis for the design of complex systems.

AKADAM is designed to combine the information obtained by utilizing different forms of analysis for the design of complex systems. In this sense, AKADAM represents and makes accessible a holistic profile of a user's declarative, procedural, and design-centered knowledge. This knowledge can then be used to create storyboards, rapid prototypes, or technological interventions within simulations.

13.4.2.1. AKADAM Methodology.

The AKADAM methodology assumes that a user is the expert in the use and application of their knowledge. Hence, the AKADAM methodology elicits knowledge in many forms that are highly intuitive for users. The three primary forms of knowledge elicitation that have been used are concept mapping, functional decomposition techniques, and interactive design storyboards (Zaff et al., 1993). Concept mapping is the cornerstone of AKADAM techniques. It begins with a cogent probe question for a subject matter expert (SME). As SMEs interact and describe their mental models as related to the probe question, a researcher represents this knowledge in a concept map structure on a whiteboard or poster paper in front of the expert. This initial map captures concepts that are valuable to the expert but also provides a facilitation mechanism to help them remember associated concepts. As SMEs begin to see the structure of concepts emerge as they talk, the concept map serves as a memory aid to spontaneously access more of their conceptual knowledge structure. This type of cognitive representation is termed a concept definition map; an example of such a map is shown in Figure 13.3.

Once the initial map is formed, the methodology may continue with a different type of map called a concept procedural map. This second style of concept mapping emphasizes event-based memory while extracting events that produce more temporal and procedural

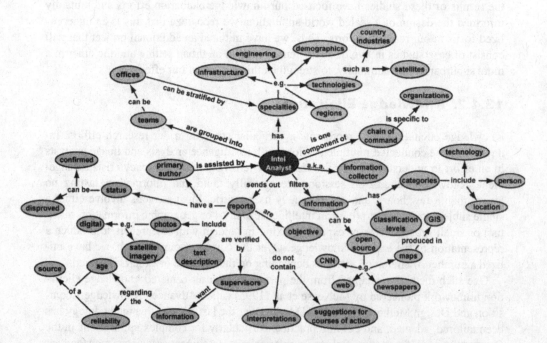

Figure 13.3. Sample concept definition map. Concepts are represented by shaded ovals while the nodes that link the concepts are shown as directional arrows. Shading is used to represent a preliminary analysis of common concepts based on SME responses.

qualities, as opposed to the basic, declarative structure of concept definition maps. In concept procedural mapping, the researcher captures the primary, sequential events for a specified scenario that was developed with the assistance of the participant. The researcher queries the SME to talk about various concepts, constraints, and processes that are resident within a given event or phase of the scenario, while tying these concepts directly into a stage, phase, or event-driven component of a scenario utilizing the same visual representation.

After their sessions and an initial analysis phase, SMEs are usually provided with a copy of their maps to directly assist in the validation process. The researchers ask the experts to review the maps for accuracy and for concepts that might evolve later in time. The research team also reviews the concept maps for further clarification and/or to develop questions that may be relevant to ask in a subsequent session. The decision to have a follow-up session frequently depends on the time, availability, and the demands of knowledge being pursued. The goal of concept mapping activities is to create concrete representations of SMEs' knowledge and work processes.

13.4.2.2. Knowledge Elicitation with Intelligence Analysts.

Both junior and senior intelligence analysts (IAs) were interviewed to access both novice and expert knowledge in this domain. All analysts had knowledge and experience in areas focusing on, but not limited to, weapons of mass destruction, counter-terrorism, counterintelligence, and human intelligence. The study was conducted in two sessions, which were held approximately two months apart. The first session featured three activities in which the IAs participated: a concept procedural mapping task; a concept definition mapping task; and a review of a simulation/experimental task currently under development. Each task was performed individually by the participants and lasted roughly 90 minutes each. For the second session, the IAs participated in two tasks. First, they reviewed and clarified the concept maps that evolved from the previous session. Second, semistructured interviews were conducted in which the IAs were given two novel scenarios that were developed by the researchers after identifying deficiencies from the first session. In the first scenario, the IAs were asked to explain how they would train their replacement. This scenario was intended to delve deeper into the important daily functions of an IA. The second scenario involved a hypothetical terrorist attack that destroyed much of the infrastructure necessary for normal IA operations. The participants were asked to provide their top five priorities for reestablishing a functional intelligence cell. This scenario was aimed at further discovery of the resources and tools that an intelligence analyst values for daily operations.

Two primary themes evolved from the concept mapping tasks from the first knowledge elicitation session. One theme was the importance of social interaction for intelligence analysts. While the function of an IA is inherently an individual knowledge construction process, there is a significant *social construction of knowledge* through collaboration and corroboration. Much of this process is emergent via information gathering, distillation of salient information fragments, and interpretation of that information via sets of rules, experience, or perhaps doctrine. Collaboration is introduced in the process of decision-making, and corroboration is essential to this process. Since much of the information gathered is measured to some degree of confidence, analysts continuously seek to confirm the validity of their sources, leading to a unique form of socialization. Much of an analyst's focus is placed on verifying the source and accuracy of the information they have gathered.

Additionally, the corroboration process tends to induce *stress,* especially when formulating reports. Analysts are particularly concerned that misinformation, knowledge gaps, or incorrect conclusions from a poorly corroborated report may end up in the hands of a policy-maker and ultimately lead to the implementation of an inappropriate policy. Thus, IAs tend to look for verification of their conclusions with other analysts. This interaction appears to reassure the analyst, especially when a consensus exists.

The second theme that emerged from the first session was the *limitations in current analyst tools*. The participants indicated that search tools and agents used to seek relevant information were the most necessary of their tools. The analysts expressed (a) concern with information overload related to the search process, including irrelevant information presented in the context of searches, and (b) the need to process this material. IAs cited a need for better databases, noting specifically that it would assist their searching process if relationships between data were recorded rather than just lists of isolated entries. This raises a desire for robust link analysis tools, where semantically and contextually related items would be linked such that the analysts would be readily able to see important connections and associations between search terms and results. In addition to providing better database search, organization, and linking tools, participants intimated their frustrations with the difficulties in *sharing information across multiple databases*. Another noted frustration was the lack of remote or alternate access of analyst resources, which is principally due to security issues with the sensitive nature of the material. The analysts mentioned that it was only recently, with the creation of the Department of Homeland Defense, that databases were allowed to be shared across agencies such as the FBI and CIA.

The scenario-driven style of the second session did not evoke any new themes but rather reinforced the themes that evolved from the first elicitation session. The first scenario, where the IAs were asked to train their replacement, reaffirmed the social theme noted above. For instance, a senior analyst remarked that one of the preliminary steps with a trainee would be introductions to other people, such as other analysts and managers. These human assets, the IA noted, were critical to the everyday operations that the trainee would experience. Further reinforcing the social theme was the emphasis that analysts would place on teaching the trainee about particular communication tools, such as the cables and e-mails sent across a wide-area network. Similarly, the IAs would stress what information was important to report (such as the credibility of a source), whom to report this information to, and how to report it.

The second scenario, where the IAs were asked what tools they would need replaced most in the unlikely event of a catastrophic loss, produced mixed results. The senior analyst was very specific, citing the need for tools to capture, search, transform, and disseminate information, as well as link analysis and *situation awareness tools*. The junior analyst indicated, however, that a pencil, paper, and decent digital camera were all that he would require. Notably, this variation could be due to the difference in experience levels between the two analysts. As the analysts discussed this scenario, their responses naturally tended toward enumerating the negative aspects of using these tools. Thus, the analysts revisited the second theme of tool limitations found in the previous session. If given the opportunity to upgrade their tools rather than replace them, the IAs indicated that they would like to have a more *intuitive search engine tool*. Similarly, the analysts indicated a desire for seamlessness, such as an analyst assistant agent that would operate "underneath" the analyst's current activities, monitoring those activities, and then providing relevant information without having to explicitly ask for it or task the agent. This highlights an analyst's need for *metacognitive support functions*.

13.4.2.3. Knowledge Elicitation with Image Analysts. Similar to the KE sessions with the intelligence analysts, interviews were conducted with several image an-

alysts and an image scientist. These experts work as part of the National Geospatial-intelligence Agency (NGA) and represent a broad range of experience within various facets of image analysis. This population of experts supplied a representative sample of *high-level experts* possessing varying degrees of experience (of at least 10 years). These experts participated in four knowledge elicitation activities, each of which was adapted from AKADAM techniques. The first activity consisted of declarative concept mapping to gain a basic structure of image analysts' work. The second activity involved a process-based knowledge elicitation technique (or procedural concept mapping) to acquire the day-to-day activities of image analysts. The third activity utilized critical incident probes to analyze how unexpected events are handled by the image analysts. The fourth activity consisted of hypothetical projections to enable the image analysts to access and utilize joint types of memories (declarative, procedural, and episodic structures). Figure 13.4 provides a graphical representation of these activities. For this application, like many of our other projects, we began with an activity designed to elicit an active initial scenario from the experts. We then used this scenario to anchor procedure-based concept mapping, as well as the remaining activities. However, prior to conducting procedure-based mapping, we first utilize concept mapping to acquire much of the *declarative structure* of an expert's mental model.

The results of the declarative concept mapping activity provided a bird's-eye perspective of the dynamics of the work environment for image analysts. We developed a general abstraction of the workflow process for image analysts by finding commonalities from each concept map elicited across all of the analysts (also known as a summary map). Note that this method of summarizing across multiple expert's map is similar to techniques employed in Zaff et al. (1993) but somewhat different from tool-based concept interpretation and summarization employed by Snyder et al. (1991). The declarative mapping activity particularly highlighted the image collection and analysis process. Formally, image analysts are responsible for scanning images of specific areas of interest. These regions are defined by military, governmental agencies, or industrial customers. Images are procured from global visualization products (i.e., satellite imagery), collected often, and examined routinely; the nature of the investigation typically determines the frequency of the collection.

Image analysts engage in what could be referred to as *holistic cognition* during this process. The analyst carefully scrutinizes the imagery with the goal of noticing any ob-

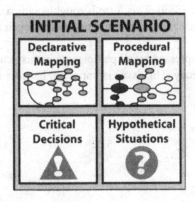

Figure 13.4. KE activities performed with image analysts.

servable differences in the successive images as compared to a baseline image. In the psychological literature, this is often classified as *perceptual differentiation*. If the analyst observes any differences, they then write a report that details the interpretations for each difference noticed. For example, if a set of circular objects were observed in the lower left corner of an image and that same set of objects were then noticed in the upper right portion of a subsequent image, the image analyst may interpret such differences as a convoy of tanks possibly heading eastward. Along with an explicit interpretation of the observed differences, image analysts will include justifications and related ramifications in addition to any environmental, economical, or military factions that might be affected (or should respond) due to their observations. This course of their activity puts dependence on an ability to *reason,* take alternate *courses of action,* and put *relevant knowledge to use.*

The procedural concept mapping activity further exacted the stages of image analyst work using the initial scenario developed prior to any KE activities. Figure 13.5 shows a visual representation of these stages. Each session began with a prompt that an initial report was received by the analyst (the first node in Figure 13.5). The task reached completion upon the generation of a new report. Note that by issuing the new report, the entire process is repeated, because a new report can also represent an initial report. For example, the analyst issuing the new report might have found some new information that another analyst uses to traverse the same process, perhaps in more depth. Similarly, by issuing the new report, other intelligence analysts might locate that report online and initiate their own process based on their job requirements and area of expertise. These iterative and recursive processes can occur in a range of time frames requiring hours, days, months, or even years. By eliciting knowledge about work using this node-based approach, this KE activity was not tied to a specific event and instead could explore generalities and specificities within each stage of image analysis.

The critical incident activity utilized a beginning stage of a critical decision method (Hoffman et al., 1998). Critical decision analysis focuses on some of the critical events and situations that analysts have run across during the course of their experience. Typically this consists of asking an SME about events that challenged their decision-making capacity and then having them explain the context, factors, and procedures that they worked with during a critical incident. This is designed to tap into more of their episodic memories to yield knowledge they used when situations were ill-defined, challenging, complex, and uncertain. The form of critical decision analysis was first presented by Flanagan (1954) but more recently has taken a formalized structure that Gary Klein and his associates have utilized in many real-world decision-making domains, termed Critical Decision Methodology (Klein et al., 1989). This form is roughly approximated as a semistructured interview technique that offers probes to progressively deepen understanding of the critical incidents.

The most focal issue expressed by all participants in this activity was the lack of experienced analysts at the agency. This issue is important because it emphasizes the need for

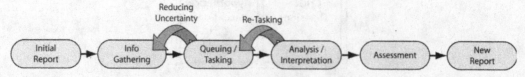

Figure 13.5. Stages of image analyst work.

strong social–organizational and institutional factors that impact image analyst work. Formal training is not the issue; however, longevity in retaining the position is the key, so having lengthy personal experience with "eyes on images" seems to be important. Collaboration is critical to ImAs and is often easily accomplished. Similarly, experienced image analysts do not prefer the use of new technologies and instead emphasize the need to have the "eyes on images" experience and deep personal knowledge when dealing with critical incidents. Tools that interfere with any of these factors will probably be rejected. This reifies the analysts' own sense of *clumsy automation* in tools, and it reifies that tools need to be highly user-centered if they are to actually work in their domain.

The final activity, hypothetical projections and situations, was designed to enable the image analysts to access and utilize joint types of memories (declarative, procedural, and episodic structures) as formulated from their real-world experiences to expound upon situations that required them to mentally simulate and project outcomes of value to operations. For this activity, "pseudo" concept maps were constructed as analysts' provided their answers. Unlike normal concept mapping activities as described above, the analysts did not provide direct interaction with or on these maps. Rather, the knowledge elicitor took notes of concepts and connections that developed as the analysts spoke. Many of the connections were developed after the session based on the elicitor's memory of the conversation. This technique may be more akin to ethnographer's note-taking and knowledge capture techniques in field study work. These maps were examined for common subject area concentrations into which the analysts' answers were appropriate matches. A noticeable similarity across the analysts was to focus on the characteristics, skills, and qualities that they would expect a trainee or replacement to have. The analysts all indicated that it would take a trainee many years to reach the level of experience needed to replace them. One analyst emphasized in particular that it would be nearly impossible to replace an analyst completely due to the established social networks, experience, and years on the job.

In conclusion, these various applications of knowledge elicitation provide in-depth knowledge, comprehension, and understanding of both individual and team-level processes inherent in counter-terrorism, albeit at differing levels. By directly working with experts, using a combination of techniques, a foundation can be provided that informs theory development, generation of scenarios for simulation of counter terrorism/crisis management, and the design of advanced *user-centered* technologies. In turn, knowledge elicitation is a crucial component of the Living Lab framework. Using what we have learned from knowledge elicitation, we can now turn to the development of scaled world simulation as a basis to uncover additional levels of expertise and cognitive processes that guide users and teams in counter-terrorism units.

13.4.3. Scaled Worlds

Human-in-the-loop simulation has produced considerable work that deals with understanding the complexities of human and team performance in complex environments. Indeed, quite an array of cognitive, social, technological, and organizational variables have been researched and subsequently used to predict performance outcomes. For the past 20 years, simulation work has encompassed a broad range of fields of practice and application domains inclusive of command and control teams, pilot teams, unmanned vehicle operators, battle management, AWACS, search and rescue planning, and emergency crisis management. Within these real-world domains, *situated problems* are experienced. These problems tend to have interrelated complexities and constraints that often limit intended outputs or outcomes. Scaled worlds are simulations designed to translate these situated problems (often described as events, scenarios, and storylines) into exploratory fields of behavior. Thus, scaled worlds are specifically intended to emulate real-world content, processes, temporal–spatial constraints, and context.

There have been several forms of scaled worlds established, sometimes from differing motivations (see Schiflett et al., 2004). The term scaled worlds can actually refer to models, simulations, or games. Using Abt's definitions (cf., Obermayer, 1964), *models* provide representations of the structure or dynamics of a thing or process; *simulations* generate an operating imitation of a real process; *games* are contests played according to rules and decided by skill, strength, or apparent luck. Within these forms of scaled worlds, reconfigurable prototypes and designs are also important because they provide insertions of new ideas or technologies that can be tested in conjunction with or in addition to the scaled world. Our research has utilized many of these entities as scaled worlds to explore teamwork [see McNeese (2003) for review]. For example, we have used fuzzy cognitive maps as dynamic models of problem-solving activity in the *Jasper* macro-context, a scaled world of a search and rescue team. Other research has led to the design and generation of research paradigms associated with simulations (e.g., team situational awareness research utilizing the CITIES simulation). Our current work in scaled worlds concerns the creation of a counter-terrorism and emergency crisis management simulation termed NeoCITIES.

Inherent in the idea of scaled worlds is the concept of fidelity. Because scaled worlds hope to emulate real worlds, but also afford experimenters explicit control over salient aspects of the simulation, the degree to which they represent the richness of the actual environment is a construct to consider carefully. When we speak of fidelity, the term must be gauged according to the degree to which (or the authenticity of) the simulation emulates, resembles, or is analogous to the phenomena in the real world. Part of the paradox encountered in scaled worlds is preserving the characteristics of real-world situated problems (e.g., emergency first responder teams) that involve human/team behavior while also maintaining control of independent and dependent variables.

Therein, scaled-world simulations and models can be thought of as analogies of the real world. Looking at analogies, one can say that they have the ability to portray either near-term or far-term similarity. Alternatively, analogies can infer surface level and/or deep structural relationships with real context. Direct observation of events in the field provides immediate exposure to the field of practice. As simulations are constructed to represent the field, various degrees of abstraction may be necessary to capture elements of the world. We provide these general comments to orient the reader as to how scaled worlds fit into the overall direction of the Living Laboratory framework. As we venture into scaled worlds, we cross over from fieldwork into the realm of development, using field observations and theory to inform the creation of a realistic analogical domain.

13.4.3.1. The NeoCITIES Scaled World.

NeoCITIES, an updated and extended simulation based on the CITIES task developed by Wellens and Ergener (1988), is a Java-based synthetic task environment designed to conduct empirical research on distributed cognition. NeoCITIES features a modular problem structure[1] that allows researchers to closely examine team behaviors, identify patterns of response to time-stressed situations, and monitor the performance outcomes of semiautonomous, spatially distributed, decision-making teams.

[1]The term *modular problem structure* indicates that investigators are able to adaptively control various parameters and problem elements within the simulation to easily alter experimental conditions

At its core, NeoCITIES is a team resource allocation problem designed to mimic the emergent situations that comprise real-life emergencies and measure decision-related outputs in a virtual environment. The simulation emulates the complex functions involved in the resource management of a city's emergency services through the joint interaction of three distinct response teams: a Police team, a Fire/EMS team, and a Hazardous Materials/Bomb Squad (Hazards) team. These three response teams are collectively referred to as a Counter-Terrorism Unit, or CTU. Participants in NeoCITIES are presented with a wide variety of overarching, emerging, dynamic, and detailed *resource allocation problem events*. These events can be simple, such as a trashcan fire in an alleyway, to fairly complex (e.g., a hostile takeover of a nuclear facility with multiple hostages). Events similarly range from isolated and mundane occurrences, to larger, more widely inclusive events that have the potential to escalate as a function of resource allocation. To solve these events, the response teams are required to meet the needs of their given constituents and develop situational awareness, while working around various problem space constraints related to the underlying emergency crisis management scenario. The majority of the information and response guidelines for creating these events were directly influenced by the results of our fieldwork with intelligence/image analysts and 911 call center employees. Translating the data obtained from our KE and ethnographic studies into events for NeoCITIES lends a sense of realism to the simulation, thereby increasing its analogous nature.

As a way of modeling teamwork, decision-making, and communication in circumstances of crisis management, the three response teams must also address events that may involve potential terrorist activities. These events are conceptually similar to those undertaken during both routine and nonroutine emergency response and law enforcement. In the case of nonroutine events, their structure is analogous to the structure of events that emerged out of analysis of our fieldwork in that they are comprised of vague, unexpected, complex, highly stressful incidents and typically occur under severe time-pressure. By following the trails of the Living Laboratory, our team of researchers has been able to design events that emulate distributed situated cognition for an emergency 911 call center, replicate responses to acts of terrorism (e.g., September 11th), and create an associated understanding of community-based resource allocation scenarios. Ultimately, the underlying terrorist-related storyline structure of NeoCITIES is informed by the results of our ethnography and knowledge elicitation efforts, as well as literature reviews and document analyses.

Data from our ethnographic studies of 911 emergency operation centers shows that employees will assume multiple roles depending on the severity of emergencies. In some instances, the employees will serve solely as call takers, collecting and filtering information provided by callers and emergency professionals on-scene; other employees allocate and acquisition resources such as vehicles or personnel. This information was used to create distinct roles for NeoCITIES participants. Thus, each NeoCITIES response team is comprised of two participants with realistic roles: an information manager (I-Mgr) and a resource manager (R-Mgr). Each role has limited capabilities, thus creating a situation where collaboration is essential in order to properly address events as they occur. Each member of the team functions via "control centers" which contain computer displays with specialized interfaces (see Figure 13.6 for sample) and communication equipment (e.g., headsets, webcams, etc.). I-Mgrs handle first-line waves of information, similar to an 911 call taker. Additionally, I-Mgrs can consult different sources of information such as protocol manuals and detailed datasets such as population records, traffic reports, and so on. R-Mgrs are responsible for allocating resources to events depending on the information

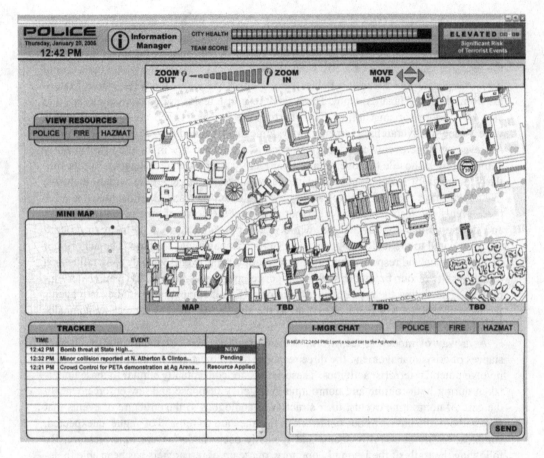

Figure 13.6. NeoCITIES Interface for a police information manager.

relayed to them by their I-Mgr teammate. Each R-Mgr has three distinct or specialized resources at their disposal that can be allocated throughout the city. For example, the Police team can employ (1) investigative units, which handle basic emergencies, (2) squad cars, which handle events such as traffic stops and robberies, and (3) Advanced Tactical Units (ATUs), which are trained to handle heavy artillery situations, such as raids or hostage standoffs.

While the roles, resources, and many of the routine events used in NeoCITIES were inspired by results from our ethnographic studies, the terrorist-related storyline and associated events are primarily the result of our knowledge elicitation session with intelligence and image analysts. This led to the inclusion of concepts into NeoCITIES such as an I-Mgr receiving cables or reports from intelligence sources, or interpreted image data from an image analyst. Many of these features are currently instantiated as "Wizard of Oz" aspects in the simulation. Future work will focus on adding intelligence or image analysts to the NeoCITIES team structure in advisory roles or automated support, such as an intelligent aid. By utilizing the NeoCITIES scaled world to understand planning and prevention of terrorist activities, a sound foundation for the design of advanced technological support can be established to enact a group-centered approach via the Living Laboratory framework.

13.4.4. Reconfigurable Prototypes

Intelligent interfaces, collaborative technologies, and other techniques may be needed to support teamwork wherein cognition can be integrated with the perceptual features that define the context of the problem. Our work in reconfigurable prototypes is represented with an initiative called an intelligent group interface (IGI). The concept of an IGI represents a new direction in the design of intelligent and adaptive user interfaces and draws heavily upon principles from human–computer interaction, artificial intelligence, cognitive science, and social psychology. Our present research proposes the design and implementation of three separate versions of the IGI, with each instantiation using a different adaptation strategy. The first form of IGI features a user-initiated adaptation (i.e., *adaptable*) strategy and will be termed IGI-U. The IGI-U utilizes interface adaptability, dynamic presentation, and user modeling. The second IGI version, referred to as IGI-S, utilizes a system-initiated (i.e., *adaptive*) adaptation strategy. Like the IGI-U, the IGI-S will have interface adaptability and user modeling as interface components. However, the IGI-S will feature plan recognition and intelligent help instead of dynamic presentation. A third IGI design is proposed that utilizes a mixed-initiative adaptation strategy, and called IGI-M. The IGI-M will combine the interface elements of the IGI-U and IGI-S, encompassing dynamic presentation, plan recognition, intelligent help, user modeling, and interface adaptability. These IGI designs are mutually informed by theories of situated cognition, team performance, and research in intelligent interfaces.

The reconfigurable prototype component of the Living Laboratory represents the future directions of our research efforts. As the scaled world NeoCITIES is instantiated as an experimental task, the various IGI designs will be used in user studies to test our theories of distributed cognition associated with the research themes listed in the introduction to this chapter. The results of these empirical studies will inform the future use of adaptation strategies in both experimental and applied settings, specifically for the domain of emergency crisis management. By determining which adaptation strategies lead to better team performance in NeoCITIES, future iterations of intelligent group interfaces, intelligent aids, and cognitive tools can focus upon new details within the particular strategies to determine further what elements most directly affect team performance. The results produced from these studies will advise prospective designs of intelligent interface technology using the feed-forward/feedback nature of the Living Laboratory approach to initiate new, more informed designs.

13.4.5. Another Example: Hurricane Management Centers

We present here an additional example of how the Living Laboratory can frame the research process. Emergency management is a complex system of interconnected agencies, guidelines, rules, and formalized structures. During an emergency, the established structures and guidelines have the potential to break down, requiring individuals to make key decisions with only the information immediately available at their fingertips. In such situations, geospatial information is often critical to making key decisions. However, the type, scale, and exact nature of the geospatial information required is generally uncertain (hidden and constrained) and highly situation-dependent. Preliminary off-site data collection and opportunistic bootstrapping (Potter et al., 2000) were used to identify target areas within the domain of emergency management where the use of geospatial information was critical to disaster response. Here, opportunistic bootstrapping includes the application of any method (e.g., document or policy analysis, social network analysis, training courses, etc.) by the knowledge elicitor prior to fieldwork with experts. This led to the selection of hurricane preparation, response, and recovery as another overarching theme in the domain of emergency crisis management to study using the Living Laboratory approach as a guide. The bootstrapping and off-site data collection phases of this project are directly tied to the problem-finding steps associated with the problem-based approach at the heart of the Living Laboratory.

Officials from hurricane management centers in South Carolina and Florida were interviewed and observed during the fieldwork phases of this project through the use of a technique known as cognitive task analysis. Cognitive task (or work) analyses (CTA/CWA) are largely concerned with collecting artifacts (e.g., documents, procedures, manuals, etc.), as well as ethnographic information and interview transcripts from experts at their work location. These types of analyses can be entirely observational or more participatory and structured in nature. The nature of CTA/CWA tends to blur the lines between traditional ethnographic studies and knowledge elicitation efforts, and as such it represents a combinatorial approach to fieldwork. The CTA procedure used for this project involved both off-site and on-site work followed by convergent, collaborative design. The goal of the off-site work was to build up the researcher's understanding of the domain of practice (e.g., emergency management in general, and hurricanes specifically) using bootstrapping methods prior to visiting with expert participants. On-site work consisted of visits to four different Emergency Operations Centers: two state-level divisions (Florida and South Carolina) and two county-level offices (Horry and Charleston Counties, SC). During these visits, a collection of knowledge elicitation exercises, including artifact collection, mission scenario creation and refinement, critical incident questioning, concept mapping, and exit questionnaires, were conducted. These sessions were performed in the tradition of the Living Laboratory using the AKADAM/COLLATA (McNeese and Rentsch, 2001) techniques.

The goal of this multifaceted procedure was to collect information that could be transformed into CTA models of the domain of practice and compiled into realistic emergency management scenarios that would guide the design of systems. The important issue to note is that the techniques were selected to maximize range of expert knowledge captured, from (1) the strictly explicit or factual knowledge that could be collected through artifacts, manuals, organizational charts, and procedures, to (2) the tacit or intuitive knowledge that is contained only within the individual emergency responders, to (3) the inferential and experiential knowledge that is imbedded within the collaborative system of emergency response among all participants.

For the extant study portion of this project, artifact information helped set the scene from which to construct an emergency response scenario. The results of concept mapping exercises were used to determine (1) who the actors or collaborating agencies were in the process of hurricane response, (2) what the common themes or stages were (e.g., decision-making, evacuation support), and (3) what the critical decision points were. The critical incident questioning yielded several other mission scenarios and variations on the initial scenario. The information captured also helped to produce dialogue excerpts between managers during hurricane response. For example, the information and planning team would work with local organizations to produce maps that could be given to groups of decision-makers in charge of determining evacuation timing, sheltering programs, and propositioning Logistical staging areas for dispensing of relief supplies. Finally, the combination of concept mapping and critical incident questioning provided depth from which to merge all of the elements together into dialogue-based storyboard scripts of the emergency management process and response activities. These results specifically inform the design of multimodal group interfaces at the Penn State GeoVISTA Center. Specifically, subsections of these scenarios have been built into iterations of a gesture/speech-enabled large screen display called DAVE_G (Dialogue-Assisted Virtual Environment for Geo-information; see Rauchert et al., 2002; Sharma et al., 2003). For more comprehensive treatments of the design and analyses from this project, we would direct the reader to further reading on this project (see Brewer, 2002, 2005).

SUMMARY

Creating useful envisioned designs for national security and counter-terrorism applications is not merely predicated upon implementing technology because it may exist, nor is it simply an allocation of results from experimental research studies. What is needed for effective prevention of terrorism is a comprehensive approach that holistically considers multiple perspectives but results in creating user-/team-centric designs to address complex problems that are often ill-defined, emergent, and uncertain across time and involve collaborative agents coordinating multiple flows of information. This chapter presents the Living Laboratory approach as a unique research program framework that focuses on envisioned designs of collaborative technology that can facilitate distributed cognition in environments where teamwork is critical and complex. The Living Laboratory has been explained and we have shown the application of the framework to selected projects in national security. This approach has enabled the cross-fertilization of ideas drawing on multiple levels of analysis, fieldwork, and experimentation to transform envisioned designs into actual artifacts for use. As these artifacts mature and develop further, it is our hope to create design interventions in actual practice. The Living Laboratory focus has afforded a deeper understanding of collaborative knowledge management in a way that leverages the development of intelligent group interfaces and collaborative suites to facilitate decision-making and situation awareness within distributed, virtual teamwork settings. As this objective continues to unfold, a completed cycle through the Living Lab will ensure triangulation of different sources of knowledge, design, and practice increasing the probability of success.

REFERENCES

Bereiter, C. (1997). Situated cognition and how to overcome it. In: *Situated Cognition: Social, Semiotic, and Psychological Perspectives,* D. Kirshner and J. A. Whitson (eds.), pp. 281–300. Hillsdale, NJ: Erlbaum.

Bransford, J. D., Goin, L. I., Hasselbring, T. S., Kinzer, C. Z., Sherwood, R. D., and Williams, S. M. (1988). Learning with technology: Theoretical and empirical perspectives. *Peabody Journal of Education* **64**(1):5–26.

Brewer, I. (2002). Cognitive systems engineering and GIScience: Lessons learned from a work domain analysis for the design of a collaborative, multimodal emergency management GIS. *GIScience 2002,* Boulder, CO.

Brewer, I. (2005). Understanding work with geospatial information in emergency management: A cognitive systems engineering approach in giscience. Unpublished doctoral dissertation, The Pennsylvania State University.

Brown, J. S., Collins, A., and Duguid, P. (1989). Situated cognition and the culture of learning. *Educational Researcher* **18**(1):32–42.

Cole, M., and Engstrom, Y. (1993). A cultural-historical approach to distributed cognition. In: *Distributed Cognitions: Psychological and Educational Considerations,* Gavriel Salomon (eds.). New York: Cambridge University Press.

Flanagan, J. C. (1954). The critical incident technique. *Psychological Bulletin* **51**(4):327–359.

Greeno, J. G., and Moore, J. L. (1993). Situativity and symbols: Response to Vera and Simon. *Cognitive Science* **17**:49–60.

Hoffman, R. R., Crandall, B., and Shadbolt, N. (1998). Use of the critical decision method to elicit expert knowledge: A case study in the methodology of cognitive task analysis. *Human Factors* **40**:254–276.

Hollnagel E., and Woods D. D. (1983) Cognitive systems engineering: New wine in new bottles. *International Journal of Man-Machine Studies* **18**:583–600.

Hutchins, E. (1995). *Cognition in the Wild.* Cambridge, MA: MIT Press.

Klein, G. A., Calderwood, R., and Macgregor, D. (1989). Critical decision method for eliciting knowledge. *IEEE Transactions on Systems, Man and Cybernetics* **19**(3):462–472.

Klein, G. A., Orassanu, J., Calderwood, R., and C. E. Zsambok (1993). *Decision Making in Action: Models and Methods.* Norwood, NJ: Ablex.

Lave, J., and Wenger, E. (1991). *Situated Learning: Legitimate Peripheral Participation.* Cambridge, UK: Cambridge University Press.

Liang, D. W., Moreland, R., and Argote, L., (1995), Group versus individual training and group performance: The mediating role of transactive memory, *Personality and Social Psychology Bulletin* **21**(4):384–393.

Luria, A. R. (1979). *The Making of Mind: A Personal Account of Soviet Psychology.* Cambridge: Harvard University Press.

McNeese, M. D. (1992). Analogical Transfer in Situated, Cooperative Learning. Unpublished doctoral dissertation. Vanderbilt University, Nashville, TN.

McNeese, M. D. (1996). An ecological perspective applied to multi-operator systems. In: *Human Factors in Organizational Design and Management*—VI, pp. 365–370. Brown and H. L. Hendrick (eds.), The Netherlands: Elsevier.

McNeese, M. D. (1998). Teamwork, team performance, and team interfaces: Historical precedence and application significance of the research at the USAF Fitts Human Engineering Division. *Proceedings of the IEEE International Symposium on Technology and Society,* pp. 161–166, IEEE Society on Social Implications of Technology, South Bend, IN.

McNeese, M. D. (2000). Socio-cognitive factors in the acquisition and transfer of knowledge. *Cognition, Technology and Work* **2**(3):164–177.

McNeese, M. D. (2001). Situated Cognition in Distributed Multi-National, Multi-Cultural Teams: A Research Plan and a Perspective. Unpublished manuscript, University Park, PA.

McNeese, M. D. (2002). Discovering how cognitive systems should be engineered for aviation domains: A developmental look at work, research, and practice. In: *Cognitive Systems Engineering in Military Aviation Environments: Avoiding Cogminutia Fragmentosa!,* pp. 79–119, M. D. McNeese and M. A. Vidulich (eds.), Wright-Patterson Air Force Base, OH: HSIAC Press.

McNeese, M. D. (2003). Metaphors and paradigms of team cognition: A twenty year perspective. In: *Proceedings of the Annual Meeting of the Human Factors and Ergonomics Society.* Santa Monica, CA: Human Factors and Ergonomics Society.

McNeese, M. D., and Brown, C. E. (1986). Large group displays and team performance: An evaluation and projection of guidelines, research, and technologies. AAMRL-TR-86-035. Armstrong Aerospace Medical Research Laboratory, Wright-Patterson Air Force Base, OH.

McNeese, M. D., Zaff, B. S., and Brown, C. E. (1992). Computer-supported collaborative work: A new agenda for human factors engineering. In: Proceedings of the IEEE National Aerospace and Electronics Conference (NAECON), pp. 681–686. Dayton, OH: IEEE, Aerospace and Electronic Systems Society.

McNeese, M. D., Zaff, B. S., Citera, M., Brown, C. E., and Whitaker, R. (1995). AKADAM: Eliciting user knowledge to support participatory ergonomics. *The International Journal of Industrial Ergonomics* 15(5):345–363.

McNeese, M. D., and Rentsch, J. (2001). Social and cognitive considerations of teamwork. In: *New Trends in Cooperative Activities: System Dynamics in Complex Environments*, M. D. McNeese, E. Salas, and M. Endsley (eds.), pp. 96–113. Santa Monica, CA: Human Factors and Ergonomics Society Press.

McNeese, M. D., Rentsch, J. R., and Perusich, K. (2000). Modeling, measuring, and mediating teamwork: The use of fuzzy cognitive maps and team member schema similarity to enhance BMC3I decision making. In: *IEEE International Conference on Systems, Man, and Cybernetics*, pp. 1081–1086. New York: Institute of Electrical and Electronic Engineers.

Obermayer, R. W. (1964). Simulations, models, and games: Sources of measurement. *Human Factors* 31:607–619.

Perusich, K., and McNeese, M. D. (1997). Using fuzzy cognitive maps for data abstraction. In: *Proceedings of the Annual Meeting of the North America Information Processing Society*, pp. 5–9. New York: IEEE Press.

Rasmussen, J., Pejtersen, A. M., and Goodstein, L. P. (1994). *Cognitive Engineering: Concepts and Applications*. New York: Wiley.

Rauschert, I., Agrawal, P., Fuhrmann, S., Brewer, I., Sharma, R., Cai, G., and MacEachren. A. (2002). Designing a user-centered, multimodal gis interface to support emergency management. In: *Proceedings of the ACM GIS 2002*, McLean, VA.

Rentsch, J. R., McNeese, M. D., Pape, L. J., Burnett, D. D., Menard, D. M., and Anesgart, M. (1998). Testing the effects of team processes on team member schema similarity and task performance: Examination of the Team Member Schema Similarity Model (Tech. Rep. No. AFRL-HE-WP-TR-1998-0070). Dayton, OH: Wright-Patterson Air Force Base, U. S. Air Force Research Laboratory, Collaborative Systems Technology Branch.

Resnick, L. B. (1991). Shared cognition: Thinking as social practice. In: L. B. Resnick, J. M. Levine, and S. D. Teasley (eds.), *Perspectives on Socially Shared Cognition*. Washington, DC: APA Books.

Salas, E., and Klein, G. (2001). Expertise and naturalistic decision making: an overview. In: *Linking Expertise and Naturalistic Decision Making*, E. Salas and G. Klein (eds.). Hillsdale, NJ: Lawrence Erlbaum.

Salomon, G. (1993). No distribution without individuals' cognition: a dynamic interactional view. In: *Distributed Cognitions: Psychological and Educational Considerations*, G. Salomon (ed.), pp. 111–138, Cambridge, UK: Cambridge University Press.

Schiflett, S. G., Elliott, L. R., Salas, E., and Coovert, M. D. (eds.) (2004). *Scaled worlds: Development, Validation and Applications*. Aldershot: Ashgate.

Schmidt, K., and Bannon, L. (1992). Taking CSCW seriously: Supporting articulation work. *Computer Supported Cooperative Work (CSCW)* 1(1–2):7–40.

Sharma, R., Yeasin, M., Krahnstoever, N., Rauschert, I., Cai, G., Brewer, I., MacEachren, A., and Sengupta., K. (2003). Speech-gesture driven multimodal interfaces for crisis management. *IEEE Special Issue on Multimodal Systems* 91(9):1327–54.

Snyder, D. E., McNeese, M. D., and Zaff, B. S. (1991). Identifying design requirements using integrated analysis structures. In: *Proceedings of the IEEE National Aerospace and Electronics Conference (NAECON)*, pp. 786–791. Dayton, OH: IEEE, Aerospace and Electronic Systems Society.

Suchman, L. A. (1987). *Plans and Situated Actions: The Problem of Human–Machine Communication*. New York: Cambridge University Press.

Vera, A. H., and Simon, H. A. (1993). Situated action: A symbolic interpretation. *Cognitive Science* 17: 7–48.

Vygotsky, L. S. (1978). *Mind in Society: The Development of Higher Psychological Processes.* Cambridge: Harvard University Press.

Wellens, A. R. (1993). Group situation awareness and distributed decision making: From military to civilian applications. In: *Individual and Group Decision Making,* N. J. Castellan, Jr. (ed.), pp. 267–291. Mahwah, NJ: Erlbaum.

Wellens, A. R., and Ergener, D. (1988). The C.I.T.I.E.S. game: A computer-based situation assessment task for studying distributed decision making. *Simulation and Games* 19(3):304–327.

Woods, D. D., Johannesen, L., Cook, R. I., and Sarter, N. B. (1994). *Behind Human Error: Cognitive Systems, Computers, and Hindsight* (state-of-the-art report). Dayton, OH: Crew Systems Ergonomic Information and Analysis Center.

Young, M. F., and McNeese, M. D. (1995). A situated cognition approach to problem solving. In: *Local Applications of the Ecological Approach to Human-Machine Systems,* P. Hancock, J. Flach, J. Caird, and K. Vincente (eds.), pp. 359–391. Hillsdale, NJ: Erlbaum.

Zaff, B. S., McNeese, M. D., and Snyder, D. E. (1993). Capturing multiple perspectives: A user-centered approach to knowledge acquisition. *Knowledge Acquisition* 5(1):79–116.

Zsambok, C. E., and Klein, G. (1997). Naturalistic Decision Making. Mahwah, NJ: Erlbaum.

Chapter 14

Agent-Based Simulations for Disaster Rescue Using the DEFACTO Coordination System

Janusz Marecki, Nathan Schurr, and Milind Tambe

14.1. INTRODUCTION

In the shadow of large-scale national and international terrorist incidents, it is critical to provide first responders and rescue personnel with tools that enable more effective and efficient disaster response. We envision future disaster response to be performed with a mixture of humans performing high-level decision-making, intelligent agents coordinating the response, and humans and robots performing key physical tasks. These heterogeneous teams of robots, agents, and people (Scerri et al., 2003) will provide the safest and most effective means for quickly responding to a disaster, such as a terrorist attack. A key aspect of such a response will be agent-assisted vehicles working together. Specifically, agents will assist the vehicles in planning routes, determining resources to use and even determining which fire to fight. Each agent only obtains local information about its surrounding, it must communicate with others to obtain additional information, and it must coordinate to ensure that maximum numbers of civilians are saved and property damage is minimized.

However, despite advances in agent technologies, human involvement will be crucial. Allowing humans to make critical decisions within a team of intelligent agents or robots is prerequisite for allowing such teams to be used in domains where they can cause physical, financial, or psychological harm. These critical decisions include not only the decisions that, for moral or political reasons, humans must be allowed to make, but also coordination decisions that humans are better at making due to access to important global knowledge, general information, or support tools.

Already, human interaction with agent teams is critical in a large number of current and future applications (Burstein et al., 1999; Fong et al., 2002; Scerri et al., 2003; Crandall et al., 2003). For example, current efforts emphasize human collaboration with robot teams in space explorations, humans teaming with robots and agents for disaster rescue,

This research written in this chapter was supported by the United States Department of Homeland Security (DHS) through the Center for Risk and Economic Analysis of Terrorism Events (CREATE). However, any opinions, findings, and conclusions or recommendations in this document are those of the author and do not necessarily reflect views of DHS.

and humans collaborating with multiple software agents for training (Dorais et al., 1998; Hill et al., 2003).

This chapter focuses on the challenge of improving the effectiveness of applications of human collaboration with agent teams. Previous work has reported encouraging progress in this arena—for example, via proxy-based integration architectures (Pynadath and Tambe, 2003), adjustable autonomy (Scerri et al., 2002; Dorais et al., 1988) and agent–human dialogue (Allen, 1995). Despite this encouraging progress, previous work suffers from two key limitations. First, when interacting with agent teams acting remotely, human effectiveness is hampered by interfaces that limit their ability to apply decision-making skills in a fast and accurate manner. Techniques that provide telepresence via video are helpful (Fong et al., 2002), but cannot provide the global situation awareness. Second, agent teams have been equipped with adjustable autonomy (AA) (Scerri et al., 2003) but not the flexibility critical in such AA. Indeed, the appropriate AA method varies from situation to situation. In some cases the human user should make most of the decisions. However, in other cases, human involvement may need to be restricted. Such flexible AA techniques have been developed in domains where humans interact with individual agents (Scerri et al., 2002), but whether they apply to situations where humans interact with agent teams is unknown.

We report on a software prototype system, DEFACTO (Demonstrating Effective Flexible Agent Coordination of Teams through Omnipresence), that enables agent–human collaboration and addresses the two shortcomings outlined above. The system incorporates state-of-the-art artificial intelligence, three-dimensional visualization, and human–interaction reasoning into a unique high-fidelity system for research into human agent coordination in complex environments. DEFACTO incorporates a visualizer that allows for the human to have an *omnipresent* interaction with remote agent teams, overcoming the first limitation described above. We refer to this as the Omni-Viewer, and it combines two modes of operation. The Navigation Mode allows for a navigable, high-quality three-dimensional (3D) visualization of the world, whereas the Allocation Mode provides a traditional two-dimensional (2D) view and a list of possible task allocations that the human may perform. Human experts can quickly absorb ongoing agent and world activity, taking advantage of both the brain's favored visual object processing skills [relative to textual search (Paivio, 1974)] and the fact that 3D representations can be innately recognizable, without the layer of interpretation required of map-like displays or raw computer logs. The Navigation mode enables the human to understand the local perspectives of each agent in conjunction with the global, system-wide perspective that is obtained in the Allocation mode.

Second, to provide flexible AA, we generalize the notion of *strategies* from single-agent single-human context (Scerri et al., 2002). In our work, agents may flexibly choose among team strategies for adjustable autonomy instead of only individual strategies; thus, depending on the situation, the agent team has the flexibility to limit human interaction, and in extreme cases it may exclude humans from the loop.

We present results from detailed experiments with DEFACTO, which reveal two major surprises. First, contrary to previous results (Scerri et al., 2003), human involvement is not always beneficial to an agent team—despite their best efforts, humans may sometimes end up hurting an agent team's performance. Second, increasing the number of agents in an agent–human team may also degrade the team performance, even though increasing the number of agents in a pure agent team under identical circumstances improves team performance. Fortunately, in both the surprising instances above, DEFACTO's flexible AA strategies alleviate such problematic situations.

14.2. DEFACTO SYSTEM DETAILS

The DEFACTO system is currently focused on illustrating the potential of future disaster-response to disasters that may arise as a result of large-scale terrorist attacks. Constructed as part of the effort at the first center for research excellence on homeland security (the CREATE center), DEFACTO is motivated by a scenario of great concern to first responders within metropolitan areas; indeed, in our consultations with the Los Angeles fire department and personnel from the CREATE center, this scenario appears to be of the greatest concern. In particular, in this scenario, a shoulder-fired missile is used to attack a very low-flying civilian jet-liner, causing the jetliner to crash into an urban area and cause a disaster on the ground. The scenario could lead to multiple fires in multiple locations, creating harm to civilians on the ground, with potentially many critically injured civilians. While there are many longer-term implications of such an attack, such as the economical impact, the psychological impact, the response of the FAA, and so on, we focus on assisting in the shorter-term first response phase.

In this section we will describe two major components of DEFACTO: the Omni-Viewer and the proxy-based teamwork (see Figure 14.1). The Omni-Viewer is an advanced human interface for interacting with an agent-assisted response effort. The Omni-Viewer provides for both global and local views of an unfolding situation, allowing a human decision-maker to acquire additional information required for a particular decision. A team of completely distributed proxies, where each proxy encapsulates advanced coordination reasoning based on the theory of teamwork, controls and coordinates agents in a simulated environment. The use of the proxy-based team brings realistic coordination complexity to the prototype and allows more realistic assessment of the interactions between hu-

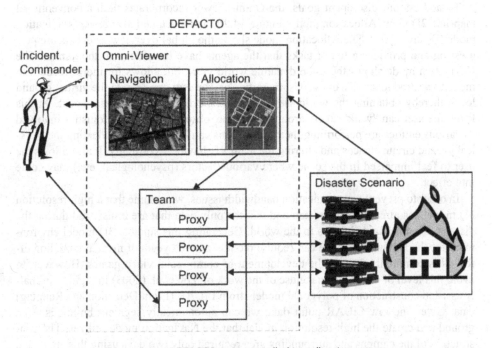

Figure 14.1. DEFACTO system applied to a disaster rescue.

mans and agent-assisted response. Currently, we have applied DEFACTO to a disaster rescue domain. The incident commander of the disaster acts as the *human user* of DE-FACTO. We focus on two urban areas: a square block that is densely covered with buildings (we use one from Kobe, Japan) and the USC campus, which is more sparsely covered with buildings. In our scenario, several buildings are initially on fire, and these fires spread to adjacent buildings if they are not quickly contained. The goal is to have a human interact with the team of fire engines in order to save the most buildings. Our overall system architecture applied to disaster response can be seen in Figure 14.1. While designed for real-world situations, DEFACTO can also be used as a training tool for incident commanders when hooked up to a simulated disaster scenario.

14.2.1. Omni-Viewer

Our goal of allowing fluid interaction between humans and agents requires a visualization system that provides the human with a global view of agent activity as well as showing the local view of a particular agent when needed. Hence, we have developed an omnipresent viewer, or Omni-Viewer, which will allow the human user diverse interaction with remote agent teams. While a global view is obtainable from a 2D map, a local perspective is best obtained from a 3D viewer, since the 3D view incorporates the perspective and occlusion effects generated by a particular viewpoint. The literature on 2D versus 3D viewers is ambiguous. For example, spatial learning of environments from virtual navigation has been found to be impaired relative to studying simple maps of the same environments (Richardson et al., 1999). On the other hand, the problem may be that many virtual environments are relatively bland and featureless. Ruddle points out that navigating virtual environments can be successful if rich, distinguishable landmarks are present (Ruddle et al., 1997).

To address our discrepant goals, the Omni-Viewer incorporates both a conventional map-like 2D view, Allocation mode (Figure 14.2d) and a detailed 3D viewer, Navigation mode (Figure 14.2c). The Allocation mode shows the global overview as events are progressing and provides a list of tasks that the agents have transferred to the human. The Navigation mode shows the same dynamic world view, but allows for more freedom to move to desired locations and views. In particular, the user can drop to the virtual ground level, thereby obtaining the world view (local perspective) of a particular agent. At this level, the user can "walk" freely around the scene, observing the local logistics involved as various entities are performing their duties. This can be helpful in evaluating the physical ground circumstances and altering the team's behavior accordingly. It also allows the user to feel immersed in the scene where various factors (psychological, etc.) may come into effect.

In order to prevent communication bandwidth issues, we assume that a high-resolution 3D model has already been created and that the only data that are transferred during the disaster are important changes to the world. Generating this suitable 3D model environment for the Navigation mode can require months or even years of manual modeling effort as is commonly seen in the development of commercial video games. However, to avoid this level of effort, we make use of the work of You et al. (2003) in rapid, minimally assisted construction of polygonal models from LiDAR (Light Detection and Ranging) data. Given the raw LiDAR point data, we can automatically segment buildings from ground and create the high-resolution model that the Navigation mode utilizes. The construction of the campus and surrounding area required only two days using this approach.

Figure 14.2. Omni-Viewer during a scenario: (a) Multiple fires start across the campus. (b) The Incident Commander uses the Navigation mode to quickly grasp the situation. (c) Navigation mode shows a closer look at one of the fires. (d) Allocation mode is used to assign a fire engine to the fire. (e) The fire engine has arrived at the fire. (f) The fire has been extinguished.

LiDAR is an effective way for any new geographic area to be easily inserted into the Omni-Viewer.

We use the JME game engine to perform the actual rendering due to its cross-platform capabilities. JME is an extensible library built on LWJGL (Light-Weight Java Game Library), which interfaces with OpenGL and OpenAL. This environment easily provided real-time rendering of the textured campus environment on mid-range commodity PCs. JME utilizes a scene graph to order the rendering of geometric entities. It provides some important features such as OBJ format model loading (which allows us to author the model and textures in a tool like Maya and load it in JME) and also various assorted effects such as particle systems for fires.

14.2.2. Proxy: Teamwork

A key hypothesis in this work is that intelligent distributed agents will be a key element of a future disaster response. Taking advantage of emerging robust, high-bandwidth communication infrastructure, we believe that a critical role of these intelligent agents will be to manage coordination between all members of the response team. Specifically, to manage the distributed response, we are using coordination algorithms inspired by theories of teamwork (Tambe, 1997) that extend the joint intentions approach to teamwork. The general coordination algorithms are encapsulated in *proxies,* with each team member having its own proxy and representing it in the team. The current version of the proxies is called *Machinetta* (Sçerri et al., 2004) and extends the successful Team-core proxies (Pynadeth and Tambe, 2003). Machinetta is implemented in Java and is freely available on the web. Notice that the concept of a reusable proxy differs from many other "multi-agent toolkits" in that it provides the coordination *algorithms* (e.g., algorithms for allocating tasks), as opposed to the *infrastructure* (e.g., APIs for reliable communication).

The Machinetta proxy consists of five main modules, three of which are domain-independent and two of which are tailored for specific domains. The three domain-independent modules are for coordination reasoning, maintaining local beliefs (state) and adjustable autonomy. The domain-specific modules are for communication between proxies and communication between a proxy and a team member (Figure 14.3). The modules interact with each other only via the local state with a blackboard design and are designed to be "plug and play", thus, for example, new adjustable autonomy algorithms can be used with existing coordination algorithms. The coordination reasoning is responsible for reasoning about interactions with other proxies, thus implementing the coordination algorithms. The adjustable autonomy algorithms reason about the interaction with the team member, providing the possibility for the team member to make any coordination decision instead of the proxy. For example, the adjustable autonomy module can reason that a decision to accept a role to rescue a civilian from a burning building should be made by the human who will go into the building rather than the proxy. In practice, the overwhelming majority of coordination decisions are made by the proxy, with only key decisions referred to team members.

Teams of proxies implement *team-oriented plans* (TOPs), which describe joint activities to be performed in terms of the individual *roles* to be performed and any constraints between those roles. Typically, TOPs are instantiated dynamically from TOP templates at runtime when preconditions associated with the templates are filled. Typically, a large team will be simultaneously executing many TOPs. For example, a disaster response team

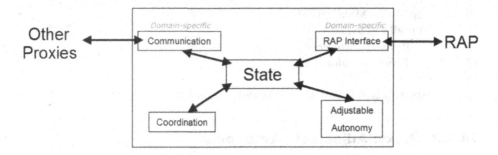

Communication: communication with other proxies
Coordination: reasoning about team plans and communication
State: the working memory of the proxy
Adjustable autonomy: reasoning about whether to act autonomously or pass control to the team member
RAP interface: communication with the team member

Figure 14.3. Proxy architecture.

might be executing multiple fight-fire TOPs. Such fight-fire TOPs might specify a break-down of fighting a fire into activities such as checking for civilians, ensuring power and gas is turned off and spraying water. Constraints between these roles will specify interactions such as required execution ordering and whether one role can be performed if another is not currently being performed. Notice that TOPs do not specify the coordination or communication required to execute a plan, and the proxy determines the coordination that should be performed.

Current versions of Machinetta include a token-based role allocation algorithm. The decision for the agent becomes whether to assign values represented by tokens it currently has to its variable or to pass the tokens on. First, the team member can choose the minimum capability the agent should have in order to assign the value. This minimum capability is referred to as the *threshold*. The threshold is calculated once (Algorithm 1, line 6 as described below), and it is attached to the token as it moves around the team.

Second, the agent must check whether the value can be assigned while respecting its local resource constraints (Algorithm 1, line 9). If the value cannot be assigned within the resource constraints of the team member, it must choose a value(s) to reject and pass on to other teammates in the form of a token(s) (Algorithm 1, line 12). The agent keeps values that maximize the use of its capabilities (performed in the MAXCAP function, Algorithm 1, line 10).

Algorithm 1. TOKENMONITOR(*Cap, Resources*)
1: $V \rightarrow \emptyset$;
2: **while** true **do**
3:     $msg \leftarrow getMsg()$
4:     $token \leftarrow msg$
5:     **if** *token.threshold = NULL* **then**
6:        $token.threshold \leftarrow$ COMPUTETHRESHOLD(*token*)
7:     **if** *token.threshold $\leq$ Cap(token.value)* **then**
8:        $V \leftarrow V \cup token.value$
9:        **if** $\Sigma_{v \in V} Resources(v) \geq agent.resource$ **then**

```
10:        out ← V – MaxCap(Values)
11:        for all v ∈ out do
12:            PassOn(newtoken(v))
13:            Values ← Values – out
14:    else
15:        PassOn(token) /* threshold > Cap(token.value) */
```

14.2.3. Proxy: Adjustable Autonomy

In this section, we focus on a key aspect of the proxy-based coordination: adjustable autonomy. Adjustable autonomy refers to an agent's ability to dynamically change its own autonomy, possibly to transfer control over a decision to a human. Previous work on adjustable autonomy could be categorized as either involving a single person interacting with a single agent (the agent itself may interact with others) or a single person directly interacting with a team. In the single-agent single-human category, the concept of flexible transfer-of-control strategy has shown promise (Scerri et al., 2002). A transfer-of-control strategy is a preplanned sequence of actions to transfer control over a decision among multiple entities. For example, an AH_1H_2 strategy implies that an agent (A) attempts a decision; if the agent fails in the decision, then the control over the decision is passed to a human H_1, and then if H_1 cannot reach a decision, then the control is passed to H_2. Since previous work focused on single-agent single-human interaction, strategies were individual agent strategies where only a single agent acted at a time.

An optimal transfer-of-control strategy optimally balances the risks of not getting a high-quality decision against the risk of costs incurred due to a delay in getting that decision. Flexibility in such strategies implies that an agent dynamically chooses the one that is optimal, based on the situation, among multiple such strategies (H_1A, AH_1, AH_1A, etc.) rather than always rigidly choosing one strategy. The notion of flexible strategies, however, has not been applied in the context of humans interacting with agent teams. Thus, a key question is whether such flexible transfer-of-control strategies are relevant in agent teams, particularly in a large-scale application such as ours.

DEFACTO aims to answer this question by implementing transfer-of-control strategies in the context of agent teams. One key advance in DEFACTO, however, is that the strategies are not limited to individual agent strategies, but also enables team-level strategies. For example, rather than transferring control from a human to a single agent, a team-level strategy could transfer control from a human to an agent team. Concretely, each proxy is provided with all strategy options; the key is to select the right strategy given the situation. An example of a team level strategy would combine A_T strategy and H strategy in order to make A_TH strategy. The default team strategy, A_T, keeps control over a decision with the agent *team* for the entire duration of the decision. The H strategy always immediately transfers control to the human. A_TH strategy is the conjunction of team level A_T strategy with H strategy. This strategy aims to significantly reduce the burden on the user by allowing the decision to first pass through all agents before finally going to the user, if the agent team fails to reach a decision.

14.3. MATHEMATICAL MODEL OF STRATEGY SELECTION

We developed a novel mathematical model for these team-level adjustable autonomy strategies in order to enable team-level strategy selection. We first quickly review background on individual strategies from Scerri et al. (2002) before presenting our team strategies. Whereas strategies in Scerri's work are based on a single decision that is sequentially passed from agent to agent, we assume that there are multiple homogeneous agents concurrently working on multiple tasks interacting with a single human user. We exploit these assumptions (which fit our domain) to obtain a reduced version of our model and simplify the computation in selecting strategies.

14.3.1. Background on Individual Strategies

A decision, d, needs to be made. There are n entities, $e_1 \ldots e_n$, who can potentially make the decision. These entities can be human users or agents. The expected quality of decisions made by each of the entities, $\mathbf{EQ} = \{EQ_{e_i,d}(t) : \mathfrak{R} \to \mathfrak{R}\}_{i=1}^n$, is known, though perhaps not exactly. $\mathbf{P} = \{P_\tau(t) : \mathfrak{R} \to \mathfrak{R}\}$ represents continuous probability distributions over the time that the entity in control will respond (with a decision of quality $EQ_{e,d}(t)$). The cost of delaying a decision until time t is denoted as $\{W : t \to R\}$. The set of possible wait-cost functions is $\mathbf{W}$. $W(t)$ is nondecreasing and is at some point in time, Γ, when the costs of waiting stop accumulating (i.e., $\forall t \geq \Gamma, \forall W \in \mathbf{W}, W(t) = W(\Gamma)$).

To calculate the expected utility (EU) of an arbitrary strategy, the model multiplies the probability of response at each instant of time with the expected utility of receiving a response at that instant, and then it sums the products. Hence, for an arbitrary continuous probability distribution, if e_c represents the entity currently in decision-making control, then we have

$$EU = \int_0^\infty P_\tau(t)EU_{e_c,d}(t) \, dt \qquad (14.1)$$

Since we are primarily interested in the effects of delay caused by transfer of control, we can decompose the expected utility of a decision at a certain instant, $EU_{e_c,d}(t)$, into two terms. The first term captures the quality of the decision, independent of delay costs, and the second captures the costs of delay: $EU_{e_c,d}(t) = EQ_{e,d}(t) - W(t)$. To calculate the EU of a strategy, the probability of response function and the wait-cost calculation must reflect the control situation at that point in the strategy. If a human, H_1, has control at time t, then $P_\tau(t)$ reflects H_1's probability of responding at t.

14.3.2. Introduction of Team-Level Strategies

A_T **Strategy:** Starting from the individual model, we introduce (depicted below) team level A_T strategy, denoted as A_T in the following way: We start with Eq. (14.2) for single agent A_T and single task d. We obtain Eq. (14.3) by discretizing time, $t = 1, \ldots, T$, and introducing set Δ of tasks. Probability of agent A_T performing a task d at time t is denoted as $P_{a,d}(t)$. Eq. (14.4) is a result of the introduction of the set of agents $AG = a_1, a_1, \ldots, a_k$. We assume the same quality of decision for each task performed by an agent and that each agent A_T has the same quality so that we can reduce $EQ_{a,d}(t)$ to $EQ(t)$. Given the assumption that each agent A_T at time step t performs one task, we have $\Sigma_{d \in \Delta} P_{a,d}(t) = 1$, which is depicted in Eq. (14.5). Then we express $\Sigma_{a=a_1}^{a_k} \Sigma_{d \in \Delta} P_{a,d}(t) \times W_{a,d}(t)$ as the total team penalty for time slice t; that is, at time slice t we subtract one penalty unit for each not completed task as seen in Eq. (14.6). Assuming penalty unit $PU = 1$ we finally obtain Eq. (14.7).

$$EU_{a,d} = \int_0^\infty P_{Ta}(t) \times (EQ_{a,d}(t) - W(t))\, dt \tag{14.2}$$

$$EU_{a,\Delta} = \sum_{t=1}^{T} \sum_{d \in \Delta} P_{a,d}(t) \times (EQ_{a,d}(t) - W(t)) \tag{14.3}$$

$$EU_{A_T,\Delta} = \sum_{t=1}^{T} \sum_{a=a_1}^{a_k} \sum_{d \in \Delta} P_{a,d}(t) \times (EQ_{a,d}(t) - W_{a,d}(t)) \tag{14.4}$$

$$EU_{A_T,\Delta,AG} = \sum_{t=1}^{T} \left(\sum_{a=a_1}^{a_k} EQ(t) - \sum_{a=a_1}^{a_k} \sum_{d \in \Delta} P_{a,d}(t) \times W_{a,d}(t) \right) \tag{14.5}$$

$$EU_{A_T,\Delta,AG} = \sum_{t=1}^{T} \left(|AG| \times EQ(t) - (|\Delta| - |AG| \times t) \times PU \right) \tag{14.6}$$

$$EU_{A_T,\Delta,AG} = |AG| \times \sum_{t=1}^{T} \left(EQ(t) - \left(\frac{|\Delta|}{AG} - t \right) \right) \tag{14.7}$$

H Strategy: The difference between (Eq. 14.8) $EU_{H,\Delta,AG}$ and (Eq. 14.7) $EU_{A_T,\Delta,AG}$ results from three key observations: First, the human is able to choose strategic decisions with higher probability, therefore his $EQ_H(t)$ is greater than $EQ(t)$ for both individual and team level A_T strategies. Second, we hypothesize that a human cannot control all the agents AG at his disposal, but due to cognitive limits will focus on a smaller subset, AG_H of agents (evidence of limits on AG_H appears later in Figure 14.6a). $|AG_H|$ should slowly converge to B, which denotes its upper limit, but never exceed AG. Each function $f(AG)$ that models AG_H should be consistent with three properties: (i) if $B \to \infty$, then $f(AG) \to AG$; (ii) $f(AG) < B$; (iii) $f(AG) < AG$. Third, there is a delay in human decision-making compared to agent decisions. We model this phenomena by shifting H to start at time slice t_H. For $t_H - 1$ time slices the team incurs a cost $|\Delta| \times (t_H - 1)$ for all incomplete tasks. By inserting $EQ_H(t)$ and AG_H into the time-shifted utility equation for A_T strategy, we obtain the H strategy [Eq. (14.8)].

$A_T H$ Strategy: The $A_T H$ strategy is a composition of H and A_T strategies [see Eq. (14.9)].

$$EU_{H,\Delta,AG} = |AG_H| \times \sum_{t=t_H}^{T} \left(EQ_H(t) - \left(\frac{|\Delta|}{AG_H} - (t - t_H) \right) \right) - |\Delta| \times (t_H - 1) \tag{14.8}$$

$$EU_{A_T H,\Delta,AG} = |AG| \times \sum_{t=1}^{t_H-1} \left(EQ(t) - \left(\frac{|\Delta|}{|AG|} - t \right) \right)$$

$$+ |AG_H| \times \sum_{t=t_H}^{T} \left(EQ_H(t) - \left(\frac{|\Delta| - |AG|}{|AG_H|} - (t - t_H) \right) \right) \tag{14.9}$$

Strategy Utility Prediction: Given our strategy equations and the assumption that $EQ_{H,\Delta,AG}$ is constant and independent of the number of agents, we plot the graphs representing strategy utilities. Figure 14.4 shows the number of agents on the x-axis and the expected utility of a strategy on the y-axis. We focus on humans with different skills: (a) low EQ_H, low B; (b) high EQ_H, low B; (c) low EQ_H, high B; (d) high EQ_H, high B. The last graph representing a human with high EQ_H and high B follows the results presented in

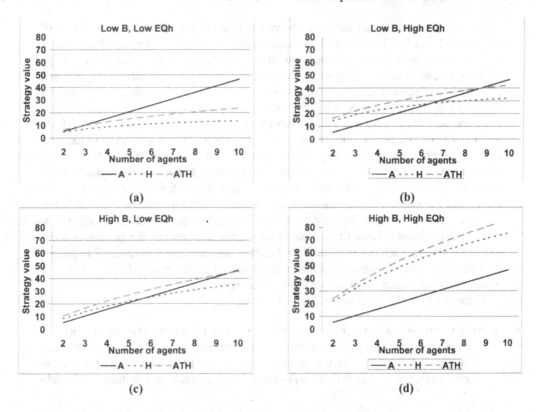

Figure 14.4. Model predictions for various users.

Ruddle et al. (1997) (and hence the expected scenario), we see the curve of AH and A_TH flattening out to eventually cross the line of A_T. Moreover, we observe that the increase in EQ_H increases the slope for AH and A_TH for small number of agents, whereas the increase of B causes the curve to maintain a slope for larger number of agents, before eventually flattening out and crossing the A_T line.

14.4. EXPERIMENTS AND EVALUATION

We performed detailed experiments with DEFACTO comparing the effectiveness of Adjustable Autonomy (AA) strategies over multiple users. In order to provide DEFACTO with a dynamic rescue domain, we chose to connect it to a simulator. We chose the previously developed RoboCup Rescue simulation environment (Kitano et al., 1999). In this simulator, fire engine agents can search the city and attempt to extinguish any fires that have started in the city. To interface with DEFACTO, each fire engine is controlled by a proxy in order to handle the coordination and execution of AA strategies. Consequently, the proxies can try to allocate fire engines to fires in a distributed manner, but can also transfer control to the more expert user. The user can then use the Omni-Viewer in Allocation mode to allocate engines to the fires that he has control over. In order to focus on the AA strategies (transferring the control of task allocation) and not have the users ability to navigate interfere with results, the Navigation mode was not used during this first set of experiments.

The results of our experiments are shown in Figure 14.5, which shows the results of subjects 1, 2, and 3, with subject 2 being more experienced in the simulation than subjects 1 and 3. Each subject was confronted with the task of aiding fire engines in saving a city hit by a disaster. For each subject, we tested three strategies, specifically, H, AH, and A_TH; their performance was compared with the completely autonomous A_T strategy. AH is an individual agent strategy, tested for comparison with A_TH, where agents act individually and pass those tasks to a human user that they cannot immediately perform. Each experiment was conducted with the same initial locations of fires and building damage. For each strategy we tested, we varied the number of fire engines between 4, 6, and 10 (this choice of numbers allowed us to observe overwhelming effects on humans). Each chart in Figure 14.5 shows the varying number of fire engines the subject controls on the x-axis, and the team performance in terms of numbers of building saved on the y-axis. For instance, strategy A_T saves 50 building with 4 fire engines controlled by a subject. The trend lines represent the best fit for 3 data points. Each data point on the graph is an average of three runs. Each run itself took 15 minutes, and each user was required to participate in 27 experiments, which, together with 2 hours of getting oriented with the system, equates to about 9 hours of experiments per volunteer.

Figure 14.5 enables us to conclude the following:

- *Human involvement with agent teams does not necessarily lead to improvement in team performance.* Contrary to expectations and prior results, human involvement does not uniformly improve team performance, as seen by human-involving strategies performing worse than the A_T strategy in some instances. For instance, for sub-

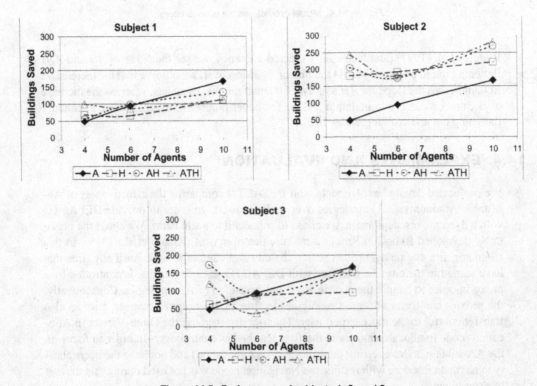

Figure 14.5. Performance of subjects 1, 2, and 3.

ject 3, human-involving strategies such as AH provide a somewhat higher quality than A_T for 4 agents, yet at higher numbers of agents, the strategy performance is lower than A_T.

- *Providing more agents at a human's command does not necessarily improve the agent team performance.* As seen for subject 2 and subject 3, increasing agents from 4 to 6 given AH and A_TH strategies is seen to degrade performance. In contrast, for the A_T strategy, the performance of the fully autonomous agent team continues to improve with additions of agents, thus indicating that the reduction in AH and A_TH performance is due to human involvement. As the number of agents increase from 6 to 10, performance of agent team following AH and A_TH strategies increases again.

- *No strategy dominates through all the experiments given varying numbers of agents.* For instance, at 4 agents, human-involving strategies dominate the A_T strategy. However, at 10 agents, the A_T strategy outperforms all possible strategies for subjects 1 and 3.

- *Complex team-level strategies are helpful in practice:* A_TH leads to improvement over H with 4 agents for all subjects, although surprising domination of AH over A_TH in some cases indicates that AH may also be a useful strategy in a team setting.

Note that the phenomena described range over multiple users, multiple runs, and multiple strategies. The most important conclusion from these figures is that *flexibility is necessary to allow for the optimal AA strategy to be applied.* The key question is then how to select the appropriate strategy for a team involving a human whose expected decision quality is EQ_H. In fact, by estimating the EQ_H of a subject by checking the "H" strategy for a small number of agents (say 4), and comparing to A_T strategy, we may begin to select the appropriate strategy for teams involving more agents. In general, higher EQ_H lets us still choose strategies involving humans for a more numerous team. For large teams, however, the number of agents AG_H effectively controlled by the human does not grow linearly, thus A_T strategy becomes dominant.

Unfortunately, the strategies including the humans and agents (AH and A_TH) for 6 agents show a noticeable decrease in performance for subjects 2 and 3 (see Figure 14.5). It would be useful to understand which factors contributed to this phenomena.

Our key predictions were that while numbers of agents increase, AG_H steadily increases and EQ_H remains constant. Thus, the dip at 6 agents is essentially affected by either AG_H or EQ_H. We first tested AG_H in our domain. The amount of effective agents, AG_H, is calculated by dividing how many total allocations each subject made by how many the A_T strategy made per agent, assuming that A_T strategy effectively uses all agents. Figure 14.6a shows the number of agents on the x-axis and the number of agents effective used, AG_H, on the y-axis; the A_T strategy, which is using all available agents, is also shown as a reference. However, the amount of effective agents is actually about the same in 4 and 6 agents. This would not account for the sharp drop we see in the performance. We then shifted our attention to the EQ_H of each subject. One reduction in EQ_H could be because subjects simply did not send as many allocations totally over the course of the experiments. This, however, is not the case as can be seen in Table 14.1, where for 6 agents the total amount of allocations given is comparable to that of 4 agents. To investigate further, we checked if the quality of human allocation had degraded. For our domain, the more fire engines that fight the same fire, the more likely it is to be extinguished and in less time. For this reason, the amount of agents that were tasked to each fire is a good indica-

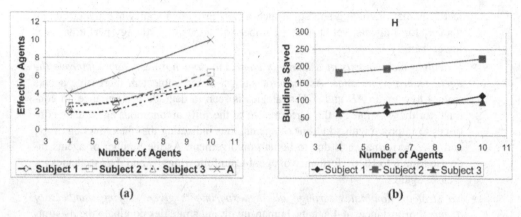

Figure 14.6. (a) AG_H and (b) H performance.

tor of the quality of allocations that the subject makes Figure 14.6b. Figure 14.7 shows the number agents on the x-axis and the average amount of fire engines allocated to each fire on the y-axis. AH and A_TH for 6 agents result in significantly less average fire engines per task (fire) and therefore less average EQ_H.

14.5. RELATED WORK

We have discussed DEFACTO throughout this chapter, however, we now provide comparisons with key previous agent software prototypes and research. Among the current tools aimed at simulating rescue environments it is important to mention products like TerraSim (TerraSim, 2005), JCATS (Lawrence Livermore National Laboratory, 2005), and EPICS (Advanced Systems Technology, 2005). TerraTools is a complete simulation database construction system for automated and rapid generation of high-fidelity 3D simulation databases from cartographic source materials. Developed by TerraSim, Inc., TerraTools provides the set of integrated tools aimed at generating various terrains, however, it is not applicable to simulate rescue operations. JCATS represents a self-contained, high-resolution joint simulation in use for entity-level training in open, urban, and subterranean environments. Developed by Lawrence Livermore National Laboratory, JCATS gives users the capability to detail the replication of small group and individual activities during a simulated operation. Although it provides a great human training environment, at this point JCATS cannot simulate intelligent agents. Finally, EPICS is a computer-based, scenario-driven, high-resolution simulation. It is used by emergency response agencies to train for emergency situations that require mul-

Table 14.1. Total Amount of Allocations Given

Strategy	H			AH			A_TH		
# of Agents	4	6	10	4	6	10	4	6	10
Subject 1	91	92	154	118	128	132	104	83	64
Subject 2	138	129	180	146	144	72	109	120	38
Subject 3	117	132	152	133	136	97	116	58	57

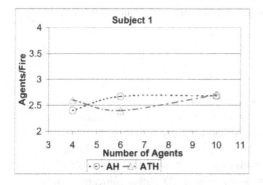
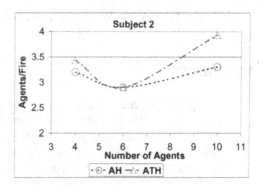

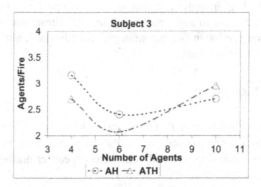

Figure 14.7. Amount of agents per fire assigned by subjects 1, 2, and 3.

ti-echelon and/or inter-agency communication and coordination. Developed by the U.S. Army Training and Doctrine Command Analysis Center, EPICS is also used for exercising communications and command and control procedures at multiple levels. Similar to JCATS, however, intelligent agents and agent–human interaction cannot be simulated by EPICS at this point.

Given our application domains, Scerri et al's work on robot-agent-person (RAP) teams for disaster rescue is likely the most closely related to DEFACTO (Scerri et al., 2003). Our work takes a significant step forward in comparison. First, the Omni-Viewer enables navigational capabilities improving human situational awareness not present in previous work. Second, we provide team-level strategies, which we experimentally verify, absent in that work. Third, we provide extensive experimentation, and illustrate that some of the conclusions reached in Scerri et al. (2003) were indeed preliminary, for example, they conclude that human involvement is always beneficial to agent team performance, while our more extensive results indicate that sometimes agent teams are better off excluding humans from the loop. Human interactions in agent teams is also investigated in Burstein et al. (1999) and You et al. (2003), and there is significant research on human interactions with robot teams (Fong et al., 2002; Crandall et al., 2003). However they do not use flexible AA strategies and/or team-level AA strategies. Furthermore, our experimental results may assist these researchers in recognizing the potential for harm that humans may cause to agent or robot team performance. Significant attention has been paid in the context of adjustable autonomy and mixed-initiative in single-agent single-human interactions

(Horvitz, 1999; Allen, 1995). However, this chapter focuses on new phenomena that arise in human interactions with agent teams.

SUMMARY

This chapter presents a large-scale prototype system, DEFACTO, that is currently focused on illustrating the potential of future disaster-response to disasters that may arise as a result of large-scale terrorist attacks. Based on a software proxy architecture and 3D visualization system, DEFACTO provides two key advances over previous work. First, DEFACTO's Omni-Viewer enables the human to both improve situational awareness and assist agents, by providing a navigable 3D view along with a 2D global allocation view. Second, DEFACTO incorporates flexible adjustable autonomy strategies, even excluding humans from the loop in extreme circumstances. We performed detailed experiments using DEFACTO, leading to some surprising results. These results illustrate that an agent team must be equipped with flexible strategies for adjustable autonomy so that the appropriate strategy can be selected.

ACKNOWLEDGMENTS

We would like to thank John P. Lewis and Nikhil Kasinadhuni for their work on the DEFACTO Navigation Viewer. Also, the help provided by Paul Scerri with the Machinetta proxy infrastructure and comments on earlier drafts of this chapter is greatly appreciated.

REFERENCES

Allen, J. F. (1995). The TRAINS project: A case study in building a conversational planning agent. *Journal of Experimental and Theoretical AI (JETAI)* **7**:7–48.

Burstein, M. H., Mulvehill, A. M., and Deutsch. S. (1999). An approach to mixed-initiative management of heterogeneous software agent teams. In: *HICSS,* p. 8055. IEEE Computer Society.

Crandall, J. W., Nielsen, C. W., and Goodrich, M. A. (2003). Towards predicting robot team performance. In: *SMC.*

Dorais, G., Bonasso, R., Kortenkamp, D., Pell, P., and Schreckenghost, D. (1998). Adjustable autonomy for human-centered autonomous systems on mars. In: *Mars.*

Fong, T., Thorpe, C., and Baur, C. (2002). Multi-robot remote driving with collaborative control. *IEEE Transactions on Industrial Electronics.*

Hill, R., Gratch, J., Marsella, S., Rickel, J., Swartout, W., and Traum, D. (2003). Virtual humans in the mission rehearsal exercise system. In: *KI Embodied Conversational Agents,.*

Horvitz, E. (1999). Principles of mixed-initiative user interfaces. In: *Proceedings of ACM SIGCHI Conference on Human Factors in Computing Systems (CHI'99),* pp. 159–166, Pittsburgh.

Kitano, H., Tadokoro, S., Noda, I., Matsubara, H., Takahashi, T., Shinjoh, A., and Shimada, S. (1999). Robocup rescue: Search and rescue in large-scale disasters as a domain for autonomous agents research. In: *IEEE SMC,* Vol. VI, pp. 739–743, Tokyo.

Lawrence Livermore National Laboratory (2005). Jcats—joint conflict and tactical simulation. In: http://www.jfcom.mil/about/fact jcats.htm.

Paivio, A. (1974). Pictures and words in visual search. *Memory & Cognition* **2**(3):515–521.

Pynadath, D. V., and Tambe, M. (2003). Automated teamwork among heterogeneous software agents and humans. *Journal of Autonomous Agents and Multi-Agent Systems (JAAMAS)* **7**:71–100.

Richardson, A., Montello, D., and Hegarty, M. (1999). Spatial knowledge acquisition from maps and from navigation in real and virtual environments. *Memory and Cognition* **27**(4):741–750.

Ruddle, R., Payne, S., and Jones, D. (1997). Navigating buildings in desktop virtual environments: Experimental investigations using extended navigational experience. *J. Experimental Psychology—Applied,* **3**(2):143–159.

Scerri, P., Liao, E., Xu, Yang, Lewis, M., Lai, G., and Sycara, K. (2004). *Theory and Algorithms for Cooperative Systems,* In: Coordinating very large groups of wide area search munitions. Singapore: World Scientific Publishing.

Scerri, P., Pynadath, D., and Tambe, M. (2002). Towards adjustable autonomy for the real world. *Journal of Artificial Intelligence Research* **17**:171–228.

Scerri, P., Pynadath, D. V., Johnson, L., Rosenbloom, P., Schurr, N., Si, M., and Tambe, M. (2003). A prototype infrastructure for distributed robot-agent-person teams. In: *AAMAS*.

Neumann, U., You, S., Hu, J., and Fox, P. (2003). Urban site modeling from lidar. In: *Proceedings, 2nd International Workshop Computer Graphics and Geometric Modeling (CGGM),* pp. 579–588.

Tambe, M. (1997). Agent architectures for flexible, practical teamwork. *National Conference on AI (AAAI97),* pp. 22–28.

Advanced Systems Technology (2005). Epics—emergency preparedness incident commander simulation. In: http://epics.astcorp.com/.

TerraSim (2005). Terratools. In: http://www.terrasim.com.

Chapter 15

Transcending the Tower of Babel: Supporting Access to Multilingual Information with Cross-Language Information Retrieval

Douglas W. Oard

15.1. INTRODUCTION

With the advent of location-independent access to massive collections of searchable content on the World Wide Web and the convergence of text, images, audio, and video in multimedia computing environments, we have come a long way toward seamless access to the information needed for commerce, security, and society. Language, however, has the potential to balkanize the information space. This chapter describes what we now know about the design of search systems that can be used to find information regardless of the language in which that information is expressed.

Figure 15.1 illustrates the nature of the challenge. The light shaded bar depicts the estimated fraction of the 943 million Web users that speak each of the world's languages as their first language; the dark shaded bar depicts the estimated fraction of the Web content that is available in those languages. It is clear that English is the dominant language of Web content. Indeed, the disparity is even sharper than it first appears, since some of the non-English content is also available in English. Of course, many people, particularly those already using the Web, have a good command of English as a second language.

At each point in history, some language has dominated commercial and intellectual pursuits in the Western world—from Greek to Latin to German, and now English. So it is not surprising to see that some degree of distributional disparity between content and the first language of Web users. Indeed, looking to the future it seems reasonable to expect that situation to persist. Growth rates for speakers depend on both (a) the fraction of speakers of that language that are presently online and (b) the viability of economic models that might extend Internet services to a larger portion of the population. In the near term, Chinese is the one language in which those factors come together to predict explosive growth, with much of the potential increase being among people who speak only Chinese. This will naturally lead to increased production of Chinese content, of course. But those increases may well be dwarfed by the continuing explosion of content in the other major languages of the industrialized world, and English in particular, for which large and wealthy markets already exist. So a thumbnail sketch of the near future would

Emergent Information Technologies and Enabling Policies for Counter-Terrorism. Edited by Popp and Yen

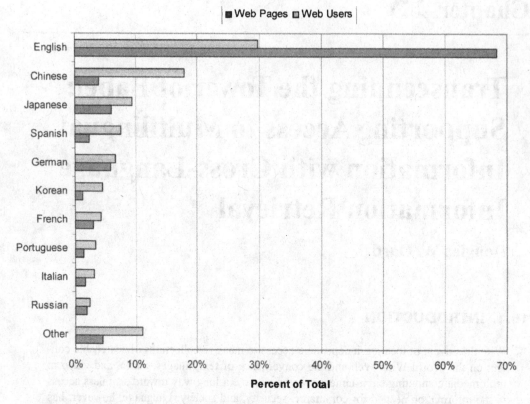

Figure 15.1. Language distribution of Web pages and the first language of Web users. (Source: Global Reach, September 2004.)

predict a significantly greater fraction of Chinese speakers that may well not be matched by proportional growth in Chinese content.

That brief review establishes the first major market for access to multilingual information access: Web search, for the two-thirds of Internet users for whom English is not their first language. And that market is growing. There are, however, two other obvious markets for Cross-Language Information Retrieval (CLIR): (1) marketing products and (2) information management for national security and law enforcement operations (referred to below generically as "security" applications). The application to marketing is fairly straightforward; speakers of English presently possess the majority of the world's wealth, so producers in every region will naturally want information about their products to be easily available to English speakers.

Security applications are the most challenging scenario for CLIR because of language diversity. Estimates vary, but there are probably about 2000 languages in common use in the world today. The public library in the New York City borough of Queens collects materials in more than 80 languages, an observation that offers some indication of the linguistic diversity with which public safety professionals must routinely cope in some major urban areas. Military operations pose even more severe challenges, both for coordination with coalition forces and for defensive or offensive information operations. The Defense Language Institute (DLI) presently trains military personnel in 31 languages for which operational needs are predictable, 13 of which were added only after the September 2001 attacks. Developing operationally significant capabilities in this way can take years, however, and our ability to predict the next flashpoint has proven to be limited. For example, DLI does not presently teach any of the four major languages spoken in Albania, but more than 5000 soldiers were required to deploy to that country on less than 30 days notice in 1999. In that case, deployment to Macedonia was originally considered, Albania was selected on March 29 after Macedonia declined to sanction the deployment, the decision to deploy to Albania was made on April 3, and operations there began on April 23 (Nardulli et al., 2002). Military forces must plan for the worst case, and with thousands of languages in the world, we simply must rely on technology to augment whatever capabilities our forces are able to bring to the fight.

It is useful to think about language technologies in two groups, those that help people find information ("access technologies") and those that help people make sense of what they have found (technologies to facilitate understanding). While the two groups are certainly coupled to some degree, this natural division results in substantial simplification in system design. The key reason for this is that search is a relatively well understood process, at least when the query and the documents are expressed in the same language. The remainder of this chapter is therefore focused on extending that capability to the cross-language case or typically referred to as Cross-Language Information Retrieval (CLIR).

This chapter is organized as follows. First, we survey CLIR to establish the present state of the art. Section 15.3 then draws those capabilities together, presenting three deployment scenarios that together illustrate the search capabilities that are now possible. Section 15.4 then presents a discussion of research investment strategies, including some prognostication on near-term commercial investments, a description of additional near-term opportunities for government investment, and identification of potentially productive investments in more basic research that could transform the opportunity space. Finally, Section 15.5 concludes the chapter with a few observations on the fundamental limitations of CLIR technology.

15.2. THE STATE OF THE ART

Ultimately, it is people (rather than machines) that seek information; Information Retrieval (IR) systems are therefore best thought of as tools that help people to find what they are looking for. Three key points help to define the scope of the field. First, the information that is sought must already exist; IR systems do not create information, all they do is help people to find it. Second, IR systems are generally designed to serve a broad range of specific information needs that cannot be anticipated in a detailed fashion when the system is designed. Third, IR systems are often employed iteratively, with searchers examining the results of one search iteration and using what they learn to refine the way in which they express their information needs. Figure 15.2 illustrates one common design for CLIR systems.

15.2.1. Evaluation

IR results cannot be "right" or "wrong" in the abstract; the degree of correctness depends upon the intent and needs of the searcher. Three simplifying assumptions are generally made when evaluating the effectiveness of an IR system. First, only a single iteration is evaluated; a fixed query is proffered and the search component produces a result set. Sec-

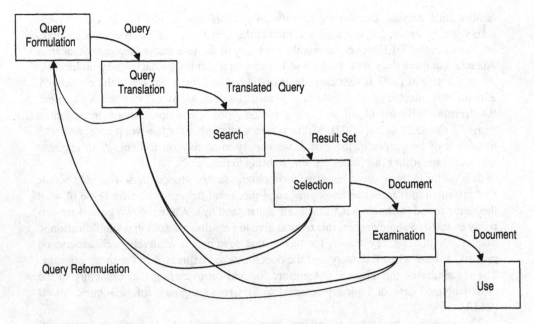

Figure 15.2. Component interaction for a CLIR system based on query translation.

ond, only the degree to which a document is on topic ("topical relevance") is assessed; this ignores factors such as authoritativeness, degree of reading difficulty, or redundancy within the result set that are also important to users in many situations. Third, topical relevance is modeled as a binary variable; every document is treated as if it is either relevant or it is not (usually, a document is treated as relevant if any substantial part of the document is relevant).

These assumptions lead to an elegant and useful formulation for IR evaluation. Systems are asked to rank the entire document set in order of decreasing probability of relevance, and the user is modeled as wishing to examine some (unknown) number of relevant documents, scanning down from the top of the list until that number of relevant documents have been found, accurately recognizing each relevant document along the way. The user's satisfaction with the results is modeled as "precision," which is defined as the fraction of the documents that were examined that turned out to be relevant. Since the number of relevant documents that the user wishes to find is not known, a uniform distribution is assumed, and an expectation (i.e., an average value) is computed. Formally, "uninterpolated average precision" for a topic is defined as the expected value (over the set of relevant documents) of the precision at the point each relevant document appears in the list. Some systems are better for one topic than another, and we do not know in advance what topic the user will ask about. This is addressed by repeating the process for several randomly selected topics (typically, 40 or more) and reporting the expectation across the topic set of the uninterpolated average precision, a value commonly referred to as "mean average precision."

It would be impractical to judge the relevance of every document in a large collection, so a sampling strategy is needed. The usual strategy is to conduct purposive sampling on a topic-by-topic basis that is focused on the relevant documents for that topic. That can be done by first pooling the top-ranked documents (typically 100) from a diverse set of (typically 10 or more) IR systems and then judging only the documents in that pool; all other documents in the collection are then treated as not relevant. Relevance judgments formed in this way may be somewhat incomplete, but they are unbiased with respect to the systems that contributed to the pools. Importantly, hold-one-out studies have shown that judgment sets constructed in this way are also unbiased with respect to other IR systems of similar design (Voorhees, 2000). Although people sometimes disagree about the topical relevance of individual documents, multi-judge studies have shown that replacing one judge's opinions with another judge's opinions rarely changes the preference order between systems. Evaluations using judgments reported in this way are therefore best reported as comparisons between contrastive system designs rather than as absolute measures of effectiveness, since different users may assess the relevance of retrieved document differently. For CLIR experiments, the reference value is typically the mean average precision achieved by a system of comparable design using queries in the same language as the documents (a "monolingual baseline").

With that as background, it is now possible to describe the effect of the known CLIR techniques in terms of this evaluation framework. Large CLIR test collections (often with more than 100,000 documents) are presently available with documents (typically, news stories) in Arabic, Bulgarian, Chinese, Dutch, English, Finish, French, German, Hungarian, Italian, Japanese, Korean, Portuguese, Russian, Spanish, and Swedish, and the results reported here are generally typical of what is seen for those languages (Braschler and Peters, 2004; Kishida et al., 2004; Oard and Gey, 2002).

15.2.2. Techniques

The basic strategy for building any IR system is to represent the documents in some way, to represent the query in some compatible way, and then to compute a score for each document using a function of the query representation and the document representation that (hopefully) assigns higher values to documents that are more likely to be relevant. Counting terms (where terms may be parts of words, full words, or sequences of words) has proven to be a remarkably useful basis for computing document representations. Three factors are typically computed: (1) term frequency (TF), the number of occurrences of a term in a document; (2) document frequency (DF), the number of documents in which a term appears; and (3) length, the total number of terms in a document. Essentially, DF is a measure of term selectivity, while the ratio between TF and length is a measure of aboutness. These factors are used to compute a weight for each term in each document, with higher TF, lower DF, and shorter length resulting in higher weights. The most effective weighting functions (e.g., Okapi BM 25) also typically transform the TF and DF factors in ways that grow more slowly than linear functions, and some systems also factor in additional sources of evidence (e.g., term proximity). The score for each document is then computed (at query time) as the sum of the weights of the query terms in that document. The documents can then be sorted in decreasing score order for presentation to the user.

CLIR applications introduce one obvious complication: The query and the documents contain terms from different languages, so direct lexical matching will often not be possible. Three basic approaches to overcoming this challenge are possible: (1) Map the document language terms into the query language, (2) map the query language terms into the document language, or (3) map both document language and query language terms into some language-neutral representation. Because each term is processed independently in a typical IR system, these mappings are typically done on a term-by-term basis. Term translation poses three challenges for system design: (a) selection of appropriate terms to translate, (b) identifying appropriate translations for each term, and (c) effectively using that translation knowledge.

Three sources of translation mappings are available to an automated system: (1) a bilingual or multilingual lexicon, (2) a bilingual or multilingual corpus, and (3) sub-word translation mapping algorithms. While all three are useful, the most effective systems rely on bilingual "parallel" corpora that contain documents written in one language and (human-prepared) translations of those documents into the other. Through automatic sentence alignment, term selection, and within-sentence term alignment, it is not only possible to compute the possible translations for a term, but also possible to estimate the probability that each possible translation would be used. Figure 15.3 shows one possible set of alignments for the first few Spanish and English words from a parallel corpus of Spanish and English proceedings of the European Parliament. For probabilities estimated in this way to be most useful, the parallel text collection should be large (so that the translation probabilities can be accurately estimated) and it should use language in a manner that is similar to the way language is used in the documents to be searched (e.g., it should be from a similar genre, with similar topical coverage). Suitable parallel text collections can often be found, since the same factors that lead to a need for CLIR typically also result in manual translation of at least some materials that are in particularly high demand (Resnik and Smith, 2003). When that is not the case, focused elicitation of the needed translations is sometimes a viable alternative (Yarowsky, 2003).

Although translation probabilities extracted from parallel text are quite useful, there are two cases in which parallel texts do not yield useful translations: (1) uncommon terms, which may not appear sufficiently often in even very large parallel text collections, and (2) terms that were introduced after the parallel text was collected. Hand-built translation lexicons (e.g., bilingual dictionaries) can be a reliable source of translation knowledge for the first case; a uniform distribution on translation probability can be assumed if no information about preferred translations is supplied with the lexicon. Newly coined terms may be missing from translation lexicons, but it is sometimes possible to predict the way in which such a term will be translated by mapping pieces of the term separately and then reassembling the translated pieces. For example, names of people are often translated from English into Chinese by sounding out the English word and then selecting Chinese characters that would be pronounced similarly (Lin and Chen, 2002). A similar approach can be used to translate multiword expressions; every known translation of each constituent word is postulated, and then a large collection of text in the target language is used to select the one combination that occurs together most often (López-Ostenero et al., 2001).

With adequate translation knowledge in hand, the translation process itself is quite straightforward. One good approach is to separately map the TF and DF evidence, allocat-

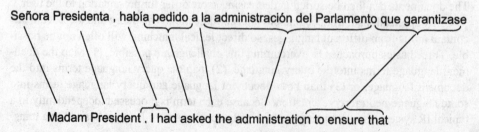

Figure 15.3. An example of aligning Spanish and English terms. (Source: EUROPARL corpus.)

ing weight across the known translations using the estimated translation probabilities (Darwish and Oard, 2003). This approach can be applied to map in either direction, and it can be helpful to merge evidence from both translation directions because the error characteristics of the two mappings are often complementary (McCarley, 1999). When well-integrated, it is possible to exceed 100% of a credible monolingual baseline system's mean average precision using these techniques. It may seem surprising at first that any cross-language technique could exceed a monolingual baseline, but this merely points up a limitation of comparative evaluation; it is difficult to introduce synonyms in monolingual systems in a manner that is comparable to the synonyms that are naturally introduced as a byproduct of translation, so (relatively weak) monolingual baselines that lack synonym expansion are often reported.

Table 15.2 shows a typical example of CLIR results based on a translation model learned from parallel European Parliament proceedings in English and French. The results for the unidirectional case were obtained using test collections developed for the Cross-Language Evaluation Forum (CLEF) using the following formulae from Darwish and Oard, (2003):

$$TF_d(e) = \sum_{f_i \in T(e)} p(f_i|e) \times TF_d(f_i) \tag{15.1}$$

$$DF(e) = \sum_{f_i \in T(e)} p(f_i|e) \times DF(f_i) \tag{15.2}$$

$$w_d(e) = \frac{TF_d(e)}{1.5\dfrac{L_d}{L_{avg}} + = TF_d(e) + 0.5} \times \log\left(\frac{N - DF(e) + 0.5}{DF(e) + 0.5}\right) \tag{15.3}$$

$$s_d = \frac{1}{|Q|} \sum_{e \in Q} w_d(e) \tag{15.4}$$

where the symbols have the meanings shown in Table 15.1. For the unidirectional case, p(fi|e) was estimated using the freely available Giza++ software using English as the source language and French as the target language. For the bidirectional case, the Giza++

Table 15.1. Factors that Affect the Score of a Document

Symbol	Meaning
S_d	Score for document d, the basis for ranking in decreasing order
Q	The set of English query terms chosen by the user
$w_d(e)$	Weight for English query term e in document d
$TF_d(f_i)$	The number of times French term f_i occurs in document d
$TF_d(e)$	Estimated number of times English term e would have occurred in a translation of d
$DF(f_i)$	The number of documents in which French term f_i occurs
$DF(e)$	Estimated number of translated documents that would have contained English term e
N	The number of documents in the collection
$T(e)$	The set of known French translations for English query term e
$p(f_i|e)$	The probability that English term e translates to French term f_i
L_d	The number of French terms in document d
L_{avg}	The average number of French terms in a document

system was run with the source and target languages swapped, the results were inverted using Bayes rule, and the results of that reversal were averaged with the function learned for the original translation order. This is now a standard technique in the design of machine translation systems because it helps to compensate for an asymmetry that Giza++ and similar systems introduce for efficiency reasons. Finally, for the monolingual case the first two equations were not needed and "f" was used in place of "e" (i.e., French queries were used).

Table 15.2 shows the results. The monolingual and bidirectional CLIR conditions were statistically indistinguishable (by a Wilcoxon signed rank test for paired samples); the retrieval effectiveness of the unidirectional CLIR condition was found to be significantly below that of the monolingual condition (by the same test, at $p < 0.05$). From this we conclude that training Giza++ in both directions is helpful, and that in this task the retrieval effectiveness in the monolingual and cross-language conditions are comparable. Note that this was achieved using parallel text from a different domain from the documents being searched, indicating that this technique is reasonably robust.

An alternative approach that does not require parallel text is the Generalized Vector Space Model (GVSM), in which each term is represented as a vector in which each element is the frequency of the term of interest in one "training document"; the length of such a vector is the number of documents in a collection. If each bilingual document is formed by conjoining a pair of comparable documents (i.e., separately authored documents writing about the same subject, one in each language), the resulting vector space will be language-neutral. A document in the collection to be indexed (or a query) can then be represented in the GVSM vector space as the sum of the vectors for each term that it contains. Further improvements can often be obtained by applying a dimensionality reduction technique (e.g., singular value decomposition) to the matrix of term vectors before computing the representations of the documents and the query; this approach is known as Latent Semantic Indexing (LSI). Because GVSM and LSI are based on document-level alignment rather than word-level alignment, it is difficult to achieve levels of effectiveness that are competitive with what could be attained using parallel text; around 70% of the mean average precision for a comparable monolingual baseline is typically reported. Useful comparable texts may be easier to obtain than useful parallel texts in some applications, however, particularly for language pairs across which little digital interaction is presently occurring for economic or social reasons. Pairing of comparable documents is needed before such collections can be used in this way, and techniques for that task have been demonstrated in restricted domains (Sheridan et al., 1998).

Comparable corpora can also be used as a basis for unsupervised adaptation of translation resources to a specific application. The basic idea is to mine a source-language collection for translatable terms that might plausibly have been included in the query (but

Table 15.2. Mean (over 151 Topics) Average Precision for Monolingual Search[a]

	Mean Average Precision
Monolingual	0.3856
Unidirectional CLIR	0.3714
Bi-directional CLIR	0.3780

[a]CLIR with English queries trained in one direction, and CLIR with English queries trained bidirectionally, searching 87,191 French news stories, scored using CLEF relevance judgments.

were not), and then to mine a target-language collection for terms that might plausibly have resulted from translation (but did not). The standard way of doing pre-translation "expansion" is to identify documents that are similar to the query in the source language collection, and then to adjust the term weights in a way that rewards presence in the highest ranked (i.e., most similar) documents. Post-translation adaptation is accomplished in the same manner (often with the addition of term reweighting), but using a large target-language collection. Because this is an unsupervised variant of the same process that systems employ when users designate a few relevant documents for query enhancement, the process is generally known as "blind" relevance feedback. A similar approach (substituting documents for queries) can also be used with document-translation architectures. Pre-translation feedback has proven to be particularly effective when the available translation resources are relatively weak (e.g., a small translation lexicon with no access to parallel text). When pre-translation and post-translation blind relevance feedback are used together with a relatively large lexicon that lacks translation probabilities, up to 90% of the mean average precision achieved by a credible monolingual baseline (without synonym expansion) has been reported. This compares favorably to the 80% relative effectiveness that is typically reported under comparable conditions without blind relevance feedback. However, when large domain-specific parallel text collections are available, blind relevance feedback offers less potential benefit.

In summary, it is now possible to build systems that accept queries in one language and rank documents written in another nearly as well as systems for which both the queries and the documents are expressed in the same language. Moreover, a range of techniques are known for optimizing the use of different types of language resources, so it is reasonable to expect that such systems can actually be constructed for real applications. It is important to recognize that these claims are based on averages, both over the topic of the query and over the position of a relevant document in the ranked list; results for individual queries and/or documents will naturally differ.

A glance back at Figure 15.2 will reveal, however, that construction of a ranked list is only one part of a complete search process. It is therefore also important to ask how well searchers can employ this capability in actual cross-language search tasks. We know from task-specific evaluations of machine translation that any reasonable translation system will often suffice to support recognition of documents that the user wishes to see (although at the cost of somewhat greater human time and effort) (Oard et al., 2004). The interaction between translation and summarization in the document selection stage has been less thoroughly studied, but anecdotal evidence from end-to-end search tasks indicate that simple combinations of summarization techniques developed for monolingual applications (e.g., extraction of fixed-length passages around query terms) and available machine translation systems works well enough. Query formulation is perhaps the least well understood area at present; interactions between vocabulary learning, concept learning, and query creation are complex, and the research reported to date has not yet fully characterized that design space. End-to-end user studies have, however, demonstrated that users can often iteratively formulate effective queries by manually entering text in the query language, and explanatory interfaces have started to appear that seek to help the user understand (and thereby better control) the cross-language search progress. Experiments with users in the loop are expensive, and thus relatively rare, but half a dozen teams have reported results, some over many years. As an example of what could be achieved as of 2004, an average of 70% of factual questions were answered correctly by searchers that could not read the document language and did not previously know the answer; that is about twice the fraction of correct answers that had been achieved by the best fully automatic cross-language question answering systems at that time (Gonzalo and Oard, 2004).

So machines can rank documents written in languages different from the query, and searchers can effectively exploit that capability for some real search tasks. The next section examines the implications of that capability by presenting three deployment scenarios that can be supported by present CLIR technology.

15.3. NEAR-TERM DEPLOYMENT SCENARIOS

Cross-language information retrieval has sometimes been uncharitably called "the problem of finding documents that you can't read." Why would someone want to do that? This section describes three scenarios in which such a capability could be useful.

15.3.1. Polyglots

Polyglots (people who are able to read several languages) are obvious candidates as CLIR system users for two reasons. First, some savings in time and effort might be realized if the searcher can formulate (and refine) their query just once, with the system then calling to their attention potentially relevant documents in any language that they can read. Depending on the number of languages involved, the results might best be displayed as separate ranked lists for each language or as a single merged list. The more significant reason that a polyglot may choose to use a CLIR system, however, is that their passive language skills (e.g., reading) and active language skills (e.g., query formulation) may not be equally well developed. In such cases, we can think of the CLIR system as a form of "language prosthesis" that can help them with query formulation and refinement. The Defense Language Transformation Roadmap calls for incorporation of language training as a regular part of professional development within the officer corps; when fully implemented, this policy will dramatically expand the number of polyglot users in the U.S. armed forces (Department of Defense, 2005).

15.3.2. Team Searching

Complex information needs are best addressed when a nuanced understanding of what is being sought can be combined with the search skills that are needed to get the best results from available systems and the language skills that are needed to make sense of what is found. These competencies need not all be present in a single individual, however. For example, search intermediaries (e.g., librarians) are often employed for high-stakes searches in fields such as medicine and law. A similar approach can be applied in the cross-language case, teaming a searcher that knows their own needs well with a skilled intermediary that has the necessary language skills to help the searcher understand (rather than simply find) the available information. Co-presence may not be essential when working in a networked environment; "remote reference services" have been the focus of considerable research recently, and tools for synchronous interaction that have already been developed (e.g., coupled displays, augmented with text chat) (Coffman, 2001) could be extended to support cross-language applications.

15.2.3. Two-Stage Triage

Scenarios that require sifting through large quantities of information in a less commonly taught language place a premium on maximizing the productivity of the small number of individuals that possess the needed language skills. In such cases, initial searches can be done using interactive CLIR systems by many skilled searchers who understand what is being sought. As promising documents are found, they can then be passed on to the few available language experts. The searchers and the language experts need not even work for the same organization; for example, promising documents might simply be submitted to a translation bureau (e.g., the National Virtual Translation Center) that will optimize the allocation of documents across the available pool of translators.

Each of these scenarios can be accomplished with the search and translation technology that is available today, but future improvements in translation technology could yield an even greater range of useful capabilities. The next section considers those possibilities.

15.4. CRAFTING AN INVESTMENT STRATEGY

Yogi Berra is credited with having observed that prediction is difficult, particularly when predicting the future. But if we are to create a rational strategy for investing government resources, we should start with some idea of what is likely to happen even without that investment. Accordingly, this section begins with a brief survey of the commercial landscape and the prognosis for near-term developments in that sector. A discussion of additional near-term investment opportunities then follows. The discussion concludes with an articulation of the fundamental challenges that remain open; those are the candidates for continued investment in basic research.

15.4.1. Commercial Prospects

The single most consequential commercial development over the past decade has been the emergence of World Wide Web indexing as a commodity product. Commercial investments in search technology are driven by two key factors: affordability and market size. Automatic language identification and on-demand machine translation are now widely available, but none of the major search engines have integrated anything but the most rudimentary cross-language search technology. Affordability is certainly not the limiting factor in this case; efficient CLIR techniques have been known for several years. Rather, the problem seems to be that the market size is perceived to be sensitive to the availability of high-quality translation services. Present on-demand machine translation services are adequate for a limited range of uses, but their translation quality (accuracy and fluency) leaves a lot to be desired, and the computational cost of the state-of-the-art "transfer method" machine translation approach used by present Web translation services is far larger than the computational cost of Web search. Broad commercial adoption of cross-language search is therefore limited far more by deficiencies in present machine translation technology than by any limitations of the CLIR technology itself.

Statistical machine translation is rapidly emerging as a practical alternative to the earlier "transfer method" approaches. Modern statistical translation systems offer two main advantages: (1) Once a statistical system has been built for one language pair, it can be extended to additional language pairs with an order of magnitude less effort than was the case for transfer-method systems (about one person-year versus about ten), and (2) statistical machine translation systems have demonstrated improved translation quality in some applications. Statistical machine translation faces two key limitations, however: (1) Research investments have focused more on translation quality than on speed, so the older "transfer method" systems are currently generally faster, and (2) deploying a statistical system requires "training data" that is representative of the materials to which it will ultimately be applied (e.g., a statistical system trained using news stories might not do as well as a "transfer method" system when used to translate text chats). Recent press reports indicate that some commercial investment is now focused on addressing these two limitations. If those efforts are successful, we could see widespread deployment of CLIR technology in Web search engines over the next few years. Other, more specialized, applications (e.g., for libraries, patents, law, and medicine) could naturally follow from the demonstrated utility of the technology that would result.

Another scenario that could result in near-term commercial adoption of CLIR technology would be close coupling of cross-language search with translation routing technology. Translation routing systems seek to automatically optimize the assignment of documents to human translators in a way that balances cost, quality (e.g., by accounting for subject matter expertise), and timeliness. Access patterns in large collection are typically highly skewed (meaning that a few documents are read by many people, and many documents may be read by nobody). If one translation routing service were to capture a significant market share, this sharply focused reuse could be exploited by cacheing translations as they are created, thus amortizing translation costs over multiple users. The resulting balance between affordability, quality, and responsiveness, when coupled with the complementary characteristics of machine translation systems, could help to push the incentive for adoption of CLIR technology past the tipping point. Some policy issues (e.g., the treatment of cached translations under international copyright conventions) may need to be worked out before that can happen, however.

15.4.2. A Near-Term Government Investment Strategy

It therefore seems likely that near-term commercial investments will ultimately yield a broader experience base with the integration of CLIR technology in realistic operational scenarios, but some targeted government investments will also likely be needed if we are to exploit the full potential that this technology offers. For example, support for cross-language team searching will require a development effort for which no likely source of commercial investment can presently be identified. Investments in several, more narrowly focused technical issues could also pay off handsomely in the near term (e.g., optimal support for query refinement in CLIR applications, effective techniques for merging result lists across languages, and closer integration of query-based summarization and machine translation technologies).

One important class of near-term investment opportunities that is almost certain not to attract commercial investment is urgent deployment of CLIR technology for new language pairs. As the Albanian example at the beginning of this chapter indicates, deployment timelines for military forces are often far shorter than commercial development timelines could possibly accommodate. In 2003, the Defense Advanced Research Projects Agency (DARPA) conducted a "surprise language" exercise in which research teams were challenged to develop machine translation, CLIR, summarization, and information extraction technology for unexpected language pairs (Oard, 2003). A preliminary 10-day effort for the Cebuano language and a large-scale 29-day effort for Hindi both indicated that usable systems could be deployed far more rapidly than had previously been demonstrated. A balanced investment strategy in which optimized systems that are built in advance to meet predictable requirements are augmented with a flexible rapid-response capability could be implemented using technology that is presently in hand. Early designs of such a system could then be improved over time as experience in actual operational settings is gained. Unless we think that the world will be a much more stable and predictable place in the near future, we would be wise to pursue such a course.

15.4.3. Investments in Basic Research

A balanced investment strategy also calls for balance between near-term and long-term investments. Advances in machine translation technology would be very highly leveraged, making that the single most important focus for longer-term investments. Clear potential exists for substantial advances in translation quality, robustness, and speed through three promising avenues: (1) exploiting massive collections of naturally occurring training data (e.g., Resnik and Smith, 2003), (2) improved models of language based on closer coupling between statistical and symbolic techniques (e.g., Chiang, 2005), and (3) adaptation to unique needs of specific application environments (e.g., Warner et al., 2004). The rapid progress in the accuracy and fluency of machine translation in recent years has been a direct consequence of the widespread adoption of affordable and insightful evaluation techniques; continued refinement of those evaluation techniques will likely be an important prerequisite to future progress as well.

The vast majority of the work to date on CLIR has assumed that that the words to be found and translated are already represented in a "character-coded" form that makes digital manipulation of those words fairly straightforward. Of course, most of the words produced by the world's 6.4 billion people are spoken rather than written. Fairly accurate automatic transcription of news broadcasts has been possible for several years, and more recently there have been substantial improvements in the accuracy of automatic transcription of conversational speech as well (Byrne et al., 2004). Integration of that speech technology with CLIR and machine translation would therefore be a highly leveraged investment. Similarly, automatic recognition of printed characters is now quite accurate, and reasonably accurate automatic transcription of handwritten text is possible in some situations. Spoken, printed, and handwritten content pose unusual challenges for interactive CLIR systems, however, because straightforward design options yield a cascade of errors (with transcription errors compounded by translation errors) (Schlesinger et al., 2001). Designing effective interactive CLIR systems requires that these issues be addressed, potentially in different ways, in at least four system components (query formulation, automated search, result list selection, and item-level examination). The proliferation of digital audio recording and digital image acquisition technology promises to move these issues to the forefront of the research agenda over the next several years.

Two other broad trends in information access technologies will also likely create important new opportunities for employment of CLIR technology: (1) search over conversational text and (2) true "text mining." Much of the investment in search and translation technology has focused on carefully written content (e.g., news stories), but the explosive growth of conversational text genre such as electronic mail, instant messaging, and "chat rooms" provides a strong incentive to understand how information access in large conversational genre collections will differ. The questions range from the most fundamental (e.g., What will people look for?), through many that are more sharply technical (e.g., How should the possibility of typographical errors be accommodated?), to some that are well beyond the scope of this chapter (What archives of instant message conversations are likely to be available?). Among the issues that will need to be addressed are mixed-language conversations, the use of sublanguage among conversational participants that share extensive context, and the consequences of informality (e.g., ungrammatical usage and iconic representations for emotions). Each of those factors promises to add complexity to the lexical mapping that underlies CLIR techniques that were originally developed for more formal genre.

The term "text mining" has been used to market a broad range of information access technologies (including, in marketing literature, ordinary query-based search systems). As a research challenge, however, it is often understood to refer to searching based on broad patterns (e.g., "find people that espouse positions on Kurdish autonomy that are rarely presented in the U.S. media") (Hearst, 1999). Satisfying information needs of that sort with any significant degree of automation can be a daunting challenge even when all the text is in the same language. Some progress in this direction has already been made, however. For example, the emerging field of visual analytics couples computational linguistics with information visualization to construct presentations that facilitate recognition of patterns in the use of language (Wong and Thomas, 2004). Multidocument summarization systems (Schiffman et al., 2002) and the closely related work on systems for automatically answering complex questions (Diekema et al., 2003) adopt an alternative approach, selecting useful snippets of text and reshaping them into text-based products that the user can then (hopefully) read for comprehension. All of these technologies rely on computational models of meaning that are necessarily weak, since the ambiguity that is central to natural language resists precise modeling. Introducing additional languages will exacerbate that challenge, compounding ambiguity of interpretation with the ambiguity that results from imprecise translation. But the ability to reason automatically across large multilingual collections would also create important new opportunities by dramatically expanding the breadth of information sources and the diversity of perspectives that could be leveraged. Extending text mining technologies to multilingual applications will therefore likely merit significant investment in the coming decade.

SUMMARY

Useful cross-language search technology is available now, and with a small set of targeted near-term investments we would be in an excellent position to leverage that important capability. As with any transformational technology, however, we must couple our thinking about the design of systems with innovative thinking about how those systems will be used. The scenarios outlined above (enhancing search capabilities for polyglot users, forming search teams with synergistic skill sets, and two-level strategies that optimize the workload for personnel with scarce language expertise) represent a first step in that direction. But true organizational innovation requires experience, and gaining experience requires that we build systems. So spiral development strategies will be a natural part of the process by which this new technologies is adopted.

Some of the technology needed to provide access to multilingual content is now quite mature. We can, for example, match content with queries across languages about as well as we can in the same language. But effective searching demands synergy between searcher and system. Sustained investment in both basic and applied research will be needed if we are to optimize that synergy over the full range of potentially important applications. There are, of course, some fundamental limits to what can be done. Existing term-based techniques for building ranked lists are far from perfect, but experience has shown that they are both useful in their present state and hard to improve upon; greater precision can certainly be achieved using techniques with greater linguistic sophistication, but only at some cost in coverage (i.e., recall) and flexibility. So now that we are able to search across languages as well as we do within the same language, focusing solely on building better ranked lists seems as if it would be a questionable investment. Instead, the time has come to refocus our efforts on the new opportunities that our past success has generated. We find ourselves at an inflection point now. Having developed the core technology for searching across languages, we are now presented with unprecedented opportunities to build deployable systems for at least the formal document genre that we have already mastered, while simultaneously beginning to explore more advanced techniques for searching conversational media in several languages and for exploratory mining of multilingual text collections.

Alvin Toffler tells us of a "third wave," a society in which information is the raw material, and the processes and systems that help people manage that information are the means of production (Toffler, 1980). Historically, men and women have sought the high ground to provide themselves with advantage as they struggle with their adversaries. In a conflict of ideas, the high ground is not to be found at the top of a hill, in the sky, or even in outer space; the high ground is the human mind. Language provides a window on the mind, and those who best command the realm of language will naturally be best advantaged in the competition of ideas. This is a challenge from which we simply cannot shrink.

REFERENCES

Braschler, M., and Peters, C. (2004). Cross-language evaluation forum: Objectives, results, achievements. *Information Retrieval* **7**(1–2):7–31.

Byrne, W., Doermann, D., Franz, M., Gustman, S., Hajic, J., Oard, D., Picheny, M., Psutka, J., Ramabhadran, B., Soergel, D., Ward, T., and Zhu, W.-J. (2004). Automated recognition of spontaneous speech for access to multilingual oral history archives. *IEEE Transactions on Speech and Audio Processing* **12**:(4)420–435.

Chiang, D. (2005). A hierarchical phrase-based model for statistical machine translation. In: *Proceedings of the 43rd Annual Meeting of the Association for Computational Linguistics*, Ann Arbor, MI.

Coffmann, S. (2001). We'll take it from here: Developments we'd like to see in virtual reference software. *Information Technology and Libraries*, **20**(3):149–153.

Kareem Darwish and Oard, D. W. (2003). Probabilistic structured query methods. In: *Proceedings of the 26th Annual ACM SIGIR Conference on Research and Development in Information Retrieval*, Toronto, Canada.

Diekema, A. R., Yilmazel, O., Chen, J., Harwell, S., He, L., and Liddy, E. D. (2003). What do you mean? Finding answers to complex questions. In: *Proceedings of the AAAI Symposium on New Directions in Question Answering*, Stanford, CA.

Department of Defense (2005). *Defense Language Translation Roadmap*.

Gonzalo, J., and Oard, D. W. (2004) iCLEF 2004 track overview. In: *Working Notes for the CLEF 2004 Workshop*, Bath, UK.

Hearst, M. A. Untangling Text Mining. (1999). In: *Proceedings of the 37th Annual Conference of the Association for Computational Linguistics*, College Park, MD.

Kishida, K., Chen, K.-hua, Lee, S., Kuriyama, K., Kando, N., Chen, H.-H., Myaeng, S. H., and Eguchi, K. (2004). Overview of the CLIR task at the fourth NTCIR workshop. In: *Proceedings of the Fourth NTCIR Workshop on Research in Information Access Technologies*, Tokyo, Japan.

Lin, W.-H., and Chen, H.-H. (2002). Backward machine transliteration by learning phonetic similarity. In: *Sixth Conference on Natural Language Learning*, Taipei, Taiwan.

López-Ostenero, F., Gonzalo, J., Penas, A., and Verdejo, F. (2001). Noun phrase translations for cross-language document selection. In: *Evaluation of Cross-Language Information Retrieval: Second Workshop of the Cross-Language Evaluation Forum,* Darmstadt, Germany.

Scott McCarley, J. (1999). Should we translate the documents or the queries in cross-language information retrieval? In: *27th Annual Meeting of the Association for Computational Linguistics,* College Park, MD.

Nardulli, B. R., Perry, W. L., Pirnie, B., Gordon, J., IV, and McGinn, J. G. (2002). *Disjointed War, Military Operations in Kosovo,* RAND.

Oard, D. W., and Gey, F. C. (2002). The TREC-2002 Arabic–English CLIR Track. In: *The Eleventh Text Retrieval Conference (TREC-2002),* Gaithersburg, MD, pp. 17–26.

Oard, D. W. (2003). The surprise language exercises. *ACM Transactions on Asian Language Information Processing* 2(2):79–84.

Oard, D. W., Gonzalo, J., Sanderson, M., López-Ostenero, F., and Wang, J. (2004). Interactive cross-language document selection," *Information Retrieval* 7(1–2):205–228.

Resnik, P., and Smith, N. A. (2003). The web as a parallel corpus. *Computational Linguistics* 29(3):349–380.

Schlesinger, C., Holland, M., and Hernandez, L. (2001). Integrating OCR and machine translation on non-traditional languages. In: *Proceedings of the 2001 Symposium on Document Image Understanding Technology,* pp. 283–287, Columbia, MD.

Schiffman, B., Nenkova, A., and McKeown, K. (2002). Experiments in multidocument summarization. In: *Proceedings of the 2002 Human Language Technology Conference,* San Diego, CA.

Sheridan, P., Ballerini, J. P., and Schäuble, P. (1998). Building a large multilingual test collection from comparable news documents. In: *Cross Language Information Retrieval,* G. Grefenstette (ed.), Chapter 11. Kluwer Academic.

Toffler, A. (1980). *The Third Wave.* Bantam Books.

Voorhees, E. M. (2000). Variations in relevance and the measurement of retrieval effectiveness. *Information Processing and Management* 36(5):697–716.

Warner, J., Ogden, B., and Holland, M. (2004). Cross-language collaboration between distributed partners using multilingual chat messaging. In: *SIGIR 2004 Workshop on New Directions for IR Evaluation: Online Conversations,* Sheffield, UK, July, pp. 9–15.

Wong, P. C., and Thomas, J. (2004). Visual analytics. *IEEE Computer Graphics and Applications* 24(5):20–21.

Yarowsky, D. (2003). Scalable elicitation of training data for machine translation. *Team TIDES,* pp. 3–4.

Chapter 16

Journey from "Analysis" to Inquiry: Technology and the Transformation of Counter-Terrorism Analysis

Aaron B. Frank and Desmond Saunders-Newton

16.1. INTRODUCTION

Decision-makers concerned with mitigating terrorist or asymmetric threats take for granted the importance of reasoned analysis. It is often assumed that "analysis" will happen with little appreciation for the twin challenges of garnering insights from massive quantities or scarce supplies of data. This chapter presents an overview of new technologies for dealing with counter-terrorism from an analytic and strategic perspective. It also establishes a linkage between developing technologies and the transformation of professional analysis and statecraft. We believe that the ability of policy-makers to successfully manage complex policy problems including, but not limited to, global terrorism will rest on the search for appropriate mental frames, operational concepts, and inclusive policy formation and implementation processes. Although this chapter is focused on the application of models of complex social systems and decision theory to counter-terrorism, we believe that concepts and methods discussed below are equally relevant to other domains.

We view *analysis* as a subset of the larger practice of *inquiry*, where inquiry is defined as the search for truth.[1] Analysis is a specific way of conducting the search—the act of separating parts from a greater "whole" in an attempt to understand a phenomenon's or event's constituent components.[2] Within the domain of counter-terrorism, analytic activities seek to provide decision-makers with *insight*, the understanding of the true nature of terrorism. Armed with insight, decision-makers should be able to prevent terrorist attacks and undermine the ability of terrorist groups to form, operate, and challenge U.S. security and interests.

---

[1] It is important to note that the term *analysis* has multiple meanings throughout this document. We attempt to differentiate between the practice of analysis and the profession of analysis. By practice, we refer to the classical, formal meaning of the term and reductionist heritage. By profession, we mean individuals whose job has been to provide information to decision-makers in order assist them in making choices. Therefore, when we discuss *analysts* and the *analytic community* we are referring to people, while when we discuss *analysis* we are referring to methodology and tradecraft.

[2] An implicit assumption associated with reducing a problem into it's important parts is the ability to reconstitute the problem into its original "whole." This reintegration process has not been effectively demonstrated for many problems.

We believe that traditional analysis is ill-equipped to provide decision-makers with the insight they seek due to the mismatch between the irreducible complexity of global terrorism and the necessary reductionism of analysis. In order to provide decision-makers with the insights they demand, the analytic community requires new technologies and methods: the professional practice of analysis must transition from analysis as classically defined to a practice of inquiry. We believe that emerging technologies provide the means for which this transformation can occur.

The broad technological and methodological approaches that we advocate below are not merely theoretical; they are being applied to the problems of state failure and counter-terrorism in a variety of efforts throughout the defense and intelligence community. At the conclusion of this chapter, we will briefly discuss one particular program that demonstrated the potential of an inquiry-based approach to analysis, the Pre-Conflict Management Tools (PCMT) Program led by the Center for Technology and National Security Policy (CTNSP) at the National Defense University (NDU).[3] PCMT provides a glimpse into the practical applications of emerging information technologies to the assessment of complex and contested strategic problems; demonstrating how tools can transition from gathering and processing large volumes of data and executing routinized, recurring organizational and managerial tasks, to assisting decision-makers in exploring the interaction between multiple, competing objectives and discovering novel threats or failure modes of candidate strategies and policies. It is this change in the practice of analysis that can help defeat global terrorism.

16.2. COUNTER-TERRORISM AT MACRO- AND MICRO-LEVELS OF ANALYSIS

Before discussing technology, it is important to consider the broader geostrategic context of terrorism as a recurring challenge to national sovereignty and international stability. Conventional views of terrorism primarily consider the particulars of group dynamics, psychology, specific tactics and technologies, and the attractiveness of specific ideological or religious motivations as causes of anti-government violence.[4] While informative, these explanations often neglect or downplay large-scale social processes that frame interactions between state institutions, legal and strategic regimes, and violent political opposition to the status quo.[5]

Macrolevel analysis of large-scale political structures and processes, such as state formation, state fragmentation, and globalization offer alternatives to the study of individual terrorist groups and personalities. These broader perspectives place the concepts of sovereignty, criminality, and ideology in prominent positions and link terrorism to broader, more diffuse issues of intrastate conflict, civil war, and state failure.[6] These alternative

---

[3]For a more detailed account of the PCMT program see Aaron B. Frank, Pre-conflict management tools: Winning the peace, *Defense and Technology Paper,* No. 11 (National Defense University, February 2005).

[4]For a variety of examples see Walter Reich (ed.), *Origins of Terrorism* (New York: Cambridge University Press, 1992); Martha Crenshaw (ed.), *Terrorism in Context* (University Park, PA: The Pennsylvania State University Press, 1995); Jessica Stern, *The Ultimate Terrorists* (Cambridge, MA; Harvard University Press, 2000); Rex A. Hudson, *Who Becomes a Terrorist and Why* (Guilford, CT: Lyons Press, 2002); and Marc Sageman, *Understanding Terror Networks* (Philadelphia: University of Pennsylvania Press, 2004).

[5]For a use view of the evolution of the modern international system from this perspective see Philip Bobbitt, *The Shield of Achilles* (New York: Anchor Books, 2003).

[6]For discussions of sovereignty, criminality, and the processes of state-formation and failure see Charles Tilly, War Making and State Making as Organized Crime, in Peter B. Evans, Detrich Rueschemeyer, and Theda Skocpel (eds.), *Bringing the State Back In* (New York: Cambridge University Press, 1985); Mohammed Ayoob,

frames are important due to their ability to contextualize terrorism, and allow it to be considered within the context of weak, warring, conflicted, rogue, and failed states. By broadening the framework within which terrorism is considered, microlevel concerns of group formation, individual recruitment, leadership, and so on, can be linked to broad geopolitical trends in the transformation of states and world systems.[7]

We believe that information technology plays an important role in the analysis of terrorism, by providing tools that formalize linkages between micro- and macrolevels of analysis. Merging these levels provides the opportunity to address the particular features of specific groups and movements while remaining cognizant of broader historical and global trends. From an analytic perspective, viewing terrorism as part of a larger political theme affects the practical aspects of data gathering, processing, organization, and coding; informs the selection of modeling methods and theoretical frames; and complicates the consideration of consequences that might result from potential strategies and policies. New technologies can significantly improve counter-terrorist activities, but more importantly they can transform the practice of strategy itself.

Our vision of emerging technology in no way undermines traditional perspectives on terrorism; it does, however, serve to provide decision-makers with a broader, deeper framework for thinking about terrorism as a phenomenon that is embedded in subtle, diffuse, macrolevel political problems.[8] In particular, we believe that linkages between micro- and macro-analytic methods provide the basis for dealing with complex problems by identifying tradeoffs between temporal and spatial scales, alternative theoretical frames, conflicting datasets, and available options (see Figure 16.1). The employment of new technological tools for analysis can help shape how decision-makers think about terrorism, better harnessing the power and effectiveness of focused, group-oriented counter-terrorist efforts by contextualizing them within deeper, nuanced perspectives on national, regional, and global problems and trends. We see strategic, technological, organizational, and conceptual change as a unified whole.

16.3. THE CRAFT AND PRACTICE OF ANALYSIS

At its heart, the craft of analysis is about the creation of knowledge and the generation of insight for the purpose of informing choice-making. Analytic communities focusing on counter-terrorism face a challenge. Their typical tools and approaches have difficulties operating across multiple levels of analysis and competing theoretical frames. More explicitly, breaking problems into constituent elements provides greater awareness of specific features at the expense of losing macroscopic context. Moreover, there is no clear way to determine the proper decomposition of the phenomenon or system, meaning that many equally valid perspectives may exist simultaneously. Thus, analysis needs to move toward inquiry, a transition that is aided through the development, explication, and exploration of models.

We believe that models play a central role in the craft and practice of analysis and inquiry. Conceptually speaking, models are stylized simplifications of real-world referents, and whether they are cognitive (closely held mental models only instantiated in people's

The Third World Security Predicament (Boulder, CO: Rienner, 1995); and Stephen D. Krasner, *Sovereignty* (Princeton, NJ: Princeton University Press, 1999).

[7]See Ray Takeyh and Nikolas Gvosdev, Do Terrorist Networks Need a Home?, in Alexander T.J. Lennon (ed.), *The Battle for Hearts and Minds: Using Soft Power to Undermine Terrorist Networks* (Cambridge, MA: MIT Press, 2003), pp. 94–107.

[8]For a discussion of the challenges that recent geopolitical trend pose to policy-makers see Robert C. Cooper, *The Breaking of Nations* (New York: Atlantic Monthly Press, 2004).

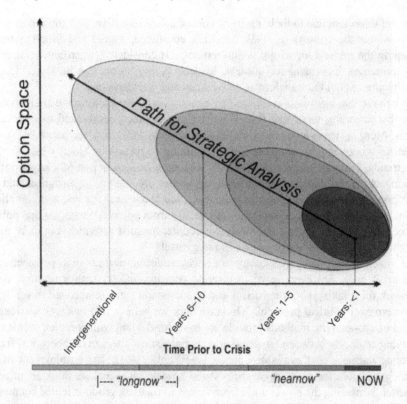

Figure 16.1. Illustrates the trade-off between available options and time prior to advent of a national crisis.

minds), mathematical, numerical, or algorithmic, models serve as a tools for understanding the world. A key feature of models is that they contain an internally consistent logic or structure of rules: They are systematic sets of conjectures about the real world.[9] The challenge for the analytic community is to formulate models that are rich in relevant real-world attributes and relations in order to be credible, as well as having the ability to manipulate these models in order to gain insights into the present and the future. Models are the artifacts of analytic craft.

If the craft of analysis produces models, then the practice of analysis refers to model exploitation for the purpose of informing decision-making—that is, choice. The notion of choice is significant because it implies that decision-makers are confronted with a set of alternative actions of nontrivial size. What option decision-makers select and the means by which they do it vary. The role of the analyst is to participate in the selection process by speculating about the costs, benefits, and consequences of alternative choices.[10]

[9]Charles A. Lave and James G. March, *An Introduction to Models in the Social Sciences* (Lanham, MD: University Press of America, 1993), pp. 3–4. For a survey of different model types used to analyze social systems see Herbert A. Simon, *Models of Discovery* (Boston: D. Reidel Publishing Company, 1977); Charles A. Lave and James G. March, *An Introduction to Models in the Social Sciences* (Lanham, MD: University Press of America, 1993); and Nigel Gilbert and Klaus G. Troitzsch, *Simulation for the Social Scientist* (Philadelphia: Open University Press, 2002).

[10]See Herbert A. Simon, *Administrative Behavior* (New York: The Free Press, 1997); David L. Weimer and Aidan R. Vining, *Policy Analysis: Concepts and Practice* (Upper Saddle River, NJ: Prentice Hall, 1999), pp. 27–34; Deborah Stone, *Policy Paradox* (New York: W.W. Norton & Company, 2002), pp. 17–34; and Hunter

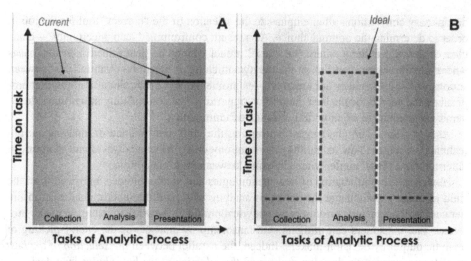

Figure 16.2. Ideal and actual depictions of how analysts spend their time.

Despite numerous texts on analytic methods, the role of ideas, models, theory, hypotheses, discussions of utility, cost, tradeoffs, optimality, robustness, and so on, the majority of the professional analyst's time is spent gathering, organizing, and preparing data for use in models and presenting model results to decision-makers.[11] The process by which analysts practice their craft (i.e., perform their job) can be described in three basic steps, (which are illustrated in Figure 16.2): (1) the gathering of relevant data, (2) the creation of insight through the use of models, and (3) the sharing and communicating of insights with other analysts and decision-makers. While these steps are simple, their general form has proven stable and are unlikely to change. However, technology can stimulate qualitative changes to the practice of analysis by reallocating the relative proportion of time spent on each step. Specifically, technologies that allow for the rapid gathering and preparation of data for use in models, and technologies that alter the way model results are communicated can affect analytic performance by increasing the time actually spent on analysis. More time means methods traditionally excluded from analysis, but regularly employed in inquiry, can be incorporated into the decision-making process.

Because of its emphasis on decision-making, the relationship between analysts and their clients or consumers of their products is paramount. Close relations between analysts and decision-makers ensure that analytic products are relevant to decision-makers concerns and sensitive to individual and organizational strengths and weaknesses. However, customer-driven analysis is often directly or indirectly influenced by a desire to maintain good relations with decision-makers and sponsors, and analysts must confront internal and external pressures to please decision-makers, potentially affecting their selection of data, models, and the presentation of outputs.

Finally, the analytic community is a highly diverse collection of individuals, organizations, and institutions employing a plethora of models, ideas, concepts, theories, and ideas that can be used to support decision-makers. While this diversity is a potential strength,

Crowther-Heyck, *Herbert A. Simon: The Bounds of Reason in Modern America* (Baltimore: The Johns Hopkins University Press, 2005), pp. 96–119.
[11]For example see David L. Weimer and Aidan R. Vining, *Policy Analysis: Concepts and Practice* (Upper Saddle River, NJ: Prentice Hall, 1999), pp. 34–35.

disciplinary conventions often emphasize the selection of the "correct" tool for the job in order to determine the optimal choice. As a result, confronting "deep uncertainty"—complex or novel problems where the "best" model cannot be determined *a priori,* cases where goal structures conflict or change dynamically, or when the relationships between actions and consequences are unknown—is problematic.[12] Professional training that emphasizes the search for the best model for supporting decision-making undermines the diversity and talents resident within the analytic community.

At first glance, the challenges confronting the craft and practice of analysis are not technical in nature. New technology does not obviously affect analyst–client relations, or determine the "best" model when choosing between multiple options.[13]

However, the combination of new technologies and methodologies borrowed from the field of inquiry can change the nature of analytic work and the institutional relationship between producers and consumers of analytical products. New relationships between producers and consumers can mitigate self-censorship by analysts or the cherry-picking of analytic output by decision-makers. Indeed, the parallel between *the selection of the best model for supporting a decision-maker* and *the selection of the best choice by a decision-maker* is an important one and is subject of the remainder of this chapter.

16.4. A NEW PERSPECTIVE ON TECHNOLOGY AND ANALYSIS

Discussing the future is difficult. Our minds naturally cling to past experiences and lessons. Therefore, it is useful to think about a potential future or scenario and then work backwards tracing the path or chain-of-events that link an imagined future to the familiar present.[14] Though brief, the vignette below reveals the extent to which developing information technologies can be a transformational catalyst, motivating a revolution in the conduct of analysis and strategic decision-making.

Imagine A World . . .

In the not so distant future, global terrorism is regarded as an anachronism, a distant memory of unfamiliar conflict. The dying gasp of global terrorism was not a military strike, not unrivaled political or economic or military power, and not the creation of world hostile to individual freedom and expression. Instead, decision-makers at the highest and lowest levels of government, industry, and community recognized that their effort to choose the optimal course of action left them vulnerable to surprise and innovation. The complexity of global terrorism and other contemporaneous challenges motivated a new way of evaluating their options. Decision-makers placed a new set of demands on their analysts.

Empowered by a new mission, analysts searched for alternative ways to evaluate the world and the choices confronting decision-makers. Rather than attempt to find the best data and the best mode, so that the best choice could be made, analysts began to collect increasingly large datasets, and generate multiple models that represented credible but conflicting theoretical frames. Armed with new libraries of data and models, analysts searched for classes of activities that fared well across the diverse mix of theoretical frames and datasets. Choices

---

[12]The concept of "deep uncertainty" has been advanced for discussing the analysis of complex systems where there is no prior way to know what the right analytical model is in advance of performing the analysis. For a discussion of "deep uncertainty" see Robert J. Lempert, Steven W. Popper, and Steven C. Bankes, *Shaping the Next One Hundred Years: New Methods for Quantitative, Long-Term Policy Analysis* (Santa Monica, CA: RAND, 2003), pp. 3–6.

[13]The parallel between *the selection of the best model for supporting a decision-maker and the selection of the best choice* is an important one, and it will be discussed in greater detail later.

[14]On the use of scenarios for exploring futures through mental simulation see Peter Schwartz, *The Art of the Long View: Planning for the Future in an Uncertain World* (New York: Doubleday, 1996).

ceased to be evaluated based on whether they were optimal given a particular set of data and a particular model, but were considered for their robustness—whether they were expected to produce favorable outcomes given uncertainty in data and dynamics.

Technology played an important role in this transition. Information technology provided the means to rapidly gather, organization, and reorganize large volumes of structured and unstructured data. Any data available in electronic form became a part of a universe of information interacting with models. Additionally, the library of models from which analysts consulted were not confined to the products of mental deduction. The library of models was augmented by inductively generated models that were conceptually unconstrained, but "fit" the data. Machine intelligence became an adjunct to human imagination by proposing theoretical frames that had a high correspondence with known data for analysts to review for conceptual credibility. Finally, computational search allowed for the simulation of unlimited combinations of choices to be simulation within unlimited combinations of models. Analysts could then focus search library of outcomes to search for classes of choices or conditions that produced particularly effective or ineffective outcomes.

Moving from optimality to robustness as an analytic criteria had a profound effect on strategy and policy. Decision-makers began to choose options that hedged against uncertainty. A desire to find robust actions motivated interagency and international cooperation because coordinated actions reduced uncertainty and allowed for the simultaneous pursuit of divergent goals. These robust strategies enabled decision-makers to shape a world where terrorism ceased to be an attractive option for voicing social and political grievance, and would-be terrorists found alternative, less costly and destructive outlets for voicing their discontent.

The vignette reveals subtle yet important changes to the profession of analysis based on maturing information technology and the demand to confront increasingly complex problems. We believe that the nature of the analytic profession is pregnant for transformation due to rapidly improving information gathering and processing tools allow analysts to rapidly assemble, organize, and re-purpose large volumes of data from any electronic source; a new generation of computational models that allow for the formalization and instantiation of a broad range of theories, including those that cannot be represented mathematically; tools that combine recursive computational simulation and search enabling the development of outcome landscapes that emphasize enhancing decision-makers' awareness of the consequences of their choices across a large range of potential futures—an emergent dialogue between humans and computers. The vignette highlights the difference between (a) technological development as the production of artifacts and (b) technological change as an engine for intellectual, organizational, and professional transformation.

We believe that this technologically enabled transformation of analysis is necessary but will not come easy. The process of creating an intellectual relationship between man and machine requires technological, methodological, and cultural change.[15] First, analysts tend to have a guarded view of electronic information sources: Deep concerns exist over determining the source's quality, authenticity, or agenda, and practical concerns over reliability of access and archival stability abound. Second, a generation of decision-makers in the field of international strategy has a distrustful view of the application of computational models and quantitative methods to what are fundamentally issues of social and political choice and agency.[16]

---

[15]See Desmond Saunders-Newton and Harold Scott, But the Computer Said! . . . A Typology for Using Computational Modeling Methods in Public Sector Decision-Making, *Social Science Computer Review*, Vol. 19, No. 1 (Spring 2001), pp. 47–65.
[16]See Harry G. Summers, *On Strategy: A Critical Analysis of the Vietnam War* (Novato, CA: Presidio Press, 1995), p. 18; and Robert J. Lempert, Steven W. Popper, and Steven C. Bankes, *Shaping the Next One Hundred Years: New Methods for Quantitative, Long-Term Policy Analysis* (Santa Monica, CA: RAND, 2003), pp. 21–23.

Most importantly, decision-makers have grown to expect more from analysts than they can offer, forgetting that some questions cannot be answered with certainty and that even the most thorough of analysis cannot eliminate the risk or responsibility of choice-making. Indeed, after a career examining decision-making, analysis, and organizations, Herbert Simon concluded that no amount of analysis or knowledge can absolve decision-makers from making hard choices, or what he considered as the constant "burden of personal ethical choice."[17] Despite these challenges, we believe that a net assessment of the analytic craft reveals the game is changing.

16.5. FROM ANALYSIS TO INQUIRY: CONTINUITY AND CHANGE IN THE USE OF MODELS

Analytic products and analysts come in a variety of shapes, sizes, and colors. Despite their differences, a common thread unites them: a desire to optimize or identify the best possible choice given a predetermined set of objectives and quantity and/or quality of resources. It is this notion of a single best choice where technological and methodological innovation can have a transformative effect.

To be sure, linking ends and means was not always the domain of analysis and reductionism. For example, strategists such as Carl von Clausewitz rejected the notion of strategic decision-making by reducing conflicting political and military systems into smaller, decomposable parts.[18] Yet, over the last five decades micro-economic decision-making models, operations research, and systems analysis came to dominate the advisory functions surrounding decision-makers in the public and private sector.[19] Though these efforts have worked well, decision-makers have remained vulnerable to surprise and overconfidence despite an ever-increasing sophistication of analytic models. The unaddressed concerns of decision-makers are the target of the transformation we envision, while the persistence of their concerns reveals the limitations of the analytic profession as currently practiced.

Decision-making in the face of global terrorism and uncertainty is a complex endeavor, yet rarely are the full implications of complexity articulated. An important feature is the lack of certainty about causal structures within the system or identifying its initial conditions from which it evolved. If decision-makers lack a full, predictive understanding of cause and effect within the system the implications of their choices cannot be known in advance, and evaluating the costs and consequences of particular choices based on the best available model may produce fragile results.[20] Confronting complexity requires better methods for exploiting models, not better models.

We believe that confronting complex problems requires a different decision-theory based on satisficing.[21] The principles of diversity, adaptiveness, and robustness, if elevat-

---

[17]See Hunter Crowther-Heyck, *Herbert A. Simon: The Bounds of Reason in Modern America* (Baltimore, MD: The Johns Hopkins University Press, 2005), p. 102.

[18]See Carl von Clausewitz, *On War* (Princeton, NJ: Princeton University Press, 1989), Michael Howard and Peter Paret, translator; and Alan Beyerchen, Clausewitz, Nonlinearity, and the Unpredictability of war, *International Security*, Vol. 17, No. 3 (Winter 1992), pp. 59–90.

[19]See Edith Stokey and Richard Zeckhauser, *A Primer for Policy Analysis* (New York: W.W. Norton & Company, 1978); and David L. Weimer and Aidan R. Vining, *Policy Analysis: Concepts and Practice* (Upper Saddle River, NJ: Prentice Hall, 1999), pp. 28–35.

[20]Herbert A. Simon, *The Sciences of the Artificial* (Cambridge, MA: MIT Press, 2001), pp. 25–37.

[21]The authors are by no means alone in this belief. Many scholars from a variety of disciplines have advocated satisficing over optimization. For examples see Robert J. Lempert and James L. Bonomo, *New Methods for Ro-*

ed over optimization and efficiency, can enable decision-makers to navigate through diverse and conflicting visions of the future contained in analytic products.[22] However, this change requires reformulating concepts and practices that have been institutionalized in the analytic community, specifically the traditional ways models are exploited.

To fully appreciate the importance of new methods for confronting deep uncertainty, a basic understanding of modeling and model-based reasoning is necessary. Regardless of their specifics, all models serve analysis by allowing them to think about problems is a structured fashion. Whether they are formal mathematical statements, computational algorithms, or theoretical and heuristic frames residing in the analyst's mind, they are systematic sets of conjectures about the real world that have immutable strengths and weaknesses.[23]

Model users often assume that models serve as analogs to real-world systems. Indeed, claiming a model to be valid implies that it is capable of serving as a reliable surrogate to a real-world referent system. Thus, many consider models to be more than technological and conceptual artifacts; they are statements about disciplinary knowledge and achievement. However, as problems shift from linear physical systems toward complex, nonlinear human systems, models cannot retain predictive or external validity.[24] The search for external validation (i.e., predictive accuracy), and mathematical elegance in dealing with linear and closed systems has biased the way complex problems are represented and what questions researchers ask when analyzing social problems.[25] As a result, many professional analysts and decision-makers fail to question whether the use of model outputs as predictive statements is he best use of use of model outputs.

Changing how models are used in the decision-making process enables analysts to capitalize on information technologies that we regard as transformative. By revisiting first-principle issues associated with the practice of modeling complex systems, along with a consideration for experimental epistemology, the analytic community is able to profit from advances in computational modeling and computer-based experimentation in order to gain insights into social behavior.[26] These approaches also suggest alternative

bust Science and Technology Planning (Santa Monica, CA: RAND, 1998); Herbert A. Simon, The Sciences of the Artificial (Cambridge, MA: MIT Press, 2001); and Robert J. Lempert, Steven W. Popper, and Steven C. Bankes, Shaping the Next One Hundred Years: New Methods for Quantitative, Long-Term Policy Analysis (Santa Monica, CA: RAND, 2003).

[22]Robert J. Lempert, Steven W. Popper, and Steven C. Bankes, Shaping the Next One Hundred Years: New Methods for Quantitative, Long-Term Policy Analysis (Santa Monica, CA: RAND, 2003), pp. 39–67.

[23]Charles A. Lave and James G. March, An Introduction to Models in the Social Sciences (Lanham, MD: University Press of America, 1993), pp. 3–4.

[24]To be fair, the fidelity of physical science models only provides the illusion of predictive accuracy—a certainty in the mechanisms between a model's inputs and outputs that displays unwavering, law-like behavior. Fortunately, their inability to perfectly reflect the real-world doesn't reduce their usefulness. However, it is useful to note that closer inspection of what models are and how they are used reveals the fragility of the view that physical science models are characterized by excessive external validity. By definition, models are simplifications of reality; they are not isomorphic with it and cannot replicate all of its intricacy and detail within their frames. Model designers must choose what features to represent and what to leave out; therefore, models should be regarded as artifacts that result from human choices regarding how to represent a problem or phenomena. See Herbert A. Simon, The Sciences of the Artificial (Cambridge, MA: MIT Press, 2001).

[25]See Desmond Saunders-Newton, Computational Social Science, Operations Research, and Effects-Based Operations: The Challenge of Inferring Effects from Dynamic Socio-Physical Systems, (McLean, VA: Military Operations Research Society, Workshop on Analyzing Effects-Based Operations, January 29, 2002); and John D. Steinbruner, The Cybernetic Theory of Decision (Princeton, NJ: Princeton University Press, 2002), 327–331.

[26]See Steven Bankes, Robert Lempert, and Steven Popper, "Making Computational Social Science Effective: Epistemology, Methodology and Technology", Social Science Computer Review, Vol. 20, No. 4 (Winter, 2002), pp. 377–388.

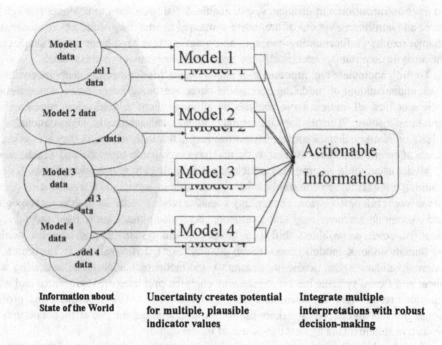

Model 1

Model 2

Model 3

Model 4

Information about
State of the World

Uncertainty creates potential
for multiple, plausible
indicator values

Integrate multiple
interpretations with robust
decision-making

Figure 16.3. Use of computational models and methods for inquiry and decision-making.[28]

performance criteria for models that are not focused on prediction as a determinant of value (external validation).

By treating models as computational experiments, as opposed to future predictions, analysis need not restrict themselves to use of validated tools. As a result, they are free to experiment with a wide variety of views, perspectives, parameters, data, and so on. The result is a search for credible computational experiments—combinations of models and data that are plausible, but whose predictive validity will never be known—that can generate landscapes of potential outcomes.[27] From these landscapes, the specific and collective merits of alternative choices can be compared based on their performance across multiple experiments. This experimental approach to policy analysis subtly changes the way analysts and their models interact, and it reorients the analytic profession toward holistic inquiry rather than reductionist analysis. The structure of this computational-based inquiry is depicted in Figure 16.3 above.

Making this transformation a reality requires technology to assist in particular analytic or methodological roles. First, technology must provide a means for (a) effectively gathering data from structured and unstructured sources and (b) automatically populating models with data. Second, computational models must be developed that can instantiate deductively generated theories of social and individual behaviors, or be inductively grown from large archives of data. Third, collections of diverse models need to be cou-

---

[27]Treating collections of models and simulations as computational experiments has been described as exploratory modeling. See Steven C. Bankes, *Exploratory Modeling and the Use of Simulation for Policy Analysis* (Santa Monica, CA: RAND, 1992); and Steve Bankes, "Exploratory Modeling for Policy Analysis", *Operations Research*, Vol. 41, No. 3 (May–June 1993), pp. 435–449.

[28]Slide modified from Evolving Logic, *Collier's Model for Predicting Civil Conflict,* Pre-conflict Management Tools Experiment, April 28, 2004. Also see www.evolvinglogic.com.

pled or integrated and simultaneously manipulated in order to generate large outcome landscapes that are responsive to parametric, theoretical uncertainty and capable of simulating numerous individual and combinations of choices. Information gleaned from this collection of technologies and models then needs to be shared and iteratively explored by a community of analysts and decision-makers, working together in order to assure themselves that the insights of inquiry are plausible and possible.

Given technological, historical, and geopolitical trends many concerns over electronic data are rapidly becoming moot. Near unlimited, inexpensive data storage, peer-to-peer networks, and so on, can ensure reliable access to electronic archives. Moreover, these virtual libraries are portable, infinitely reproducible, and increasingly diverse in their content as a larger and larger portion of the global population gains access to electronic media.[29] While these trends can obviate the technical concerns over working from electronic sources, they tend to amplify concerns over data quality. However, data quality issues can be addressed through (a) computational search across parameter settings and (b) networks of human filters culling databases for information that is not regarded as credible.

Moving beyond the issues of quality, the repurposing of data into model-relevant information is a needed development for transforming the analytic community. This is not about data quantification, an act that results in the loss of information, but is instead about the maintenance of relevant contextual information that is important to the modeling process. Thus massive amounts of "potential" data, as well as theories resident in academic journals, new articles, blogs, and so on, that allow for alternative approaches for framing this data, are not currently or easily exploited by existing analytic tools. Data tools that can support gather and contextualize structured and unstructured information for a variety of purposes are needed in order to exploit the ever-growing electronic universe of information.

Effectively accessing and using more data than has been traditionally handled by analysts is only the beginning of their transformation. Technologies for exploiting a vast array of models simultaneously are also in demand. Many analysts have expressed concerns regarding the use of models of social and individual behavior due their simplicity and inability to capture the more nuanced and sophisticated behaviors of their subjects. However, as noted earlier, this does not suggest that insights cannot be gained from even the simplest of models. Reasoning from collections of models, or collections of computational experiments, allows for the artifacts of simplification and assumptions to be documented and compared. While technology cannot solve legitimate concerns over simplicity, it can provide new interfaces for evaluating, combining, and manipulating models, thereby shifting the burden of generating insights off of individual models onto collections of models each possessing different strengths and weaknesses. Addressing these issues also allows for the coupling of models of different types, perspectives, and levels of analysis together.

Finally, the transformation of the analytic community includes the creation of collaborative workspaces where humans and machine intelligences share the designs, inputs, and outputs of computational experiments. Harvesting insights across a diverse ecology of analytics ensures that while no one analyst or model is capable of providing the correct assessment of how the world will evolve over time, a diverse population will consider more possibilities than a small insular group, and someone, or some model, will identify a tra-

---

[29]See Peter Lyman, Hal R. Varian, James Dunn, Aleksey Strygin, and Kirsten Swearingen, *How Much Information? 2003* (Berkley, CA, University of California at Berkley, 2003) available at http://www.sims.berkeley.edu/research/projects/how-much-info-2003/.

jectory that is similar to what actually unfolds. Put differently, rather than forcing the analysts to move toward consensus, the community's strength will come from a cacophony of voices together provide a typography of outcomes from which choices that robust across many possible futures are identified.

16.6. PEERING INTO THE FUTURE: PCMT AND TRANSFORMATIVE ANALYSIS

The PCMT program at NDU provided a glimpse into the practical applications of the technologies and methods discussed above to the problems of state failure, civil war, and counter-terrorism. The PCMT program was a proof of concept study that developed a prototype system, a system that is still under development and growing in functionality. While technologically immature, its operational significance was immediately recognized. PCMT's experiments revealed many important lessons about technological trends and thrusts, while numerous exercises with analysts and decision-makers provided an opportunity to learn what features users demanded and found useful. PCMT's nascent software and developing concepts demonstrated how new capabilities can transform the way decision-makers and analysts interact in order to deal with complex strategic problems.

Technologically, PCMT incorporated a variety of information technologies. The system itself was a collection of interrelated components that supported the decision-making process from the collection of information and identification of potential problems through policy analysis and development, resulting in the implementation and monitoring of robust strategies. A simplified diagram of the PCMT architecture is depicted in Figure 16.4.

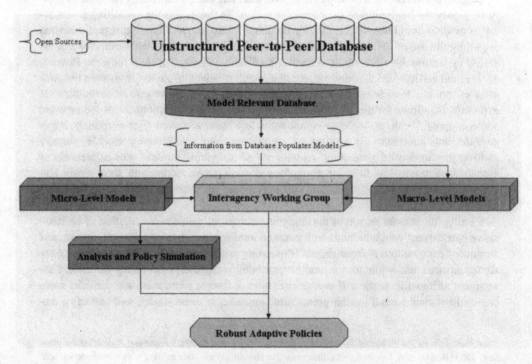

Figure 16.4. Overview of the PCMT architecture.

First, PCMT's underlying architecture employed a variety of information collection tools that automated the collection of structured and unstructured data. Although the proof of concept primarily worked from news wires, the data infrastructure was also capable of gathering and processing journals, blogs, or any other text-based digital source. Moreover, the data itself were stored in a peer-to-peer database that allowed for multi-level security and the maintenance of metadata such as date produced, date collected, data source, and copyright information. This structure ensured that the database was highly scalable and secure and could facilitate the storage and use of data from free and subscription services.

PCMT's peer-to-peer database was only part of the data management tools. The database was capable of growing rapidly due to its computational nature; in one day the automated data gathering tools collected more than 60,000 articles on Central Asia.[30] In order to make sense of the massive, dynamically changing dataset, PCMT broke from traditional analytic convention. First, no single, ontological structure was imposed on the data. Rather, the database was designed to dynamically restructure itself in conjunction with an array of analytic models. Because each model required different types and formats of data, the base data were dynamically reconfigured to support the ontology that each model desired. As new models are introduced into PCMT's analytic suite (discussed below), new instructions are given to the database regarding the specific ontology the models require.

A second innovation regarding PCMT's database was the role of human users. Traditionally, large datasets are carefully cured, normalized, and validated prior to publishing. PCMT's vision was based on gathering all available information, regardless of quality or format, and then notifying networks of interested users that new data was available. These data would then be evaluated by subject matter experts in the relevant domain, and ranked. These rankings would then be attached to the data itself, allowing analysts to run models based on specific datasets, such as all data provided from a particular source or set of sources, data ranked as especially good by expert judgment, or data "blessed" by particular institutions. The combination of automated data collection, dynamically reconfigurable ontologies, and expert evaluation allows analysts to (a) forego their search for the "best" individual model and (b) search across collections of assumptions about initial conditions, dynamics (alternative theories of cause and effect), costs, and utility.

New technologies for data gathering and organization allow for changes in analysis to occur. PCMT's modeling suite allowed analysts to (a) conduct a dialogue between data and theory in order to generate insights and (b) search for strategies that were robust in spite of structural and parametric uncertainty. During the proof of concept, analysts had access to a suite composed of seven operational models: Fund for Peace's Conflict Assessment System Tool (CAST), along with six instantiations of greed and grievance models developed by Paul Collier and his colleagues from the World Bank Group.[31]

The use of multiple models within an exploratory modeling environment allowed collections of diverse analysts, each with different assumptions and goals, to identify how divergent assessments about the region and international system (i.e., beliefs about the what constituted the "best" model) produced alternative notions of an optimal strategy. However, by abandoning the search for optimal solutions in favor of robust, adaptive ones, inter-

---

[30]Figure provided by the Institute for Physical Sciences and DARPA.

[31]For information on the CAST model see www.fundforpeace.org. For information on the World Bank Group's greed and grievance models see Paul Collier, Lani Elliot, Håvard Hegre, Anke Hoeffler, Marta Reynal-Querol, and Nicholas Sambanis, *Breaking the Conflict Trap* (Washington, DC: World Bank and Oxford University Press, 2003).

agency representatives were able to identify actions that performed well across all of the available models.

PCMT's experimentation revealed that models were not simply talking to analysts, but that they were allowing for a dialogue. For example, in one case the model suggested the effectiveness of a given policy option, but a user suggested that the input data may not be accurate. A simple change in the input data revealed that the proposed policy ceased to be effective under alternative conditions, conditions that the group considered plausible even though not empirically verified. Although this example was simple, the ability to search across combinations of assumptions about parameters and theoretical frames through computational means suggested that automating the search would allow for millions of excursions to be explored, lifting the burden of asking the right question or running the right excursion off of analysts and placing them onto the computer. Analysts only needed to explore collections of outcomes that were interesting and then evaluate the specific conditions that produced them. Modeling and simulation allowed for analysis to transition from a deductive activity into an inductive one.

Armed with deep insight into the regions structure and potential futures, insights that could only be achieved through the consideration of multiple, competing models, analysts and decision-makers in PCMT's exercises were able to consider a large number of policy options. Moreover, because the modeling environment elicited divergent perspectives and objectives, the generation of robust strategies encouraged cooperation and expanded the area of decision-making brought under analytic control. While issues requiring political negotiation and compromise remained, this space was constrained and unnecessary battles over problems that could be addressed through robust strategies did not absorb the attention and energy of decision-makers. Because computational tools created an interactive environment, model-based analysis and the presentation of analytic products were fused. The linear progression between data gathering, modeling and simulation, and presentation became iterative, and the relationship between analysts and decision-makers was transformed.

SUMMARY

The PCMT program marks a notable beginning to an analytic journey, a journey that will transform the way professional analysts work and interact with decision-makers—a journey enabled, though not determined, by enabling technologies. Although many of the ideas expressed in this chapter regarding the use models, satisficing, robustness, and so on, have been used by the analytic community in the past, their application has been idiosyncratic, employed by the most skillful, creative, and inquisitive analysts. These concepts have been far more difficult to institutionalize in educational programs, training curricula, and mentoring within the community. The unfortunate side effect of this lack of institutionalization has been the near myth-like belief that tools used to analyze a system's components are equally applicable to the system as a whole. Misplaced confidence in analytic tools, at the expense of larger, broader inquiry, has left decision-makers vulnerable to surprise and unable to resolve multiple, competing objectives analytically.

We believe that technological trends are creating new opportunities for the analytic community. The ability to rapidly gather and organize large datasets, instantiate an ever-increasing array of theories in computational form, inductively generate models, automate the population of models with data, and perform searches across outcomes spaces generated through the use of multiple, competing models and dataset can change how models are used. These new technological capabilities provide the analytic community with an ability to incorporate inquiry into their work and improve their ability to support decision-makers when confronting classes of problems against which reductionist tools fail to generate adequate insight.

An inquiry-based approach to the use of models, along with a decision-theoretic approach specifically designed to search across large collections of computational experiments, can dramatically improve decision-making without the presence of a single, validated model. A transparent logic that couples model inputs, model logic, and insights enables analysts to produce collections of future scenarios with varying qualitative and quantitative properties. Thus, the ability to explore multiple futures arising from a suite of models provides analysts with (a) a window into the possible and (b) a unique ability to consider the consequences of candidate actions within this universe of potential futures that is unrivaled in today's world yet within the grasp of developing technologies and methods.

Chapter 17

Behavioral Network Analysis for Terrorist Detection

Seth A. Greenblatt, Thayne Coffman, and Sherry E. Marcus

17.1. INTRODUCTION

In the last 50 years, modern international terrorism has been manifested in a variety of ways—from the attempted assassination of General Eisenhower by the Nazis, to the terrorist strategies of the KGB, the plane hijackings of the 1970s, the activities of the PLO and Hezbollah, the 1988 bombing of Flight 103 over Lockerbie, Scotland, and the terrorism of Al Qaeda and 9/11. However, more recently the asymmetric threat has been elevated to a higher priority by the American military not only because of 9/11, but also because of civilian operations. One needs only to look at the number of American military casualties in Iraq to understand the significance of the asymmetric threat. U.S. adversaries, such as Al Qaeda, are exploiting terrorism and insurgencies to wear down U.S. resolve and erode public support for the global war on terrorism. What is different in this situation is that unlike international terrorist organizations of the past, Al Qaeda is not currently affiliated with any nation state. Therefore, this war requires new approaches, new perspectives, and a different mindset from that which the United States brought to previous conflicts.

In this section, we will discuss asymmetric threat detection technology based upon the *Terrorist Modus Operandi Detection System* (TMODS) framework that is in use in the Intelligence and Defense communities, followed by a discussion of the application of social network analysis to terrorist detection.

In Sections 17.2 and 17.3, we will describe the nature of asymmetric tactical threats and the evolving tactics used by our adversaries to motivate our technical approach. Section 17.4 discusses TMODS in detail. Finally, in Section 17.5 we present some conclusions and directions for future research.

17.2. EMERGING ASYMMETRIC TACTICAL THREATS

In order to motivate our specific approach to asymmetric threat detection technology, we first point out some recently emerging facts:

The research reported in this chapter was managed by the Air Force Research Laboratory in Rome, NY. The views and conclusions contained in this document are those of the authors and should not be interpreted as necessarily representing the official policies, either expressed or implied, of Rome Laboratory, the United States Air Force, or the United States Government.

- Al Qaeda states that it is a stronger organization today than it was on 9/11. A key Al Qaeda leader points out that before 9/11 they were able to carry out an attack once per year, and now they are able to carry out two attacks per year.[1]

- A Singaporean cell was recently detected with plans to (1) hijack a plane loaded with passengers and deliberately crash it into a tower and (2) dispatch multiple truck bombs to destroy U.S. military and diplomatic facilities. While the modus operandi was similar to the 9/11 and USS Cole plots, the plotters were, on average, a group of middle-aged, married, and educated Singaporeans. The Singaporean group had a common goal for the creation of a global Caliphate state and a genuine hatred of the west. Although the Singaporean cell was a distinct terrorist group from Al Qaeda, they had known connections to bin Laden's organization.[2] As one can see from this example, terrorist cell members are not necessarily North African or Arab, and they cannot be stereotyped by race, sex, or citizenship.

- According to the International Institute for Strategic Studies (IISS), a cadre of at least 18,000 individuals who trained in Al Qaeda's Afghanistan camps between 1996 and 2001 are today theoretically positioned in some 60 countries throughout the world. Al Qaeda uses these resources to gather intelligence, plan attacks, and survey targets throughout the world.[3] Thus, Al Qaeda possesses a "fifth column" whose capabilities have yet to be determined.

- Again according to IISS, the cost of terrorism is relatively low. The Bali bombing of 2002 cost $35,000, the USS Cole Operation cost $50,000, and the 9/11 attacks cost $500,000. Thus, because of the relatively low cost amount involved in these attacks, large amounts of cash are not necessary to conduct operations against high value targets. The American destruction of facilities in Afghanistan forced Al Qaeda to decentralize and inadvertently decreased Al Qaeda's financial burden of supporting a physical base of operations.[4]

The Singaporean cell represents a change from the 9/11 asymmetric attacks: The men involved in these attacks are supporters of Al Qaeda, but are not necessarily members. While the main participants of the Madrid cell are believed to be Moroccan, logistical and financial supporters come from a variety of regions.[5] In these ways and others, terrorism has become less centralized with more opaque command and control relationships, and Al Qaeda has transformed their itself into more of a concept than an organization held together by a loosely networked transnational membership.

17.3. THE INTELLIGENCE PROCESS

In the previous section, we briefly outlined a portion of the asymmetric threat problem space. Modern terrorist organizations are not affiliated with a single nation state, are loosely networked across transnational borders, cannot be identified by demographics,

---

[1]Dana Priest and Walter Pincus, "New Target and Tone: Message Shows Al Qaeda's Adaptability", Washington Post, 16 April 2004; and Geoffrey Nunberg, "Bin Laden's Low Tech Weapon", New York Times, 18 April 2004.
[2]Hoffman, Bruce, The Rand Corporation, "The Changing Face of Qaeda", Studies in Conflict and Terrorism, 27:549-560; 2004.
[3]International Institute for Strategic Studies, Strategic Survey, 2003/4 Oxford University Press 2004 page 6
[4]Ibid.
[5]http://www.answers.com/main/ntquery;jsessionid=9ptjm3eeoria0?method=4&dsid=2222&dekey=Aftermath+of+the+11+March+2004+Madrid+attacks&gwp=8&curtab=2222_1&sbid=lc02a

and have active intelligence operations within our borders. To understand the technology required to fight this asymmetric threat, we also must understand the circumstances in which an analyst detects asymmetric threats.

An intelligence analyst's job is to answer policy-makers' questions on a given subject. The questions may be broad and open-ended (e.g., What economic factors shape the foreign policy of Iran?), or they may be very specific (e.g., Is a terrorist planning to strike the Washington Monument?). Answering these questions often requires the analyst to predict future events. There are literally thousands of pieces of information available on each subject, and they invariably contain incomplete and contradictory evidence on the situation. Making reliable predictions with limited and contradictory evidence is an incredibly challenging task. Many analysts are turning to new graph-based analysis approaches to help them perform their jobs better. These new approaches are an interdisciplinary combination of mathematical graph theory, anthropology, and sociology.

Intelligence analysts are faced with the problem of finding very small warning signs of upcoming threats within mountains of data. When analysts are required to understand a complex uncertain situation, one of the techniques they use most often is to simply draw a diagram of the situation. These diagrams are *Attributed Relational Graphs* (ARGs), an extension of the abstract directed graph from mathematics. In these graphs, nodes represent people, organizations, objects, or events. Edges represent relationships like interaction, ownership, or trust. Attributes store the details of each node and edge, such as a person's name or an interaction's time of occurrence. Early on, these graphs were drawn and searched manually—on posters, chalk boards, or whiteboards. More recently, these graphs have been drawn and visualized digitally, but search and analysis must still be done by hand.

While analysts track many pieces of evidence, most evidence is completely innocent when viewed individually. Many people rent trucks, buy fertilizer, or take pictures of public monuments, and in isolation these actions are not remarkable. In contrast, the *combination* of those events performed by the same person or group could signal a threat to public safety. Graphs focus analysts' attention on the relationships between pieces of information, helping them see emerging event patterns and the big picture of evolving situations.

The analyst's problem is often not a lack of information, but rather information overload. Analysts lack the tools that can effectively locate the relatively few bits of *relevant* information and support reasoning over that information. In the next section, we will show how the Terrorist Modus Operandi Detection System, or TMODS, helps the analyst solve the first problem—sifting through a mountain of data to find the small subset that is indicative of threatening activity. This activity is often suspicious not because of the characteristics of a single actor, but because of the dynamics *amongst* a group of actors. In contrast with databases and spreadsheets, which tend to facilitate reasoning over the characteristics of individual actors, graph-based representations facilitate reasoning over the relationships between actors. TMODS leverages the power of graph-based representations to provide unique capabilities to today's intelligence analyst.

17.4. TERRORIST MODUS OPERANDI DETECTION SYSTEM (TMODS)

TMODS automates the tasks of searching for and analyzing instances of particular threatening activity patterns. With TMODS, the analyst can define an ARG to represent the pattern of threatening activity he or she is looking for. TMODS then automates the search for that *Threat Pattern* through an *Input Graph* representing the large volume of observed data. TMODS pinpoints the subsets of data that match the threat pattern defined by the analyst, transforming an arduous manual search into an efficient automated tool. It is important to note that the activity graph analyzed by TMODS can be derived from multiple sources, allowing for an analysis of information across several domains without extra effort.

TMODS is a distributed Java software application that has been under development by 21st Century Technologies since October 2001. Before we describe TMODS capabilities in further detail, a brief overview of *Graph Matching* is provided below.

Graph matching is often known as *Subgraph Isomorphism* (Diestel, 2000; LaPaugh and Rivest), and it is a well-known problem in graph theory. Informally, graph matching finds subsets of a large *Input Graph* that are "equivalent to" a *Pattern Graph* (*Threat Pattern*). These sections of the input graph, called *Matches*, are "equivalent" in the sense that their nodes and edges correspond one-to-one with those in the pattern graph. Figure 17.1 illustrates a sample pattern graph and an inexact match highlighted within one possible input graph. The match is inexact because there is a missing edge between Bill and Acme Inc.

As defined formally, subgraph isomorphism is an "*NP*" *Complete Problem* (no known polynomial-time solution exists) first identified in 1978. An *Adjacency Matrix* is one representation for an abstract graph. For a graph $G = (N, E)$ with nodes in set N and edges in

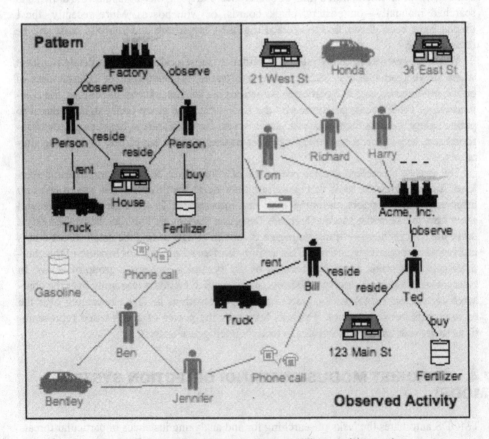

Figure 17.1. Inexact match to a pattern graph in an activity graph.

set E, the adjacency matrix is a matrix where each element $G(i, j)$ equals 1 if there is an edge from node n_p to node n_j, and 0 otherwise. Inputs to the subgraph isomorphism problem are a pattern graph with adjacency matrix G_p, and an input graph with adjacency matrix G_i. The solutions to the problem (the matches) are expressed in the form of a *Permutation Matrix*, M, such that $G_p = MG_iM^T$. Because M is a permutation matrix, elements of M must be in the set $\{0, 1\}$ and M may have at most one nonzero element in each row and column.

TMODS turns its ability to solve the subgraph isomorphism problem into a powerful tool for intelligence analysts. Figure 17.2 shows a typical usage scenario for TMODS. First, the analyst defines a pattern graph to represent activity they consider threatening based on past results or an idea they have about a potential threat. The analyst also specifies a set of data sources from which TMODS imports and fuses information on observed activity to form the input graph. The analyst then selects, configures, and executes the search algorithms. TMODS highlights matches to the threat pattern against surrounding activity in the input graph. Finally, the analyst views the set of matches and decides (possibly based on further investigation) which need to be acted on.

In the asymmetric threat detection domain there is a core set of graph patterns that are of general interest to the Counter-Terrorist (CT) analyst because they represent known

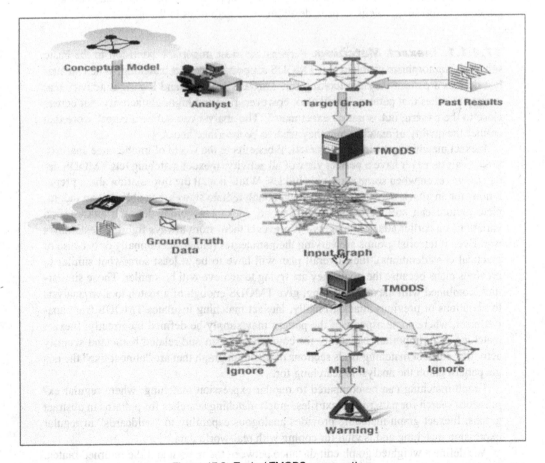

Figure 17.2. Typical TMODS usage pattern.

methods of illicit operations. In many such transactions, there are a multitude of middle-men or "front organizations or persons" used to shield and protect the leaders involved. These graph patterns may be implemented as (1) the movement of money or physical ob-jects between several organizations and persons over a period of time, (2) the shipment of physical assets between multiple or "front" countries to deflect suspicion of those assets, or (3) the churning of identifies for a specific individual. The key point behind the devel-opment of these patterns is that there are really only a handful of methods in which an or-ganization or individual can operate covertly. These graph patterns are genuinely differ-ent from that of normal business activity. This is true not only for terrorist detection, but also for narcotics detection and transnational criminal activity. While TMODS will never detect all these patterns nor will the analyst be able to define all possible threat patterns in advance, the ability to detect deviations from known threat patterns, within a reasonable period of time, is a significant achievement. Analysts have the ability to draw graph pat-terns that are stored within TMODS; and as graph patterns are matched, alerts are sent to the analyst.

17.4.1. TMODS Extensions to Standard Graph Matching

TMODS capabilities have been extended beyond approximations to the standard sub-graph isomorphism problem, to provide additional capabilities to the analyst.

17.4.1.1. Inexact Matching.
Perhaps the most important extension to the basic subgraph isomorphism problem that TMODS supports is inexact matching. When an ana-lyst defines a pattern they are looking for, TMODS will find and highlight activity that exactly matches that pattern. It will also, however, find and highlight activity that comes close to the pattern, but is not an exact match. The analyst can define a cutoff score that defines the quality of matches that they wish to be informed about.

Inexact matching provides huge practical benefits in the world of intelligence analysis. First, analysts never have a perfect view of all activity. Inexact matching lets TMODS de-tect threats even when some activity is hidden. While not all the information about prepa-rations for an attack may be present, often enough telltale signs are visible that an incom-plete picture can still be constructed. Second, inexact matching lets the analyst find variations on earlier attack strategies—it prevents them from always fighting yesterday's war. Even if terrorist groups are varying their strategies (either intentionally or because of practical considerations), their overall plan will have to be at least somewhat similar to previous plans because the goals they are trying to achieve will be similar. Those similar-ities, combined with inexact matching, give TMODS enough of a match to alert analysts to variations of previous attacks. Finally, inexact matching insulates TMODS from ana-lyst error, where some aspects of the pattern may simply be defined incorrectly. Inexact matching is an important capability for counter-terrorism and related homeland security activities. Inexact matching finds sections of the input graph that are "almost like" the tar-get pattern graph the analyst is searching for.

Graph matching can be compared to regular expression matching; where regular ex-pressions search for patterns in text files, graph matching searches for patterns in abstract graphs. Inexact graph matching provides analogous capability to "wildcards" in regular expression matching and is vital for coping with real-world data.

We define a weighted graph edit distance between the pattern and the returned match, formally defining the similarity measure. Figure 17.3 shows an abstract representation of the progression from an exact match to inexact matches. Inexact matches may have missing edges or nodes, missing or incorrect attribute values, missing or incorrect edge labels, or any combination of these. *Partial Graph Matches* refer to a subset of the pattern graph identified within the input graph. Figure 17.4 shows screenshots of TMODS inexact matching capability for a nuclear trafficking application. Based on the weighted edit distance criteria, a 95% match in this case represents an inexact match on an edge attribute (e.g., in the target pattern we are looking for an "arrest" edge attribute, and in the pattern returned by TMODS we find "killer" as the edge attribute).

However, the ranking is still high because we are able to find a connection between two entities. In the 90% match case, we can only indirectly (through an intermediate node) link a "weapon" to an individual, and thus the ranking is lower at 90%. TMODS has the capability to allow the analyst to assign ranking criteria for inexact matches.

17.4.1.2. Multiple Choices and Abstractions. TMODS patterns support variations on how the pattern may be instantiated. For example, a communication between two individuals might be achieved through e-mail, a face-to-face meeting, or a phone call. For an analyst's particular purposes, the medium through which the communication occurred may not matter. TMODS lets the analyst define multiple alternative graphs for each pattern, called *choices*. Regardless of which choice graph was matched, the match is represented by its *abstraction*, which defines the salient aspects of the match (usually a subset of the full match information). In our previous example, for instance, the salient information is likely the identities of the two people involved. Regardless of how they communicated—be it e-mail, meeting, or phone call—the analyst can define the pattern such that their matches would be presented uniformly.

17.4.1.3. Hierarchical Patterns. TMODS allows analysts to define patterns that are built from other patterns. Rather than requiring analysts to describe their entire pattern in one graph, TMODS lets the analyst modularize their patterns.

Figure 17.5 shows an example from counter-terrorism domain, where the pattern actually represents a composition of multiple graph-based patterns. When combined with TMODS' capabilities for multiple choices and abstractions, the ability to match hierarchical patterns is extremely powerful. Take, for example, the problem of representing a "murder for hire" in a pattern. All such contract killings will have a customer, a killer, and a victim, but aside from that, there may be a wide variety of possible instantiations. The customer may plan the killing directly with the killer, or the planning may be done

Exact vs. inexact matching

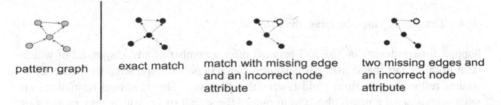

| pattern graph | exact match | match with missing edge and an incorrect node attribute | two missing edges and an incorrect node attribute |

Figure 17.3. Exact versus inexact graph matching.

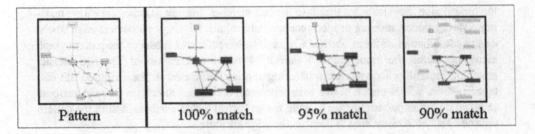

Figure 17.4. TMODS exact and inexact matching capability.

through a middleman. Planning might entail a single communication or a number of communications, and each communication could be made through any number of media. The combination of multiple choices, abstractions, and the ability to define hierarchical patterns lets TMODS represent extremely complicated and varied activity patterns while controlling algorithmic complexity and the complexity presented to the user. In one specific model of contract killings, TMODS was able to represent 13,000,000 different variations on how a contract kill could be executed. The top-level pattern had 11 subpatterns with a total of 31 choices, and each instantiation had an average of 75 total nodes. The use of hierarchical patterns changes an exponential complexity into an additive complexity, to great advantage. A discussion of specific algorithms used can be found under the upcoming Algorithms section.

TMODS is able to process approximately 900K graph elements per hour using an average desktop computer (i.e., 3-GHz Pentium 4). A previous benchmark exercise, in a specific problem domain, showed that TMODS can achieve 55% recall and 71.6% precision in search results at the stated processing rate; these results are without fusion algorithms. With fusion algorithms added, TMODS achieves 83.8% recall and 65% precision.

17.4.1.4. Constraints. TMODS lets the analyst define *constraints* between attribute values on nodes and edges. Constraints restrict the relationships between attributes of actors, events, or relationships. Using constraints, the analyst can restrict timing and relative ordering and can represent stateful threat patterns. In a counter-terrorism context, constraints can be used to specify restrictions like:

- "The event must have occurred within 50 miles of Houston."
- "The intelligence must have come from a reliable source in country X."
- "The person observed must belong to the same organization as person Y."
- "The money must come from an organization with at least $10 MM/year in income."
- "The quantity must be larger than 10,000."

Support for constraints in TMODS patterns offer a number of advantages, all of which stem from the fact that constraints make the TMODS pattern representation richer. Constraints refine the pattern to yield fewer false positives. The additional restrictions on what is considered a match also help to reduce the search space, which reduces memory requirements and required search time.

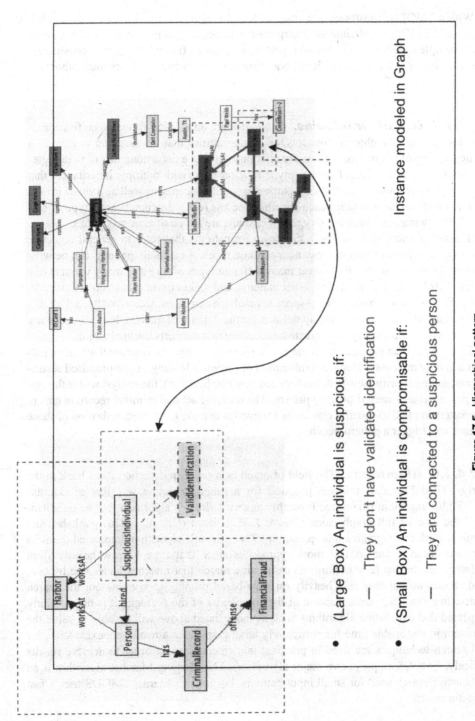

Figure 17.5. Hierarchical pattern.

- **(Large Box)** An individual is suspicious if:
  - They don't have validated identification
- **(Small Box)** An individual is compromisable if:
  - They are connected to a suspicious person

Instance modeled in Graph

Within TMODS, constraints are attached to individual patterns. Under the default be-havior of TMODS, constraints are interpreted as patterns used in a search. In the case of large, complex searches that may be repeated, it is more efficient to compile constraints. The built-in compiler generates Java code from constraints and compiles them automati-cally.

17.4.1.5. Use of Ontologies.

Ontologies are an explicit formal specification of how to represent the objects, concepts, and other entities that are assumed to exist in a particular area of interest, as well as the relationships that exist among them.[7] Ontologies can be thought of as a set of type–subtype relationships (with multiple inheritance) that define a classification hierarchy for a particular set of concepts, as well as a set of invari-ants about what characteristics each specific type has (e.g., "Mammals are a type of ani-mal," "Every mammal breathes oxygen," "Humans are a type of mammal," etc.).

The use of ontologies in TMODS allows for patterns that refer to general object or event types, instead of specific instances of those types. As a result, patterns can be writ-ten very generally, so that they cover many different types of threat or many variants of a threat. This lets the analyst define fewer patterns, and makes those patterns more flexible. For performance purposes, domain-specific ontologies are used. Occasionally, a TMODS user can use an ontology previously defined for the domain of interest, but it is necessary to work with a domain expert to create an ontology that supports the application.

Figure 17.6 is an example from the counter-terrorism domain. Instead of writing a pat-tern that only matches a specific combination of activities leading to compromised securi-ty (and having to write new patterns for each new combination), the analyst writes the sin-gle *generic compromised security* pattern. The criminal act and criminal record events in the pattern are tied to specific classes in a terrorism ontology. Any specialization of those classes will trigger a pattern match.

17.4.1.6. Algorithms.

The field of graph isomorphism detection dates back to the early 1970s. The most relevant proposal for a general solution was that of Berztiss (1973); his algorithm performed favorably against Ullman's algorithm, but he only han-dled the case of full graph isomorphism. J. R. Ullman (Ullman, 1976) published the seminal work in subgraph isomorphism in 1976. Ullman's algorithm dominated the field for two decades, and in fact most approaches since that time borrow heavily from Ullman, first in that they perform an exhaustive search that matches nodes one by one, and second in that they rely heavily on edge-based pruning to winnow out the search space. In a practical sense, because of the complexity of the problem, it is not currently expected that exhaustive algorithms such as those listed above will be able to solve the problem in reasonable time for particularly large graphs. As a result, nonexhaustive, lo-cal search techniques are used in practical implementations in order to achieve results quickly. TMODS employs two major algorithms. The Merging Matches algorithm is an exhaustive search used for small input patterns. For larger patterns, TMODS uses a fast genetic search.

17.4.1.7. Merging Matches.

Merging Matches is a novel algorithm to search for matches with small to medium-sized input patterns. It is a complete search; that is, the

---

[7]http://dictionary.reference.com/search?q=ontology.

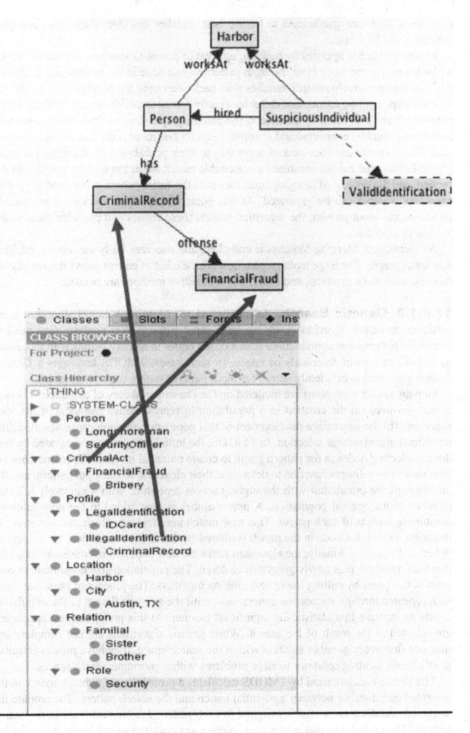

Figure 17.6. Subset of a terrorist ontology.

matches it finds are guaranteed to be the best matches possible. Any other potential matches must be worse.

Merging Matches operates by building up a list of potential matches. The initial entries to the list match one node from the input pattern to one node in the pattern graph. The algorithm then iteratively merges matches with each other until the best matches are found. At each step, any two entries that differ by exactly one node are combined if all the nodes they match are connected by an edge in the pattern graph. The resulting entry is guaranteed to be internally connected and to contain exactly one more node than either of its parents. These entries are then ranked according to their probability of matching the input graph. Entries that cannot constitute a reasonable match under the best circumstances are pruned, and the process of merging continues until the entire pattern is matched or no new candidate matches can be generated. At this point, if any of the entries are reasonably similar to the input pattern, the algorithm selects these entries and provides them to the analyst to examine.

As mentioned, Merging Matches is complete, and executes fairly quickly for medium size input graphs. For large input graphs, however, the list of entries grows too rapidly for this approach to be practical, and other, less exhaustive methods are needed.

17.4.1.8. Genetic Search. As mentioned, the Merging Matches algorithm is insufficient to handle searches involving large input patterns. Yet analysts may need to search for patterns that contain more than a dozen nodes in activity graphs with thousands of nodes and tens of thousands of edges. In such cases, TMODS leverages a *Genetic Search* algorithm to efficiently search for input patterns within the activity graph.

Genetic search algorithms are modeled on the Darwinian theory of evolution. This approach involves (a) the creation of a population of representative members of the state space and (b) the successive development of this population through processes modeling reproduction and natural selection. In TMODS, the initial population is generated by randomly selecting nodes in the pattern graph to create potential matches. These matches are then ranked by a fitness function to determine their closeness to the input pattern, and the members of the population with the highest scores reproduce with a randomly selected member of the general population. A new member is next added to the population by combining aspects of each parent. This new match may undergo stochastic variation, or mutation, in which a node in the match is altered so that it does not reflect the content of either of the parents. Finally, the algorithm ranks the new population, consisting of all the previous members plus newly generated children. The population size is maintained constant at this point by culling the lowest ranking members. The process of reproduction is then repeated through successive generations, until the average fitness of the population ceases to increase in a statistically significant manner. At this point, the best specimens are selected as the result of the search. While genetic algorithms are not complete and may not find every possible solution within the search space, they have proven effective at efficiently locating solutions to large problems within enormous search spaces.

The fitness measure used by TMODS calculates a probability of a match based on the weighted edit distance between a potential match and the search pattern. To compute the weighted edit distance, a cost is assigned to each node, edge, and attribute in the search pattern. The probability that a generated pattern matches the search input is a ratio between the total cost of all nodes, edges, and attributes and the cost of those elements that the potential match lacks. Some attributes in the search pattern may be designated as required, in which case the probability of a match is zero unless these necessary attributes are present.

Distributed Genetic Search. TMODS distributes its genetic search over several processes to increase the speed and completeness of the search. TMODS assigns a limited search domain to each process, potentially running on different computer systems. These limited domains require a particular node or nodes in the pattern graph to be included at a fixed position in any potential match. Each process then performs its own genetic search on the limited domain, and if any of its candidate matches are reasonably similar to the input pattern, the process returns its findings. Once all subordinate processes have reported their results, TMODS passes on all acceptable matches to the analyst.

This distributed approach performs several searches at once on multiple processors, delivering final results much faster. The efficiency of TMODS' search is further enhanced by using a reduced candidate set (the set of possible matches to a pattern), which allows the exclusion of many possible matches without an actual search, so that considerably less computation will have to be performed.

17.4.1.9. Candidate Set Reduction Optimization. When searching for a pattern match within a graph, there are many possible combinations that do not need to be considered. In general, it is only worthwhile to search for matches that are connected— that is, matches for which there exists at least one path between any two constituent nodes. At each stage of the search, TMODS uses a reduced candidate set constructed to preserve this principle of connectedness. Once a potential match contains one node, the search only needs to consider as possibilities those nodes that are reachable from the matched node within a number of steps less than or equal to the maximum distance between any two nodes in the pattern. In practice, this optimization greatly improves the efficiency of the search without a significant loss in completeness.

17.4.2. Other TMODS Capabilities

While the core technologies of TMODS are stable and mature, new facilities continue to be added to complement TMODS ability to detect threatening patterns. Two major recent additions are statistical classification and analysis based on Social Network Analysis (SNA) and pattern layering.

17.4.2.1. Social Network Analysis. *Social Network Analysis* (SNA) is a technique used by intelligence analysts to detect abnormal patterns of social interaction (Coffman and Marcus, 2004; Scott, 2000; Wasserman and Faust, 1994). SNA arose out of the study of social structure within the fields of social psychology and social anthropology in the 1930s (Wasserman and Faust, 1994). It can be used to investigate kinship patterns, community structure, or the organization of other formal and informal networks such as corporations, filial groups, or computer networks.

Social network analysts typically represent the social network as a graph. In its simplest form, a social network graph (sometimes called an "activity graph") contains nodes representing actors (generally people or organizations) and edges representing relationships or communications between the actors. Analysts then reason about the individual actors and the network as a whole through graph-theoretic approaches, including SNA metrics that take different values at different nodes in the graph. This approach is similar to and compatible with TMODS other graph matching technology.

Central problems in SNA include determining the functional roles of individuals and organizations in a social network (e.g., gatekeepers, leaders, followers) and diagnosing network-wide conditions. For example, studies of interlocking directorships among leading corporate enterprises in the 1960s have shown that banks were the most central enterprises in the network.

TMODS SNA Capabilities. TMODS has been developed to identify characteristics that differentiate normal social networks from those used for illicit activity. Many of these characteristics are quantifiable with multivariate SNA metrics. For example, in legitimate organizations, there are usually many redundant communication paths between individuals. If an individual wants to get information to A, they may contact her directly, or go through B or C. Covert organizations generally do not have many paths of communications flow between individuals. Redundant paths lead to increased risk of exposure or capture. Redundancy is one of many properties that TMODS can recognize, represent, and exploit.

TMODS can compute the functional roles of individuals in a social network and diagnose network-wide conditions or states. Different individuals in a social network fulfill different roles. Examples of intuitive roles include leaders, followers, regulators, "popular people," and early adopters. Other roles that are less intuitive but are still common in both normal and covert/abnormal social networks include bridges, hubs, gatekeepers, and pulse-takers.

Much of our work in SNA metrics focuses on distilling complex aspects of a communications graph into simple numerical measures, which can then be used with traditional statistical pattern classification techniques to categorize activity as threatening or nonthreatening. TMODS can then measure communications efficiency and redundancy, identify which participants are 'central' to the communication structure, and single-out those groups of participants that form tightly knit cliques. SNA metrics are a unique approach to quantifying and analyzing human interpersonal (or online) communication that provide TMODS with novel detection abilities.

17.4.2.2. Event Detection via Social Network Analysis. The unifying goal of the various applications of SNA described above is to quickly differentiate between threatening and nonthreatening activity. These approaches use abnormal group structure, behavior, and communication patterns as the indicators of threatening activity. In some cases, static SNA is sufficient to characterize a group's structure as normal or abnormal. In other cases, dynamic SNA is required to differentiate between normal and abnormal group structure and behavior, based on a group's evolution over time. These approaches require user-specified *a priori* models (which are often but not always available) of both normal and abnormal behavior; equivalently, they require labeled training data. This places them in the general category of supervised learning algorithms. When we do not have a sufficient amount of labeled training data we must use unsupervised learning techniques, which perform the task of *event detection* (also called *anomaly detection*).

The goal of SNA event detection is to flag any significant changes in a group's communication patterns, without requiring users to specify *a priori* models for normal or abnormal behavior. Where supervised learning techniques perform the task of "Tell me which groups behave in this particular way," SNA event detection performs the task of "Tell me if any group begins to significantly change its behavior." As described in the sections above and in many counter-terrorism studies, the lead-up to major terrorist events is almost always preceded by significant changes in the threat group's communication behavior. SNA event detection finds these internal indicators and gives the intelligence analyst the chance to alert decision-makers in time for preemptive action.

The application of SNA event detection to predicting terrorist activity is very similar to the application of SNA event detection to detecting anomalous digital network behavior. SNA event detection begins by tracking the SNA metric values of various groups over time, just as it is done for dynamic SNA. The left half of Figure 17.7 shows two visualization of multivariate SNA metric values gathered over time for one actor. The figure shows a time-series view and a scatter-plot view.

As information is gathered over time, TMODS automatically builds its own models of normal behavior for the groups being observed, without requiring user input. This is currently done using online clustering algorithms, including the Leader–Follower algorithm and variations of K-Means Clustering. Future work could include the use of neural networks or other machine learning techniques to build these behavior models. The current behavior models group observed metric values into clusters, each of which describe a normal "mode" of operation for the group.

The right half of Figure 17.7 shows SNA metric values grouped into clusters (with cluster membership designated by color). This is TMODS' model of behavior for one or more groups. The figure also shows five points (circled) that, while assigned to clusters, do not fit those assignments well. These are the anomalies we are looking for—a previously unmanifested communication pattern that may indicate internal threats.

There are a number of approaches for deciding if an alert should be raised, given observations and a learned behavior model. If an online clustering algorithm like Leader–Follower is used, any attempt by the algorithm to introduce a new cluster (after an initial training period) is, by definition, the algorithm deciding that the existing model does not fit the newly observed data, and it is thus an anomaly. We could also reason about the data's distance from existing cluster centers. We could fit Gaussian (or other) probability densities to the clusters and declare that any points falling outside X% of the volume of the combined probability density surface are anomalous. This particular approach has the advantage that we can explicitly set our expected false alarm rate. Neural networks, in contrast, return an explicit normal or anomalous characterization directly.

Supervised learning algorithms are used when we have labeled training data, and unsupervised learning algorithms are used when we have unlabeled training data. TMODS has capabilities for both, allowing us to perform semi-supervised learning, often called learning with a critic. As TMODS raises detections via the unsupervised event detection algorithms, the analyst will make a case-by-case decision on whether the detection is a true or false positive. This feedback can be incorporated in the event detection algorithms to tune or train them to improve their results. Ultimately, this set of case-by-case decisions and corresponding evidence will constitute a labeled training dataset, which can be used by our static and dynamic analysis methods.

SUMMARY

TMODS provides the intelligence analyst with a reliable mechanism to extract relevant data out of a flood of facts and relationships. Its novel capability to quickly and effectively locate patterns within data from multiple sources allows intelligence professionals to focus on analyzing potential threats without being overwhelmed by false alarms. Inexact matching keeps the analyst abreast of changing threats in a constantly shifting environment. In essence, TMODS helps the analyst with information overload and allows him to do his job more effectively and confidently. By combining *Graph Matching* techniques (such as *Inexact Matching* and *Merging Matches*) with *Social Network Analysis Models*

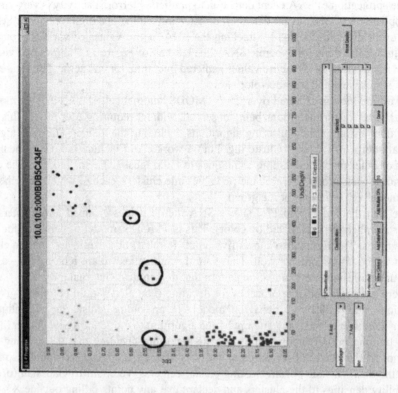

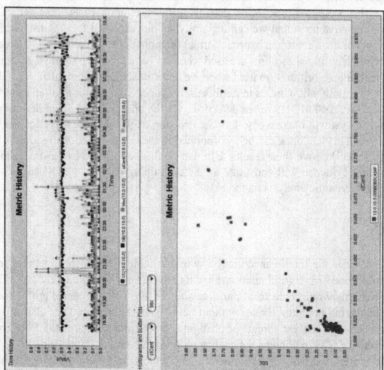

Figure 17.7. SNA Event detection (*left*) two views of SNA metric history (*right*) clustering and anomaly detection.

and *Genetic Algorithms,* TMODS provides the means to greatly improve situational awareness and threat identification.

Building upon the current work, we plan to model a wider range of terrorist and insurgent behavior, together with a framework for simulating these models. We also plan to develop the capability to automatically learn graph patterns and SNA metric signatures corresponding to the modeled behavior. These new capabilities will allow the analyst, policy-maker, and warfighter to react more quickly to potential threats, allowing for minimal loss of life on both sides.

REFERENCES

Berztiss, A. T. (1973). A backtrack procedure for isomorphism of directed graphs. *Journal of the ACM* **20**(3):365–377.

Coffman, T., Greenblatt, S., and, Marcus, S. (2004). Graph-based technologies for intelligence analysis. *Communications of the ACM* **47**(3):45–47.

Coffman, T., and Marcus, S. (2004). Pattern Classification in Social Network Analysis: A Case Study. *Proceedings of the 2004 IEEE Aerospace Conference,* March 6–13.

Cordella, L. P., Foggia, P., Sansone, C., and Vento, M. (2001). An improved algorithm for matching large graphs. In: *Proceedings of the 3rd IAPR-TC-15 International Workshop on Graph-Based Representations,* Italy, pp. 149–159.

Corneil, D. G., and Gotlieb, C. C. (1970). An efficient algorithm for graph isomorphism. *Journal of the ACM* **17**(1):51–64.

Diestel, R. (2000). *Graph Theory.* New York: Springer-Verlag.

LaPaugh, A. S., and Rivest, R. R. (1978). *The Subgraph Homeomorphism Problem.*

Marcus, S., and Coffman, T. (2002). *Terrorist Modus Operandi Discovery System 1.0: Functionality, Examples, and Value,* 21st Century Technologies internal publication.

Messmer, B. T. (1995). Efficient graph matching algorithms for preprocessed model graphs. Ph.D. thesis, Institut fur Informatik und Angewandte Matheatik, Universitat Bern, Switzerland.

Scott, J. (2000). *Social Network Analysis, A Handbook,* 2nd edition., London: Sage Publications.

Ullman. J. R. (1976). An algorithm for subgraph isomorphism. *Journal of the ACM* **23**(1):31–42.

Wasserman, S., and Faust, K. (1994). *Social Network Analysis: Methods and Applications.* New York: Cambridge University Press.

Chapter 18

Detecting Terrorist Activities in the Twenty-First Century: A Theory of Detection for Transactional Networks

Tom Mifflin, Chris Boner, Greg Godfrey, and Michael Greenblatt

18.1. INTRODUCTION

Detecting terrorist or insurgent operations is fundamentally different from detecting the operations of traditional military opponents. In the past, a credible opponent was associated with a particular country. The enemy had an array of military assets such as tanks and planes, uniformed troops, and localized bases of operation. Monitoring these military assets was the key to detecting threat activities. Traditionally, this has involved measuring radar or acoustic emissions, intercepting dedicated military communications, observing troop and weapons movements, and detecting chemical or radiological materials.

The fundamental unit of information for determining an enemy's activities was a contact or report, such as a radar return, an ELINT hit, or a sonar contact that emanated from the enemy's dedicated military assets. The requirement to anticipate the enemy's moves and the nature of the information led to the development of a theory of detection, tracking, and data association known as *data fusion*.

By contrast, today's terrorist enemy is fundamentally poor with respect to traditional military assets. They are not localized to a particular country or region. Most of their tangible assets are commercially available. The main asset that a terrorist or insurgent organization possesses is their network of terrorists or insurgents. The network enables terrorists to plan and communicate covertly, to recruit new members, to acquire assets and expertise, to move money and assets where needed, and to carry out attacks. Executing these tasks leaves *signatures* in data—structures of interrelated transactions and associations. Yet, terrorists tend to use the same media and infrastructure that are used by the general public, so these signatures are often buried in an immense sea of background *noise*—data about transactions from legitimate activities and associations that are not relevant to detecting threats.

Signatures constitute more than a simple trail of evidence to be followed. The *structure* of the network of data—how interrelated pieces of evidence fit together—contains much of the exploitable information. This differs dramatically from classical data fusion applications that process sensor reports or signals sequentially and assume conditional independence when fusing. In the structured, linked data environment of counter-terrorism, signal processing requires connecting interrelated pieces of data and distinguishing threat signatures from noise. This process is often referred to as *link analysis.*

Commercially available link analysis tools such as Analyst Notebook™ and Visual Links™ are useful visualization aids. They offer a suite of automated layout algorithms and network exploration features that help analysts to monitor known threat organizations, to extend and refine knowledge about their support networks, and to detect their threat activities. To be effective counter-terrorism tools, however, network data must be winnowed down carefully to, at most, thousands of links among hundreds of entities, most of which are relevant to detecting threat relationships and activities. Users of these tools are constrained by the amount of data they can view on a monitor, the degree to which threat signatures stand out from background noise, and the *signal-to-noise* ratio of the data—that is, the proportion of entities and links that are relevant to detecting threats.

Most transactional data sources today, however, are massive with very low signal-to-noise ratios. For example, James Bamford documented that NSA listening posts pick up tens of millions of communications *each hour,* including e-mails, faxes, data transfers, telephone calls, and other media (Bamford, 2001). Bank databases of financial transactions and phone company call records are also enormous and composed almost entirely of legitimate transactions. Link analysis tools of today that rely on network visualization cannot be applied to these massive data sources. New link discovery technologies are needed to extract threat signatures and relevant networks from the data. To be effective, these technologies must exploit differences between threat signatures and signature-like structures that arise from noise to efficiently explore massive amounts of data and to discriminate between threat and non-threat networks.

Optimizing performance—maximizing detections while minimizing false alarms—requires a theory of detection on structured, linked data. A mathematical theory of detection was developed and applied successfully to a variety of signal processing problems, including detecting objects using radar and sonar signals, speech recognition, image processing, detecting disorders using biomedical data, and detecting underground oil deposits using seismology. Each involves characterizing both signal and noise and deriving formulas to compute optimal detection statistics. For binary detection problems, Neyman and Pearson proved that the likelihood ratio is an optimal detection statistic (DeGroot, 1970; Neyman–Pearson Lemma). That is, deciding whether to call detections by comparing the value of the statistic to a threshold yields the maximum possible detection rate for the associated false alarm rate.

The mathematical investigations within this chapter were inspired by the following, somewhat vague, questions: Is it possible to detect signatures of threat activity within massive amounts of noisy, transactional data? How does this detection problem differ from more classical signal processing detection problems, which often assume conditional independence of the data (typically, signals or sensor reports)? What constitutes a mathematical theory of detection on structured, linked data?

A key component is that transactional "noise" differs fundamentally from the noise models typically used in classical signal processing applications. Complex patterns, even those that resemble planned activities by the enemy, can arise from noise. As the level of noise increases, the number of random occurrences of a particular pattern of transactions can grow exponentially, making false alarm rates unmanageable. Thus, as in most detection problems, simply understanding the nature of the transactional signal is not sufficient. To optimize the search for threat signatures and the discrimination between signal and noise, one must understand and model the transactional noise.

A thorough review of graph theory literature suggests that these questions have yet to be investigated by the research community. Members of the intelligence community describe massive transactional data sources with "low signal-to-noise ratio" and allude to the challenge of "connecting the dots," "finding a needle in a haystack," or "piecing together a needle from a stack of needle pieces." Our goal in this chapter is to derive a theory within which we precisely define these metaphors for detection in structured, linked data.

To derive a formal theory of detection for graph-like structures, we sought background noise models for which it could be tractable to derive formulas for detection statistics and to prove theorems that bound performance—the ability to discover "threat" network structures and to discriminate them from false alarm structures that arise from noise.

To illustrate the mechanics of the theory, we start by modeling transactional noise using the simple, but somewhat unrealistic, Erdös–Rényi random graph model $G(n, p)$. Even with this simple noise model, estimating the likelihood that a particular signature will arise from background noise can defy intuition. Section 18.2 illustrates counterintuitive phenomena for the $G(n, p)$ noise model. Section 18.3 builds the foundation for a theory of threat network detection for the $G(n, p)$ noise model. We present a closed-form expression for the likelihood ratio statistic, an optimal statistic to discriminate between networks of data that consist entirely of noise and those that include threat signatures as well. We generalize the likelihood ratio statistic formula to models in which some transactions remain unobserved or hidden.

Section 18.4 describes several more realistic network and transactional data models that have drawn the attention of the research community recently. These network models include the popular "small-world" networks, collaboration networks, and others that are more representative of real-world social networks. We define the most common network metrics and measures relevant to building models that reflect realism. Although no theory of detection exists currently for these more realistic models, we summarize several proven properties of these models that will provide a foundation for future detection research.

18.2. SUBGRAPH STRUCTURES EMERGING FROM NETWORK "NOISE"

The purpose of this section is to highlight characteristics and phenomena of transactional noise in a relatively simple context. We represent a set of transactional data as a simple graph in which edges are undirected, generic transactions between two entities. Using a standard random graph noise model, we can answer questions such as:

1. What graph structures rarely arise from background noise?
2. What graph structures commonly arise from background noise?
3. How does the occurrence rate of a graph structure vary with increasing noise?
4. What measures and statistics best characterize the structure of a graph for the purposes of
   (a) optimizing the strategy to search for instances of the graph in the data and
   (b) quantifying the difficulty of a particular detection problem?

While there are several standard random graph models, this section restricts the discussion to the Erdös–Rényi random graph model. Let $G(n, p)$ denote the model for generating a random graph among n entities in which each edge (of the $n(n-1)/2$ possible edges) is instantiated independently with probability p. An instantiation of $G(n, p)$ represents uncorrelated transactional noise.

In a counter-terrorism application, one might want to detect instances of a particular pattern of transactions that is believed to indicate enemy activity. In the context of this model, that goal translates into finding subgraphs of a particular type or pattern (to be mathematically rigorous, the goal is to find subgraphs in a particular isomorphism class). The pattern of transactions is analogous to a signature in a standard detection problem. The enemy's activities may have multiple signatures or indicators of its existence, each of which would be a candidate subgraph for which to search. The suitability of a candidate signature depends on the nature of the background noise transactions. For example, a subgraph that arises commonly from the noise would be a poor choice for a subgraph signature.

The following theorem by Paul Erdös, one of the seminal results of random graph theory, provides a formula for computing a statistic that quantifies the "rarity" of a subgraph of $G(n, p)$.

Theorem 18.1 (Erdös [Bollobás, 1998, pp. 218–219]). Let H be a subgraph with k vertices and $e(H)$ edges. The expected number of subgraphs of type H in a random graph $G = G(n, p)$ is

$$E[X_H(G)] = \frac{n_k}{a(H)} p^{e(H)} \qquad (18.1)$$

where n_k is the kth falling factorial $n(n-1)\cdots(n-k+1)$ and $a(H)$ is the size of the automorphism group of H.

The automorphism group of H, aut(H), is the set of permutations of vertices of H that preserve adjacency relations. The quotient $n_k/a(H)$ is the number of possible distinct subgraphs of type H among n vertices. Theorem 18.1 provides a closed-form expression for the expected number of subgraphs of a given type in terms of the number of possible subgraphs, the number of subgraph edges, and the edge probability.

Quantifying the "rarity" of a subgraph using the expected number from Theorem 18.1 leads to findings that may appear counterintuitive. For example, Figure 18.1 illustrates four simple subgraphs for the random graph model $G(n, p)$ with $n = 1000$ and $p = 1/500$.

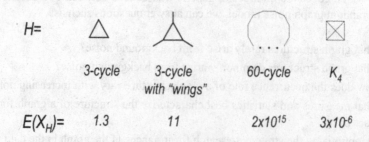

Figure 18.1. Expected number of subgraphs for $G(1000, 0.002)$.

It may seem surprising that the expected number of "winged" 3-cycles is greater than the expected number of 3-cycles since each subgraph of the former type must contain the latter. The missing insight is that each triangle may be a subgraph of multiple winged triangles. For $n = 1000$ and $p = 1/500$, the expected number of wings on each triangle vertex is two. Thus, the expected number of winged triangles for each distinct triangle is 2^3, or eight.

One might also guess (incorrectly) that the expected number of 60-cycles is less than the expected number of 3-cycles in an instantiation of $G(1000, 0.002)$ because the 60-cycle has a greater number of edges and the improbability (just 1 in 500) of each edge. However, the Erdös formula reveals that the expected number of 60-cycles is fifteen orders of magnitude greater than the number of 3-cycles. The clarifying insight is that the number of possible 60-cycles within a 1000-node graph, roughly 10^{177}, is far greater than the number of possible 3-cycles, roughly 10^8.

It is worthwhile to briefly discuss the role of symmetry in the frequency or rarity of particular types of subgraphs. Recall that the automorphism group of a subgroup H is the set of vertex permutations that preserve adjacency relations in H. For example, the automorphism group $aut(K_m)$ of a complete graph K_m is the symmetric group S_m with $m!$ elements. The automorphism group $aut(C_m)$ of an m-cycle C_m is the dihedral group D_m with $2m$ elements. The size of the automorphism group alone can greatly affect the frequency or rarity of a particular type of subgraph. In Figure 18.2, each subgraph has 75 edges and 75 vertices. Hence, the automorphism group size is the only factor that contributes to differences in the expected numbers of subgraphs in a random graph $G(1000, 0.002)$.

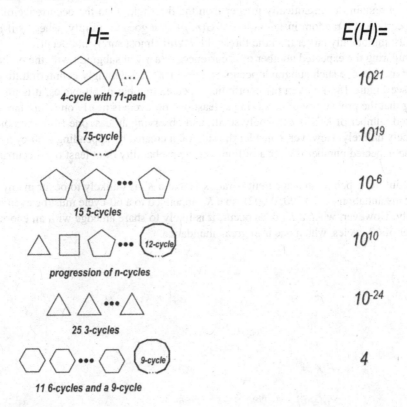

H=   *E(H)=*

4-cycle with 71-path 10^{21}

75-cycle 10^{19}

15 5-cycles 10^{-6}

progression of n-cycles 10^{10}

25 3-cycles 10^{-24}

11 6-cycles and a 9-cycle   4

Figure 18.2. Some graphs with 75 edges and 75 vertices and their expected number of occurrences in $G(1000, 0.002)$.

It is well known that for any finite group G, there exists a graph H with $aut(H) = G$. On the other hand, for large n, most subgraphs of a graph of order n will have a trivial automorphism group. Lauri and Scapellato (2003) provide a good reference additional information about graph automorphisms.

Another measure of "rarity" is the probability that at least one subgraph of a given type arises from background noise. Bollobás proved that the existence or nonexistence of a particular subgraph depends almost entirely on its maximum density.

Definition 18.1. The *maximum density* of a graph F is

$$m(F) = \max\left\{ \frac{e(H)}{v(H)} : H \subseteq F, v(H) > 0 \right\}$$

where $e(H)$ is the number of edges of H and $v(H)$ is the number of vertices of H.

Theorem 18.2 (Skokan, 2003, p. 56). For an arbitrary graph F with at least one edge,

$$\lim_{n \to \infty} P(G(n, p) \supseteq F) = \begin{Bmatrix} 0 \ if p = n^{-1/m(F)} \\ 1 \ if p \ ? \ n^{-1/m(F)} \end{Bmatrix}$$

Theorem 18.2 says that there is a threshold probability for each subgraph F. If the parameter p remains asymptotically greater than the threshold, then the occurrence of F is nearly certain in a random instantiation of $G(n, p)$ as n goes to infinity, whereas if p remains asymptotically larger than the threshold, F will almost surely not occur.

Comparing the expected number of occurrences of a given subgraph with the probability that at least one such subgraph occurs can also lead to seemingly counterintuitive results (see Figure 18.3). Given the enormous expected number of 60-cycles, it is not surprising that the probability of observing at least one 60-cycle is nearly one. Similarly, the expected number of K_4's is extremely small, and observing at least one from the noise is extremely unlikely. However, consider the subgraph created by appending a 60-cycle to a K_4. The expected number is over a billion, yet the probability of at least one occurring is nearly zero.

The intuition behind this apparent paradox is that a K_4 is unlikely to occur in any particular instantiation of $G(1000, 0.002)$, so a K_4 appended to a 60-cycle must be even more unlikely. However, when a K_4 does occur, it is likely to share an edge with an enormous number of 60-cycles, which occur in great abundance.

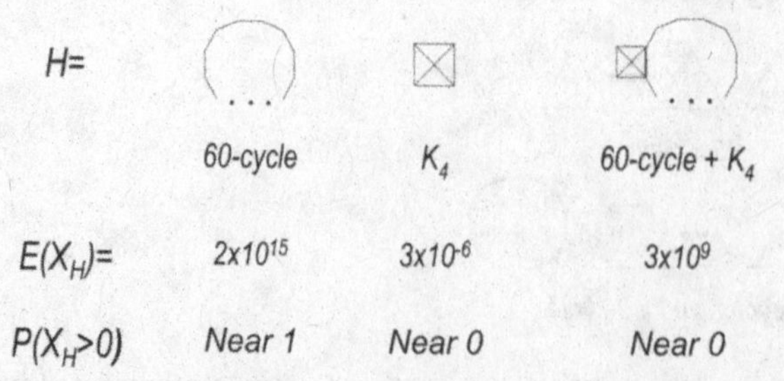

$H=$	60-cycle	K_4	60-cycle + K_4
$E(X_H)=$	2×10^{15}	3×10^{-6}	3×10^{9}
$P(X_H > 0)$	Near 1	Near 0	Near 0

Figure 18.3. Expected number and probability of existence for three subgraphs of G(1000, 0.002).

18.3. A THEORY OF DETECTION ON RANDOM GRAPHS

The previous section examined two metrics for quantifying how likely a complex structure is to arise from background noise transactions. This section extends these ideas to derive a closed-form expression for the optimal statistic for deciding whether a complex structure arose from simple background noise transactions or a threat activity.

How can we detect a network of insurgents or terrorists when their transactions are buried in a vast tangled mass of legitimate transactions? The Neyman–Pearson lemma says that for binary detection problems, the optimal detection statistic is the likelihood ratio,

$$\Lambda(evidence) = \frac{P(evidence \mid target\ present)}{P(evidence \mid target\ not\ present)} \quad (18.2)$$

A simple notion of an enemy network "target" is a pattern or subgraph of transactions associated with an enemy activity.

With the detection problem in mind, we formulate a new random graph model for a threat subgraph H embedded in a noise graph. We define the *prescribed subgraph process* $G_H(n, p)$ as follows: Choose a subgraph of type H at random from the set of all subgraphs of type H among n vertices. Then connect the remaining potential edges among the n vertices independently with probability p.

Viewing H as the target graph model, $G_H(n, p)$ is a model for simulating a single target instance in a noisy environment. In this model, the prescribed subgraph of type H is the only target; any other subgraph of type H arises through some combination of simple noise and the prescribed target subgraph.

We seek a criterion for determining whether an observed graph J was generated according to $G_H(n, p)$ or $G(n, p)$. That is, when does J constitute sufficient evidence to "call a detection" for the presence of a target? The optimal statistic on which to base this decision is the likelihood ratio

$$\Lambda_H(J) = \frac{P(J \mid target\ present)}{P(J \mid no\ target)} = \frac{P(Z = J \mid Z \sim G_H(n, p))}{P(Y = J \mid Y \sim G(n, p))} \quad (18.3)$$

The following theorem, proven by Boner, Godfrey, and Mifflin, is the first detection theory result in a structured, linked data environment.

Theorem 18.3 (Mifflin et al., 2004). Let $G = G(n, p)$ and let H denote the target graph. The likelihood ratio of an observed subgraph J is

$$\Lambda_H(J) = \frac{X_H(J)}{E[X_H(G)]} \quad (18.4)$$

where $X_H(J)$ is the number subgraphs of type H in J.

The denominator of Eq. (18.4) is the expected number of subgraphs of type H in an instance of the pure noise model $G = G(n, p)$. This can be computed from the Erdös equation (18.1). The numerator will be, in general, much harder to calculate. Determining whether there are any subgraphs of type H contained in an observed graph J is an instance of the subgraph isomorphism problem, which is known to be NP-complete (Gary and Johnson, 1979). However, algorithms exist that can solve the vast majority of these problems extremely efficiently. Still, counting the number of distinct subgraphs of type H contained in J could prove to be challenging.

To complicate matters further, actual intelligence collection has some unreliability. For example, not every transaction will be observed in the data. This can be modeled by applying an "observability filter" to each instantiated random graph. Let $G(n, p, q)$ and $G_H(n, p, q)$ denote models for generating random graphs by first generating instances of $G(n, p)$ or $G_H(n, p)$, respectively, and then selecting each edge independently with probability q. Theorem 18.4 generalizes Theorem 18.3 by deriving the likelihood ratio statistic $\Lambda_q(J)$ for an observed graph J when not all transactions are observed:

$$\Lambda_q(J) = \frac{P(Z = J \mid Z \sim G_H(n, p, q))}{P(Y = J \mid Y \sim G(n, p, q))}$$

Theorem 18.4 (Skokan 2003). The likelihood ratio statistic for discriminating between the random graph processes $G_H(n, p, q)$ and $G(n, p, q)$ is

$$\Lambda_q(J) = \sum_{J' \supseteq J} w(J') \Lambda(J') \qquad (18.5)$$

where the sum is taken over all supergraphs J' of J among the n vertices, $\Lambda(J')$ is the likelihood ratio for discriminating between $G_H(n, p)$ and $G(n, p)$, and

$$w(J') = \left(\frac{(1-q)p}{1-p} \right)^{e(J')-e(J)} \left(\frac{1-pq}{1-p} \right)^{\binom{n}{2}-e(J)} \qquad (18.6)$$

Skokan provides an algorithm for enumerating the supergraphs J' of any subgraph J and proves that their weights $w(J')$ sum to one (Skokan, 2003). One interpretation of this result is that the detection of a terrorist operation when not all transactions are observed requires hypothesis management. Each $J' \supset J$ represents a different hypothesis for the actual set of ground truth transactions.

Although Theorem 18.4 generalizes the likelihood ratio formula to partially observable transactional data, it still assumes a simple model of uncorrelated background noise. In the following sections, we describe a more general set of random graph models that address some of these shortcomings. No theory of detection currently exists for these models, but research attention has only started and a number of properties have been proven, some of which we summarize below.

18.4. BEYOND SIMPLE RANDOM GRAPH MODELS

Although the random graph model $G(n, p)$ has been shown to be tractable analytically, it is probably not sufficiently accurate for modeling an actual transactional network. The reason is that most real networks are highly nonrandom, so many of the results that hold for random graphs do not hold for real-life networks, and vice versa. For example, consider the degree distribution of vertices. The degree of a vertex in a graph is the number of other vertices that are connected to that vertex via an edge. For the random graph model $G(n, p)$, the degree distribution of the vertices can be shown to follow a binomial distribution, which is well-approximated by a Poisson distribution for large n. In fact, when n is large (as is typical in such models), the expected number of vertices with degree k is approximately $z^k e^{-z}/k!$. Here, z denotes the average degree of a vertex of a graph drawn from $G(n, p)$.

On the other hand, the degree distributions of real-life networks tend to follow power-law distributions. Namely, there are positive numbers A and b such that the expected fraction of graph vertices having degree k is approximately Ak^{-b}. That is, the total number of vertices of degree k is approximately $Ak^{-b}n$. Viewed as a function of k, $Ak^{-b}n$ behaves quite differently from $z^k e^{-z}/k!$. Namely, the function $Ak^{-b}n$ trails off as an inverse polynomial, while $z^k e^{-z}/k!$ increases as k increases from 0 to np, and then decreases exponentially for larger k.

Another measure that is noticeably different between random graphs and most real-life networks is the *clustering coefficient*. The clustering coefficient of a vertex measures the interrelatedness of its neighbors. It is the ratio of the number of edges that connect two neighbors of the vertex to the number of possible edges between neighbors of the vertex. The clustering coefficient of a graph is the average clustering coefficient across all vertices.

In a random graph, the probability that two neighbors of a vertex are connected is the same as the probability of an edge between any other pair of vertices. This, of course, is not true of most real-life networks. For example, two people with a common friend are more likely to be friends with each other than two randomly selected individuals. Similarly, two web pages that contain links to a third web page are more likely to contain links to each other than two web pages that do not have links to a common web page. In general, a high clustering coefficient means that there are multiple communities or groups in which members tend to be connected with many other members of that same group. A low clustering coefficient means that connections are more random, with $G(n, p)$ representing the extreme case.

In view of this, one might question the practical value of developing a theory of detection that assumes a random graph noise model $G(n, p)$. The hope, however, is that the methods and results derived using these simpler, more tractable models will guide the development of a theory of detection for more realistic network noise models. Although more work is needed, we believe that assuming the random graph noise model $G(n, p)$ is better than making no assumptions and ignoring altogether the potential impact and structure of network noise. Assuming a simple random graph noise model to guide the detection of threat networks is analogous to the common practice of assuming Gaussian white noise in more classical signal processing applications such as detecting and tracking submarines.

Moving toward more realistic network noise models, there are several methods for randomly generating graphs with degree distributions, clustering coefficients, and other graph metrics that are more consistent with real-world networks. Even though these models are quite general, the inductive procedures for defining these networks share a probabilistic structure with the $G(n, p)$ model. This similarity extends to ideas and approaches for analyzing the networks, and someday it may lead to a general theory of detection for these more realistic classes of models.

There is no "best" way to construct a general network model; one chooses a model based on the desired characteristics of the resulting network. Furthermore, this subject is still quite recent, so more useful probabilistic network constructions may be discovered. We start by describing one of the more popular models, namely the "small-world" network model proposed by Watts and Strogatz (1998).

18.4.1. Watts and Strogatz "Small-World" Models

The small-world model starts with the empirical observation that many large networks have a small diameter. This means that despite the size of the network, one may travel from any one vertex of the network to any other by traversing only a relatively small number of edges. This notion was popularized by the Guare play "Six Degrees of Separation," which suggested that an unattached person could find his or her soul mate through a sequence of at most six connections through friends, despite the enormous size of the graph whose vertices consist of all living human beings.

Watts and Strogatz (1998) construct small world graphs that have small diameters and large clustering coefficients, in accordance with the behavior of real networks. This is done as follows (see Figure 18.4). Start with n vertices, labeled as $1, 2, \ldots, n$, arranged clockwise in a circle, so that after vertex n we are back to vertex 1 again. Choose a number r, and join two vertices with an edge if their index difference modulo n is at most r. The expected clustering coefficient for this graph is $3(r - 1)/2(2r - 1)$, which goes to 3/4 (which is quite large) for large r. In contract, the expected diameter of this graph is $n/2r$, which goes to zero for large r. Thus, these small world graphs have a high clustering coefficient and low diameter, consistent with real-life network models.

Strogatz and Watts describe a procedure that reduces the diameter while increasing the randomness of the model (see Figure 18.5). First, select a fixed number p between 0 and 1. For each edge in the original graph, select a uniform random number between 0 and 1. If this random number is greater than p, then do nothing. If the random number is less than or equal to p, then remove the edge and connect two vertices chosen at random with an edge. This adds some randomness to the graph.

Setting $p = 0$ leads to the same nonrandom small world graph with which we started. Setting $p = 1$ leads to graphs that look more like Erdös–Rényi random graphs. Graphs generated with intermediate values of p fall between these two extremes of randomness. As p increases from zero, the diameter of the graph decreases quickly, a property shared by many real networks. In fact, introducing even a small number of random edges causes the diameter of the graph to decrease to $O(\log n)$.

Although the Strogatz–Watts model has a number of desirable characteristics, it has some disadvantages. Among these, the initial nonrandom graph has a very specific structure, and there is no particular reason to believe that real-life networks are derived from a base graph with such characteristics or from any particular base graph at all. Several interesting classes of networks have been proposed that have appropriate clustering coefficients, diameters, degree distributions, and so on, but are not restricted by a fixed initial

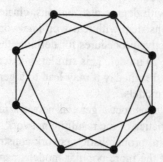

Figure 18.4. First stage of the Strogatz–Watts construction with $n = 8, r = 2$.

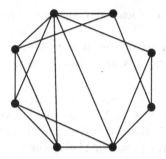

Figure 18.5. Strogatz–Watts model with $n = 8$, $r = 2$ after edge removals and replacements.

graph. Many of these networks are *scale-invariant;* that is, the network "looks" the same when viewed close-up as it does from a distance. Many networks, both natural and man-made, have some type of scale-invariance. For example, graphs whose degree distributions follow a power law exhibit scale-invariance, and some researchers use this property to define scale-invariance.

18.4.2. Albert–Barabási Inductive Models

Albert and Barabási initiated a set of popular nonrandom network models (Barabási and Albert, 1999). Although their original formulation was not defined with a mathematical rigor, more recent variations have done so. The idea is as follows. Start with a small, initial graph, typically constructed by hand, that has the degree distribution desired in a much larger network. The Albert–Barabási method enlarges the graph iteratively with minimal changes to the degree distribution. The end product is a graph that satisfies a power law with high probability, resembles the initial graph in many cases, and shares characteristics of real networks.

The details of the Albert–Barabási induction are as follows. Suppose that the initial graph G_0 has k vertices. Select a number m that is the number of new edges to be added at each stage of the process. At the nth stage, add a new vertex v_n and add m new edges from v_n to the other $k + n - 1$ vertices. Add the edges one at a time, where the probability of connecting vertex v_n with vertex v is proportional to one plus the degree of v at the $(n - 1)$st stage.

To make this procedure more intuitive, consider the network representation of the World Wide Web. Each vertex represents a website, and an edge between two vertices denotes a link between the two sites. As the World Wide Web expands and new links are created, websites with more links are more likely to get new links. It is reasonable to suggest that the rate at which a website gets more links is proportional to the number of links it already has. In relation to counter-terrorism, this has ties to the development of social networks. Those who have rich social networks tend to grow their networks faster than those who do not.

There is no guarantee that the degree distribution of the final graph will match that of the original graph G_0. It merely implies that as the graph grows, the degree distribution is unlikely to change significantly from stage to stage. In fact, it would be extremely difficult to set up any inductive procedure that matches the degree distribution exactly. The Albert–Barabási method provides a probabilistic method for constructing networks with degree distributions and other characteristics consistent with empirically observed networks.

The choice of the integer m determines the nature of the power law that the graph is highly likely to satisfy, as described by the following theorem:

Theorem 18.5 (Bollobás, Riordan, Spencer, Tusnady; Theorem 18.6 [Bornholdt and Schuster, 2001, Chapter 1]). Let $N(m, n, d)$ be the number of vertices of degree d in an Albert–Barabási graph with n vertices and with m edges being added at each stage. Then for each $\varepsilon > 0$, as n goes to infinity, the following holds with probability 1:

$$(1 - \varepsilon)\frac{2m(m + 1)}{d(d + 1)(d + 2)} \leq \frac{N(m, n, d)}{n} \leq (1 + \varepsilon)\frac{2m(m + 1)}{d(d + 1)(d + 2)} \qquad (18.7)$$

for each d with $0 \leq d + m \leq n^{1/15}$.

Next, we show an example of how these probabilistic Albert–Barabási models could be used to search for terrorists. Consider a network that models phone calls made by some segment of the population during some time period. Specifically, the vertices represent a collection of telephone numbers, and an edge connecting two of these vertices signifies a phone call made between the two associated telephone numbers during that specified time period. Suppose we are searching for a small terrorist cell of three members who communicate via three phone numbers in the graph. Suppose further that we have good reason to believe that those three phone numbers have been making calls only to each other and not to any other phone numbers in the graph. Geometrically, our search is for a triangle in the graph that is disconnected from the rest of the graph.

A few natural questions arise. For one, how common are such isolated triangles? Specifically, given the number of vertices and edges in the graph, what is the chance that there are only a few isolated triangles? If only a few are expected, then we could devise an algorithm to find them. On the other hand, if there was a 90% chance that there were more than 5000 triangles, then we should try to narrow down the graph further before attempting to find the terrorist cell. Fortunately, a number of theorems exist that help answer this question for the Albert–Barabási model. The first theorem states how many triangles one expects to appear in a graph on average (the issue of how many of these triangles are isolated must be addressed separately).

Theorem 18.6 (Bollobás; Theorem 18.14, Chapter 1 [Bornholdt and Schuster, 2003]). Let $G_{(m,n)}$ denote the Albert–Barabási model with n vertices and with m edges added at each stage, starting with an initial configuration with one vertex and one loop. The expected number of triangles in $G_{(m,n)}$ as n goes to infinity is given by

$$(1 + o(1))\frac{m(m - 1)(m + 1)}{48}(\log n)^3 \qquad (18.8)$$

The above theorem is good news for the terrorist search problem. It says that the number of triangles increases only as the cube of the logarithm of the number of nodes. The expected number of isolated triangles should be substantially smaller. The initial configuration with a single vertex and the loop is important, based on the following theorem:

Theorem 18.7 (Bollobás; Theorem 18.5, Chapter 1 [Bornholdt and Schuster, 2003]). Suppose $f(n)$, $n \geq 2$, is any integer valued function with $f(2) = 0$ and $f(n) \leq f(n + 1) \leq f(n) + 1$ for every $n \geq 2$, such that $f(n)$ goes to infinity as n goes to infinity. Then there is an initial configuration G_0 such that with probability one, the nth stage of the graph obtained by the Albert–Barabási procedure with $m = 2$ has $f(n)$ triangles for all sufficiently large n.

Another way of stating Theorem 18.7 is that any increasing integer function that increases more slowly than $f(n) = n$ is a possible number of triangles for an Albert–Barabási model with $m = 2$, for sufficiently large values of n. For example, one could have n^a triangles for any $a \leq 1$, as well as $(\log n)^b$ for any $b > 0$. In fact, one could even have $6n^a (\log n)^b + 2n^c (\log n)^d$ triangles for $a \leq 1$, $c \leq 1$ if desired. Keep in mind that while unusual configurations can occur, they may rely on an unnatural initial configuration G_0. Theorem 18.7 illustrates the flexibility of the Albert–Barabási model by saying that one can fit the Albert–Barabási model to give the correct number of triangles for any network of interest.

Another natural question to ask is whether analogues to Theorem 18.6 exist for subgraphs other than triangles. For example, consider modeling a terrorist cell as a collection of vertices all connected to each other, one of which (the "leader") is connected to the outside. Is there a way to count the expected number of these configurations for an Albert–Barabási graph? There is a general procedure for counting graphs for the Albert–Barabási model $G_{(m,n)}$. However, it requires a complicated inductive procedure and explicit results are hard to come by. Even when $m = 1$, things are difficult (see Theorem 18.13 [Bornholdt and Schuster, Chapter 1]). However, there is a generalization of Theorem 18.6 for counting k-cycles for any k. Recall that a k-cycle is the graph where k vertices are arranged in a circle and each vertex is connected to two neighbors.

Theorem 18.8 (Bollobás; Theorem 18.15 [Bornholdt and Schuster, 2003, Chapter 1]). Let $k \geq 3$ be fixed. The expected number of k-cycles in $G_{(m,n)}$ is of the form

$$(1 + o(1))C_{m,k}(\log n)^k \tag{18.9}$$

as n goes to infinity with $m \geq 2$ fixed. Here $C_{m,k}$ is a positive constant such that $C_{m,k} \sim m^k$ as m goes to infinity.

The graph models $G_{(m,n)}$ also satisfy desirable small-world properties, including that $G_{(m,n)}$ is usually connected and has an explicit bound on its diameter:

Theorem 18.9 (Bollobás; Theorem 18.18 [Bornholdt and Schuster, 2003, Chapter 1]). Fix an integer $m \geq 2$ and a positive real number ε. Then as n goes to infinity, the probability that $G_{(m,n)}$ is connected goes to 1. Furthermore, for n sufficiently large we also have

$$(1 - \varepsilon) \log n / \log(\log n) \leq \text{diam}(G_{(m,n)}) \leq (1 + \varepsilon) \log n / \log(\log n) \tag{18.10}$$

Heuristically, this says that the diameter of the typical $G_{(m,n)}$ grows slightly slower than $\log n$ as n gets big, so that diameters above a few dozen will be rare when the number of vertices is comparable to that of real networks.

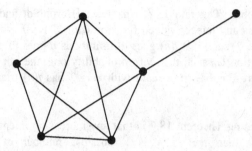

Figure 18.6. Graph representation of a terrorist cell.

Another virtue of the graphs $G_{(m,n)}$ is the wide range of possible clustering coefficients for different values of m:

Theorem 18.10 (Bollobás; Theorem 18.12, Chapter 1 in [Bornholdt and Schuster, 2003]). Let $m \geq 1$ be fixed. The expected value of the clustering coefficient $C(G_{(m,n)})$ of $G_{(m,n)}$ satisfies the following, as n goes to infinity:

$$E(C(G_{(m,n)}): \quad \frac{m-1}{8} \frac{(\log n)^2}{n} \tag{18.11}$$

18.4.3 Bender–Canfield Models

There is another probabilistic way of constructing realistic graphs that is markedly different from the Albert–Barabási model. This method has been described a few times in the literature, but its earliest appearance appears to be from Bender and Canfield (1978). In this model, one specifies in advance a vector k such that each element k_i will be the degree of the vertex v_i, for $i = 1$ to n. Frequently, one chooses k_i by sampling the desired degree distribution. Next, assign to each vertex v_i a total of k_i "stubs". A stub signifies the end of an edge that will go from vertex v_i to one of the other vertices. Now, connect the stubs to each other at random. The result is a probabilistically-generated graph that has the exact degree distribution specified in advance. The only requirement on the k_i is that their sum is even, so no stubs will remain unmatched at the end. Notice that this construction allows a vertex to connect to itself and permits more than one edge to connect the same pair of vertices (the fraction of such anomalous edges is typically small).

Newman describes several interesting consequences of the Bender–Canfield construction (Bornholdt and Schuster, 2003, Chapter 2), some of which are made mathematically rigorous. For example, there is an explicit formula for the expected number of vertices that can be reached from a particular vertex by moving through exactly two edges. This is known as the second neighbor problem, the results of which can lead to asymptotic formulas for the expected clustering coefficient as the number of vertices goes to infinity.

Let p_k denote the probability that a vertex has degree k. Choosing one of the n vertices at random, the expected number of vertices that can be reached starting at that vertex and traversing exactly m distinct edges (asymptotically as $n \to \infty$) (Bornholdt and Schuster, 2003, Chapter 2.2) is

$$z_1 = \langle k \rangle = \sum_k k p_k$$

$$z_2 = \langle k^2 \rangle - \langle k \rangle = \sum_k k^2 p_k - \sum_k k p_k = \sum_k k(k-1)p_k \qquad (18.12)$$

$$z_m = \frac{\langle k^2 \rangle - \langle k \rangle}{\langle k \rangle} z_{m-1} = \frac{z_2}{z_1} z_{m-1} = \left(\frac{z_2}{z_1}\right)^{m-1} z_1 = \frac{z_2^{m-1}}{z_1^{m-1}}$$

Note that the random graph model $G(n, p)$ can be viewed as a special case of the Bender–Canfield model. Namely, when constructing a Bender–Canfield graph, one can choose the degrees k_i by taking a random sample from the binomial degree distribution of the vertices of $G(n, p)$. The result is a randomly selected $G(n, p)$.

18.4.4. Collaboration Networks

Newman has made many other recent contributions to the science of networks (Newman, 2003; Newman and Park, 2003), including networks with arbitrary degree distribution, social network models and networks for modeling epidemics. Another contribution has been a systematic study of "collaboration networks," which are bipartite graphs with the top vertices representing groups and the bottom vertices representing individuals. Figure 18.7 illustrates a collaboration network and the projected unipartite graph; this is an adaptation of Figure 18.1 in Newman and Park (2003).

Collaboration networks are useful for group detection problems, and they have provided useful analyses of companies and their boards of directors and movies and their casts. In terms of random graph characteristics, the projected unipartite graph associated with a collaboration network typically has a higher clustering coefficient than Erdös–Rényi random graph models.

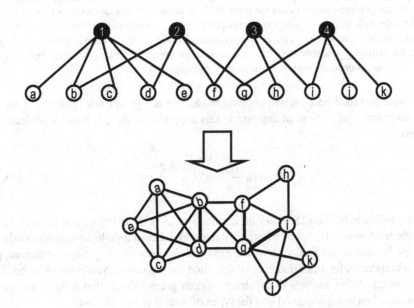

Figure 18.7. A collaboration network and unipartite projection.

18.4.5. Other Probability Network Models

There have been various other models devised to deal with specific cases, or to deal with more general scenarios than the ones typically used for the Albert–Barabási or Bender–Canfield models. One generalization of the Albert–Barabási model is the Buckley–Osthus model (Buckley and Osthus, 2004), which is also an inductive model. The Albert–Barabási model adds a new vertex v_n at the nth stage and connects m new edges to v_n, where the probability of connecting an existing vertex v_k to v_n is proportional to $\deg(v_k) + 1$.

The Buckley–Osthus model also adds a new vertex v_n at the nth stage and connects m new edges to v_n. However, the probability of connecting an existing vertex v_k to v_n is proportional to $\deg(v_k) + c_k m$. The constant c_k can be viewed as the "attractiveness" or "pull" of vertex v_k. Often the constant c_k is assumed to be independent of k. If $m = 1$ and $c_k = 1$ for all k, then the model reduces to the Albert–Barabási graph $G_{(1,n)}$. Buckley and Osthus also show that their model obeys a power law and thus is a reasonable model of real networks (Buckley and Osthus, 2004).

Another interesting network model is the copying model of Kumar, Raghavan, Rajagopalan, Sivakumar, Tomkins, and Upfal (Kumar et al., 2000), excerpted below:

> The linear growth copying model is parameterized by a copy factor $0 < \alpha < 1$ and a constant out-degree $d \geq 1$. At each time step, one vertex u is added, and u is then given d out-links for some constant d. To generate the out-links, we begin by choosing a "prototype" vertex p uniformly from the old vertices. The ith out-link of u is then chosen as follows. With probability α, the destination is chosen uniformly at random from the old vertices, and with the remaining probability the out-link is taken to be the ith out-link of p. Thus, the prototype is chosen once in advance. The d out-links are chosen by α-biased independent coin flips, either randomly from the old vertices or by copying the corresponding out-link of the prototype.
>
> The intuition behind this model is the following. When an author decides to create a new web page, the author is likely to have some topic in mind. The choice of prototype represents the choice of topic—larger topics are more likely to be chosen. The Bernoulli copying events reflect the following intuition: a new viewpoint about the topic will probably link to many pages "within" the topic (i.e., pages already linked to by existing resource lists about the topic), but will also probably introduce a new spin on the topic, linking to some new pages whose connection to the topic was previously unrecognized.

They show that the linear growth copying model obeys a power law. Namely, if $N_{n,r}$ denotes the number of vertices of degree r in this model when the graph has n vertices, then we have

$$\lim_{n \to \infty} \frac{N_{n,r}}{n} = C_\alpha r^{-\frac{2-\infty}{1-\infty}} \tag{18.13}$$

The models in Section 18.4 play an important role in the development of realistic, yet tractable models of terrorist or insurgency networks. Being able to compute directly and put tight bounds on metrics, such as the expected diameter or clustering coefficient, provides a foundation for a future theory of detection for more realistic networks. In addition, these metrics allows analysts to construct random graph models that reflect the types of operational data being observed and the types of threats to be addressed.

SUMMARY

Countering threats posed by today's adversaries requires new link discovery technologies that can process massive amounts of structured, linked data to extract threat signatures and to discriminate between threat and non-threat networks of data. To do so optimally requires a theory of detection that establishes optimal detection statistics and explicit formulas for these statistics. The results in this chapter build a foundation for a theory of detection using simple random graph noise models, just as signal processing applications started years ago assuming unrealistic Gaussian white noise. A general theory of detection for transactional networks is in its research infancy, but we have identified several, more realistic network noise models to which a mathematical theory of detection can and should be extended.

REFERENCES

Bamford, J. (2001). *Body of Secrets*. New York: Random House.

Barabási, A.-L., and Albert, R. (1999). Emergence of scaling in random networks. *Science* **286**:509–512.

Bender, E. A., and Canfield, E. R. (1978). The asymptotic number of labeled graphs with given degree sequences. *Journal of Combinatorial Theory A* 24:296–307.

Bollobás, B. (1998). *Modern Graph Theory*, New York: Springer.

Bornholdt, S., and Schuster, H. G. (eds.). (2003). *Handbook of Graphs and Networks, from the Genome to the Internet*. New York: Wiley-VCH.

Buckley, P. G., and Osthus, D. (2004). Popularity based random graph models leading to a scale-free degree sequence. *Discrete Mathematics* **282**:53–68.

DeGroot, M. (1970). *Optimal Statistical Decisions*. New York: McGraw-Hill.

Garey, M., and Johnson, D. (1979). *Computers and Intractability: A Guide to the Theory of NP-Completeness*. New York: W. H. Freeman and Company.

Kay, S. (1998). *Fundamentals of Statistical Signal Processing: Detection Theory*, Vol. II. Prentice Hall.

Kumar, R., Raghavan, P., Rajagopalan, S., Sivakumar, D., Tomkins, A., and Upfal, E. (2000). Stochastic models for the web graph. *FOCS*.

Lauri, J., and Scapellato, R. (2003). *Topics in Graph Automorphisms and Reconstructions*, Cambridge, England: Cambridge University Press.

Mifflin, T., Boner, C., Godfrey, G., and Skokan, J. (2004). A random graph model for terrorist transactions. *2004 IEEE Aerospace Conference Proceedings*, March 7–12.

Newman, M. E. J. (2003). The structure and function of complex networks. *SIAM Review* **45**:167–256.

Newman, M. E. J., and Park, J. (2003). Why social networks are different from other types of networks. *Phys. Rev. E* **68**:036122.

Skokan, J. (2003). Likelihood ratio for random graphs with imperfect observability. Metron working paper.

Watts, D. J. (1999). *Small Worlds: The Dynamics of Networks Between Order and Randomness*. Princeton, NJ: Princeton University Press.

Watts, D. J., and Strogatz, S. H. (1998). Collective dynamics 'of small-world' networks. *Nature* **393**:440–442.

Chapter 19

Social Network Analysis via Matrix Decompositions

D. B. Skillicorn

19.1. INTRODUCTION

Social network analysis (SNA) explores the structure of groups in human society by (a) modeling individuals, places, and objects as nodes of a graph, and (b) placing links between nodes to represent relations among them. In the simplest case, all of the nodes represent the same entities—for example, people—and the edges represent a simple relation, perhaps that the two people involved know each other. From such a graph, we could estimate how sociable each person is from the number of other people that they know. If we change the graph so that an edge represents the flow of information from one person to another (perhaps a graph based on e-mails among the individuals), then the graph provides a sense of how information flows: Do most people pass information on to a few others, or are there a small number of people who are almost totally responsible for communication? Does the flow of information match the supposed structure of the group, or does it somehow crosscut it? If the nodes describe different kinds of entities, then there can be a wider range of connections. For example, if the nodes represent individuals and bank accounts, then we can connect individuals to other individuals as before, but we can also connect individuals to bank accounts which they have used. Bank accounts used by more than one person create an *indirect* link between the individuals which can often be revealing when there is no corresponding direct link. This kind of exploration of graph structures is sometimes also called *Link Analysis* or *Network Mining*.

Several different kinds of analyses can be carried out on such a graph. Important subgroups can be identified because their members are all connected to one another (in graph terms, they form a clique). People of importance can be identified because they appear naturally in the "middle" of a graph (centrality). Particular substructures of interest can also be identified—for example, communication chains or unusual combinations of people and objects (Jensen and Neville, 2003; Krebs, 2002; van Meter, 2002).

Social network analysis has been applied to both terrorist and criminal networks. For example, Baker and Faulkner (1993) relate location in a criminal network to length of eventual sentence in an analysis of fraud in the electrical industry; Sageman uses SNA to validate his division of al Qaeda members into four classes: leadership, core Arab, South-East Asian, and Maghreb (Sageman, 2004).

19.1.1. The Challenge

Transnational terrorism groups present a new problem for the countries against whom their actions are directed, usually characterized as *asymmetric* or *fourth-generation warfare* (Shultz and Vogt, 2004). Unlike the case of military conflicts between nations, such terrorist groups have a membership that is hard to define, few visible fixed targets, the ability to operate across borders relatively freely, and independent sources of funding, removing indirect ways to pressure them via sponsors. The resources that must be expended by both sides differ by several orders of magnitude: Around 25 men and expenditures estimated to be only ~$500,000 were sufficient for al Qaeda to attack the World Trade Center. In contrast, U.S. spending in response is at least $100 billion (Corbin, 2002; United States Government, 2004).

Counter-terrorism efforts face corresponding difficulties in attempting to detect and preempt attacks. A metaphor suggested for al Qaeda is that it is a venture capitalist for terror (Gunaratna, 2003); proposals for attacks are brought to the leadership, and those that are approved receive support in the form of training and financing. This means that attackers may have only minimal contact with the main part of the organization until quite close to the time an attack is mounted. This suggests that *every* contact with known al Qaeda members, no matter how fleeting, needs to be treated as significant. The transnational nature of al Qaeda also makes it clear that a profile of a "typical" al Qaeda member does not exist—and there is some evidence that the group is trying to recruit members who appear even less like a hypothetical Salafist terrorist.

Al Qaeda is only the most visible of a number of movements whose grievance extends beyond a single geographical region, whose aim is not simple visibility for their cause, and who have discovered that nation-states are vulnerable to asymmetric warfare attacks. Counter-terrorism technologies will, sadly, be of use even when al Qaeda has been defeated.

19.1.2. Social Network Analysis Technology

The techniques of social network analysis have some limitations as tools to explore the graphs that model social groups. First, it is not straightforward to extract "higher-order" information—that is, information that is associated not with a connected pair of objects but with a larger set. For example, suppose we consider a particular node of the graph, and its neighbors two steps away. These neighbors may be connected to each other or they may not, but in many cases the difference might be important. See, for example, Priebe's use of scan statistics in the graph of Enron e-mails (Priebe, 2005). Social network techniques do not easily distinguish these different possibilities.

Second, it is not easy to introduce and use information that is not naturally associated with edges of the graph—for example, demographic information. Suppose that we know the ages of people who are represented by nodes of the network. There is no natural way to discover patterns such as the fact that people of the same age are more likely to be connected.

Third, social network analysis typically depends on the *precise* connection structure of the graph, so that small changes in the graph may produce large changes in its properties. This is a problem because the graph that is analyzed is almost never the "real" graph—some edges are missing because some information was never captured (or perhaps was wrong).

In this chapter, we show to how to use the technology of *matrix decompositions* to extract more information from a graph than standard social analysis tools are able to do. We use three such decompositions:

1. Singular value decomposition (SVD). Although SVD is commonly used for dimension reduction, we use it both as a graph partitioning tool (an approach known as *spectral graph partitioning*) and as a way to detect the most anomalous, and hence most interesting, nodes in a graph. SVD transforms data based on correlation between edges rather than exact matches of edge attributes, and thus it can extract structure that is incomplete. It also does not require prespecification of the structures of interest, a property that is critical in a counter-terrorism setting because it is impossible to predict *all* patterns of potential interest.

2. Semidiscrete decomposition (SDD). SDD partitions data into subsets with similar attribute values, in the process creating an unsupervised hierarchical classification tree. Hence it is a clustering tool that works in a different way to both SVD and metric-based clusterers such as *k*-means that are, in any case, unreliable for datasets with a large number of attributes.

3. Independent component analysis (ICA). ICA partitions data into the least Gaussian components possible. In a graph context, this amounts to selecting components that are the most like cliques as possible. ICA is good at finding small, tightly clustered groups of nodes.

These techniques largely avoid the weaknesses of conventional social network analysis: They include higher-order correlation information, they can use extra information associated with both edges and nodes, and they are robust in the presence of missing values (because these are often implied indirectly by other values) and wrong values (because correlation rather than equality is the basic comparator).

We illustrate the application of these methods on a dataset containing information about 366 members of al Qaeda (current as of the beginning of 2004). The dataset contains typical relationship information, such as members who are related, who are friends, or who have encountered one another since joining the organization. However, it also contains demographic information (age, countries of origin and joining the group, education and marital status, etc.) and we are able to include this information in our analysis.

19.2. MATRIX DECOMPOSITIONS

We begin with a dataset containing information about *n* objects (people in our context), with *m* attributes about each one. There are three different kinds of attributes that might appear in such a representation of a dataset. The first are attributes that describe connections between an object and all of the other objects. For this, we will use an adjacency representation: The friendships among the 366 people in the al Qaeda dataset will be represented by 366 different attributes, with a 0 value at position *ij* indicating that persons *i* and *j* are not friends, and a 1 value indicating that they are. Of course, this part of the dataset will typically be sparse (i.e., mostly 0s) because most people have many fewer than 366 friends. The second kind of attribute values are categorical, that is, they come from a fixed set of choices such as marital status (single, married, separated, divorced). The third kind of attribute values are numeric—for example age.

Such a dataset is naturally viewed as a matrix, A, with n rows and m columns. A *matrix decomposition* expresses the matrix A as a product of other, simpler matrices in a way that reveals A's structure. Hence a typical matrix decomposition can be expressed as a matrix equation:

$$A = CSF \tag{19.1}$$

where C is $n \times m$, S is an $m \times m$ diagonal matrix (off-diagonal entries are all 0), and F is $m \times m$. Typically, the sizes of the matrices on the right-hand side are restricted by taking only the first k columns of C, the top left-hand $k \times k$ submatrix of S, and the first k rows of F (where k is smaller than both n and m). This truncation forces the decomposition to represent the data more compactly. The product of these truncated matrices gives a matrix of the same size as the original A, so we can write an equation for the truncated decomposition as

$$A \approx C_{n \times k} S_{k \times k} F_{k \times m} \tag{19.2}$$

Expectation–Maximization (EM) is a powerful technique for clustering data objects, given a set of probability distributions from which they are supposed to have come. Matrix decompositions are related to EM, with each different decomposition imposing extra conditions on the underlying distributions and thus on the way in which the clustering implicit in the matrix decomposition is done.

There are several different ways to interpret a matrix decomposition, and each sheds different light on the underlying data. In the *factor* interpretation, the rows of F are interpreted as underlying or latent factors and the entries of C are interpreted as ways to mix these factors to produce the observed data. The diagonal entries of S are *weights,* whose magnitude gives the relative importance of each factor. This interpretation is common in the social sciences, where it is known as *factor analysis.* Sometimes the factors can be regarded as axes in some space, in which case the entries of C are coordinates of points in this space.

The (outer) product of the ith column of C, the ith entry on the diagonal of S, and the i row of F is a matrix of the same shape as A, and in fact A can be expressed as the pointwise sum of all of these matrices. This allows a *layer* interpretation of the decomposition. A is obtained by sandwiching all of the outer-product matrices together, and thus each of them can be regarded as making some contribution to all of the values of A. Once again, the magnitude of the diagonal element provides information about how important each layer is to the total dataset. This interpretation can be particularly revealing when each entry in the original dataset can be thought of as being there because of a combination of different processes, each of which has made some contribution to the observed value.

19.2.1. Singular Value Decomposition (SVD)

SVD transforms data in a way that converts correlation to proximity (Golub and van Loan, 1996; Stewart, 1992). In the decomposition

$$A = USV' \tag{19.3}$$

U and V are each orthogonal matrices (the prime indicates transposition), and the diagonal entries of S, called the singular values, are nonincreasing.

Because V is orthogonal, a geometric interpretation is natural. The rows of U can be understood as the coordinates of points corresponding to the objects. The axes of the transformed space are such that the greatest variation in the original data lies along the direction of the first axis (the first column of V), the greatest remaining variation along the second axis, and so on. Hence truncating at some k gives a representation in a lower-dimensional space that captures the correlative structure of the entire matrix as accurately as possible. In other words, the first k elements of each row of U are a set of coordinates in a k-dimensional space. If $k = 2$ or 3, then each object can be represented by a point in two- or three-dimensional space.

SVD is a numerical technique, so the relative magnitudes of the matrix entries matter—larger values are automatically treated as more significant. To avoid being misled by the units in which the attributes are expressed, it is conventional to scale the data by (a) subtracting the mean of each column from all of that column's entries (zero centring) and (b) scaling the values so that the standard deviation of the values around that mean is 1. If this form of scaling is not done, the first dimension of the transformed space represents the average magnitude of the data overall and is typically of less interest. However, when the data represent, for example, the adjacency matrix of a graph, the attribute entries are all naturally in the same "units" and thus it is not necessary to scale the entries.

The SVD is completely symmetric with respect to rows and columns of the original matrix, so that all of the analysis that can be done for objects can trivially be repeated for the attributes as well.

SVD can be used in a number of ways to analyze a dataset:

- **Dimensionality Reduction.** This is the most common use of SVD in data analysis since it provides a way to reduce high-dimensional data (i.e., with many attributes) to lower dimension, losing as little information as possible in the process. When the original data contain noise, this dimensionality reduction can be regarded as denoising as well.

  One of the benefits of dimensionality reduction is that choosing $k = 2$ or 3 allows the rows of U to be plotted. This often makes it possible to understand the most significant structure of a dataset by visual inspection.

- **Clustering.** In a transformed and truncated space, the relationships among the points have been clarified and consequently clustering might be expected to work more effectively. There are, broadly, two approaches, although each contains many competing variants. The first is to use metric-based clustering—for example, a standard algorithm such as k-means—in the new space. The k-means algorithm chooses starting centers for each cluster, allocates each object to the center to which it is closest, recalculates centers as the centroids of the new clusters, reallocates objects to their closest centroid, and repeats until the process converges. Distances are not well-behaved in high-dimensional spaces, so k-means can often be effective in a space of truncated dimension when it would not have been if applied to the raw data.

  The second approach to clustering is to use the properties of SVD directly in an approach called spectral clustering (Kannan et al., 2000). For example, those points which lie in the cone around the first transformed axis (those whose dot product with the axis is less than 1/2) are placed in one cluster; those with the same property with respect to the second axis are placed in the second cluster, and so on. This produces k clusters, of which the last one is the "everything else" cluster. In some settings, it is obviously correct to include in each cluster the points that lie within the cone corresponding to the negative direction of each axis as well. These points are negatively correlated with the others with which they are being lumped, but they are correlated nevertheless. In low dimensions, no formal clustering algorithm is required because the clusters can usually be seen in a visualization.

When the matrix represents the adjacency matrix of a graph, the clustering produced by SVD is often similar to the clique structure of the graph.

- **Ranking Objects by Their Interestingness.** We have already explained that each row of U can be identified with a point in a k-dimensional space. Suppose that an arrow is drawn from the origin of the space to each of these points. Then the angles between these vectors reveal the correlation among the points. Two points that are strongly *positively* correlated will have vectors that are close together. Their dot products, which correspond to the cosine of the angle between the vectors, will be large and positive. Two points that are strongly *negatively* correlated will point in almost opposite directions, and will have a dot product that is large and negative. Two points that are uncorrelated should have a dot product that is close to zero, and it here that a problem arises. One way in which such a dot product can arise is that the two vectors are almost at right angles to each other. However, typically the number of available dimensions (k) is much smaller than the number of uncorrelated points (which could be n). There is another way in which the dot product can be close to zero and that is that the point itself is close to the origin. Hence points that are uncorrelated with most of the other points will tend to be placed near the origin. For similar reasons, a point that is correlated with almost all of the other points will also tend to be placed near the origin.

  Hence in the transformed space, points that are located far from the origin correspond to objects that are interesting in the sense that their correlations with the other objects are unusual. Conversely, points that are close to the origin correspond to objects that are less interesting, either because they are randomly correlated with other objects, or correlated similarly with all of them. Ranking the objects in order of the distance of their points from the origin allows the most interesting objects to be selected. Of course, the *direction* in which interesting points lie is also important.

  Because SVD is symmetric with respect to objects and attributes, exactly the same idea can be used to discover the relative interestingness of the attributes.

19.2.2. Semidiscrete Decomposition (SDD)

SDD (Kolda and O'Leary, 1998; O'Leary and Peleg, 1983) decomposes a matrix A as

$$A = XDY \qquad (19.4)$$

where the entries of X and Y are from $\{-1, 0, +1\}$ and D is a diagonal matrix with nonincreasing entries.

The natural interpretation of SDD is the layered one based on the outer product matrices. The product of the ith column of X and the ith row of Y is a matrix which contains rectilinearly aligned patterns of -1s and $+1$s (a stencil) against a background of 0s. The corresponding element of the diagonal of D indicates the weight associated with positions indicated in the stencil. The locations where there is a $+1$ correspond to positive values of this magnitude and those where there is a -1 correspond to negative values of this magnitude.

Hence, whereas SVD analyzes the data in a geometric space, SDD analyzes the data within the matrix itself. Imagine the matrix as a surface where, at each of the *ij* locations, there is a tower whose height corresponds to the magnitude of the entry in that location. Locations containing negative values are represented as basements whose depth depends on the magnitudes of the values. SDD decomposes the matrix into components, each of which is a set of rectilinearly aligned locations with similar (positive or negative) magnitudes. In other words, if SDD were applied to the downtown area of a large city, a component might pick out all the buildings of, say, roughly 30 stories.

The values in the X matrix provide an unsupervised hierarchical classification of the objects. Those objects whose entry in the first column of X are +1 are in one branch, while those whose entries are −1 are in an opposite branch. Those objects whose entries are 0 are in yet a third branch, so that the classification tree is ternary. The values in the second column of X provide a ternary subclassification for each of the three branches at the top level, and this process can be extended as far as required. The first column of X divides the objects into three groups, the second column divides each of these groups into 3 subgroups for a total of 9 groups, the third column into 27 groups, and so on.

Although SDD was originally developed as a storage-efficient analogue of SVD, there is no necessary link between the classifications each produces. When the data naturally cluster into many small, well-separated clusters, SDD and SVD tend to agree. It also often happens that the top-level classification from SDD is aligned with the first axis of SVD, so that the +1 points are at one extremity and the −1 points are at the other—but this will not always be the case.

19.2.3. Independent Component Analysis (ICA)

ICA (Bach and Jordan, 2002; Hyvärinen, 1999; Hyvärinen and Oja, 2000; Ng et al., 2001) decomposes the data matrix, A, into components that are as statistically independent as possible (in contrast to SVD which decomposes the data into components that are *linearly independent*). We use the FastICA algorithm for convenience.

The ICA of a matrix A is

$$A = WH \tag{19.5}$$

(note that there is no "weight" matrix in this case, and hence no natural ordering on the components). H represents the statistically independent factors, and W represents the way in which these factors must be mixed to recreate A.

19.3. AL QAEDA DATASET

We will illustrate the power of these matrix decomposition techniques by using them to investigate the structures and relationships within al Qaeda (2009), to the extent that they are publicly known. We use a dataset collected by Marc Sageman from a wide variety of public sources. The dataset contains information about 366 members of al Qaeda as of the beginning of 2004. The available attributes are shown in Table 19.1.

Many of these attributes are demographic in nature, but several describe the links among al Qaeda members in various categories. Of course, there are many missing values because not all information is publicly available.

Table 19.1. Dataset Attributes

Short name	Year joined the jihad
Full name	Age joined the jihad
Date of birth	Place joined the jihad
Place of birth	Country joined the jihad
Youth national status	Acquaintance links
Family socioeconomic status	Friend links
Religious background	Nuclear family links
Educational achievement	Relative links
Type of education	Religious leader
Occupation	Ties not in sample
Marital status	Role in organization
Children	Operation(s) involved
Social background	Fate
	Links after joining

We also use a subset of the dataset, a link or adjacency matrix containing all of the links among members, whether as family, relatives, friends, or contacts within the group. This matrix has a row and column for each individual, and the ijth entry of the matrix is 0 if there is no known link between individual i and individual j; otherwise its value represents the number of different kinds of connections between that pair of individuals. This matrix represents the graph in which there is a node for each individual and an edge between nodes whenever there is a known relationship. The graph of these relationships has 366 nodes (of course) and 2171 edges. The maximum degree of the graph, the largest number of known connections of one person to all of the others, is 44 (but of course this number is probably higher in reality). The mean degree—that is, the typical number of people that a given person is connected to—is 6.44. (This value for the mean degree is interesting because it matches the rule of thumb that members of any group must have connections to about 6 others if they are to remain part of the group.) The diameter of the graph, the length of the path of connections between the two most remote individuals, is 11. This is a relatively large value for a group of this size and probably reflects both a long geographical reach and some attention to security issues.

Table 19.2 gives the Bavelas–Leavitt centrality values that exceed 220. For each node, this measure is the ratio of the sum of all of the shortest paths to and from that node to the sum of all of the shortest paths in the entire dataset. Accordingly, it measures how close the node is to the center of the graph of links in some notional space. Although the centrality values for group leaders are somewhat higher than those of the others around them, these numbers show that al Qaeda has a relatively decentralized structure.

Many of the members with high scores are the leadership of al Qaeda as expected. However, there are several surprises: Hada, Harithi, Ayiri, Aktas, Faruq, Ramda, Melouk, Trabeisi, and Bahaiah. Examination of the data suggests that these members get such high centrality scores because they have links to Osama bin Laden and several others of the top leadership. In the absence of other knowledge, this complicates the use of a centrality measure as an analysis device because it does not distinguish well between the important leadership and those with little importance but who are directly connected to the leadership. (Of course, this is further complicated by the fact that such people may be hangers-on, but may also be *eminences grises*.)

Table 19.2. Al Qaeda Members with High Bavelas–Leavitt Centrality

Name	BL Centrality	Name	BL Centrality
bin Laden	298	Jarrah	234
Zawahiri	240	Shehhi	235
Banshiri	226	Mihdhar	220
M Atef	254	Hada	227
Sheikh Omar	222	Harithi	227
Islambuli	230	Ayiri	232
Zubaydah	260	Aktas	222
Makkawi	242	Sungkar	229
Hawsawi	227	Hambali	253
Taha	230	Faruq	233
KSM	250	Ramda	251
Zarqawi	221	Melouk	220
Qatada	221	Doha	225
Hage	221	Trabelsi	244
Khadr	222	Moussaoui	235
Ghayth	224	Bahaiah	229
Khallad	241	Khabab	228
Shah	232	Khalifah	227
Atta	246	Tabarak	222
Shibh	260		

The University of Arizona group have analyzed this dataset and used multidimensional scaling to produce a picture of the group's connectivity (Jie Xu, personal communication, 2004). This shows that the dataset is naturally clustered into 13 almost-cliques, with about 60 members not allocated to a single clique. In subsequent work (Qin et al., 2005) they have used standard social network analysis measures, small-world graph measures, and the PageRank algorithm used by Google to extract structure from the same dataset. However, they are unable to include demographic information in their analysis.

A graph of the links within al Qaeda is maintained by Intelcenter and can be viewed on their website (www.intelcenter.com/linkanalysis.html). While the graph is compend actionable information from it.

19.4. ANALYSIS USING MATRIX DECOMPOSITIONS

19.4.1. Using the Links Between Individuals

In this section we consider only the results of enhanced social network analysis; that is, we consider the graph of relationships among al Qaeda members, but not demographic information. The base dataset is a 366 × 366 adjacency matrix representing the graph that includes connections who are acquaintances, family, friends, relations, and contacts after joining.

Figure 19.1 shows a three-dimensional (truncated) view of the relationships among al Qaeda members extracted from their links. The axes here correspond to coordinates with respect to the first three axes of the transformed space; axis $U1$ corresponds to the values from the first column of U, and so on. The most obvious fact is that there is a clear division into three (perhaps four) clusters. This radial pattern is typical: Those points at the

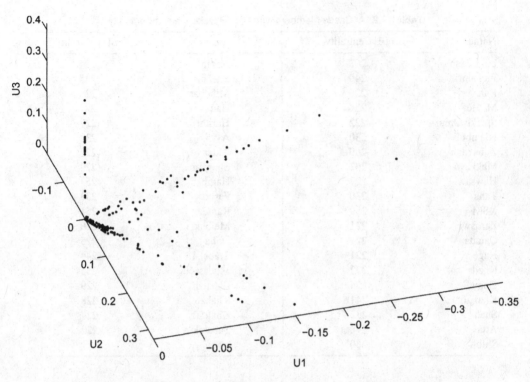

Figure 19.1. SVD plot of al Qaeda members using only relationship attributes.

extremities represent individuals with the most interesting connections to the rest of the group. Many members are either connected in limited ways, or little is known about them. All such members resemble each other, and thus they tend to be located close to the origin.

The structure is made clearer by adding name labels (we follow Sageman's usage) and removing points (and so individuals) that are located close to the origin. Figure 19.2 shows those points that are more than 1.5 times the median distance from the origin, while Figure 19.3 removes even more points. It now becomes possible to identify the visible structure.

There are three clusters in these figures: a group of Algerians arranged vertically in the figures; a group of South East (SE) Asian members stretching to the right; and a group of leaders and some core Arabs toward the front. It is clear from these figures that Hambali plays a pivotal connecting role between the SE Asian group and the leadership group. In fact, the separation into two parallel lines of the leadership group is entirely due to whether or not they have a link to Hambali. The fact that Hambali is well-connected is obvious from the raw data, but it is not so obvious how integral these connections are to holding al Qaeda together. The strong presence of the Algerian cluster is slightly surprising; while these members have been active over a long period, they are not obviously the most important members of al Qaeda's European operations in the raw data.

Each of the clusters arranges the more important members farthest from the origin as expected. Notice that bin Laden is not the most extremal member of the leadership cluster; this appears to be partly due to good tradecraft (he is not directly involved in operations) and to relative inactivity over the past few years. Note that Figure 19.3 selects the highest profile al Qaeda members well.

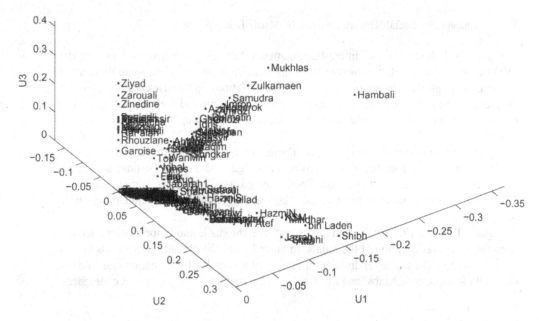

Figure 19.2. SVD plot of 143 interesting members (greater than 1.5 times the median distance from the origin) labeled with short identifiers.

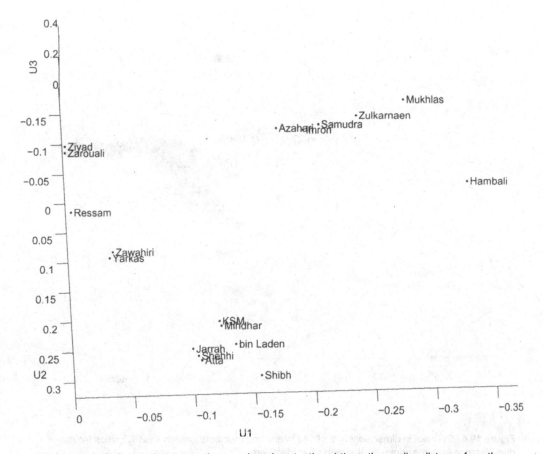

Figure 19.3. SVD plot of 18 interesting members (greater than 4 times the median distance from the origin) labeled with short identifiers.

Figure 19.4 shows the 143 interesting members, but using dimensions 4 to 6 of the SVD (in other words, relationships in less-important dimensions). Here again there are 3 clusters, although they do not bear the same close relationship to attack teams (although the group to the right are in fact the September 2001 attackers and their support group). It is clear, once again, that the most important members of the group are placed far from the origin.

Figure 19.5 overlays the SVD plot in dimensions 1–3 with information about which cultural group each member comes from. This figure shows the strong, separated, groups from the Middle East and from South East Asia. Although the vertical group are different from everyone else, most of the Maghreb/Algerian/French members resemble core Arabs.

Figures 19.6 and 19.7 are the same plots, but with the shade and shape labeling derived from the SDD classification of the points. In other words, the division into groups here is *fully automatic*. The top-level division in Figure 19.6 is coded by shade: on one side the important leaders, core Arabs, and SE Asians; in the middle the majority of the members;

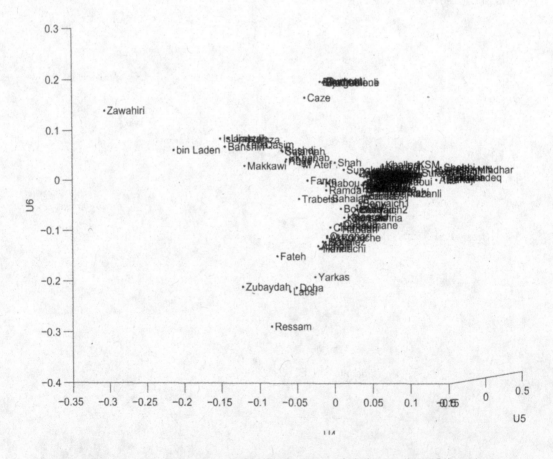

Figure 19.4. SVD plot in dimensions 4–6 of 143 interesting members (greater than 1.5 times the median distance from the origin) labeled with short identifiers.

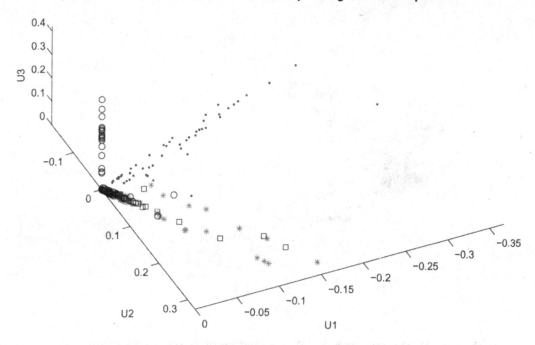

Figure 19.5. SVD plot showing cultural group membership (squares—leadership; stars—core Arabs; circles—Maghreb; dots—S.E. Asian).

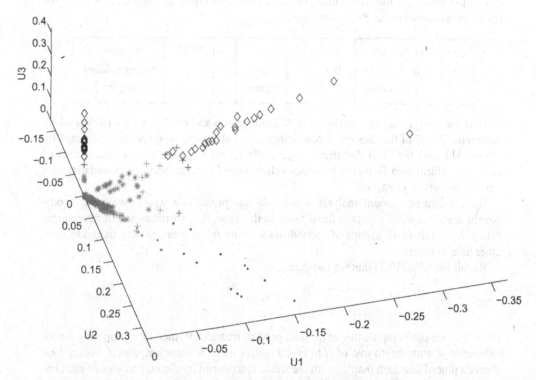

Figure 19.6. SVD plot of members with SDD shade and shape labeling, showing extra boundary information.

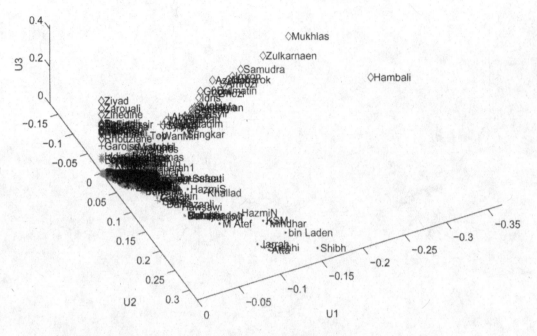

Figure 19.7. SVD plot of members with SDD color and shape labeling and short identifiers.

and on the other side the Algerians. The subsequent two levels are indicated by the symbol shape as shown in the following table:

+1	+1	dot	0	+1	+	−1	+1	diamond
+1	0	circle	0	0	star	−1	0	triangle down
+1	−1	cross	0	−1	square	−1	−1	triangle up

Here the similarities are between the Algerian group and the SE Asians (indicated by diamonds). In all of the clusters, a few marginal members can be discerned, indicated by pluses. Although the SDD classification generally agrees with that of SVD, the benefit of the extra information is that it provides substructure: a better view of boundaries and more detail within clusters.

Independent component analysis is naturally interpreted in a layered way: Each component describes some aspect of the dataset. In this case, ICA works as an effective clique detector. It finds small groups of individuals who are much more closely linked to each other than to others.

Recall from Eq.(19.5) that we compute

$$A = WH$$

From this, we can compute the set of outer product matrices formed by multiplying the ith column of W with the ith row of H to give a matrix with the same shape as A. Figure 19.8 shows a plot of one such matrix, with the shade determined by the magnitudes of each entry of the matrix. A clearly defined group is visible. Because, in this dataset, the rows of the original dataset have been organized in rough groups, the clique of connected individ-

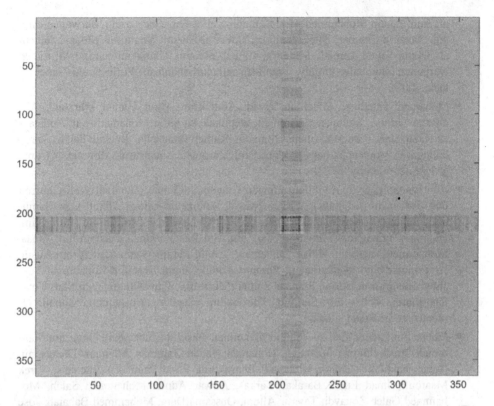

Figure 19.8. An example of an outer product matrix from the ICA of the relationship matrix. The presence of a small, connected group is easily visible.

uals discovered by ICA happens to be located almost contiguously in the figure, but this will not always be the case.

We can extract the individuals associated with each outer product group from such a matrix, even when they do not occur in such nicely contiguous rows. We apply a threshold function to the outer product matrix (in this case, 0.2 of the maximum value) to produce a 0–1 matrix. We then list those objects (individuals) with a 1 anywhere in their row. This selects individuals who have enough association that they form a tightly knit group.

Recall that ICA does not impose an importance ordering on components (at least not directly), so we cannot extract the most "important" clusters first. Some clusters that do arise from the dataset are:

- Christophe Caze, Lionel Dumont, Rachid Souimdi, Saad el Aihar, Amar Djouina, Mouloud Bougelane, Hassan Zemiri, Hocine Bendaoui, Seddick Benbahlouh, Laifa Khabou, Fateh Kamal (Groupe Roubaix, France 1994).

- Rachid Ramda, Ah Touchent, Boulem Bensaid, Safe Bourada, Smain Ait Alt Belkacem, Mohamed Drici, Ah ben Fatoum, David Vallat, Khaled Kelkal, Karim Koussa, Adelkader Maameri, Abdelkader Bouhadjar, Nasserdine Slimani, Farid Melouk, Ahmed Zaoui (France 1995).

- Osama bin Laden, Mohammed Atef, Mustafa Ahmed al-Hawsawi, Khalid Sheikh Mohammed, Waleed Tawfiq bin Attash, Mohamadou Ould Slahi, Mamoun Darkazanii, Mohammad bin Nasser Belfas, Mounir al-Motassadeq, Abdal Ghani Mzoudi, Said Bahaji, Mohammed Atta, Ramzi bin al-Shibh, Ziad Jarrah, Marwan el-She-hhi, Zakarya Essabar, Hani Hanjour, Nawaf al-Hazmi, Khalid al-Mihdar, Saleem al-Hazmi, Fayez Ahmad el-Shehri, Ahmed al-Nami, Christian Ganczarski, Encep Nurjaman (Hambali) (largely organizers and participants of World Trade Center attack, 2001).

- Mohamed Zinedine, Abdelilah Ziyad, Abdelkrim Afkir, Hamel Marzoug, Abdeslam Garoise, Radouane Hammadi, Stephane Ait Iddir, Mohamed Azil, Abdelaziz Rhouzlane, Abderrah-mane Boujedii, Kamel Benakcha, Rachid Falah, Tarek Falahm El Moustapha ben Haddou, Farid Zarouali, Abderrazak Mountassir (same group identified by SVD).

- Abu Bakar Baasyir, Abdullah Sungkar, Encep Nurjaman (Hambali), Alt Ghufron bin Nurhasyim (Mukhlas), Yassin Syawal, Rahman al-Ghozi, Abdul Aziz (Samudra), Enjang Bastaman (Jabir), Amrozi bin Nurhasyim, Ah Imron bin Nurhasyim, Hutomo Pamungkus (Mobarok), Faiz bin Abu Bakar Bafana, Hasyim bin Abbas, Mohammed Nasir bin Abbas (Sulaeman), Abdul Rahim Ayub, Azahari bin Husin, Arts Sumarsomo (Zulkarnaen), Suranto Abdul Ghoni, Noordin Mohammad Top, Jhoni Hendrawan (Idris), Pranata Yudha (Mustofa), Wan Min bin Wan Mat, Umar Dul Matin, Abbas Edy Setiono, Thoriqudin (Rusdan), Mustaquim, Muhajir (JI members, SE Asian attacks).

- Osama bin Laden, Zain al-Abidin Mohammed Hussein (Zubaydah), Omar ibn Mahmoud Omar Othman (Qatada), Mohamed Heidar Zammar, Mamoun Darkazanii, Amar Makhlulif (Doha), Mohamed Bensakhria, Essid Sami ben Khemais, Tarek Maaroufi, Imad Eddin Barakat Yarkas, Anwar Adnan Mohammad Salah, Mohammed Galeb Zouaydi, Tayssir Alluni, Oussama Dara, Mohammed Bahaiah, Jose Luis Galan Gonzalez, Abdelaziz Benyaich, Salahed-dine Benyaich, Said Chedadi, Driss Chebli, Najib Chaid Mohamed, Mohamed Fizazi (North African and European attacks).

- Zain al-Abidin Mohammed Hussein (Zubaydah), Safe Bourada, Laifa Khabou, Fateh Kamel, Abdellah Ouzgar, Zoheir Choulah, Said Atmani, Abderraouf Hannachi, Ahmed Ressam, Mustapha Labsi, Mourad Ikhlef, Adel Boumezbeur, Samit Ait Mohamed, Abdel Majit Dahoumane, Mokhtar Haouari, Amar Makhlulif (Doha), Yacine Akhnouche, Omar Chaabani (Jaafar), Rabah Kadri, Slimane Khalfaoui, Hassan Zemiri, Adil Charkaoui (Los Angeles millennium attack).

Other groups include (a) those involved with early attacks in Egypt and the early leadership of al Qaeda and (b) those involved in the Casablanca attack in 2003.
The interesting things about these groups are the following:

- Although they are based purely on relationship data, they correspond well to the groups who have carried out terrorist attacks. This shows that al Qaeda's functional structure (who plans, leads, and carries out an attack) is heavily derived from existing familial and relationship connections among its members. (Although some group link structure is present in the raw data, it is by no means enough to determine attack groups.)

- Several people appear in multiple groups, thus revealing their role as the glue that binds disparate groups together. Notice that many groups with close geographical and relationship ties still include one or two members of the al Qaeda leadership, showing how long-distance relationships maintain overall group cohesiveness.

- There are some individuals who ought, on the face of it, to appear as members of a group but do not. This may happen simply because not enough is known about them, so they appear to be relatively unconnected. However, it is also possible that such people are deliberately trying to lie low, so it may be useful to apply extra scrutiny to them.

The choice of threshold affects the tightness of the boundary of each cluster: Increasing the threshold reduces the membership of each cluster and removes some apparently anomalous individuals. The question of appropriate choice of threshold has not yet been examined in a systematic way.

A sense of the overall clustering implied by the ICA can be obtained by examining images of the W and H matrices. Each column of the W matrix corresponds to one component, and thus in this case refers to one group (Figure 19.9). The presence of high values in a column indicates objects that are associated with this component (recall that the organization of the data has placed similar people in adjacent rows already, which is why the clusters are so obvious). For example, column 1 reveals the cluster at rows ~230–250, and column 3 reveals the cluster at rows ~60–80 but with some weaker connections to the leadership (early rows).

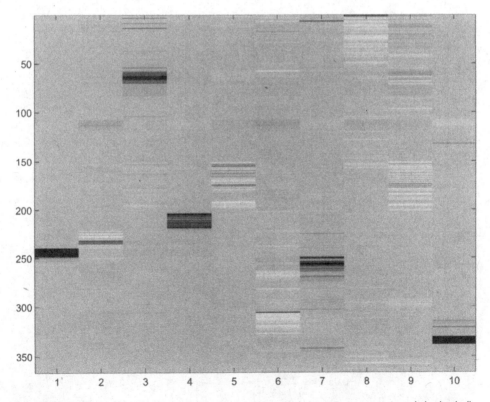

Figure 19.9. Image of the W matrix. Each column corresponds to one component, and shades indicate the magnitude of the matrix elements. In each column we can see large entries corresponding to a group.

19.4.2. Using Demographic and Relational Information

We now add demographic information including: year of birth (dob), country of birth (birthplace), cultural group (clump), national status (natstatus), socioeconomic status (fses), religious background (religbgnd), type of school attended (school), education level attained (educ), type of education (edtype), occupation (occup), marital status (married), number of children (kids), possession of a criminal background (crimbgnd), year of joining al Qaeda (yrjoin), age at joining al Qaeda (agejoin), place at which member joined (placejoin), country in which member joined (country join), fate, and year left the group (yrleft) usually by death. The number of demographic attributes and their amount of variation they show produces plots with much less clustering.

Figure 19.10 shows the basic clustering among al Qaeda members based on SVD. It is clear that the group is fairly homogeneous, except for a distinct cluster towards the bottom of the figure. As we shall see, this cluster represents a subgroup of members who have a stronger religious background and religious education than the majority.

Analysis of the attributes, plotted in Figure 19.11, shows that dimension 1 captures the variation in educational attainment, dimension 2 captures variations in locations such as where members were born and joined the organization, and dimension 3 captures differences in religious background and schooling.

These relationships among the dimensions in the attribute space must necessarily be consistent with the relationships among members in the object space. Figures 19.12 and

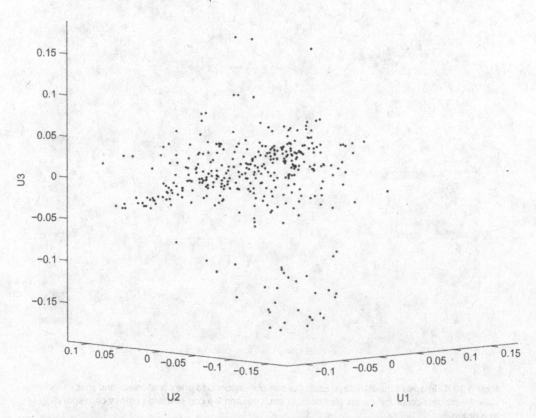

Figure 19.10. SVD plot of al Qaeda members using both demographic and relationship attributes.

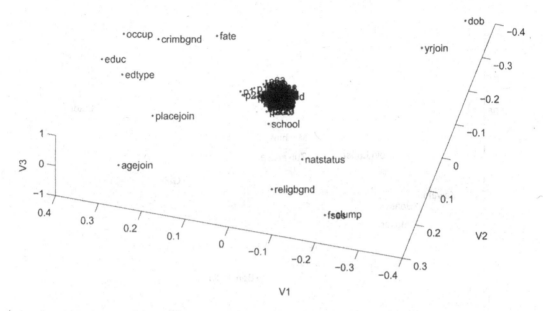

Figure 19.11. SVD plot of dataset attributes, showing the relationships among them. The large cluster of attributes in the center are associated with explicit relationships among members.

19.13 show the most unusual members, projected in different dimensions. We can see that, for example, al-Zawahiri and bin Laden are well-educated while Omar Khadr and Abdul Karim Khadr are not (separation along axis Ul). The second dimension captures differences in country of birth and country in which the member joined the jihad. Since the countries are coded alphabetically, this reveals no absolute information about the structure of al Qaeda, although it may reveal some relative information. For example, Abdallah ibn Mohammad al-Rashoud was born and joined the jihad in Saudi Arabia, while Chellali Benchellali was born in Algeria and joined in France and Wadih el-Hage was born in Lebanon and joined in Afghanistan.

Figure 19.13 shows the relationship between education and religious background. Now the vertical dimension represents degree of religious background: Hage is a non-Muslim with a secular education, and Mukhlas and Zulkarnaen are from a religious background and are pupils of a Madrassa. In the lower left-hand corner, note the small cluster of members who are both religious and highly educated: Sheikh Omar Abdel Rahman, who has a doctorate; and Abu Bakar Baasyir and Abdullah Sungkar, who both have Master's degrees.

The size of the singular values (the diagonal of S) give some indication of the relative importance of the factors corresponding to each dimension. These values are 13.5, 11.9, and 9.6, indicating that education is about 40% more important as an explanation for variation among al Qaeda members than religious background (13.5/9.6).

Figure 19.14 shows the effect of cultural background. It is clear that the leaders (squares) are slightly different from the remainder of the members, but this is not surprising because of the group's history. Its leaders come from similar backgrounds and are of a similar age. There are very little difference between the characteristics of the other

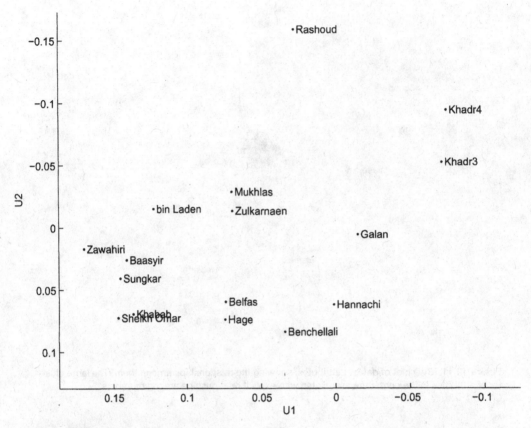

Figure 19.12. SVD plot of 16 interesting members (greater than 1.5 times the median distance from the origin) in dimensions 1 and 2. Dimension 1 represents variation in education; dimension 2 represents variation in place of origin.

groups, although the Maghreb members (circles) show some systematic differences from the core Arab (stars) members.

Figure 19.15 shows an SVD overlaid with information obtained from SDD. In this case, we have used a more powerful combination of the two matrix decompositions called the JSS methodology: SVD is applied to the data matrix, A, the decomposition is truncated at some k, and the component matrices are multiplied to give a modified version of A. SDD is then applied to the correlation matrix obtained from the modified version of A. This correlation matrix captures higher-order correlation information and tends to provide a clearer picture of complex data than applying SDD directly to A.

It is clear from the figure that the extra information agrees with the clustering given by SVD. Note that the group of well-educated, religious members is captured as a subgroup. It is also noticeable that the well-educated cluster displays more variability than the matching cluster of less-educated members. There are substantial overlaps between the well-educated cluster and the group's leadership, providing further evidence that the stereotype of terrorists as ignorant, brain-washed, or psychotic does not apply to al Qaeda.

ICA is not useful on the demographic data because it tends to select small groups who resemble each other on the basis of a few demographic attributes—which is misleading and is obvious from the raw data.

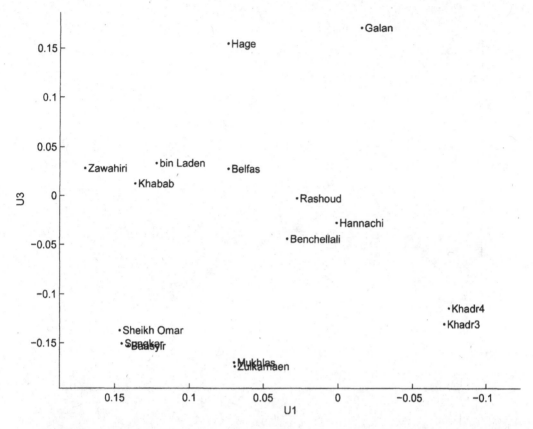

Figure 19.13. SVD plot of 16 interesting members (greater than 1.5 times the median distance from the origin) in dimensions 1 and 3. Dimension 1 represents variation in education; dimension 3 represents variation in religious background.

19.5. DISCUSSION

19.5.1. Methodology

We can see from these results that the major benefit of SVD is its ability to select and order objects (in this case al Qaeda members) from most to least interesting. This is partly because al Qaeda is a fairly homogeneous organization, so that there are few significant demographic clusters within it. Even the clustering visible in the relationship data is important only for the more unusual/important members—most of the rank and file are quite similar. SDD allows more detailed and discriminative analysis, because it is able to provide boundaries between subgroups more precisely.

The major benefit of ICA is its ability to find and select closely coupled groups of individuals. Unlike a traditional clique-discovery algorithm, ICA allows an individual to participate in several groupings, which is both more flexible and more realistic.

A number of parameter choices were made in these algorithms: the number of dimensions at which to truncate the SVD for visualization, and for preparation for SDD, the scaling of the array entry magnitudes for SDD, the boundaries for considering objects interesting, the number of components used for ICA, and the thresholds used for using ICA

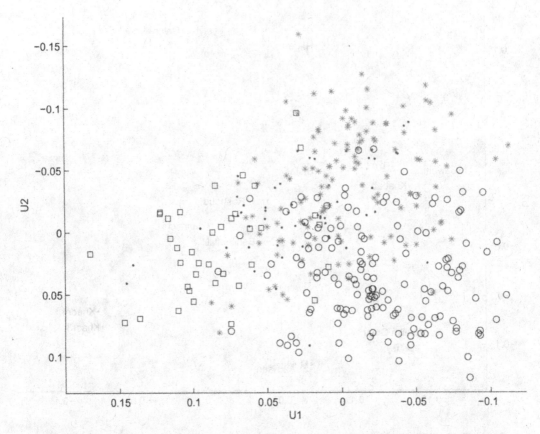

Figure 19.14. SVD plot based on both relationship and demographic data, showing cultural group membership (squares—leadership; stars—core Arabs; circles—Maghreb; dots—S.E. Asian).

components to select groups of members. Sensible values for all of these were chosen, but other structures might conceivably be revealed by other parameter choices. At present, no principled ways to choose these parameters are known.

A major advantage of matrix decompositions over typical social network analysis and link analysis tools is complexity. The matrix decompositions used here have complexities that are typically cubic in n, the number of people being considered. However, when the data are sparse, as relationship data usually are, this can be reduced to linear, which remains feasible even for much, much larger datasets. In contrast, measures such as centrality have complexities that are at least cubic in n and often worse (because they often consider all paths in a graph). Furthermore, the software tools used for social networks analysis often assume quite small networks and thus are not optimized for datasets even of this size, let alone larger ones.

Social network analysis also has a number of other drawbacks. First, such analyses are at the mercy of their graph-drawing algorithms, which may create a misleading impression of the importance of an individual through an accident of placement. Second, the individuals to which attention is drawn are those with many connections. This is useful, but is easily extracted from the raw data and fails to show either centrality measures or higher-order connections. Third, the graphs quickly become large, so that only small pieces can be seen at a time. This makes it hard to extract global information or see large-scale

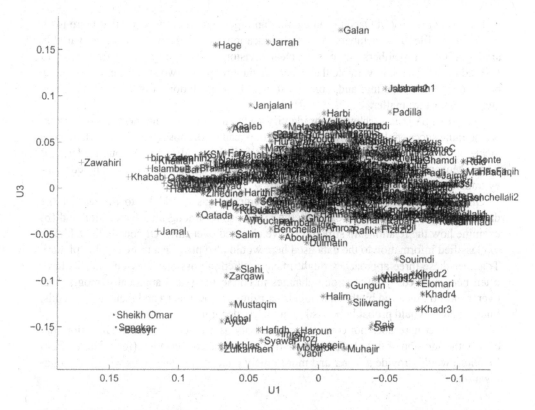

Figure 19.15. SVD plot with SDD color and shape labeling, using both demographic and relationship data.

patterns. Hence, although visualization via social network analysis plays to human strengths in seeing patterns, the size and complexity of the graphs involves tends to make this difficult to achieve in practice.

19.5.2. al Qaeda

It is clear from this analysis that al Qaeda is better regarded as a loose confederation of groups with related aims than as a hierarchically controlled, functionally organized single group. Repeatedly, the structure that emerges from considering relationships among members matches the structure related to groups that have carried out attacks. In al Qaeda, it is who you know, not what you know, that determines your role in the organization. This observation has also been made by Sageman (2004), Gunaratna (2003), and others.

The difference between the three cultural groupings—core Arabs, South East Asian muslims, and European/Maghreb muslims—is also strong, as is the fact that the leadership is not only made up of core Arabs, but is also much more tightly bound to this group than to the others. In fact, it is surprising that there are not more people who play the role of Hambali in connecting groups together—surprising enough that it raises the question of whether there are in fact such people, either not captured at all in this dataset or about whom not enough is known to elicit this role.

It is also clear that al Qaeda is an egalitarian organization in the sense that there is no particular profile to its members. Although education level is the most important variable among al Qaeda members, there is no clear division across the spectrum from most to least educated. The only variable that separates the group into two subclusters is religious background and schooling; and, contrary to popular expectation, it is the more religious cluster that is the smaller.

The use of SVD as a technique for identifying the most interesting members of a group is also quite successful at identifying either group leaders or those with an important technical role. For example, Figure 19.2 identifies both bin Laden, an obvious leader, and Ramzi Mohammad Abdullah bin al-Shibh, a more technical operative (who handled money transfers for the September 2001 attacks).

Other possible analyses using matrix decompositions would be to (a) restrict the dataset to those still alive and examine the relationships among the organization and (b) examine how the relationship structures have changed over time. Of course, the addition of classified information to the data used here would also provide a more reliable picture. Together these three approaches might make prediction possible: Previous attacks have often been marked by quite strong changes in connectivity and apparent demographics over a short time period by the individuals carrying out the attacks and their support cells. Such changes would probably be visible in matrix decomposition plots.

The dataset here does not consider connectivity as a function of communication, but clearly the addition of links based on e-mail or telephone conversation (for example, from Echelon) would provide a better and more timely picture of connections within the organization.

SUMMARY

Transnational terrorist groups such as al Qaeda present new challenges for Counterterrorism. Like all terrorist groups, their members and actions are hard to see against the background of innocent groups and activities. Al Qaeda has demonstrated that a group formed as very loose federations can still be effective, creating a new requirement to detect sporadic or short-lived links to create a workable defense.

We have shown how matrix decomposition techniques can be used to enhance link and social network analysis. These techniques are more revealing than clique detection and centrality measures, less reliant on exact data, and more efficient to compute.

While we discover nothing particularly new about al Qaeda, existing knowledge is replicated from much less data. In particular, the techniques we have used are able to detect and rank the importance of members of the group solely based on their relationships. This is a powerful addition to the arsenal of counter-terrorism data analysis techniques.

ACKNOWLEDGMENTS

I am deeply grateful to Marc Sageman for making the al Qaeda dataset available.

REFERENCES

Bach, F. R., and Jordan, M. I. (2002). Finding clusters in Independent Component Analysis. Technical Report UCB/CSD-02-1209, Computer Science Division, University of California, Berkeley.

Baker, W. E., and Faulkner, R. B. (1993). The social organization of conspiracy: Illegal networks in the heavy electrical equipment industry. *American Sociological Review,* **58:**837–860.

Corbin, J. (2002). *Al-Qaeda: In Search of the Terror Network that Threatens the World.* Thunder's Mouth Press.

Golub, G. H., and van Loan, C. F. (1996). *Matrix Computations,* 3rd edition. Johns Hopkins University Press.

United States Government. (2004). *Final Report of the National Commission on Terrorist Attacks Upon the United States.*

Gunaratna, R. (2003). *Inside al Qaeda,* 3rd edition. Berkley Publishing Group.

Hyvärinen, A. (1999). Survey on independent component analysis. *Neural Computing Surveys* **2:**94–128.

Hyvärinen, A., and Oja, E. (2000). Independent component analysis: Algorithms and applications. *Neural Networks* **13**(4-5):411–430.

Jensen, D., and Neville, J. (2003). Data mining in social networks. Invited presentation to the National Academy of Sciences Workshop on Dynamic Social Network Modeling and Analysis.

Kannan, R., Vempala, S., and Vetta, A. (2000). On clusterings: Good, bad and spectral. In: *Proceedings of the 41st Foundations of Computer Science (FOCS '00),* p. 367.

Kolda, G., and O'Leary, D. P. (1998). A semi-discrete matrix decomposition for latent semantic indexing in information retrieval. *ACM Transactions on Information Systems* **16:**322–346.

Krebs, V. E. (2002). Mapping networks of terrorist cells. *Connections* **24**(3):43–52.

McConnell, S., and Skillicorn, D. B. (2002). Semidiscrete decomposition: A bump hunting technique. In: *Australasian Data Mining Workshop,* pp. 75–82.

Ng, A. Y., Zheng, A. X., and Jordan, M. I. (2001). Link analysis, eigenvectors and stability. In: *Proceedings of the Seventeenth International Joint Conference on Artificial Intelligence (IJCAI-01),* pp. 903–910.

O'Leary, D. P., and Peleg, S. (1983). Digital image compression by outer product expansion. *IEEE Transactions on Communications* **31:**441–444.

Priebe, C. (2005). Scan statistics on Enron graphs. In: *Workshop on Link Analysis, Counterterrorism and Security, SIAM International Conference on Data Mining,* pp. 23–32.

Qin, J., Xu, J., Hu, D., Sageman, M., and Chen, H. (2005). Analyzing terrorist networks: A case study of the global salafi jihad network. In: *Intelligence and Security Informatics, IEEE International Conference on Intelligence and Security Informatics, ISI 2005, Atlanta, GA, USA, May 19–20,* pp. 287–304. Springer-Verlag Lecture Notes in Computer Science LNCS 3495.

Sageman, M. (2004). *Understanding Terror Networks.* Philadelphia: University of Pennsylvania Press.

Shultz, R. H., and Vogt, A. (2004). The real intelligence failure on 9/11 and the case for a doctrine of striking first. In: R. D. Howard and R. L. Sawyer (eds.). *Terrorism and Counterterrorism: Understanding the New security Environment,* pp. 405–428. Hightstown, NJ: McGraw-Hill Dushkin.

Stewart, G. W. (1992). On the Early History of the Singular Value Decomposition. Technical Report TR-2855, University of Maryland, Department of Computer Science.

van Meter, K. M. (2002). Terrorists/liberators: Researching and dealing with adversary social networks. *Connections* **24**(3):66–78.

Chapter 20

Legal Standards for Data Mining

Fred H. Cate[1]

20.1. INTRODUCTION

Data mining is a promising tool in the fight against terrorism. It already plays a number of important roles in counter-terrorism including locating known suspects, identifying and tracking suspicious financial and other transactions, and facilitating background checks. Rapid increases in the power and speed of computing technologies, the capacity of data storage, and the reach of networks have added exponentially to both the volume of data available for possible use and the ability of the government to meaningfully examine them. As a result, as discussed elsewhere in this volume, new data mining applications are likely to play increasingly important roles in fighting terrorism.

Government data mining also poses significant issues for individual privacy and other civil liberties. Proposals for enhanced government data mining have provoked serious controversy, beginning with the first large-scale computerized government benefits databases created by the then Department of Health, Education and Welfare. More recently, public concern over proposals for Total Information Awareness (TIA) and second-generation Computer-Assisted Passenger Profiling System (CAPPS) was sufficient to block at least public development of these systems.

One of the major contributors to the controversies over government data mining is the absence of clear legal standards. Forty years ago the lack of relevant law was understandable: The technologies were new, their capacity was largely unknown, and the types of legal issues they might raise were novel. Today, it is inexplicable and threatens to undermine both privacy and security.

The situation is exacerbated by the Supreme Court's 1976 decision in *United States v. Miller* that there can be no reasonable expectation of privacy in information held by a third party, so the Fourth Amendment does not apply to the government's seizure of such data.[2] With the growth in digital technologies and networks and the resulting proliferation of digital data, the *Miller* decision today means that the government faces few, if any, constitutional limitations when it seeks the personal data maintained by banks, credit card issuers, brokers, airlines, rental car companies, hospitals, insurers, Internet service providers, real estate agents, telephone companies, publishers, libraries, educators, employers, and information brokers. According to the Supreme Court, it does not matter whether the information sought by the government was disclosed to a third party as a nec-

---

[1]The author gratefully acknowledges the generous aid of P. Rosenzweig and K. A. Taipale and the excellent research assistance of David Scott Dickinson and Lindsey Ann Rodgers. The author alone is responsible for any errors or omissions.
[2]United States v. Miller, 425 U.S. 435 (1976).

essary part of a consumer transaction, provided to a third party "on the assumption that it will be used only for a limited purpose," or conveyed pursuant to a "confidence" that it will not be shared at all.[3] The government is still free to seize it, and the Fourth Amendment imposes no limits on either its collection or use.

Congress reacted to *Miller* and subsequent cases by enacting statutory protections for customer financial records held by financial institutions and other sectoral statutes,[4] but these laws offer limited protection and do not apply to the terabytes of other personal data maintained by third parties today. So, while most individuals believe that the government is constitutionally prohibited from seizing their personal information without a warrant, granted by a judge, based on probable cause, the reality is that the government is only restricted from obtaining that information directly from the individuals to which it pertains.

The massive volume of data about individuals and the ease with which they are collected, aggregated, and shared means that the private sector often holds a treasure trove of information to which the government desires access as part of its counter-terrorism efforts. Often those data are already collected together by private-sector service providers and data aggregators. The exponential growth in detailed personal information that third parties possess, the ease of access to that information, and the absence of constitutional protections for such data have greatly reduced the government's need to seek information directly from the individuals to which it pertains. Instead, the government can often obtain—whether by seizure or purchase—the same or an even wider and more revealing supply of data from third parties, thereby avoiding entirely the need to comply with the Fourth Amendment. As a result, the barrier that the Fourth Amendment historically interposed between the government and data about individuals has been greatly reduced and may soon be eliminated effectively. Congress' failure to respond with broad legislation has resulted in a situation in which the vast majority of personal data about individuals is now accessible to the government without legal limit and contrary to the public's expectations.

Moreover, the growing importance of new forms of data mining to fight terrorism is enhancing the government's interest in third-party data. No longer does the government just want occasional access to a narrow range of records for specific searches for information about identified individuals. Instead, new data-mining programs would require broad access to vast amounts of third-party records about people who have done nothing to warrant attention in an effort to detect relationships and patterns of behavior that might highlight terrorist activities. Even if the Supreme Court had not decided *Miller* or otherwise excluded personal information held by third parties from the protection of the Fourth Amendment, Congress would still need to create a legislative framework for these new and very different data mining activities. *Miller* only exacerbates the need for that framework which, to date, Congress has declined to provide.

The absence of a coherent legal regime applicable to data mining significantly undercuts the confidence of the public and of policy-makers that it will be carried out with appropriate attention to protecting privacy and other civil liberties. That absence denies government officials charged with fighting terrorism guidance as to what is and is not acceptable conduct. It interferes with businesses, universities, and other possessors of potentially relevant databases knowing when they can legally share information with the government. And it is threatening individual privacy while slowing the development of new and promising data-mining programs, undermining research into this potentially im-

---

[3]Id. at 443 (citation omitted).
[4]Right to Financial Privacy Act, 12 U.S.C. §§ 3401-3422. See notes 51-63 and accompany text.

portant weapon in the war on terrorism, and hampering the data sharing that is key to national security. This is an untenable situation for both protecting privacy and fighting terrorism.

This chapter examines the Supreme Court's exclusion of government mining of third-party data from the privacy protection of the Fourth Amendment, Congress' failure to fill the gap left by the Court's jurisprudence or to otherwise respond to the growing use of data mining in counter-terrorism by specifying its appropriate roles and limits, and the resulting threat to privacy and security. Even as other technologies, such as anonymized data matching, help reduce the impact of government data mining on privacy and other civil liberties, legal rules will still be necessary to allow those technologies to reach their full potential, protect privacy in settings they do not reach, build public confidence in appropriate data mining, enhance national security, facilitate more rational and consistent policy-making, and foster further innovation.

20.2. WHAT IS DATA MINING?

"Data mining" is defined in many different ways, but most have in common the elements of searches of one or more databases of personally identifiable information by or on behalf of the government. Data mining in the anti-terrorism context usually involves third-party data that have been provided voluntarily, purchased or seized by the government, or reported to the government in compliance with routine reporting requirements. It may also involve the use of data previously collected by the government for other purposes.

Dramatic advances in information technology have greatly enhanced the government's ability to search vast quantities of data for the purpose of identifying people who meet specific criteria or otherwise present unusual patterns of activities. These technologies have exponentially increased the volume of data available about individuals and greatly reduced the financial and other obstacles to retaining, sharing, and exploiting those data in both the public and private sector. They also have eliminated the need to physically combine disparate data sets to be able to search them simultaneously.

Government data mining in general is widespread and expanding. A 2004 report by the Government Accountability Office found 42 federal departments—including every cabinet-level agency that responded to the GAO's survey—engaged in (88), or were planning to engage in (34), 122 data-mining efforts involving personal information.[5] Thirty-six of those involve accessing data from the private sector; 46 involve sharing data among federal agencies.[6]

Data mining is increasingly being looked to as a tool to combat terrorism. For example, in 2002 the Defense Advanced Research Projects Agency in the Department of Defense launched "Total Information Awareness"—later renamed "Terrorism Information Awareness"—a research and development program that included technologies to search personally identifiable transaction records and recognize patterns across separate databases for the purpose of combating terrorism.[7] The Advanced Research and Development Activity center, based in the National Security Agency in DOD, has a project—Novel Intelligence from Massive Data—to develop tools to examine large quantities of data to "re-

[5]U.S. General Accounting Office, *Data Mining: Federal Efforts Cover a Wide Range of Uses* (GAO-04-548), May 2004, at 3, 27-64, Tables 2-25.
[6]Id. at 3.
[7]U.S. Department of Defense, Technology and Privacy Advisory Committee, *Safeguarding Privacy in the Fight Against Terrorism* 15-20 (Mar. 2004).

veal new indicators, issues, and/or threats that would not otherwise have been found due to the massiveness of the data."[8]

Army defense contractor Torch Concepts, with the assistance of DOD and the Transportation Security Administration, obtained millions of passenger records from U.S. airlines in 2003 to study how data profiling can be used to identify high-risk passengers.[9] The TSA also worked to develop the second generation of the Computer-Assisted Passenger Prescreening System to compare airline passenger names with private- and public-sector databases to assess the level of risk a passenger might pose.[10] In the Homeland Security Act, signed into law in November 2002, Congress required the new Department of Homeland Security to "establish and utilize . . . data-mining and other advanced analytical tools," to "access, receive, and analyze data detect and identify threats of terrorism against the United States."[11]

These are just a handful of the more prominent and controversial publicly disclosed projects since the terrorist attacks of September 11, 2001. These projects are far removed from traditional inquiries to locate information about a particular individual. Criminal investigators have long made use of "subject-based" data mining to look for information about a specific individual. These inquiries start with *known* suspects and search for information about them and the people with whom they interact. The law applicable to such searches is quite complex, but fairly well settled.

Many new government data mining programs, especially in the counter-terrorism arena, feature "pattern-based" searches. These involve developing models of what criminal or terrorist behavior might look like and then examining databases for similar patterns. The GAO, for example, defines "data mining" as "the application of database technology and techniques—such as statistical analysis and modeling—to uncover hidden patterns and subtle relationships in data and to infer rules that allow for the prediction of future results."[12] The Federal Agency Data-Mining Reporting Act would require that the search or analysis of the database(s) be intended "to find a predictive pattern indicating terrorist or criminal activity."[13]

The power of data-mining technology and the range of data to which the government has access have contributed to blurring the line between subject- and pattern-based searches. The broader the search criteria, and the more people other than actual criminals or terrorists who will be identified by those criteria, the more pattern-like these searches become. Even when a subject-based search starts with a known suspect, it can be transformed into a pattern-based search as investigators target individuals for investigation solely because of apparently innocent connections with the suspect. The more tenuous the connection, the more like a pattern-based search it becomes. Moreover, even searches that are not pattern-based raise similar significant issues if they use third-party data from the private sector or data previously collected by the government for other purposes. Whether pattern- or subject-based, "data mining," as the term is used in this chapter, involves the government's access to and use of personal information about

[8]See <ic-arda.org>.

[9]Department of Homeland Security Privacy Office, *Report to the Public on Events Surrounding jetBlue Data Transfer—Findings and Recommendations* (Feb. 20, 2004).

[10]Privacy Act; System of Records, 68 Fed. Reg. 45,265 (2003) (DHS, TSA) (interim final notice); U.S. General Accounting Office, Computer-Assisted Passenger Prescreening System Faces Significant Implementation Challenges (GAO-04-385), Feb. 2004.

[11]Homeland Security Act of 2002, Pub. L. No. 107-296, §§ 201(d)(1), (d)(14) (Nov. 25, 2002).

[12]GAO *Data Mining* Report, supra at 4.

[13]S1169, Federal Data-Mining Reporting Act, 109th Cong., 1st Sess. (2005).

people who have done nothing warrant suspicion in an effort to identify those individuals who do.

20.3. CONSTITUTIONAL PROTECTION FOR INFORMATION PRIVACY

20.3.1. The Fourth Amendment

Historically, the primary constitutional limit on the government's ability to obtain personal information about individuals is the Fourth Amendment:

> The right of the people to be secure in their persons, houses, papers, and effects, against unreasonable searches and seizures, shall not be violated, and no Warrants shall issue, but upon probable cause, supported by Oath or affirmation, and particularly describing the place to be searched, and the persons or things to be seized.[14]

The Fourth Amendment does not purport to keep the government from conducting searches or seizing personal information; it only prohibits "unreasonable" searches and seizures. The Supreme Court interprets the Fourth Amendment also to require that searches be conducted only with a warrant issued by a court, even though this is not a requirement contained in the amendment itself.[15] For a court to issue a warrant, the government must show "probable cause" that a crime has been or is likely to be committed and that the information sought is germane to that crime. The Supreme Court also generally requires that the government provide the subject of a search with contemporaneous notice of the search.[16]

The Fourth Amendment applies to (a) searches and surveillance conducted for domestic law enforcement purposes within the United States and (b) those conducted outside of the United States if they involve U.S. citizens (although not necessarily permanent resident aliens). The Fourth Amendment also applies to searches and surveillance conducted for national security and intelligence purposes within the United States if they involve U.S. persons who do not have a connection to a foreign power.[17] The Supreme Court has not yet addressed whether the Fourth Amendment applies to searches and surveillance for national security and intelligence purposes that involve U.S. persons who are connected to a foreign power or are conducted wholly outside of the United States.[18] Lower courts have found, however, that there is an exception to the Fourth Amendment's warrant requirement for searches conducted for intelligence purposes within the United States that involve only non-U.S. persons or agents of foreign powers.[19]

Where it does apply, while the protection afforded by the Fourth Amendment can be considerable, it is not absolute. The Supreme Court has determined, for example, that warrants are not required to search or seize items in the "plain view" of a law enforcement

---

[14]U.S. Constitution amend. IV.

[15]Akihl Reed Amar, *The Constitution and Criminal Procedure* 3–4 (1997).

[16]Richards v. Wisconsin, 520 U.S. 385 (1997).

[17]U.S. v. U.S. District Court for the Eastern District of Michigan, 407 U.S. 297 (1972) (commonly referred to as the *Keith* decision).

[18]Jeffrey H. Smith and Elizabeth L. Howe, "Federal Legal Constraints on Electronic Surveillance," Markle Foundation Task Force on National Security in the Information Age, *Protecting America's Freedom in the Information Age* 133 (2002).

[19]See U.S. v. Bin Laden, 126 F. Supp. 2d 264, 271–72 (S.D.N.Y. 2000).

officer,[20] for searches that are conducted incidental to valid arrests,[21] and for searches specially authorized by the Attorney General or the President involving foreign threats of "immediate and grave peril" to national security.[22] Moreover, the Fourth Amendment poses no limits on how the government may use information, provided that it has been obtained legally. So personal data seized by the government in compliance with the Fourth Amendment may later be used in a context for which the data could not have been obtained consistent with the Fourth Amendment.

The Fourth Amendment prohibits only "unreasonable" searches and seizures, but is silent about what makes a search or seizure "unreasonable." In his 1967 concurrence in *Katz v. United States,* Justice Harlan wrote that reasonableness was defined by both the individual's "actual," subjective expectation of privacy and by an objective expectation that was "one that society was prepared to recognize as 'reasonable.' "[23] The Court adopted that test for determining what was "private" within the meaning of the Fourth Amendment in 1968 and continues to apply it today.

20.3.2. The *Miller–Smith* Exclusion of Third-Party Records

The Supreme Court held in 1976 in *United States v. Miller*[24] that there can be no reasonable expectation of privacy in information held by a third party. The case involved canceled checks, to which, the Court noted, "respondent can assert neither ownership nor possession."[25] Such documents "contain only information voluntarily conveyed to the banks and exposed to their employees in the ordinary course of business,"[26] and therefore the Court found that the Fourth Amendment is not implicated when the government sought access to them:

> The depositor takes the risk, in revealing his affairs to another, that the information will be conveyed by that person to the Government. This Court has held repeatedly that the Fourth Amendment does not prohibit the obtaining of information revealed to a third party and conveyed by him to Government authorities, even if the information is revealed on the assumption that it will be used only for a limited purpose and the confidence placed in the third party will not be betrayed.[27]

Congress reacted to the decision by enacting modest statutory protection for customer financial records held by financial institutions,[28] but there is no constitutional protection for financial records or any other personal information that has been disclosed to third parties. As a result, the government can collect even the most sensitive information from a third party without a warrant and without risk that the search may be found unreasonable under the Fourth Amendment.

The Court reinforced its holding in *Miller* in the 1979 case of *Smith v. Maryland,* involving information about (as opposed to the content of) telephone calls.[29] The Supreme

---

[20]Coolidge v. New Hampshire, 403 U.S. 443 (1971).
[21]U.S. v. Edwards, 415 U.S. 800 (1974).
[22]68 *American Jurisprudence 2d,* Searches and Seizures § 104 (1993); Smith & Howe, supra at 136, no. 16.
[23]389 U.S. 347, 361 (1967).
[24]United States v. Miller, 425 U.S. 435 (1976).
[25]Id. at 440.
[26]Id. at 442.
[27]Id. at 443 (citation omitted).
[28]Right to Financial Privacy Act, 12 U.S.C. §§ 3401–3422. See notes 51–53 and accompanying text.
[29]442 U.S. 735 (1979).

Court found that the Fourth Amendment is inapplicable to telecommunications "attributes" (e.g., the number dialed, the time the call was placed, the duration of the call, etc.), because that information is necessarily conveyed to, or observable by, third parties involved in connecting the call.[30] "[T]elephone users, in sum, typically know that they must convey numerical information to the phone company; that the phone company has facilities for recording this information; and that the phone company does in fact record this information for a variety of legitimate business purposes."[31]

As a result, under the Fourth Amendment, the use of "pen registers" (to record outgoing call information) and "trap and trace" devices (to record in-coming call information) does not require a warrant because they only collect information about the call that is necessarily disclosed to others. As with information disclosed to financial institutions, Congress reacted to the Supreme Court's decision by creating a statutory warrant requirement for pen registers,[32] but the Constitution does not apply.

The third-party exemption from the Fourth Amendment made little sense in the two cases in which it was created. Individuals who write checks and dial telephone calls do not "voluntarily" convey information to third parties. They have no choice but to convey the information if they wish to use what in the 1970s were the overwhelmingly dominant means of making large-value payments or communicating over physical distances.

Moreover, and more importantly, the information collected and stored by banks and telephone companies is subject to explicit or implicit promises that it will not be further disclosed. Most customers would be astonished to find their checks or telephone billing records printed in the newspaper. As a result of those promises and the experience of individuals, the expectation that such information would be private was objectively reasonable and widely shared. The Court's decisions to the contrary, while they served important law enforcement objectives, made little logical or practical sense and did not reflect the expectations of either the public or policy-makers, as demonstrated by the fact that Congress responded so quickly to both with gap-filling legislation.

Irrespective of whether *Miller* and *Smith* were correctly decided, however, excluding records held by third parties from the protection of the Fourth Amendment makes no sense today because of the extraordinary increase in both the volume and sensitivity of information about individuals necessarily held by third parties. Professor Daniel Solove writes: "We are becoming a society of records, and these records are not held by us, but by third parties."[33] He offers these examples:

> [L]ife in modern society demands that we enter into numerous relationships with professionals (doctors, lawyers, accountants), businesses (restaurants, video rental stores), merchants (bookstores, mail catalog companies), publishing companies (magazines, newspapers), organizations (charities), financial institutions (banks, investment firms, credit card companies), landlords, employers, and other entities (insurance companies, security companies, travel agencies, car rental companies, hotels). Our relationships with all of these entities generate records containing personal information necessary to establish an account and record of our transactions, preferences, purchases, and activities.[34]

Thanks to the proliferation of digital technologies and networks such as the Internet, and tremendous advances in the capacity of storage devices and parallel decreases in their

---

[30]442 U.S. 735 (1979).

[31]Id. at 743.

[32]18 U.S.C. §§ 3121, 1841. See notes 51–53 and accompanying text.

[33]Daniel J. Solove, Digital Dossiers and the Dissipation of Fourth Amendment Privacy, 75 *Southern California Law Review* 1083, 1089 (2002).

[34]Id.

cost and physical size, those records are linked and shared more widely and stored far longer than ever before, often without the individual consumer's knowledge or consent.

In addition, as more everyday activities move online, records contain more detailed information about individuals' behavior. No longer do merchants record data only on what individuals buy and how they pay for their purchases. Instead, those data include every detail of what we look at, the books we read, the movies we watch, the music we listen to, the games we play, and the places we visit. Instead of comparatively barebones data about the checks individuals write and telephone calls we place, the government today has access unrestricted by the Fourth Amendment to private-sector records on every detail of how we live our lives.

The robustness of these records is difficult to overestimate and is not limited to settings involving commercial transactions. For example, computers track every moment of most employees' days. Digital time clocks and entry keys record physical movements. Computers store work product, e-mail, and Internet browsing records—often in keystroke-by-keystroke detail, as more and more employees use technologies to monitor employee behavior. E-mail and voice mail are stored digitally. Even the content of telephone conversations may be recorded.

Also, the ubiquitous nature of data collection and observation is not limited to the workplace. Digital devices for paying tolls, computer diagnostic equipment in car engines, and global positioning services that are increasingly common on passenger vehicles record every mile driven. Cellular telephones and personal digital assistants record not only call and appointment information, but location as well, and transmit this information to service providers. ISPs record online activities, digital cable and satellite record what we watch and when, alarm systems record when we enter and leave our homes, and all of these data are held by third parties.

All indications are that this is just the beginning. Broadband Internet access into homes has not only increased the personal activities we now engage in online, but also created new and successful markets for remote computer back-up and online photo, e-mail, and music storage services. With Voice-Over IP telephone service, digital phone calls are becoming indistinguishable from digital documents: Both can be stored and accessed remotely. Global positioning technologies are appearing in more and more products, and Radio-Frequency Identification Tags are beginning to be used to identify high-end consumer goods, pets, and even people.

Moreover, those records may be held by more private parties than ever before. Digital transactions are likely to be observed by more parties. Data about online browsing or purchases are accessible not only to the consumer and merchants directly involved in the transaction, but also to their ISPs, the provider of the payment mechanism (for example, a credit card company), and the company that delivers the merchandise. The everyday use of a credit card or ATM card involves the disclosure of personal financial information to multiple entities.

In addition, digital networks have facilitated the growth of vigorous outsourcing markets, so information provided to one company is increasingly likely to be processed by a separate institution. Customer service may be provided by another. And all of those entities may store their data with still another. Personal information is available from all of these. For example, many employers contract with separate ISPs. Information on browsing habits of employees is available to both the employer and the ISP. If an employee buys an airline ticket through an online travel service, such as Travelocity or Expedia, the information concerning that transaction will be available to the employer, the ISP, the travel service, the airline, and the provider of the payment mechanism, at a minimum.

The government would hardly need to visit all of these businesses separately, however, to gather personal information. A handful of service providers already process, or have access to, the large majority of credit and debit card transactions, ATM withdrawals, airline and rental car reservations, and Internet access. As demonstrated by the 2005 security breach at Atlanta-based CardSystems that revealed sensitive information about as many as 40 million Visa, MasterCard, Discover, and American Express customers,[35] there is no need to go to each of these companies separately for information on their customers when one service provider can supply the same data.

Moreover, there are information aggregation businesses in the private sector that already combine personal data from thousands of private-sector sources and public records. ChoicePoint, Acxiom, LexisNexis, the three national credit bureaus, and dozens of other companies maintain rich repositories of information about virtually every adult in the country. These records are updated daily by a steady stream of incoming data. These businesses supply this information, for a fee, to private- and public-sector customers for a variety of valuable uses. One of the common threads among most of the antiterrorist data-mining programs that have been made public to date is their reliance—intended or actual—on these aggregators. Why seize data from many separate entities or even service providers when much the same information can be bought from one?

The *Miller* exclusion from the Fourth Amendment of information disclosed to third parties means that all of this information, no matter how sensitive or how revealing of a person's health, finances, tastes, or convictions, is available to the government without constitutional limit. The government's demand need not be reasonable, no warrant is necessary, and no judicial authorization or oversight is required. Moreover, it appears not to matter how explicitly confidentiality was promised by the third party as a condition of providing the information. Those promises and contractual provisions may restrict the ability of the third party to volunteer the information, although as Professor Solove notes, most privacy policies today are written to permit voluntary disclosures to the government,[36] but privacy promises have no effect on the power of the government to obtain the information.

Finally, technological developments over the past 40 years have both (a) ensured that the data are in digital form and therefore more likely to be of use to the government and (b) put increasingly powerful tools in the hands of the government to be able to use those data. Millions of records stored on index cards were not likely to be of much use to the government. The cost of duplicating, transporting, storing, and using them would have been in most cases prohibitive. In electronic format, however, those costs are comparatively negligible. So while the impact of *Miller* in 1976 was primarily limited to government requests for specific records about identified individuals, today *Miller* allows the government to obtain the raw material for broad-based data mining.

This is a significant difference. The 1970s searches involved demands for information about individuals who had already done something to warrant the government's attention. Whether or not the suspicious activity amounted to "probable cause," there was at least some reason to suspect a particular person. Today, because of major technological and related changes, the government has not only the power under the Fourth Amendment to ask for everything about everybody, but increasingly the practical ability to do something with that information. As a result, as part of its ongoing fight against terrorism, the government

[35]Eric Dash, "68,000 MasterCard Accounts Are at High Risk in Breach," *New York Times,* June 19, 2005, at A22.
[36]Solove, supra at 1098–1100.

increasingly desires access to broad swaths of information about people who have done nothing to warrant suspicion. This new practical power offers potentially valuable new weapons in the war against a nearly invisible terrorist foe. But that power, especially in the absence of constitutional oversight, also raises important legal and political questions.

Advances in technologies, and the development of new products and services in response to those changes, have significantly expanded the scope of the *Miller* exclusion of records held by third parties from the protection of the Fourth Amendment. Today there are vastly more personal data in the hands of third parties, they are far more revealing, and they are much more readily accessible than was the case in the 1970s. Moreover, for the first time, the government has the practical ability to exploit huge datasets. As a result, the scope of the *Miller* decision has been greatly expanded, and the balance between the government's power to obtain personal data and the privacy rights of individuals has been fundamentally altered.

20.4. CONGRESSIONAL ROLES

While the Supreme Court identifies and interprets constitutional boundaries between the government and the citizenry, Congress establishes statutory boundaries and rules that the government must follow to cross them. The congressional roles are vital because of the breadth of Congress' power and its ability to provide detailed, prospective guidance to the public and to government officials about the seizure of personal information.

That guidance is also necessary to address the consensual and regulatory collection, use, storage, and disclosure of personal data. While the government has constitutionally unlimited power to search and seize third-party records, it is more likely to seek those records through routine reporting requirements or purchase, or by reusing data already collected by the government through these means for other purposes. Historically, the Fourth Amendment has played no role in restricting these activities. Moreover, as we have seen, the Fourth Amendment plays no role once information has been lawfully collected in determining how it is to be used, stored, or disclosed. These are significant omissions that legislation is well-suited to address.

As a result, even if the Supreme Court had not excluded third-party records from the protection of the Fourth Amendment in *Miller*, congressional action would still be critical because of the need to provide a legal structure for the government's collection of information through means other than seizure, and for its use, storage, and dissemination of that information. This is especially true in the face of technological advances that have exponentially increased the volume of data available about individuals, greatly reduced the financial and other obstacles to sharing and exploiting those data, and significantly enhanced the government's ability to search vast quantities of data for the purpose of identifying people who meet specific criteria or otherwise present unusual patterns of activities. These changes have resulted in a new environment and new challenges that require new rules. It is the responsibility of Congress to provide them.

20.4.1. The Privacy Act

Congress first regulated how the government collects and uses personal information in the Privacy Act of 1974.[37] In the early 1970s, mounting concerns about computerized data-

---

[37]5 U.S.C. § 552a.

bases prompted the government to examine the issues they raised—technological and legal—by appointing an Advisory Committee on Automated Personal Data Systems in the Department of Health, Education and Welfare. In 1973, the Advisory Committee issued its report, *Records, Computers and the Rights of Citizens*[38] Congress responded the following year with the Privacy Act.

The Privacy Act requires federal agencies to store only relevant and necessary personal information and only for purposes required to be accomplished by statute or executive order; collect information to the extent possible from the data subject; maintain records that are accurate, complete, timely, and relevant; and establish administrative, physical, and technical safeguards to protect the security of records.[39] The Privacy Act also prohibits disclosure, even to other government agencies, of personally identifiable information in any record contained in a "system of records," except pursuant to a written request by or with the written consent of the data subject, or pursuant to a specific exception.[40] Agencies must log disclosures of records and, in some cases, inform the subjects of such disclosures when they occur. Under the Act, data subjects must be able to access and copy their records, each agency must establish a procedure for amendment of records, and refusals by agencies to amend their records are subject to judicial review. Agencies must publish a notice of the existence, character, and accessibility of their record systems.[41] Finally, individuals may seek legal redress if an agency denies them access to their records.

The Privacy Act is less protective of privacy than may first appear, because of numerous broad exceptions.[42] Twelve of these are expressly provided for in the Act itself. For example, information contained in an agency's records can be disclosed for "civil or criminal law enforcement activity if the activity is authorized by law."[43] An agency can disclose its records to officers and employees within the agency itself, the Bureau of the Census, the National Archives, Congress, the Comptroller General, and consumer reporting agencies.[44] Information subject to disclosure under the Freedom of Information Act is exempted from the Privacy Act.[45] And under the "routine use" exemption,[46] federal agencies are permitted to disclose personal information so long as the nature and scope of the routine use was previously published in the Federal Register and the disclosure of data was "for a purpose which is compatible with the purpose for which it was collected." According to OMB, "compatibility" covers uses that are either (1) functionally equivalent or (2) necessary and proper.[47]

Moreover, the Privacy Act applies only to information maintained in a "system of records."[48] The Act defines "system of records" as a "group of any records under the con-

---

[38]U.S. Department of Health, Education and Welfare, Report of the Secretary's Advisory Committee on Automated Personal Data Systems, Records, Computer, and the Rights of Citizens (1973).
[39]Id.
[40]Id. § 552a(b).
[41]Id. § 552a(e)(4).
[42]Sean Fogarty and Daniel R. Ortiz, "Limitations Upon Interagency Information Sharing: The Privacy Act of 1974," Markle Foundation Task Force, *Protecting America's Freedom in the Information Age, supra* at 127, 128.
[43]Id. § 552a (b)(7).
[44]5 U.S.C. § 552a(b),
[45]Id. § 552a (b)(2)
[46]Id. § 552a (b)(3).
[47]Privacy Act of 1974; Guidance on the Privacy, Act Implications of "Call Detail" Programs to Manage Employees' Use of the Government's Telecommunications Systems, 52 Fed. Reg. 12,900, 12,993 (1987) (OMB) (publication of guidance in final form); see generally Fogarty & Ortiz, supra at 129–130.
[48]5 U.S.C. § 552a(b).

trol of any agency from which information is retrieved by the name of the individual or by some identifying number, symbol, or other identifying particular assigned to the individual."[49] The U.S. Court of Appeals for the District of Columbia Circuit held that "retrieval capability is not sufficient to create a system of records. . . . 'To be in a system of records, a record must . . . in practice [be] retrieved by an individual's name or other personal identifier.' "[50] This is unlikely to be the case with new antiterrorism databases and data-mining programs. They are more likely to involve searches for people who fit within certain patterns, rather than inquiries by name or other personal identifier.

As a result, the Privacy Act plays little role in providing guidance for government data mining activities or limiting the government's power to collect personal data from third parties. In fact, the framework created by the Privacy Act, which was designed more than 30 years ago primarily for personnel records and benefits files, would appear to be altogether ill-suited for regulating counter-terrorism data mining. Like many laws relating to information, it has become outdated and outmoded by the passage of time and dramatic technological change.

20.4.2. The Response to *Miller* and *Smith*

Congress responded to *United States v. Miller* and *Smith v. Maryland* with specific statutes designed to address the vacuum created by the Supreme Court's decisions. The Right to Financial Privacy Act, enacted in 1978, two years after *Miller*, regulates how federal agencies may obtain financial records from financial institutions.[51] The Electronic Communications Privacy Act, enacted in 1986, seven years after *Smith*, broadly regulates electronic surveillance, including the use of pen registers and trap and trace devices.[52]

Neither statute provides the level of protection that would have been required under the Fourth Amendment, and both contain a number of exceptions. The Right to Financial Privacy Act, for example, does not restrict disclosures to state or local governments or private entities, nor does it apply to the federal government obtaining financial information from other third parties. Even in the limited area where it does apply, the Act allows the federal government to seize personal financial information pursuant to an administrative subpoena, judicial subpoena, search warrant, or formal written request. The Electronic Communications Privacy Act allows the government to obtain a judicial order authorizing the use of a pen register or trap and trace device upon a mere certification that the "information likely to be obtained is relevant to an ongoing 'criminal investigation.' "[53]

Nevertheless, despite their weaknesses, both statutes do impose some substantive limits on the government's power to seize financial and calling attribute information and they do impose discipline on the government by specifying procedures to be followed. In short, the statutes help guard against the "unreasonable" searches and seizures that the Fourth Amendment, had it applied, would have prohibited.

This sectoral approach is not limited to financial and communications records, although other sectoral protections are often weaker, especially following post-9/11 amendments. For example, the Cable Act of 1984 prohibits cable companies from providing the

---

[49]Id. § 552a(a)(5).
[50]Henke v. United States DOC, 83 F.3d 1453, 1461 (D.C. Cir. 1996) (quoting Bartel v. F.A.A., 725 F.2d 1403, 1408 No. 10 (D.C. Cir. 1984)).
[51]12 U.S.C. §§ 3401–3422.
[52]18 U.S.C. §§ 3121, 1841.
[53]Id. §§ 3122–23.

government with personally identifiable information about their customers, unless the government presents a court order.[54] The USA Patriot Act, adopted in the immediate aftermath of the September 11 attacks, amended this provision to apply only to records about cable television service and not other services—such as Internet or telephone—that a cable operator might provide.[55] The Video Privacy Protection Act prohibits video rental companies from disclosing personally identifiable information about their customers unless the government presents a search warrant, court order, or grand jury subpoena.[56] The Family Education Rights and Privacy Act of 1974 contains a similar provision applicable to educational records.[57]

The Fair Credit Reporting Act, enacted in 1970, permits disclosure of credit information only for statutorily specified purposes.[58] One of those purposes is "in response to the order of a court having jurisdiction to issue such an order, or a subpoena issued in connection with proceedings before a Federal grand jury."[59] In addition, consumer reporting agencies may freely furnish identifying information (e.g., "name, address, former addresses, places of employment, or former places of employment") to the government.[60] The Act was amended following the September 11 terrorist attacks to permit virtually unlimited disclosures to the government for counter-terrorism purposes. All that is required is a "written certification" that the request information is "necessary for the agency's conduct or such investigation, activity or analysis."[61]

In 2001, the Department of Health and Human Services adopted rules, specifically authorized by Congress, protecting the privacy of personal health information.[62] Those rules, while restrictive on their face, in reality permit broad disclosure of personal health information to the government "in the course of any judicial or administrative proceeding," "in response to an order of a court or administrative tribunal," "in response to a subpoena, discovery request, or other lawful process," "as required by law," "in compliance with . . . a court order or court-ordered warrant, or a subpoena or summons issued by a judicial officer," "in compliance with . . . a grand jury subpoena," and "in compliance with . . . an administrative request, including an administrative subpoena or summons, a civil or an authorized investigative demand, or similar process."[63]

These statutes and rules apply in limited areas; where they do apply they impose few substantive limits, although some procedural discipline, on government access to third-party data.

20.4.3. The Response to Data Mining

In 1988, Congress passed the Computer Matching and Privacy Protection Act as an amendment to the Privacy Act.[64] The new law responded to the growth in early forms of

[54]47 U.S.C. § 551.
[55]Uniting and Strengthening America by Providing Appropriate Tools Required to Intercept and Obstruct Terrorism Act of 2001, Pub. L. No. 107-56, 115 Stat. 272, Title II, § 211 (2001).
[56]18 U.S.C. § 2710.
[57]20 U.S.C. § 1232g.
[58]15 U.S.C. § 1681b.
[59]Id. § 1681b(a)(1).
[60]Id. § 1681f.
[61]Id. §§ 1681u, 1681v.
[62]*Standards for Privacy of Individually Identifiable Health Information,* 65 Fed. Reg. 82,462 (2000) (HHS, final rule) (codified at 45 C.F.R. pt. 160, §§ 164.502, 164.506).
[63]45 C.F.R. § 164.512.
[64]Pub L. No. 100-503 (1988) (codified at 5 U.S.C. §§ 552a(a)(8), 552a(o)–(r)).

data mining within the federal government and the reality that the broad exceptions to the Privacy Act, and particularly the growing view of agency officials, the Office of Management and Budget, and even courts that data matching constituted a "routine use of data" and therefore was exempt from the Privacy Act,[65] rendered the Privacy Act inadequate to respond to data mining.

The Computer Matching and Privacy Protection Act provides a series of procedural requirements, such as written agreements between agencies that share data for matching,[66] before an agency can disclose personal information for data mining. These requirements deal only with federal agencies supplying—not obtaining—records for data mining.[67] Moreover, they only apply to data mining for the purpose of "establishing or verifying the eligibility of, or continuing compliance with statutory and regulatory requirements by, applicants for, recipients or beneficiaries of, participants in, or providers of service with respect to, cash or in-kind assistance or payments under Federal benefit programs" or "recouping payment or delinquent debts under such Federal benefit programs" or "Federal personnel or payroll systems of records."[68] Counter-terrorism data mining does not fit within the definition of activities covered by the statute. Moreover, the Act specifically excludes data mining for "law enforcement," "foreign counterintelligence," and "background checks."[69]

As of 1988, then, Congress had responded to the Supreme Court's decisions in *Miller* and *Smith* and the growth of federal data mining with sectoral statutes imposing modest limits on the government's ability to seize personal data from third parties and with a statute imposing procedural limits on the ability of the government to share data for data mining in connection with federal benefits or payroll programs. The 1988 law was effectively Congress' last word on the subject prior to post-9/11 developments. Laws and regulations enacted since then have either ignored government data mining entirely or failed to provide any structure for when data mining is appropriate and how it should be conducted. Moreover, counter-terrorism laws and even so-called "privacy" laws have actually weakened the protections against government seizure of personal data held by third parties. As a result the government now has the technological capability, incentive, and authority to engage in data mining, ready access to a virtually unlimited store of personal data on which to work, and no legal or policy framework to guide its data-mining activities.

20.5. THE CURRENT POLICY-MAKING MORASS

20.5.1. The Immediate Post-9/11 Response

The terrorist attacks of September 11 focused the attention of national security officials and policy-makers on the importance of effective data mining to combat terrorism. In the immediate aftermath of the attacks, government officials turned to private-sector data as never before in an effort to identify the perpetrators and track down their co-conspirators. The government sought information from credit card companies, banks, airlines, rental

---

[65]Office of Technology Assessment, Congress of the United States, *Electronic Record Systems and Individual Privacy* 57 (1986).
[66]5 U.S.C. § 552a (o).
[67]Id. § 552a (o)(1).
[68]Id. § 552a(a)(8)(A).
[69]Id. §§ 552a (a)(8)(B)(iii), (B)(v)(vi).

car agencies, flight training schools, and colleges. Law enforcement officials sought information on large or suspicious financial transactions, and on any accounts involving suspected terrorists, not just from U.S. banks, but from all U.S. financial institutions and even from foreign banks that do business in the United States. Private-sector data, it became clear, was a treasure trove of information that could and would be used to identify and trace the activities of the 19 hijackers and their accomplices.

As shock and recovery efforts gave way to inquiries into why the attacks had not been prevented, it became clear that U.S. counter-terrorism and law enforcement officials had failed to connect important pieces of information stored in disparate government agencies.[70] Moreover, with the clarity of 20–20 hindsight, newspaper and magazine articles showed the myriad connections among the 19 hijackers available from largely nonsensitive private-sector data. Two of the terrorists—Nawaf Alhazmi and Khalid Almihdhar, flying under their real names on September 11—were on a State Department watch list. Data analysis expert Valdis Krebs first showed the 9-11 terrorist network connections, such as a third hijacker used the same address as Alhazmi. Two others, including Muhammad Atta, shared a residence with Almihdhar. Five others had the same phone number as Atta. Another had the same frequent-flier number as Almihdhar.[71] How could we have failed to spot such now-obvious connections? What could be done to ensure that never happened again? Government inquiries and private-sector task forces stressed the need to "connect the dots."

The government's authority to centralize or more effectively share data it collects through traditional intelligence and law enforcement information-gathering methods has been greatly enhanced. Section 203 of the USA Patriot Act amended federal law to allow intelligence information gathered in grand jury proceedings and from wiretaps to be shared with any federal law enforcement, intelligence, immigration, or national defense personnel.[72] In the case of grand jury information, the government must notify the court after disclosure.[73]

Legislative proposals emerged from many sources, some of which were ultimately adopted, to centralize the dozen or more terrorist watch lists maintained by separate federal agencies. Government intelligence data were also brought together initially under a Terrorist Threat Integration Center and then, following the recommendations of the 9/11 Commission, under the National Counterterrorism Center. Ultimately, intelligence operations themselves were made subject to a new Director of National Intelligence.[74]

Efforts to enhance the collection and use of private-sector data have been more fractured and controversial. The USA Patriot Act imposed significant new reporting requirements on financial institutions. The Act expanded the power of the Treasury Department's Financial Crimes Enforcement Network (FinCEN) to require financial institutions to report suspected money laundering or terrorist activities by their customers.[75] The Act also mandated new "Know Your Customer" rules which require financial institutions to

[70]See, for example, *Joint Inquiry into Intelligence Community Activities before and after the Terrorist Attacks of September 11, 2001,* Report of the U.S. Senate Select Committee on Intelligence and U.S. House Permanent Select Committee on Intelligence, S. Rept. No. 107- 351, H. Rep. No. 107-792, 107th Congress, 2d Session (2002), at xv–xvi.

[71]http://www.orgnet.com/hijackers.html

[72]Pub. L. No. 107-56, Title II, § 203.

[73]Id.

[74]Intelligence Reform and Terrorism Prevention Act of 2004, Pub. L. No. 108-458, 118 Stat. 3638 (Dec. 17, 2004).

[75]Financial Crimes Enforcement Network; Special Information Sharing Procedures to Deter Money Laundering and Terrorist Activity, 67 Fed. Reg. 60,579 (2002) (Treasury) (final rule).

(1) verify the identity of any person seeking to open an account, (2) maintain records of the information used to verify the person's identity, (3) determine whether the person appears on any list of known or suspected terrorists or terrorist organizations, and (4) report to the government if they do.[76]

Under section 215 of the USA Patriot Act, the Director of the FBI or a high-level designee of the Director may apply for an order from the Foreign Intelligence Surveillance Court requiring the production of any tangible things (including books, records, papers, documents, and other items) for an investigation to protect against international terrorism or clandestine intelligence activities.[77] The only substantive limit on obtaining section 215 orders is that the investigation of a U.S. citizen or permanent legal resident may not be "conducted solely upon the basis of activities protected by the first amendment to the Constitution."[78] The orders are issued and executed in secret, and the statute prohibits the recipient of a section 215 order from disclosing its existence to anyone.[79]

The following year, in November 2002, Congress enacted the Homeland Security Act establishing DHS.[80] Section 201 of the law requires DHS to:

- "access, receive, and analyze law enforcement information, intelligence information, and other information from agencies of the Federal Government, State and local government agencies (including law enforcement agencies), and private sector entities, and to integrate such information";
- "request additional information from other agencies of the Federal Government, State and local government agencies, and the private sector relating to threats of terrorism in the United States, or relating to other areas of responsibility assigned by the Secretary, including the entry into cooperative agreements through the Secretary to obtain such information"; and
- "establish and utilize, in conjunction with the chief information officer of the Department, a secure communications and information technology infrastructure, including data-mining and other advanced analytical tools, in order to access, receive, and analyze data and information in furtherance of the responsibilities under this section, and to disseminate information acquired and analyzed by the Department, as appropriate."[81]

This positive command from Congress to access private-sector data and engage in data mining in the fight against terrorism could hardly have been more explicit, but it was soon contradicted by Congress' response to another counter-terrorism data-mining initiative.

20.5.2. Total Information Awareness

In April 2002, the Director of the Defense Advanced Research Projects Agency testified before the Senate Armed Services Committee about a new research program: Total Infor-

---

[76]Transactions and Customer Identification Programs, 68 Fed. Reg. 25,089 (2003) (Treasury, Comptroller of the Currency, Office of Thrift Supervision, Federal Reserve System, Federal Deposit Insurance Corporation, National Credit Union Administration, Commodity Futures Trading Commission, Securities and Exchange Commission) (final rules and proposed rule).

[77]Pub. L. No. 107-56, Title II, § 215.

[78]Id.

[79]Id. If not reauthorized by Congress, this section will sunset on December 31, 2005.

[80]Homeland Security Act of 2002, Pub. L. No. 107-296 (Nov. 25, 2002).

[81]Id. §§ 201(d)(1), (d)(13), (d)(14).

mation Awareness.[82] In August, Admiral John Poindexter, director of DARPA's Information Awareness Office (IAS), described TIA at the DARPATech 2002 Conference, and his Deputy, Dr. Robert Popp, spoke publicly often about the goals and objectives of TIA and IAO. Admiral Poindexter described the need to "become much more efficient and more clever in the ways we find new sources of data, mine information from the new and old, generate information, make it available for analysis, convert it to knowledge, and create actionable options."[83] To accomplish these purposes, he articulated the need for a "much more systematic approach."[84] "Total Information Awareness—a prototype system—is our answer."[85]

In numerous speeches given in 2002, Poindexter and Popp both noted a key hypothesis that required research was exploring "one of the significant new data sources that needs to be mined to discover and track terrorists"—the "transaction space."[86] "If terrorist organizations are going to plan and execute attacks against the United States, their people must engage in transactions and they will leave signatures in this information space."[87] He then showed a slide of transaction data that included "Communications, Financial, Education, Travel, Medical, Veterinary, Country Entry, Place/Event Entry, Transportation, Housing, Critical Resources, and Government" records. He also noted the importance of protecting privacy.

In November 2002, at the height of the debate over enactment of the Homeland Security Act, public controversy erupted over TIA and its impact on privacy, sparked in large part by a *New York Times* column by William Safire.[88] In the seven months between the initial disclosure of TIA and Safire's column, only 12 press reports had appeared about the program. In the next 30 days, the press carried 285 stories.[89]

In December 2002, the Assistant to the Secretary of Defense for Intelligence Oversight conducted an internal review of TIA and related programs. The review concluded that no legal obligations or "rights of United States persons" had been violated.[90] Opposition to TIA, however, continued to mount. In late 2002 Senators Charles E. Grassley (R-Iowa), Chuck Hagel (R-Neb.), and Bill Nelson (D-Fla.) wrote to the DOD Inspector General asking him to review TIA. On January 10, 2003, the Inspector General announced an audit of TIA, including "an examination of safeguards regarding the protection of privacy and civil liberties."[91]

Congress did not wait for the results of the audit. On February 13, 2003, Congress adopted the Consolidated Appropriations Resolution.[92] The bill contained an amendment proposed by Senator Ron Wyden (D-Ore.) prohibiting the expenditure of funds on TIA unless the Secretary of Defense, the Director of the Central Intelligence Agency, and the

---

[82]*Fiscal 2003 Defense Request: Combating Terrorism,* Hearing before the Senate Armed Services Committee, April 10, 2002 (statement of Dr. Tony Tether).

[83]John Poindexter, Overview of the Information Awareness Office, prepared remarks for delivery at DARPATech 2002, Anaheim, CA, Aug. 2, 2002, at 1; Robert Popp Interview, E. Jonietz, "Total Information Overload," *MIT Technology Review,* July 2003.

[84]Id.

[85]Id. at 2.

[86]Id.

[87]Id.

[88]William Safire, "You Are a Suspect," *New York Times,* Nov. 14, 2002, at A35.

[89]*TAPAC Report,* supra at 16.

[90]Statement of George B. Lotz, II, Assistant to the Secretary of Defense (Intelligence Oversight), to TAPAC, July 22, 2003, at 2.

[91]Letter from Joseph E. Schmitz, DOD Inspector General, to Senator Charles E. Grassley, Chairman, Committee on Finance, Jan. 17, 2003).

[92]Consolidated Appropriations Resolution, Pub. L. No. 108-7, Division M, § 111(b) (Feb. 24, 2003).

Attorney General jointly reported to Congress within 90 days of the enactment of the law about the development of TIA, its likely efficacy, the laws applicable to it, and its likely impact on civil liberties. The amendment also prohibited deployment of TIA in connection with data about U.S. persons without specific congressional authorization.[93]

Secretary of Defense Donald Rumsfeld sought to diffuse congressional tension by appointing two committees in February 2003. One was an internal oversight board to establish "policies and procedures for use within DOD of TIA-developed tools" and "protocols for transferring these capabilities to entities outside DOD . . . in accordance with existing privacy protection laws and policies."[94]

The other committee was the Technology and Privacy Advisory Committee, the members of which were eight prominent lawyers, including four former senior officials from democratic administrations and two from republican administrations.[95] The Secretary charged TAPAC with examining "the use of advanced information technologies to help identify terrorists before they act."[96]

The report specified by the Wyden Amendment was delivered to Congress on May 20, 2003.[97] The report described an array of TIA and TIA-related programs. With regard to TIA itself, the report eschewed earlier descriptions of a "virtual, centralized grand database." DARPA wrote that "the TIA Program is not attempting to create or access a centralized database that will store information gathered from various publicly or privately held databases."[98] Instead, the report focused on technological tools. Some of those tools would help the government

> imagine the types of terrorist attacks that might be carried out against the United States at home or abroad. They would develop scenarios for these attacks and determine what kind of planning and preparation activities would have to be carried out in order to conduct these attacks. . . . The red team would determine the types of transactions that would have to be carried out to perform these activities. . . . These transactions would form a pattern that may be discernable in certain databases to which the U.S. Government would have lawful access.[99]

The report also addressed other tools for secure collaborative problem solving, creating more structured and automated ways of organizing and searching data, enhancing the ability to detect and understand links between different individuals and groups, presenting data in easier-to-understand ways that make important connections easier to visualize, and improving decision making and the ways in which decision-making processes draw on stored data.[100]

The report also identified technological tools that were being developed as part of TIA to enhance privacy protection. For example, the Genisys Privacy Protection Program "aims to provide *security with privacy* by providing certain critical data to analysts while controlling access to unauthorized information, enforcing laws and policies through software mechanisms, and ensuring that any misuse of data can be quickly detected and addressed."[101] DARPA had begun funding research into privacy enhancing technologies from the start of the TIA program in March 2002.

---

[93]S. Amend. 59 to H.J. Res. 2 (Jan. 23, 2003).

[94]U.S. Department of Defense, Total Information Awareness (TIA) Update, News Release 060-03 (Feb. 7, 2003).

[95]Establishment of the Technology and Privacy Advisory Committee, 68 Fed. Reg. 11,384 (2003) (DOD, notice).

[96]U.S. Department of Defense, Technology and Privacy Advisory Committee Charter (Mar. 25, 2003).

[97]Report to Congress Regarding the Terrorism Information Awareness Program (May 20, 2003).

[98]Id., Detailed Information, supra at 27.

[99]Id. at 14.

[100]Id., Executive Summary, at 2-3.

[101]Id., Detailed Information, at 6.

With regard to the privacy issues posed by TIA and related programs, the report provided the following:

> The Department of Defense's TIA research and development efforts address both privacy and civil liberties in the following ways:
>
> - The Department of Defense must fully comply with the laws and regulations governing intelligence activities and all other laws that protect the privacy and constitutional rights of U.S. persons.
> - As an integral part of its research, TIA program itself is seeking to develop new technologies that will safeguard the privacy of U.S. persons.
> - TIA's research and testing activities are conducted using either real intelligence information that the federal government has already legally obtained, or artificial synthetic information that, ipso facto, does not implicate the privacy interests of U.S. persons.[102]

Neither the report nor the appointment of TAPAC was sufficient to sway Congress. On September 25, 2003, Congress passed the Department of Defense Appropriations Act, 2004.[103] Section 8131 of the Act terminated funding for TIA, with the exception of "processing, analysis, and collaboration tools for counter-terrorism foreign intelligence"[104] specified in a classified annex to the Act. Under the Act, those tools may be used by DOD only in connection with "lawful military operations of the United States conducted outside the United States" or "lawful foreign intelligence activities conducted wholly overseas, or wholly against non-United States citizens."[105]

In its report accompanying the Act, the Conference Committee directed that the IAO itself be terminated immediately.[106] The Act thus closed the IAO, further research on privacy enhancing technologies, and further publicly disclosed research on data mining, while keeping open the possibility of counter-terrorism data mining programs being developed outside of DARPA in secret.[107]

On December 12, 2003, the DOD Inspector General released the results of his audit of TIA. The audit concluded that "although the DARPA development of TIA-type technologies could prove valuable in combating terrorism, DARPA could have better addressed the sensitivity of the technology to minimize the possibility for Governmental abuse of power and to help ensure the successful transition of the technology into an operational environment."[108]

With specific regard to privacy, the audit found that DARPA failed to perform any form of privacy impact assessment, did not involve appropriate privacy and legal experts, and "focused on development of new technology rather than on the policies, procedures, and legal implications associated with the operational use of technology."[109] The report acknowledged that DARPA was sponsoring "research of privacy safeguards and options that would balance security and privacy issues," but found that such measures "were not

---

[102]Id., Executive Summary, at 3.

[103]Department of Defense Appropriations Act, 2004, Pub. L. No. 108-84 (Sept. 25, 2003).

[104]Id. § 8183(a).

[105]Id. § 8183(b). The President stated in his signing statement that the classified annex "accompanies but is not incorporated as a part of the Act" and therefore would be considered by the President as merely "advisory in effect." Statement on Signing the Department of Defense Appropriations Act, 2004 (Oct. 6, 2003).

[106]Conference Report on Making Appropriations for the Department of Defense for the Fiscal Year Ending September 30, 2004, and for Other Purposes, House Rpt.108-283 (2003).

[107]See note 141 and accompanying text.

[108]Department of Defense, Office of the Inspector General, *Information Technology Management: Terrorism Information Awareness Program* (D-2004-033) 4 (2003).

[109]Id.

as comprehensive as a privacy impact assessment would have been in scrutinizing TIA technology."[110]

On May 18, 2004, TAPAC released its report. The report described TIA as a "flawed effort to achieve worthwhile ends,"[111] but the report went on to "conclude that advanced information technology—including data mining—is a vital tool in the fight against terrorism."[112] "Technological tools to help analyze data and focus human analysts' attention on critical relationships and patterns of conduct are clearly needed."[113]

The TAPAC report stressed the inadequacy of law applicable to data mining. Describing the law as "disjointed," "inconsistent," and "outdated," the Committee wrote: "Current laws are often inadequate to address the new and difficult challenges presented by dramatic developments in information technologies. And that inadequacy will only become more acute as the store of digital data and the ability to search it continue to expand dramatically in the future."[114] Enacting a new regulatory structure, the report continued, is necessary both to "protect civil liberties" and to "empower those responsible for defending our nation to use advanced information technologies—including data mining—appropriately and effectively."[115] "It is time to update the law to respond to new challenges."[116]

TAPAC proposed the outline for that new legal structure applicable to anti-terrorist or law enforcement data mining conducted by the government. Under that framework, government data mining would require:

- written authorization by agency heads;
- compliance with minimum technical requirements for data-mining systems (including data minimization, data anonymization, creation of an audit trail; security and access controls, and training for personnel involved in data mining);
- special protections for data mining involving databases from other government agencies or from private industry;
- programmatic authorization from the Foreign Intelligence Surveillance Court before engaging in data mining that involves personally identifiable information concerning U.S. persons that has not been anonymized, and case-by-case authorization from the Court before reidentifying previously anonymized information concerning U.S. persons; and
- regular audits to ensure compliance.[117]

Certain data would be excluded from these new requirements, such as data mining that is limited to foreign intelligence that does not involve U.S. persons; data mining concerning federal government employees in connection with their employment; data mining that is based on particularized suspicion; and searches to identify or locate a specific individual (e.g., a suspected terrorist) from airline or cruise ship passenger manifests or other lists of names or other nonsensitive information about U.S. persons.[118] The report also

---

[110]Id. at 9.
[111]*TAPAC Report,* supra at 43.
[112]Id. at 7.
[113]Id. at 48.
[114]Id. at 6.
[115]Id.
[116]Id.
[117]Id. at 49-52.
[118]Id. at 46–47.

recommended that data mining that is limited to information that is routinely available without charge or subscription to the public—on the Internet, in telephone directories, or in public records to the extent authorized by law—should be subject to "only the requirements that it be conducted pursuant to the written authorization of the agency head and auditing for compliance."[119]

The "special protections" for data mining involving third-party databases from private industry recommended by TAPAC included:

- The agency engaging in the data mining should take into account the purpose for which the data were collected, their age, and the conditions under which they have been stored and protected when determining whether the proposed data mining is likely to be effective.
- If data are to be used for purposes that are inconsistent with those for which the data were originally collected, the agency should specifically evaluate whether the inconsistent use is justified and whether the data are appropriate for such use.
- Data should be left in place whenever possible. If this is impossible, they should be returned or destroyed as soon as practicable.
- Government agencies should not encourage any person voluntarily to provide data in violation of the terms and conditions (usually reflected in a privacy policy) under which they were collected.
- Government agencies should seek data in the order provided by Executive Order 12333: from or with the consent of the data subject, from publicly available sources, from proprietary sources, through a method requiring authorization less than probable cause (e.g., a pen register or trap and trace device), through a method requiring a warrant, and finally through a method requiring a wiretap order.
- Private entities that provide data to the government upon request or subject to judicial process should be indemnified for any liability that results from the government's acquisition or use of the data.
- Private entities that provide data to the government upon request or subject to judicial process should be reasonably compensated for the costs they incur in complying with the government's request or order.[120]

The TAPAC report met with modest support from both the political left and right, but to date neither the Administration nor the Congress has taken any action on the committee's recommendations concerning a new legal framework for government data mining. The gap created by *Miller* and *Smith* remains unaddressed more than 25 years later.

20.6. THE NEED FOR STANDARDS

The controversy surrounding TIA and other counter-terrorism data mining projects illustrates the need for Congress and the Administration to establish legal standards for when personal information may be obtained from third parties and how it may be used. Although such standards serve many valuable purposes, six warrant special attention.

[119]Id. at 47.
[120]Id. at 50–51.

20.6.1. Protect Privacy and Other Civil Liberties

Government data mining, and especially of personal information obtained from third parties, threatens the privacy that is at the core of the relationship between the government and the citizenry. The Court's failure to extend the protections of the Fourth Amendment to personal data maintained by third parties, combined with the technological changes that result in more and increasingly revealing information being necessarily disclosed to and stored by third parties, threaten to vitiate those protections entirely. Moreover, the government's new practical ability to analyze vast amounts of disparate data rapidly and affordably threaten to extend government surveillance to every aspect of daily life. TAPAC wrote: "Government data mining presents special risks to informational privacy. If conducted without an adequate predicate, it has the potential to be a 21st-century equivalent of general searches, which the authors of the Bill of Rights were so concerned to protect against."[121]

Updating the law to respond to these new challenges is a daunting, but urgent, challenge. On one side is the risk of failing to identify and deter terrorist attacks. On the other are the civil liberties put at risk by data mining. The impact of data mining on civil liberties may not be immediately obvious, but awareness that the government may, without probable cause or other specific authorization, obtain access to myriad, distributed stores of information about individuals is likely to alter their behavior. The original motto of the TIA program—*Scientia Est Potentia*—is certainly correct: "knowledge is power." Knowledge that the government is observing data we generate through thousands of ordinary activities can alter the way people live their lives and interact with others. This is not always a bad outcome.

However, knowledge of that power can cause people to change their behavior to be more consistent with a perceived social norm, to mask their behavior, and to reduce their activities or participation in society to avoid the surveillance. Vice President Hubert Humphrey observed almost 40 years ago: "[We] act differently if we believe we are being observed. If we can never be sure whether or not we are being watched and listened to, all our actions will be altered and our very character will change."[122] The threats posed by government data mining in a democracy are not merely to information privacy, but to other civil liberties, including freedom of expression, association, and religion.

Alexander Hamilton wrote in Federalist Paper 8 in 1787, exhorting the people of New York to ratify the Constitution, that "safety from external danger is the most powerful director of national conduct. Even the ardent love of liberty will, after a time, give way to its dictates."[123] "The violent destruction of life and property incident to war, the continual effort and alarm attendant on a state of continual danger," Hamilton warned, "will compel nations the most attached to liberty to resort for repose and security to institutions which have a tendency to destroy their civil and political rights. To be more safe, they at length become willing to run the risk of being less free."[124]

20.6.2. Enhance Public, Policy-Maker, Press, and Private-Sector Confidence

Privacy and national security are also inherently linked because there are limits as to how much of the former the public is willing to trade in pursuit of the latter. The clear lesson of

---

[121]Id. at 49.

[122]Hubert H. Humphrey, Foreword to Edward V. Long, *The Intruders* at viii (1967).

[123]Alexander Hamilton, The Consequences of Hostilities Between the States (Federalist Paper 8), *New York Packet,* Nov. 20, 1787.

[124]Id.

the series of controversies over data mining programs is that the American people will rebel and policy-makers will change direction in an instant if they believe that privacy is being threatened too much or unnecessarily.

With TIA, as we have seen, Congress restricted development and then terminated funding entirely, at least from the public budget.[125] But other programs have been similarly retarded by a privacy backlash. In response to public and political pressure, CAPPS II was scaled back and the data-mining aspects limited merely to verifying identify and determining if a passenger is on a government terrorist watch list. Delta Air Lines withdrew from a pilot program after it was threatened with a boycott.

"MATRIX" (Multistate Anti-Terrorism Information Exchange)—designed "to link law enforcement records across states with other government and private-sector databases" and to "find patterns and links among people and events faster than ever before"—has been hard hit by privacy concerns.[126] At its height, 16 states were participating in MATRIX, which is funded by the Justice Department and DHS. Partly in response to privacy issues, all but five states have withdrawn.[127]

The experience of companies who participated voluntarily in a test of how data profiling can be used to identify high-risk passengers has been particularly illuminating. With the assistance of DOD and TSA, Army defense contractor Torch Concepts obtained millions of passenger records from U.S. airlines to help test the system it was designing.[128] For many of the passengers, Torch Concepts was able to buy demographic information including data on gender, occupation, income, Social Security number, home ownership, years at current residence, number of children and adults in the household, and vehicles.[129] Now, JetBlue, Northwest, and American, all of whom provided passenger data for the test, face multiple class-action lawsuits under a variety of federal and state laws, as does Acxiom, the supplier of the third-party demographic data.

Section 215 of the USA Patriot Act is under renewed attack for fear that it may be used to seize broad collections of data about the reading habits of people who have done nothing to warrant the government's attention. On June 21, 2005, the *New York Times* editorialized that "law enforcement should be able to get information, including library records, about specific individuals it reasonably suspects of a crime," but that the law as currently written "allows requests for library records for large numbers of people without any reason to believe they are involved in illegal activity."[130] According to the *Times,* this goes too far: "Fishing expeditions of this kind invade people's privacy and threaten to bring people under suspicion based on what they read."[131] Some members of Congress appear to agree. On June 15, the House of Representatives voted to prohibit the use of section 215 to obtain "circulation records, library patron lists, book sales records or book customer lists" altogether.[132]

---

[125]Department of Defense Appropriations Act, 2004, Pub. L. No. 108-84, § 8183 (Sept. 25, 2003).

[126]Thomas C. Greene, A Back Door to Poindexter's Orwellian Dream, *The Register,* Sept. 24, 2003; Robert O'Harrow, Jr., U.S. Backs Florida's New Counterterrorism Database, *Washington Post,* Aug. 6, 2003, at A1; see also http://www.matrix-at.org/.

[127]Chris Maag, The Matrix: An Expensive Government Program Was Doomed from the start, *Cleveland Scene* (Ohio), Mar. 9, 2005.

[128]Sara Kehaulani Goo, Airlines Confirm Giving Passenger Data to FBI After 9/11, *Washington Post,* May 2, 2004, at A14.

[129]Department of Homeland Security Privacy Office, *Report to the Public on Events Surrounding jetBlue Data Transfer—Findings and Recommendations* (Feb. 20, 2004).

[130]Fishing in the Card Catalogs, *New York Times,* June 21, 2005, at A20.

[131]Id.

[132]Richard B. Schmitt, House Weakens Patriot Act's "Library Provision," *Los Angeles Times,* June 16, 2005, at A1.

While the retreat from each of these programs may have been justified in the circumstances, collectively they raise the specter that valuable tools for enhancing security may have been compromised. Moreover, the public outcry over these programs has made the government wary of security programs that involve data matching and industry hesitant to share personal data with the government.

Promises by proponents of all of these data-mining projects that they were "adhering to the law" did little to quell the controversies, because the law is so limited and uncertain. Inadequate or unclear privacy laws are slowing the development of new and promising data mining programs, they are undermining research into this important weapon in the war on terrorism, and they are hampering the very data sharing that the 9/11 Commission recommended. Clear rules would facilitate accountability, public and policy-maker confidence, and the willingness of the private sector to provide data for lawful counter-terrorism uses. The absence of those rules undermines efforts to protect privacy and security.

20.6.3. Enhance Security

Good privacy protection not only can help build support for data mining and other tools to enhance security, it can also contribute to making those tools more effective. For example, data integrity—ensuring that data are accurate, complete, up-to-date, and appropriately stored and linked—is a key privacy principle. But it clearly enhances security as well. Legal obligations requiring data integrity inevitably make those data more useful for security application as well.

In March 2003 the Justice Department exempted the FBI's National Crime Information Center from the Privacy Act's requirements that data be "accurate, relevant, timely and complete,"[133] and in August 2003 the DHS exempted the TSA's passenger screening database from the Privacy Act's requirements that government records include only "relevant and necessary" personal information.[134] These efforts to avoid privacy obligations raise important security issues as well. Mismatched data and misidentified individuals pose serious risks for both privacy and security.

Similarly, the DOD Inspector General's December 2003 audit of TIA concluded that DOD's failure to consider privacy adequacy during the early development of TIA led the Department to "risk spending funds to develop systems that may not be either deployable or used to their fullest potential without costly revision."[135] The report noted that this was particularly true with regard to the potential deployment of TIA for law enforcement: "DARPA need[ed] to consider how TIA will be used in terms of law enforcement to ensure that privacy is built into the developmental process."[136] Greater consideration of how the technology might be used would not only have served privacy, but also likely contributed to making TIA more useful as well.

As this example suggests, privacy protections often build discipline into counter-terrorism efforts that serves other laudatory purposes. By making the government stop and justify its effort to a senior official, a congressional committee, or a federal judge, warrant requirements and other privacy protections often help bring focus and precision to law enforcement and national security efforts. In point of fact, courts rarely refuse requests for

---

[133]*Privacy Act of 1974; Implementation,* 68 Federal Register 14140 (2003) (DOJ, final rule).

[134]*Privacy Act of 1974: Implementation of Exemption,* 68 Federal Register 49410 (2003) (DHS, final rule).

[135]OIG Terrorism Information Awareness Program Report, supra at 4.

[136]Id. at 7.

judicial authorization to conduct surveillance. For example, between 1968 and 2003, courts approved a total of 30,692 wiretap orders (10,506 federal and 20,186 state)—all but 32 sought by the government.[137] Between 1979 and 2003, Foreign Intelligence Surveillance Court judges approved 16,971 FISA warrants—all but five that the Attorney General had sought.[138] As government officials often note, one reason for these high success rates is the quality of internal decision-making that the requirement to obtain judicial authorization requires.

As TAPAC noted in the introduction to its recommendations for new privacy protections:

> Our conclusion, therefore, that data mining concerning U.S. persons inevitably raises privacy issues, does not in any way suggest that the government should not have the power to engage in data mining, subject to appropriate legal and technological protections. Quite the contrary, we believe that those protections are essential *so that* the government can engage in appropriate data mining when necessary to fight terrorism and defend our nation. And we believe that those protections are needed to provide clear guidance to DOD personnel engaged in anti-terrorism activities.[139]

20.6.4. Improve Policy-Making

One of the most striking lessons from Congress' response to TIA and other data-mining programs is that the absence of a clear regulatory regime for data mining contributed to erratic and inconsistent behavior by policy-makers. Clear standards are necessary not only to help guide the actions of counter-terrorism personnel, but also to help guide policy-makers as well.

After all, it was only three months after Congress required DHS to engage in data mining with private-sector data that it prohibited DOD from deploying data mining tools within the United States, collecting or using data about U.S. persons, or developing other elements of TIA, including translation software, networks to link the intelligence community, and other tools that had few, if any, privacy implications.[140] Seven months later, Congress blocked the development of TIA entirely, but then established rules for how classified funding for TIA might be used. TIA's opponents in Congress and the privacy advocacy community proudly claimed that they had "killed" TIA, but the statutory language suggests that they had merely driven it from public view.[141] Moreover, President Bush stated in his signing statement that the classified annex "accompanies but is not incorporated as a part of the Act" and therefore would be considered by the President as merely "advisory in effect."[142] Ironically, the part of TIA that Congress did eliminate entirely was the funding for the development of privacy enhancing technologies.

[137]Administrative Office of the United States Courts, *2003 Wiretap Report,* tab. 7; Electronic Privacy Information Center, Title III Electronic Surveillance 1968–2002.

[138]Center for Democracy and Technology, The Nature and Scope of Governmental Electronic Surveillance Activity (June 2004); Electronic Privacy Information Center, Foreign Intelligence Surveillance Act Orders 1979–2002.

[139]*TAPAC Report,* supra at 48.

[140]S. Amend. 59 to H.J. Res. 2 (Jan. 23, 2003).

[141]See K. A. Taipale, Data Mining and Domestic Security: Connecting The Dots to Make Sense of Data, *Columbia Science and Technology Law Review* 1, 48, n. 96 (2003) ("The former TIA projects Genisys and Genoa II are believed to be included in the classified annex to the Defense Appropriations Bill," citing to the statement of Major General Paul Nielson before TAPAC, Nov. 20, 2003).

[142]Statement on Signing the Department of Defense Appropriations Act, 2004 (Oct. 6, 2003).

The immediate result, therefore, of congressional intervention was to drive the development and deployment of data mining at DOD from public view, relieve it of the statutory restrictions that had previously applied to it, block funding for research into privacy enhancing technologies, and undermine the policy debate over the appropriate roles for and limits of data mining. Law and technology scholar K. A. Taipale writes:

> At first hailed as a "victory" for civil liberties, it has become increasingly apparent that the defunding [of TIA] is likely to be a pyrrhic victory. . . . [N]ot proceeding with a focused government research and development project (in which Congressional oversight and a public debate could determine appropriate rules and procedures for use of these technologies and, importantly, ensure the development of privacy protecting technical features to support such policies) is likely to result in little security and, ultimately, brittle privacy protection.
>
> Indeed, following the demise of IAO and TIA, it has become clear that similar data aggregation and automated analysis projects exist throughout various agencies and departments not subject to easy review.[143]

Congress' inconsistent treatment of similar technologies confuses the public and government officials charged with following these widely varying statutes. It runs the risk of compromising the protection of both national security and information privacy. And it is the inevitable result of the absence of clear legal structure concerning data mining and access to third-party data.

20.6.5. Facilitate Innovation and Research

The inconsistency that results from the absence of a legal framework may have its longest-term effect on the innovation and research that is necessary to improve the accuracy and effectiveness of data mining, enhance privacy protections, and develop next generation tools for fighting terrorism.

TAPAC explicitly recognized the importance of research into technological and other tools for making data mining more precise and accurate and for protecting privacy. One unfortunate consequence of Congress blocking further public development of TIA was to prohibit further research by DARPA into both data mining and privacy.

Congress' inconsistency and the controversy that data-mining projects have provoked in the absence of strong legal protections for privacy are likely to undermine forward-looking research elsewhere as well. After all, what federal funding agency would invest seriously in an area where Congress had already acted to ban research once, and what investigator would invest her career in research on such a politically sensitive subject? It is instructive to remember that DARPA funded the development of the precursor of the Internet as a secure tool for connecting defense researchers. Where would the World Wide Web be today if Congress, at the infancy of ARAPNet in the 1960s, had prohibited further research because the emerging technologically posed a clear threat to privacy?

Clear standards are necessary to support the investment of financial, institutional, and human resources in often risky research that may not pay dividends for decades. But that type of research is essential to counter-terrorism efforts and to finding better ways of protecting privacy.

---

[143]Taipale, supra at 4 (citations omitted).

20.6.6. Make New Technologies Work

Some observers suggest that the issues presented by data mining will be resolved by technologies, not by law or policy. There are indeed technologies emerging, some of which, such as anonymous entity resolution and immutable audit trails, are both very promising and described elsewhere in this volume. But even the best technological solutions will still require a legal framework in which to operate, and the absence of that framework may not only slow their development and deployment, as described above, but make them entirely unworkable.

Anonymous entity resolution is a perfect example. This technology makes it possible to standardize and match data that are completely anonymized through a one-way hash function. Only when there is a match between datasets—for example, a terrorist watch list and a list of airline passengers—would the government be entitled to seek the underlying, personally identifiable information from the data source. The technology protects privacy, enhances the accuracy of matches, and promises to facilitate the sharing of information likely to enhance national security.

However, it will work only if the private sector is willing to share its data with the government, and to anonymize it appropriately before doing so. After the experiences of Jet-Blue, Northwest, and American, companies might understandably require some legal comfort before they are going to share even anonymized data.

There is going to be a need for rules about when and through what process the government may seek the underlying data. This is the key question that the Court's *Miller* decision and Congress' inaction have left unanswered. That void will have to be filled before the public will have confidence in the system. There will also need to be rules to help protect the system. While anonymous entity resolution systems are very secure, they can still be challenged by relentless attacks (for example, through so-called "dictionary attacks," where one party runs thousands of queries against another party's anonymized data in an effort to pierce the anonymization). We will need laws that stop users of the system from engaging in conduct designed to defeat the privacy protection it provides.

Similarly, technologies that create immutable audit trails hold great promise for monitoring access to data and ensuring that rules are followed, but there will need to be legal standards for when immutable audit trail technologies are used, who holds the audit trail data, and who can obtain access to them.

Information technologies, far from eliminating the need for law, actually exacerbate it. The failure of Congress and the Administration to adopt a coherent legal framework applicable to data mining threatens not only to eliminate the useful role of law in protection privacy and fighting terrorism, but to reduce the effectiveness of technologies as well. Moreover, there will always be gaps left by technological protections that law will be essential to fill.

SUMMARY

In *Miller v. United States* and subsequent cases the Supreme Court created a broad gap in the privacy protection provided by the Fourth Amendment by finding that the government's seizure of personal information from third parties is outside of the scope of the Fourth Amendment. As a result, the government's behavior need not be reasonable nor is any judicial authorization required when the government searches or seizes personal information held by third parties.

As striking as the Court's decision was in 1976, in the face of 29 years of technological developments since then, it today means that the government has at its disposal an extraordinary array of personal data that individuals necessarily deposit in the hands of third parties as we live our daily lives. As we rely more and more on technologies, that situation will only increase, until the Fourth Amendment is entirely swallowed up by the *Miller* exclusion. Although Congress has responded with specific, sectoral statutes, these are limited in their scope and in the protections they create. As a result, the government's ability to seize data from third parties is effectively unregulated.

Until recently, the government has had little practical use for massive datasets from the private sector. Significant advances in data-mining technologies, however, now make it possible for the government to conduct sophisticated analysis, rapidly and affordably, of disparate databases without ever physically bringing the data together. These technologies allow the government to move beyond looking for data on specific people to search data about millions of Americans in the search for patterns of activity, subtle relationships, and inferences about future behavior. These technologies and the terrorist attacks of September 11 mean that the government now has both the ability and the motivation to use huge arrays of private-sector data about individuals who have done nothing to warrant government attention.

Even if *Miller* had not excluded these records from the protection of the Fourth Amendment, there would still be a critical need for Congress to establish a legal framework for the appropriate use of data mining. To date, Congress has failed to respond to this challenge. In fact, Congress has behaved erratically toward data mining, requiring and encouraging it in some settings and prohibiting it in others.

There is an urgent need for Congress and the Administration to address this situation by creating clear legal standards for government data mining, especially when it involves access to third-party data. It is beyond the scope of this chapter to try to articulate the content of those standards. There have been many efforts to do so, including the work of TAPAC, the Markle Foundation Task Force on National Security in the Information Age, the Cantigny Conference on Counterterrorism Technology and Privacy organized by the Standing Committee on Law and National Security of the American Bar Association,[144] think tanks and advocacy groups concerned with national security and civil liberties issues, and individuals, including other contributors to this volume.

Standards for government data mining and access to third-party data are essential to protect privacy, build public confidence in appropriate data mining, enhance national security, facilitate more rational and consistent policymaking, foster innovation, and help new technologies for protecting privacy and security reach their full potential.

---

[144]The Cantigny Principles on Technology, Terrorism, and Privacy, *National Security Law Report,* Feb. 2005, at 14.

Chapter 21

Privacy and Consequences: Legal and Policy Structures for Implementing New Counter-Terrorism Technologies and Protecting Civil Liberty

Paul Rosenzweig

21.1. INTRODUCTION

New twenty-first-century technologies (ranging from data mining, to link analysis and data integration, to biometrics, to new encryption techniques) have much to offer in achieving the compelling national goal of preventing terrorism. The other chapters in this book demonstrate that proposition clearly at a technological level.[1]

But all the new technology in the world will be of little use if partisan political considerations or an unwarranted fear of the loss of individual liberty prevent the deployment of new systems. And there is substantial political resistance to many of the new technologies—the demise of Terrorism Information Awareness is but one cautionary tale. That resistance arises from legitimate fears: Government access to and use of personal information raises concerns about the protection of civil liberties, privacy, and due process. Given the limited applicability of current privacy laws to the modern digital data environment, resolving this conflict will require the adoption of new policies for collection, access, use, disclosure, and retention of information, as well as for redress and oversight.

[1]This chapter is based upon a talk entitled "Privacy and Consequence—Protecting Liberty in the Cyberworld" delivered at the Indiana University Center for Applied Cybersecurity Research (IUCACR) on November 11, 2004. Small portions of this Chapter also appeared in James Jay Carafano and Paul Rosenzweig, *Winning the Long War: Lessons from the Cold War for Defeating Terrorism and Preserving Freedom* (2005) and are derived from earlier publications by the author. I am grateful to James Dempsey, Stephen Dycus, Jeff Jonas, Nuala O'-Connor Kelly, Heather MacDonald, John Poindexter, Robert Popp, and especially K. A. Taipale and the participants at the IUCACR seminar for their contributions to my education and/or thoughtful comments on this work, though they, of course, bear no responsibility for any errors that might remain. The author serves as Chairman of the Department of Homeland Security Data Privacy and Integrity Advisory Committee. The views expressed herein are those of the author alone and do not reflect the views of the Committee or any other governmental entity.

Thus, this chapter asks a practical, concrete question: Can the new technologies be developed, deployed, implemented, and operated in a manner that allows them to be used as an effective anti-terrorism tool while ensuring that there is minimal risk that use of the toolset will infringe upon American civil liberties?

Some believe this goal is not possible to achieve. Civil libertarians believe that the technologies are "Big Brother" projects that ought to be terminated. They begin with the truism that no technology is foolproof: Every new technology will inevitably generate errors, and mistakes will be made. And, as with the development of any new technology, risks exist for the misuse and abuse of the new tools being developed. From this, critics conclude that the risks of potential error or abuse are so great that all development of many new technologies (such as Terrorism Information Awareness, MATRIX, or biometric identification) should be abandoned. To buttress their claim that these systems should be abandoned, critics parade a host of unanswered questions. Among them: Who will be trusted to operate the systems? What will the oversight be? What will be the collateral consequences for individuals identified as terrorist suspects?

These questions are posed as if they have no answers when all that is true is that for a system under development, they have no answers . . . yet. The same is true of any new developmental program, and our experience tells us that these implementation issues are generally capable of being resolved.

But to hear civil libertarians ask these questions is to suppose that they believe there are no feasible, practical answers. And if that were so, then all should be rightly concerned, because the provision of adequate checking mechanisms and safeguards ought to be an absolute precondition to the deployment of any new technological system that pose a potential threat to civil liberties.

The thesis of this chapter, however, is that practical answers to the problem of oversight can, and must, be crafted. In fact, there are a number of analogous oversight and implementation structures already in existence that can be borrowed and suitably modified to the new technologies. Thus, new enabling technologies can and should be developed if the technology proves usable, *if and only if* the accompanying limitations are also developed and deployed. This can be done in a manner that renders them effective, while posing minimal risks to American liberties, if the system is crafted carefully with built-in safeguards to check the possibilities of error or abuse. This chapter is an effort to sketch out precisely what those safeguards ought to be and how they might impact the most prominent proposed new technologies.

But even more important than its specific recommendations, this chapter is an exhortation to technology developers—*consider privacy at the start of any system development.* Privacy protection methods and code (such as immutable audits, or selective revelation techniques) need to be built into new systems from the beginning, both as a matter of good policy and as a matter of good politics. If privacy is treated as an "add on" for a new technological development, then it is likely that development will fail.

With appropriate safeguards, twenty-first-century technologies can be safely implemented. Failing to make the effort poses grave risks and is an irresponsible abdication of responsibility. As six former top-ranking professionals in America's security services have observed, we face two problems: both a need for better analysis and, more critically, "improved espionage, to provide the essential missing intelligence." In their view, while there was "certainly a lack of dot-connecting before September 11," the more critical failure was that "[t]here were too few useful dots."[2] Technology can help to answer both of these needs.

---

[2]Robert Bryant et al., America Needs More Spies, *Economist,* July 12, 2003, at 30.

Indeed, resistance to new technology poses practical dangers. As the Congressional Joint Inquiry into the events of September 11 pointed out in noting systemic failures that played a role in the inability to prevent the terrorist attacks:

> 4. Finding: While technology remains one of this nation's greatest advantages, it has not been fully and most effectively applied in support of U.S. counterterrorism efforts. Persistent problems in this area included a lack of collaboration between Intelligence Community agencies [and] *a reluctance to develop and implement new technical capabilities aggressively.* . . .[3]

It is important not to repeat that mistake.

21.2. A CONCEPTION OF PRIVACY AND LIBERTY

To simply state rules for appropriately implementing new information technologies is easy. To justify those rules as the proper ones for protecting liberty and privacy is less so and requires, in the first instance, that we begin from basic principles and ask questions about the nature of privacy and liberty. And to answer those questions, in a sense, requires us to answer the age-old philosophical question: If a tree falls in the woods and nobody is there to hear it, does it make a sound? Or, in a modern formulation: If individually identifiable data are examined but there are no consequences, has anything happened?

21.2.1. What Is Privacy?

First let's define some terms: What is the "privacy" right that we talk about when we discuss the use of twenty-first-century information technologies? Is it different from the conception of privacy that arises in the "real" physical world?

In 1976, Phil Kurland of the University of Chicago wrote a small, seminal discussion of privacy entitled "The Private I."[4] There he identified three different types of privacy that one might be talking about. The first of these was the concept of privacy as "autonomy"—that is, the right of an individual to do whatever he or she wants, irrespective of who knows that it is being done. Examples of this concept of privacy would include contemporary debates about abortion or gay marriage—and those conceptions are, for the most part, not germane to a discussion of the new cybertechnologies.

A second conception of privacy is the privacy that is really the demand for complete secrecy—in other words, the capacity not to have anyone know what an individual is doing at all, in any way at all. Examples of this form of privacy are common in America. They include freedom of religious conscience, as well as the right to generally conduct activities in ones own home without scrutiny from anyone, neighbor or government. That concept of privacy is of limited interest in the new technological sphere (at least as it relates to knowledge discovery and information sharing technologies) and makes its appear-

---

[3]*Report of the Joint Inquiry Into the Terrorist Attacks of September 11, 2001,* House Permanent Select Committee on Intelligence and Senate Select Committee on Intelligence, 107th Cong., 2nd Sess., S. Rept. No. 107–351 and H. Rept. No. 107–792, Dec. 2002, p. xvi, *available at* http://www.fas.org/irp/congress/2002_rpt/911rept.pdf (emphasis supplied). The Joint Inquiry also critiqued the lack of adequate analytical tools, *id.* at Finding 5, and the lack of a single means of coordinating disparate counterterrorism databases, *id.* at Findings 9 & 10.

[4]*See* Phillip Kurland, The Private I, *University of Chicago Magazine*, Autumn 1976, at 8 (characterizing three facets of privacy, broadly characterized as anonymity, secrecy, and autonomy) (quoted in Whalen v. Roe, 429 U.S. 589, 599 n.24 (1977)).

ance, if at all, only as we consider issues related to encryption technologies and their dissemination amongst the public.

The conception of privacy that most applies to the new information technology regime is the idea of anonymity—that is, the ability to expose one's actions in public but not be subject to identification or scrutiny. The information data-space is suffused with information of this sort—bank account transactions, phone records, airplane reservations, and Smartcard travel logs, to name but a few. They constitute the core of transactions and electronic signature or verification information available in cyberspace. The anonymity that one has in respect of these transactions is not terribly different from "real"-world anonymity—consider the act of driving a car. It is done in public, but one is generally not subject to routine identification and scrutiny.

Notably, this conception of anonymity has come to be viewed as our birthright, in part because, in practice, the veil of anonymity has often proven impossible to pierce. Justice Stevens once called that the "practical obscurity" that comes from knowing that disparate records about your conduct cannot be collated and accessed.[5] Who among us, for example, when young, did not deliberately neglect a speeding ticket, confident that the failure to pay would not be correlated with a driver's license renewal application?

Today, of course, technological advances are eroding that practical obscurity. And thus, we face directly the question of what this concept of privacy as anonymity really means in a world where data in distributed databases can be readily examined.

To begin with, we should recognize that this form of anonymity is actually a relatively modern invention. It is the product of mass urbanization as a result of which the information technology of "personal knowledge" could not keep up with the population growth of the industrial urban environment. Contrast that with the circumstances of a small medieval town. In such a town, one's business was known to everyone, and the most effective (though often error-prone) information network was the town gossip and the knitting circle. In effect, the migration from Old Wexfordshire to London created the conditions that give rise to privacy of the anonymity form.

Yet the new technological erosion of anonymity is in some sense even more troubling than the lack of anonymity in a small town: At least in a small town information disclosed about an individual would generally be placed within the context of general knowledge about the individual, often with ameliorating effect. The loss of anonymity in the mass information context arguably produces a less favorable construct, namely, information without context.

21.2.2. Privacy as a "Right"

The change is sufficiently dramatic that, today, most Americans consider this form of anonymous privacy to be a "right." And the characterization as a "right" has very important legal implications. Typically, rights can't be taken away from you without your consent or some supra-governmental act—we do not deny the right to vote, for example, except to those who are not registered or have forfeited the right. And generally, rights injuries are compensated even without actual damages—the injury is to the right itself.

---

[5]For example, Justice Dept. v. Reporters Committee, 489 U.S. 749, 780 (1989) ("There is a vast difference between public records that might be found after a diligent search . . . and a computerized summary located in a single clearing house."). Notably valuation of this practical limitation on governmental efficiency is in tension with another strand of the Framers' conception: One of the purposes of the constitutional structure was to ensure "energy in the Executive." *See* Federalist No. 70 ("Energy in the executive is a leading character in the definition of good government.").

Most significantly, rights are absolutes. You either have them or you don't—there is no gray. This aspect of the conception of "rights" is particularly notable in the Constitutional understanding of privacy of the anonymity form. The law in that area is clear and has been since the 1970s. *Katz v United States* defined the Constitutional (not statutory) privilege against scrutiny (as reflected in the Fourth Amendment) as a "reasonable expectation of privacy"—that is, an expectation that society is willing to recognize.[6]

This right has been narrowly construed by the courts. In their view the prevailing social rule is that any exposure of personal information to the public waives the right completely; in other words, there is no such thing as graduated or partial revelation, and privacy rights are only of the pure *secrecy* form. Thus, as a Constitutional matter, one has no privacy right in information voluntarily disclosed to others. When one tells the bank about deposits or withdrawals, he effectively waive all rights (as a Constitutional matter) to limit the further dissemination of that information.[7] Similarly, when one "tells" an ISP the node address from which one is accessing the Internet, that information, likewise, is not generally considered protected against further dissemination.[8]

One response to this line of decisions is to create privacy rights by statute. These are, in effect, modified anonymity statutes—they define situations where one can exercise some control over dissemination of information about individual information, providing a limited and limitable anonymity. Congress has done this—for example, in the laws governing medical privacy.[9] But virtually all such laws have a law enforcement/national security exception written into them—so, in the context of a terrorism investigation the government can usually get individual information from a third party without the third party's permission, and under certain prescribed circumstances without even any notice to the individual.

In other words, though the idea of a right is a very strong formulation in principle, in practice the protections that "rights talk" provides to individuals are exceedingly weak. From a governmental perspective the Constitution places very few limits on the authority of the government to access data in cyberspace—in part because of the legal premise that all privacy expectations are checked at the Internet portal door. Whatever limits there are, are either statutory (though we have thus far chosen to create few such limits) or political (if we choose to use that form of influence).[10]

21.2.3. Privacy as Consequence

This is exceedingly unsatisfactory and calls for a new way of thinking about privacy. The way to more concretely and thoughtfully answer the conundrum of privacy in the cyber-

[6]Katz v. U.S., 389 U.S. 347 (1967).

[7]U.S. v. Miller, 425 U.S. 435, 443 (1973).

[8]Smith v. Maryland, 442 U.S. 735, 744 (1979) ("when he used his phone, petitioner voluntarily conveyed numerical information to the telephone company"). This understanding of the scope of the Fourth Amendment is based upon an outdated vision of technology. In an era of Voice-Over Internet Protocols and off-site stored communications such as G-mail, it might well prove untenable. In the absence of reconsideration by the Supreme Court, however, it remains the prevailing law. Thus, this paper is an effort to outline a suitable theory that would support a statutory mechanism to fill the gap between law and reality.

[9]Substantial new privacy protections for medical information were added to federal law by the Heath Insurance Portability and Accountability Act, §§ 262, 264 Pub. L. No. 104–191 (1996).

[10]The political system's approach to privacy-related issues is sometimes schizophrenic. At times, it responds to public hysteria and overreaction, leading to the premature termination of promising research. But because political attention is transient, it also often leads to unexamined conduct without adequate oversight. The demise of TIA, its fracturing into the classified budget, and the apparent termination of funding for its privacy-related technologies are a cautionary tale of this schizophrenic approach.

world is to look to the non-cyberworld for analogs that create procedural, rather than definitional, protections.

Earlier we posited that anonymity was, in effect, the ability to walk through the world unexamined. That was, however, not strictly accurate, because our conduct is examined numerous times every day. Sometimes the examination is by a private individual—one may notice that the individual sitting next to them on the train is wearing a wedding ring. Other routine examinations are by governmental authorities—the policeman in the car or on the beat who watches the street or the security camera at the bank or airport, for example.

So what we really must mean by anonymity is not a pure form of privacy akin to secrecy. Rather what we mean—and this is the answer to the thesis question—is that even though one's conduct is examined, routinely and regularly, both with and without one's knowledge, *nothing adverse should happen to you without good cause.* In other words, the veil of anonymity (previously protected by our "practical obscurity") that is now so readily pierced by technology must be protected, instead, by rules that limit when the piercing may happen as a means of protecting privacy and preventing governmental abuse. To put it more precisely, the key to this conception of privacy is that privacy's principal virtue is as a limitation on consequence. If there are no unjustified consequences (that is, consequences that are the product of abuse or error), then, under this vision, there is no effect on a cognizable liberty/privacy interest. In other words, if nobody is there to hear the tree, it really doesn't make a sound.

The appeal of this model is that it is, by and large, the model we already have for government/personal interactions in the physical world. The rule is not that the police can't observe you—it is that they require authorization of some form, from some authority in order to be permitted to engage in certain types of interactions (what are here identified as "consequences"). The police cannot stop you to question you without "reasonable suspicion"; cannot arrest you without "probable cause"; cannot search your house without "probable cause"; and cannot examine a corporation's business records about you without a showing of "relevance" to an ongoing investigation.[11] We can map the same rules-based model—of authorization linked to consequence—as the appropriate one for the cyberworld.

21.2.4. Does Observation Create Consequence?

The most frequent objection to this conception of privacy as consequence is the argument that mere knowledge that one's conduct is examined by others effects behavior and thus that, even in the absence of official consequences, examination has effects. In other words, some say that observation creates its own consequence of altered behavior—sort of like Niels Bohr's theory of quantum mechanics measurement applied to human conduct.[12] This response also contends, either explicitly or implicitly, that the effects are adverse—that the paradigm for liberty is a life free of examination and that any self-editing is, as a matter of principle, wrong.

[11]Terry v. Ohio, 392 U.S. 1 (1968); United States v. Watson, 423 U.S. 411 (1976); Illinois v. Gates, 462 U.S. 213 (1983); U.S. Const. Amend. IV; U.S. v. R. Enters., Inc., 498 U.S. 292 (1991). To be sure, there are some exceptions to these general rules, but nonetheless, their existence establishes the presumption of a rules-based system, from which derogations are to be identified.

[12]According to Bohr, the act of measuring a quantum particle affected the particle. See Nils Bohr, Quantum Mechanics and Physical Reality, *Nature* 136:1025–1026 (1935). ("The procedure of measurement has an essential influence on the conditions on which the very definition of the physical quantities in question rests.") This conclusion is an outgrowth of the somewhat more famous Heisenberg uncertainty principle, positing that one cannot know accurately both the position and velocity of a quantum particle.

Closely examined, however, this objection is unpersuasive. First, some self-editing is good. To the extent the fact of scrutiny deters criminal or terrorist behavior, society is improved. So it can't be that those defending the privacy principle of an unexamined life are defending a capacity to engage in wrongful conduct of the sort at issue here.[13]

Rather, they must be defending the capacity to engage in nonharmful conduct that they would be deterred from engaging in (it is said) by the fact of scrutiny. One example might be the exercise of the right of political protest. Another might be the capacity to engage in behavior that is in some way socially "unacceptable" but not necessarily unlawful—a professor having a relationship with a student, for example. We can see this fear most prominently in the refrain that new knowledge discovery technologies will create an "electronic dossier" on every American.

But why would the fact of scrutiny have the consequence of altered behavior in cases such as these? For some of these behaviors, the problem is not governmental scrutiny, but the fact of public exposure in any form—the pure secrecy form of privacy. Ridicule and disdain are, after all, powerful social mechanisms. But this dataset of socially disdained behavior is exceedingly unlikely to have any relevance to any terrorism investigation. And so, we can and should envision the construction of new technological systems with strong software and legal/policy prohibitions that place the examination of such social behavior off limits absent a compelling showing of need.

For many of the other behaviors, however, it cannot be that exposure of conduct to public scrutiny generally alters the behavior. Almost all of the behavior we are talking about—credit card purchases, bank transactions, phone transactions, and political protest—is already known to someone. So for these actions—a portion of which will be at the core of any new cybertechnology applications—the issue is not about the secrecy aspect of privacy.

To be clear, our conception of anonymity might also have some aspects of a "starting over" mentality in America—the idea that you can escape your reputation by moving and turning over a new leaf. Clearly, to the extent true information about you is available in cyberspace, you cannot escape your reputation.[14] And, to be sure, the ability to do so does have some utility and value—a fresh start can produce good results. But its utility is limited—both because it stands in opposition to the disclosure of true information and because, as a practical matter, increased commercial use of knowledge discovery techniques will limit this ability in the future quite strongly.[15]

Thus, when it is stripped down, at the core of the anonymity objection there must be

---

[13]An interesting corollary to the development of new technologies is that they will, inevitably require a much better (and narrower) definition of "wrongful conduct." As technology trends towards perfect enforcement (thus rendering the deterrence component of enforcement less relevant), society will need to re-examine its definition of what constitutes a "wrong." To put it prosaically, in a world where we could identify every Senator who had illegally smoked a Cuban cigar, or every individual who had exceeded the speed limit by the least amount, we might well need to change our definition of those acts as wrongful. Increasingly, we will need to enhance autonomy by decreasing the sphere of governmental authority. For example, Julie Cohen, Examined Lives: Informational Privacy and the Subject as Object, 52 Stan. L. Rev. 1373 (2000).

[14]*Cf.* Gates v. Discovery Comm. Inc., 34 Cal. 4th 679, 21 Cal.Rptr.3d 663, 101 P.3d 552, (2004) (no libel action for publication of true information). My colleague K. A. Taipale of the Center for Advanced Studies first called this conception to my attention. *See* K. A. Taipale, Technology, "Security and Privacy: The Fear of Frankenstein, the Mythology of Privacy, and the Lessons of King Ludd," 7 Yale J. L. & Tech. 123, 9 Intl. J. Comm. L. & Tech. 8 (Dec. 2004).

[15]It may also conflict with First Amendment principles, since it would serve to limit ones right to convey a true, negative fact to a third party. The limitation is especially problematic if the third party is about to engage in some transaction with the individual to whom the information refers—a situation where the utility of communication the information is likely to outweigh the privacy interests of the individual.

something about the nature of governmental scrutiny of otherwise public behavior that makes a particular difference. And that something has to be the prospect of governmental action, not the fear of scrutiny by itself. And more particularly, since deterrence of wrongdoing is a public good, it must be the prospect of government misuse—that is, identifying the wrong person by accident, or a willful misuse of technology to target (for example) an Administration's political opponents or publicly "out" the concealed social behavior of someone.

To see this most clearly, let's indulge in a simple thought experiment—imagine a perfect technology (clearly one beyond our current capabilities). Imagine a technology that was:

- 100% accurate in identifying wrong doers (i.e., it never had a false negative);
- 100% accurate in not mistakenly identifying as wrongdoers those who had done no wrong (i.e., it never had a false positive);
- 100% comprehensive in ensuring that the identity of those innocents whose conduct was examined in doing the sorting just described was never disclosed to any government agent, but rather perfectly wiped from memory after scanning;
- 100% automated on the front end, so that no human scrutiny occurs; and
- 100% perfect in preventing any mistaken or deliberate misuse of the system.

In other words, imagine a system where the consequences of identification were perfectly aligned with objective reality and with absolute protection for all innocent behavior. In such a system, would anyone have a plausible objection to the proposed knowledge discovery system? One can conceive of none (at least where the system is directed at harms, such as terrorism, that are uniformly acknowledged as wrongful conduct). Thus, we can conclusively reject the notion that observation, by itself, creates a consequence.

In doing so, however, we must acknowledge the importance of public perception. Because that perception can warp reality, the following can be stated: To a very real degree, public acceptance of lack of anonymity can derive from a misperception that anonymity persists to a greater degree than it actually does. Conversely, public rejection of enhanced information technologies may arise from a misperception about the prevalence of consequences and the absence of effective checks on abuse. In the long run, however, misperception is an unstable situation. It results in policy-making by anecdote and an irrational approach to vital public concerns. And so the better approach lies in education, explicit public consideration of privacy issues, and their direct consideration in the design and development of new technologies.

21.3. BUILDING THE LEGAL AND POLICY STRUCTURES

Thus, at long last, we come to what lies at the root of the objection to new technology that manipulates data about individuals—the necessity to address the perception that it is imperfect and susceptible of abuse and misuse. And surely, nobody can deny the truth of that claim, because we know that the perfect system described is impossible to construct. And we also know—through quite a bit of history—that men and women are imperfect creatures, capable of error and of ill-intentioned action. Thus, the fact of observation only has a real consequence because we fear the misuse of the observational result.

But the answer to the "problem of abuse" is not prohibition. We don't, for example, disarm the police, even though we know that police weapons can and have been misused—especially in the context of terrorism investigations (to whose uniqueness we will return). The better answer is the traditional American one of checks and balances—authority combined with responsibility. Power and oversight. It's an unwieldy system—it won't create the perfect technology hypothesized. But it is the best, most workable model we have.

So, what does that mean in practice? How should a link analysis or knowledge discovery system or a cybersecurity system using personal information or biometrics be built in a way that is consistent with this understanding conception of privacy?[16] What checks and balances should be built into new technology systems at the front end?

Herewith are seven basic principles (with, naturally, some subprinciples) that can and should be incorporated in any new system manipulating personally identifiable information.

21.3.1. Neutrality

First, any new technology should be "neutral"; that is, it should "build in" existing legal and policy limitations on access to individually identifiable information or third-party data and not be seen as a reason to alter existing legal régimes. In mapping the rules of consequence that exist in the physical world into the cyberworld the rules should, where feasible, be hard-wired or programmed in, not an add-on later.

For example, when we talk about individually identifiable data held by a commercial third-party data holder, the rule in the physical world is that the third-party data holder has an opportunity to object to the request and have its propriety adjudicated by a neutral third-party decision-maker (i.e., a judge).[17] The right way to build, for example, a new cybersecurity system that requires access to such data would incorporate that same rule into the software design.

Similarly, existing rules recognize a substantial difference between non-content "traffic" information and the content of a message. Law enforcement, for example, can get the phone numbers a person calls without a warrant. But they need a warrant to gain access to the content of his communications. And, intelligence investigators can obtain the header information on an e-mail easily (though some dispute whether the "Subject" line should be treated as traffic information or content), but to get the body of the message requires a warrant.[18]

One strongly suspects that much of the analysis that will go into creating better cybersecurity walls, tracking down hackers, and linking information databases will be of the

---

[16]Of course, the first question is whether the new technology will work. The thrust of the other chapters in this book and the work of others in the field (e.g., David Jensen, Matthew Rattigan, Hannah Blau, Information Awareness: A Prospective Technical Assessment, SIGKDD '03 August 2003) is that the prospects for success are real, though tentative. The purpose of this chapter is, therefore, twofold: (1) to identify control mechanisms that ought to be incorporated directly in the architecture of any new system where possible and practicable and (2) to reassure those who have legitimate concerns about the misuse of new technologies that means of controlling misuse while fostering appropriate advances do exist.

[17]Fed. R. Crm. P. 17; U.S. v. R. Enters., Inc., 498 U.S. 292 (1991). There is ongoing debate concerning whether certain provisions of law prohibit such third-party challenges. See Doe v. Ashcroft, 334 F.Supp.2d 471 (S.D.N.Y. 2004) (declaring National Security Letter provisions, 18 U.S.C. § 2709, unconstitutional for lack of right to challenge). To the extent the law does not allow such challenges, it is suspect—but the question of whether such challenges should, or should not, be permitted ought to be independently determined on the merits, outside the context of enabling technological implementations.

[18]Compare 18 U.S.C. §§ 3121–23 (authorizing access to pen register/trap and trace phone record information by certification of need) with 18 U.S.C. §§ 2516–18 (authorizing access to content of communications on showing of probable cause made to a court); see also Electronic Communications Privacy Act of 1986, Pub. L. No. 99-508, 100 Stat. 1848 (extending content protections to e-mail).

"traffic" variety. The fact that X called Y phone number, known to be used by a terrorist (or accessed the Internet using an account known to have been used by a terrorist), will be the initial item of interest, rather than knowing the content of that phone conversation or internet communication. This suggests that a process of selective revelation is the most appropriate mode of cyber-analysis—a two-step process (even in fully automated systems) where non-content analysis that is more readily approved (and less intrusive) precedes access to content, just as in the "real" world.

21.3.2. Minimize Intrusiveness

Second, new technologies should minimize intrusiveness to the extent practicable consistent with achieving their counter-terrorism objectives.[19] Depending upon the context, this principle might mean the following:

1. Ensuring that entry of individually identifiable information into the system is voluntary, where possible. To be sure, some systems involving, for example, access to controlled locations will not be voluntary. But where feasible, the degree of intrusiveness is lessened if individuals have the option of foregoing the benefit if they do not wish to be scrutinized.

2. Whether voluntary, or involuntary, the use of any new system should be overt, rather than covert, where possible. Thus, one should be particularly skeptical of programs that operate without the knowledge of those upon whom they act. To be sure, in a national security environment, secrecy may at times be necessary—but any new technology should seek to minimize those occasions and maximize disclosure.

3. Information technologies are more readily used, and accepted by the public, when used for the verification of information rather than as an independent source of identification. To take but one example, biometric systems are better suited for a one-to-one match ensuring that the individual in question is who he says he is and has the requisite authorization to engage in the activity in question. Biometrics are both less practically useful, and more problematic as a matter of policy, when they are used in a one-to-many fashion to pierce an individual's anonymity without the justification inherent in, for example, seeking access to a particular location.

4. As a corollary, to these principles, information technologies are generally more appropriately used to generate investigative leads than to identify individuals for specific action. Consider again the analogy to the law enforcement context, where the standard for the initiation of an investigation of a particular individual is minimal. No judicial authorization is needed for a government agent to initiate, for example, surveillance of a suspected drug dealer. All that is generally required is some executive determination of the general reliability of the source of the predication and, within the context of a particular agency, approval for initiation of an investigation from some executive authority.

Subject-oriented queries of this sort, using, for example, knowledge discovery technology is best understood as enhancing the efficiency of the information gathering process. But it should not be seen as an end in itself—just as in the physical world, the enhanced scrutiny must produce tangible results before adverse consequences beyond the fact of scrutiny should be allowed to be imposed.

5. Access to information already in the possession of the government is more readily

---

[19]These principles were first developed in Paul Rosenzweig, Alane Kochems and Ari Schwartz, Biometric Technologies: Security, Legal, and Policy Implications, Legal Memorandum No. 12 (The Heritage Foundation 2004).

accepted than is access to information in the private domain because once the information is lawfully collected, the public generally accepts its use within governmental systems. Similarly, government access to information in the private domain that is freely available to the public (for example, Yellow Pages listings or Google searches) is relatively unproblematic. The greatest problems will arise when (or if) the government seeks access to private commercial information that is not otherwise broadly available to the public.

6. Data and information are better maintained in a distributed architecture than in a centralized system. To be sure, some applications will require centralization of information—but the impulse to centralization should be resisted where possible because in a centralized database there is a greater possibility of abuse. A single repository of information provides, for example, an inviting target for a hacker and a brittle cybersecurity redoubt. By contrast, distributed databases, though sometimes less efficient, are also less easily compromised.

So, for example, when constructing a biometric system of identification for access to a secure facility, or for authorization to use a particular system, the preferred methodology (if feasible for the particular application) is to use a form of "match-on-card" technology where the biometric identifier is verified at a distributed site, rather than through transmission to a centralized database containing all the known biometrics available.

7. Finally, where possible, individually identifiable information should be anonymized or rendered pseudononymous and disaggregated so that individual activity is not routinely scrutinized. Frequently, the pattern analysis or the link that needs to be discovered can be examined without knowing the individual identity of the subject of the investigation, so long as the subject is uniquely identified. One can imagine many ways in which this form of anonymization can be achieved; as one example, it may be possible to use "one-way hashes" of lists that require comparison, allowing each list holder to maintain security of the list, and piercing the veil of anonymity thus created only in instances where a match occurs. Disney can compare its list of visitors with the Terrorist Screening Center's watch list, and neither need disclose the contents of the list. If, and only if, a match occurs, would Disney be obliged to disclose the identity and characteristics of the record associated with the individual identified.[20]

Protection of individual anonymity can be even further enhanced under this model. Mirroring the rules regarding identification in the real world, we could, for example, protect privacy by ensuring that individual identities are not disclosed without the approval of a neutral third-party decision-maker such as a judicial officer who determines the necessity for this disclosure based upon some defined standard of proof. Then those involved in high-level policy determinations can regulate the use of the system by imposing greater or lesser requirements for the degree of proof necessary before the veil of anonymity is torn away.

21.3.3. Intermediate Not Ultimate Consequence

Third, where appropriate, the consequence of identification by a new technology should not be presumptive; that is, it should not lead directly to the ultimate consequence (e.g., arrest, denial of access). Rather, such identification is generally best seen as a cause for additional investigation, not punitive government action. Considered in this light, we develop an understanding that knowledge discovery used for "subject-based" inquiries is

---

[20]James X. Dempsey and Paul Rosenzweig, Technologies that Can Protect Privacy as Information Is Shared to Combat Terrorism, Legal Memorandum No. 11 (The Heritage Foundation 2004).

really just an improved form of information sharing and link analysis. In this formulation, knowledge discovery is generally less likely to be subject of abuse since it more closely follows the traditional forms of police investigation and thus may appropriately lead in short order to ultimate consequences.

"Pattern-based" analysis also has a paradigm in the physical world. For example, the Compstat program in New York City uses pattern analysis to (a) identify emerging crime patterns allowing the police to direct scares enforcement resources to at-risk areas or (b) address emerging crime patterns before they become entrenched—all to the great benefit of its citizens.[21] Thus, pattern analysis recapitulates in automated and enhanced form the commonplace human behavior of seeing patterns in discrete objects[22]—whether stars in the sky, the repetitive pacing of a man casing a store for robbery on the ground,[23] or bank transactions in cyberspace. But, while useful in the aggregate, many remain skeptical of its ability to identify particular individuals for scrutiny. Given the comparatively greater potential for false positives in the context of pattern-based analysis, we should be especially vigilant in ensuring that the consequences of such identification are limited to investigative, rather than ultimate results.

21.3.4. Audits and Oversight

Fourth, any new technology should have strong technological audit and oversight mechanisms to prevent against abuse built in. The only way to ensure public acceptance of a new technology is to build in processes that demonstrate the certainty of punishment for misuse. Most of this will need to be based upon the inclusion of technological means in the design of a new system. New technologies should, for example, be tamper proof or at a minimum tamper evident. They should include automated and continuous audit functions that (a) log all activity for later review and (b) incorporate routine review as a means of uncovering misuse.

21.3.5. Accountability

Fifth, new technologies should be used in a manner that insures accountability of the Executive to the Legislative for its development and use. For example, we can conceive of systems that require authorization by a publicly appointed and accountable official before they are deployed, and perhaps used, and that involve periodic oversight of their basic architecture and effectiveness. Here, again, the real-world paradigm maps well. Just as a police chief wouldn't institute new rules for physical interactions with citizens in a manner that forestalled review by the city council, a new technology should not be developed under the guise of an intelligence program and deployed without appropriate consideration by those elected officials who are responsive to public concerns.

21.3.6. The Necessity of Redress Mechanisms

Sixth, we must provide a robust legal mechanism for the correction of false-positive identifications. People's gravest fear is being misidentified by an automated system. The

---

[21]For a short overview of Compstat and a description of its spread throughout the United States, see Shaila K. Dewan, "New York's Gospel of Policing by Data Spreads Across U.S.," *NY Times* (Apr. 28, 2004).
[22]See Heather MacDonald, What We Don't Know Can Hurt Us, *City Journal* (Spring 2004). (describing use of pattern analysis techniques for star pattern analysis).
[23]Terry v. Ohio, 392 U.S. 1 (1968).

prospect of not being allowed to fly, or of being subject to covert surveillance based on electronic records, scares them.

Of course, the same possibility exists in the "real world"—individuals become subjects of suspicion incorrectly all the time. What makes the difference is that in a cybersystem, the "suspicion" may persist—both because the records generating the suspicion are often persistent and uncorrected and especially because the subject of the suspicion is a broad concern for preempting future attacks that is likely to be lest susceptible of refutation. By contrast in the real world, law enforcement eventually comes to a conclusion and "clears" the suspect of connection to a specific prior criminal act.

Hence, here, at last, the direct map from the real world to the cyber world may break down. As a result, rather than relying on the inherent nature of investigative methods to correct false positives, we will need a formal process—including both administrative and, if necessary, judicial mechanisms—for resolving ambiguities and concerns discerned by new knowledge discovery technologies.

We should recognize that the greatest difficulties of all in developing new technologies may lie in the construction of such a process. For one thing, it must act in many instances, nimbly and quickly—especially, for example, in real-time contexts like clearing passengers for flights. For another, it must itself have protections against being spoofed, lest terrorists go through the clearing process to get "clean" before committing wrongful acts.

But equally problematic, the process will likely not be able to meet our traditional standards of complete transparency in an adversarial context because often disclosure of the methodology and algorithms that lie behind a new information technology will destroy their utility for identifying suspicious individuals. Yet, the failure to disclose this information will deprive the effected individual of a full and fair opportunity to contest his identification.

In short, an effective redress mechanism will need to answer the following questions: How much information about himself can an individual see? What will be the forum and mechanism for disputing and correcting alleged inaccuracies in that information? What mechanisms will there be to purge old records? What sort of notification should an individual receive when information about him has led to a loss of a privilege (e.g. employment in a secure capacity, or ability to travel)?

What will be necessary is a concept of calibrated, or graduated and partial transparency, where alternate mechanisms of resolution are used. Those are fairly rare in American legal structures and will require careful thought.[24] By and large, however, these mechanisms will be external to the new technologies themselves. They are relevant to the development of technology, however, first in demonstrating the need for audit mechanisms that will provide accurate data correction capabilities and, more importantly, in emphasizing the need for technological development to go forward in tandem with parallel policy development because the absence of an answer to the redress question may doom even the most advantageous new technology.

21.3.7. People and Policy

Finally, we must recognize that besides the process we build into any new technology, there are people. Here, too, technological development will benefit from attention to ex-

---

[24]For a detailed consideration of what a redress mechanism should look like in the context of watch list identification, *see* Paul Rosenzweig and Jeff Jonas, Correcting False Positives: Redress and the Watch List Conundrum, Legal Memorandum No. 17 (The Heritage Foundation June 2005).

ternal policy content because, as new information technologies are deployed, we must create a culture of heightened accountability and oversight. This will include: internal policy controls and training; administrative oversight of the use of technology through, for example, Inspectors General or a Privacy Board[25]; enhanced congressional oversight through the intelligence committees; and, ultimately, civil and, if necessary criminal penalties for abuse.

We know that this sort of effort can be successful. One example is the modern NSA. In the 1970s Congressional investigations concluded that the NSA had misused its surveillance powers, conducting improper surveillance of American citizens.[26] Since that time, although it is a substantial training and oversight effort, NSA has developed a corporate culture that strongly controls potentially abusive behavior.[27] It isn't easy—controlling abuse requires a continuous and sustained commitment, something rare in our political culture. But it is possible.

21.4. THE NATURE OF PRIVACY IN THE POST-9/11 WORLD

To conclude the consideration of the question, we need to understand two final points regarding the nature of privacy: its multivariate nature and its lack of an "absolute" quality. These properties were of relatively little importance when the subject matter of most governmental inquiry was simple criminal behavior. But in the post-9/11 world, where the threat of terrorism is substantially greater, these properties take on a new significance.

21.4.1. Multivariate Privacy

In the post-9/11 world we have, inevitably, seen changes in many of the ways in which government interacts with its citizens—often in derogation of privacy interests. But it is important to recognize that privacy takes many forms. Consider some of the changes and how they have affected privacy. First, there is an increase in what we might call the "citadelization" of America—more barricades, more check points, and so on. This is especially true in cities like New York and Washington that are thought to be prominent terrorist targets. There is also an increase in public surveillance—more cameras and more police on the streets, routinely watching citizen behavior. And then there is a decrease in pure physical privacy: At airports we take off shoes; new mothers are stopped because their breast pump attracts attention from the screeners; and recent tragedies have led to even more intrusive physical screening.

Finally, of course, there are potential intrusions into electronic privacy. As knowledge discovery and link analysis techniques take hold, and as increased information

---

[25]For example, a Privacy and Civil Liberties Board was created by Intelligence Reform and Terrorism Prevention Act of 2004, Pub. L. No. 108-458, § 1061 (2004).

[26]See *Intelligence Activities and the Rights of Americans, Book II, Final Report of the Select Committee to Study Governmental Operations with Respect to Intelligence Activities Together with Additional, Supplemental, and Separate Views*, S. Rep. No. 755, 94th Cong., 2d Sess. (1976) (Church Committee Reports); *Recommendations of the Final Report of the House Select Committee on Intelligence*, H.R. Rep. 833, 94th Cong., 2d Sess. (1976) (Pike Committee Reports). The Church Committee Reports, but not the Pike Committee Reports, were made public, but the latter were eventually leaked, and both sets of reports, comprising many volumes, are available online.

[27]See Joel F. Brenner, Information Oversight: Practical Lessons from Foreign Intelligence, Heritage Lecture No. 851 (2004). There is a risk, of course, that stringent rules may create rigidity within an organization. Thus, some flexibility needs to be maintained. By and large, however, suitable rules actually promote useful activities by affording those who act on our behalf with a "safe harbor" of approved conduct.

sharing capacity erodes the "practical obscurity" that used to prevail, the public are finding, increasingly, that information about their conduct is more readily available to the government.

The key point to take from this brief summary is that, given the multivariate nature of privacy interests at stake, many of the questions we are facing are not questions of privacy invasion *vel non*. Reductions in privacy are, in at least some instances, inevitable. There is, for example, no prospect of returning to a pre-9/11 system of passenger screening, much less to the 1980s when you could fly anonymously and pay cash on flights.[28]

So the principal policy issue to be considered will be privacy tradeoffs—more electronic privacy at the airport will probably mean less physical privacy, and vice versa. And different people will have different values for different aspect of privacy—some would readily trade a little electronic privacy in order to avoid a full random search of their luggage.[29] And, when risk assessment through information technology demonstrates little risk, the use of scarce resources to conduct a full physical screening is simply a waste.

Of equal importance, many will accommodate greater or lesser tolerance for invasions of privacy depending on the perceived imminence of actual harm—thus privacy protections may also vary as the threat environment changes (allowing, for example, greater intrusions under a "code red" threat level and less when the threat diminishes).

Thus the multivariate nature of privacy is one property of information that those building systems in the cyberworld should take into account because, if privacy valuations are to be built into cybersystems, and if privacy is multivariate, such that the designer's assessment of the proper privacy regime may differ from that of the user(s) and effected third parties, then the decision about the privacy principles to be built into a new system should be made in the most representative way possible, rather than the least representative.

In the Federal context, this means we should prefer Congress over the Executive Branch in setting privacy rules. And either of those institutions is preferable to the unelected and unrepresentative Judicial branch, which, in this context, is ill-suited to rendering broad societal judgments of the sort at issue. Ideally, legislative consideration of these questions should be required before any new technology that potentially infringes on civil liberties is deployed.

Another implication from the multivariate nature of privacy is also clear: Since privacy values vary, where possible the optimal design of a new system should allow individual choice between equally effective options. If, for example, I want to join the TSA's registered traveler program and you don't, that's fine.[30] That choice may mean that you get more physical screening more frequently, but that's a fair choice to require. Of course there is a possibility that the choices will trend so far in one direction (e.g., everyone electing to be a trusted traveler) that the minority choice of more physical screening will come at a higher cost or premium. That is, however, unlikely on the current state of American psyche. And, if it becomes a reality, it will be the natural product of a free market.

---

[28]A recent challenge raising precisely this point has, thus far, been rejected. *See* Gilmore v. Ashcroft, 2004 WL 603530 (N.D.Cal. 2004).

[29]For an discussion of this principle, *see* Paul Rosenzweig, "The Transportation Security Administration's Computer-Assisted Passenger Prescreening System (CAPPS II)," Testimony Before the United States House of Representatives, Committee on Transportation & Infrastructure, Subcommittee on Aviation (March 17, 2004).

[30]The TSA is experimenting with a trusted traveler program that will allow passengers who submit to a significant background investigation to speed their way through airports with limited or alternative physical screening. The program is widely popular: Travelocity reports, for example, that 43% of frequent travelers (with more than 5 trips per year) favor the program. *See* Travel Security Update (Feb. 2002) (available at http://media.corporate-ir.net/media_files/NSD/TVLY/presentations/tvly_022502/sld001.htm).

21.4.2. Privacy as a Nonabsolute Value

Finally, let us consider the single most important property of the privacy interest—its nonabsolute nature. Or as we might rephrase the question: Does the fact that we are talking about terrorism prevention make a difference?

If you think that privacy is an absolute value, never to be compromised, then your answer clearly would be "no." And there are some who see privacy as an absolute value, never to be compromised. They see the virtue of anonymity not in the lack of consequences but in some mystical, ontological argument for the right to lead a life free from scrutiny. This view supports a belief in the ability, for example, to fly a plane paying cash or using a false name. There is little basis for debate with those who hold this view, because it is, ultimately, a faith belief of the sort that is not falsifiable.[31] But we can say that this view is not the view held by the majority, and, more importantly, that to effectuate it, those who hold this view must impose it ubiquitously on those who see privacy as a nonabsolute value.

The better answer to the question of whether terrorism makes a difference is, or ought to be, "yes." Consider the following—again mapping to existing physical world analysis: Law enforcement has a paradigm for its proof requirements—"it is better that 10 guilty go free than that 1 innocent be mistakenly punished."[32] This aphorism expresses a preference for false negatives and a deep aversion to false positives. It is embodied in the rule that convictions can only be based upon proof "beyond a reasonable doubt."[33] But the expression of this proof rule also admits that the "liberty" interest involved (i.e., physical freedom) is not something we absolutely protect—it can be taken from a citizen, without his consent if necessary, if he violates certain rules deemed socially necessary.

The same understanding is, or ought to be, true of privacy of the anonymity sort. Consider how terrorism and data surveillance change the paradigm. Now it is expressed as: "Better that 10 terrorists go free than that 1 innocent have his electronic data examined." Note that both sides of the equation have changed.

On one side of the equation the potential for harm has greatly increased, because the danger from terrorism is much greater than that from common crime.[34] And the infringement on liberty (screening versus imprisonment) is much less. And so, we have a sense that the solution to the equation should change as well. No longer is the "beyond a reasonable doubt" standard appropriate as would be necessary to justify a deprivation of liberty. But rather a more appropriate standard is something of the form "when there is a reasonable basis for suspicion" to justify an action effecting the privacy interest.[35]

---

[31]See, e.g., Anthony Flew, Theology and Falsification in Anthony Flew and Alastair MacIntyre, eds., *New Essays in Philosophical Theology* (London: SCM Press, 1955; New York: Macmillan, 1964).

[32]See, e.g., Furman v. Georgia, 408 U.S. 238, 367 n.158 (1972) (Marshall, J., concurring). The aphorism has its source in 4 Blackstone, Commentaries, ch. 27, at 358 (Wait & Co. 1907).

[33]"In a criminal case . . . we do not view the social disutility of convicting an innocent man as equivalent to the disutility of acquitting someone who is guilty. . . . [T]he reasonable doubt standard is bottomed on a fundamental value determination of our society that it is far worse to convict an innocent man than to let a guilty man go free." In re: Winship, 397 U.S. 357, 372 (1970) (Harlan, J., concurring).

[34]Harvard professor Graham Allison has estimated that there is a 50/50 chance that a nuclear device will be exploded by terrorists in the United States within the next 10 years. *See* Graham Allison, *Nuclear Terrorism: The Ultimate Preventable Catastrophe* (2004). Even if this estimate is off by a factor of 100, it is still a risk of a unique magnitude.

[35]As noted earlier, the change is not only contextual, but variable. Individual technological applications may pose different questions when applied in a low-threat environment (where blanket rules may be appropriate) from those relevant in a high-threat environment (where greater flexibility might be necessary).

Of course, the formulation of the new paradigm is not strictly accurate. It really isn't "one" innocent whose data are screened, but many millions. But so long as that is the only consequence, and so long as any other consequences flow not from the examination of information records by itself but only from the independent determination of the "reasonable basis," then the costs on the right-hand side of the equation are relatively modest .

Finally, note that the fact that it is a new equation suggests strongly that any new technology should be deployed within the context of counter-terrorism and with a recognition that many balances struck in that context would be struck differently, in the context of traditional law enforcement. And so the last principle: To guard against "mission creep," one should be especially wary of the instinct to use new enabling technologies in nonterrorism contexts.

To be sure, the Counter-terrorism/Law Enforcement line may be difficult to police in practice. The same technologies will uncover identity forgers or system hackers whether or not their intent is terrorist or criminal or mere mischief. The key to guarding against mission creep abuse will be development of mechanisms for assessing the intent of those who use the new technologies—a strong front "gate" if you will, before the new technologies may be applied.

SUMMARY

In any event, what we really know is that to solve the new terrorism/privacy equation, we need to know more than we do now. We need to know how effective a new technology will be. We need to know the frequency with which it might misidentify individuals for examination. We need to know what "gates" for the imposition of consequences will be built into the system. And we need to know what error-correction mechanisms there will be.

But none of these can be determined without much more testing and development. So we know that the only really wrong answer is to stop the testing of these new systems now. If the government does not develop them, the private sector and the academy surely will.[36]

In short, we must realize that there are no iron-clad guarantees against abuse. But prohibition on new technology developments is surely the wrong answer. We cannot act with an over-wrought sense of fear. While we must be cautious, John Locke, the seventeenth-century philosopher who greatly influenced the Founding Fathers, was correct when he wrote: "In all states of created beings, capable of laws, where there is no law there is no freedom. For liberty is to be free from the restraint and violence from others; which cannot be where there is no law; and is not, as we are told, a liberty for every man to do what he lists."[37] Thus, the obligation of the government is a dual one: to protect civil safety and security against violence *and* to preserve civil liberty.

In reviewing what we have done and what we should do in the future, we must be guided by the realization that this is not a zero-sum game. We can achieve both goals—

[36]See Robert O'Harrow, Jr., Bahamas Firm Screens Personal Data to Assess Risk, *Washington Post* (Oct. 16, 2004) (new firm formed in Bahamas for data analysis in part to avoid US privacy laws); Eric Lichtblau, Homeland Security Department Experiments with New Tool to Track Financial Crime, *New York Times* (Dec. 12, 2004) (describing new British program for tracking financial transactions); *see generally,* K. A. Taipale, Data Mining and Domestic Security: Connecting the Dots to Make Sense of Data, 5 *Colum. Sci. & Tech. L. Rev.* 2 (2003) (describing potential commercialization phenomenon generally).

[37]John Locke, *Two Treatises of Government* 305 (Peter Laslett, ed., 1988).

liberty and security—to an appreciable degree. The key is empowering government, while exercising oversight. So long as we keep a vigilant eye on police authority and so long as the debate about governmental conduct is a vibrant part of the American dialogue, the risk of excessive encroachment on our fundamental liberties is remote. The only real danger lies in silence and leaving policies unexamined.

Chapter 22

Designing Technical Systems to Support Policy: Enterprise Architecture, Policy Appliances, and Civil Liberties

K. A. Taipale

22.1. INTRODUCTION

It has become cliché to describe the relationship between security and liberty as one requiring the achievement of some optimal balance between two competing and irreconcilable needs. But such cliché is metaphorically misleading. There is no fulcrum point—as is implicit in the balance metaphor—at which point the correct amount of security and liberty can be achieved. Security and liberty are not dichotomous rivals to be traded one for another in a zero sum game as the notion of balance suggests or as the *enragés* of the public debate would have. Rather, security and liberty are dual obligations of a liberal republic, and each must be maximized within the constraints imposed by the other.[1]

The events and subsequent investigations of 9/11 have highlighted the national security need for better information management and for new technologies and techniques to improve collection, information sharing, and data analysis in counter-terrorism applications. The need to manage vast data volumes and better "connect the dots" is uncontroverted and has been explicitly set out in a series of executive orders, presidential directives, national strategy documents, committee reports, and legislation.[2]

---

[1]K. A. Taipale, Data Mining and Domestic Security: Connecting the Dots to Make Sense of Data, 5 *Colum. Sci. & Tech. L. Rev.* 2 at no. 6 (1993) [hereinafter, Taipale, Data Mining], citing Thomas Powers, Can We Be Secure and Free? 151 Public Interest 3, 5 (Spring 2003); *see also* K. A. Taipale, Technology, Security, and Privacy: The Fear of Frankenstein, the Mythology of Privacy, and the Lessons of King Ludd, 7 *Yale J. L. & Tech.* at 5 (Dec. 2004) [hereinafter, Taipale, Frankenstein].

[2]See, e.g., Executive Order 13356 (2004); Presidential Directive, Strengthening Information Sharing, Access, and Integration B Organizational, Management, and Policy Development Structures for Creating the Terrorism Information Sharing Environment, June 2, 2005; National Strategy for Homeland Security at 55 (2002); The National Commission on Terrorist Attacks Upon the United States, The 9/11 Report §13.3 (2004); Intelligence Reform and Terrorism Prevention Act of 2004, Pub. L. No.108-458, §1016.

However, emergent information technologies that can enable such improved information management and analysis processes—technologies like those described in this book—also challenge traditional policy doctrines and legal structures premised in part on protecting individual liberty by maintaining *privacy* through the "practical obscurity" arising from inefficiencies in information acquisition, access, management, and analysis.[3] Thus, to some observers, improving the ability of government agencies to "connect the dots" is seen to be in political conflict with the notion of keeping the power to "connect the dots" out of any one hand, particularly that of the central government.[4] The result, as evidenced in the public debate, is a presumed implacable antagonism between security and privacy.

Fortunately, we do not need to resolve this Jacobin discordance in order to design information systems with technical features that can support a broad range of policies to mitigate privacy concerns and still meet security needs. Indeed, there is no inherent *technical* design conflict at all between security and privacy because the technical features required to support privacy policy are in large part the same technologies required to meet operational information assurance and data security needs in national security or law enforcement information sharing applications. Both national security and privacy policy require (i) that shared information be *useful* (that is, that data are accurate, reliable, and timely, and that it can be updated or corrected as needed) and (ii) that information be *used appropriately* according to policy rules. Technical features to support these concordant policy needs in information systems include rules-based processing, selective disclosure, data quality assurance, error correction, and strong authorization, logging, and audit functions (to control and record what information goes where, under what constraints, and who has access to it).

This chapter discusses policy-enabling systems design based on an *enterprise architecture* to support *knowledge management* (a life-cycle approach to managing information from production to consumption as a product to support business process needs) and *due process* (procedures to protect civil liberties). This architecture includes *policy appliances* (technical control mechanisms to enforce policy rules and ensure accountability in information systems),[5] interacting with *smart data* (data that carry with them contextual relevant terms for their own use) and *intelligent agents* (queries that are self-credentialed, authenticating, or contextually adaptive). See Figures 22.1 and 22.2. It is beyond the scope of this chapter to detail specific technology development or current research avenues in depth, or to exhaustively examine information management strategies or developments. Rather, this chapter provides an overview of the relationship between emerging policy process models and technical design choice in order to better understand the interdependence of technical architecture and policy implementation.

---

[3]See *Department of Justice v. Reporters Committee for Freedom of Press,* 489 U.S. 749, 780 (1989) (recognizing a legally protected interest in the "practical obscurity" of inefficient paper-based record systems).

[4]See, e.g., Kathleen Sullivan, Under a Watchful Eye: Incursions on Personal Privacy, in *The War on Our Freedoms* (Richard C. Leone et al., eds., 2003).

[5]See Taipale, Frankenstein, supra note 1 at 56-58 (discussing "privacy appliances" to enforce rules and provide accountability). The concept of privacy appliances originated with the DARPA Total Information Awareness project. See presentation by Dr. John Poindexter, Director, Information Awareness Office (IAO), Defense Advanced Research Projects Agency (DARPA), at DARPA-Tech 2002 Conference, Anaheim, CA (Aug. 2, 2002); Dr. Robert Popp interview, E. Jonietz, "Total Information Overload,: *MIT Technology Review,* July 2003. ISAT 2002 Study, Security with Privacy (Dec. 13, 2002); and IAO Report to Congress Regarding the Terrorism Information Awareness Program at A-13 (May 20, 2003) in response to Consolidated Appropriations Resolution, 2003, No.108-7, Division M, §111(b) [signed Feb. 20, 2003].

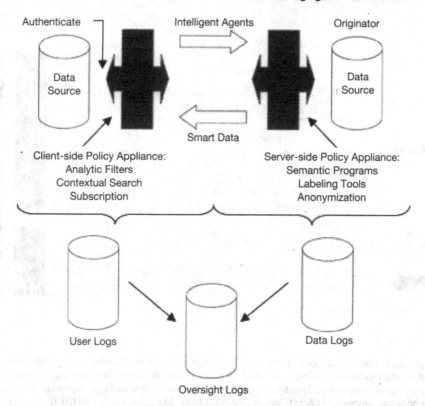

Figure 22.1. Policy management architecture. An *enterprise architecture* for *knowledge management* (an information product approach) and *due process* (civil liberties protections) that includes *policy appliances* (technical control mechanisms to enforce policy rules and ensure accountability) interacting with *smart data* (data that carry with them contextual relevant terms for their own use) and *intelligent agents* (queries that are self-credentialed, authenticating, or contextually adaptive).

22.2. CHANGING BASE CONDITIONS

New technologies do not determine human fates; instead, they alter the spectrum of potentialities within which people act.[6] Thus, information technologies alone cannot provide security, nor can they destroy liberty or intrude on privacy; rather, they enable or constrain potential developments or implementations, and thereby may facilitate or inhibit a particular policy or affect a technology's adoption within that or another policy framework. Code may not be law, but it can bound what policy can do.[7] Thus, technologists need to understand policy requirements and associated policy *process models* in order to design systems that can enable familiar policy mechanisms, procedures, and doctrines (or their analogues) to function under novel, technology-enabled conditions.

---

[6]Robert McClintock and K. A. Taipale, *Educating America for the 21st Century,* Institute for Learning Technologies (Columbia University) at 2 (1994).

[7]See Lawrence Lessig, Code and Other Laws of Cyberspace 3-8 (1999) ("[Code] constitute[s] a set of constraints on how you behave. . . . The code or . . . architecture . . . constrain[s] some behavior by making other behavior possible, or impossible"). *Id.* at 89. Lessig writes that behavior is controlled (regulated or constrained) through a dynamic interaction of legal rules, social norms, market forces and architecture (or code). *Id.* at 83-99.

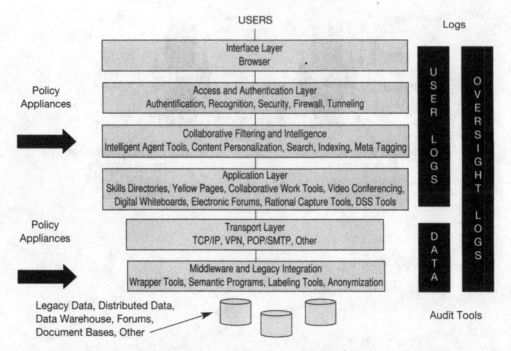

Figure 22.2. Policy management stack. An *enterprise architecture* showing *policy appliances* (technical control mechanisms to enforce policy rules and ensure accountability) and *logging functions* in network stack relationship. This figure builds on the seven-layer knowledge management architecture originally suggested in Amrit Tiwana, The Knowledge Management Toolkit (2000).

In the context of counter-terrorism, technologies like those described in this book can help allocate scarce security resources to more effective uses. The primary challenge to *liberty* from these uses, however, comes not from the technology itself but rather from the shift to *preemptive* security strategies necessitated by the changed nature of the threat presented by transnational terrorism. The primary challenge to *privacy* (upon which we rely in part to protect individual liberty) comes from the *efficiencies* enabled by new information processing technologies for the collection, sharing, and automated analysis of data in support of such preemptive strategies.[8] Designing systems to address these challenges requires an understanding of the nature of the fundamental change to the governing security, information, and privacy paradigms (and the related process models) enabled by new information technologies, as well as how technology design decisions intersect with existing policy mechanisms to mitigate or exacerbate the effects of such changes.

22.2.1. The Changing Nature of the Threat and Preemption

The traditional line between reactive law enforcement policies and preemptive national security strategies is blurring because the seed value—that is, the initiating force—of potentially catastrophic outcomes has devolved from the nation state (the traditional target

---

[8]Note that the same characteristics of efficiency that challenge existing privacy policy—in particular, the ability to share and analyze information independent of the original purpose of collection and beyond the control of the original data "owner"—also affect operational security and information assurance requirements.

of national security power) to organized but stateless groups (the traditional target of law enforcement power). Organized groups of stateless actors (and soon perhaps even individuals) have the capacity to inflict the kind of catastrophic outcomes that can threaten national survival by undermining the public confidence that maintains the economic and political systems in modern Western democracies.[9] In simple terms, the threat to national security is no longer confined only to other nation-states. Thus, there exists a political consensus, at least with regard to these types of threats, to take a preemptive rather than reactive approach. "Terrorism cannot be treated as a reactive law enforcement issue, in which we wait until after the bad guys pull the trigger before we stop them."[10] The policy debate, then, is not about preemption itself (even the most strident civil libertarians concede the need to identify and stop terrorists before they act) but instead revolves around what new process model—that is, what strategies, what implementations, and what supporting technologies or techniques—are to be employed in this endeavor. And, because the exercise of law enforcement power and national security power has previously been governed by disparate—and potentially irreconcilable—doctrines and laws, this blurring also requires determining which set of existing principles, or what new principles, will govern these developments.

22.2.1.1. The Need for Surveillance.
Preemption of terrorist attacks that can occur at any place and any time requires *actionable intelligence*—that is, information useful to anticipate and counter future events. Since organized terrorism generally requires communications and precursor behaviors likely evidenced by transactions or interactions recorded in databases, counter-terrorism intelligence in part requires *surveillance* or *analysis* of communications and transactions to uncover evidence of organization, relationships, or other relevant patterns of behavior indicative or predictive of potential threats, so that additional law enforcement or security resources or actions can then be increasingly selectively focused on such threats. The technologies discussed in this book generally are tools to help selectively focus scarce analytic, security, or law enforcement resources on more likely threats in order to preempt terrorist attacks; that is, they are tools to help produce actionable intelligence.

22.2.1.2. The Dissolving Perimeter of Defense.
Another characteristic of the changing nature of the threat is that the perimeter of defense is dissolving. The traditional "line at the border"-based defense, useful against other nation-states, is insufficient against an enemy that moves easily across and within borders and hides among the general population, taking advantage of an open society to mask their own organization and activities. The national security challenge is no longer just to defend against outsiders but to identify and investigate potentially malicious actors from within the general populace—so-called "in-liers."[11] Effective preemption, therefore, requires that potential attackers be identified from the background population and neutralized before they can act without undermining or compromising the liberty of the vast majority of innocent people.

---

[9]See K. A. Taipale, Losing the War on Terror, *World Policy Journal* (forthcoming 2005).

[10]Editorial, The Limits of Hindsight, *Wall St. J.*, July 28, 2003, at A10. See also U.S. Department of Justice, Fact Sheet: Shifting from Prosecution to Prevention, Redesigning the Justice Department to Prevent Future Acts of Terrorism (May 29, 2002).

[11]Comments by Ted Senator, DARPA, at *Roundtable on Data Mining,* Center for Democracy and Technology and Heritage Foundation, Washington, DC (Dec. 2003).

22.2.1.3. The Challenge of Preemption. Thus, the real challenge to liberty comes from the need to act preemptively against a proved parlous adversary who hides among the general population as part of their strategic and tactical doctrine, thereby ne-. cessitating a new domestic security process model that includes some method of screening the general population in order to allocate investigative or other security resources to more likely targets by differentiating likely threats from unlikely threats before they act. This new process model blurs existing distinctions in law and policy rules that have traditionally governed reactive law enforcement and proactive national security power under disparate and conflicting principles. The policy questions raised by preemption as they relate to liberty are:

- First, how is such screening or scrutiny going to be managed (that is, under what procedures is actionable intelligence going to be developed and what tools or techniques may be employed against what data under what constraints)?

- Second, what procedures will govern further government action based on such intelligence (that is, what predicate is required for, and what consequences flow from, acting on such intelligence, and how are such predicate and consequence established, authorized, and reviewed)?[12]

The technical design questions involve determining how systems architecture can facilitate (or hinder) control over such decisions and help enforce, as well as monitor, agreed-upon policies.

22.2.2. New Information Technologies, New Economics, and New Efficiencies

Vast data volumes and limited resources are overwhelming the capacity of law enforcement and intelligence agencies to identify relevant information and develop useful counter-terrorism intelligence. The intelligence community collects enormous amounts of raw data every day, but much of it cannot be analyzed on a timely basis (or ever) because of parochial information management practices and scarce analytical resources. There are many examples set forth in the 9/11 commission report[13] and elsewhere in which planned terrorist activities went undetected despite the fact that evidence to expose them existed within intelligence agency files—but the relevant evidence was just one needle in a huge haystack or, worse, many pieces of a single needle scattered among many silos of hay. In addition to information collected directly by intelligence agencies, terabytes of commercial communication and transaction records are also being created each day. Furthermore, both intelligence and commercial data stores are increasing not only in size (the number of records or objects in the database), but also in dimensionality (the number of fields or attributes to an object). Finally, an almost infinite amount of "open source" information exists in the public domain—some of which is highly relevant to counter-terrorism intelligence. The "practical obscurity" of earlier, less efficient paper-based records systems has been replaced by an "obscurity by volume" in which human analytic abilities are no longer able to manage the size and di-

---

[12]Determining predicate and developing standards is particularly relevant where counterterrorism sanctions that may not be subject to traditional judicial due process procedures are employed—for example, imposing travel restrictions or deportation for unrelated infractions.

[13]National Commission on Terrorist Attacks Upon the United States, *Final Report* (July 2004).

mensionality of current data collection methods or availability. Thus, the need for more efficient collection, sharing, and analytic capabilities through computational automation is driven by a practical (and unrelenting) imperative.

Some might argue that one solution to vast data volumes is to decrease the inputs—that is, to be more selective about data acquisition or access. However, this approach ignores two vital points: First, in the context of counter-terrorism it is usually not possible to determine *a priori* what information is useful, and second, the economics of digital information collection and storage have changed in ways that make growth in data volume inevitable. Unlike in the paper-based world, the cost of data retention in digital systems is now less than the cost of selective deletion. Because technical means of information acquisition, storage, and processing are capital-intensive not labor- or physical space-intensive, the cost per unit of information has and will continue to decrease. Thus, data are accumulated and retained for potential future relevance or usefulness because a search after the fact for relevant information is a more efficient or cost-effective strategy than editing or preselecting for relevance before storage. Likewise, the cost of indiscriminate data collection is generally less than the cost of selective acquisition or collection. These trends ensure that we face an inevitable future of more—not less—data.

Therefore, if data largely "exist" or are increasingly attainable at lower cost, the operational question is how to better allocate limited human analytic, law enforcement, or security attention to more relevant information (and the answer lies in part in developing better collection, sharing, and analysis technologies as described elsewhere in this book) and the policy question is how to ensure that such allocation of selective attention is effective for security purposes without unduly compromising civil liberties.

Thus, we have the paradox of technology-driven change in this area: On the one hand, the vast data volumes that result from efficiencies in collection and storage technologies lead to a high collective expectation of privacy (that is, government cannot watch *everyone*), but, on the other hand, improvements in information sharing and analysis technologies result in a low individual expectation of privacy (that is, government can selectively watch or focus on *anyone*). The policy debate is over how we allocate the social cost or burden of such selective attention between society and the individual—or between security and privacy—particularly as new information technologies lower the cost of selectively focusing attention.

An illustrative example of how technology interacts with policy in allocating this burden is to compare the different approaches idealized in the development and use of *Carnivore* and *Echelon*. Carnivore was an FBI-developed analytic filtering technology—essentially a specialized packet sniffer—that was to be deployed at an ISP pursuant to a court authorized warrant to 'tap' e-mail communications by collecting only the information subject to or authorized under the warrant. (The FBI has since replaced Carnivore with commercial software to accomplish the same task.)[14] The Carnivore approach places the burden on government to identify and narrowly circumscribe the relevance of particular information or information source prior to collection. Echelon, on the other hand, is an NSA project that indiscriminately intercepts communications signals for filtering by key-

---

[14]"Carnivore" was the original name chosen by its developers because it was designed to "get at the meat of the investigation," that is, to retrieve only the relevant data subject to court order. After much public criticism of the program, the FBI renamed the system DCS-1000. For more information about Carnivore, *see Carnivore Diagnostic Tool,* Testimony of Donald M. Kerr, Assistant Director, Laboratory Division, FBI, United States Senate, The Committee on the Judiciary (Sept. 6, 2000). The FBI has since replaced Carnivore with commercial software.

word.[15] The burden with Echelon is arguably on the data subjects whose communications are being intercepted and analyzed without the need for government showing that any particular information or source is relevant through legal or other process prior to content analysis. Regardless of the actual particulars of these examples, the illustrative thing to consider is that moving the technical locus of data analysis and policy interaction can shift the burden between government and individual (or, indirectly, between security and privacy). In the case of Carnivore the technical analytic capability is narrowly circumscribed by policy prior to collection, thus putting the burden (a higher cost of selectively focusing attention) on the FBI to predetermine what information is likely useful for a particular purpose, but, in the case of Echelon, the analytic capabilities (and thus the costs of selective attention) are applied after interception without any prior determination of specific relevance. What this example helps illustrate is that systems architecture—that is, where within the process model technical mechanisms are deployed and interact with policy—has substantive policy implications.

The same considerations are relevant in designing distributed information environments in which data sharing, data access, and data analysis—not collection—are the primary concern. Technical design decisions about where in systems architecture a particular policy intervention is enabled, controlled, or enforced (as well as the related information flow design choices) can have substantive impact on the efficacy or consequence of such policy (and its relative allocation of burden). Additionally, determining who has technical control over intervention mechanisms will have policy implications for authorization, administration, and oversight.

22.2.3. Privacy and Due Process in a Changed World

A policy of preemption based on actionable intelligence threatens liberty because it challenges two interwoven doctrinal protective mechanisms habitually relied upon to shield individuals from the power of the government—*privacy* and *due process*. In this context, privacy is about maintaining a default state in which the government is precluded from knowing a particular thing about a specific individual, and due process governs the process whereby the government may intrude on that default state to gain particular knowledge and what the government can do with that knowledge once it has it. For purposes of our analysis, privacy is about the *disclosure* of information and due process is about the *fairness of its use* (that is, the fairness of the process by which government initially focuses on (or accesses) information and subsequently uses unclosed information to affect individual liberty). In both cases the issue is about the allocation of the power that comes from the knowing a particular thing.

22.2.3.1. Privacy. Although privacy interests are said to be as "old as civilization" itself (references to privacy interests can be found in the Qur'an and the Old Testament),

---

[15]The existence of Echelon has been disputed and the details of the program are classified. Most public accounts describe a process in which communications are flagged by certain keywords.*See* http://www.fas.org/irp/program/process/echelon.htm. *See also* European Parliament, Temporary Committee on the ECHELON Interception System, *Report on the existence of a global system for the interception of private and commercial communications (ECHELON interception system)* (2001/2098(INI)) (July 11, 2001). Although both Carnivore and Echelon could be described as analytic filtering applications, for purposes of the example, Echelon is not as burdened by process (cost) at intake; that is, it intercepts all communications for processing—as is Carnivore, which is subject to an *a priori* showing of potential relevance through articulation of specific predicate under legal process prior to data collection.

the modern notion of a legally protected privacy right is a relatively recent, and illusive, conception—in the main a creature of twentieth-century legal developments. The very notion of privacy itself is subject to a wide range of interpretations and supporting theories. However, it is beyond the scope of this chapter—nor is it necessary for our purposes—to definitely define privacy or reconcile the competing views.[16] In general, privacy *law* can be said to have developed in response to new technologies. As emerging technologies have challenged existing doctrines through new forms of intrusion, new principles have emerged and new laws created. Thus, it is instructive to examine how current technologies challenge existing privacy principles by understanding what technical characteristics don't easily fit under traditional analysis.

In the first Supreme Court ruling to explicitly recognize information privacy rights, the Court noted in passing at least three facets of privacy.[17] These facets can be seen to correspond with the notions of *secrecy, anonymity,* and *autonomy*

- Secrecy is the interest in not having information revealed or exposed,
- Anonymity is the interest in not having information attributed to the individual.
- Autonomy is the interest in the individual being free from the consequences of disclosure or attribution of information.

Despite this nuanced footnote reference to the complexity of privacy interests, however, the Court in practice has rooted its jurisprudential conception of Fourth Amendment[18] privacy protections more narrowly in the simple notion of *secrecy* maintained through *concealment,*[19] and has generally extended such protection only in cases where there is a finding of both a subjective and objective "reasonable expectation of privacy" against intrusion or disclosure.[20] Thus, it is generally well established that the Fourth Amendment does not prohibit the government from obtaining and using information that was voluntarily given to a third party and then conveyed by that party to government authorities because there can be no reasonable *subjective* expectation of privacy for information that has already been shared.[21] The emergence of ubiquitous electronic record keeping, however, challenges the intellectual underpinnings of this doctrine. In an information environment in which vast amounts of personal information is maintained by third parties in public and private sector databases, and the very nature of the medium requires that data be shared with, maintained by, or exposed to such third parties, over-reliance on "secrecy" as the linchpin of Fourth Amendment protection leads to no protection at all. Furthermore, the need to show an *objective* reasonable expectation means, in practice, that the more ubiquitous that an intrusive technology becomes, the less protection afforded because there can be no objective reasonable expectation of privacy from a technology that is

---

[16]See Taipale, supra note 1, at 50-57 (for an overview of privacy law development and competing views).

[17]Whalen v. Roe, 429 U.S. 589, 599 n. 24 (1977).

[18]U.S. Const. amend. IV: The right of the people to be secure in their persons, houses, papers, and effects, against unreasonable searches and seizures, shall not be violated, and no Warrants shall issue, but upon probable cause, supported by Oath or affirmation, and particularly describing the place to be searched, and the persons or things to be seized.

[19]Daniel J. Solove, *Digital Dossiers and the Dissipation of Fourth Amendment Privacy,* 75 S. CAL. L. REV. 1083, 1086 (critiquing the Supreme Court's conceptualization of privacy premised on "a form of total secrecy" and safeguarding only "intimate information that individuals carefully conceal.")

[20]Katz v. United States, 389 U.S. 347, 361 (1967) (holding that the use of a wiretap requires a warrant under the fourth amendment and setting forth the two part "expectations of privacy" test).

[21]United States v. Miller, 425 U.S. 435, 441-443 (1976) (holding that financial records held by third party are not entitled to Fourth Amendment protection).

widespread. Thus, we have the paradoxical downward spiral in Fourth Amendment protections: To function in an information-based society with obligatory electronic record keeping requires sharing information with third parties (including government) for some purposes, thus eliminating any *subjective* expectations of privacy for that particular information for any subsequent purpose, and the general widespread sharing and disclosing of information itself abates any *objective* expectations of privacy for electronic records. However, because technological developments challenge the very underlying intellectual basis for this "third-party rule," it is ultimately inadequate to argue that there simply is no reasonable expectation for privacy in electronic records and—to paraphrase Scott McNeely—we should "get over it."[22]

Rather, in response to these developments, several commentators have called for a reconceptualization of privacy based not so much on secrecy or concealment but on ownership of personal information protected by property-like rights of control[23]—in particular, over secondary uses.[24] However, this concern with the appropriateness of *use* of personally relevant information (rather than on a continued fixation on *concealment*) means—at least to me—that the policy issue is less about privacy (that is, less but privacy as confidentiality—the secrecy of or non-access to data) than it is about due process,[25] thus requiring a different language of analysis and debate.

22.2.3.2. Due Process. *Due process* is the means for ensuring fairness in a system[26]—for our purposes, the fairness of the use of information. Determining whether some action provides due process is generally a function of analyzing four factors: the reasonableness of the *predicate* for the action, the *practicality* of alternatives, the severity and *consequences* of the intrusion, and the procedures for *error control*. In the context of using counter-terrorism technologies in support of preemptive strategies, there are two related processes (or government activities) to be considered against these factors: first, the ecumenic use of information sharing and data analysis to develop actionable intelligence (that is, general surveillance, dataveillance, or analysis); second, the reliance on such intelligence to increasingly focus resources on particular threats and ultimately individuals (that is, acting on such intelligence). The former requires determining whether (and under what terms) it is reasonable for government to access available information based on a known but undifferentiated threat (that is, on a generalized predicate), and the latter involves determining whether (and under what terms) it is reasonable for government to take further action against specific individual(s) (and the procedures under which those actions are authorized, administered, and reviewed) based on specific predicate developed

---

[22]Scott McNeely, Chief Executive Officer, Sun Microsystems, famously stated in 1999 that consumers "have no privacy" and should "get over it."

[23]*See*, e.g., Pamela Samuelson, Privacy as Intellectual Property? 52 *Stan. L. Rev.* 1125, 1127 (2000); Jerry Kang, Information Privacy in Cyberspace Transactions, 50 *Stan. L. Rev.* 1193, 1246-94 (1998); Lawrence Lessig, Privacy as Property, 69 *Soc. Res.* 247, 247 and n.1 (2002).

[24]*Cf.*, e.g., the "Fair Information Practices" (as first set forth in U.S. Department of Health, Education and Welfare, *Records, Computers and the Rights of Citizens* at 61–62 (1973) that explicitly state that data not be used for other or subsequent purposes without the data subject's consent; *see also OECD Guidelines on the Protection of Privacy and Transborder Flows of Personal Data* at Use Limitation Principle and para. 10 (1980); Information Infrastructure Task Force, Information Policy Committee, Privacy Working Group, *Privacy and the National Information Infrastructure: Principles for Providing and Using Personal Information* at § II.D (1995); *The European Union Directive on the Protection of Personal Data* at arts. 6–7 (1995).

[25]Taipale, Frankenstein, supra note 1, at 146–152.

[26]See generally Ronald Dworkin, *Law's Empire* (1986).

through general observation or as a result of nonparticular analysis. It is beyond the scope of this chapter to fully explore these issues or the legal framework within which these factors are to be considered.[27] Rather, it is sufficient to note how technical development factors interact with due process concerns.

22.2.3.3. Due Process, Surveillance, and the Development of Actionable Intelligence.
Traditionally, domestic surveillance has been managed under rules based on *place* and *time* and the reasonableness of government intrusion on *expectations* of privacy to "search or seize" (that is, collect) information in that place or time. As noted above, these traditional rules are rooted in the conception of *privacy-as-secrecy-based-on-concealment*—an all-or-nothing approach in which the policy control mechanisms are concerned only with the circumstances under which government can initially acquire that which was previously concealed. Once information is unclosed (either because it was revealed to a third party or because government has followed the appropriate procedure to obtain it for a particular purpose), the information is no longer subject to any Constitutional restriction on its further or subsequent use for any purposes (it may, of course, be subject to further statutory protections).

A ubiquitous networked information environment, however, challenges the very premise itself of space- and time-based regulation over collection (not just the *reasonable expectations* doctrine as discussed above). This challenge is especially complicated when it is control over access to otherwise available information—rather than the "collection" of concealed information—that is being considered. Furthermore, in networked systems, information is always proximate (that is, it can be accessed from anywhere) and is no longer transient (that is, it generally remains available and easily accessible even after its primary use). These two characteristics undermine protections afforded by (or procedures based on) inefficiencies of previous record systems in which geographic distance made information access inconvenient and the passage of time provided ephemerality for most information, or where the place or time of initial search or seizure of concealed information governed collection methodologies (that is, where policy controlled access to "private space" or time).

The problem of access versus collection (and thus with place- and time-based regulation) is particularly acute for secondary uses of available information—that is, uses or access to information for purposes beyond or different than the purpose for which the information was originally disclosed, recorded, or collected. In a paper-based record system the ability to go back, find, and reuse or analyze information for secondary purposes (or to surveil that which was previously not observed) is severely limited due to inefficiencies in storage, access, and analysis (and the nontrivial economics of overcoming these inefficiencies), but such reuse is virtually unrestricted (and has little marginal cost) in databases of electronic records. In counter-terrorism intelligence, this secondary use problem (and related privacy concerns) manifests itself particularly with regard to the access to or use of data routinely collected by government in the course of providing ordinary services, or in accessing commercially available data. Among the concerns is that the trivial cost of automated access and analysis will overcome protections previously afforded by the economics of inefficiency (economics that required a conscious and justifiable commitment of resources to overcome), thus leading to widespread "fishing expeditions."

---

[27]But see, e.g., K. A. Taipale, Frankenstein, supra note 1, at 187-197 (discussing the four factors of due process in the context of information systems, counterterrorism, and the need for analysis based on a *calculus of reasonableness*).

For some, this potential for fishing expeditions—that is, looking through *available* information for *potentially* relevant information (as opposed to seeking *particular* information based on a *specific* predicate)—violates a presumed absolute Fourth Amendment requirement for individualized suspicion before government can generally observe (or analyze) evidence of individual behavior. However, there is no such irreducible requirement under existing Supreme Court precedent,[28] nor would such a doctrine be a practical (or reasonable) policy, because it would prevent *any* preemptive or proactive law enforcement strategies, including assigning police officers to high crime areas or otherwise using crime statistics or experience to allocate resources. I have addressed these issues elsewhere, in particular with respect to data-mining or other pattern-based analysis,[29] and it is beyond the scope of this chapter to reiterate those arguments here. Suffice it to say that data analysis, including data-mining or pattern-based analysis, is not inherently constitutionally suspect any more so than observing suspicious behavior on a street corner—in both cases the pertinent policy issue is whether the particular data space ought properly be observed, by whom, under what conditions, and for what purposes and to what consequence (that is, is it reasonable under the totality of the circumstances). To a large extent, the appropriateness of the observation (that is, whether it is both reasonable for general use and meets standards for due process in particular application) will depend on assessing the efficacy of the methodology in the context of the four due process factors (predicate, alternatives, consequences, and error control) set forth above, on the one hand, and the peculiar circumstances of its use, on the other.

Nevertheless, for purposes of designing or developing technical systems—including those for information sharing or automated analysis—it does not need to be determined *a priori* what data may be accessed by any particular person, in any particular place, for any particular purpose, or under any particular circumstance. Rather, by recognizing that access control policy (and supporting technical infrastructure) will be needed to substitute for existing place- and time-based policy rules governing collection, systems architectures can be developed that provide technical controls (that is, allows policy intervention) in analogous situations or by substituting other mechanisms. For example, technical means to control access to remote data through authentication or authorization technologies—that is, who can access what data and when—can be designed and built into systems regardless of what those policy rules are (and, assuming such technical features are built in, then policy can be developed over time to meet changing circumstance). Moreover, effective user authentication, together with logging and audit, can also offset to some degree the real-world procedural requirements for proving (or *articulating*) individual predicates in formal legal proceedings prior to taking certain action since access, query, and analysis actions (and the investigative sequence leading up to them) are subject to review after the fact on the basis of immutable and nonrepudiable records. Since one of the primary due process purposes of requiring prior articulation of individual predicate is to avoid post-hoc rationalization for selective focus, an immutable record of investigative procedures documenting the basis for increasingly individualized suspicion may help mitigate this concern for individualized predicate. Relevant design (and related policy) issues that will affect such policy implementation and enforcement include how such authorization mechanisms and logging are to be controlled, managed, and overseen (for example, who physically controls log files, or are the logs discoverable by the data subject in subsequent proceedings?).

---

[28]United States v. Martinez-Fuerte, 428 U.S. 543, 561 (1976) ("the Fourth amendment imposes no irreducible requirement of [individualized] suspicion").

[29]See, e.g., Taipale, Data Mining, *supra* note 1, and Taipale, Frankenstein, supra note 1.

22.2.3.4. *Due Process, Government Action, and Individual Consequence.*

It seems forgone that government will—and should, subject to appropriate procedures—have access to available information that can help prevent catastrophic events. Indeed, it would be an unusual policy that demanded accountability from its representatives for being unable to prevent terrorist acts yet denied them access to the information to do so—particularly if such information were already available in government databases or easily available in the private sector. In any case, as noted above, privacy protection based on preventing collection based simply on maintaining absolute secrecy is a brittle civil liberties policy anyway since any disclosure—whether to third parties or under some authorized access for a particular purpose—results in complete termination of any protections for subsequent or unrelated purposes. Furthermore, it is unlikely that "blinding" government to available information based on a fetish for secrecy can—or should—provide an adequate basis for protecting national security or civil liberties in the information age, and the policy debate (as well as legal analysis) should move beyond the issue of simple disclosure or access to that of controlled consequence. A more pragmatic—and ultimately, more protective—paradigm than secrecy for automated processing might be constructed by examining how privacy based on controlling *anonymity*—that is, controlling the *attribution* of data to an individual identity—might be used to help protect *autonomy,* the core civil liberty for which privacy based on secrecy has been the until now bulwark mechanism.

Based on the changed nature of the threat and the resulting need for preemptive counter-terrorism strategies, some form of data surveillance or analysis of generally available information is inevitable (albeit circumscribed according to some appropriately agreed rules enforced through access controls, logging, and other mechanisms); thus, policy rules governing the consequences of such access will increasingly be the mechanisms relied on for protecting civil liberties. The policy issue will be to determine what consequences may (fairly) accrue to the individual from government access to available information and how are those consequences to be managed—that is, according to what standard, authorization, and review. (For example, by what authority and under what standard of proof or review can government deny an individual the right to travel based on appearing on a watch list?)

Again, from a technical design perspective, it is unnecessary to determine precisely what predicates for what further actions may be required, or to what standard these consequences are to be reviewed. Rather, it is the need for intervention and review itself that should to be taken into account in systems design. The policy question is to determine what standard for intervention or review is appropriate—that is, to determine the *due process model;* also, the technical design requirements are to design systems that support such policy by providing opportunities for interventions in information flows that allow related policy procedures to function at various places along the flow of information in the context of its use.

Here it should again be pointed out that determining predicate requirements—that is, setting the policy standards for authorizing further action at any stage—is a dependant variable that needs to be considered against the practical alternatives, the consequences of the action, and the procedures for error correction as noted above. Since these criteria are contextual, and may be variable under the particular circumstances under which they are to be applied, no system design should contemplate rigid policy rule enforcement; that is, policy rules should not be hard-coded in architecture to provide only for a one-policy-fits-all standard. Thus, policy appliances that mediate access to, or constrain the use of, information should be developed to support myriad—and at times seemingly contradictory—policies [for example, selective disclosure mechanisms should be designed to support both (a) disclosure of appropriate information and (b) concealment of inappropriate information.

22.2.4. Protecting Liberty by Selectively Controlling Attribution

Due process in a general sense requires that in order for government to focus increasingly selective attention on a specific individual, some form of *predicate* may be required; that is, at some point of intrusion some reasonable basis of justification for taking some further action(s) must exist. Thus, the government commonly must have duly observed or otherwise come into the possession of some information that meets some due process standard (for example, *probable cause or reasonable suspicion*) in order to exercise legitimate authority to (a) collect more information about a particular individual in an intrusive way (for example, through an authorized search or wiretap, where there is a reasonable expectation of privacy) or (b) deprive that individual of liberty (for example, by arrest). As a general rule, the greater the intrusion on individual liberty, the higher the standard for predicate. So, too, the contrapose should hold: The lesser the discriminative intrusion or consequence, the lesser the need for specific predicate. In any case, as already discussed, the Constitutional need for specific predicate (that is, individualized suspicion) is not irreducible. Thus, there is no absolute requirement for presenting individual predicate for general preemptive policing strategies that are properly—and reasonably—based on a generalized predicate.

And, as noted above, reasonableness (due process) is to be judged according to the government interests at stakes, the practicality of alternatives, the severity of the intrusion or the consequences, and the procedures for error correction. So, for example, analysis of general crime statistics is a sufficient and proper basis for focusing law enforcement resources on a nonspecific but likely threat—say, assigning additional officers to a high crime area or staking out a particular class of target where they can observe the general public and look for suspicious behavior. Furthermore, in conducting such general observations, experientially derived generalized patterns (for example, the matching of drug courier profiles), can properly be used as the predicate to individualized suspicion (thus as a legally sufficient basis for follow-up investigation—even physical searching or arrest—of matched individuals). So, too, observed anomalies in data or traffic—if probative—ought to be sufficient predicate for a subsequent follow-up investigation that is increasingly individualized on the data subject, assuming, of course, that (a) the state interest is compelling, (b) the practical alternatives are limited, (c) the consequences are restrained, and (d) robust review and error correction procedures are provided.

Nevertheless, some argue that even the initial act of analyzing aggregated data itself should require some individualized predicate lest we "alter the way that government investigations typically occur."[30] According to this view, data analysis or data matching "investigates everyone, and most people who are investigated are innocent."[31] I've previously set forth my disaccord with these views[32]: The first statement conflates "investigations" with policing (thus conveniently ignoring the practical reality, prevalence, and appropriateness of preemptive policing strategies to allocate resources), and the second

---

[30]Solove, Digital Dossiers, supra note 19 at 1109.

[31]Priscilla M. Regan, Legislating Privacy 90 (1995).

[32]See, e.g., Taipale, Data Mining, supra note 1; Taipale, Frankenstein, supra note 1.

carries the smuggled—but in my view controverted—assumption that data analysis (even of records evidencing *public* behavior) is somehow *inherently* and *qualitatively* different from traditional observation (and thus a greater intrusion). Neither view seems unconditionally warranted; in particular, the former ignores the practical necessity for effective allocation of resources against recognized but nonspecific threats based on a generalized predicate, and the latter ignores the relative consequences of alternative intrusions (ignores, for example, that the alternative to a minimal data scan might be an intrusive physical search). As noted earlier, due process analysis requires determining the reasonableness of a predicate requirement not in the abstract, but by reference to the practical alternatives, the severity of consequences or intrusion, and the procedures for error correction.

However, for purposes of this chapter it is not necessary to reargue this case nor to conclude that one view or the other is correct; instead, systems designers can accommodate the requirement for individualized predicate by controlling *data attribution* through *selective disclosure*—that is, for example, by providing intervention points for policy application before the results of analyzed data are attributed to any particular individual (thus, prior to triggering any individual consequences). Such strategies are premised on separating *knowledge of behavior* from *knowledge of identity* prior to or during processing based on the *anonymization* of data (for data sharing, matching, and analysis applications) and the *pseudonymization* of identity (for identification and collection applications) and can enable familiar due process procedures (or their analogues) to function.[33] Results from a generalized preliminary data analysis can then be used, much like the drug courier profile, to establish individual predicate before additional information is disclosed, including identity (and such further disclosure would only occur under proscribed policy constraints and acceptable confidence intervals and would be subject to whatever administrative or judicial procedures determined appropriate). The result of such an approach is not to negate the privacy concerns, but rather to use technical means to conform their mitigation to existing doctrines and familiar due process procedures and analysis.

22.2.5. Data Quality and Error Correction

As noted above, there are two fundamental systems requirements for any information management system to conform to both national security and civil liberties policy needs: first, that systems provide opportunities to ensure that shared data are useful, and, second, that shared data is used appropriately and in accordance with policy rules. The prior sections generally have discussed due process policy issues relating to information use, including the need to assess the reasonableness of due process by reference to four factors: the predicate for action, the alternatives, the consequences, and the procedures for error control. In this section, we discuss error control—assuring data quality and providing mechanisms for error correction.

In calling for increased information sharing for counter-terrorism purposes, it is common to suggest that among the information management problems to be overcome to produce better intelligence is that of *originator control*—the policy under which shared information cannot be passed on or used by the recipient without the concurrence of the originator. Indeed, Executive Order 13356 specifically states that "terrorism information

---

[33]See Taipale, Frankenstein, supra note 1, for a more detailed discussion of these strategies in the context of identification, data aggregation and data analysis, and collection technologies.

[is] to be shared free of originator controls." Although it seems clear that, in practice, originator control has become a bureaucratic impediment to effective sharing and intelligence production, the rationale for originator control is not the product solely of some parochial bureaucratic desire to protect turf; rather, it is a sound concept of information management to ensure data quality and data security. The justification for originator control is based on the legitimate notion that in the traditional intelligence production model the entity with the most understanding of, and investment in, the accuracy and security of any particular information is its originator, and that such entity is therefore the best party to ensure its accuracy, keep it up-to-date, judge its reliability in context, and protect its methods of production. Originator control serves as a bureaucratic means to tether information to its producer, allowing for controlled use and the potential for recall or error correction—it allows the originating party to exert ongoing control (or knowledge of use) over information it shares. If existing procedural or organizational rules enforcing bureaucratic originator control as a means to ensure data quality and data security are to be eliminated, then some alternative means of meeting these needs will have to be developed within the new intelligence production process model as well, and systems architecture design will be required to accommodate and support such process needs.

To use information effectively for counterterrorism—in particular, to generate actionable intelligence from data as generally discussed above—requires that the quality of data be considered in order to avoid garbage-in garbage-out. Data quality in this context, however, goes beyond simple accuracy to include assessment of its reliability, timeliness, and usefulness for a particular purpose. The concern for data quality is also a civil liberties concern—indeed, much of the opposition to technological developments in this area is premised on the problem of "false positives" generated from bad data. Data reliability is also a particular concern when data are repurposed for other uses, especially when data are collected for purposes requiring a low standard of accuracy (for example, commercial direct marketing uses where the consequences of error are slight) but used for purposes demanding a higher standard (for example, counter-terrorism purposes where the consequences may be to deprive a subject of liberty). (Note that the availability in networked information systems of data to be repurposed itself undercuts in part the effectiveness of originator control for data quality purposes because there may be a mismatch between the originator and consumer data quality needs.)

Data security is also a concern. In this context, data security goes beyond simply ensuring its *confidentiality,* but also protecting the process of its production (including its sources and *methods*). Disclosures of sources and methods can jeopardize operational assets and intelligence programs, but can also impact the civil rights of others (for example, the identity of confidential sources or information about innocent third parties that is disclosed collaterally). Again, the widespread sharing of information subject to different producer and consumer security needs requires developing a new information management process that takes these issues into account.

An important component of ensuring data quality, of course, is error correction. Error correction requires procedures to discover inaccuracies, as well as mechanisms to update information or correct errors. In the context of complex systems and multiple uses (and reuses) of information, error correction must also ensure that derivative products based on out-of-date or erroneous information can be updated or corrected. Any system designed to produce useful intelligence needs robust mechanisms to update or correct information even after it has been shared or used for other purposes. Some method to tether information and its subsequent uses to the original data source must be incorporated. Design solutions including a distributed information architecture based on directories, pointers, and web services, in which the original data remains within the data "owners" control, have been suggested to address these issues.

Obviously, similar mechanisms for error correction are required to protect civil liberties. In this context, the problem is compounded by the fact that the data subject—who may be the party with the most interest in correcting a particular error relating to their own data—may never be in a position to know that the inaccurate data exists. There are significant policy issues that will need to be worked out over time through both political and legal processes regarding how data quality issues are to be resolved and due process maintained. Obviously, secret or classified intelligence data cannot be shared with data subjects directly for error discovery, however, it may be possible that "feeder" data—that is, data in nonclassified government databases or available from commercial sources that are used in the production of actionable intelligence—can be, or should be, subject to analogous protections as that provided in the Fair Credit Reporting Act (FCRA) for consumer credit data. Such procedures might enable data subjects to query these sources and could provide procedures to update or correct errors. Furthermore, even intelligence data files or records might be subject to the Freedom of Information Act or other similar disclosure procedures after some period of time or when operational security no longer requires secrecy. Additional policy questions that will need to be resolved are whether query data themselves, access logs, or other meta-data become subject to the same information management procedures or rules as the underlying data. For example, under FRCA, credit inquiries themselves become part of the credit report subject to the requirements of the Act, including disclosure. (And, note that under FRCA, even national security investigations are subject to disclosure after completion of the investigation.) Whether intelligence or law enforcement queries, logs, or metadata would—or should—become subject to the same rules governing the underlying information are issues that will need to be resolved in particular contexts and with respect to different kinds and different sources of information.

Robust error control is an absolute requirement for meeting due process needs in information process and architecture. As noted above, the requirement for predicate is analytically related (in terms of due process) to the adequacy of error control. Thus, robust error control may alleviate or lessen the need for individualized predicate prior to general data analysis, however, lack of such control would argue for increased predicate requirements and against generalized analysis.

We do not need to resolve these issues here. For purposes of overall systems design, data quality and error correction features are requirements to support both intelligence production processes and civil liberties due process and, therefore, must be built into information sharing architectures.

22.3. SYSTEMS ARCHITECTURE

This chapter argues that there is no technical design conflict between national security and civil liberties needs because technical systems requirements to protect civil liberties are essentially the same as those required to meet operational needs in managing information flows in order to produce actionable intelligence for counter-terrorism. Furthermore, we have suggested that actually determining what specific policy rules may be required to protect civil liberties in any particular application or circumstance (that is, determining the precise standards for due process) is not required prior to systems design (or application research and development) if the need for policy intervention itself is incorporated into the technology design. Indeed, specific policy rules should be kept out of systems and tools design altogether because policy rules are highly contextual and circumstance specific in application. Designing technical systems that can enable myriad and competing policy procedures to function in support of divergent process needs—including civil liberties protections—requires building in intervention points and providing control mechanisms over information flows.

In particular, we propose an overarching *enterprise architecture* designed to guide systems and applications development to support *knowledge management* and *due process* across multiple connected networks and systems.[34] Such a design is based on *policy appliances* (technical control mechanisms to enforce policy rules and ensure accountability), interacting with *smart data* (data that carry with it contextual relevant terms for its own use) and *intelligent agents* (queries that are self-credentialed, authenticating, or contextually adaptive). See Figure 22.1 (showing an idealized view of policy appliance topography between client and server) and Figure 22.2 (showing the relative position of these mechanisms in the network stack). It should be emphasized that the suggested architecture is not a design blueprint for any particular system—there is no single system that will meet either security or civil liberties needs. Instead, we set out our proposal as a reference model against which technology and policy development can be assessed.

Furthermore, we suggest that such mechanisms would generally function best in a distributed information environment premised not solely on *information sharing,* but rather on sharing *information availability* through the use of directories, pointers, and web services in which producers would *publish* information availability and consumers would *subscribe* according to their individual needs. Such a publish-and-subscribe information model would enable policy appliances to mediate information flows of shared data according to on-demand information needs, matching information accuracy, relevance, timeliness, and policy needs more closely with user needs and allowing original data owners to maintain control over data for purposes of ensuring data quality and security. This would also allow systems with varying information management needs to interact or coexist; for example, systems for managing classified information can exchange availability information with lesser classification networks without compromising information security. Likewise, the availability of sensitive personal information can be made known without compromising the underlying privacy interests except subject to appropriate procedures (an authorized need to know).

Under this approach, once an initial need for information access was established (and authenticated or authorized), these policy appliances would mediate query access or data exchange. For example, semantic programs could evaluate query needs in context by interrogating intelligent agents (queries that are self-credentialed, authenticating, or contextually adaptive) before returning data that were labeled on-the-fly with contextually relevant metadata (that is, data about the underlying data, for example, the original source, date or time of origin, expiry information, reliability, and other relevance assessments). Such devices could also mediate data security and civil liberties needs, for example, by returning only "cleansed" data—unclassified data in the case of security or de-identified data in the case of civil liberties—based on assessing the credentials and authority of a particular query. (Note that many institutional sharing arrangements will be negotiated, either technically or as policy, on a global bases—for example, agency to agency or database owner to user. We are not suggesting that every data exchange be initiated *de novo,*

---

[34]See Markle Foundation Taskforce on National Security in the Information Age, *Creating a Trusted Information Network for Homeland Security* (2003).

but whatever information management practices are developed and agreed upon can be monitored or enforced through technical means.)

Developing rule-based policy appliances to mediate queries and data exchange requires further research in intelligent agents, proof carrying code, data labeling (DRM), and analytic filtering tools, as well as in entity resolution, contextual search, searching on encrypted data, and one-way hashing technologies, among others. Semantic programs and applications that can contextually label data at ingestion or in response to particular queries or within use needs will be required to manage scaling requisites. Additional development requirements include a common language for expressing policy rules across systems, general computer and network security, user authentication, encryption, and compliance checking and reporting technologies.

Control and accountability over policy appliances will be a key determinant in policy implementation and enforcement. Immutable and nonrepudiable logs will be necessary to ensure accountability and compliance for both operational and civil liberties policy needs. Thus, physical control over logs and their use is a significant policy issue, not just a technical decision. Figures 22.1 and 22.2 suggest an architecture in which additional oversight log functions are designed to collect and aggregate user and data logs from both client and server (or producer and consumer) for subsequent monitoring and compliance audit by a supra-authority. The tracking of where information flows and who used it for what purposes provides opportunities for robust data error control, as well as access and use policy compliance. (In addition, such integrated logging is a also a requirement for system self-awareness, which can facilitate the production of additional intelligence by correlating disparate analysis or query of related data.) However, significant policy issues regarding authorities, security, and civil liberties will need to be resolved to develop these functions. Additionally, further technical research in immutable logging, audit tools, and self-reporting data will be required.

SUMMARY

Meeting security needs and protecting civil liberties are dual obligations of the civil state, and neither can be neglected for the other. This chapter has suggested that there is no inherent technical design conflict in developing information systems to support the requirements of both. It is not the intent of this chapter to proffer precise technical solutions or research avenues for ultimate resolution; however, we have proposed a generic architecture around which policy makers, information managers, and systems architects can begin to develop a shared understanding. In addition, we have examined the intersection of certain civil liberty policy concerns with national security needs and technical developments in order to illustrate their interdependence.

Index

About the Editors

Robert L. Popp is currently executive vice president of Aptima, Inc. of Woburn, Massachusetts, a provider of human-centered technology solutions to industry and government by applying advanced principles in social and cognitive sciences coupled with quantitative and computational methods from mathematics, computer science, and engineering. Formerly the deputy director of the Information Exploitation Office (IXO) at the Defense Advanced Research Projects Agency (DARPA), Dr. Popp oversaw R&D programs focused on sensing, exploitation and C4ISR systems to improve U.S. military capabilities in combat operations; he also managed programs addressing post-Cold War strategic problems and challenges for pre- and post-conflict stability operations. While at DARPA, Dr. Popp also served as deputy director of the Information Awareness Office (IAO), where he assisted Director John Poindexter, retired Admiral and former National Security advisor to President Ronald Reagan, oversee R&D programs focused on information technology solutions for counter-terrorism, foreign intelligence and other national security concerns, including the Total Information Awareness (TIA) program. Dr. Popp was an adjunct professor of computer science at the University of Connecticut and a lecturer at Boston University, a visiting research scientist at the Air Force Research Labs in Rome, New York, and held senior positions with defense contractors Alphatech (now BAE) and BBN. Dr. Popp received his Bachelor of Arts and Master of Arts degrees in computer science from Boston University (summa cum laude, Phi Beta Kappa) and his Ph.D. degree in electrical engineering from the University of Connecticut. He has authored or co-authored 5 book chapters, more than 70 scholarly technical papers in refereed journals and conferences, and holds 2 patents. Currently serving as an associate editor for the *IEEE Transactions on Systems, Man and Cybernetics (SMC),* and the *Journal of Advances in Information Fusion,* Dr. Popp is a member of the Defense Science Board (DSB), a senior associate for the Center for Strategic and International Studies (CSIS), a member of the Association for Computing Machinery (ACM), the American Association for the Advancement of Science (AAAS), a senior member of the IEEE, a founding fellow of the University of Connecticut's Academy of Distinguished Engineers, and a lifetime member of HOG—Harley Owners Group.

John Yen is university professor and professor-in-charge of the College of Information Sciences and Technology at the Pennsylvania State University, University Park, Pennsylvania. Like other faculty members of the college, he is interested in multidisciplinary research and innovative education related to information and communication technologies, the human contexts of their uses, and their impacts on people. In particular, he and his research team have focused on developing agent-based collaborative technologies that assist human decision-making teams by anticipating and sharing relevant information and knowledge. Dr. Yen received his Ph.D. degree in computer science from the University of California, Berkeley in 1986. He has published more than 100 technical papers in journals, conference proceedings, and edited volumes. Dr. Yen is a member of the editorial boards of several international journals on intelligent systems. He received an NSF Young Investigator Award in 1992 and is a Fellow of IEEE.